"Innovation
is here defined as any thought, behavior, or
thing that is new because it is qualitatively
different from existing forms," says the author
(p. 7). He has explored innovations in six
main cultures. Five of these are ethnic groups:
European broadly considered, three western
American Indian tribes, and the Palauans of
Micronesia. The sixth group is religious, the
Shakers. But his principal interest is the
incidence of new thoughts, behaviors and
things rather than the cultures themselves, and
he has organized his unique book under four
major headings:
1. The Setting
2. Incentives to Innovation
3. Innovative Processes
4. Acceptance and Rejection

H. G. Barnett is Professor of Anthropology
at the University of Oregon.

McGRAW-HILL PAPERBACKS
PROBLEMS OF CIVILIZATION

Prices subject to change without notice.

Innovation:
The Basis of
Cultural Change

H. G. Barnett

McGraw-Hill Book Company, Inc.
New York   Toronto   London

IV

INNOVATION : THE BASIS OF CULTURAL CHANGE

Library of Congress Catalog Card Number: 52–9439

EDITOR'S INTRODUCTION

The practice of prefacing a text or technical book with a few kind and hopeful words by the one who has functioned as editor has fallen largely into disuse. Perhaps, on the whole, it is well that this is so. But I have personally so much enjoyed and profited from the reading of the manuscript of *Innovation,* and, above all, I have been so much impressed with the intellectual integrity of the author that I am anxious to serve as advocate for his innovation.

Were it not that the phrase has been worn out through misuse, I should be content to say that the theories here developed constitute "a major contribution to the social sciences." As it is, I shall say just that in more and different words.

It is a rather curious fact that, although science is systematized knowledge, the extension of scientific knowledge seems, on the surface at least, to be quite random and erratic. Scientists, like other humans, are subject to faddy excitements; and they often converge on a single problem or method, with the result that it becomes, for a time, the fashionable realm in which to labor. The frontier of a scientific discipline, the demarkation between the known and the still to be discovered, is as a consequence a line of skirmish rather than one of frontal assault. Here and there are points of deep penetration, where the advance was rapid; but here and there also are pockets of ignorance which represent problems that have been passed by, either because they were unusually resistant to solution or else because for some reason or other they never became popular areas of inquiry.

The theory expounded in this book deals with a problem that has long been neglected by social scientists: the processes by which, and the conditions under which, men devise new additions to their culture. This theory constitutes a scientific innovation; in terms of the above metaphor, it straightens one section of the line between our knowledge of and our ignorance about matters social. And it may, indeed it should, provide a base for many new points of penetration into the vast unknown that lies before us.

Not since Gabriel Tarde's *Les Lois de l'Imitation* (1895) has there been any real attempt to formulate a theoretical explanation of the innovative process and of the individual and social circumstances involved therein. Tarde's theory of invention was only a dependent by-product of his all-inclusive law of imitation, by which he sought to explain social continuities. His "law of imitation" was soon discarded by social psychologists and others in favor of vastly more complex and nonparticularistic theories of socialization. Yet, oddly, his theory of invention persisted unchallenged and unchanged. It became so much incorporated in the social science subculture that most subsequent comments on the innovative process have until now been little more than a paraphrasing of one or more of the ideas that Tarde advanced.

The long, and at times bitter, controversy among anthropologists over the roles of diffusion and of independent invention in the development of culture provoked many excellent factual studies of specific inventions and their diffusion, but it did not produce a new theory of the innovative process. Sociologists and social historians have in a number of instances attempted to trace the development of some particular technique or organizational form, and for the past thirty-odd years the former have been much concerned with the impact on social organization of new mechanical devices. But no important effort has been made by either sociologists or social historians to explain the emergence of such new devices. Psychologists, and to a lesser extent sociologists, have in some instances attempted to single out one or another of the crude correlates of inventors as a class, and experiments in the field of learning have greatly extended our understanding of the motivational and other factors involved in behavior. But, again, no theory of innovation per se has been advanced.

In effect, then, what has been happening is that our knowledge of actual innovations has been growing in a fragmentary way for more than half a century, a period during which, however, our understanding of the innovative process has advanced hardly at all. Such a condition of affairs provides an opportunity favorable to theoretical synthesis, to the appearance of an innovation. And that is exactly what *Innovation* is.

The concepts advanced in this book have only a faint historical relation to Tarde's theory of invention. They are new, in the limited sense that any innovation is new. They have, clearly, been synthesized out of the relevant accumulated knowledge of anthropology, sociology, and psychology. And, further, they have been given a preliminary testing against a variety of factual settings. Together they constitute what may be characterized as a general theory of innovation; but each is in its own right what Robert Merton has so aptly termed a "theory of the middle range," *i.e.,* a theory that can be further tested and can serve as a working hypothesis for empirical investigations.

As a synthesis of our present knowledge and a base from which new investigations can take off, this book comes at a most opportune time. Particularly since the Second World War, anthropologists have become increasingly interested in social change, an interest which is encompassed by the rubric "cultural dynamics." And of late years sociologists have added to their long-standing concern with the historical "lag" between the rates of technical and organizational change a concern with the possible consequences to science and science-based technology of such organizational developments as the constant expansion of governmental functions, especially of military subsidy of scientific research. It is commonly assumed that many of the changes taking place in our social order are reducing the individual incentives for innovation and creating a climate hostile to the acceptance of such innovations as do occur. Thus the most trenchant argument advanced by the defenders of private medicine is that under bureaucratic organization medical practices would tend to be frozen and, ultimately, medical science would stagnate.

That the acute functional disequilibriums of all modern societies, and of all those in the throes of becoming modern, can be resolved only through innovative endeavor would seem to be self-evident. But we simply do not know, whatever we may believe, whether any or all of the various current trends in organizational development—themselves often innovations—will foster or discourage the innovative process. *Innovation* provides us with the conceptual tools for a wide variety of scientific attacks upon this general problem; it is my personal hope that it will also provide the stimulus for the application of these tools to what is, I think, the most urgent practical problem of our age.

R. T. LaPiere

Stanford, Calif.
October, 1952

CONTENTS

INTRODUCTION

1

In the chapters which follow an attempt has been made to formulate a general theory of the nature of innovation and to analyze the conditions for, and the immediate social consequences of, the appearance of novel ideas. It seems that any innovation, when it is understood as a mental phenomenon, conforms to one of a limited number of reaction patterns irrespective of the contents of the ideas that are embodied in the mental reactions. The conception of a new idea is not a specific, unitary phenomenon; it is the result of a particular conjunction of psychological processes, none of which, when taken alone, is peculiar to the pattern of thought that is essential to the conception of a novelty. There is, in other words, no innovative "faculty," nor is there any specifically creative instrument that is possessed by some men and not by others.

Certain conditions are obviously more propitious than others for the occurrence of new ideas. Favorable and unfavorable conditions have, moreover, social as well as personal determinants. These two major kinds of influences, together with subordinate variables that affect innovative potentials in each, are considered in the sections that deal with the cultural backgrounds of the innovators and with their individual histories and motivations.

The attention given to the social consequences of innovations is confined for the most part to an analysis of the factors that influence their acceptance or rejection. Incidental reference is made to the demands for change that the acceptance of an innovation imposes on the rest of a culture. No effort is made to study either the ramifications or the cumulative results of acceptance. Hence the analysis stops short of a discussion of trends, drifts, tendencies, cycles, and other formulations based upon the coordinates of time, location, and quantity.

The same is true of the treatment of innovations themselves. They, rather than combinations of them, are taken as the complexes to be analyzed and compared. They are not studied as components in patterns of change, or viewed as steps in an evolutionary sequence, or dealt with as events localized in time and place. In short, the present approach to innovation and its consequences is neither historical nor statistical. The aim has been to describe processes rather than substance, universals rather than singularities. Common conditions and consistent mechanisms have been sought in the hope of establishing regularities in the functioning of cultural change.

2

The empirical data for the study have been drawn from six main sources. They have been accumulated since 1938 as a part of a research program directed toward an analysis of cultural change. Since the goal has been to generalize upon innovative behavior and to define the conditions and the limitations upon its manifestations, the research has been conditioned by the premise that it could not be restricted to one cultural continuum. If the conclusions are to have universal validity—that is, to be true regardless of when or where change occurs—then it is indispensable to make as many intertime, interplace, and intercultural comparisons as possible.

The six sources mentioned comprise the total cultures of five ethnic groups, plus material on the changes that have taken place in a certain religious cult over a sixty-year period. The selection of the ethnic groups was determined to some extent by expediency, but beyond that by a desire to assure variation in the sample. There are important differences among the ethnic groups with respect to both their cultural inventories and the historical events that have affected them during the past hundred years. The cult was included to contribute still further to the diversity of the data. It represents a distinct cultural phenomenon, a self-contained one that passed across several cultural boundaries in the course of its development. The fact that it is a purely religious phenomenon, an ideological structure with supernatural elements and sanctions, set particularly difficult problems in analysis. It was believed that if there are any special innovative processes or any exclusive conditions for them, the history of this cult would serve to bring them out.

Of the five ethnic groups from which data on change have been taken, the one best known to the author, the American, has understandably contributed the most. Greater familiarity with it naturally has provided greater insight into the meanings and values of its changes, and its extensive communication system and written records have enlarged the range and multiplicity of particulars available far beyond that possible with the other four groups. While data that is specifically American will be found to predominate, there is also much that is taken from other manifestations of European culture. The European tradition has many extensions, including the American; and while they reveal significant temporal and geographical variations, there is a skeleton of characteristics common to them all and a basis for common understanding that is found to be lacking when we turn to societies with entirely different and historically unconnected developments.

In relation to the Euro-American material it will be noticed that little attention is given to the landmarks of technological progress that are usually dealt with in histories of invention. There are several reasons for this cursory treatment. One is that the kind of information which is pertinent to an analysis such as the present one is all too often lacking or untrustworthy in the existing records concerning the major inventions of the past. Too many critical questions about them and their creators require answers that can never be given at this late date. Another reason stems from a theoretical position and a didactic purpose. It is commonly supposed that inventions are extraordinary achievements of rare and brilliant individuals, and consequently that at any one period in history few of them appear. A contrary view is taken in this book, and partly with the idea of substantiating it, examples of little-noticed contemporary inventions are chosen in preference to the famous few the arbitrary selection of which has resulted in a distorted perspective of human ingenuity. Innovations—even important ones—are everyday commonplaces, a fact which needs to be demonstrated by an emphasis upon nonspectacular and homely illustrations. Still another reason lies back of the slighting not only of outstanding inventions like steamboats and cotton gins but of technological innovations generally. Because man-made objects have an extramental existence, it is deceptively easy to formulate a theory of innovation that will purport to describe their conception. It is much easier to explain them as things than as ideas. At the same time, treating them exclusively as things defined by the possession of material properties can produce nothing but a special and ancillary theory of innovation that puts their conception in an artificial category distinct from that of new ideas without material representations. Even when things are treated as mental constructs it is easier to deal with them than with abstract ideas. The real challenge for a general theory of innovation lies in the realm of behavior, belief, and concept. If such a theory can be shown to hold in the sphere of the purely intangible, no less than with respect to the ideas of things, a significant advance will have been made beyond existing psychological studies of mechanical innovations. The emphasis upon nonmaterial creations in certain later chapters is to be viewed in this light. Social, behavioral, and ideological constructs are neither more nor less important than thing constructs; but they are more in need of precise and thoroughgoing analysis on the order of that which characterizes the scientific treatment of things.

Three of the other ethnic groups studied are Indian tribes located in the western part of the United States. They are known as the Yurok, the Tsimshian, and the Yakima. The Yurok live in the northwestern corner of California at the mouth of the Klamath River. Aboriginally they depended almost entirely upon fishing for their subsistence. Their social and political organizations were comparatively simple, but they were quite conscious of class distinctions based upon family connection and inherited wealth. The changes that have taken place in the material and nonmaterial aspects of their culture since their first contacts with the whites in the 1850's were investigated in 1938.

Two years later the Tsimshian were visited with the same goal in mind. These Indians formerly lived in villages scattered along the Skeena River in

British Columbia. Since their contacts with European traders in the 1830's many of them have lived on a reserve at Port Simpson near the river's mouth. They, too, were a fishing people without livestock or a knowledge of farming. Their social organization, however, was considerably more complex than was that of the Yurok. In further distinction with the Yurok, and with ourselves, they reckoned kinship and inheritance by matrilineal clan affiliation. Social stratification was pronounced and was signalized by numerous invidious privileges that were inherited in the female line.

The Yakima were investigated in 1942. The Indians who have been given this name are really a conglomeration of culturally related tribes that have occupied a large reservation in south central Washington since the end of the so-called Yakima wars in the late 1850's. They relied to a considerable extent upon fish for food, but they were also hunters and collectors of wild plant foods. Early in historic times they acquired the horse and a good bit of the culture that developed around the use of this animal among the Indians of the Western great plains. They were loosely organized politically and were without clans or inherited class differentiations. On the whole their way of life was less involved and less imaginative than was that of either the Yurok or the Tsimshian. By that comparison it was lacking in exotic emphases and dominant orientations.

All these Indian groups have been greatly affected by the pressures of our civilization. The changes in their customs that have been induced by alien influences have proceeded so far and so rapidly that at present very little that is distinctly native remains in their thought and behavior. This is not true of the fifth ethnic group, the Palauans, who are an island people living in the southwestern part of Micronesia. They were studied over a period of nine months in 1947–1948. Although they have had rather continuous contacts with Europeans and Asiatics since the eighteenth century, the Palauans have retained a good part of their aboriginal culture. They subsist, as their ancestors did at the time of their discovery by Europeans, by tropical farming and fishing. They are acquainted with Occidental technology and its artifacts, and also with some of the institutions of the Japanese and the Americans; but these foreign elements are as yet in the process of being tested and absorbed. Although their social, political, and religious institutions have been modified and reduced in their complexity, they are still exceedingly intricate and difficult for an outsider to understand. Palauan culture presents a basic pattern that is entirely unrelated historically to the Indian examples, and in addition it affords materials for the study of the effects of a succession of dissimilar alien contacts. Since the latter part of the last century the Palauans have had to adjust to the varying cultural models of first the Germans, then the Japanese, and now the Americans. Each of these foreign patterns has left its imprint upon native life.

The religious cult to which frequent reference will be made is known as the Indian Shaker cult. In origin, at least, it is not related to the sect of Believers in Christ's Second Appearing, also known as the Shakers, which was established at New Lebanon, New York, in 1774 by its founder, Ann Lee. The Indian Shaker religion is one of the numerous messianic cults that have emerged among native peoples whose life patterns have disintegrated under the pressures of advancing Western civilization and who find some measure of compensation and security in the promises of the prophets who are likely to arise among them during such periods of crisis. John Slocum, the founder of the Indian Shaker religion, was such a prophet, the unwitting vehicle of the despair, the fears, and the hopes of the detribalized and partially Christianized communities of Indians who were scattered around the southern shores of Puget Sound, in Washington, toward the end of the last century. According to his followers, he died, probably in November of 1881, went to heaven, and then returned to life with a message of peace and salvation for the Indian people. Individual accounts of these events naturally vary. The one which follows is a summary of a statement obtained in 1943 from Mrs. Annie James, Slocum's wife's younger sister, who was an eyewitness to his "resurrection."

Mrs. James, who was between eight and ten years of age at the time, understood that the ostensible cause of Slocum's death was a broken neck resulting from a logging accident, but according to rumor it was actually due to the machinations of an Indian medicine man or shaman. Slocum had been "dead" for several hours and his body was lying on view during a wake when the assembled mourners were horrified to see him move. He at first stirred gently under his shroud, then began to push the sheet away from his face. He sat up, rubbing the back of his neck and moving his head from side to side. Then he began to speak. He asked his wife, Mary, for a clean sheet, and for some water with which to wash himself. He wrapped the clean sheet around him and told Mary to get rid of his clothes and the bedding on which he had been lying—the things associated with his "death." After that he addressed everyone in the room, asking them to shake hands with him. He asked them to kneel while he prayed. Then he began to preach to them. He said that he had a message from God; that he had been "up above" but had been stopped at a "gate" and told that he must come back to earth. He was told that he must explain to the people that gambling, drinking, and Indian doctoring were bad; that they must learn to pray before eating or going to bed and after getting up each morning; that they must cross themselves on all these occasions; that they must confess their sins; and that they must go to church on Thursdays and Sundays. He added that he was to teach the Indian people more about these things and that he would need a church. They were therefore to build one for him by the next Sunday.

Slocum gained a small following and preached in the church that had been constructed for him. Before long, however, his followers began to lose interest, and he seems to have lacked faith himself. He grew lax in avoiding the very temptations against which he had cautioned his listeners. Within a year he had fallen into his old habits of drinking and gambling. Then he became ill, and eventually his condition was so serious that he was expected to die. Slocum's father insisted upon calling upon a medicine man for help, but Mary Slocum refused to permit this. Apparently she remained steadfast in her belief in her husband's divine inspiration. His father nevertheless forced the issue and sent for a shaman despite Mary's vigorous protests. This contest between Slocum's father and his wife emerged, in part, out of a long and complicated background of mutual hostility, which need not be detailed here. Suffice it to say that Mary was unnerved by the crisis. When Slocum's unconscious body was taken into the presence of the shaman she left the house and began to collect her husband's logging implements, crying all the while. Her young sister, Annie, followed her. Mary showed unnatural strength in handling Slocum's heavy tackle; but as she started to wash her face in a nearby creek, she fainted. Annie screamed for help, and others came and carried Mary into the house. She was trembling and moaning, and when she regained consciousness her head and hands were twitching. In this state she began to demand that her husband be taken from the shaman who had started to work on him. Slocum's nose had started to bleed, and that caused even more consternation. Mary's wild appearance and frantic demands frightened everyone and they did as she asked. She requested that certain people, mostly relatives, station themselves around Slocum's prostrate body, holding lighted candles as they extended their arms over him. She gave her brother a hand bell that Slocum was accustomed to use in his church services and told him to ring it continuously. Praying and weeping, she began to twitch and jerk her head and limbs more violently.

No one knows how long this hysterical performance lasted, but when it was over it was observed that Slocum's nose had ceased to bleed. That was the beginning of "shaking"; for it was deduced that Mary's trembling ecstasy was a manifestation of divine purpose. It was instinct with supernatural healing power. It was the fulfillment of a promise given Slocum by God, a promise that if he and other Indians believed and were faithful they would receive a "medicine" that would be free and far superior to the false and evil incantations of the shaman. It was the answer to the desperate needs of many people, and before long it seemed that "everybody was shaking."

Thus shaking gave new life to Slocum's gospel. It was also instrumental in taking the leadership out of his hands and transferring it first to his wife and then to an aggressive nucleus of early converts led by a man known as Mud Bay Louis. Reports of the marvelous cures effected by shaking spread rapidly to adjacent Indian groups, and many individuals who came to the meetings near Shelton, Washington, were engulfed in the emotional atmosphere and carried away by the constant bell ringing, the singing, and the steady tramping of participants' feet that had come to characterize a healing service. They, too, fell to shaking in the manner set by Mary's original seizure.

Missionaries and reservation superintendents tried to suppress the movement, sometimes by the use of force; but this attempt only made martyrs of its protagonists and caused it to spread to more distant groups. In 1892 James Wickersham, an attorney in Olympia, came to the rescue of the cult's members. He helped them organize a church and supported them against their persecutors. In 1910 Milton Giles, another sympathizer living in Olympia, assisted in drawing a legal document that made the Shaker church a corporation in the state of Washington. From that time until about 1927 new congregations continued to be formed in Indian communities over most of the Pacific Northwest. Since 1930 missionizing progress has been slight, but at present the cult has an active membership extending from Duncan, British Columbia, almost to Eureka, California. In the course of its spread to different Indian groups, and also in its continuous development in communities near its point of origin, the Shaker religion has undergone numerous changes in ritual and belief. It is these changes that attract our attention.

In addition to the materials just reviewed some data reported upon by other investigators have been used. No attempt has been made, however, to cover the literature systematically or to correlate the conclusions or interpretations of different observers. In general, observed data rather than an author's interpretation of them have been cited. Even this has been done with some misgivings. At best it is risky to presume to interpret the observations of another person, and such interpreting should be done with reservations when it is grounded solely upon the implicit rather than the explicit statements of a published account. Citations from the reports of other collectors of primary data on cultural change are given with a full appreciation of this caution. If an observer and I disagree on our interpretations of his data, there can be no argument between us. More than likely he is right.

3

An innovation is here defined as any thought, behavior, or thing that is new because it is qualitatively different from existing forms. Strictly speaking, every innovation is an idea, or a constellation of ideas; but some innovations by their nature must remain mental organizations only, whereas others may be given overt and tangible expression. "Innovation" is therefore a comprehensive term covering all kinds of mental constructs, whether they can be given sensible representation or not. A novelty is understood in the same way; hence, "innovation" and "novelty" are hereafter used synonymously, the choice of one term over the other being dictated solely by lexical propriety. To a limited extent "invention" is also used as a synonym for "innovation." There would be no objection to a consistent equation of these two terms were it not that popular usage puts a more restricted meaning upon invention than is intended for the word innovation. For most people an invention is a thing, and the label seems inappropriate when applied to novel behavior patterns, theories, and social relations. While maintaining that there is no psychological distinction between the conception of a new object and a new act or theory, the present study retains the conventional implications of the term "invention." When it is used it means simply a technological innovation, a new thing. Custom has also governed the use of the term "discovery." It is fruitless to try to establish a rigorous and meaningful distinction between "discovery" and "invention," and nothing is to be gained by redefining the two words. On the contrary, communication is facilitated by conforming to ordinary usage. Beyond this purpose no significance should be attached to the differential employment of "invention" and "discovery." Both are names for innovations.

Some authors attempt to draw a distinction between "basic" and "derived" or "elaborating" inventions. While this approach may have some value, it is likely to be more misleading than enlightening. This is definitely so if it alleges or suggests that there are two kinds of inventions and that they result from different conditions and mental processes. It is impossible to characterize major and minor concepts in terms of the concepts themselves, yet this approach is likely to carry that implication. Actually when such a distinction is made it rests on other grounds, and the evaluation is to a large extent subjective. If "basic" means "important," any attempt to use the characteristics of inventions themselves as a measure of their relative importance turns out to be an estimate of the attitudes toward them, and this estimate varies by individual and with context. The same novelty will be regarded in one situation as trivial, whereas in another it will assume major significance. The devising of a whistle to call farm hands to dinner might strike most people as a rather unimportant novelty, although it would not if its purpose were to announce dinner to formally invited guests. A new type of wrench would undoubtedly be regarded as more important by a mechanic than by a lawyer; and new technological developments generally are more highly valued by Americans than by many other people.

There are objective grounds for saying that one invention is more basic than another if the criterion is the social effects that they have; but this cannot be adduced from the qualities which characterize them. If it could, we would be much wiser than we are about the future consequences of a given innovation. Also, if by basic and derived it is meant that some inventions provide a stimulus for more subsequent inventions than do others, there is an unquestioned basis for making a distinction. But, again, this has nothing to do with the properties of the inventions themselves; or at least none that can be demonstrated in advance of developments. If new ideas do have such inherent qualities they appear only in retrospect, which means that external factors play a necessary part in determining what they are. It is, in fact, evident that the time-place setting of an invention instills it with whatever possibilities it might have for future development.

All in all the distinction between basic and secondary inventions is an artificial one that contributes more confusion than clarity to an understanding of cultural change. All innovations have antecedents. All are therefore derived from others. Consequently, each one may be considered to be an elaboration, even though not all are basic to others. Certainly in point of creative processes, which is our main concern here, there is no difference between an invention such as the wheel that has subsequently entered into the creation of many others and one such as the hairpin that has figured in relatively few developments. The conception of something new is independent of the consequences of its conception.

This conclusion is related to the contention that new ideas are a much more common occurrence than they are usually supposed to be. Unless some arbitrary and external standard is set up, it is not possible to segregrate what we laud as inventions from other new ideas. Whether a novelty is striking or shocking or is a minor or a major departure from previous patterns has nothing to do with the mental processes which brought the idea of it into existence. The innovative act is the same; "radical" or "minor" are expressions of attitudes toward certain of its consequences. When this evaluative attitude is discounted, it will appear that innovations, whether major or minor, whether of private or public significance, and whether of ephemeral or lasting utility, are constantly being made. Everyone is an innovator, whether popular definitions allow him that recognition or not.

In defining an innovation as something that is qualitatively new, emphasis is placed upon reorganization rather than upon quantitative variation as the criterion of a novelty. Innovation does not result from the addition or subtraction of parts. It takes place only when there is a recombination of them. Psychologically this is a process of substitution, not one of addition or subtraction, although the product, the novelty, may be described as having a greater or lesser number of parts than some antecedent form. The essence of change, however, lies in the restructuring of the parts so that a new pattern results, a pattern the distinctness of which cannot be characterized merely in terms of an increase or decrease in the number of its component elements. This limitation clearly excludes from the category of innovations the many instances of change that consist solely of a multiplication or an extension of the dimensions of an existing thing. The manipulation of parts that can be treated as mathematical units produces an entirely different result from that which occurs when incommensurable variables are added, dropped, or interchanged.

While quantitative variations in themselves are not to be reckoned as innovations, it is true that they may be employed with innovative results. Such employment is, in fact, a very common occurrence. The requirement, again, is reorganization, which can be entirely independent of numerical variation. Thus, the man who increases the size or number of sails on a boat has created nothing qualitatively new if quantity alone, and not proportion or arrangement, is involved. If, however, an added sail is so placed that the configuration it forms with others is different, there has been an innovation. The same applies to the sail itself; changing its size is not innovative, whereas changing its shape by disproportionate extensions is. The addition of one molecule of water to another produces nothing qualitatively new, but the addition of one atom of oxygen to H_2O does. The removal of one of the four legs of a stool is not in itself innovative. It becomes so if the arrangement of the remaining three legs is altered so that a tripod support, for example, replaces the original four-post pattern. In all such instances of innovation, even though quantitative changes are necessarily involved, those changes are not the critical factor. The definitive characteristic of a novelty is its newness with respect to the interrelationships of its parts, not their number. Irrespective of whether or not quantitative changes are entailed, all innovations are qualitative departures from habitual patterns.

The materials for all innovations come from two major sources. There is, first of all, the cultural inventory that is available to the innovator. This includes all the ideas of things, techniques, behaviors, and ideas that he knows to pertain to human beings, whether they belong only to his own particular ethnic group or to others. Then there are the nonartificial elements of the innovator's experience, those that exist independent of human ingenuity or control. They include, most obviously, the objects and phenomena of nature. But they also include the natural man himself, his physical and mental attributes, as a thing or other part of the inescapably given universe of phenomena. It is important to bear this fact in mind, for innovators do treat human beings as they do other objects in nature. They invent by drawing upon the physical properties of man as they do by using the physical properties of iron and heat. Furthermore, they manipulate the psychical and psychosomatic attributes of themselves as they do the immaterial aspects of the rest of their experience. They take, as their material, ideas and the ideas of ideas. They treat persons not only as objects but as volitional, feeling, vacillating elements. The manipulation of these intangibles is indeed the height of innovative ingenuity.

4

It is possible to discuss cultural change in terms of the addition, elimination, substitution, or hybridization of traits and complexes. As a general characterization of what takes place, this is well enough; but it is only a statement of results, not a definition of process. It is descriptive, not explanatory. It states that such and such element is an addition, but it does not explain how or why that element came to be such. Such a procedure can, therefore, rarely offer grounds for anything more than ex post facto summaries, and this leaves much to be desired if the aim is to establish generalizations regarding cultural change. What is needed are answers to the questions of why, which, when, and how—under what conditions and within what limits are certain traits and not others added, or subtracted, or fused with others. It is difficult to escape the conclusion that this is a sociopsychological problem.

There has been much discussion of the subject of a science of culture. Among the many students who have attacked the problem of establishing an approach to the subject, a sharp division of opinion has manifested itself. Most anthropologists have taken the position that cultural data are *sui generis* and that, if any hope exists for the foundation of a science of custom, it must operate with its own materials and solely within the framework of concepts developed to deal with their interrelationships. To the other school of thought belong those who see small prospects of success in this approach to a social science and insist upon describing its materials in terms of another level of discourse, either the psychological or physiological. For them, the only adequate and realistic explanation of human behavior is to be found in the functions of the human mind.

The two points of view are not as incompatible as they at first seem to be. There is no doubt that the study of custom constitutes a special discipline, and that nothing is to be gained and much lost by attempting to "reduce" its data to mental, physical, or chemical reactions as such. At the same time it is pertinent to ask of those who propose to operate on a detached level of custom just what they understand by cultural facts. All will agree, presumably, that cultural facts are intangibles. They are not to be equated with objects, even though they sometimes give rise to them. They are and must be ideas. In no other way can there be continuity in a cultural tradition, for chairs, tables, and governmental forms neither beget nor cause their like. Nor can one conceive of a system of relationships between things, acts, and forms, *as such,* that differs from the science of physics, chemistry, and related disciplines. It is, therefore, difficult to understand what the materials of the cultural scientist might be unless they are composed of the immaterial representations of these objects and behaviors. It must also be true that the only possible locus for the existence of the representations is in the mind. Furthermore, the only system of interrelations that can develop among these mental modes of things are those that take shape in accordance with the potentialities of mental action. In other words, ideas interact with ideas according to psychological laws and not some other. In the last analysis, then, it is incumbent upon the cultural scientist to work with ideas.

This does not mean, however, that we are thrown back on the study of laboratory psychology, however much this may be of assistance in some instances. As it is generally practiced, psychology is the investigation of individual or group variation within a range of norms that have been established in large measure by a common cultural inheritance. In other words, psychology typically, traditionally, and often unwittingly, discounts the cultural constant in a definition of its problems. The anthropologist, on the other hand, begins with the fact of cultural variability; and his problems develop around the permutations of that factor with others. He must also deal with individual human mental reactions if he is to deal with anything real. But his primary concern is with the socialized aspect of ideas instead of with the idiosyncratic. The idea-in-common is the proper area for his exploration, for this is culture. About such shared ideas it is appropriate for him to ask all the questions with which he as an anthropologist is familiar: when, where, and how do they come into being, how are they transmitted, how do they affect one another, why do they differ from one locality to another, how are they related to individual and group biology, and so on to indefinite length. In all this inquiry the questions and the problems remain unchanged, but we have localized our search for the answers to them and have come to grips with the real motive force that makes culture the dynamic phenomenon that it is. Any other approach makes it a sterile, static, and mystical entity, unsuitable for scientific investigation.

Cultural explanations of human behavior can be given, but they always imply or necessitate psychological assumptions. They presuppose certain attitudes or other mental connections that are the real explanatory elements in the observed relationships between behavioral patterns. One institution may be said to explain another only by granting the existence of such psychological sets in the thinking of those whose culture contains the institutions. Observations may disclose that in societies where it is the custom for a man to marry the widow of his deceased older brother it is also commonly the custom for him to be allowed considerable familiarity with her while her husband lives, and it may be inferred that the first custom explains the second. It can do so, however, only if a certain psychological postulate is granted; namely, that in the thinking of those who practice both customs probable future marriage with a particular person is warrant for a moderate degree of sexual license preliminary to the event. If this connection or one comparable with it does not exist in the minds of those who adhere to the two customs, there is no connection between them at all, even if there is a positive statistical correlation between their occurrences. The same holds for correlations and alleged connections between any other institutions. The linkages between them—if there are any—are psychological; and if they exist, they must reside in the individual minds of participants, irrespective of the inferences and deductions of an outsider.

Those who maintain that one institution can be explained solely in terms of another can do so only by committing the observer's error of projecting constructions upon the material which they are intent upon describing. This fallacy takes several forms. In one the observer theorizes and organizes his data in accordance with the norms in which he has been trained and which he has unwittingly come to regard as natural, inescapable, and real. Accordingly, logical constructs and familiar abstractions take the place of empirical referents in explanations of other peoples' behavior. One observer reports, for example, that among certain African tribes women have been much more receptive to Christianity than have men. In explanation we are told that women have traditionally played a prominent part in native "religion," so it is to be expected that they would occupy leading roles in the "corresponding sphere" in the introduced European culture. By this reasoning African ancestor veneration and related practices are equated with Christianity under the rubric of "religion" to explain the readiness with which the women, as contrasted with the men, have accepted Christian teachings. Yet it is certain that the natives themselves have not equated the two systems of belief, as missionary experience and other evidence in abundance go to show.

Reification is another aspect of the observer's error whereby there is a confusion of the properties of things with the properties of ideas about them. It lies in supposing that projected abstractions behave like things—but like very special things because the characteristics of their relationships and interactions conform neither to psychological principles nor to the physical and chemical laws of things. In this way, concepts of the observer are alleged to have relationships that are proper only to things. In explanation of certain correlations it is said, for example, that one institution "supports" or "clashes" with another and therefore may or may not coexist with it. Thus, "agriculture," an abstraction, conflicts with "pastoral nomadism," another abstraction. Or "communal ownership" is inimical to "private ownership"— two logical constructs no matter how clearly they are defined. Or it is maintained that ideas do not "fit" each other or a system; hence, human sacrifice or idolatry is "incompatible" with Christianity. Clearly ideas cannot exert physical pressures upon each other as can two stones, or fit together like jigsaw pieces; and even less certainly so when they are edited and imposed upon an observational field from the projection room of an external observer's mind. Nor is this censure to be escaped by defending these explanatory terms as mere figures of speech. The real error lies in treating ideas as things.

This same fallacy leads to an unconscious substantiation of analogies so that one set of data insensibly and improperly come to assume the characteristics of some parallel that was introduced to elucidate them. Before the interpreter or his readers are aware of it, the relations which exist between one set of data are accepted as valid for another. Thus, culture, an abstraction, is made to grow, decay, and die like an organism. Or it exerts pressures and compulsions on the individual like a thing: it has mass and inertia and moves along like a stream, irrespective of the individual and quite independent of his will or understanding. Parts of it may even grow fatigued or exhaust their inherent possibilities for growth and cease to develop. It is not to the point to reiterate that these expressions are just pedagogical devices and that they propose nothing but analogies—when they are actually used as explanations, and as the only explanations, of certain cultural facts. It is misleading to insist that they are only verbal exigencies and yet to infer, deduce, and construct theories upon them as if they were real. It undermines confidence to be told that there really is no supraindividual current of culture and at the same time to be told that we all are awash in one. It would help to be told that this stream is an anthropologist's abstraction and that we are not influenced at all by it but by our own individual motives and ideas.

So insidious and specious is this error of projection that it has been used in all innocence to vindicate itself. In fact, anthropologists have characteristically resorted to its false assurances to assert their occupational independence from the psychologists. This declaration has as its keynote the proposition that knowing all that it is possible to know about individual psychology will not tell us anything about the nature or functioning of culture. Thus, in many so-called primitive societies it is the custom for a man to avoid his mother-in-law's person and to have no direct social relations with her. If, the argument runs, this avoidance pattern were due to psychological necessity and if, as we believe, all human beings are equipped with the same, or nearly the same, mental apparatus, then the mother-in-law taboo should be found among all societies of mankind. When so stated and accepted, this reasoning is unassailable; but in reality it misrepresents the issue. The real question is not why married men in some societies fail to avoid their wife's mother but why some do not have mothers-in-law. The issue is not whether all human beings avoid the same social object but whether in all societies there are the same social objects, such object, in this case, being a mother-in-law. The crux of the problem, then, is not a psychological reaction but a definition of social entities. In short, a wife's mother is an entirely different social construct in one society than in some others, and we should therefore not expect attitudes, whatever they may be, to coincide. Properly stated, the mother-in-law taboo has universal validity; namely, that individuals everywhere treat certain other individuals in specified ways, including avoidance, if and when these other persons, wives' mothers, are psychological and not mere structural equivalents. Again, the ethnologist's error lies in imposing his own equation upon elements in a kinship nexus, an equation which is alien to the thinking of the human subjects whose behavior he strives to interpret. By thus obviously eliminating the thought processes of the subjects and being unaware of the substitution of his own for them, he is able to deny the necessity for psychological interpretations of custom.

It should be evident that the anthropologist need not abandon his field of culture to the clinician, or even "reduce" his cultural data to a psychological level. In truth, demonstrable cultural facts are never anything else but ideas. We can appreciate this if we keep in mind the fact that the anthropologist is really talking about the idea of a chair instead of a four-legged object of wood when he speaks of it as an element of culture. In dealing with culture we are inevitably dealing with multi-individual ideas, that is, with ideas shared by more than one person. But this sharing does not take the ideas into a new plane. It does not make them supraindividual with an autonomy of their own. They are no different from any other ideas. They have the same place of residence, and they are subject to the same principles of thinking as idiosyncratic ideas. They do not act with forces and features of their own, and assuredly they do not behave like wind or stone.

The argument for a sociopsychological view of culture applies with special force to the problem of change. No matter how this problem is viewed, it takes on an ultimate mental reference. It is, for instance, often said that an invention is the expression of a need. This statement can have no meaning when it is applied to the abstraction called culture, for a culture never needed anything. To maintain otherwise is to take an ethnocentric standpoint and evaluate the observed objective facts in accordance with some stated or unannounced norm. This assertion would hold even if it were a question of whether the "need" were vital to the existence of the culture of a particular people and the failure to respond to it appropriately would mean the extinction of the group. A need is by no means identical with an absence. A need is a psychological experience, and it only clouds our view to project this feeling upon a system of things. Even "a people" is incapable of this experience, for the concept of "a people" is again an abstraction. Unless we are to accept the group-mind concept, there is no locus to which we can refer the existence of a need in this sense.

Institutional explanations of change, like institutional explanations of correlations, must assume a psychological foundation in the motivations of the people who initiate and support the changes. Thus, it has been reported that the incidence of theft has increased in certain Melanesian communities since prohibitions upon sorcery have been made effective by European administrators. There is no reason to doubt the development of this inverse relation between the two practices; and it may be taken as an adequate explanation of the change that has taken place—unless we contend that it is the practices rather than the native thinking fundamental to them that are responsible for the observed facts. Indeed, the formula "sorcery reduction equals theft increase" has meaning only in terms of certain psychological certainties or postulates relative to native thinking. At a minimum it must be assumed that the official ban upon sorcery has lessened the fear of supernatural venge- ance for theft, and that this fear of supernatural punishment was more effec- tive in constraining thievery than are the legal sanctions instituted by the administering secular authority. Unless some such native reasoning is ad- mitted, by implication or otherwise, sorcery is unrelated to theft, even if they can be shown to co-vary in a single community. As we know, "figures can prove anything," and the reason, as far as human behavior is concerned, is that they treat with consequences and not with the mental linkages between them.

With reference to the mechanics of invention the same conclusion must hold. Every innovation is a combination of ideas. The only bonds between its parts in a cultural setting are mental connections; they are instituted with the first individual mind to envisage them, and they dissolve with the last individual mind to retain a recollection of them. The mental content is socially defined; its substance is, in major part, dictated by tradition. But the manner of treating this content, of grasping it, altering it, and reordering it, is inevitably dictated by the potentialities and the liabilities of the machine which does the manipulating; namely, the individual mind.

The constant reference to ideas as the mediating and essential element in it should not be taken to mean that innovation is always a deliberate and a closely reasoned process. It definitely is not, as a large part of subsequent chapters will illustrate. Thousands of innovations are unpremeditated, and innumerable others are both unplanned and unwanted. Many appear upon impulse, and multitudes go unnoticed by either their creators or anyone else. All this makes them no less individual and no less ordained by psychological necessities, however little we may know of these complexities.

Innovation, then, must be subject to the rules of thinking and feeling, and any theory of invention must take this fact into account. In fact, such a theory should be a formulation of the rules of thinking as they pertain to the origins of new combinations of thought. This is at once a psychical and a cultural phenomenon, because the content of a thought predisposes the part it will play with respect to others. Its custom-determined substance will determine just which one of the possible mental reaction patterns it will pro- voke. Understood in this way, there can be no legitimate distinction between the psychological and the cultural approaches to the problem of cultural change.

Part One: The Setting

CHAPTER I

THE PROTAGONISTS

Everyman. It usually happens that those who concern themselves with innovation begin with, or come to accept, one of two antithetical propositions relative to human inventiveness. It does not matter whether their point of view is founded upon general impressions or careful study; in either case they find themselves impelled to believe that human beings are fundamentally creative, or that they are not. Almost always they are prepared to argue for or against the statement that man is by nature a mentally lazy and complacent creature who has to be shocked or forced into the conception and the acceptance of a new idea.

Those who take the affirmative in this argument have been impressed with the creeping pace of cultural change, with the infrequent appearance of "basic" inventions, and with the vigorous and violent resistance that typically greets departures from tradition. They point to the slow and painful accumulation of new ideas over the millennia spanned by human history, and to the inclination that men have for imitating others instead of formulating and adopting novel and more effective ways to meet their own special needs. Their opponents assert that these evaluations magnify unflattering human characteristics and ignore the multitude of unsung, unrecorded, and abandoned ideas that have appeared in all ages and conditions of society. They protest the evaluative nature of the concept of a "basic" invention. They stress the unlimited diversity which characterizes cultural developments within broad areas of similarity and adduce illustrations of the wide range of responses to environmental challenges made by different ethnic groups. They counter the charge of "slavish imitation" by calling attention to the universal and persistent phenomenon of individual variation within the latitudes of any group norm. They admit that new ideas are usually resisted but point out that in spite of this deterrent they continue to occur.

Division of opinion upon this question naturally produces contrary interpretations of the same facts. To those who maintain that new ideas are rare, inventors are in some measure always geniuses. They are exceptional individuals with uncommon intellectual capacities and strong motivations. They are the creators of the "significant" departures. Their "basic" innovations

17

usually initiate a series of new developments that have had to await a foundation. These sequels are merely "elaborations" and "improvements" made
by lesser men—skillful and enterprising, perhaps, but without the vision of
the genius. The advocates of inventiveness look upon these distinctions as
subjective estimates of men and their ideas. They can discover, they assert,
no objective means to distinguish a "basic" invention from any other, none
for measuring degrees of novelty among new ideas as far as the ideas themselves are concerned. Radicalism to them is a measure of the reaction to a
new idea, not of the degree of its intellectual saltation.

Students of the history of cultural growth have been forced to answer the
question of human inventiveness in their efforts to interpret the meaning of
multiple occurrences of the same phenomenon in different ethnic groups.
When an institution or an artifact is found distributed among several groups
it is possible to maintain either that the duplication has been due to its independent development in each one or several of the groups, or that the idea
of it has been spread by, or diffused from, its originators in one locality to
their offshoots or their imitators in other areas. There have been extremists
on both sides of this argument, those who have attempted to find a common
origin for every occurrence of an institution, and those who have seen them
as repeated manifestations of the psychic qualities common to all men. The
latter view was implicit in the approach of the evolutionary school of ethnologists who at the end of the last century maintained that "the like work-
ings of men's minds under like conditions" produce cultural parallels as
often as the conditions are repeated. The opposite extreme is embodied in
diffusionistic schemes that have been formulated in Germany and England.
The proponents of the *kulturhistorische* and the heliolithic theories of cultural growth adhere to the doctrine of human uninventiveness as an essential adjunct to their explanation of cultural parallels. To them, things and
institutions that are the same have a single origin simply because they could
not have been invented more than once. American ethnologists have adopted
positions in between these extremes, declaring that each instance of a parallel
must be decided alone and upon evidence apart from the question of inventiveness. Nevertheless, in practice most of these students also evince a predisposition to accept one point of view or the other in the weighing of the
evidence.

It must be evident that the issue of inventiveness hangs upon the definition of it. If the devising of a log raft is an invention, there have certainly
been more inventors than if the term is limited to things like bicycles and
bathtubs. If inventiveness be granted to the man who conceives of a lawn-
mower but denied the individual who first thinks of connecting a gasoline
motor with it, we should not only have fewer geniuses to consider but would
be forced in honesty and in confusion to recast our patent regulations. If we
are disposed to withhold the label unless a new idea becomes incorporated

in a culture, we shall be talking about something else than human originality, something more restricted and often less novel. If we were to leave the definition to popular consensus, we should be dealing with a protean concept which itself varies by era and by society.

Definitions are not as important as the facts they presume to classify. Anyone is free to make his own and to go on, alone or with support, from there. They are instruments, not ends, and their sole value lies in the consequences that flow from the insights they permit. Most definitions of invention block rather than open the way to an understanding of cultural change because they place the emphasis, not upon change itself, but upon estimates of its significance. They rate individual variation in terms of its degree, in terms of attitudes toward it, or in terms of its cultural consequences. Now, all these things are important and worthy of serious attention, but they tell us nothing about the sources or characteristics of ideological or behavioral variation. A vast amount of such variation is ignored because it does not fall within the arbitrarily established range of novelty. It is passed over if it does not elicit comment, or if it is not repeated or imitated, or if it otherwise is without lasting effects. The problem of change is thus shunted into the problem of measuring it.

If our concern is with the origins of differential behavior and its characteristics, then it is advisable to take all of it into account without prejudgment of its cultural worth. Once this is done, it becomes evident that nothing is more common or certain than individual variability in concept and reaction. Such differentiation, moreover, is the only source of those aberrations that are chosen because of their social significance to merit the label of innovation. But giving them this name does not make them different from those variations which pass without a trace. Their fate is something apart from their origins, even though the latter might be provoked by ideas concerning the former. Change as such is a universal phenomenon. Human beings have an infinite capacity for responding divergently—just how divergently will concern us from now on. But in this ultimate sense of being deviant every individual is an innovator many times over.

Every individual is basically innovative for two reasons. No two stimuli to which he reacts are ever identical. They may be more or less alike, and it may require an expert analysis to detect the differences between them; but the variables which affect their presence and their organization inevitably make them distinct in some way. When an individual steps across the traditionally accepted boundaries of sameness and treats two different things as the same, he is displaying originality; and inevitably there are degrees of this as there are degrees of difference between the stimuli prompting him. The second reason for diversified reactions is that no one ever entirely or minutely duplicates his responses to what he regards as the same stimulus. Inevitably an organism is altered by its own responses; it is not the same after responding as it was before. This is so even when the reactions follow upon each other immediately; a person does not react to a second loud noise or drink of water as he did to the first. Changes in his reactions are even more evident when the passage of a long interval of time brings about physiological, emotional, and intellectual transformations in an individual. And responding differently to the same stimulus is also counted as original when it overrides the cultural dictates which make prescribed allowances for it. This dynamic situation is pregnant with novelty; and it is continually bearing strange fruit, as anyone may observe by close attention to his own behavior and that of his associates.

While it is true that novel reactions are routine phenomena in the experience of every man, it is at the same time undoubtedly true that individuals differ in their propensities and abilities to veer across the normal boundaries of acceptable deviation. It is a commonplace that some people are more inventive than others. Individuals differ in the frequency with which they depart from the norms of behavior, in the character of their preferences for doing so, and in the uniqueness of their divergent ideas. The characteristics of their immediate cultural setting have a great deal to do with this. As will be pointed out in the next chapter, opportunity differentials that are compounded of time and place factors in experience provide a partial explanation of individual variability in innovative potential. Equally important, however, are those individual peculiarities that are less directly and less certainly dependent upon the cultural background for their organizations. It is unnecessary to raise here the moot question concerning the extent to which these idiosyncrasies are biologically determined. It is sufficient to recognize that human beings, beyond the age of infancy at least, exhibit differences in what we call character and personality, and that these differences predispose some of them to a hesitant and retractile attitude toward experimentation with the new, while others are much more adventurous and intrepid. In short, some people, for whatever reason, are temperamentally more conservative than others. Some are more likely than others to think of something that will generally be regarded as new.

As far as innovation is concerned, individual differences are evident in the ability to conceive of something beyond the limits of the conventional range of routine variation. This ability is dependent upon a number of factors to be considered later; among them are the capacity for meaningful observation, the ability to retain knowledge in memory, and, above all, the faculty to analyze the data of everyday experience and recombine them in new patterns. Innovative capacity is at times equally dependent upon attitudes toward existing modes. Individuals display different degrees of satisfaction with them, different degrees of tolerance of them under stress, and different degrees of detachment or emotional involvement with them, as well as different degrees of distrust of anything that might take their place.

In consequence of these factors individuals do react differently to the same situation, and some are certain to respond with greater originality than are others. Given any set of circumstances, some individuals will be constrained to the orbit of the customary more certainly and more securely than will others. Individual variability in this respect is unquestioned. At the same time, it is only a special aspect of the more general and universal phenomenon of idiosyncratic deviation. Within conventional limits individual deviation is inevitable; for excursions beyond those limits special conditions are necessary.

Primitives. Most Europeans and Americans, priding themselves upon the complexity of their civilization, are predisposed to belittle the intellectual accomplishments of vast numbers of people in other parts of the world. Impressed, and rightly so, by the enormous difference between their cultural inventories and those of the so-called primitive peoples, they are prompted to explain the disparity on biological grounds. Some have maintained that the mental equipment of the primitive is near the animal level. In their view the savage's perceptive powers are keener than those of civilized man, but his ability to remember the past, to imagine the absent, to envisage future possibilities, and to think abstractly are definitely limited. He is often pictured as being naïve and childlike in his emotional reactions, his lack of self-discipline, his simple tastes, and his gullibility. He is said to be impulsive and unreflective, lacking in the ability to free himself from the limitations of immediate and materialistic considerations.

Others who take a dim view of primitive innovative capacities stress his conformance to tribal standards and find in this an effective deterrent to original thinking. Those who emphasize this point depict the savage enchained by his own rules of behavior. He is a "slave to custom," bound by mental necessity to conform to group standards even though they are irrational and dangerous to his health and sanity. It is supposed that his unwavering adherence to custom is an actuality, and that this trait is a mark of the primitive mind. It is regarded as a mental disability that forestalls change.

Cultures differ, not only in the number of elements into which they can be divided, but also in their qualitative characteristics. Some people believe that this variation exists because primitives think in ways that are not only simpler than those of the European but also distinctly different. It is affirmed that primitives do not reason or that, if they do, their minds are not governed by rules of consistency or logic. Stress is laid upon their irrational behavior, their inability to see distinctions that are obvious to the civilized man, and their insistence upon dichotomies which do not exist in more sophisticated philosophies. Lévy-Bruhl holds that the primitive mind operates upon a plan that is peculiar to it. It is "prelogical." The native makes no distinction between himself and other objects in nature. All things are imbued with a mystical essence which is their only real and significant property. Speaking of the primitive man's remarkable knowledge of nature, Lévy-Bruhl writes,[1]

Yet the primitive, with all this somewhat exact knowledge that he possesses and utilizes, scarcely troubles about extending and investigating it. He is content with transmitting it as he has himself received it. While not failing to realize its practical value, he does not appraise it as we should do. The objective characteristics which permit of our differentiating beings very like each other, are of slight importance to him unless they bear a mystic significance. He makes use of the knowledge, often a very exact one, that he possesses, but only exceptionally is he interested in it, for it plays an altogether subordinate part in his actual doings. It is especially upon the power or powers, the mysterious, invisible, and every-where present forces, that the success or failure of his hunting, fishing, agriculture, and in fact, of all the enterprises in which he may engage, depends. These it is that he must endeavour to subjugate, appease, and incline to his cause.

There are very few ethnologists who can agree with Lévy-Bruhl, or with others who find differences between the mentalities of primitives and modern men. No objective evidence exists to support the view; and there is much to demonstrate that, if differences do exist, they must be minute, so inconsiderable that they cannot explain the observable differences in cultural inventories, or the great variety of attitudes toward change found in different times and places among the same ethnic group. Conclusions to the contrary have been due to superficial observations, ethnocentrism, and philosophical speculation.

It soon becomes apparent to one who takes a dispassionate and unbiased view of the subject that modern man is as irrational and prelogical as any known primitive; that primitives are to be found in varying proportions in all contemporary societies, civilized or otherwise; and that the thralldom of custom is nowhere more apparent than in the stultification of individualism in the more sophisticated circles of modern society. Unfortunately, when judgment is passed upon primitive man, extremes are selected for comparison. The bow and arrow is set off against the machine gun—which few Americans know how to use and still fewer know how to make. At the same time the fact that our great-grandfathers—who presumably had a mentality no more primitive than our own—lived without benefit of this and other features of modern civilization is overlooked. The essential truth is that degree of cultural elaboration is in no way directly correlated with ethnic differences in mental ability.

Despite the differences in complexity between primitive and sophisticated cultures, the impartial student of the subject will find abundant evidence of innovative ability in tribal societies. Modern Occidental civilization is out-

[1] Lucien Lévy-Bruhl, The "Soul" of the Primitive (trans. by Lilian A. Clare). New York: The Macmillan Company, 1928, p. 20. Permission of The Macmillan Company.

standing in its technological achievements; its inventors have far surpassed the accomplishments of any other people at any time. Yet even in this aspect of culture, which is only one of many, primitives have not been wanting in ingenuity. In fact, many of their material inventions must be rated as admirable by any standards, and the rest reveal no lack of imagination and abstract thinking.

Ethnographic literature contains a wealth of illustrations in support of this contention. The food-getting devices of such lowly primitives as the Bushmen of Africa, the Australian aborigines, and the Semang of the Malay Peninsula testify to a fact that is virtually a truism; namely, that men living in a hand-to-hand struggle with nature must be clever to survive. Their game traps and stalking techniques, their use of fish poisons, boomerangs, and blowguns and their extraction of noxious and poisonous elements from wild plant foods are achievements of real insight and skill.

The Eskimos were a Stone, or Bone, Age people when first discovered by Europeans; and they were and still are supremely inventive by our own standards. Lacking wood and stone in many places, they made extensive use of bone and ivory for their utensils. They made a variety of specialized tools and implements that not only were admirably suited to their purposes but were artistically shaped and decorated—objects such as bow drills, shoe cleats, snow goggles, needles, buoys, seal lures and detectors, sledge runners, blood stoppers, and skewers. They made excellent composite whale harpoons, bird arrows, bows, and fishhooks. Their snow houses are unique. The snow blocks of which they are composed are laid in a spiraled course so that the building achieves the structural stability of a masonry dome without the use of a keystone. Their skin boat, the kayak, challenges comparison with any craft that could be designed to answer the purposes that it serves. The same is true of their tough, warm, and well-tailored skin clothing. Their material culture is admirably adapted to their habitat, so much so that civilized man has frequently found that his solutions to arctic living are inferior to theirs.

Primitive man has not found the tropics as enervating as some theorists would have us believe. The native inhabitants of tropic latitudes wisely refrain from exhausting activities, but this is not the equivalent of existing in a state of complacent lethargy. They, no less than civilized man, have substituted cleverness for brawn; and, like the Eskimo, they have exploited their environment and adapted themselves to it in amazing ways. The natives who lived in the Amazon basin and adjacent areas in South America were in many respects among the most backward of the American Indians. Yet at the time of their discovery by Europeans they were unique in their possession of some bits of useful knowledge, and they shared with some other groups still more which it is believed they discovered for themselves. Their staple food was manioc, the plant from which we get tapioca. They raised two varieties, one of which was poisonous. In order to make the poisonous root edible they had perfected several means of ridding it of the prussic acid that it contains. One technique made use of an extensible tubular squeezer of basketwork which, when it was stretched, compressed the pulp in it. Other extraction processes included fermentation and roasting. They had learned to make use of several poisons for their blowgun darts, among them the deadly curare, the pakuru-neara, and the secretion from a certain frog. They were familiar with such narcotics as parica, caapi, and cohoba snuff; with medicinals like copaiba, carap oil, balsam of umiri, and guarana tea; and with useful resins like karamanni, carnauba, and caranna waxes. They used cayenne pepper not only as a condiment but as a siege weapon by burning the plant so that its fumes were wafted over the palisaded village of their enemies. They were the discoverers of the rubber of modern commerce as well as several other latexes with elastic properties. They made balls, rings, waterproof fabrics, and enema syringes of rubber. They also invented the hammock. They made use of signal drums, reinforced their pottery by an ingenious use of sponge spicules, and shrank enemy heads after the skull and other parts had been removed with a minimum of incisions.

As for abstract thought, the cosmological conceptions of the Maori of New Zealand were as metaphysical and as beautifully expressed as any of our own. As would be expected, not all the people understood them or even had the opportunity to do so. The esoteric cult of the god Io was confined to the nobility, and the god's priests were of the highest and most exclusive order. Io was conceived to be a supreme being with ineffable powers and attributes. He was without shape or residence. He did not interfere in the affairs of men and was not propitiated. His name could not be uttered except by his priests at specified times and places, and then only with some qualifier to denote one of his numerous attributes. He was the core of all gods, greater than all of them, the parent of heaven, earth, and men, and without parents himself. He was the source of all knowledge and thought and volition, unseen and knowable only as a radiant light, permanent, immutable, and omniscient.

An understanding of the profundity and subtlety of Maori thinking may be obtained from the following recital [2] which, it will appear, embodies a recondite evolutionary conception of creation. The beginnings, preceding the advent of human beings, are here conceived to have taken place in five stages or cosmic ages. The first, as related in the first stanza, comprises the birth of consciousness and desire. Next came the emergence of sensation, created by an articulation of consciousness and desire; then the genesis and evolution of matter; and finally, and less mystically, the establishment of the firmament, followed by the appearance of the earth in the form of the islands named in the closing lines of the account.

[2] Richard Taylor, *Te Ika A Maui; or New Zealand and Its Inhabitants.* London: W. MacIntosh, 1870, pp. 109–111.

From the conception the increase,
From the increase the swelling,
From the swelling the thought,
From the thought the remembrance
From the remembrance, the consciousness, the desire.

The word became fruitful;
It dwelt with the feeble glimmering;
It brought forth night:
The great night, the long night,
The lowest night, the loftiest night,
The thick night to be felt,
The night to be touched, the night unseen.
The night following on,
The night ending in death.

From the nothing the begetting,
From the nothing the increase,
From the nothing the abundance,
The power of increasing, the living breath;
It dwelt with the empty space,
It produced the atmosphere which is above us.

The atmosphere which floats above the earth,
The great firmament above us, the spread-out space
    dwelt with the early dawn,
Then the moon sprang forth;
The atmosphere above dwelt with the glowing sky.
Forthwith was produced the sun;
They were thrown up above as the chief eyes of heaven;
Then the heavens became light,
The early dawn, the early day,
The midday. The blaze of day from the sky.

The sky which floats above the earth,
Dwelt with Hawaiki,
And produced Taporapora,
Tauware nikau and Kukupara,
Wawauatea and Wiwhi te rangi ora.

This philosophical expression is not a unique specimen. Other Maori chants evidence the same concern with ultimate origins. The trait is, in fact, a well-established one all over Polynesia.[3] Nor is the ability to systematize abstract ideas confined to this primitive area. Several American Indians, among them the Bella Coola, are well known for their systematic concep-

[3] Paul Radin, *Primitive Man as Philosopher*. New York: Appleton-Century-Crofts, Inc., 1927, Chap. 16.

tions of the universe. Theirs are not as refined as are those of the Maori, but they betoken a speculative interest in imponderables.

This is not the place to document primitive inventions in detail. A few synoptic treatments of the subject are available that should dispel skepticism about the savage's ability to meet his material needs in efficient and original ways.[4] Apart from that, it is well to remember that the essentials, and many of the particulars, of our own culture were devised or discovered by peoples who, on other grounds at least, are labeled primitive. The domestication of plants and animals is ancient but not coextensive with human existence; which is to say that agriculture and animal husbandry are inventions made by men a few thousand years ago. All our basic plant foods and all our economically useful animals are old domesticates; contemporary man has added nothing to the list except hybrids. With metallurgy the situation is somewhat different, thanks to modern chemistry and physics. Still the use of free copper and gold goes back to 4000 B.C. in Egypt; and small groups of people around the Black Sea were smelting iron as early as 1400 B.C. The ceramic arts are older than agriculture and have been carried to a high degree of perfection both technically and artistically by many peoples in remote times and places. The textile arts are likewise old in origin and widespread. Primitive peoples have employed a remarkable variety of materials for weaving, including cotton, wool, silk, and hemp; and they have utilized most if not all of the modern techniques. The Incas of Peru produced embroideries, gauzes, voiles, and nets, the technical excellence and beauty of which have not been surpassed. Writing, though somewhat late by comparison with these other developments except metallurgy, still has a respectable antiquity and was developed in several societies which in the popular view are seldom reckoned as civilized: Egyptians, Sumerians, Chinese, Indus, Mayans, and Aztecs. Our calendar system derives from an early Egyptian form, and our week was evolved in the Near East perhaps a century before the birth of Christ. The Chinese were using rag paper by the end of the first century A.D. and gunpowder in warfare by the end of the thirteenth. The Egyptians made glass and erected heavy stone masonry by 3000 B.C. The arch, so essential to our architecture until the advent of steel frames, and the wheel, upon which so much of our mechanistic age depends, both appear in history at about the same time (3400 B.C.) in the remains of Sumerian cities in Mesopotamia. Aside from these basic ingredients of our culture there are hundreds of particular discoveries and inventions of primitives to which we have fallen heir. All our narcotics, alcoholic drinks, natural dyes, adhesives, and spices and many of our medicinal herbs are ancient and come from remote corners of the primitive world. Those who adhere to a distinction be-

[4] Otis Mason, *The Origins of Invention*. London: W. Scott, Ltd., 1895. See also "Primitive Travel and Transportation," *U.S. National Museum Annual Report for 1894,* Washington, D.C., 1896, pp. 237–593; and several other studies by Mason.

tween basic and improving inventions could make a good case for primitive man the inventor versus modern man the elaborator.

Black, White, Red, and Yellow. Closely related to the view that primitives have inferior innovative capacities is the notion that there are racial differences in this respect. The two ideas are not distinguishable in the thinking of those who assume that there is a correlation between an alleged degree of mental development and an alleged degree of cultural advance. Beginning with a comparative evaluation of cultures, it is reasoned that the differences noted are due to qualities that are a function of racial differentiation. In other words, it is said that there are average and limiting potentials characteristic of ethnic groups because of their ancestry. Under this interpretation, "primitive" means biologically unspecialized or underdeveloped, not necessarily historically prior. Hence the limited achievements of some contemporary races as well as those of ancestral groups are believed to be due to inborn mental disabilities.

This is an old, recurrent, and widely disseminated view. It is founded upon several presuppositions, and its acceptance as a demonstrated fact permits some far-reaching inferences. One of the assumptions upon which it rests is that cultural complexity can be taken as a measure of mental complexity, that what a people think about is an index of how well or how poorly they can think. This is at best a proposition of circumscribed validity. Setting aside the intricate question of the connection between mind content and the mental processes that deal with it, other involvements remain that render the thesis untenable in indiscriminate cross-cultural comparisons. When it is used to grade racial groups, auxiliary hypotheses are required that vitiate whatever validity the thesis might have in interindividual comparisons within the same cultural milieu. Within a single society some indication of individual mental capacities may be had if there is a constancy of intellectual environment, interest, and motivation. Ordinarily, these constants are lacking in cross-racial comparisons. Interests are highly variable among societies of mankind, just as they are among individuals in one society; and it cannot be reasoned that a selection of one interest and an ignorance of another is in itself a criterion of thinking ability. It is indefensible to conclude that the Fijians are incapable of inventing a gasoline engine because they have not done so, just as it is unreasonable to contend that an illiterate American is innately incapable of reading a book because he has never done so. What a people have done is not to be taken automatically as a measure of what they can do. Further inquiry must be made in order to settle this question.

Inferences concerning racial capacities that are based upon cultural comparisons entail the additional assumption that cultures can be objectively evaluated. It must be taken for granted that there is some criterion by which intellectual achievements can be measured if they are to be used as a test of innovative ability. This is a natural assumption, natural in the sense that most people in most societies tacitly make it. But the difficulty comes when it appears that the character of the yardstick varies from society to society. Ethnocentrism is a universal phenomenon, and most people believe that the value systems of their own group are axiomatic and unassailable. It is true that American culture is more complex than many others, in certain aspects at least. But it is not true that all mankind regards this as a proper measure of perfection. If the striving for greater elaboration and complexity were a universal human ideal, we should have some basis for judging the native abilities of racial groups to achieve it. Failing this constant, we are not justified in drawing any positive conclusions about superior and inferior innovative capacities. We are free to rate cultures according to this standard if we please, but we should be prepared to expect to be rated ourselves on different premises and with equal logic.

When George III of Great Britain sent an embassy to China to ask for trading privileges, the Emperor Chien Lung sent him the following disdainful reply: [5]

You, O King, live beyond the confines of many seas. Nevertheless, impelled by your humble desire to partake of the benefits of our civilization, you have dispatched a mission respectfully bearing your memorial. To show your devotion you have also sent offerings of your country's produce. I have perused your memorial. The earnest terms in which it is couched reveals a respectful humility on your part, which is highly praiseworthy. . . . Our Celestial Empire possesses all things in prolific abundance and lacks no product within its own borders. There is, therefore, no need to import the manufactures of outside barbarians in exchange for our own produce. But as the tea, silk, and porcelain, which the Celestial Empire produces, are absolute necessities to European nations and to yourselves, we have permitted, as a signal mark of favor, that foreign business houses [at Canton] be supplied, and your country thus participate in our beneficence. . . . As your Ambassador can see for himself, we possess all things. I set no value on objects strange or ingenious, and I have no use for your country's manufactures. . . . I do not forget the lonely remoteness of your island, cut off from the world by intervening wastes of sea, and I overlook your excusable ignorance of the usages of our Celestial Empire. I have consequently commanded my Minister to enlighten your Ambassador on the subject. . . . It behooves you, O King, to respect our wishes and to display even greater devotion and loyalty in the future, so that by perpetual submission to our throne, you may secure peace and prosperity for your country hereafter. Tremble and obey!

Cultures have qualitative as well as quantitative differences, and more than one yardstick may appropriately be applied to them to measure the mental capacities of their creators. Standards of evaluation are relative, and they are indeed unassailable unless we are prepared to maintain that all men

[5] A. L. Warnshuis, *The New York Times,* Feb. 28, 1926, Sec. 8, p. 15.

after all value the same thing to the same degree. In any event, it is not defensible to stigmatize a person or a group of people for failure to do something which he or they have lacked the opportunity to do or have regarded as not worth doing.

The concept of race is an equally deceptive variable in the incautious linkage of mental endowment with cultural achievement. It may be true that individuals inherit special talents and facilities as well as general abilities, but it is a long step from this view to the admission that the groups of mankind that we call races collectively exhibit differences in this respect. At the present time there is no general agreement upon a definition of "race," even among impartial scholars of the subject, much less among those who have partisan purposes in exploiting their private interpretations of it. The usual method of measuring and classifying populations on the basis of their external appearances is at best a sorting device that leaves many odds and ends of humanity without a niche in the scheme. The application of statistics to the measurements refines the procedure but does not make the material more amenable to the treatment. Above all, this morphological approach to racial classification can tell us very little about actual inheritance patterns, for it deals with phenotypes, not with genotypes, the essential data of inheritance. It deals with genetic symptoms rather than with genetic composition itself. Hair form, skin color, nose shape, and head proportions are epiphenomena which make inheritance patterns manifest, but they are not the patterns themselves. In consequence, a growing number of physical anthropologists are now insisting upon a more meaningful approach to the concept of race.[6] Perhaps in time we shall have one that is founded upon the principles of Mendelian inheritance. Then we may be in a position to assess the relative mental endowments of biologically related groups of humanity. Just now we have no warrant for doing so.

Volumes have been written to prove and disprove the contention that races are equally endowed mentally. In the end the fundamental question has remained unanswered, for the reasons given above and one other. Collective innate abilities cannot be measured unless the group measured is a real biological unit; neither is it possible to measure inborn qualities if they cannot be isolated from the acquired. So far no method or test has been devised that will measure only the innate capabilities of an individual. Constitution and behavior are always compounded of nature and nurture—if indeed there is any empirical distinction between the two components. A large number and variety of physiological and psychological tests have been given to individual representatives of different races. The results do not justify the conclusion that there are racial differences; neither do they permit

[6] M. F. Ashley Montagu, *An Introduction to Physical Anthropology*. Springfield, Ill.: Charles C Thomas, 1945, Chap. 5.

us to say unequivocally that there are not.[7] They do not tell us anything about inborn qualities, but they do highlight the difficulties of the problem. Their principal, and by no means insignificant, value lies in their refutation of the doctrinaire assertions of those who insist upon racial inequality without the support of experimental evidence. From this standpoint the tests are valuable precisely because they have utilized phenotypes as racial criteria, for these are what the uninstructed layman uses. Race to him means a given combination of skin color, eye color, stature, etc. To have shown that these conjunctions of attributes are insignificant from the standpoint of the mental abilities of an individual is a long step forward.

The conclusion to be drawn from the foregoing analysis of the doctrine of racial inequalities is that no ethnic group has yet been shown to have a monopoly upon originality because of its biological endowments. A direct approach to the question, by a comparative study of culture itself, leads to the same conclusion. Unfortunately the comparisons that are usually made present an unbalanced picture that is due to an unwitting or a deliberate bias in time perspective. The evaluations about which we hear most have been made by western Europeans and their colonial descendants. The date is the present, when the star of the Occident is in its ascendancy and its followers have made themselves the masters and arbiters of the lifeways of the people with whom they compare themselves. It might, of course, be argued on the Darwinian principle of the survival of the fittest that this ascendancy is proof of racial superiority, except that it is a relatively recent phenomenon that is not correlated with any demonstrable change in the biological composition of Europeans a generation prior to A.D. 1492. The truth is that a European mastery of large parts of the globe has been due more to the possession of gunpowder and iron—both non-European inventions—than to racial superiority. Comparisons dating from the period just before the destructive effects of Western civilization made themselves felt would be more justifiable. Our historical records contain many illustrations of the fact that Europe then was not much in advance of many other parts of the world that were conquered by its representatives.

When Cortez reached the Aztec city of Tenochtitlàn in 1519, he and his men were understandably astonished at the artistic, industrial, and governmental achievements of its builders. They found a Venicelike city, built upon an artificial island in Lake Texcoco, which in its material aspects was not inferior to a great many European cities of the time. It contained temples, pyramids, and palaces of stone, broad causeways, and aqueducts connecting it with the mainland. It was a wealthy mercantile center with trade relations ramifying over most of southern Mexico and beyond. It was the seat of a

---

[7] Otto Klineberg, *Race Differences*. New York: Harper & Brothers, 1935.

militaristic government which drew regular tribute from surrounding areas in the valley of Mexico and in varying degrees exercised hegemony over outlying regions in the present states of Veracruz, Guerrero, and Oaxaca. Its citizenry included farmers; skilled workers in wood, stone, gold, copper, obsidian, turquoise, and feathers; a wealthy and privileged merchant guild; a priesthood serving a multitude of gods according to a complex religious calendar; a trained professional soldiery for whom special inducements were offered; and a select group of judicial officials who administered a strict legal code. There were twenty schools within the city for the children of common people and others for the nobility. There priests gave moral, religious, and vocational instruction to children above the age of six, who lived under their strict discipline.

The crowds of people that assembled to witness Cortez's entry into Tenochtitlàn made a deep impression upon Bernal Díaz, the chronicler of the event, even as did the splendor of Montezuma's palace and his personal appointments. Díaz doubtless magnified the opulence of the scenes that he witnessed, but there is no question that he was amazed by the contrast between what he had expected and what he found. He relates that Montezuma's cooks had thirty different ways of preparing meats for his table and that "above 300 dishes were dressed, and for his guards, above a thousand." Montezuma's table was covered with white cloths; and servants presented him with water and napkins for his hands. He had numerous attendants and entertainers while at dinner. His palace comprised an armory, a treasury of gold and precious stones, and a zoological garden.[8]

His gardens, which were of great extent, were irrigated by canals of running water, and shaded with every variety of trees. In them were baths of cut stone, pavilions for feasting or retirement, and theaters for shows, and for the dancers and singers; all were kept in the most exact order, by a number of laborers constantly employed. There were market places where all kinds of vegetable products, domestic animals, textiles, gold ornaments, writing paper, and even slaves were traded. [In Atzcapotzalco] were the shops and manufacturies of all of their gold and silver smiths whose works in these metals, and in jewelry, when they were brought to Spain, surprised our ablest artists. Their painters we may also judge of by what we now see, for there are three Indians in Mexico, who are named Marcos de Aquino, Juan de la Cruz, and Crespillo, who, if they had lived with Apeles in ancient times, or were compared with Michael Angelo or Berruguete in modern times, would not be held inferior to them. . . . The women of the family of the great Montezuma also, of all ranks, were extremely ingenious in these works, and constantly employed; as was a certain description of females who lived together in the manner of nuns.

[8] Bernal Díaz del Castillo, *The True History of the Conquest of Mexico* (trans. by Maurice Keating). New York: Robert M. McBride & Company, 1927, pp. 172 and 175. Quoted by permission of Crown Publishers.

The Aztecs were not the sole creators of their civilization. No people ever is. They were the heirs of their remarkable predecessors in the same general area, the Mayans and the Toltecs; but the Aztecs added to their cultural heritage and gave it a distinctive cast. That their descendants are no longer the peers of the descendants of their conquerors is less a matter of race than it is of greed and inhumanity.

According to the generally accepted system of classification, the Aztecs, like the rest of the American Indians, belong to a subdivision of the Mongoloid race. The creative abilities of their distant relatives, the Chinese, can scarcely be questioned regardless of their strangeness for the Occidental mind. China as a political entity was already ancient when most of the European nations came into existence, and its cultural foundations were laid centuries before the birth of Christ. It was still an intellectually vigorous nation when Marco Polo served in the government of Kublai Khan and returned to Venice to tell his compatriots of the many wonders that he had seen.

Chinese talents have been directed toward the cultivation of the humanities rather than the sciences. Chinese scholars have been concerned with ethics, history, and literature; with the definition of interpersonal rights and duties; with poetry, drama, and painting; with scholasticism, writing, and books; with casuistry and social and moral philosophy. The Chinese early developed an extensive bureaucratic system which was backed by a civil-servant tradition that was based upon sheer academic learning. Their dynastic and other histories go back to the ninth century B.C. They invented printing, long before it was known in Europe, by using first block prints, then movable type of clay and metals. The oldest known printed book is in their language. They have long shown an interest in demographic problems and were the first nation to keep census records. Their records reveal that under the Han dynasty a century or two after the beginning of the Christian Era their kingdom contained about as many subjects as did western and central Europe at the time the New World was discovered. Despite their emphasis upon knowledge for its own sake, they made a remarkable number of purely utilitarian inventions and discoveries: silk, hemp, playing cards, paper money, coins, gunpowder, porcelain, writing paper, and cast iron—not to mention a great variety of cultivated food plants and medicinals. Their numbers, the strength of their traditions, the essential merit of their original ideas, and their ability to repulse or absorb invaders have carried them into the contemporary period as a culturally autonomous ethnic group.

While a knowledge of history may condition advocates of racial inequalities to make concessions in favor of the Chinese, there is little information outside ethnographic literature to support a case for the Negro. Most people either doubt or deny that there has ever been a Negro civilization worthy of the name. If by this it is meant that there has never been a Negro state ranking in power and influence with modern nations, or a native industrialized growth in Negro Africa comparable to our machine age, then there can be no argument. Of course, the same is true of many subgroups of the Caucasian race. On the other hand, if we are interested not only in ingenuity in developing political power and influence, but in inventiveness of any sort, the achievements of the African Negroes as a whole, and of particular groups, must be rated as considerable even by modern European standards. Perhaps their artistic talents need not be emphasized, for allowances are usually made for them. Most large museums now contain products of the industrial arts of native groups that give evidence of excellent craftsmanship as well as inspiration in conception. Work in leather, clay, iron, wood, textiles, bronze, ivory, and the precious metals, especially in western Africa, is ancient, local in origin, and skillfully executed. Other achievements, however, are not so well known. Few people, for example, realize that the inhabitants of the upper Volta and Niger Rivers possess an old written literature of considerable refinement. It is not a lay literature. It has been developed by Negro scholars. It reflects an interest in learning for its own sake and shows no lack of subtlety in thinking. In part, this literature is written in Arabic, the traditional medium of learned discourse in this region, because for many centuries the people there have had both direct and indirect contacts with Mohammedan centers to the north and east. In consequence, many Mohammedanized Negroes in the remote hinterland of French West Africa compose works on law, theology, and history, both in prose and verse, using elegant Arabic. In this same region there also exists a more truly indigenous literature written in alphabets of local invention. The best known of these systems of writing is the one that has been in use for a century or more among the Vai people who live on the frontiers of Liberia and Sierra Leone.

It is not generally appreciated that Africans have a flair for political organization. Kingdoms and empires embodying complex administrative and judicial systems of control have been rather typical of the whole continent except for its desert and deep forest areas. Often African kings have ruled over thousands of subjects through an administrative hierarchy that was scarcely less complex than many found at the present time elsewhere. The kingdoms of Uganda, Mossi, Dahomey, and Benin come to mind because of their recent significance for the Europeans. The tradition, however, is an old and well-established one. We know from Arabian sources that there have been a succession of kingdoms of considerable power and extent in the region of the French Sudan. The Ghana Empire was founded to the west of Timbuktu in the fourth century and persisted until the fourteenth. In the meantime others rose to challenge its hegemony, among them the Diara, the Soso, and the Songhoy. The most renowned was the Mandingo State with its capital at Kangaba on the upper Niger River. This state began its rise to prominence in the seventh century and still exists, headed by rulers of the same dynasty as in the beginning. The peak of its power came between 1300 and 1350, when it controlled most of what is now the French Sudan. Several of its kings made pilgrimages to Mecca, the first in 1050, to return with elements of Mohammedan learning. The Arab geographer Ibn Batuta, who visited the Mandingo capital in 1352–1353, found it at the apogee of its influence. According to Delafosse,[9]

He has left us a detailed and apparently scrupulous account of his travels in which he is pleased to testify to the fine administration of the State, its prosperity, the courtesy and the discipline of its officials and provincial governors, the excellent condition of public finance, the luxury and the rigorous and complicated ceremonial of the royal receptions, the respect accorded to the decisions of justice and to the authority of the sovereign. In reading his account, one has the impression that the Mandingo Empire was a real State, whose organization and civilization could be compared to those of the Mussulman kingdoms or indeed to the Christian kingdoms of the same epoch.

Tribes, Cities, and States. It is sobering to reflect that inventive preeminence is a fleeting possession of ethnic groups when the total span of human cultural development is viewed in retrospect. Physical anthropologists subdivide the contemporary Caucasian population of Europe and the Mediterranean border of Asia and Africa into at least three subraces, the Nordic, the Alpine, and the Mediterranean. Most of them would add still others, such as the Armenoid and the Dinaric, to account for physical types found in the Balkans and the adjacent Near East. To the layman all these people may be simply Caucasians, with perhaps some doubt about the Egyptians, the Hebrews, the Turks, and other non-European peoples; or he may choose to confuse race with language or nationality and find even more races in the area than does the anthropologist. Whatever view one takes, it should be evident from a study of the cultural development in this area that race has had nothing to do with cultural leadership. The rise and fall of nations has gone on irrespective of race, however defined. Political, social, and economic preeminence has passed from one group to another; and part and parcel of such leadership has been an efflorescence of innovation in one or another aspect of culture.

For fully 2,000 years, from 3500 to 1500 B.C., all Europe was a cultural wilderness by comparison with developments in Asia and North Africa, and for centuries thereafter its central and northern sections lagged far behind its southeastern Aegean border. During those twenty centuries, and perhaps for some seven more, the only people who could be called civilized lived in the valleys of the Nile, the Tigris-Euphrates, and the Indus Rivers and, from

---

[9] Maurice Delafosse, *The Negroes of Africa* (trans. by F. Fligelman). Washington, D.C.: Associated Publishers, 1931, pp. 66–67. Quoted by permission of Associated Publishers.

1500 B.C. on, in the Honan Province of China, where the late but fully developed Bronze Age Shang culture appeared. Beginning as early as 5000 B.C. in Egypt and Mesopotamia, these Afro-Asiatic culture centers evolved a sophisticated urbanized society that was not approximated, even in attenuated form, in central Europe until a century or two before the birth of Christ. The concentrations of population in these areas were supported by intensive agriculture and the use of domesticated animals. By 3000 B.C. there were large cities of mud brick, glazed brick, or stone masonry in the Fertile Crescent and in India. The Indus builders incorporated stairways and bathrooms in their dwellings, and their cities were provided with sewer systems. Bronze metallurgy and pottery making were highly developed skills in all these centers. Writing was likewise fully developed; and in Egypt and Babylonia libraries were assembled which now tell us much about the life, the laws, the commerce, and the literary interests of the day. Works of art in bronze, stone, clay, and semiprecious stones were of such quality that they are still valued for their artistry alone. In Mesopotamia and Egypt, at least, the city dwellers were diversified in occupation and social position. There were elaborate and powerful priesthoods and divine or divinely sanctioned kings. The priesthoods and the temples were maintained by taxation, or, as in Babylonia, by land-grant privileges which were converted into liquid wealth through rentals and loans at interest. The Babylonian priests developed astrology, discovered five of the planets, formulated the zodiac, and made predictions of eclipses. Organized commerce was especially active in Mesopotamia. There the interest in goods and trading, in property and finance, was so general that a refined and integrated system of weights and measures was required. Quantities, time, and space were divided into 12's and multiples thereof; and it is from this duodecimal system that the Western world has derived its concepts of feet, ounces, hours, and angular measurements. The Neo-Babylonians under Nebuchadnezzar also conceived the idea of zero, as the Hindus did a thousand years later.

All in all these Afro-Asiatic cultures, especially those of Mesopotamia, had a distinctly modern flavor. In many respects they were closer to contemporary European standards than a good part of the rest of the world is today. From 3000 to 1250 B.C. Crete also participated in the cultural expansion of the Near East. Her growth was related to that of Egypt and Mesopotamia, as they were to each other; but Crete had its special characteristics, just as they did. The Minoans developed a distinctive form of writing and an indigenous naturalistic art style. Their artisans worked in bronze, gold, clay, ivory, and stone, manufacturing objects for trade with other parts of the Mediterranean world. They built palaces with armories, stairways, galleries, tile drain pipes, frescoed walls, and colonnaded halls. They were a wealthy, clever, and prosperous people.

The city-states of the Egyptians and the Sumerians, which had their beginnings around 3500 B.C., eventually became incorporated into kingdoms
and empires. When the last revival of the failing empire of the Egyptians
collapsed under Persian assault in 525 B.C., and the Persians in turn fell before Alexander in 330 B.C., the greatest days of the people of the Near East
were over. The impressive civilizations which they fostered did not vanish;
they merely lost their drive as political forces. Cultural leadership passed into
the rough but eager hands of the barbarians who were pressing down upon
the Mediterranean from the north. They took what they wanted from the
ancient culture centers and ignored or destroyed the rest. The most important, and the most strategically situated, of these ruder people were the early
Greeks. They began to participate in Mediterranean civilization through its
Cretan manifestation in Mycenae around 1800 B.C.; but they were slow in
achieving leadership after the destruction of Minoan Crete around 1250. It
was close to 400 years before they began their spectacular rise.

At this juncture it may be more to the point to shift our attention exclusively to the history of scientific invention and discovery, because the greatest
emphasis is usually placed upon this kind of innovation in discussions of
racial or national abilities. A convenient summary of innovation in this category has been assembled by Sorokin, who has relied mainly upon the comprehensive compilations of Darmstaedter. Sorokin's tabulations of the data
reveal clearly the phenomenon that we are discussing; namely, the rise and
fall of national leadership in cultural elaboration. The Greeks, of course, were
the first to achieve scientific prominence in Europe. The greatest number
of their inventions and discoveries came between 600 and 200 B.C., with a
notable peak between 400 and 300. From that climax Greek discoveries declined in number, though there was a slight revival in the first century A.D.
The latter fluctuation was coincident with a slightly more marked upswing
of science in Rome between 100 B.C. and A.D. 100. Roman contributions are
reckoned as fewer and less sustained in time, though it should not be overlooked that discoveries made by persons of Greek origin after 146 B.C. owed
no small measure of their amplitude to Roman patronage and encouragement. Nevertheless, scientific development came to a standstill under the
Romans, and with their political collapse under the invasions of the Goths
and the Vandals it ceased to flourish anywhere in Europe for centuries.

The Arabians, playing much the same role as the Romans had previously,
eventually took over where the Greeks had left off. Not all the scientific discoveries attributed to the Arabs were actually made by them, but they fostered philosophy and the sciences, and the active literature of the time was
in their tongue. This fact has left some slight imprint upon our language;
such words as algebra, alcohol, and alchemy recall this phase in the history
of science. It took the Arabs about a century after their conquest of the Near

East to become acquainted with Greek and Roman science. They did not begin to be productive themselves until about A.D. 800; but from then until about 1050 they made outstanding contributions in almost every branch of science known at the time: astronomy, geography, medicine, mathematics, pharmacology, chemistry, mechanics, and optics. Arab science in Spain and Morocco got started a century or more later than it did in the east, and its rise and fall there was less significant and briefer. Its peak in the west seems to have occurred between A.D. 1150 and 1200.

Except for the contributions of the Arabs there was little scientific growth in or around Europe from the seventh to the fourteenth centuries. England, France, Italy, and Germany contributed about equally to the meager stock that was accumulated up until the second half of the thirteenth century. Then Italy assumed the leadership and maintained it until the middle of the seventeenth century, when the other three countries pressed ahead with England pacing the rest. During the second quarter of the nineteenth century Germany, which had not been far behind England, stepped into the lead and maintained it through the first decade of the twentieth century. In the meantime, other interesting developments had been taking place. Spain and Portugal experienced brief surges of scientific activity from 1300 to 1525; and during this period Spain outdistanced England, France, and Germany, and for brief intervals surpassed Italy. The Americans began to make a small showing against the European backdrop soon after they gained their independence. By 1900 the United States had equaled the scientific output of France, and by 1910 it was decidedly in advance of both England and France. Russia, too, was late in starting, but by 1900 it began to show signs of acceleration.[10]

It does not matter whether or not some other estimate of inventiveness would alter the details of the picture that Sorokin's data present. For present purposes it does not matter whether Italy led England during a certain period of history or vice versa. The point to be stressed is that there have been fluctuations in scientific productivity and that one ethnic group after another has experienced them. As one nation reaches its climax and goes into a decline, another experiences the beginnings of its comparatively brief day of intellectual leadership. Or it may be, as in the case of the Arabs and the Greeks before them, that an interval of "dark ages" will separate one spurt from another. However this may be, it is evident that no race or national group has exhibited the sustained and unbroken productivity that would inevitably follow if intellectual superiority were simply a matter of biological inheritance. Even within the confines of Europe, inbred strains, if not races, are multiple and diverse. No one of them has even approximated

[10] Pitirim Sorokin, *Social and Cultural Dynamics,* American Sociological Series. New York: American Book Company, 1937, Vol. 2, pp. 148–150.

a cultural constancy to match the persistence of its biological characteristics. Rise and decline is a feature of culture, not of head conformation or eye color. Throughout history as we know it, intellectual leadership has shifted from group to group, irrespective of their genetic compositions, and presumably it will continue to do so in the future.

CHAPTER II

THE CULTURAL BACKGROUND

All cultural changes are initiated by individuals. The stimulus for a new idea or a new behavior is consequently always specific to a given individual. Sometimes, however, it is generalized so that it bears upon several individuals, or it becomes more intense or recurrent so that it affects some individuals more acutely than it does others. In any event, conditions external to the individual have a marked effect upon his innovative potential and upon the potential of the group in which he lives. With a shift of conditions in the experience of an individual, or with an alteration in the conditions that affect one society at different times in its history, or with a diversification of the conditions that affect different societies, there must go a variation in innovative possibilities.

It is with these conditions that we shall be concerned in this and the next chapter, not with the innovator's personality, predispositions, or abilities. For the most part these externals are not of a person's own making. In a sense they are impersonal and supraindividual. They include the aspects of the natural environment that are clearly independent of human manipulation. More importantly, they include cultural constructs that have come to be what they are irrespective of any given individual's will or effort. Most of any person's cultural environment falls in this category. Each of us is able to make some slight modifications in the cultural milieu in which we live, and some individuals make significant changes; but we all begin with a body of ideas and a range of things and behaviors that have been assembled and integrated by our predecessors long before we are able to comprehend them. The complexity and the orientations of this traditional inventory inevitably have a determinative effect upon the interests, the competencies, and the innovative potentials of the members of any society.

For the present, the conditions to be discussed will include only those which have a bearing upon the initiation of a cultural change, and not those which relate to the acceptance of one that already has been conceived and proposed for adoption. When factors contributing to the acceptance or rejection of a new idea are touched upon in this chapter, as they are in the discussion of imitation, they will be treated only to the extent that they can be shown to contribute to the development of some other new idea. Many of the conditions affecting the inception of new ideas are, of course, also relevant to a consideration of their acceptance. They will be treated separately, however, because it is important to keep the phenomena of creation and acceptance distinct.

The Accumulation of Ideas. The size and complexity of the cultural inventory that is available to an innovator establishes limits within which he must function. The state of knowledge and the degree of its elaboration during his day, the range and kind of artifacts, techniques, and instruments that he can use, make some new developments possible and others impossible. The mere accumulation of things and ideas provides more material with which to work. A sizable inventory allows for more new combinations and permits more different avenues of approach in problem solution than does a small one.

Some societies are much richer than others in cultural possessions; hence their members have an initial advantage that is denied individuals in less well endowed societies. The Australian aborigines and the pygmies of Africa have a minimum of technological devices. It is not to be expected that a member of either group, regardless of his ability, would invent a photoelectric cell or evolve a theory of world government. The same may be said of our own ancestors of a few hundred years ago. Einstein could scarcely have developed his theory of relativity had he lived in the Neolithic age, nor could the atomic bomb have been invented in the days of Newton. The cultural base must provide the materials for further development. If the necessary ingredients are not contained in the inventory that is available, a new idea involving them is obviously impossible.

Sometimes the question of availability of innovative resources relates to the intellectual perspective of the innovator. His cultural horizon may be limited to the knowledge that exists only within his own society, or it may extend beyond to include the knowledge that is known to adjacent or remote groups in other parts of the world. This is a matter to be considered later, but we may note now that facility and extent of communication influence the accumulation of ideas. With well-developed channels of communication there goes a greater possibility of building up intellectual resources.

The fact that ideas do or do not accumulate has cultural implications in itself. A noticeable accumulation presupposes an interest in assembling and preserving ideas and things of the past. In societies wherein this interest is manifest the development of something new does not mean the elimination of the old; instead it is added to the old as an alternative, or at least a knowledge of the old is preserved in the memory or in the written records of the people. Even if the old is no longer functional, it exists as a part of the inventory and may be revived. In short, accumulation results from a building upon the past, not a discarding of it; and the amount of past development conditions the amount and variety of what can be done at present.

There are marked differences between societies in this matter of an interest in the past. To some extent it is correlated with the existence or non-existence of written records, but this is not the sole determiner. Some people simply do not care about the achievements of their forefathers; or they care only to the extent that the activities of their ancestors provide amusing and interesting material for speculation and storytelling.

The Concentration of Ideas. Important as it is, the accumulation of ideas provides only a minimum condition for innovation. If the elements of the cultural inventory remain disparate and disconnected in time and place, the situation is no more propitious for innovation than it is when the resources of the society are scanty. The cultural materials that provide the basis for a new conception must come to a focus in the mind of some individual. There must be a concentration of ideas in the personal experience of the innovator.

Cultural complexity is not the equivalent of idea concentration, although they are likely to be confused. Because of the necessity of classifying their data, anthropologists and sociologists are in the habit of speaking of the culture of a given people, meaning by this the totality of customs to be found among the group, not just those that are shared by all its members. Thus, we speak of American culture, Fijian culture, or Eskimo culture and would include under these headings all the learned behaviors that can be discovered among people we call Americans, Fijians, or Eskimos, provided they are not confined solely to one individual. This usage is justified on the grounds that there are some things known in some fashion to all the adult members within each of these populations; there is an abstracted common denominator of behaviors, ideas, and things that is said to be Pan-American, Pan-Fijian, or Pan-Eskimo. While this or some similar classification principle is essential, and while it has use and validity for historical and comparative purposes, it gives only a minimum of information about the idea system of any given individual in a society. Consequently it tells us nothing of the innovative possibilities that exist within it. Ideas do not mix or rearrange themselves. This process must take place in some one mind. The concentration of ideas within a stated geographical boundary among a certain number of people is concentration on the abstract plane of the observer's synthesis. Unless the same focusing also occurs in the mind of a single person living in the area, it has no relevance as a condition favoring the creation of new ideas; only in this way can innovations be stimulated by a multiplicity and a variety of existing ideas. The mere physical propinquity of many people with a multitude of ideas will not result in an ideational enrichment. That is an individual function.

The foregoing remarks may seem to be obvious. They have implications, however, that are sometimes overlooked. We are accustomed to saying or believing that Americans have a prodigious cultural inventory. If anyone were to attempt to itemize it in the technological field alone, the task would seem to be endless. This difficulty is significant, for it will appear at once that no single individual actually experiences the entire range of things that should be included in such a catalogue. No one even knows about them all. A multitude of the items would be as alien to any cataloguer as are the customs of another ethnic group, such as the Chinese. Very few Americans know "how the other half lives"; most of them know little about the wide regional differences that exist within the political boundaries of the United States. Still fewer have any conception of the intricacies of such specialties as medicine, law, physics, and chemistry; and no one comprehends the complexities of all of them. American culture, in other words, is a concept, not a fact in the experience of individuals who call themselves Americans. Their mental richness is far less than is implied by the abstraction called American culture. Group complexity is meaningless as far as innovation is concerned; the complexity of individual knowledge is the pertinent consideration.

The concentration of ideas means, then, their localization in a particular mind; and with reference to the topic being discussed, it means that breadth and depth of personal knowledge and experience constitute a factor in innovation. The more a man knows about a given set of data, or about diverse sets of data, the more likely he is to develop something new. Professional inventors say that to be successful in their field a man must have a good memory, a large fund of facts, a thorough knowledge of his subject, and a practical mind. Rossman's inquiry among 710 professionals revealed that they placed knowledge and memory near the top of their list, after the requirements of perseverance and imagination. They also regarded the lack of knowledge as a major obstacle in inventing, rating it second to the lack of capital.[1]

The ideal of breadth and depth of knowledge does not mean that innovation is confined to specialists and encyclopedists. It means only that added resources multiply the chances that new thoughts will occur, and that resources may be increased by intensive and extensive explorations. It means, too, that innovation is impossible for an individual beyond the limits of his understanding of his experiences. Breadth and depth of ideas increase the frequency with which anyone is likely to conceive of something new; hence the importance of fact accumulation for those who make their living by inventing. By the same token it is an auspicious condition for acceleration in cultural change.

Some societies provide more opportunity for a concentration of ideas than do others and, consequently, a more stimulating climate for change. Where there are any cultural or natural barriers to an exchange of ideas, there will be proportionately less opportunity for their mixing and remodeling. Thus, the physical isolation of people, for whatever cause, hinders their intercommunication and therefore the concentration of ideas. Institutions that encour-

---

[1] Joseph Rossman, *The Psychology of the Inventor*. Washington, D.C.: Inventor's Publishing Co., 1931, pp. 40 and 162.

age secrecy and exclusiveness have the same effect. Some societies sanction professional and other secrets; or foster exclusive organizations such as trade unions and fraternal orders; or restrict social intercourse; or curtail the free flow of information; or force selected segments of the cultural inventory through inheritance channels or other artificial avenues. Among some people there is a tradition of learning, a stimulation of curiosity, and a nurturing of the quest for new and diverse knowledge. In a few parts of the world, libraries, publication centers, schools, and apprentice systems have been developed for the wide dissemination and perpetuation of ideas. On the other hand, in many societies the acquisition of knowledge is a privilege of the few who are selected either formally or indirectly by economic or inheritance preferences.

The Collaboration of Effort. The likelihood that a new idea will develop is enhanced if several individuals are simultaneously and cooperatively exploring the same possibility. A collaboration of effort not only pools the concentration of ideas of several individuals, but also increases the chances that one of them will solve their common problem. Moreover, their interactions are mutually stimulating. The views of one collaborator are an impetus to new ideas by the others. Then, too, their integrated thinking adds to the possibility of a solution; for in many instances complex problems require so much experimentation, or such a diversity of approach and training, that one man cannot hope to meet all the requirements.

Collaboration, like the accumulation and the concentration of ideas, is not a natural phenomenon; it does not take place inevitably or haphazardly. It is culturally induced and sanctioned. There is more or less of it in different times and places and under different societal conditions. It may be encouraged or discouraged; or there may be no well-conceptualized attitude toward it at all. In many primitive societies cooperation is highly valued in one or another area of activity. Sometimes it is restricted to certain occasions or to specific areas, such as the economic. In other societies it is quite generally operative. Porteus found that many of the Australian natives to whom he gave mental tests were genuinely puzzled to find that he was not very cooperative because he would not help them solve the test problems. To a person whose whole life pattern was infused with concepts of mutual help and cooperation this minor assistance seemed the least that could be expected.

There are specific mechanisms and devices in some societies for the encouragement and realization of collaboration, and there are others of which it takes advantage. In our own society, and those of western Europe, where the scientific tradition has been so firmly implanted, there are numerous institutions which encourage the collaboration of effort in scientific discovery and invention. Professional associations, study groups, clubs, and cults are organized for the interchange of ideas. Symposia, conferences, workshops, institutes, municipal councils, and a host of other meetings are called to solve emergency and other common problems. In addition, we have numerous publications to announce the results of researches and to publicize new knowledge and new theories. Furthermore, at the present time there is an emphasis upon cooperative research, especially upon interdisciplinary attacks upon problems that bear upon the interests of groups of specialists.

Among the devices used in collaborative efforts in our culture may be mentioned the standardizations of techniques, measurements, and terminologies. All these add to precision in reporting scientific ideas; they also make new ideas comprehensible across ethnic and linguistic boundaries. This is the great advantage that mathematics has for science; it is universally intelligible among all workers in the field. Such recording and communicating devices facilitate the exchange of information and give a common base line and background for scientific discovery everywhere. They permit and encourage collaboration where in practice there is none.

There is organized, closely integrated, and mutually directed collaboration, and there is collaboration of the most informal kind. The latter is not often considered in this connection; and, strictly speaking, "collaboration" may not be an acceptable term for it. But the results are the same, and the conditions for it are parallel with conditions for intimate collaboration. It is impersonal and indirect. The individuals who participate in it often do not know each other; they have never met and there is no direct communication between them. Yet they know of the work of each other; or they are familiar with what is common knowledge in the field; or their thinking is directed and circumscribed by the same conditions, such as the demands of a given problem.

Informal collaboration is the explanation for numerous instances of independent and often simultaneous inventions. Ogburn and Thomas have compiled a list of almost 150 of these parallels.[2] The list is impressive, and the phenomenon itself is startling upon first acquaintance with it; but the cause is not so mysterious as it is sometimes made to appear. To say that simultaneous inventions are made because, and not until, the time is right for them is no explanation at all. To consider them to be the manifestation of supraindividual social forces is to translate the discussion of them into a realm of abstraction that exists only in the mind of the objective observer. As we have seen, the wherewithal for an invention must preexist the conception of it; but an accumulation of the necessary materials for it does not predetermine it any more than the existence of brick and mortar determines that a building shall be constructed. Culture does not determine or cause anything. Ideas about it may and do.

[2] W. F. Ogburn, *Social Change*. New York: The Viking Press, Inc., 1938, pp. 90–102.

The repeated occurrence of parallel ideas thus takes on a more realistic aspect when we appreciate that the great majority of men who independently invent or discover the same thing are in effect collaborators. It is true that they are physically separated from each other, but they are nevertheless in communication. There is no essential difference between the celebrated independent conception of natural selection as an explanation for evolution by Darwin and Wallace and the invention of the atomic bomb that was made by several men working in intimate and daily association with each other. Darwin and Wallace did not have to exchange ideas; they got them from the same source.

The duplicate inventions that are frequently cited from the history of science have been made possible by the development of the cultural mechanisms already mentioned. Chief among them are the various communication devices, such as instruction techniques, printing, and libraries. Through these devices a common fund of knowledge becomes widely spread, questions are asked, and curiosity is evoked. More men are made potential inventors simply because more of them are thinking about the same things in the same way.

In part, too, independent inventions derive from the limitations that are imposed by the conditions of the problem, its conventional conceptualization, and the range of techniques that are currently available and are considered appropriate to meet its demands. The resort to clichés, the drawing upon a common stock of knowledge for the development of something new, is bound to result in duplication sometime; and the more frequent the attempts to find a solution to a problem, the more numerous will be the duplications. This conjunction of events was well illustrated recently when a certain author of young people's stories about a horse called Black Stallion asked his readers to suggest a name for a female offspring of the horse hero. He received 50,000 letters from youthful admirers, eighteen of whom suggested the name "Black Minx." [3] In the runoff for the prize awarded for this name the contestants were asked to write their reasons for suggesting it. It is obvious from their replies that they envisaged the stereotype of an attractive and heroic colt, and that this was linked in their minds, as in the minds of thousands of other Americans, with the popular meanings associated with the word "minx." Some of the young contestants used the dictionary to aid them in their search for a name; others undoubtedly used their parents as an equally original source for their new ideas. In any event, they were all in contact, although they did not realize it; and all were constrained by conventional thinking. All were indirectly collaborating. Convergent innovation within a single cultural network takes place under the same controls and illusions, as will appear more fully later.

[3] *Life*, Feb. 13, 1950, pp. 59–60.

The Conjunction of Differences. Teggart, the historian, has insisted that the "great advances of mankind have been due, not to the mere aggregation, assemblage, or acquisition of disparate ideas, but to the emergence of a certain type of mental activity which is set up by the opposition of different idea systems." [4] In his opinion the borrowing of ideas by one group from another has acted only as a leveler of customs; new ideas, he says, arise only when the clash of ideas provokes comparisons and critical discussions of the differences. The individual is thereby released from the trammels of tradition and is able to express himself in the organization of new customs.

Teggart's theory of cultural growth is open to criticism on several counts, but it contains a solid kernel of truth. It is unquestionable that the apposition of alternate values, things, and usages can bring about an entirely new concept that is qualitatively distinct from either of the alternatives. Furthermore, the conjunction of such differences can be a stimulus for the emergence of some new idea deriving from them. The difference itself induces change.

Teggart's thesis envisages the interplay of differences only on the ethnic-group level. He was concerned with the vast panorama of history and with the clashing and commingling of nations and diverse groups of humanity. The apposition of differences in such cases is, of course, very marked; but it is equally significant for change, although less obvious, within the microcosm of a single society. The differences that exist across caste and class lines are sometimes as productive of innovations as are the collisions of disparate peoples. Interfamilial differences within the same community are likewise important sources of change. And finally, differences between individuals, even those who are members of the same family, necessitate mutual adjustments on the idiosyncratic level that may or may not develop into behaviors shared with others. This level of contrasts is certainly not insignificant.

There are a variety of culturally defined conditions which either facilitate or obstruct the conjunction of differences. Any custom which encourages the mingling of people with variant habits provides an opportunity for a mutual appraisal of their differences. Market places do this in both modern and primitive societies. The regular trading places of the American Indians along the Columbia River and those of the natives of certain parts of Melanesia and western Africa, as well as the commercial centers of the eastern Mediterranean area, brought together groups of people with decidedly different customs. Even in western Europe and the United States the cultural differences between rural and urban life patterns that appear at farmers' markets are not insignificant from the standpoint of change.

The presence of itinerant or resident traders in foreign lands is, by its very nature, an instrument for the presentation of contrasts, if not in the behavior

[4] Frederick Teggart, *The Processes of History.* New Haven: Yale University Press, 1918, p. 112.

of the trader himself, then certainly in the wares that he imports. The activities of merchants, especially in connection with the expansion of European civilization into technologically backward parts of the world, have had revolutionary effects, and very frequently they have been productive of local innovations. European traders among the natives of the Americas, Africa, and the Pacific Islands spearheaded the invasion of an entirely new way of life. They and the commercial interests that sponsored them have had comparable effects upon oriental peoples, such as the Chinese, the Japanese, and the Hindus. Less extreme but still important contrasts have been presented by traders in many other times and places—by the Arabs in the Far East, by the Aztecs among their neighbors, and by Neolithic merchants along the Danube River, to mention only a few.

Missionary endeavor has had effects comparable to the commercial activities of traders. Because it also represents an effort to extend the range of one system of ideas at the expense of another, it has highlighted contrasts in customs, not infrequently with innovative consequences. The penetration of Christian missionaries into remote parts of the world comes to mind in this connection. Yet Mohammedanism and Buddhism, two other proselytizing religions, have had equally important effects in terms of the number of people who have been reached by them. All three are dedicated to an expanding frontier that necessarily poses a conjunction of differences. Each asserts a claim to the only truth and declares that idea systems in conflict with it must be reduced. Because they are similarly dedicated, we must also include in this category the activities of social-welfare workers and social and political reformers, as well as the conflicting claims of subsidiary sects and cults within the three world-embracing religions just mentioned. Alleviation or betterment programs inherently involve a juxtaposition of differences, even though their aims may concern quite different aspects of culture.

Customs and ideologies which sanction the protected passage of individuals across ethnic boundaries encourage the juxtaposition of cultural differences. Trade relations are one example, but there are many others. In some parts of the world intermarriage between members of groups speaking different languages and having other divergent customs happens quite often. It is most common in Europe and America at the present time, but it has by no means been confined to these areas or to modern times. Its cultural effects are always significant, not only because of the habit adjustments required of the spouses, but from the standpoint of their children as well. The same requirements can assume major importance in marriages between individuals of different classes in the same society. The custom of exchanging ambassadors and other ethnic-group representatives, which is well established among the nations of the world at the present time but is not unique to them, also conjoins differences. Even more important is the modern custom of emigration and expatriation, whereby the citizens of one nation take up permanent residence in another. This, more than anything else, has made Americans, geographically isolated as they are, conscious of differences in custom.

The institutions of slavery and wage-labor recruitment among foreign populations have brought cultural contrasts to the attention of various people since prehistoric times. The slaves and the laborers, if not the masters, have been made acutely aware of such differences. Technical slavery is no longer the cultural mixer it once was, but ethnic groups continue to be dislocated and dispersed under an involuntary system very like it. Cross-ethnic labor recruiting on a voluntary basis is an active force in the conjunction of differences. It is common practice over much of South Africa; and annually Mexican and Caribbean laborers are brought into the United States under special provisions. Until recently, too, it was a widespread and culturally important practice all over the Pacific Island area. A good proportion of the larger Pacific Islands have mixed populations that are a result of a system of indentured labor; and many others have mixed cultures as a consequence of the well-established custom whereby young men spend a year or more away from their home villages working for white men.

The urge for exploration and adventure has brought about many isolated instances of conjunction. This urge is a cultural variable. Comparatively few people in world history have cultivated it. Most of them have inculcated a sedentary attitude, usually for the good reason that it would be suicidal to stray beyond home boundaries. The pioneer spirit was once a characteristic trait of the Polynesians in contrast with most of the other inhabitants of the Pacific Islands; and it marks a distinctive difference between the southern and the northern Chinese. It has manifested itself most prominently in recent centuries among Europeans, sometimes combined with the ideal of scientific research and exploration, sometimes with commercialism, sometimes with a spirit of rebellion. In any event, the lure of new lands has brought escapists, exploiters, and adventurers face to face with contrasting customs, and it has opened up entirely new cultural vistas to the backward populations of the world.

This brings us to conquest and colonization as mechanisms for the conjunction of differences. They are ancient and appealing practices, but they are certainly not instinctive. Not all societies resort to them, even in economic extremity—the historic Eskimos and aboriginal Australians did not—but they have had tremendous consequences for most of the world's population. They have resulted not only in the incidental juxtaposition of differences, but in the magnification of them through the militant insistence upon changes in native customs by the members of invading ethnic groups. Teggart maintains that migrations and collisions of groups of people have been essential for the genesis of new ideas. Only in this way can there be the "break-up of crystallized systems of organization and of thought" that is necessary for real cultural advance. Teggart's position is extreme and certainly speculative. Friction and social disruption are not essential to new ideas, although they may help. Like the other mechanisms that have been mentioned, they bring together materials for the construction of something new.

The results of the conjunction of differences are no more automatic than are the results of the accumulation and concentration of ideas. The reactions to differences may take one of three forms, and there are cultural determinants for each, as well as for the particular patterns within them. An alternative custom may be rejected forthwith, or it may be accepted in one of two ways. We shall consider the conditions for rejection and the psychological and cultural involvements of acceptance in a subsequent chapter. The purpose at the moment is to point out that acceptance can take two courses and that the conditions for their functioning are traditionally defined. In the one case the purpose of the acceptor is to imitate some alien form, thus producing a copy; in the other he attempts a compromise between the alien form and one of his own, thus initiating a syncretism. In both instances there is a conjunction of differences, and in both something new is produced.

Imitation inevitably produces a modification of the prototype even though the copyist makes a diligent effort to be faithful to his model. The deviations may go unrealized or unregarded both by the copyist and by other people. There can be good and bad copies, some being more like the original than others and so valued because of their fidelity. It may require an expert to detect the differences, as in counterfeiting, but this is a matter of greater or lesser degrees in exactitude. All imitations must entail some discrepancy, even when a person tries to imitate himself. An individual's signature varies from one occasion to the next, despite his efforts to make it identical. It varies noticeably over a period of years. That is one reason why banks ask their patrons to provide them with current signatures from time to time.

Reproductive variation occurs in all aspects of culture. It is evident from casual observation and from uncontrolled studies of the phenomenon. It appears in handicraft, in news reporting, in rumors, in artistic designs, in stories, and in songs. It is a commonplace in the experience of ethnologists. It has also been studied experimentally under controlled conditions. Many years ago Balfour called attention to the remarkable consequences of a series of reproductions of a drawing by a series of individuals. He gave the first individual a picture of a snail crawling over a twig and asked him to copy it. The second individual was not allowed to see the original but was asked to make a copy of the drawing of the first person, and so on through a series of fourteen individuals. The final sketch looked nothing like the original; it resembled a bird with some heavy nondescript appendages that could not be called legs.[5] Bartlett amplified this technique and made a thorough analysis of his results.[6]

More will be said of reproductive variation in later chapters. The point to be made here is that the departures from the original made in imitation are not haphazard. They take shape under the dual controls of the thing that is copied and the idea conceived of it by the copier. For any given individual the deviations from the objective prototype vary within specific limits. These limits are determined by the previous experience and training of the copyist; more specifically, by the system of values by which he formulates his estimates of what constitutes equivalence, and by his conviction of the need for precision in any given case of copying. His deviations are governed by a preformed system that is dependent upon his personal, including his cultural, background. Thus, there is always a conjunction of differences, even in the closest imitation. They are the values of the originator of the thing to be copied and the values of the copyist.

Since reproductive variation is an individual matter, the greater the number of people who are induced to copy, and the more often they do so, the more variation there will be. Innovation, then, in so far as it relates to imitation, thus becomes a function of the encouragement or discouragement of copying. And since imitation is channelized differently in different societies, there are certain to be different manifestations of variability.

The amount of imitation that is sanctioned in a society is an important consideration. The Samoans deplored it in almost all aspects of their culture.[7] Americans avoid it in many aspects, but emphasize its virtues in others, especially where questions of "truth" and the social graces are concerned. We have recognized institutions which cultivate or take advantage of the ideal it represents. Our customs of gossiping and carrying tales and rumors are trivial but highly satisfying perseverations of an imitative pattern. Our moral tales, like those of other peoples, are expected to inspire the ideal of imitation.

The channelization of imitation has many ramifications. There is, first of all, a cultural definition of paragons, a designation of whom one shall imitate. American parents take pride in knowing that their children are like themselves; they expect their offspring to model upon themselves, and they bristle if a child justifies his aberrant behavior by saying that the Joneses do it that way. In most societies, even though it is expected that children will model on their parents, there is a distinction between adult and child pat-

[5] Henry Balfour, *The Evolution of Decorative Art*. London: Percival and Co., 1893, pp. 24–30.

[6] F. C. Bartlett, *Remembering. A Study in Experimental and Social Psychology*. New York: Cambridge University Press, 1932, p. 118.

[7] Margaret Mead, "The Role of the Individual in Samoan Culture," *Journal of the Royal Anthropological Institute of Great Britain and Ireland*, 1928, 58:481–495.

terns of behavior; a young person is supposed to act his age by imitating other children, not grown-ups. There are numerous other patterns of inter-individual imitations that are approved, such as the student copying his teacher, the child aping older playmates, and the devoted friend modeling upon his favorite associate.

Culture heroes serve or are expected to serve as paragons. Moses, George Washington, Abraham Lincoln, and Quetzalcoatl are examples. These figures, half real and half fictional, epitomize the cultural ideals of a group. According to popular beliefs, they are the makers or the givers of the good things in life. In their role as culture heroes their foibles are ignored or translated into harmless and ingratiating weaknesses and their virtues are magnified. Even entirely fictional characters make paragons. They are more ideally suited to this role than are mere human beings, who are tied and tarnished by their spotty manifestations of the heroic. True heroes can be exquisitely and continuously good or evil. They make consuming ideals. The adoration of movie and radio stars in the United States makes fashion models of Hollywood heroines and accounts for the hold on young minds that is exercised by Roy Rogers and Hopalong Cassidy.

History reveals that the members of one ethnic or subethnic group frequently become paragons for another. Almost always a certain amount of eclecticism standardizes the imitative pattern that results. Thus, for many years, and to some extent even at the present time, Americans admired and copied French fashions and French artists; but scientists, especially the applied scientists, looked to the Germans for leadership in chemistry and physics. During one period of their history the Japanese imitated the humanistic accomplishments of the Chinese; at a later time they turned to copy the industrialism of the United States. During my youth many of the people of Arizona were eager imitators of the Californians, especially those living in Los Angeles. It was the ambition of every young person of my acquaintance to be able to "go to the coast" and brag about it ever after. Our parents did the same.

The behaviors and possessions of upper classes and castes within a society commonly become the focus of goal striving by their inferiors. Minority groups in the United States, in the Pacific Islands, and in South Africa struggle in devious ways not only to gain the privileges of the majority group members, but to imitate their ideals in dress, gesture, and social convention. Even under a rigid caste system members of inferior groups make attempts to acquire status by imitating their superiors, even to the extent, as in India, of their assuming some of the disabilities and restraints upon behavior that symbolize superior status. Thus the members of a local segment of a caste might restrict their social intercourse or increase the number of their food taboos in order to acquire merit in the eyes of other castes.

This emulation has been one of the most persistent reasons for the splitting of castes in India.

Just as there are channels and facilitators for imitation, so there are blocks and penalties. One of the most interesting obstacles is the tradition of non-imitation. This is a cultural outlook which not only dictates tolerance of ethnic differences but insists upon a mutual preservation of them. A well-documented example comes from Guatemala, where cultural diversity is the norm and where it goes to the ultimate length of township autonomy in culture. There each township or *municipio* maintains its distinctive dress, religious beliefs, and economic pursuits. The diversity is not the result of isolation, for the members of each *municipio* maintain trade and visiting relations with the members of others and are fully aware of their differences.[8] In parts of Melanesia the same situation prevails. There, too, cultural diversity is the rule, especially with respect to material goods. It is most evident in the subdivision of economic production. Frequently one village produces only one artifact or food which must be traded for practically everything else that is needed. There is thus a symbiotic relationship between adjacent villages that is supported by an indispensable system of trade relationships.[9] Mutual dependence was not the rule among the Yurok, Karok, and Hupa Indians of northwestern California, but they had a clearly defined concept of cultural segregation from each other and from their other neighbors. They shared the belief that in the beginning of time the Creator had given them their world of customs, and that was the end of it. Their culture was not to be changed. Other peoples might have been given their customs by the Creator, too. The Indians were not sure about that; but they were certain that no good could come of their imitating the ways of foreigners. Their convictions, however, could not prevail in the teeth of the white man's aggressive insistence to the contrary.

Group pride is also a barrier to imitation. Perhaps there was a good proportion of this ingredient in the attitude of the Yurok and their ideological congeners. It motivates all ethnic groups to some extent. All people find superior merit in their own way of life, even though they complain about certain aspects of it. That fact makes them selectively imitative. They choose their paragons and want to shop around among the offerings of those they choose. Group pride, with its concomitant refusal to imitate except in superficial ways, is more marked in some cultural traditions than in others. The Americans and the British are superlative nonimitators. They expect the rest of the world to catch up with them. The Palauans, even though they have debased themselves before the Japanese and the Americans, are inveterate

---

[8] Sol Tax, "World View and Social Relations in Guatemala," *American Anthropologist,* 1941, 43:29.

[9] Margaret Mead, *Growing Up in New Guinea.* New York: William Morrow & Company, Inc., 1930, pp. 295–298.

critics of their backward cousins, the Yapese. And within Palau itself the inhabitants of other districts scoff at the hillbilly habits of the people of Ngerchelong at the northernmost point of the largest island in the chain.

Class consciousness also bars the way to imitation. Upper-class members discourage and penalize "passing" by their social inferiors. Social climbers are scoffed at everywhere, and in some places they are physically punished. Minority group members must not be presumptuous; parvenus are snubbed and obstructed. In Palau, age is a critical determinant of social privilege. An older person always takes precedence over a younger member of the community, unless there are complicating circumstances. Young men may not carry pouches for their valuables because they are not supposed to have any, and they may not eat with their elders or with Americans. These and other symbols of high status are denied them, and they are punished in subtle but effective ways for their temerity if they defy the rules.

The discrepancies that occur in imitation are necessarily individualized. Usually they are treated as minor and insignificant. The variations from the prototype are regarded as equivalents; they revolve about a norm and are considered "for all practical purposes" to be the same. There is, however, a hierarchy of norms. There are idiosyncratic norms, which are defined by variations in individual repetitions of behavior as they fluctuate from day to day and from occasion to occasion. There are also familial norms, within the orbit of which the variations of closely associated individuals ride. Beyond that there are class, local-group, and ethnic-group boundaries.

On each level the departures may be regarded as mere variants, accidental and insignificant in the total picture. They may be so regarded if interest in them is merely for purposes of classification. But if the phenomenon of change is the focus of attention, it is evident that the departures constitute a continuous series of innovations. This fact naturally becomes more obvious when we compare cross-familial, cross-class, or cross-ethnic imitations. In all cases the intent of the protagonist is to copy, but in cross-ethnic imitations the results are often strikingly innovative. The reason is the greater disparity of the differences that are conjoined.

The picturesque speech transformations that take place in consequence of imitations across linguistic boundaries are an everyday experience of many people. The alterations in accent, in word order, and in phonetic substitutions strike the provincial listener with special force. Ideological metamorphoses are equally striking. The meeting of the Hellenic and Indic cultures in the Punjab in the third century B.C. produced an art style out of their contrasting norms. The Gandhara art of this period was a fusion of Greek and Buddhist ideas. An even more instructive example has recently been provided by an artistic program inaugurated by the Catholic Church. Some years ago Vatican officials conceived that a lasting testimony to the universality of the Church could be made through having artists the world over express their understanding of the teachings of the Church in their local media. Communications were sent to 600 Catholic missions asking for examples of local art, whether by converts or by pagans, that embodied some Christian motif. The numerous interpretations of Christian themes and religious figures are most illuminating. The student of comparative art will find no difficulty in assigning provenience to the individual characterizations of the same subject matter. They embody in striking ways the customs and the artistic conventions of the ethnic groups to which the artists belong.[10]

Some of the experiments of Bartlett reveal the same distortive influences of cultural imperatives in verbal material. In one experimental series he gave his English subjects a supernatural tale taken directly from the mythology of the Kwakiutl Indians of Vancouver Island, and then required them to relate the story from memory at subsequent intervals. During the course of these reproductions the story of "The War of the Ghosts" lost practically all its characteristic features. Most significantly, it lost them in favor of interpolations and alterations that made the story more comprehensible to its English tellers. The Englishmen unwittingly remodeled the tale under the demands of their own contrasting cultural norms.[11]

The compromise reaction to contrasts exhibits no essential difference in its results. The difference between compromise and imitation lies in the attitudes of the acceptors. The willingness to copy is a phenomenon that is psychologically distinct from the willingness to adjust or compound differences. In the one case there is an unconscious distortion of the conflicting model because of an absence of awareness of the contrast; in the other the conflict is overt, and there is a conscious adaptation of the opposing idea in terms of some indigenous counterpart. Syncretisms are deliberate amalgamations or hybridizations.

As with imitation, there are culturally established conditions which encourage and discourage syncretisms. There are, for example, value systems, such as our own, which assign merit to arbitration and compromise in case of conflicts. There are others in which this reaction would be interpreted as weakness or self-debasement and would be treated as such. To some extent syncretisms must occur in all societies upon one level of interaction or another or in one context or another. Innovative compromises often result from the apposition of incompatible policies, programs, political platforms, and other contrarieties that stem from diverse interests.

A willingness to resort to compromise appears in communication systems that are devised to reach across linguistic barriers. Lingua francas which incorporate elements of the speech peculiarities of two mutually unintelligible languages have been repeatedly evolved under the mutual desire to transact business. Hybrid dialects such as pidgin English, Hindustani, the beach-la-

[10] *Life,* Sept. 4, 1950, pp. 63–66.
[11] Bartlett, *op. cit.,* pp. 63*ff.*

mar of New Guinea, and the Chinook jargon of the north Pacific coast of America represent efforts by members of different ethnic groups to understand each other, if only out of mutually selfish interests. Bilingualism, with its many innovative crudities, is more imitation than syncretism; but it, too, is often a kind of compromise with necessity, as most Americans will attest.

The fusion of religious forms and beliefs is the type instance of syncretism. Some religions are much more tolerant of such dilution or adulteration than are others. Early Christianity was markedly receptive. Catholicism in its ministrations to native groups in remote parts of the world still is. Usually Protestantism has not been. The Samoans and some other Polynesians have absorbed Christianity into their native system without very much disruption of it. Palauan religion has collapsed under no more pressure by the alien form. The New World Negroes, in both the United States and Brazil, have evolved an interesting and a highly syncretized combination of their ancient African beliefs and Christianity.[12]

Another encouragement for syncretism is the readiness of some people to accept cross-cultural equations, not as a concession, but out of a genuine appreciation for the value of certain contrasting forms. Sometimes the things that are valued and accepted are trivial and reflect merely an interest in the exotic, as in the American pastime of collecting souvenirs. Nevertheless, the predisposition is a culturally sanctioned one. Souvenirs are incomprehensible to many of the people upon whom Americans descend. And the incorporation of souvenirs is certainly innovative, as when bows and arrows are hung over mantels, Navajo rugs are used as draperies, and the hula dance is staged for men over eighteen only.

More genuine cross-cultural validations seek to preserve the essence and the meaning of the adopted forms, and they are to be found only among individuals who undertake a more sympathetic understanding of alien customs. This, too, is a cultivated and standardized attitude. An illustration of it is the policy of the United States Bureau of Indian Affairs from about 1932 until the present. During this period efforts have been made to restore Indian dignity and to revive Indian customs for the virtues that they inherently contain. For the Indian who was already partially assimilated, the idea came too late for him to participate in the benefits that it was designed to bestow; half white man and hoping to conceal the rest, he did not want to become an Indian all over again, because for too long he had been made to feel that there were no virtues in his heritage. This policy of encouraging cultural pluralism, with its attendant emphasis upon the essential merits of alternate standards, has also been adopted by the American administration in the Trust Territory of the Pacific. It is the approach to the treatment of

[12] Melville Herskovits, *Man and His Works*. New York: Alfred A. Knopf, Inc., 1948, pp. 570–572.

dependent peoples that many anthropologists advocate. It is also the solution to the dilemma of the Jews that was militantly espoused by Lewin.[13]

The ideals of collaboration, imitation, and compromise account in large measure for the importance of population size and density as factors in cultural growth. The number of people in a society is in itself a neutral factor. It is a biological fact, and it alone leads to nothing cultural. A large population wherein individual members remain intellectually isolated or antipathetic is not more productive of innovation than is a small group. In fact it is only an agglomeration of small groups, with no more potential for cultural elaboration than the potential of its most active subdivision. But if, through the dissemination of ideas, concentrations are built up and collaboration and imitation come into play, the larger the number of individuals involved, the greater will be the certainty that new ideas will appear.

The Expectation of Change. Innovation flourishes in an atmosphere of anticipation of it. If the members of a society expect something new it is more likely to appear than if it is unforeseen and unheralded. The chance frequency will be augmented in proportion to the number of expectant individuals. It is like seeing ghosts at midnight. The greater the number of people who expect to see them, the more frequently they will be seen.

In some societies there is a tradition of expecting change. The anticipation is a conscious belief that change is going to take place. It is a cultivated attitude with variable limits and areas of relevance, depending upon the society. Most often it is limited to selected aspects of the culture. Among ourselves there is a very general expectation that change is certain in our technology, in our art forms, in our women's fashions, and to some extent (slang) in our language. We do not anticipate it in our religion, in our political structure, or in our family organization. We may individually and privately hope for change in these latter areas, but we do not really expect it. The Zuñi Indians of New Mexico are even more restrictive in their anticipations. They neither hope for nor anticipate changes in any part of their culture, and they are resolute against any suggestion of the idea. They are extremely ethnocentric and are uninterested in the world around them; they, in fact, regard their village as the center of the world. Their philosophy recalls that of the Yurok Indians. The Navajo, who live close to the Zuñi, take another view. They expect new developments in their culture; and their history, in so far as it is known, reveals that they have been receivers and adapters of alien customs throughout the period of their occupation of their present habitat. They welcome change, accepting it as a realistic adjustment to the world around them.[14] The Samoans are also

---

[13] Kurt Lewin, *Resolving Social Conflicts.* New York: Harper & Brothers, 1948, pp. 159ff.

[14] John Adair and Evon Vogt, "Navaho and Zuñi Veterans: A Study of Contrasting Modes of Culture Change," *American Anthropologist,* 1949, 51:547–561.

anticipators of change, but in a way different from that of the Navajo. They expect each individual among them to be unique in everything that he does. Imitation is deplored. Every woman has her own design for tapa cloth, even different designs for each piece and the opposite ends of the same piece. Every person is expected to improvise songs and dance steps for himself. Likewise for house builders, tattooers, and other specialists. The expectation of deviation even extends to religion and political organization, both for individuals and villages. Innovation is the rule, and in consequence the innovator receives only passing recognition. He is merely doing what is expected of him.[15]

This brings up another point, namely, that the expectation of change always envisages limits upon its operation. Change is expected only between certain minimal and maximal boundaries. It is constrained by traditional conceptions of propriety, and by traditional definitions of what constitutes newness. If it falls below the minimum, it is regarded as nothing new, as a mere variant, even though to the objective observer this pronouncement may seem entirely arbitrary. On the other hand, if it goes beyond the limits of expectation, it will be greeted with varying degrees of resistance, as happens when someone suggests a significant change in our social or political structure.

The restraints upon innovative activity are commonplace observations in comparative ethnological studies. The Samoan instance affords an excellent illustration. The innovations that loom so large to the Samoan are trivial if not imperceptible to the casual alien observer. Moreover, one who takes the trouble to analyze them finds that they all fall within the framework of a limited pattern. Toleration is within an extremely narrow range, and variations are correspondingly minute. The same can be said of women's fashion changes in our history. The annual variations in dress that are so greatly valued by our women of fashion are quite minute; they assume significant proportions only because attention is consciously directed toward them. Few men recognize the differences, except in dress lengths and breadths, from year to year precisely because it requires close attention to detect them. A radical departure would be definitely unstylish, beyond the bounds of expected change. As Kroeber, who has made a study of fashion changes over several centuries, says:[16]

. . . it is remarkable how virtually all changes of fashion, alike in Classical, Western, and East Asiatic costume, have consistently operated each within the basic dress pattern of its own civilization. Fashion creates a thousand bizarre forms and extravagances; but it never has produced, among Occidentals, a man's type of dress based on toga instead of trousers, nor a woman's with a Japanese silhouette.

[15] Mead, "The Role of the Individual in Samoan Culture," *loc. cit.*

[16] A. L. Kroeber, *Anthropology.* New York: Harcourt, Brace and Company, Inc., 1948, pp. 332–333.

Intensive studies, comparable to Kroeber's, have been made in other areas of artistic creation. Bunzel's analysis of Pueblo Indian pottery making reveals the same psychology.[17] Potters prided themselves upon their artistic freedom and fancied that their products were unique to themselves. Some of them claimed to have dreamed their decorative designs or to have envisioned them in sudden flashes of insight. The student of southwestern Indian pottery, however, finds that the departures are in reality only a reworking of traditional elements on a very limited scale. The same conclusions are to be drawn from O'Neale's study of Yurok and Karok Indian basketry.[18]

The testimonials and the preachments of Shakers are said by them to be spontaneously and divinely inspired. They say that you do not need to think about what you are going to say before you address a congregation; words will come to you when you get on your feet and begin to talk. This is certainly so, and there is no wonder about it; for all the exhortations follow a pattern that is apparent to anyone who has heard a few of them. The illusion of complete originality is due to the magnification of the freedoms permitted within a very narrow range.

The Palauans have an annual dance, performed solely for amusement, that combines a set of separate movements by two lines of young men or by two lines of young women. Each movement in the series must be new each year. Any one of the dancers may invent a figure or a movement, and all are encouraged to do so. The creator teaches the others his dance and they perform it in unison. In 1948 the new dances that I witnessed were novelties only in that they combined and recombined figures and steps drawn from alien sources and from other native performances. One of them was called the "one-step." It was executed by each dancer holding his hands as if he were grasping a partner close to him while he took one side-step after another. The "two-step" inventor had the dancer place his hands on his hips while he side-stepped around a square. Inquiry revealed that these posturings and maneuvers, or a semblance of them, had been learned from the Japanese, who had learned them from the Americans. Other dance movements betrayed the stimulus of the free motion pictures that the natives had been seeing at the naval station in Koror. To the dance steps seen in these pictures, and to certain purely Japanese ingredients, were added some of the most typical and recurring motifs in the aboriginal repertoire. Further analysis of these dances would not be appropriate at this juncture; it is enough to say that the Palauans, struggling under the requirement of novelty, were, like the Samoans and our fashion designers, much impressed by their own ingenuity.

[17] Ruth Bunzel, *The Pueblo Potter*. New York: Columbia University Press, 1929.
[18] L. M. O'Neale, "Yurok-Karok Basket Weavers," *University of California Publications in American Archaeology and Ethnology,* 32 (No. 1):1–182.

Not all expected cultural change is universally welcomed. Often it is deplored or dreaded by certain segments of a society. Typically the aged deplore a rate of change that upsets the norms of their youth. This plaint of the elders is well known to the majority of the young people of the United States. Most of them have heard diatribes against contemporary courting and child-rearing patterns, female behavior, progressive education, and the pernicious effects of the movies upon our morals. The critics of these things expect even more change to take place. Some refuse to accommodate themselves to it, some are resigned to it, and others say that they are glad that they will not be here to witness it. Immigrants to this country find it equally difficult to accept changes in behavior that bring their children into accord with American patterns and estrange them from their own; but most of these parents also regard such changes as inevitable.

Comparable attitudes develop among the members of societies that have been overwhelmed by alien customs as a result of conquest. The Palauans expect change in their culture and most of them are resigned to it; some gladly welcome it. This attitude is in harmony with their history. It appears that they have always been politically unsettled, and conquest and penalization for defeat are not new to them. Since the discovery of the islands by Europeans they have taken their domination by foreign peoples as a matter of course; it is a prerogative that goes to the victor. They are philosophical about the changes that have been introduced by the successive occupations of their homeland by Germans, Japanese, and Americans. Having read a few Japanese-language newspapers published in Honolulu since the war, some of them ask, "Who will be next? The Russians?"

In other subjugated groups the shock of conquest could not be harmonized with such a philosophy; or, even more commonly, the shock has been much more severe than in Palau. In such cases change is certainly expected, but in defeatism. Some dependent people accept the inevitable in despair, some with resignation, and others with bitterness.

The fact that a people expects change and yet does not welcome it does not mean that they are at the mercy of "social forces" over which they have no control. It may mean that they are at the mercy of other people whose ideas are opposed to theirs. Or, as frequently happens, it may mean that they have themselves made one choice that excludes another. It is doubtful whether any case could be found in which an anticipated change is not wanted by anyone. Its advocates may be members of a majority group or of a powerful minority, or they may be foreigners who are determined to impose their will upon their subordinates. But, in any event, the course of change is humanly conceived and directed; the anticipation of it takes form precisely because some individuals of superior influence or power are sponsoring it.

Stating that unwelcome anticipation may be self-initiated seems to be a contradictory formulation of the facts, but it is a common phenomenon nonetheless. After all, it seems quite human for a person to want to have his cake and eat it too. At least we can understand other people who respond in this way to the threatened loss of a cherished custom. Aboriginally the Yurok cultivated a variety of indigenous tobacco which they smoked for pleasure and also used upon ritual occasions. Over the years since the introduction of commercial tobacco by the white man they have gradually abandoned the planting of the native species. At the present time not more than one or two old men make an attempt at its cultivation; and very few individuals can get any of it for use in surviving rituals, such as those still considered to be necessary by some people for the healing of the sick. When these individuals are queried about their dilemma, they agree that they could still plant the native form; but they go on to point out that doing so is a lot of trouble, and that as far as taste goes they prefer the commercial brands of tobacco. In brief, their value system has changed. They have acquired a preference for the white man's tobacco and for his method of getting it. Obviously, it is easier to go to the store and buy tobacco than it is to plant and tend it—if you have the money.

It is usual for people to blame other causes for dilemmas that result from their uncomfortable or compromising choices. At one time the Palauans made excellent outrigger canoes from the trunks of large hardwood trees. These craft were propelled by paddles and sails, and their speed and beauty excited the admiration of many of the Europeans who saw them. The Palauans started to abandon their manufacture as soon as they began to use European boats. Inferior canoe types continued to be made until the Second World War; but the end came when the Japanese destroyed all that they could find during the siege of the islands by the Americans in 1945. At present only an occasional old man will be found making a canoe. The young men, and most of the older ones, too, want rowboats at least, and Diesel motors with them if it is at all possible. In consequence, few people have any kind of transportation at all. This situation was serious in 1947, and everyone complained about it. When the men were urged to build canoes, their response was that there were no more big trees. They had told themselves this so often that they had really come to believe it, so they were made uncomfortable when it was pointed out that there were such trees here and there, especially back in the hills. But getting those trees would be too difficult, they said, thereby relieving their discomfort with an argument that any civilized man could readily appreciate. The truth is, of course, that they no more want outrigger canoes than Americans want horses and buggies.

The passing of native Palauan carpentry offers a parallel case. Palauan men once spent much of their time in large and well-constructed club-houses that were reserved for groups of age mates. These buildings were erected and maintained at considerable expense and labor. Each village had at least one, and more often from two to six. Their importance as retreats and as gossip and work centers began to decline when the German authorities put restrictions upon the amount of time that men could spend in them. Now there are not more than a half dozen in the whole islands, a circumstance that saddens the older men who have spent many hours of their lives working, sleeping, and relaxing in them. When they are asked why new ones are not built or old ones reconstructed, they say that the Palauan population has declined to such an extent that there are too few men in a village to undertake the erection of a clubhouse and too few to enjoy it. When it is pointed out that anciently all small villages did have clubhouses, and when still other excuses are met, the real reason is finally admitted; namely, that too few people are interested enough in the old-style buildings to expend the necessary labor to build one.

These observations recall Rivers's contention that the use of objects may be abandoned for social and religious reasons, even though it seems that they would be indispensable to their users. He cites evidence to show that the natives of the Torres Islands have lost the art of canoe making because of the loss of skilled craftsmen whose knowledge was essential to the task. While acknowledging material causes for some losses of this kind, he emphasizes the importance of the nonmaterial.[19] It is true that some cultural changes may be forced by the withholding action of an environment, just as they may be prohibited by alien masters or other human agents with supreme power. Useful material objects have undoubtedly been lost in this way in many instances of colonization or expatriate residence. But an equal number have just as certainly been voluntarily abandoned, even though the stimulus has come from a negative aspect of the new habitat. They have been gradually abandoned because they have been relegated to the status of second choices by offerings in a new environment, just as new preferences develop in a changing culture.

Natural circumstances do not provide conditions sufficient to account for human behavior. In the last analysis social conditions do not either. The fundamental condition is the desire or nondesire of a person or a group of persons. For this reason Rivers's thesis, laudable as it is, does not put the emphasis where it should be. His suggestion that canoe making became a lost art in the Torres Islands perhaps as a result of some calamity that depleted the population and killed off the priest-craftsmen presumes a more direct connection between the two factors than actually exists. Even assuming the

[19] W. H. R. Rivers, "The Disappearance of Useful Arts," *Festskrift Tillägnad Edvard Westermarck*. Helsingfors, 1912, pp. 109–130.

occurrence of a catastrophe so sudden, violent, and selective as to cut down all the practicing canoe makers, it would be difficult to understand why there would not be apprentices more or less competent to take over the task during the emergency if it were considered important. Makeshifts are resorted to, even when esoteric lore is concerned, if the demand for them is imperative. On the other hand, the passing of a craft like canoe making at one fell stroke can be understood if there are no neophytes or others sincerely interested in perpetuating it. And this would be understandable if few people wanted canoes, or if some other profession or activity were more attractive and less burdensome than canoe making so that men have come to shun it. In either case the art would already have become moribund at the time of the calamity. Most people, or at least the key individuals in the demand situation, must already have anticipated the extinction of the craft, although they may have done so reluctantly.

The anticipation of an unwanted change, then, will not necessarily alert a people to forestall it. One reason is that desires are individual and not group attributes. A people cannot be said to want anything. Another reason is that wants are relative, and the priority of one desire often requires the denial of another. A custom may be abandoned either because its adherents prefer some alternative to it or because they prefer some alternative to a custom that is indispensable to its perpetuation.

A general expectation of change may be active, or it may exist at a low ebb, because of certain indoctrinated attitudes. The predisposition to order events in a historical sequence is one stimulus to anticipation. The application of a historical perspective, and the urge to link events in a temporal series, is not a pronounced trait in most societies. All people do, of course, see events against a time scale. But not all take an interest in doing this, nor in speculating upon its meaning, if they do indeed see any meaning in it at all. The temporal world for such people is spanned by their lifetimes, and their universe is often a very personal one. History as such, especially the history of impersonal or abstract concepts, is beyond their purview. Some cultural change is everywhere inevitable; but at times and in places it is so insensible that to a people who are lacking in time perspective it is not apparent. Discrete events are not aligned on a scale of past and present in a way to induce the concept of change; past and present are not conjoined with enough persistence or regularity for the phenomenon to make an impression and be conceptualized for future reference. Not having experienced change, the members of such societies do not expect any.

Another determinative of expectation that may be related to the foregoing is a philosophy which expresses the view that change is natural, inevitable, or morally good. Our philosophy contrasts with that of many primitive peoples in this respect. In its popular manifestations it has much in common with that of the Hindus, as the following quotation from the writings of an Indian scholar indicates:[20]

The most important generalization that is particularly relevant to Indian conditions is that mutations arise occasionally in culture due to the magnetic influence of great personalities. The Hindus postulate in their cosmologies a kind of see-saw movement in culture history; the rise and decline of culture follow one another with the regularity of the seasons; in fact there is much in common between this concept of the Hindu philosophers and that of Spengler, but with this difference that the former are more optimistic and believe that saviours appear at the needed moment to give an upward thrust to the forces that lead to human welfare. "For upholding dharma and its re-establishment I am born every epoch" says the Lord in the Bhagavad Gita. The importance of the part played by some outstanding personality in making qualitative changes in culture (mutations) and giving it a new direction and new sets of values transcending the bounds imposed by the existing limitations, is a factor in the history of culture that has not been given sufficient consideration. . . . The Sanskrit saying "the king is the creator of the Age" is centuries old. The wise king, according to Hindu belief, is the creator of the age, and is vested with the authority to modify existing practices to suit changed situations. If he creates the Krita (golden) age in the Kali (dark) age he gets salvation.

An expectation of change is also cultivated by the "problem" concept, especially as it relates to human behavior. Americans and Europeans especially are indoctrinated with this cultural perspective. We are concerned with all sorts of situations which we interpret as being unnecessary. They are not, we think, an essential part of the natural order. They are, in fact, disorders of the natural or man-made universe. They are eradicable discomforts or social evils. They need not or should not be; hence we should do something to alter them to conform to our specifications. Instead of accepting things as they are because they have always been that way, as many people do, we seek to change them. Problems are such an important stimuli to change because we make them out of the substance of our wishes. We have become accustomed to ask for solutions almost as freely and as often as the reality in our experience conflicts with our hopes.

Finally, there is the notion of progress as a stimulus to the expectation of change. This concept, too, is almost unique to European civilization and its offshoots. It is, moreover, a relatively recent development in our cultural history, having taken its rise about the end of the seventeenth century in Europe.[21] It is the loadstone of our ambition, and we make it the justifica-

[20] A. Aiyappan, "Theories of Culture Change and Culture Contact." In J. P. Mills (ed.), *Essays in Anthropology Presented to Rai Bahadur Sarat Chandra Roy.* Lucknow, pp. 46–48.

[21] Frederick Teggart, *Theory of History.* New Haven: Yale University Press, 1925, Chap. 8.

tion for the changes we hope for and suggest. It is our rationalization for the attitude of superiority that we hold with respect to most of the world's population. It is a philosophical interpretation of change, a moral polarization of cultural transitions in terms of better or worse, advance or stagnation. While it is thus merely an evaluation of change and is more often subjective than not, it is nonetheless a powerful incentive to change because of its moral and transcendent implications. It holds that advancement is natural, is certain, and has an unlimited future on the way to ultimate but far distant perfection. It reasons that, since we should always aim at perfection and since there are no finite limits to progress, we must always be prepared to accept change.

CHAPTER III

THE CULTURAL BACKGROUND
(CONTINUED)

The Dependence upon Authority. There is a positive correlation between individualism and innovative potential. The greater the freedom of the individual to explore his world of experience and to organize its elements in accordance with his private interpretation of his sense impressions, the greater the likelihood of new ideas coming into being. Contrariwise, the more the reliance upon authoritative dictates, the less the frequency of new conceptualizations. When individuals are taught to revere and fear authority as the ultimate source of the good, the true, and the proper, they cannot be expected to have variant notions. When they are indoctrinated with the virtue of dependency, the ideals of curiosity, personal inquiry, and evaluation are denigrated; and whole blocks and societies of individuals become nucleated into single ranges of possibilities.

The dependency attitude is variable by society, as well as by individuals within a society. Some persons are voluntarily more dependent than others, but this raises questions of another order than those being considered here. For the time being, our concern is with conditions that inspire shared attitudes and predispositions. These group conditions regulate the ranges for dependency, its orientation, and its intensity. The requirements are never absolute and complete. They stipulate dependency for certain situations and for certain individuals. At the same time, individual independence of thought and action is encouraged in other contexts.

Restrictions upon individual inquiry and decision may be either consciously or unconsciously imposed. Deliberate measures may be instituted by internal or external agents of power, in which case the limitations upon individualism are consciously appreciated, at least by their sponsors. On the other hand, there are cultural dead spots, determined by the mores of a people, wherein free inquiry is voluntarily avoided. Such areas, like those of sex, humanitarian ideals, and patriotism in our own society, are posted by the authority of tradition. To probe them is considered to be indelicate, sacrilegious, or inhuman. All societies have their bestial preserves, proscribed to all but the lost and the damned.

The dependence upon authority is intimately associated with other cultural inflections. It is inherent in the process of socialization, but this takes on various colorings and emphases in different societies. The long process of indoctrinating the young with group standards in accordance with parental interpretations of them is by nature an authoritarian mechanism. The aim of the elders is to inculcate norms, and this must mean the ignoring or overriding of individual differences in attempts to level them. The aim of standardization is never fully realized, and is perhaps scarcely ever fully intended. Individual differences always remain, but the program is basically and severely delimitative of personal whim and preference. And it is ex cathedra. It does not tolerate rational inquiry. It maintains itself by fiat and coercion.

Although socialization as such is an authoritarian device, it varies by society in the range and in the intensity of its application. In other words, children are given more freedom of individual expression in some ethnic groups than in others; and there are lesser and greater emphases upon strict adherence to the norm in the same behavioral field when one group is compared with others. We, for example, encourage imagination and experimentation on the part of our children in much of their play but not in matters of sex. The Polynesians, however, included this aspect of behavior in their permissive area. Various interpretations of adulthood also reveal themselves as cultures are compared; there are shorter or longer periods of juvenile dependency and of unquestioning submission to the authority of the elders. Most primitive societies hasten to confer the status of adulthood early in life, commonly making it coincide with physical maturity. We postpone it until long after that event. The native Australians and the Palauans go to the extreme of keeping most individuals in a dependency status most of their lives. Finally, it is to be noted that there are differences in the matter of dependency with respect to the treatment of the sexes. Men and women may be treated the same, as they were in many American Indian tribes, especially the Iroquois; or women may be made subservient to their fathers, brothers, and husbands throughout their lifetimes, as they are in Japan, Palau, and parts of New Guinea.

The dependence upon authority is correlated with the development of specialized knowledge in particular fields. This is an almost necessary linkage, because the mass of the people must accept the views of specialists on complex matters the details of which are mysteries to them. The more intricate the knowledge, the greater must be the dependence, if there is any appeal to the specialists at all. People everywhere must take the word of their prophets and their medicine men. American culture, with its multiplication of specialties and the extreme complication of many of them, offers a good example. Few of us are competent to judge the merits of vaccination on the basis of personal inquiry and research. Not one in a thousand of us has made a study of the process or a controlled check upon its efficacy. Nevertheless the majority of us accept the assurances of the specialists that it will give us immunity. Similarly, very few of us know how to forecast

the weather or repair automobiles, radios, or clocks. We ar
the diagnoses and the good faith of trained men in these fiel
plans and for the continued functioning or the trade-in values
clocks and radios that we own. Illustrations could be multipli
Indeed, because of specialization, Americans are constantly lis
voice of authority from some quarter. This dependence has bec   a habit
with us. As a people we have an almost slavish regard for "experts" in
any field. We call upon them in our courts, appeal to them for advice in
formulating our laws, and are swayed in our politics and in our philosophies
by them. There are even professional experts in fields like news evaluation,
personnel advising, industrial management, child rearing, and vocational
guidance. All this dependence on experts contrasts with the situation found
in less elaborated cultural systems, where most men are jacks of almost all
trades.

There are certain areas of culture that appear to be more desirable or
suitable for authoritative controls than others. This may be because these
fields offer the greatest returns to power seekers; or because they are areas
wherein dependency is most humanly appealing; or simply because they are
so all-inclusive that any idea or behavior must fall within one or the other
of them as they are defined. However this may be, it has happened repeatedly that authoritative systems have emerged in government, science, and
religion.

Under authoritative political systems the emphasis is upon the establishment of a dogmatic social philosophy. The dependent subjects are urged or
coerced into submission to the dictates of those in control in accordance with
a theory which apotheosizes the paternalistic virtues of the select few and
minimizes the intellectual abilities of the masses. Often the parent-child
parallel is manifest or latent in this philosophy. The leader-elders know
what is best for their spiritual children. Hence, the techniques of regimentation, obscurantism, and corrective punishment for the misguided or the will-
fully perverse are justified. As far as innovation is concerned, the results are
negativistic. That is well recognized in authoritarian regimes. Regimentation
and obscurantism are designed to suppress or depress individualistic thinking because it is likely to be subversive of the existing order. When the Inca
Roca founded the school for nobles at Cuzco sometime after the middle of
the thirteenth century, he is alleged to have said that "the children of the
common people should not learn the sciences, which should be known only
by the nobles, lest the lower classes should become proud and endanger the
commonwealth." [1] He was the ruler of one of the most completely paternalistic governments on record and certainly one of the most interesting

[1] Philip A. Means, *Ancient Civilizations of the Andes*. New York: Charles Scribner's
Sons, 1931, p. 305.

ᴊm the standpoint of its appearance in time. The idea, if not the wording, of his dictate is familiar to us from recent developments in European history.

There are, of course, all degrees of state paternalism. In its extreme form it is usually associated with the conquest of one group by another, although even in the relationships between the victors and the vanquished there are all degrees of freedom allowed to subservient populations. The colonial governments of modern times have experimented with all sorts of authoritarianism under the pressure of enlightened self-interest and the periodic surges of conscience called humanitarianism.

Political thought control does not have an absolutely dampening effect upon individual thought. It sets the limits for discovery and innovation but does not outlaw them altogether. It forbids antithetical social innovations; but it encourages and even subsidizes new ideas that further its own ends in the social, the technological, and the humanistic fields. Witness the Nazi fictions relative to the racial superiority of the Aryans and the Russian version of the history of inventions. Nor can it be denied that the Nazis were inventive in warfare and in the technology that contributes to its success. The Inca state offers parallels in other departments of culture. The members of the Inca nobility were unquestionably brilliant administrators; and they subsidized some of the most remarkable industries known to the primitive world, among them the artistic weaving of cloth and the manufacture of metal objects. Authoritarianism in government, like authoritarianism in anything else, sets the goals and the limits of ingenuity rather than suppressing it completely.

All of us like to believe that science is free of dogmatism, and most of us do. The scientific ideal calls for an eagerness for truth, no matter what it may be, and consequently for open-mindedness toward new ideas. The impartial observer, however, will find that this ideal is less frequently realized in practice than is generally claimed and supposed. Most scientists are not the dispassionate seekers after truth that their self-concept and their popular stereotype demands. Their emotional involvements with their scientific ideas are complex, and some of these involvements will be considered in the chapters on the acceptance and rejection of innovations. For the present we are concerned with the dependence upon authority as an extrinsic consideration in the evaluation of new scientific ideas; and we are to note that judgments based upon this criterion commonly result in the discouragement and suppression of unorthodox views. In other words, new ideas are frequently scouted by scientists, not because of their intrinsic merits but because they do not conform to existing doctrine.

The period of the combined Dark and Middle Ages in Europe is notorious for its ignorance of natural phenomena and for its lack of original thinking in science. The ignorance and the folkloristic character of the natural history of the period are not to be wondered at, for Europe did not descend into the Dark Ages; with the exception of a small corner, it was already in that state when Rome fell. It simply remained there until it was able to assimilate the learning of the Greeks and their immediate cultural heirs. This process took a long time, and the approach was through a reverence for the authority of Aristotle, Galen, and Avicenna. It may be said that this dependence upon pronouncement as a guide to belief was due to the domination of learning by the Church, but this does not in itself explain the essential aspect of the dependence. It helps one to understand why the devout accepted the dicta of the learned clerics, but not why the latter accepted those of the learned pagans. Essentially the attitude had nothing to do with religion. It was a cultural value of the times. The informed men of that day were scholastics; they were dedicated to the study of books, not nature. They were given to metaphysics and logic, not observation. They valued niceties and subtleties of reasoning rather than the testimony of the senses. Above all, they sought and believed they could achieve finality and absolutism in place of change and relativism. This is the essence of dogmatism; and while it was idealized in the Middle Ages it is not peculiar to that era nor to theologians.

Murray's study of nineteenth-century scientific theories is relevant at this point.[2] His aim has been to show that important new ideas of so recent a date were almost without exception ignored or rejected by the scientific fraternity itself because they did not conform to one or another of the accepted doctrines of the leaders of opinion. The observations and discoveries of Jenner, Simpson, Lyell, Pasteur, Darwin, Lister, Helmholtz, Metchnikoff, and scores of lesser contributors were greeted with disdain or incredulity. Repeatedly their critics refused even to be shown. Helmholtz, for example, had difficulty getting physiologists to pay any attention to his ophthalmoscope; one believed it would be dangerous to admit "naked light" into a diseased eye, while another felt that the instrument might be useful to an oculist with poor vision but that he himself had no need of it. Most illuminating of all is the fact that one dogma fell only to be replaced by another. The upstart view of one generation became the inviolable creed of the next, and not infrequently this metamorphosis took place in the career of a single individual.

It would be unrealistic to believe that dogmatism in science ended in 1900. Even if we did not have such flagrant examples as the Nazi doctrine of "Aryan" racial supremacy and the Communist credo of dialectic materialism, it would not be difficult to point to less publicized instances. They are known to every discipline in small or large degree. Every area of knowledge at the present time has its "big names" whose opinions in science and out of it carry weight and prevail over the views of lesser lights just because

[2] Robert H. Murray, *Science and Scientists in the Nineteenth Century*. London, 1925.

they are recognized authorities. Some men are jealous of these prerogatives, some not. It is as easy to be pontifical in the scientific domain as in any other, especially after a lifetime of dedication to the proof of an idea.

Religion is not necessarily the authoritarian phenomenon that it is sometimes supposed to be. It can be thoroughly dogmatic, and there are many instances of its having been so. Dogmatism is a frequent concomitant of a systematized creed and a well-institutionalized priestly hierarchy. The essential condition is unified control with a discipline that is dedicated to its unquestioning support. This condition directly parallels the requirement for an authoritative secular administration. In both instances it is necessary that there be only one source of truth and that the source be accorded enough power to enforce its dictates. In religion this condition has been met by the exclusionist faiths, those which assert that their founder has the only true insight into divine word and purpose. These faiths characteristically declare that their founders were divinely appointed and are the givers of the law as ordained by God. The pronouncements of venerated leaders are alleged to be due to divine inspiration and are not to be tampered with. The authoritarian bias is strengthened by the development of a priesthood and an organized church, for these things increase the values at stake in any threatened disruption of the system. Heretical views may not be tolerated, not only because they are contrary to inveterate truths, but because they threaten the economic and the ideological commitments of the church fathers.

The burden of the foregoing remarks is that authoritarianism is not an intrinsic aspect of religion. In many cases considerable latitude is permitted the individual in his interpretation of spiritual benefits and requirements. There are always bounds to his interpretation in this as in any other aspect of culture, but they may be only the limitations that are imposed by cultural perspectives. In other words, individuals may be constrained in their concept of the supernatural, just as they are in technology and in art, by the conventional thought channels of their group rather than by any formally established prescriptions and prohibitions. Within the universe of what is considered to be religion the individual may have the same sense of utter freedom of interpretation that the Palauan dancer has.

Shakerism has this characteristic and the appeal that accompanies it. The cult has only a very weakly developed dogmatic component, and none which asserts that an absolute and final truth has been revealed. This characteristic stems in part from a lack of decisive and impressive leadership but more definitely from the character of the cult itself. Its appeal lies in its permissiveness, which is comparable to that of a revival meeting. In consequence there is an almost total lack of restraint upon individual interpretations of tenet and ritual. Anyone may introduce a change under the sanction of an intuitive demand called a "gift." A host of changes have been suggested and many of them followed because of personal tastes and preferences. One

Yakima man now living is responsible for at least seven innovations concerning belief and ritual that have been accepted by other members of the church.

The Shaker example points to the crux of the question of innovative freedom. The existence of standards of behavior presumes that they are supported by some authoritative controls. The belief system which sustains these controls may permit a wide or a narrow range of individual interpretations. Tradition may allow flexibility or deny it; but in either case, if the belief system or the control mechanism that it supports is weakened or eliminated, the individual is thrown upon his own resources to innovate or accept some other dogma.

The collapse of controls during periods of social and political upheaval opens the way for innovation. The confusion attending conquest, civil strife, and economic booms and depressions offers auspicious circumstances for the emergence of new ideas, many of them predatory. Revolutions and coups do not in themselves breed the idea of political change. The aim of rebels is to institute changes that they have already formulated in their minds. The revolution is an attempt to put preconceived ideas into practice. Nevertheless, the instability of the transition period offers multiple opportunities for the exercise of ingenuity. There is a premium upon initiative and resource. Crises develop by the hour, and unprecedented and unexpected situations arise that demand individual and novel decisions. The expediences developed by modern subversive activities and the devices of resistance and underground movements during the Second World War and since attest to the inventive stimulus of chaotic situations. A spy is "on his own," and he must be ingenious to survive.

Frontier unsettlement and boom-town disorganization offer auspicious circumstances for the inception and the acceptance of new ideas. The land rush into Oklahoma when the territory was opened for white settlement, the gold rushes to California and to Alaska, and the oil booms in Texas and Oklahoma invited and forced men to live by their wits. All, or almost all, traditional controls were relaxed or abandoned. Men took custom into their own hands and devised a means of living as best they could with others from diverse walks and conditions of life who were eager to do the same. Improvisations, extemporizations, and trials and errors were the rules of action.

On a much-reduced but nonetheless significant scale the same thing happened during the Second World War. There was a tremendous shifting and churning of the American population while the conflict lasted, and the stirring has not been quieted yet. Millions of men served in the armed forces, there to meet and be compelled to get along with others whose ways were diverse beyond their previous realization. Thousands of civilians changed their residences, their routine habits, and their ideas about other people, cities, and customs. Families were disrupted, women worked as they never had before, new friendships and entirely new communities of strangers were formed. All these developments were new in themselves, but in addition the individuals who were involved had to make adjustments to meet the new conditions. The total effect of this vast mixing of people is not yet apparent and will not be for a long time, but it is certain to be significant. Part of the changes were due to the apposition of divergent value systems, *i.e.*, to the conjunction of differences. Fully as many were due to the relaxation of controls. The two go together. The relaxed controls were multiple and often very subtle; not the least among them were those of family and provincial allegiances.

The effect of all such situations in which there is an abandonment or a withdrawal of authoritative controls is to cut the individual adrift from his moorings. He loses his orientation points, and he must take new bearings in order not to drift aimlessly and anxiously. The microcosm in which he has lived has been destructuralized and is not habitable in that condition. He strains to give it some organization and some meaning, and in so doing he innovates or accepts the definition of the situation offered by others. Or, still more often, he and his associates work out a solution together. Sherif's experimental data upon the compulsive urge to reconstitute a disorganized experiential field will be discussed in another place, but it is relevant at this point, too.

The Competition of Rivals. Modern businessmen incline to the view that competition is an essential spur to progress. This idea has overtones of the "economic man" theory of labor, if it is not an offshoot of it. Its implication is that human beings are inherently lazy and, unless they are forced to exert themselves by the economic threat of rivals, they will relax in a rut. In so far as the theory singles out competition to the exclusion of other incentives to labor, it is certainly in error. There are many other inducements to increased activity and to raising the level of aspiration of the individual. There is no denying, however, that within the frame of reference implied by the proposition competition is a stimulus of great importance.

Competition is a potent incentive when mutually desirable rewards are allocated on the basis of performance. In such situations it is productive not only of increased effort but also of distinctly new kinds of effort to achieve greater shares of the reward. It stimulates innovation as well as prolonged and intensified effort along conventional lines. It can do this, not only in struggles for economic rewards, but in contests for favors, prestige, adherents, and power. Sometimes the competition is strictly individualized. On the other hand, it may require the cooperation of individuals organized into political parties, clubs, sects, factions, schools of thought, or ethnic groups.

The pressure of competition may inspire innovation in several ways. If it does no more, it always accentuates the rivalry situation by polarizing the differences between the contestants. It sets them apart and prepares the way for reciprocally interacting withdrawal mechanisms that are characterized by greater or less novelty in their conception. Sometimes the only new thing that develops is a magnification of some original distinction between the rivals, a quantitative elaboration of something that already exists. Bateson calls this "schismogenesis." He distinguishes between the cumulative antithesis of rivals, which he calls symmetrical differentiation, and the progressive elaboration of distinctions between nonrivals, which he calls complementary differentiation. Thus, the boasting of competitors, if unrestrained, would lead to more and more self-glorification and perhaps ultimately to open conflict. In complementary differentiation, if a display of exhibitionism on the part of one person calls for admiration on the part of another, each reaction may be a stimulus for the further magnification of the other.[3] In such instances nothing qualitatively new has been conceived. In the end there is simply more of the same. The total situation has been altered, however, and this must not be overlooked in a study of change.

Differentials that are developed under the stimulus of competition may be qualitatively distinct. New ideas that are produced under such circumstances often have as their main purpose the further differentiation of rivals. These novelties are never creations out of nothing. Like other innovations, either they are due to the reworking of old elements in the rivalry situation or they are importations, that is, ideas previously considered appropriate to other situations. The devising of distinguishing insignia, slogans, names, gestures, and rituals is a familiar tactic of competitive groups of all descriptions. The early Christians, in their efforts to dissociate themselves from the Jews, renounced circumcision, blood sacrifice, and many purification rites and instituted baptism, communion, the Trinity, Sunday as a day of rest, and the cross as a symbol. Protestantism has not only rejected many features of the Catholic Church but has gone on to develop tenets and rituals of its own, such as predestination, unitarianism, and revival meetings. Christian missionaries of all sects make a deliberate effort to prevent a confusion of their faith with local native religions, and in so doing they are often innovative. The first Catholic missionaries around Puget Sound called the sacraments "medicines" in their attempts to translate their meaning to the Indians. One priest, Father Blanchet, invented the so-called "Catholic ladder," a device for pictorially presenting the history of the Christian religion to the natives.

Fraternal organizations have their characteristic rituals, gestures, and insignia that requires some degree of ingenuity in their conception if they are to be made different from those of their rivals. Very often there are only very minor differences between these symbols, but they loom large to those who wish to draw distinctions, and they are magnified for the benefit of out-

[3] Gregory Bateson, "Culture Contact and Schismogenesis," *Man*, 1935, 199:181.

siders. Political factions make the most of the same principle in their appeals for popular support. In addition, they concoct alluring or inflammatory slogans to stir the populace to action against opponents: "Tippecanoe and Tyler Too," "The Full Dinner Pail," "A Car in Every Garage," and "The New Deal."

Another innovative formula calls for the spreading of damaging rumors, canards, and fictions about opponents—mudslinging, it is popularly called. The Protestants who were competing with the Catholics for Indian converts around Puget Sound toward the end of the nineteenth century stressed their puritanical moral code and magnified the Catholic departures from it. One Presbyterian missionary accused the priests of encouraging the use of spirituous liquors among the Indians and once exhibited for the enlightenment of his congregation a regenerated parishioner who, he said, had fallen from grace under Catholic tutelage. He and other Protestants in the area at the time publicly deplored the evils of quick conversions for which they belabored the Catholics. The issue of puritanism has had important political repercussions on a national scale in the United States. Cleveland's campaign for the presidency in 1884 was aided by the slogan "Rum, Romanism, and Rebellion," which damaged his opponent James G. Blaine.

Missionaries have been prone to falsify the meaning and the intent of native religious practices in order to eliminate them. In the past, at least, Christians have been disposed to refer to all native religious conceptions as nonsense and to attribute only the basest motives to shamans and magicians. The Shakers have been slandered by a variety of fictitious notions. On their side they have an enviable defamation mechanism at their disposal in their visions and "gifts," admirably suited as it is to the expression of divinely sanctioned prejudices. As a result they have often made damaging allegations about outsiders and each other and have compiled private histories of the cult that are colored by their individual enmities and preferences.

Opposites are particular manifestations of contrasts, and they are especially effective in distinguishing rivals. This segregative device makes the issues clear-cut, and when distinction is an advantage it will be exploited. Thus, the Shakers are inveterate foes of shamans and have made repeated efforts to isolate themselves from them. In the eyes of the cult's members they themselves are all that is good, and the medicine man is all that is bad. Their curing power comes from above, the medicine man's from below, or theirs from the right and his from the left. The medicine man cures for money; the Shakers will accept no pay for their services. The medicine man kills out of malice or for pay, while they will only heal. Mary Slocum, the wife of the cult's founder, became a bitter rival of another Indian called Mud Bay Louis in the contest for cult leadership. She advocated changes upon several occasions that were the opposites of his "teachings," such as black "garments" instead of white and a clockwise instead of a counterclockwise ritual circuit of the church room.

Advertising slogans, within the limits of nonlibelous distinctions, draw invidious contrasts between the products of rival companies. The less explicit the suggested inferiority of competitive brands the better, both from a legal and from a psychological standpoint. The potential consumer thus may read as much into the slogan as he wishes, and the steady customer may identify himself with the superlative qualities of the product of his intelligent choice. Hence the effectiveness of such slogans as "All *We* Sell Is the Goods," "We Are Tobacco Men, Not Medicine Men," "The Salt That Is *All* Salt," "Ask the Man Who Owns One," and "Gush, the *Richer* Milk."

All the foregoing discussion relates to innovations which serve to differentiate the competitors themselves. Apart from this well-exploited area, there is the one wherein their activities give substance to their competitive claims. Within it occurs the kind of innovation that is generally considered in discussions of the subject; and it is the one which, we all hope, pays off in the long run. In this area of invention, superior performance is the goal; that is, superior as determined by commonly accepted scales of value as they apply to specific achievements. Instruments or techniques are sought which, by their comparative excellence, will give them an advantage over existing mechanisms for achieving the same result. They strive to be more reasonable, rapid, economical, beautiful, honorific, adequate, efficient, scientific, protective, tasteful—in fact, more anything to the discomfort of rivals who advocate alternatives.

Competition has given direction to the effort behind modern technological developments. It has reached its zenith in subsidized research programs in the United States. At the present time all large automotive, petroleum, electrical, metallurgical, and pharmaceutical concerns employ research staffs to create new products that will give their makers a commercial advantage over their competitors. The goals of the researchers are changes that will conform to the ideal of improvement or progress. The same efforts are evident in the mercantile world, in college offerings, and in regional and city planning when economic considerations enter. Advertising techniques themselves have evolved under the competitive stimulus.

Competition for prestige has produced a wide range of novelties. Innovative efforts under this impetus naturally depend upon current and acceptable values relative to prestige credit. In American society, as in many others, wealth is the symbol of, and the essential qualification for, social preeminence and, to a large extent, political power. Consequently, many novel devices for the exhibition of wealth have been evolved. Several remarkable techniques have been created to further the ostentatious display and waste of wealth: imported clothing, exotic foods and drinks, bizarre and costly entertainments, custom-built cars, lavish tipping, ubiquitous servants, private swimming pools and gymnasiums, etc. The Kwakiutl Indians also valued wealth and accorded social position and power to those who were most extravagant with it. They exploited the potlatch as a mechanism for competition and the ostentatious display of wealth. Basically the potlatch was an institution for the reciprocal exchange of gifts upon specified occasions, but the Kwakiutl exhibited considerable ingenuity in their invention of several ramifications and elaborations upon this fundamental idea.[4]

Wealth is, of course, not the only means of achieving status, nor is it the only one that has been brought within the framework of competitive innovation. Fighting ability has in some societies assumed major importance, while hunting skill or oratorical ability has been prized in others. In all cases new techniques and instruments for achieving success under competition have been evolved. The warfare pattern of the Indians of the Great Plains and the political warfare in our own society provide illustrations.

Competition can also lead to imitation. Native populations the world over have adopted guns when they have been able to do so in order to fight on equal terms with the Europeans. Some white men adopted the Indian custom of scalping and in turn passed the idea along to still other Indian groups who previously had been unacquainted with the practice. In order to reach a goal competitors often adopt the methods of each other; you "must fight fire with fire." In itself such borrowing creates nothing new; but, as we have seen, the borrowed object or technique is inevitably modified in the process of imitation. The modification may be unconscious or it may be deliberate. The industrial ideas that Japan adopted from the United States under the stimulus to compete with the Western world were altered to fit Japanese standards. Similarly for the westernization of Turkey. Kemal Ataturk felt the need to bring his country into the orbit of western Europe in order to maintain its life as a nation to be reckoned with in world councils. He imported many Western ideas, but they had to be modified to integrate with the rest of Turkish culture. Sometimes competition encourages imitative attempts that are deliberately innovative. The aim in patent infringement is just this, and so are efforts to mislead the public in the deceptive labeling of commodities. In both cases the intention of the imitator is to engage in competition with some existing article by creating a likeness of it that is near enough to the original to serve the interests of competition yet is dissimilar enough to avoid the legal charge of duplication.

Competition exists everywhere in some degree, but the amount and variety of it is conditioned to a large extent by tradition. There are ethnic differences in the extent to which it is encouraged, tolerated, or merely expected. Americans frown upon it within the circle of individuals who are

[4] H. G. Barnett, "The Nature of the Potlatch," *American Anthropologist*, 1938, 40 (No. 3):349–358.

considered to be blood relatives and between husband and wife, yet it exists in those areas. We deplore sibling competition for parental favors and for rewards outside the family except in a spirit of fun. We consider it to be appropriate in most other fields. It is evident in the struggle for economic, political, artistic, and social rewards; it occurs in play-group situations, athletics, education, and in membership recruiting of many kinds. It is considered to be inappropriate in religion, and for the most part it is absent within any given sect; but competition between religious groups of different persuasions is notorious just because people, even those who engage in it, deplore it. The Dobuans expect hostility and competition between all individuals except those who are related to each other through their mothers. Man and wife, father and child, are in continuous and ugly rivalry throughout the whole period of their intimate association in family life. Every advantage that is gained is at the expense of some rival. The Zuñi Indians, by contrast, consider rivalry unbecoming in almost any situation. Their ideal is cooperation and mutual aid. They advocate the humble acceptance of leadership as an obligation to the community, not as a means of self-aggrandizement.[5]

Incentives to competition are culturally determined. Where it is a pronounced feature of a people's life, the young are trained to engage in it. They are taught to take pride in their individual abilities, to measure themselves against others, and to try their powers in contests with their fellows. The stress upon individualism gives a further coloring and emphasis to this ideal. If a person is taught that he is personally responsible for his fate and that he must rely upon himself alone in the struggle for rewards, he will be inclined to press his interests at the expense of others. And the more positive the insistence upon self-sufficiency, the more keen and brutal will be the competition. Patterns of child treatment also encourage or discourage competition. If parents show preferences, either consciously or unconsciously, for the first child, or for the last, rivalries are almost certain to develop among the children. If, in addition, interfamily competition is a marked trait in the society, as it is in the United States, children will be pitted very early in contests with the children of other families, whether in pride of possession, manners, talent, or precocity. The ego projection of parents results in their engaging in vicarious struggles with their neighbors upon any issues that affect their pride. Threats of deprivation, loss of favor and power, are also incentives to competition, even in societies where no pattern exists for its expression. Contrariwise a system of rewards may also provide incentives.

There are as many deterrents upon the play of competition as there are incentives to it. Its unrestricted functioning is curtailed in some places by

[5] Ruth Benedict, *Patterns of Culture*. Boston: Houghton Mifflin Company, 1934, Chaps. 4 and 5.

ethical considerations. We are familiar with this kind of moderator in our rules of fair play and in our codes of business ethics. The rules that are adhered to in these instances are self-imposed, although in most cases they are motivated by an enlightened self-interest. They assert that there are limits to what one may do in order to achieve his goal if it is not to be an empty accomplishment, for the violator of the rule can expect to be scorned and avoided in the future even though he may get the reward he sought. In American society there are also legal controls upon unrestricted competition, such as Federal laws upholding food and drug standards, local regulations concerning building permits, and standardizations of weights and measurements.

Class or other social group discriminations act as barriers to competition. The members of minority groups may be handicapped in unobtrusive ways, or subtle pressures may be exerted upon them to force them out of the competitive field. The threat of physical punishment has the same effect, and not infrequently it is used for this purpose. In many instances the members of one class cannot compete with the members of another, not because they are intimidated, but because their economic, educational, or other circumstances place them at a disadvantage in comparison with the more favored members of other classes. The uneducated man is handicapped in his job pursuit on certain levels; and the man with small capital cannot compete with well-endowed organizations, regardless of his business abilities.

Specialized training of any sort reduces the number of competitors who may realistically hope for success in the area where it is demanded, and persons without the necessary qualifications do not even try for the rewards that it offers. To be sure, competition may prevail among the specialists; but it is so demanding that novices disqualify themselves. In most instances, as in the legal, artistic, and medical professions in American society, untrained persons never think of becoming competitors of the specialists. Even in amateur sports, games, and a variety of quiz contests, many individuals eliminate themselves if it is suggested that they become contestants. They regard those who have already entered or are likely to enter the competition as being "out of my class." Professionalism and other manifestations of specialized training automatically reduce the number of candidates for any reward to a relatively small and select proportion of the total population.

The humiliation that failure brings is another deterrent to competition, and this to a large extent is culturally determined. The Manus people of the Admiralty Islands train their children for self-sufficiency and self-confidence. They watch over their infants very carefully and assist them in every way, taking care to give them no cause for anxiety or distrust of the adult world. Young people are encouraged to be always more proficient, but they are not pampered or shamed when they fail. In consequence, the Manus child enters adolescence without feelings of inferiority, ready to undertake anything with an aggressive self-assurance of success. "He grows up to be an adult wholly admirable from a physical standpoint, skilled, alert, fearless, resourceful in the face of emergency, reliable under strain." [6] The Palauans are the diametric opposite. They are timid and uncertain of themselves. They never know just where they stand, and it is easy to shake their self-confidence. They are not trained for leadership or the responsibilities of adult life, and most individuals avoid both. The majority avoid the making of decisions, because doing so is the prerogative of the few and being presumptuous in this regard can bring only criticism.

The public aspect of competition has much to do with the willingness to engage in it. If humiliation attaches to failure, the less conspicuous it is the better from the standpoint of encouraging participation in contests. The dramatization of a contest has a terrifying effect upon those who have been sensitized to defeat. Preoccupation with the possibility of failure and the prevision of it in a public spectacle are enough to cause them to renounce any thoughts of competing. Furthermore, the intimacy of the contest situation wherein the competitors are vis-à-vis is doubly repellent to the person who has been made uncertain of himself. Confronted by his rival, he feels very acutely the nightmare of his self-doubts. In societies where such anxieties are induced, secret or anonymous competition is likely to engage a larger segment of the population than are publicized contests.

As has been implied in reference to the Palauans and others, the fostering of a dependent attitude depresses the level of competitive intensity. The theory that the individual is helpless to meet his needs by his own efforts is not calculated to promote the competitive urge. On the contrary it induces, if it does not advocate, complacency and disinterest in change. The impartial apportionment of benefits as natural rights rather than as rewards for striving eliminates the need for competition even as it dissipates the need for initiative. Paternalistic states, like indulgent fathers, must be rich in resources and in confidence to perpetuate for posterity the advantages they have gained.

Monopolistic practices obstruct competition and sometimes are initiated for that purpose. Trade monopolies are ancient and primitive. So are controls over services and means of production. Sometimes exclusive controls are inherited, sometimes granted, sometimes usurped, sometimes acquired by purchase. Aztec merchants were given the foreign-trade monopoly and many additional special privileges by their city-state. They constituted a subethnic unit of their own and lived in luxury. Samoan house builders, who were organized into very effective trade unions using strike and boycott techniques, claimed their privileged status by divine institution. Trusts and

[6] Margaret Mead, *Growing Up in New Guinea*. New York: William Morrow & Company, Inc., p. 47.

cartels in modern industry and the closed shop, collective bargaining, and industry-wide organizations among laborers restrict competition in the interests of greater and assured common benefits. The practice of acquiring patent rights to inventions for the sole purpose of suppressing them to protect investments is a direct means of blocking change through eliminating competitive possibilities. Monopolistic practices as such are not necessarily deterrents to innovation. In fact they encourage new ideas within controlled limits.[7] On the other hand, they are directed toward minimizing the total number of innovations by reducing the number of individuals who may hope to profit from their new ideas.

The Deprivation of Essentials. The terms in this heading must be defined before it can have real meaning. "Deprivation," as the word is used here, refers to the elimination of something that a person believes he has the right to expect. It includes the expropriation of some good that was once available and also the withdrawal of the promise of some good that has not been realized but has been enjoyed in anticipation. Furthermore, we must include in the discussion of this incentive to innovation not only actual deprivation but the threat of it. "Essentials" is an entirely relative term. It takes on meaning only in the light of the system of values of a specific ethnic group. An essential is something which a particular group of people consider to be imperative for their survival or continued functioning in a customary and valued manner. Essentials are therefore highly particularistic and culturally determined. A people do not have a need for "food," which is an abstraction. They need a specific kind or kinds of food, and frequently they elect to perish rather than consume that which is considered food by some other group. The need for rest and relaxation is universal only in the sense that these words comprehend particular phenomena known to most or all people; any individual who can be designated demands a particular kind of rest in a particular way and at particular times. The concept of essentials must have this meaning in a study of behavior; otherwise it is worthless for an understanding of motivation.

Although essentials are specifics, there are a number of specifics that are given the rating of an essential by diverse ethnic groups. The repeated coincidence of these evaluations brings it about that several recurring conditions are widely regarded as deprivations or as preludes to them. Wars, conquests, famines, epidemics, land alienations, economic losses, captivities, exploitations, exterminations, and discriminations are in varying degrees alarming to practically all people, if they are not indeed considered to be disastrous. Almost universally the apprehension is greatest when life itself is endangered, although there are philosophies, such as the Hindu, wherein the pains

[7] Colum S. Gilfillan, *The Sociology of Invention*. Chicago: Follett Publishing Co., 1935, pp. 55–58, 115–117.

and even the extinction of physical existence are as nothing when compared with spiritual pollution and degradation. Human life, even one's own life, is not everywhere valued the same.

It is often impossible to say whether a crisis has actually incubated a certain idea or whether it has merely provided the opportunity for its realization. It frequently happens that an idea is conceived in leisure but is not developed to the point of being practicable, or is abandoned or ignored by others, until a crisis calls attention to it and creates a demand for it. Even more often the utility of a new idea is not envisioned until a crisis suggests some application of it. It is treated, even by its formulator, as an academically interesting discovery or merely as a curiosity at the time of its conception. Or, finally, an idea that makes its appearance in a time of crisis may have been borrowed from some other ethnic group or from a past era in the history of the same group. It is then reapplied or adapted to meet contemporary circumstances. Some of the most important weapons of modern warfare certainly have had origins before the time when they were developed to meet the needs of war, among them the airplane, the submarine, and the atomic bomb. The same is true of nontechnological ideas that are drawn upon in times of turmoil and crisis, such as those embodied in the "New Deal."

In one respect old ideas that are revived or borrowed to meet a crisis must be classed as innovations. If they have been borrowed or taken out of other contexts of time and place, they must almost inevitably be modified to conform to existing modes and requirements. The use of body armor by medieval knights might suggest its use today, but it is clear that the same type of body covering would not satisfy protective needs in modern warfare. And as for previously conceived but unused ideas, their launching almost always requires some alteration of the initial formulation before they become useful. In the course of instituting any idea, whether it concerns a thing or an abstraction, problems are raised and tests must be made that in themselves demand ingenuity. Rarely will an idea of any sort be workable or entirely defensible as it is first conceived. It has to be put to the practical test and this almost always results in modification. Sometimes the alterations are so thoroughgoing that the initial idea bears but slight resemblance to the final product.

These complications suggest caution against an overemphasis upon the role of deprivation in innovation. It is certainly important; but the part that it plays is essentially passive, like that of the other conditions that have been considered. Natural or social calamities do not themselves produce human responses to them. Beyond that, even the feeling of deprivation will not automatically lead to relief. Necessity, even when it is understood as the deprivation of an essential—which it usually is not—is the mother of invention only to a limited degree. It may be, but frequently it is not. And it may only offer the opportunity for the expression of an old idea or for some readaptation of one conceived under other necessities, if they can be so called. The deprivation incentive is of variable force, and the response to it is likewise variable.

A crisis as such is neither wholly nor certainly productive of the new. Neither is it unequivocally inimical to it. Some of the same considerations are pertinent here that were noticed in connection with competition and the dependence upon authority. The over-all effect of a crisis situation is restrictive, as is a retreat from competition and a reliance upon authority. The personal freedom to experience and to explore widely can be constrained by anxieties as well as by the design of social pressures, cultivated ignorance, and legal coercives. Leisure is unquestionably a most important condition for an unhampered manipulation of ideas, and this approach to innovation has been extremely productive. Any cultural device or natural condition which frees the individual from the tensions of personal insecurity, such as the relief from the necessity to provide food, shelter, and protection, frees his mind for other thoughts, thoughts that may be entirely irrelevant and inconsequential as far as his immediate needs are concerned. Freedom from pressing want is essential to an exuberance of new ideas. Hence the importance of subsidized research, sinecured study, and patronized dabbling. Hence also the stimulus of political stability and social consolidation. Judging from some of the analyses that have been made, the periods of greatest national prosperity and world leadership in other respects have been correlated with an efflorescence of new ideas.[8]

Freedom from biological necessity is essential for the speculative mind. The threat of physical extinction, whether from war, pestilence, or hunger, constrains the free flight of fancy. So does the requirement that the thinking be practical; that is, directed toward producing a stipulated effect. If a compendium of the thoughts of men conceived in leisure were available for reference, it would be far more efficient to refer to it for solutions to practical problems than to set the best minds of the day to work upon them. Leisured speculation is of high value, and it may be that in one way or another it always plays a part in innovation.

Under the pressure of deprivation the attention of the individual is focused upon it to the exclusion, relatively speaking, of innovative thoughts about other matters. There is a shrinking of the range of choice for innovative exploration. The range may be voluntarily constricted, delimited by popular consensus, or demanded by legislation or fiat. Threats to the individual or his group revoke his freedom to seek freely and conscript his mental resources to face the emergency. Necessity demands that efforts be made to reach a specific, not just any, goal. Consequently few innovations occur outside the premium area, although there may be an increase within it.

[8] Pitirim Sorokin, *Social and Cultural Dynamics,* American Sociology Series. New York: American Book Company, 1937, Vol. 2, Chap. 3.

Rossman's study of war and invention reveals the degree of interrelationship between these variables.[9] He investigated the effect of the First World War stimulus upon inventive activities in several European countries and the United States, using patent-office records. His summary indicates a spurt of activity coincident with the war, inasmuch as there was a noticeable increase in the number of patents applied for by comparison with the prewar period. At the same time the total number of patents *granted* decreased considerably during the war years, 16 per cent in the United States and 40 per cent in England. The increase in the number of patents applied for, combined with the decrease in the number granted, suggests, for one thing, that the heightening of the activity was to a considerable degree unrealistically directed. A large proportion of the new ideas were impractical, trivial, or in the crackpot category. They were indications of panic or of premature or immature thought given free reign and asylum in an emergency. Others of those that were rejected probably duplicated previous inventions and suggest the effects of indirect collaboration. An analysis of the patents granted shows that the increased activity was war-stimulated and emergency-restricted. The number granted that concerned weapons and war increased almost three times over the prewar level in the United States and doubled the prewar number in England. The shrinkage of genuinely useful and nonduplicating ideas during the war, combined with the increased number proposing solutions to emergency problems, supports the view that crises are stimulating at the point of pressure but distractive in other areas. There is an intensification and a narrowing of innovative activity, with much of it being misspent.

There are individual and group differences in reactions to emergencies and security threats. Because of generally accepted norms, ethnic groups, or subethnic groups such as classes or sects or age groups, respond in characteristic and different ways to the same stimulus. Some react with detachment, stolidity, and coolness; others with frenzy or belligerency. If it is normal for the people in a given society to lead protected lives without responsibilities, a large proportion of them will very probably respond to disaster by withdrawing, by regressing to infantile behavior, or by resorting to daydreams of wish fulfillment.[10] In our culture women are more inclined to react hysterically to a crisis than are men. Individuals with narrow ranges of experience and little training in objective thinking have only a limited number of responses to any given situation at their command. Their restricted frame of reference makes them more susceptible to first impressions and to suggestions, however fantastic such reactions may be even to them, because they

[9] Joseph Rossman, "War and Invention," *American Journal of Sociology,* 1931, 36:625–633.
[10] David Krech and Richard Crutchfield, *Theory and Problems of Social Psychology.* New York: McGraw-Hill Book Company, Inc., 1948, pp. 64–65.

are unable to set the impression or the suggestion in a realistic context. The naïve and the uneducated therefore characteristically respond to crises in unrealistic ways. The hoax of the radio play called "The Invasion from Mars" spread panic among such people. They lacked a factual inventory upon which they could draw in order to evaluate the suggestion dramatically made in the play that the earth had been invaded by men from another planet. They had no generalized framework of knowledge by which they could check the possibility. Consequently they accepted the suggestion and had no more rational solution to the threat of the impending catastrophe than to run aimlessly about or to pack their belongings and sit and wait for the inevitable.[11]

The factor of the personal immediacy of the deprivation has a bearing upon individual reactions to it. If a person can be isolated from it by some cultural buffer, he can think more circumspectly, no matter what his inclinations might be when face to face with the threat. If he can, for example, be protected by others, as research workers are in modern warfare, the situation simulates in microcosm the placid state of the noncrisis situation. There are urgency and specificity of assignments, both deterrents to innovation as such; but there are subsidy, protection, encouragement, and collaboration to compensate for those disadvantages. The stimulus to invention under such conditions of simulated leisure can be quite effective.

By contrast, if the threat of deprivation must be faced directly and immediately and the degree of personal involvement is great, innovations will also result, but most of them will not be rewarding. In modern psychological terminology, they would not reduce the tension set up by the urge to accomplish the goal. Individuals differ in their capacities to shield their rational processes; but if the intensity of the threat is great enough, it can disorganize even the most resistant mental system. Most people can withstand destruction in one quarter if they can salvage the rest of their values. If one anchor holds, there can still be hope and rational analysis. But if all is threatened—self, loved ones, and way of life—panic and irrational behavior ensue. This is the meaning of the reactions of those who lost their reason when they were convinced the Martians had attacked the earth. That event literally marked the end of the world for them. All was lost, and there was nothing reasonable to do. So they prayed, gathered their loved ones about them, made provisions for an aimless trip, ran, or wanted to run and were transfixed. The very extravagance of the interpretation of the situation and some of the reactions to it were innovative, but they did not alleviate the anxiety. The new ideas did not meet the demands of the situation which had given rise to them.

[11] Hadley Cantril, "The Invasion from Mars." In T. M. Newcomb and E. L. Hartley (eds.), *Readings in Social Psychology*. New York: Henry Holt and Company, Inc., 1947, pp. 619–628.

There are therefore two kinds of innovative reactions to extreme crises. One contributes to survival while the other only gives the illusion of doing so; one employs materialistic instruments to accomplish its rational ends, the other resorts to fantasy thinking and employs supernaturalistic devices. Each has several aspects that can be illustrated by repeated instances from the histories of different peoples. In labeling the one adjustment realistic and the other fantastic there is no implication that success always attaches to the first and that failure is inevitable for the second. Supernatural techniques for survival can be effective if they oppose other supernatural techniques only, and they may be effective, although inadequate, even when they oppose materialistic forces. Realistic adaptions can also be effective but inadequate.

Realistic opposition to human enemies, to choose but one example, has inspired innumerable innovations for aggression and defense. Aside from the uncounted number of weapons that have been constructed from Paleolithic times onward, there is an almost equally endless variety of offensive and defensive stratagems that have been designed to overcome, circumvent, harass, confuse, or demoralize an enemy. To be included in the list of such tactics are ambush, infiltration, guerilla activities, sabotage, passive resistance, feints, coded messages, propaganda, and all else that now comes within the meaning of the term "psychological warfare." Realistic strengtheners include treaties, alliances, confederations, the development of substitute foods and materials, rationing, formal training in warfare, requisitioning, taxation, and conscription—all new ideas to many peoples. Morale builders include rallies, news censorship, payments for war service, the awarding of honors and special privileges to those who sacrifice or contribute the most, and an emphasis upon the righteousness of the cause being championed.

The last-mentioned technique frequently results in innovation, even though it might be supposed to be a constant feature of a given conflict. Rationalizations and other conscious and unconscious fictions are evolved to justify resistance to the enemy. It is maintained, for example, that he represents the forces of evil and symbolizes the end of civilization. At times the struggle comes to be epitomized in the fervent advocacy of some symbol of the threatened way of life; the defenders of a cultural heritage may foresee its extinction if the enemy forces prevail, or it may already be moribund or almost entirely abandoned. Gandhi's advocacy of the ascetic life, his use of native dress, and his hand spinning were effective weapons against the encroachment of British industrialism in India. Aboriginally the Yakima Indians of Washington lived in long multifamily dwellings. Now their homes are like those of their white neighbors, but they maintain a "long house" for their ceremonials. These buildings and the ceremonies held in them are the symbols of the unity and of the opposition of a strong conservative minority who oppose assimilation by the whites. In Palau the Modekne cult mobilized the antiforeign sentiments of the natives and championed a revival of belief in the old religious concepts and the use of wooden dishes and other outmoded artifacts.

Even in these instances of a clinging to the present, or of a reaching back into the past, there is novelty quite as much as if the familiar idea had been borrowed from some other ethnic group. In addition, it often happens that the symbolic trait, whether resuscitated or current, is elaborated upon or extended so that it spreads into new contexts. The ecstatic trembling of the Shakers was vigorously opposed by Christian missionaries; and the Protestants railed against the use of lighted candles in their services and their making the sign of the cross. Opposition to these practices only served to intensify the Shakers' adherence to them. Shaking, crossing, and candles became symbolic of their resistance, and they proceeded to find new contexts for the employment of these signatures.

In fantasy reactions to extreme threats by enemies, aggression and defense depend upon wishful thinking and the employment of magic and prayer. These responses are not absent from the situations just described, but in such cases they are not the principal sources of relief. In other instances they play the predominant role. Usually this happens only when the realistic measures at the disposal of a people are patently inadequate. This development is often a sequel to extended armed conflict which reduces the vanquished group to the status of an embittered but impotent minority. The homeland of the conquered has been invaded and expropriated, their leaders punished, their culture disrupted, and their values destroyed. They are disillusioned and hopeless until a new kind of leader appears, a prophet who has a message of salvation given to him by divine inspiration. He claims to have the supernatural power to lead his people out of bondage and to return to them their lost paradise, if only they will follow the injunctions of their spiritual sponsor. Thus arises a messianic cult to combat the oppressor with faith and magic.[12]

Messianic cults have appeared among oppressed groups in all parts of the world. They have been a rather regular phenomenon on the colonial frontiers of expanding European civilization in North America, South America, Africa, and in many of the islands of the Pacific. Usually they have a meteoric career, but some have existed in modified and moderated form for several years. They are still popping up. Some, like the American Indian "Ghost Dance," depend almost solely upon supernatural means for a restoration of the aboriginal way of life. Their leaders scoff at the use of physical force and recommend amulets, ritual performances, and an ecstatic faith, declaring that the weapons of the enemy cannot prevail against these defenses and the intervention of God on their behalf. Other movements with a marked

[12] Ralph Linton, "Nativistic Movements," *American Anthropologist,* 1943, 45 (No. 2):230–240.

emphasis upon supernatural support for their cause still make realistic use of armed force to win it. The names of their leaders—Joan of Arc, Pontiac, Tecumseh, Sitting Bull, the Fifth Monarchy Men—are more likely to appear in the history books.[13]

Land alienation and its equivalent, migration, force some cultural readjustments if the dispossessed group is to survive. At the very least adjustments must be made to accommodate for the absence of essentials that were relied upon in the old habitat. The accommodation could mean only a loss. But usually it also results in the utilization of the unfamiliar foods and materials of the new land, adaptations to the climate and the terrain, and, if the new land is inhabitated, the development of economic, social, and political arrangements with the indigenous population. Rarely will the innovations be restricted to those that are directly concerned with the physical aspects of the new home. On the contrary, the removal itself usually has an unsettling effect that manifests itself in changes throughout the culture. Migrants and dispossessed populations are characteristically receptive to new ideas, whether those ideas are developed by their own members or suggested by outsiders.

The Hindus who have been settled in Fiji under the indentured labor system now have relatively little in common with their congeners in the homeland. Caste prejudices have been altered considerably. High- and low-caste members mingle in schools and public assemblies, and all drink water from the same sources. Caste membership no longer defines occupation. Life is not sacrosanct as in orthodox Hindu belief; the immigrants still do not kill cows, but they are not so meticulous about pests. The men have abandoned the loincloth and the turban to wear shirts and shorts. The women have been more conservative in their dress, but they no longer take care to conceal their faces.[14] To some extent these changes may have been induced by the living conditions forced upon the laborers. Very likely, too, a great many of the immigrants were of low caste to begin with and had more to gain than to lose by their deviations. Nevertheless, the removal to a new setting made the changes more acceptable as well as impelling.

One band of Sioux Indians, forced by the Federal government to move from Minnesota after some fatal disturbances in 1865, settled in northern Nebraska. Disease destroyed a third of their number during their first years in the new land; but once they became adjusted to the white man's culture, they rapidly assimilated it. By 1878 they had become the successful farmers of large tracts of land, the owners of substantial homes, and the publishers

[13] James Mooney, "The Ghost-dance Religion," Bureau of American Ethnology, *14th Annual Report, 1892–93,* Washington, D.C., 1896, Part 2, pp. 928–947.

[14] John Wesley Coulter, *Fiji, Little India of the Pacific,* Chicago: University of Chicago Press, 1942, pp. 101–103.

of a newspaper in their own language. Government officials heralded them as models to be imitated by other Indian groups.[15]

The forced or voluntary alteration of the economic base of a people in consequence of removal to a new land plays a part in the changes that take place in other aspects of their culture, but this is not the crucial factor. The natives of Bikini Island, who were evacuated to make way for the atomic-bomb tests in 1946, suffered extreme privation during their stay on Rongerik. The food resources of their new home were inadequate and the island was strange and fearsome to them. To meet a starvation crisis they abandoned their traditional land-ownership pattern and their system of government. They organized a council with powers to apportion all labor and all food and prepared their food in four cooking centers for the 167 people. In 1948 they were moved to the more productive island of Kili, where they are now in the process of again reorganizing their lives. It appears certain that the pattern which will evolve there will not be the one they knew in 1945. They learned much about American ways during an interlude on Kwajalein, and they display reluctance to return to the feudalistic type of government which formerly kept them subservient to a nonresident superior chief of the western Marshall Islands. And as yet they have not decided to return to the old system of land tenure. The determinative factors are not economic compulsives. They are the associations that the Bikinians have had with the Americans.[16]

Two other instances are informative in this connection. The Todas of southern India are a pastoral people who subsist upon the milk of their buffalo herds and the rice and millet that they obtain from their neighbors the Badagas. They are almost solely preoccupied with the pasturing and milking of their buffaloes and with the rituals associated with these animals. Dairymen-priests maintain sacred herds of buffaloes, and Toda religion centers about their veneration. The British have taken care not to interfere with Toda culture, but the building of a military station in their vicinity required the removal of one clan to neighboring pasture lands. The new pasture was adequate for the needs of the group, but its sacred dairy spot, its temple, lies beneath the cantonment parade grounds. The deprivation of this essential has caused this clan to abandon buffalo-cult rituals along with many of its associated features. The dispossessed clan members have begun to cultivate potatoes and raise cattle along with their buffaloes.[17]

The American Indians who now live on the Yakima reservation in Washington are the remnants of several tribes who were gathered there after 1855.

[15] U.S. Indian Office, Commissioner of Indian Affairs, *Annual Report for 1877*, p. 99.

[16] Leonard Mason, "The Bikinians: A Transplanted Population," *Human Organization*, 1950, 9 (No. 1):5–15.

[17] David G. Mandelbaum, "Culture Change among the Nilgiri Tribes," *American Anthropologist*, 1941, 43 (No. 1):22–23.

Aboriginally all of them were fishers, hunters, and gatherers of wild-plant foods. To a considerable degree they still are, but some individuals among them have become successful farmers as well. It is significant that the majority of the farmers are the descendants of Indians who were evacuated from adjacent areas. The traditional possessors of the land are ultraconservatives, not only with respect to land use but in other ways. The other Indians call them the "Toppenish Bunch" in reference to a creek that aboriginally was their point of concentration. They form the nucleus of a stiff resistance to assimilation. They still wear moccasins and the men braid their long hair. They are members of the so-called Pom Pom cult, which maintains its vitality through a stimulation of antiwhite sentiment.

The real reason why innovation appears with deprivation is the one given in the discussion of the failure of authoritative controls; namely, that a familiar universe of associations and sanctions has been distorted or destroyed and must be reorganized. The wrenching away of any control mechanism, including the natural environment, requires a reorientation. Unsettlement for any cause creates a fluid condition in which the old values are no longer operative. With the old sanctions and compulsives gone or of doubtful validity, the way is open for the creation and the acceptance of new interpretations.

There are other innovative adaptations to extreme deprivations. Compromises, syncretisms, imitations, and sublimations are alternative reactions to the loss of essentials, especially when an ethnic group does not or cannot react to threat in concert or with coordinated efforts. Individualism then takes over, and new forms that are privately satisfying evolve to compensate for the loss. The exhibitionistic innovations of members of unorganized ethnic groups, depressed classes, and minority groups illustrate the point. They, too, find themselves in a destructured world as a result of deprivation and have to build to obtain a substitute.

The Modification of a Dominant Correlate. Some cultural changes not yet considered are derived, incidental, unforeseen, and even unwanted. They are in a sense forced as a result of a change in some other part of the cultural nexus. The initial and dominant change is the focus of attention. It may have been instituted by some member of the in-group, imposed by a conquering group, or voluntarily adopted from an outside source. It may demand the concomitant introduction of other ideas or things to support it or simply necessitate a dislocation in the indigenous culture to make way for its accommodation alone. In any event, other changes follow its introduction in a chain-reaction effect.

We shall touch upon this phenomenon again in discussing incentives, but it deserves separate consideration here. The reason for it is that a culture is made up of interdependent ideas. A culture is not a jumble or a mere assemblage of customs. The linkages between its parts may be strong or weak, and there are many ideas that are not directly related to each other at all. Still, the whole is a complex such that no concept is an isolate and each element through its associates participates in the characteristics of the whole. Consequently if there is a change in one sector of the culture, there must be some reflection of the change elsewhere in those idea-sets that are correlated in some way with it. The initial alteration is what is here referred to as the modification of a dominant. Dominance in this sense refers not to the importance of one idea with respect to others, but only to its role as a prime mover. And the point to be made is that one change sets up a propitious and even a compelling condition for others. The more changes there are, the more must follow in their train. Consequently, any situation which promotes innovation or diffusion multiplies the potentialities for change far beyond the number of initial ideas themselves.

In some instances there is no distinction between this condition for innovation and the deprivation of an essential. If an essential is taken away, its loss will inevitably result in modifications of its former correlates. Or if the essential is altered or replaced by some other good, that change will force concomitant changes elsewhere. However, the modification of a correlate is a much more inclusive phenomenon; it occurs regardless of deprivation whenever something new is invented or adopted. In another sense the reaction to deprivation is more inclusive, particularly if there is only a threat of it. Then the innovative reactions are designed to stay the challenge and preserve the essential.

Ogburn's analyses of the effects of the radio, the automobile, and the airplane upon American culture is an impressive demonstration of the reactive effects of single changes. He lists 150 effects of the radio.[18] They interlace American culture, spreading out from primary, secondary, and tertiary activators like the roots and rootlets of a tree. The near effects appear to have little relationship to the ultimate ones, but they are connected through a series of intermediate stimuli. One of the subordinate effects of the radio, for instance, is the increased interest that it has stimulated in the relatively minor area of sports. Yet, this has its own consequents which ramify into many other areas: the reputation of star athletes is further magnified, football coaches become nationally prominent and higher salaried, athletes are drawn from a wider segment of the population, small colleges and those not stressing athletics are placed at a disadvantage in the competition for students, and so on. Ogburn's list of fifteen of these effects could be extended, and each one of them can be shown to have its own derivatives. It is, in fact, doubtful whether there can be any real end to the consequents and the repercussions in such a series.

[18] W. F. Ogburn and Colum S. Gilfillan, "The Influence of Invention and Discovery." In *Recent Social Trends in the United States.* New York: McGraw-Hill Book Company, Inc., 1933, Vol. 1, p. 153.

The chain effect is most evident when there is a physical incompatibility between some correlate of the displaced thing or behavior and that which displaces it. Many early railroads had narrow-gauge tracks that would not accommodate pullman cars. The adoption of the larger cars required that existing tracks, roadbeds, and bridges be widened and strengthened. The development of larger and heavier automobiles in recent years, especially busses and freighting trucks, has necessitated the same kind of changes in highway construction. A great many Palauan customs are naturally correlated with the size and shape of their aboriginal dwellings. The old-type house was as much as 35 feet long, with an open fireplace near one end and no partitions. It could easily accommodate twenty-five or thirty people, and upon many occasions it was necessary for it to do so. Meals were always eaten indoors, and visitors at feasts often filled the room. Etiquette demanded that the men who were invited to such feasts sit and receive their food portions in ranked order and that no man turn his back upon another. Custom also required family reunions at certain times. A girl anticipating her first child had to bring her husband to live in the home of her maternal uncle for three months just prior to her delivery. Birth, marriage, and death ceremonies called for the congregation of the families concerned in a specified house. At the present time very few of the large houses remain. Most of the Palauans live in small two- or three-room houses built on the Japanese or American style. They still attempt to carry on with the customs just mentioned, but some departures are physically necessary. Visitors now crowd into the small houses and sit packed together all over the floor area. They have to disregard the insult of having to look at a neighbor's back and take their food in any way that they can in order to get it. Girls whose uncles still insist upon it bring their husbands for only a token visit of a few days sometime before the birth of their child, or afterwards if it is more convenient.

The Palauans are incessant betel chewers—and spitters. Their native-style dwellings and clubhouses had several doors and numerous cracks in the floors to accommodate this habit. New-style buildings, especially the Quonset huts now being erected for chiefs' dwellings and council chambers, have precipitated a minor crisis on this score. The two doors that the Quonsets usually have are premium locations. A few chewers may find a knothole in the floor; but since most floors are made of plywood, this carry-over does not offer much hope or relief for the majority. The alternative that occurred to some genius in our village was to use tin cans from my garbage dump for spittoons. Unless the Palauans now receive more canned goods than they did then, this is not likely to be a permanent solution to the problem. Tin cans have their own dominant correlate.

Physical necessity has forced or is forcing many other Palauan customs to be ignored or modified. The Germans required every adult native to plant a certain number of coconut trees, and they put other restrictions upon the natives' leisure. The Japanese increased the pressure for more work and less idleness. The consequences have naturally been fatal to many aboriginal behavior patterns. To mention only one: ceremonials, dances, and other native group pastimes have been abandoned, curtailed, or restricted to weekends. Aboriginally chiefs were wealthy and powerful because they controlled most of the native type of money that was essential for social and political functioning. Nowadays only American money will buy some of the most desirable kinds of goods and services. The old chiefs rarely have an opportunity to earn any of this, while the young men do. As a result the chiefs are threatened with a loss of power incidental to their having accepted the new kind of valuable. They want the money as much as anyone but not the consequences its adoption has brought in its train. They must accept or work out new means to perpetuate their controls, such as requisitioning money from their younger dependents and accepting the support of their position by the government or converting to a new definition of leadership, one founded on the possession of American money. Both these things are happening in individual cases.

Instances of this sort, drawn from primitive and modern cultures alike, could be cited indefinitely. Aboriginally the Yakima maintained their ethnic unity by a mode of life that cultivated an interdependence among the families living in one village. As has been previously mentioned, they lived in long narrow dwellings that accommodated several conjugal families. The members of the village participated in many social and economic activities as a group. They had common interests and an intimate knowledge of the affairs of one other. They all turned their unruly children over to a village disciplinarian. When they began to live in houses patterned after those of the white man, all these things began to disappear. Conjugal families living in scattered homes could no longer have maintained the sense of belonging that went with village life, even if there had not been other forces operating to dispel it. Intimate and daily communication was more difficult, and group solidarity was dissipated. Along with this change went numerous other derived changes.

The Yakima instance parallels developments in our own culture that have been stimulated by the growth of urban life, especially in metropolitan centers. Apartment-house dwellers have been forced to adapt their living pattern to the crowded conditions imposed by their living quarters. Limitations are placed upon family size and composition; furniture and household appliances have been modified to save space; the keeping of pets has taken on a characteristic pattern; and a reliance upon laundry and other professional services has been encouraged if not forced.

Physical necessity is only one condition for concomitant modification. The phenomenon is in reality unrelated to the properties of material things;

it is an ideological reaction, not a physical one. Impropriety of association is often as compelling a reason for the modification of correlates as is physical incompatibility. Whether the impetus for an adjustive alteration is mechanical or psychological necessity, the modification itself is due to an idea.

Persons as well as things act as dominants. Their personalities, ideas, and ambitions regulate the character of their thing and person associates quite as much as do the size, shape, and strength of their bodies. Consequently, with a change in the personnel of a social or artifactual context, demands are, as a rule, made for a correlative modification of the context. Stated more simply, each individual has his own preferences and seeks to establish them along with himself. New tenants bring new furniture and a different pattern of demands upon their landlord and their neighbors. A new workman or a new playmate makes adjustive demands upon others in a work or play group, as well as being required to make concessions himself. Not infrequently these mutual adjustments are new to both parties. Typically a change in administrators brings a "house cleaning"; things and subordinate personnel get rearranged and dislodged from their accustomed niches.

Since 1945 the Palauans have been going through an anxious period of making tentative adjustments to the change from Japanese to American occupational personnel. Extensive modifications of their interpersonal behavior patterns have been necessitated by the differences between Japanese and American culture and by the unfamiliar characteristics of the American administrator. Not knowing precisely what has been expected of them in particular situations, the natives have had to experiment with ideas and behaviors to find those that will achieve their purposes. Very often their interpretation of an American regulation or expectation or their understanding of an American behavior has been novel if not bizarre from the American standpoint. Their adjustments to the new elements have been made more difficult, as well as innovative, by the lack of any direct means of communication with individual Americans, for there have been only a few bilingual individuals to mediate between the two cultures.

Profound social and economic changes have followed upon the indoctrination of one ethnic group with the values of another. The acceptance of one idea entails the acceptance of some correlate which supports or complements it. Merely imparting bits of academic or technical knowledge opens up an ever-expanding vista of linked ideas that contradict or overshadow more limited perspectives. The knowledge that the world is round and that it is populated by millions of other people with diverse customs is infinitely unsettling to a person who has grown up with a provincial view of his place in nature. Instruction in a language like French or English with a vast literature in science, geography, and history can have revolutionary effects. In any integrated system of knowledge the mastering of one segment becomes a vehicle for the coverage of the rest. Moving under its own momentum, it may have remarkable effects; but when it is impelled by the proselytizing zeal of an outsider, it can completely disrupt an alien culture upon which it impinges.

The concatenation of causes and effects that are initiated by schoolroom indoctrination not infrequently leaves its well-meaning initiator aghast and uncomprehending of the part he has played in the ultimate results. Missionary teachers, concentrating upon the impressionable minds of the children of an alien group, seek to implant the divergent values of their own world view while ignoring or belittling those of the group they are intent upon enlightening. Implicitly or explicitly they give their pupils to understand that the ideas of their parents are misguided, naïve, evil, or dangerous. Very few of them in the past have foreseen the far-reaching consequences of such instruction. Few have been prepared to face the fact that teaching a child that his father's ideas are foolish leads to a bankruptcy of parental discipline and to an irreparable rift between the two génerations; and that these breaches lead to severe emotional disturbances which manifest themselves in the violence, irresponsibility, and aimless despair of bereft and insecure people. This sequence of events has occurred with the regularity of a natural law in all parts of the world where systematic education has aimed at the weaning away of children from the idea systems of their elders. And this has been the favored approach, endorsed as it is by the common-sense realization that adults make discouraging pupils, especially when their prejudices are assailed.

Education has other entrained effects that are repercussive. Wherever it has been the intention of a master group to keep its dependent people subservient, reaction has developed against their education, because, as the Inca Roca observed, it makes them restless. Planters and other residents in the New Guinea mandate in the 1920's were opposed to education for the local native. An official investigator reported that it was alleged that schooling "makes the native more cunning, generates and develops evil qualities, makes him disinclined to work, and renders him a less pliant instrument." [19] The change which comes about in a person as a result of his education requires concomitant adjustments in his thing and idea associations and in his interpersonal relations. He makes new demands upon his social and artifactual environment. Employers, administrators, and fellow associates face the necessity of working out new patterns in dealing with him. Paternalism, deception, circumvention, and exploitation, if they continue to be practiced at all, must be modified to parallel the change from ignorance to literacy and increased sophistication.

[19] B. J. McKenna, "Report on Native Education," *Annual Report to the League of Nations on the Administration of New Guinea, 1929–30,* Canberra, Australia.

Literacy has created a schism in the Shaker church. For many years very few of the leaders of the cult could read. This was a disadvantage which they felt keenly in the years of their oppression by hostile whites. Two men, James Wickersham and Milton Giles, came to their rescue and enabled them to get legal recognition for their church. With the passing of this crisis the need for literate and sophisticated leadership was no longer imperative; but since then an increasing number of converts have been schooled in the fundamentals of American education and have inevitably introduced a new perspective on some of the traditional concepts of the older members of the church. Gradually they have sought to develop a new type of leadership. They want leaders who are literate, look and behave like white men, and, more than anything else, can deal with hostile whites on equal terms. This has been the fundamental issue in the schism, although it has not been formulated in these terms. Rather, the contest between the conservative and the progressive factions has centered about a division of opinion concerning the source of their spiritual guidance. The conservatives insist that now, as in the past, direct inspiration from God is indispensable and sufficient for the good life and eternal salvation. The progressives admit the value of inspiration, but make it secondary to the teachings of the Bible. The opposing views precipitated an open controversy in 1927, and between 1931 and 1935 they resulted in the election of two bishops, each claiming a mandate for supreme leadership in the church. Since then a series of court actions, partisan elections, boycotts, and local withdrawals from the conflict have only aggravated the confusion. Regardless of the eventual outcome of the struggle, the entrained effects of these developments are certain to modify the traditional aspects of the cult.

Part Two: The Incentives to Innovation

CHAPTER IV

SELF-WANTS

Terminology. There are incentives for innovation, just as there are motivations for any other action. They may be treated within more than one conceptual framework, but it is essential that some position concerning them be taken. The "why" of innovation is an inescapable question. It is also one of the most difficult aspects of the problem and one of the two that have been treated only very superficially. The analysis is admittedly a formidable task, the more baffling and confusing the deeper the probing goes.

At present psychologists are inclined to explain human activity as being due to specific motive forces that they call drives, instigators, or needs. The propulsive force is looked upon as an organized energy set that is directed toward some particular goal, the gaining of which results in satisfaction. Under this interpretation a need or a drive is a tension in the psychological or neural field which seeks readjustment. It is an unstable arrangement of forces that is due to stresses set up by a given complex of stimuli. The achievement of the goal toward which it is oriented is the means of relieving the stress and restoring the balance of forces. If a given response results in a stable reorganization, the drive for further response is reduced or dissipated. If not, the tension remains and continues to express itself by efforts to relieve it. Thus, hunger is a drive or a need or an instigation to such action as will produce the kind of food that will quiet it; fears and anxieties are stresses with resultants or vectors directed toward specific action complexes.[1]

Some psychologists, as well as many laymen, distinguish between conscious and unconscious motivation. Some also subdivide needs into wants and demands. Wants are those tensions that are autochthonous or spontaneously created under controls within the organism. They are the self-ordered drives. Demands are externally organized pressures, such as the requirements of conscience, the urge to complete a task, or the pressure to fulfill a social obligation. They carry the impression of being imposed even though their immediate source is recognized as being internal.[2]

---

[1] David Krech and Richard S. Crutchfield, *Theory and Problems of Social Psychology*. New York: McGraw-Hill Book Company, Inc., 1948, pp. 40–50.

[2] *Ibid.*, pp. 42–43.

Usually the incentives for innovation are phrased as needs. A new idea is said to be conceived because there is a need for it; it is the answer to some want, lack, or demand. It would be difficult to defend a categorical denial of this interpretation. In one sense or another it is true that people do what they do because they need to. However, there are certain objections to the indiscriminate use of the term "need" as an explanatory concept in innovation. For one thing, it is a much-abused word in popular usage. It becomes quite meaningless when it is applied to a group of people, as it usually is. It loses whatever validity it may have when it is said that necessity is the mother of invention, or that airplanes were not invented until they were needed, or that people in backward areas of the world need the advantages of an industrial economy. Such judgments are ex post facto, evaluative, and ethnocentric. They presume that wants are supraindividual and inherent in social systems, that one aspect of culture requires something else for its balance, support, or completion. The truth is that a group of people that we call a society needs nothing, because it is not an organism. It has no desires, because it is an abstraction; and it has no lacks, except by gratuitous comparisons with other societies. American family life needs greater binding forces only because a condition can be conceived by someone in which it might profit by them; the Hottentots need sewing machines only because we have them, and we need them only because we have become accustomed to them. Needs, in short, are relative to time and place and are highly particularistic.

The concept of need has application only with reference to the individual. A need is a psychological state that can have a locus only in individual minds. It has, moreover, an intimate and personal quality about it. It is suffused with feeling, so that there is a keen appreciation of self-involvement in it. That, in fact, is what gives a need its motivational force. True, the feeling may be assumed, sublimated, or transferred, or it may be a vicarious one; but it is a feeling and means nothing in the abstract. A need must be inwardly sensed by the individual, which is to say that it cannot be imputed to him by an observer on the basis of the latter's experience. Its existence can be ascertained by introspection, inferred from goal-directed behavior, or deduced from a cessation of such behavior.

Even though we confine our use of the term to individuals, "need" has connotations that should be rejected in an objective analysis of innovation. For many people the word has overtones of the absolute and the indispensable. It suggests that a critical condition exists for the organism which, if not ministered to, will have deleterious effects. By implication it posits an ideal or a desirable state which must be maintained or restored lest disaster befall. It is, in brief, a normative and evaluative term by common usage; it implies or tacitly asserts that some adjustments are good and others bad for the individual or his group regardless of his estimate of their worth. The projection of such arbitrary standards upon goal-directed behavior affords but limited insight into the motivation for innovation. Generally it gives better hindsight than foresight and it may be quite misleading as a guide to an understanding of incentives. That which is calamitous to one person is not necessarily so for another, especially if the two have been reared in different traditions. Even if indispensability is accepted as an incentive to action, its functioning may not entail any psychological component. Man needs food to survive, it is true; but in certain instances this amounts to no more than a statement of a biological fact, not a mental one. Not only men but non-conscious organisms like plants need food, too. It is a chemical, not a psychological necessity. It is one thing to say that a person is aware that certain things are indispensable for his existence, and another to say that he needs them even if he does not know it. There is an important difference between saying that a man needs a drink of water when he is thirsty and that he needs proteins, calcium, and vitamins when he is hungry.

In the present state of our knowledge of human motivation it seems wisest to avoid as many a priori conceptions and traditional connotations attaching to its terminology as we can. In particular, more gain than loss will accrue if we allow for as much flexibility as possible in defining drives and needs until we know more about them. Perhaps it would also be better to avoid the imputation of purpose in them, especially if we mean anything more by purpose than organization and direction in mental sets. We do have, nonetheless, to deal with directed behavior and specifically with the "why" of it. It is obvious that there are bendings of efforts; there are concentrations and channelizations of energy. It is clear, too, that these orientations and focusings are felt. Just what they are in their demonstrable characteristics is uncertain; but some terminology is essential if we are going to discuss them.

In the following analysis preference is given to the term "want" as a label for incentive to innovation, without its being assigned any special meaning beyond that given to it in naïve popular usage. This is because "want" is more clearly assertive of the personal element in motivation than "need" is and because it has fewer of the objectionable overtones just mentioned. At the same time, the term "want" is not used to the exclusion of other terms. It has been employed when it seemed to fit the context according to the dictates of ordinary linguistic habits. When other expressions such as "needs," "tendencies," "predispositions," "desires," "demands," or "urges" have seemed more appropriate, they have been used with no shift in meaning intended. In other words, the incentives that mobilize innovative resources have not been analyzed. They are assumed to exist, but their nature and origin is not made the object of inquiry.

While wants are accepted as "givens" for the purposes at hand, it is not to be understood that they are assumed to be innate or preformed constellations of forces. It is not necessary to think of them as primordial or autochthonous orientations that are part of the physical endowment of the individual. They are not necessarily instincts as that term is generally understood. In fact, a good case can be made out for the view that wants, desires, and needs are spontaneously organized mental and emotional sets that nucleate about specific complexes of stimuli. Far from being innate, they may be synthesized and manufactured out of an amorphous reserve of energy under the pressure of repeated stimulation. A given stimulus may build up configurations of nervous energy that are peculiar to it and responsive only to it. While not identical with Lewin's view, this interpretation, like his, makes allowance for the important fact that wants and desires have formative preludes that only gradually lead to crystallization. There are intervals, long or short, of mobilization. As Lewin says, we may need to revise our ideas about a direct connection between motivation and action. Frequently there is a demonstrable interval of decision.[3]

For our purposes it is not essential to adopt a position on this question or on others relating to the nature of motivation. We could, if we chose, treat the data of the next three chapters behavioristically. The activities are observationally true regardless of the character, origin, or even the existence of incentives for them. Thus it remains true that people exhibit restlessness and random activity and that this sometimes results in singular action systems, irrespective of want or purpose. Similarly, it is undeniable that the memory of a past event can be distortive, regardless of a need or a desire for either the distortion or its products.

The subordination of particular innovative reactions under one heading rather than another in the following pages is primarily a device for convenience in presentation. Some ordering of the data is essential, and their complexity and subtlety defy any neat compartmentalization of them. Any specific activity has a variety of facets and might as well be placed in one category as another as long as one of its aspects is relevant. The larger categories subsume particulars that are more or less equivalent, but it could be maintained that there should be more or fewer of them without altering the character of the particulars. The subdivisions of wants and the characterization of the types of innovations associated with them are not to be considered rigid or final. They provide a rationale for understanding the inception of new ideas, but do not provide a support or a justification for them. Other organizations and interpretations of innovative responses might be just as reasonably offered, and the validity of the facts would stand.

The same may be said of the specific psychological mechanisms credited with satisfying wants. They have been drawn upon in order to integrate the study of innovation with known or assumed mental processes. They, and the premises upon which they rest, are not fundamental to the present analysis of

[3] Kurt Lewin, "Group Decision and Social Change." In Theodore M. Newcomb and Eugene L. Hartley (eds.), *Readings in Social Psychology*. New York: Henry Holt and Company, Inc., 1947, p. 336.

innovation. They could be abandoned and others substituted in their place without modifying the data or vitiating the argument. In fact, the observed facts do not always answer the requirements of a given mechanism; they could with equal reason be said to be an inflection or a ramification of some other process. Furthermore, some doubt exists about the adequacy of such conceptualizations as "projection" and "aggression" as explanatory ideas. They are often used as tents to cover a veritable circus of tenuously related behaviors. Interpretations of what constitutes aggressive behavior and its causes vary by investigator, and some interpretations seem as curious as the behaviors they propose to comprehend. Fortunately, again, these matters are not fundamental to what follows.

Credit Wants. In many instances people strive deliberately for novelty with the recognized purpose of receiving credit for their cleverness. They seek gratification through the recognition of their abilities by their fellows. The expressions of the desired recognition are traditionally defined. Tokens of esteem may be in the form of formal or informal praises, favors, prizes, or immunities; or they may be in the nature of grants of wealth or power status. Whatever the symbols of acclaim, the self-centered innovator makes their acquisition his goal. His aim is not to be confused with the desire for success, which may be realized opportunistically by any means at hand. Neither is it to be confused with the desire for change itself. The prestige-seeking innovator has chosen novelty as a means to success, and he is interested in change only incidentally. His primary urge is for recognition, and he finds that the exercise of his creative abilities is the most suitable and rewarding device at his disposal. First and foremost he wants to be appreciated as a clever person.

There are several inflections upon this desire. There is, first of all, the wish to be different for the sake of being distinct from the common run of humanity. This incentive is probably universal to some extent, but the frequency of its appearance is subject to traditional controls. In some societies it is discouraged altogether or is reserved for a few individuals selected by hereditary right or otherwise. American culture, with its great emphasis upon individualism, is at the opposite extreme. With us a premium is placed upon individual differences over a wide but by no means all-inclusive range of endeavors. We value originality in things far more than in abstract ideas. Among things, emphasis is placed upon novelty in intimate possessions, such as clothes, body ornamentation (among women), houses, automobiles, and foods. Among ideas, praises are reserved for originality in the arts and crafts, the professional skills, and in economic enterprises but are withheld from novelty in religious, social, and political thinking. Within the approved areas, ego-oriented experimentation manifests itself in a host of minor variations upon widespread patterns, as in women's dress styles, dwelling architecture, and interior decoration. For the favored few in this category, ego demands are realized through the highly developed art of publicity seeking and press-agentry exploitation. On the other hand, the iconoclasts operate in the prohibited areas. They achieve distinction by shocking their prosaic fellows with their unorthodox ideas. Whether they believe in them or not is irrelevant. They delight in tilting with the philistines quite as much as in achieving prestige for their *avant-garde* ideas. Sometimes it is difficult to say which of the two motives is prior or predominant with them, but in any case they do not shun their reputations as new thinkers. Somewhere on the borderline are the eccentrics and the bohemians. Their motives are mixed, but not the least among them is the desire to attract attention. "Ideas are like shirts," says the artist Picabia, "they get dirty after a while and then you have to change them." Perhaps, but this artist has no doubt noticed that the extravagances of his shirt changes, as much as anything else, have kept him in the artistic eye.[4]

The desire for exclusive rights to a new idea is an important incentive to creativeness because of the valuable emoluments that go with them. In this instance credit is expressed by the granting of certain privileges with respect to the use of a new idea, and the grant is important because it permits the innovator to capitalize upon his ingenuity. In short, it is the value that the idea has for other people that is the main consideration. The demands of others for the new idea provide the innovator with the means to satisfy his other wants, most of which are entirely unrelated to his need for novelty. The latter is incidental to his desire for subsistence, prestige, or power. Copyrights and patents are thus means to translate creative credit into means to obtain other wants.

Credit of this kind is of particular importance in the motivations of professional inventors. The rules of the patent system establish a foundation for a legal defense of rights to new ideas. The assumption upon which this control rests is that an innovator should be accorded recognition for his achievement in terms of prestige or wealth or both. There is also the implied assumption that these rewards are the essential if not the most important incentives for invention.

It is unquestionable that the inventors of things who apply for patents on them are motivated by the hope of reward at some stage in their thinking. Otherwise there would be no point in obtaining a patent. The real question is whether this is the primary incentive. It doubtless is with a few amateurs, but not with all of them. The novice who seriously contemplates entering the professional field is spurred by it. He has the encouragement of the popular fancy, which pictures inventors as geniuses who make a lot of money and acquire lasting fame on the Edison pattern. This idea is perpetuated by benign and anecdotal fictions about great inventors, and it is deliberately

⁴ *Time,* Apr. 10, 1950.

fostered by certain interests which stand to gain by it financially. Among the latter the least reprehensible are the magazines which, through their advertisements, fire the enthusiasm of would-be inventors with prospects of fame and fortune. The most pernicious influences are the lures set out for the unwary by unscrupulous patent lawyers and idea pirates.

Experienced inventors are not deceived by these enticements, although many of them have entered their profession by this route and a fair proportion of them continue to be motivated by the desire for personal gain in some form. Rossman's questionnaire, sent to 710 men who had obtained patents for their inventions, revealed that, in point of the frequency of the motives they mention, the desire for financial gain came third and the desire for prestige seventh. The most frequently mentioned motive was the "love of inventing," and the second most frequent was the "desire to improve." The meaning of these self-ratings is not altogether clear, especially when it is borne in mind that all subjects were patentees and, furthermore, that the same study revealed that 38 per cent of those questioned earned their living by inventing and another 22 per cent did so partially.[5] With over 60 per cent of these professionals obtaining some financial reward for their new ideas, it would seem that this is a more important motive than is indicated by their introspections. It could still have been a secondary consideration for many, however, and doubtless was for some. In any event, it is evident that not even all professional inventors need the lure of material rewards and prestige. Most of them have discovered that these are illusions anyway.

Another aspect of credit wants is the desire to be imitated. This reward is sufficient for some innovators, because their demand for ego satisfaction assumes the form of a need to lead and influence others. Passive acknowledgement of their creative abilities is not enough for them, and monetary considerations are irrelevant. Their fundamental craving is for power, and they exploit the admiration that inventive genius inspires to gain a following. Thus, the cult leaders and the founders of various schools of thought who pride themselves upon their popularity are less interested in the merits of their ideas than in the favorable impression that they themselves make. With some of them, as with stylists and fashion designers, the desire for imitation is mixed with financial considerations. Pseudo scientists and didactic writers and painters are often more clearly motivated by the urge to establish a coterie of devoted admirers and imitators. Social leaders who maintain the equivalent of salons satisfy their ego demands in the same way. It is quite natural that this desire should often take shape, if it has not already existed, in the complex of incentives which inspire men to teach, especially on the collegiate level. The nature of their position is such that it offers ideal possibilities for the emergence or the encouragement of the incentive to set forth

[5] Joseph Rossman, *The Psychology of the Inventor*. Washington, D.C.: Inventor's Publishing Co., 1931, pp. 152 and 157.

new ideas on teaching methods or on idea substance. The desire for admiration is universal, and few academicians fail to rejoice at least secretly in the
inescapable fact that they are able to leave the peculiar imprint of their thinking upon their students. Some make the most of this unique opportunity.

Innovative credit wants can assume the complexion of a desire for self-
vindication. They come into play when a person feels that he must qualify
himself for a role to which he aspires and which is impossible for him by
artless and forthright methods. A situation of this sort develops when the
need for attention, justification, and praise exceeds the limitations imposed by
factual and commonplace approaches. A resourceful individual in this position will resort to colorings, fabrications, and improvisations to vindicate
himself, and some people make a habit of doing this. All of us are prone
to react in this fashion when we are placed at a disadvantage and feel that
our ego is threatened. We may embellish the truth and manufacture evidence
out of righteous indignation, put on a front to come up to some private
standard of accomplishment, or adopt attitudes and behaviors to challenge
the derogatory estimates of others. This incentive may be observed in operation in a minor but instructive way when an individual senses that others
are skeptical of or unimpressed by what he has to say. In order to redeem
himself, he may embroider, exaggerate, or entirely recast the facts of which
he speaks. Inept raconteurs of jokes and stories and self-conscious narrators
of their own experiences often salvage their self-esteem by coloring and remodeling the facts that are available to them. In making themselves more
entertaining, credible, or worth listening to, they consciously alter their
accounts.

Distortions due to this incentive are also potent elements in rumor
spreading. A rumor always contains information of considerable interest.
The teller is therefore the center of attention; and the listener, by his eagerness, magnifies the teller's feelings of importance. This heightening of ego
consciousness is, in fact, a primary motivation in rumor transmission. A
rumor is further characterized by the fact that it is compounded of incomplete and uncertain data. In order to justify his concern with and his
credence in a rumor, the teller frequently feels impelled to substantiate or
color it. The rumormonger, who engages in this activity for the ego gratification that it affords him, is prepared to authenticate his accounts by particular-
izing, by adding confirmatory evidence, or by implying or asserting private
knowledge of the information which he conveys. His need to feel important
forces him to falsify.

While the conscious desire for credit thus plays an important part in innovation, it is not the preeminent incentive that it is sometimes supposed to
be. On the whole we are inclined to overemphasize the stimulus of social
approval in this connection. Several observations which attest to a disregard
of public rewards are pertinent for an evaluation of its importance.

In the first place, it is a well-recognized fact that not all new ideas receive a public welcome. On the contrary, many are rejected and their proponents scoffed at or reprobated. This is to some extent true of the majority of inventions, but it is a marked public reaction to new ideas in the conservative aspects of a culture, as in the religious field among us. Despite this deterrent, new ideas constantly appear, even when the innovator fully anticipates the disfavor that he brings upon himself. Indeed most innovators soon learn, if they do not already know, that rewards, if they come at all, must be won by auxiliary means, irrespective of the intrinsic merits of their ideas.

Secondly, many innovations are made without any thought of credit. In accidental inventions, for example, the idea of a reward, if it occurs, is an afterthought. Likewise for the products of the subliminal motivations to be discussed shortly. Discoverers and amateur inventors who create to satisfy their own personal wants must also be only incidentally or secondarily concerned with credit. Beyond that, there are numerous inventors who are not proud of their creations and who do not even want to be remembered for them. They desire the effects of their fabrications but not the recognition that they are fabrications. This is true of the artifices for self-justification, protection, and orientation and for many others to be discussed subsequently. Evasions, misrepresentations, and other manipulations of things, people, and the truth that are conceived for selfish ends rarely aim at recognition for the talents of their authors. In general, no matter how original a man's devices to achieve asocial ends, he is more likely to become infamous than famous because of them, and he knows it.

Thirdly, some innovators disavow or reject credit for valuable ideas. It must be admitted that under certain circumstances this is merely a culturally dictated pretension: a manifestation of false modesty; a subscription to the socially valued ideals of sportsmanship, altruism, or cooperation; or a lip service to the social deprecation of materialistic self-seeking. The person who makes a point of disclaiming credit when he knows that he deserves it may sense that more good is going to accrue to him just because he belittles his own talents. His sincerity is not in question; he simply recognizes that it is more advantageous for him to conform to ideals than to fight them. On the other hand, there are innovators who really do not want credit for their desirable ideas. Some make a point of concealing their identity. The real motive of such people is not always as selfless as at first appears; but it cannot be denied that some really seek the anonymity that they ask for. There are people who are more concerned with bestowing the benefits of their ideas upon others than in acquiring fame or fortune for themselves. Missionaries and social reformers who devote their lives to the service of others give their ideas freely and without thought of reward; and a study of the careers of such people leaves no question about the necessity for ingenuity on their part. Working under privation and in strange situations, they have had to devise an untold number of expedients. Those that we know about are merely samples that give us the right to suppose that there have been multitudes of others. Even in the history of the development of Occidental technology, there have been many instances of inventors who have disclaimed rewards, especially financial rewards, for their ideas. One example was Christopher Sholes, "the father of the modern typewriter." He was never interested in the financial success of the machine that he helped to build. He wanted to make written communication simpler and the work that it entails easier.[6]

Finally, in by far the majority of cases there has been relatively little possibility of assigning credit to an innovator. The full meaning of this observation appears when the world as a whole is taken into account. Millions of inventions and discoveries have been made by individuals in world history without credit aims being attached to them. This is not because such ideas have not been worth while, but because the concept of assigning credit has so often been weak or absent. In many societies the amount of prestige that goes with the conception of a new idea is so small, the granting of it so uncertain, and its duration so fleeting that it can hardly be expected to function as an incentive. Commonly there is no tradition of bestowing awards for novelties, and there are therefore no mechanisms for claiming or securing them. This is not to say that originality is not appreciated, but only that some people regard it as something to be taken for granted and shared rather than signalized and rewarded. And even though praise or passing acknowledgment may be granted, substantial rewards for ingenuity are the exception rather than the rule. Our knowledge that most Americans are encouraged to strive for any goal if it carries a financial reward and our belief that they should do so are reflections of the generic cultural bias that postulates individual recognition as an essential condition for any labor. The patent system is an outgrowth of our dedication to the ideals of individualism and progress. It testifies to our emphasis upon the importance of the individual and to our materialistic bent. It subscribes to our conviction that, since new ideas are valuable, their authors are entitled to credit, especially to credit in the form of a financial reward. These orientations are facts, so it is expectable that patent regulations should meet the desire for rewards and that they should encourage efforts on the part of some people.

Our conclusion must be, then, that the conscious desire for credit is an important motivation to invention but that it is not universally operative in all societies or in all aspects of culture in a single society. Its appeal varies by culture, by culture trait, and by individual. Furthermore, men create in spite of it and even in defiance of it. They must be motivated by stronger or by more subtle needs.

[6] Waldemar Kaempffert, *A Popular History of American Invention*. New York: Charles Scribner's Sons, 1924, Vol. I, p. 276.

Peripheral Subliminal Wants. Because they are sensitive to stimulation and because the stimuli to which they react are incessant, human beings, like other organisms, are almost constantly impelled to make numerous simultaneous adjustments to a fluid interplay of motive forces. The kaleidoscopic shiftings, the shadings and the fluctuations of internal and external influences, produce an endless ferment of activity in the individual. Some of his wants are gross and involve his whole organic system, others are localized; some are consciously apprehended, and a great many others are sensed only peripherally and subliminally.

It is with the last-mentioned wants and the discernible responses to them that we are concerned at this point. While a large number of these urges are within the reach of conscious realization and control, for the most part they run their intricate courses independent of it. They waver between autonomy and dependency upon conscious directives. They are constantly building up and discharging nervous-energy potentials irrespective of the conscious preoccupations of the individual. They can be transient and self-liquidating; each satisfies some microcosmic purpose of the organism, then gives way to fresh demands. When these subliminal wants of the organism are lulled, stayed, or depressed, their overt manifestations are proportionately reduced; when they are stimulated, they result in disquiet, nervousness, and restlessness. Also, some organisms act as if they enjoy stimulation. Whether or not they can be said to want it, they appear to seek it for the satisfaction that it gives in and of itself. This at any rate is the simplest explanation of the random exploratory probings that are engaged in by individuals of many animal species. If some motivational explanation of them is called for, it might be suggested that they are manifestations of a desire to ease muscular and psychic tensions; perhaps more fundamentally they are means to release impounded energy. They increase in frequency and in intensity with unrest, excitement, and mental stress.

To be included in this category are the numerous and diversified probings, doodlings, fingerings, and pokings that people engage in with their various body parts and anything that might be grasped by them. These activities are, from an objective standpoint, exploratory and manipulative, though most often they lack any such conceptualization on the part of the actor. For the most part they are unorganized, aimless, and unpremeditated. They are not pursued with reference to anything done in the past or with relation to accomplishment. They are performed absent-mindedly and without regard to whether they are aberrant. They are individualized; and once accomplished, they must be rated as innovations, although myriads of them never achieve that accolade. Only an infinitely small fraction ever acquire enough significance to lift them out of the mass. The innovator himself only very rarely considers his absent-minded act important enough to warrant a repetition, and still more rarely do others follow him when he does.

In spite of the high mortality rate on these subliminal discoveries, the importance of the source should not be underestimated. The insight to perceive the implications of a random act can have personal survival value for the innovator, and upon occasion it has given men the key to problems of considerable importance to others. Edison's realization that carbon answered the requirements of his incandescent lamp filament is reported to have come as a result of his distracted toying with materials on his workbench. Like many other problem solutions, his was preceded by a baffling series of failures. He and others before him had experimented with the incandescent properties of a variety of substances, including carbon strips and rods. None of them proved to be durable enough to be practicable as resistance elements in lamps. Edison continued his search for an appropriate substance but at the same time worked on other projects. One was aimed at the development of a better telephone carbon transmitter. In his experiments with the transmitter he made use of lampblack, and one day he vacantly rolled a pinch of this together with some tar that was on his table. The resulting thread recalled his problem of resistance elements in lamps, and the thought occurred that a carbon element of this kind might meet the requirements. He then began the long series of experiments with carbon residues which eventually produced a filament that had commercial possibilities.[7]

The inception of the backward-folding airplane wing is also reported to have been a by-product of doodling. Its inventor was Leroy Grumman, who undertook the problem of constructing a collapsible wing to save space on carrier decks and transports. Upward-folding wings were already in use, but Grumman wanted for his planes "the kind that birds have"; he wanted them to "break at the shoulder," twist from the horizontal to the vertical plane, and rest flat against the fuselage of the aircraft. He found the solution while absent-mindedly fingering a paper clip and an eraser that lay upon his desk. The story of this has been told by Howard W. Blakeslee, science editor for the Associated Press, in these words: [8]

One afternoon he [Grumman] absently picked up the paper clip and the eraser, one of the long flat variety, fiddled with them as he thought. When he looked down, he saw that he had thrust the eraser through the paper clip, the two forming the semblance of a plane, the eraser the wings, the clip the fuselage. Grumman noticed that he was twisting the eraser back and forth, and that the side which went back was suggestive of a folding bird's wing. He removed the eraser and laid it on his desk. From his pocket he drew a pen knife. He carefully severed the eraser across the middle. Then he whittled one of the halves to the bevel of a plane wing. This half he put into the clip, like a wing. When the beveled ob-

[7] Abbott Payson Usher, *A History of Mechanical Inventions*. New York: McGraw-Hill Book Company, Inc., 1929, p. 18.

[8] Howard W. Blakeslee, "The Folding Wing: What It Means to Our Carriers," *Washington Post*, Apr. 15, 1944.

ject was swung backward, it also turned slightly sidewise like the slant of a bird's wing. He did a little figuring, and then went to the design room, to the chief aeronautical engineer, Bill Schwendler, and L. A. (Jake) Swirbul, Grumman vice president and general manager. "I think," he said, "we have the answer for the folding wing."

Almost certainly many toys, games, and other means of amusement have come into existence as a result of some idle manipulation of the hands or feet or of things that chanced to be near them. In fact, all of us have invented little private games for ourselves and our children in just this way. It is a common pastime, and doubtless there exist or have existed a multitude of amusements restricted to family circles that go back to such beginnings. Very often their originators, while protesting to outsiders that these games are silly, with a little encouragement can be induced to acknowledge their authorship.

Random activity is a well-recognized prelude to problem solutions and discoveries among experimental animals. At this point we must distinguish between goal-directed and incidental random activity. The food-seeking ant that makes innumerable tentative efforts and eventually finds its way into a cupboard or the hungry rat that presses a food-delivering lever has certainly made discoveries. But these trial-and-error and accidental approaches are random only in the sense that they are irregular. From the standpoint of motivation their curves of success or failure are straight lines, even though they are jagged behaviorally speaking. We shall consider them later. Subliminal random activity, as the term is intended here, eventuates in discoveries that are tangential to the dominant preoccupation at the moment, not an integral part of it. Its motivation is subsidary and peripheral. It may be that subhuman animals are capable of making discoveries in this way. Perhaps some of the inventions of Köhler's apes could be included here. It would depend upon the extent to which the activities that produced them were collateral to the dominant interests of the ape at the moment.[9]

Impulsive acts are other manifestations of subliminal and peripheral drives. They are not entirely distinct from the absent-minded exercises just discussed, but they are less diffuse and less continuous. They are more discrete, intense, self-contained, and obtrusive, and hence more definitive in their characteristics and durations. As is the case with absent-minded discoveries, either the impulsive act itself or the unpremeditated effect that it has upon something else may constitute the innovation. In any event, the impulsive act, like the more random manipulative one, is peripherally aroused and may be only subliminally gratifying. The act itself satisfies and dissipates the want.

[9] Wolfgang Köhler, *The Mentality of Apes* (trans. by Ella Winter). New York: Harcourt, Brace and Company, Inc., 1925.

In so far as observation goes, some impulses are reactions to internal stimuli. They are muscular or mental adjustments to inward stresses. Others are set off by an external stimulus; that is, there is some demonstrable cue or a specific activator for them. Either an isolated stimulus or a total situation, such as a room or a crowd, may trigger impulsive reactions. In some instances they erupt as sudden releases of pent-up wants; in others they seem to be spontaneously mobilized energy releases in the nature of reflexes. All expend energy, but some do it primarily to discharge an excess while others have a conserving effect in that they thwart or constrain expenditure in another quarter of the organic system.

A remarkably large number of traditional acts bear evidences of impulsive origins, but in most cases it is impossible to demonstrate that they have in fact come into existence in this way. This area of behavior as a source of innovations has been slighted, so much so that it may be considered speculative to suggest it. Nevertheless, some instances that appear to be beyond question may be cited, and still others of the same nature may be suggested for inclusion in the category despite our lack of knowledge concerning the circumstances of their origins.

Shakerism is replete with ritual elements that began as impulsive acts. The phenomenon of shaking itself is an excellent example. Mary Slocum, the wife of the founder of the cult, was its originator. At its inception it was a gross manifestation of hysteria, resulting from her intense and sustained anxiety and grief over the prolonged illness and anticipated death of her husband. Much to the consternation of the other Indians who were attending her sick husband, she was seized by an uncontrollable trembling of her head and hands. While in this state she wailed and prayed incoherently over his unconscious body. She, and later others, attributed his recovery to the presence of divine power that was evidenced by her shaking. Since that time all Shakers have striven to induce these ecstatic convulsions. They have become the mark and the emotional release of adherents to the faith. Within this framework innumerable individual variations have appeared, many of which have become standard practices. In other words, the trance state has erupted repeatedly in impulsive acts that have become crystallized into accepted ritual elements. All the specific hand manipulations of individuals "under power" that are supposed to have curative value have surely originated in this spontaneous fashion. As one observes a group of Shakers trembling and milling about a patient, there at first appears to be no order or convention in their "laying on of hands," and they will say that they are aware of none in their transported state. Yet a little study will make it evident that their hand movements are standardized and that there are a limited number of patterns which they follow. They can be analyzed and described. Moreover, for some ritual acts now current, positive information detailing their inception is available, principally because the impulsive aberrations of their originators were denounced as unorthodox. There are accounts of other spontaneous acts that did not weather criticism and failed to become elements in the Shaker behavior system. At one time there was an acrimonious controversy over the direction of the ritual circuit of the church or sickroom, whether it should be clockwise or counterclockwise. Understandably each side rested its argument upon divine sanction, but the interesting point to us is that divine guidance was alleged in each case to have manifested itself in the actions of specific individuals while they were in a trance. Mary Slocum's impulsive precedent was appealed to by one faction, while a certain new convert's spectacular reversal was pointed to by the other. It is probable that the entire complex of activities exhibited by Shakers "under power" has been elaborated by impulsive creation.

The Shaker data suggest that conventionalized trance behaviors elsewhere have had similar origins. The spectacular demonstrations of insensitivity to pain by Hindu fakirs, Tahitian fire-walkers, and certain Christian anchorites could well be perseverations of impulses incidental to an abnormal mental state. So could the patterned contortions and symbolic acts of shamanistic healers and spiritualistic diviners; their pointings, gropings, talking in tongues, table tappings, and tent shakings bear the imprint of rationalized reflexes. The mimicry compulsion that is such a pronounced feature of hysterical seizures in northern Siberia and on the Malay Peninsula is peripheral to the main interest of the afflicted person at the time that the uncontrollable urge to imitate something or someone overcomes him.[10] Intricate as the behavior is, it is spasmodic, disruptive, and close to the reflex level. The custom of running amok is of the same involuntary character and very likely has its roots in unpremeditated aggressive acts in emotionally unstable individuals. The frenzied kris dances of the Balinese have the earmarks of an elaborated impulse. The "exercises" of the participants in the religious frenzy known as the Kentucky Revival were orgies of impulsive behavior. Those who were inspired at its camp meetings barked like dogs, leaped around like frogs, jerked and twisted like spastics, and rolled on the ground like senseless creatures.[11]

It should be kept in mind that all these phenomena are patterned behaviors. They are well-recognized stereotypes within specific cultural traditions. They have had beginnings, imitations, and elaborations. Their inceptions, like their ultimate culminations, probably rested upon an impulse or a series of impulses.

Only a minority of impulsive acts spring out of abnormal mental states and remain connected with them. The development of Shaker ritual and

[10] M. A. Czaplicka, *Aboriginal Siberia*. New York: Oxford University Press, 1914, Chap. 15.

[11] James Mooney, "The Ghost-dance Religion," *Bureau of American Ethnology, 14th Annual Report, 1892–93*. Washington, D.C., 1896, Part 2, pp. 942–944.

ideology again offers illustrations. The testimonials and the exhortations of ardent members have been pregnant with unpremeditated novelties in phrasing, in idea, and in gesture. Some of these spontaneous innovations have been imitated and so preserved, others were abortive or remained as idiosyncrasies. Once, while exhorting a congregation, a Yakima man was suddenly impelled to disrobe himself. He was preaching upon sin and the spiritual purity of newborn infants. He felt that his disrobing was a dramatic way to testify to his yearning to shed his sins symbolically before God. He had only one known imitator, a woman. The idea was too shocking to become popular. Another minister, a vigorous "stomper," tried unsuccessfully to speed up the tempo of the rhythmic tramping that is such an important emotional stimulus at certain points in Shaker services. Another convert, carried away by contrition, felt compelled to stand before church congregations and give lurid descriptions of his sins, to the embarrassment of those who made a distinction between testimonials of regeneration and the intimate confession of sins to ministers in private. Shakerism, like some other religious movements, has encouraged impulsive aberrations, whether in trance or otherwise, because its dogma validates inspiration, which is necessarily an individualistic phenomenon. Anyone may justify a spontaneous innovation by appeal to divine sanction. Such departures are "gifts" or "teachings" that invite but do not require adherence by believers. In short, differentiation through inspiration is the norm; there is a premium upon diversity, and sharing is not a measure of the effectiveness of innovation.

Outside this special field, which in itself offers sufficient justification for the consideration of impulsive activity as a source of innovation, there are surely other examples. It is not too much to suppose that many of the customs which we and other people accept in a matter of fact way have had their origins in nonrational avoidances, compulsions, obsessions, and phobias. Doubtless many of the taboos, charms, gestures, and mannerisms that are a part of the daily life of many people are to be understood as conventionalizations of subliminal needs. Acts of courage, defiance, devotion, and self-sacrifice are frequently precipitated spontaneously out of crisis situations and become models for others. It is also possible that patterns of self-destruction such as our suicide pacts and pledges, the "voluntary death" decisions of the Chukchi of Siberia, and the "Crazy Dog" vows of the Crow Indians have taken shape under the impetus of some one or a few spectacular eruptions of melancholia and seemingly irremediable despair.[12]

Random and impulsive activities vary in their frequency, intensity, duration, urgency, and degree of awareness. These variables depend upon the

[12] Czaplicka, *op. cit.*, pp. 317–318. Robert H. Lowie, *The Crow Indians*. New York: Farrar & Company, 1935, pp. 331–334.

amount of tension to which the individual is subjected and the vigor of his stimulation. They fluctuate with his physical and mental state; some situations, such as those with which he is unfamiliar, augment his tensions and hence his subliminal needs to release them. By custom, the individual is allowed greater freedom to fulfill these needs in some social situations than in others, and the members of some social groups are frequently more restrained than others. Typically members of the elite classes and others on their best behavior exercise greater control over their impulsive acts and random behaviors.

Central Subliminal Wants. Some subliminal wants are integral to other wants of the individual. They contribute to some of the most fundamental demands that he can experience, even if only vaguely and indirectly. They are central, not only in the sense that they are not tangential to other needs, but because they embody the individual's conception of himself and are his means of self-realization, self-assertion, and self-constancy. They provide him with indispensable mechanisms for establishing and maintaining himself as an integrated, continuing entity, the same now as in the past and continuing into the future. We are not dealing here merely with what is often called the need for self-preservation. The motivations go deeper than that. Perhaps they could be summed up under the caption of the need for self-definition.

The importance of this category of incentives lies in the fact that every individual has to react in some fashion to stimulation. If the stimulus is real, that is, sensed by the individual in question, there must be some response to it that is characteristic of him. Even though he reacts negatively by excluding, resisting, or refusing to acknowledge stimulation, he is nevertheless reacting. His need to do so is compelling and definitive; for he is in the beginning of his existence confronted with an unorganized mass of sensory stimuli, internal and external, out of which he must make some sense. He must perforce nucleate himself out of the welter of sensations and formulate a conception of himself. He needs to isolate and identify himself if he is to be an individual. He has the further need to formulate in some fashion his ideas about other things, people, situations, and ideas. In this extremely complex and confusing process he inevitably develops a personality with its own colorings and with its singular functional compulsions to filter experience. He develops ideas about himself, biases, moods, and attitudes that make him an entity. We need not ask whether he wants or needs, in a voluntaristic sense, to do all this—whether he has some yearning to thread his way through the "blooming, buzzing, confusion" to some satisfying end, or whether he is free to choose his course. The objective fact is that he acts as if he were strongly motivated to bring order into his personal chaos. And it is undeniably true that he must do so if he is to survive by his own efforts.

In speaking of these ego wants or self-wants as subliminal it is not meant that they are inaccessible to the conscious mind. They are knowable to the individual by probing, and often they press over the threshold of awareness by themselves. Apprehension of them ranges all the way from a complete unawareness of their persuasive demands and effects to an acute distress and the terror of insanity with their frustration. Recognition of their demands varies between one's not knowing that he is being himself to an aggressive assertion of it; from uneasiness over memory lapses to self-persecution over bad judgments; from bland ignorance of the self to pride in it or disgust with it.

There are innumerable human documents which attest to the central character of self-wants. These wants come to the surface when they are thwarted and attended by nightmarish sensations of unreality. Upon the failure or withdrawal of their satisfaction the very existence of the self is threatened. Bettelheim's description of his and other prisoners' reactions under persecution in Nazi concentration camps vividly illustrates the fundamental need for preservation of ego integrity and constancy. He relates that observations made upon himself and others were deliberately contrived by him to prevent the destruction of his personality. They were his private means of retaining his hold upon reality under the shocks and indignities of the brutal treatment to which he was subjected. He found himself unconsciously using other safeguards as well, such as an attitude of detachment from the things that were happening to him, which enabled him to "remain alive and unchanged." [13]

The importance of self-wants for innovation relates to the fact that they place the individual's imprint upon all his perceptions. His understandings of other things are inevitably colored by his understanding of himself. In order to preserve his identity, if for no other reason, he is faced with the necessity of organizing the field of his experience at every moment. He does this in terms of his sociopsychological self, an entity that is the product of a unique life history in a unique social microcosm. He is continuously, and largely unconsciously, casting his environment in the mold of his past experiences through a dynamic interaction between its components and his self-conception. He must perforce classify and interpret himself as well as other things; and since no two things (including himself) are ever identical from one moment to the next, he is constantly grouping together sensory and ideological data that are different. Perceptual organization is not a photographic process. It is fundamentally an innovative act; it is an interactive, adjustive relationship between the perceiver and the thing perceived. The two together make up a dynamic creative whole. The extent to which the

[13] Bruno Bettelheim, "Individual and Mass Behavior in Extreme Situations," *Journal of Abnormal and Social Psychology*, 1943, 38:417–452.

individual realizes this relationship ranges from complete ignorance of it in routine responses to frustration and withdrawal from "impossible" decisions and dilemmas.

These private moldings of the phenomenal world and the demands for them are ever-present occurrences. They are obvious upon introspection and appear also upon casual observation of others. In addition, there exists a voluminous literature upon controlled experiments that attest to their operation.[14] Their consequences are always innovative in some degree, and they in part explain "Everyman, the inventor." They are one of the many instances of ever-present phenomena that merely have a special significance for the study of innovation; they are routine occurrences with spectacular facets.

Central subliminal wants may be discussed under several headings, each treating of some particular aspect of the demand for integrity of the self. All operate under an unconscious desire to assert, stabilize, and maintain the ego; but each illuminates some need facet with consequences distinct enough to warrant their separate considerations. There may be a greater or a lesser number of them than are noticed below. That is not a critical question, since our interest is only in pointing out that such needs do exist and in illustrating their innovative potential.

One such need is for orientation or structuralization. If an individual is to function as a psychological whole, he must work out some adjustment with his experiences. He must feel or know that he stands in some relationship with his natural and social environment; he must orient his ego in some fashion with respect to his ideas and the ideas of other people. A great variety of self-placement scales are manifested in explicit or implicit beliefs, attitudes, evaluations, and judgments. The placements occur in all dimensions, including the temporal, spatial, and social. The relationships of the self to other phenomena may be positive, being expressed in preferences, interests, identifications, and participations; or they may be negative and so be manifested as neglect, avoidance, dislike, unconcern, or withdrawal. Whatever expression it may take, the individual's appreciation of himself is organized and structured with reference to the other data of his experience. That gives his ego reality, constancy, and protection.

Not only must a person orient himself; if he is to survive in a universe of unremitting sense impressions, he must order them; he must discover and assign relationships between them. Again, the placement series, their dimensions, and the relationships appropriate to them are multiplex. The confusion and uncertainty which characterize an individual's estimate of certain areas of his experience may prove too baffling for resolution, and it fre-

[14] See bibliography in Jerome S. Bruner and Cecile C. Goodman, "Value and Need as Organizing Factors in Perception," *Journal of Abnormal and Social Psychology*, 1947, 42:33–44.

quently happens that he either ignores the demands that his estimate places upon him or finally abandons his attempts to make any sense out of them. But if circumstances require that he deal with the situation, it cannot remain chaotic and undifferentiated. It has to assume some recognizable characteristics. In particular, perception demands some structuring of the perceived field, a fact that is demonstrated by the psychological effects of ambiguous figures. An observer presented with such a visual stimulus organizes it in one way or another. There may be reorganizations, and one interpretation may fluctuate with another; but both cannot coexist. One cannot see an outline as the boundary of a continent and the borders of an ocean at the same time. Most importantly, some interpretation must be made if the observer is sufficiently motivated to attend to the stimulus.

The point here is that these compulsive perceptual organizations may be highly individualized. Moreover, their peculiarities commonly become stabilized to such an extent that a given individual can actually perceive no other organization than the one he has himself achieved. For a person who has once visualized an ambiguous figure in one way, a deliberate effort is necessary if he is to see it in any other way, and often he is unable to do so. This is not only true of such trivial things as experimental drawings; it holds for ambiguous life situations as well. In consequence there are innumerable private interpretations of the same social, political, and historical data. These idiosyncratic organizations of experience are unquestionably innovative, and like any invention they invite concurrence and imitation by others. In short, they may initiate a trend and in time become a custom-decreed fact.

That such developments are more than a matter of speculation has been shown by Sherif's experiments. He employed the autokinetic effect to ascertain what an observer would do when he was required to define the characteristics of an objectively unstabilized stimulus field. A fixed point of light was presented to his subjects in an otherwise totally dark room, and they were requested to estimate how far the spot of light moved. Because under such circumstances a light appears to move, even though it is stationary, the estimates given were necessarily indicators of subjective evaluations. The question was, Would they exhibit any consistency in individual or in group situations? Sherif's results are pertinent to our consideration of the subliminal demands for orientation because they reveal that, when an individual is deprived of any objective means of stabilizing his perceptions, he will establish an internal point of reference for this purpose. This internal orientation point is peculiar to himself and becomes, after a few repetitions, as standardized as if it had an objective referent. Once established, it will serve him upon subsequent occasions. Furthermore, when groups of individuals are presented with a similarly unstructured field, they will, as a group, establish a hypothetical reference point and an organization of their perceptions based upon it that are peculiar to them and distinct from the norms evolved by other groups. If, then, an individual of such a group is presented with a comparable situation alone, he perceives it in terms of the group norm; his evaluations, established as one of a group, persist when he is no longer acting as a member of it. Contrariwise, several individuals who have privately established their orientation points and structured their fields tend to alter their individual constructs under the influence of group estimates so that they more closely approximate one another. The degree of conformance is not so great as when all began without preconceptions, but the group effect is undeniable. Both individuals and groups, then, unconsciously manufacture norms under the need to stabilize their sense impressions.[15]

As Sherif points out, these experimental results have wider and more important implications. He says that [16]

. . . when a group of individuals faces a new, unstable situation and has no previously established interests or opinions regarding the situation, the result is not chaos; a common norm arises and the situation is structured in relation to the common norm. Once the common norm is established, later the separate individuals keep on perceiving it in terms of the frame of reference which was once the norm of the group.

Any unstructured situation, such as an emergency, a social or a political crisis, or a meeting of strangers, summons the need for some kind of solution to bring order out of fluidity or uncertainty if an individual or a group is to deal with it effectively. Natural catastrophes have the same unsettling effect, and out of them emerge new leaders and new ideas. Some of the tentative efforts may fail through their unacceptability to others, or because they do not meet the needs of the situation. Nonetheless, there has been innovation. This fact is the psychological justification for including the deprivation of essentials and independence of authority in our survey of settings for change. They are propitious circumstances for innovation because they provoke destructuralized situations that demand a reformulation.

The subliminal striving for meaning is another important central need of the ego system. This want is closely related to orientation needs, as they have been discussed, and in some instances it would be difficult to assign a given reaction unequivocally to the one or the other category. They are intimately linked because both are drawn into an individual's unconscious struggle to understand his universe in terms of what he already knows. He configurates it and reads meanings into it in the light of the only possible frames of reference available to him; namely, those provided by his

[15] Muzafer Sherif, *The Psychology of Social Norms.* New York: Harper & Brothers, 1936, Chap. 6.

[16] *Ibid.,* p. 111.

past experiences. New experiences must be integrated with the old. They must be drawn into the matrix of the known before they can have any significance. Otherwise they remain utterly alien, detached, and incomprehensible. In short, they must have meaning if the individual is to deal with them; and if they appear to be lacking in meaning, he consciously or unconsciously assigns some significance to them.

This urge to rationalize the irrational is a well-known human reaction on the conscious level. Human beings everywhere evince a tendency to respond in this way when the logic of their routine behaviors is questioned. Still more insistent and subtle are their subliminal urges to do the same thing under the pressure of their own hidden doubts and quandaries. This insidious demand for meaning is significant from the standpoint of innovation. because it to some extent inevitably distorts the stimulus data. The necessity of fitting a sensation into the framework of the known entails some degree of individual coloring, filtering, and evaluation. The observer molds his new experiences to suit his needs and in so doing makes of them something that, in objective fact or to others, they are not. This distortion is minimal and may have no discernible consequences when the evaluations of different individuals of the same social group are compared. Except for the unusual individual, the recognized innovator, their judgments are conformable. They vary only within an accepted range of interpretations. Disparities become more frequent and more evident the less constrained a person is by the conventional definition given the thing, idea, or behavior in question. The freer he is of automatic acceptance of traditional interpretations, the more novel, incomprehensible, amusing, extravagant, or repellent the meanings that he reads in are likely to be. The freest of all is the person who is confronted with an isolated alien form, one which does not carry with it any clue to its meaning in the culture of its origin. Hence, the bizarre and "freewheeling" interpretations of the stranger and the ignorant person. Hence, the curious (to us) adaptations of European trade goods and castoff articles made by natives in remote areas, the perverted (to them) interpretations that superficial observers give to their customs, and the "fresh insight" that scientific workers in one discipline bring to their analysis of problems in another. Ignorance is quite as much of an advantage in innovation as is brilliance when the urge to read in meaning is active. From the standpoint of established custom—and that is the only basis for evaluation—it is as truly creative, albeit unwittingly, as is abundant knowledge.

Bartlett has emphasized the importance of the subliminal demand for meaning in his experiments upon remembering. The urge and its creative consequences were most evident in the reports of his subjects when they were asked to read and subsequently to reproduce exactly certain strange and outlandish verbal material. Striking illustrations of it occurred when his sophisticated English subjects were given a short myth of an American

Indian tribe with the understanding that they were to recall it accurately later on. To a European this story, called "The War of the Ghosts," is jerky, puzzling, and incoherent. Its episodes do not seem to have much logical connection, strange objects are mentioned, there are references of uncertain significance, and a supernatural aura surrounds the whole. All these shortcomings (from the Englishman's viewpoint) were rectified in the series of reproductions from memory. In the retelling the story was shortened and made more consistent internally; familiar phraseology was substituted for the unfamiliar; content was altered so that "canoes," for example, became "boats"; and explanatory connectives were introduced to give point to the episodes and to the conversation of the characters. In brief, the myth was unconsciously reworked to give it more meaning to a modern European and less to the Indian. The original story was scarcely recognizable in the final products of the serial reproductions after a lapse of months.[17]

Bartlett calls the subliminal want that we are here discussing the "effort after meaning." It comes into play because every experience presents the observer with a problem that he knowingly or not recognizes as such and to which he must, knowingly or not, find a solution in terms of the value systems established in his personal experience.

Because this task factor is always present, it is fitting to speak of every human cognitive reaction—perceiving, imaging, remembering, thinking and reasoning —as an *effort after meaning*. Certain of the tendencies which the subject brings with him into the situation with which he is called upon to deal are utilized so as to make his reaction the "easiest," or the least disagreeable, or the quickest and least obstructed that is at the time possible. When we try to discover how this is done we find that always it is by an effort to connect what is given with something else. Thus, the immediately present "stands for" something not immediately present, and "meaning," in a psychological sense, has its origin. As we have seen, in certain cases of great structural simplicity, or of structural regularity, or of extreme familiarity, the immediate data are at once fitted to, or matched with, a perceptual pattern which appears to be pre-existent so far as the particular perceptual act is concerned. This pre-formed setting, scheme, or pattern is utilized in a completely unreflecting, unanalytical and unwitting manner. Because it is utilized the immediate perceptual data have meaning, can be dealt with, and are assimilated.[18]

As this quotation from Bartlett implies, the compulsion to read in meanings is not confined to materials from alien cultures. It operates at all times, only more so with data that are fragmentary, incoherent, or inconsistent for any reason. It is this characteristic of the stimulus field which causes the effort after meaning to join forces with the demand for orientation and

[17] F. C. Bartlett, *Remembering. A Study in Experimental and Social Psychology.* New York: Cambridge University Press, 1932, Chap. 5.
[18] *Ibid.,* pp. 44–45.

structuralization. Ambiguous universes summon the need for meaning as well as the desire for certainty and fixity.

The results of an effort after meaning are quite evident in the accounts of the origin of the Shaker religion that were given by people who knew of it only by hearsay. The distortions that occur are the more flagrant the less the specific knowledge of the particular historian. Rumor spreading offers an equally instructive and better known illustration of the same process. Rumors are by their nature fragmentary and ambiguous. They present a set of allegations that are insufficiently structured to be satisfying to the listener; they contain uncertainties, probabilities, and contradictions. Their nature is, moreover, such that they provoke high interest; their subject matter fixates concern and motivates the teller and the listener to find the utmost of meaning in the little that they know for certain. The purveyor of the story strives to give more reason and certainty to his report than it possessed when he heard it. Its incompleteness and its indefiniteness are unbearable; they call for certification and assurance. Hence mere probabilities, possibilities, guesses, and conditional propositions become metamorphosed, often insensibly, into certainties, facts, and asseverations. The meaningless becomes meaningful, and the unstructured becomes structured. There are, as has been mentioned, other motivations involved in rumor spreading and the creativeness that goes with it; but the chaotic character of the rumor content, combined with its high interest value, evokes the remodeling forces of meaning and orientation wants as well.

Still another creative force is inherent in the subliminal drive for ego domination of a perceptual or a cognitive field of experience. This urge is manifest, for one thing, in the interest selection of the individual by which he achieves a kind of ego coloration of all that he senses. He tends to magnify those aspects of it with which he in some way identifies himself and slights, overlooks, or implicitly belittles those that do not interest him, that he cannot understand, and that detract from his estimate of himself. This incentive is also related to the need for orientation, for it is one of the forces which contribute to the structuralization of objective and ideological referents.

The interest selection and emphasis that take place under this demand are evident in many experimental situations. In their study of the psychology of rumor, Allport and Postman have noted the importance of distortions that are due to what they call the process of assimilation, "which has to do with the powerful attractive force exerted upon rumor by habits, interests, and sentiments existing in the listener's mind." They list several varieties of assimilation as they relate to individual and group bias of one type or another and illustrate them with examples from their experimental data. Thus, under the heading of "assimilation to interest" they note that when a picture containing some subordinate detail of a woman's dress was described from hearsay and memory by one woman for another in a successive series of retellings, the description became in the end a "story exclusively about dresses." This did not happen when men were the reporters. Similarly, when a picture involving policemen was described by one police officer for another in a series, the final account came to center about police interests read into the picture, and the story as a whole became protective of and partial to them. More striking alterations occurred when racial stereotypes were involved in pictorial stimuli. One scene depicted a white man holding an open razor while engaged in what might be interpreted as an argument with an apologetic Negro. The authors report that in more than half the serial reproductions of this scene the final description had the Negro holding the razor, and in some it was stated that he was brandishing it or otherwise threatening the white man.[19]

It is unnecessary to detail further the distortive effects of the process of ego coloration. Suffice it to say that it is a recognized phenomenon and that its unwitting modifications have diagnostic value for ascertaining deep-seated motivations and conflicts in certain individuals. This fact is exploited in the use of the so-called projective tests. Beyond that, it remains to be stressed that coloration is innovative, and that from its small beginnings important cultural consequences can develop. Not only the fates of individual men but the tempers and prejudices of groups of them have been affected by it. Factionalism and strife crystallize around its figments. So do value judgments and precedents. Courtroom testimony notoriously dramatizes its operation. Schools of thought and interpretations of history emerge under its spotlights. It is not surprising that those who have pressed the case for the environmental determinism of culture have been geographers and that those who argue for an economic interpretation of history have strong personal biases for simplistic structuralizations of the tangle of forces in which they find themselves.

The history of ethnological theory is most instructive from this standpoint. The extent to which men, including the present author, have propounded theories of cultural development solely because of the accidents of their preoccupation with selected ranges of its subject matter offers an object lesson that is worth the study of every professional ethnologist. Apart from their conscious motivations, it should be realized that to a considerable degree G. Elliot Smith's heliolithic theory was determined by the accident of his immersion in Egyptian culture, Fritz Graebner's Kulturkreise sequences by his familiarity with Pacific Island cultures, Bronislaw Malinowski's functional view by his intimate acquaintance with the Trobriand Islanders, L. H. Morgan's stages of culture by his firsthand acquaintance with

[19] Gordon W. Allport and Leo J. Postman, "The Basic Psychology of Rumor," *Transactions of the New York Academy of Sciences,* 1945, Series II, 8:61–81.

the Iroquois, and Franz Boas's skepticism of cultural regularities by his familiarity with the diversity of American Indian cultures. There is no question about the brilliance and the sincerity of these men, but in retrospect it is evident that the views of all of them have been colored by the circumstances that led to their special interests and by their identifications with those interests. In varying degrees all of us are subject to the same frailty of subliminal bias. It is naïve to suppose that we can escape it, and it is equally naïve to underestimate its importance for new ideas.

Egocentricity is another aspect of ego domination, not always to be distinguished from coloration. The urge to interpret things in terms of one's self has had important cultural consequences. It is responsible to a large extent for the common human proclivity for personifying nature so that trees, winds, and celestial bodies are believed to have volition, souls, and procreative powers. In other words, it gives rise to animism and to all that is entailed by that belief. The process is not a simple one, but the tendency to project self-characteristics springs from an intimate knowledge of them and from an overweening preoccupation with them. The same unconscious exaltation of the ego results in the tendency revealed by all of us to read our motivations and values into the acts of other people, with all the misunderstandings that become consolidated around such perversions. Ethnic-group antipathies are very often mobilized by this ego dominance and its frequent concomitant, ego defense. Finally, it may be noted that the insidious demands of ego dominance often lead, in reputable scientific analysis, to the observer's fallacy.

Another of the innovative central and subliminal wants is for protection. Very often the ego under threat responds in an unconsciously defensive manner. Much has been written and said about inner defensive mechanisms, but nothing, it seems, about their innovative characteristics. Usually they are treated as maladaptive; that is, as bad because of their unhygienic and asocial implications. They may be so considered because they are makeshift responses. They do not resolve permanently the difficulty in which the individual finds himself; his tensions and anxieties remain to spring up another time. But laying aside this important consideration, we cannot disregard the fact that the devices to which a person resorts to shield his ego are often ingenious, if not colorful or spectacular. And, as always in our discussion, it is to be kept in mind that these improvisations can become standardized and accepted by others than the originator. Some become custom and some not. Moreover, they can give rise to inferences and theories and have other socially significant effects.

One innovative aspect of ego defense is exhibited in the subliminal rejection of guilt. This defense may be accomplished by the projection of unpraiseworthy traits upon others. It often happens that if external conditions threaten the ego concept by forcing the individual to admit an unacceptable fault, he unconsciously attributes it to an appropriate scapegoat. Thus, a person who is sensitive about his slovenliness, laziness, or improvidence may exhibit an ingenious facility for projecting these attributes upon those who have no redress against the imputation. This is a typical reaction when an ethnic minority is available as a target for displaced hostility.[20] People who have repressed prejudices of any sort are prone to impute them to others whom they dislike. Equally common in our day are the fictitious vilifications of ideological opponents that bolster the inward uncertainties of the self. The smear campaigns that take shape when reputations are at stake frequently can tell us more about the character weaknesses of the attacker than about those of the attacked. The same is true of the probings and exposés of morals censors.

Guilt may also be rejected by a kind of subconscious hairsplitting. If there is a threat of identification with some reprehensible attribute, it is sometimes avoided by the individual's inventing some difference between it and that which characterizes him. This reaction was demonstrated by the so-called Mr. Biggott experiments. In them, subjects with certain prejudices were shown cartoons lampooning characters who had attitudes comparable to their own. The experiment was planned in the hope that by thus exposing prejudice the subject would reject his own rather than be identified with Mr. Biggott. The results were unexpected. The subjects did refuse to identify themselves with the socially disapproved characters in the cartoons; but, still clinging to their prejudices, they exhibited considerable ingenuity in manufacturing distinctions between themselves and the characters. Some scoffed at a defect in Mr. Biggott's bias in such a way as to deprecate his stand and enhance theirs. Some used the scapegoat technique: Mr. Biggott was a Jew, a foreigner, a Communist, or a labor agitator. Whatever his recourse, the prejudiced observer preserved his self-conception by unconsciously and cleverly denying that the socially undesirable trait could be attributed to him.[21]

The ego may even be shielded by a fictitious assumption of guilt. In this way the vulnerable individual may, so to speak, beat his potential attackers to the punch and save the sting of their reproaches. This mechanism is protective because the self-accuser who employs it to guard his weaknesses does not actually believe in his condemnations. Often the charges that he lays against himself are unrealistic; and even though he experiences genuine humiliation under his own criticism, he cannot tolerate attacks by others.[22] Neuroticism of this or of any other description cannot be ignored as a source

[20] E. Frenkel-Brunswik and R. N. Sanford, "Some Personality Factors in Anti-Semitism," *Journal of Psychology*, 1945, 20:271–291.

[21] E. Cooper and M. Jahoda, "The Evasion of Propaganda: How Prejudiced People Respond to Anti-prejudice Propaganda," *Journal of Psychology*, 1947, 23:15–25.

[22] Karen Horney, *The Neurotic Personality of Our Time*. New York: W. W. Norton & Company, 1937, pp. 230ff.

of innovation, especially when it is kept in mind that personality traits of any sort may structure certain social situations to conform to their demands and so establish an acceptable role for other individuals with the same predispositions. Thus, even if it cannot be shown that the self-mortification feature of certain fundamentalistic branches of Christianity has been created by neurotics, the religious sanction of the practice without doubt provides a haven and a rostrum for its further elaboration by those who do in fact fall within this category.

Finally, selective learning and selective forgetting are mechanisms that can be called upon in defense of the ego; and they, too, may set precedents in their distortions of reality. Experiments have indicated that subjects in test situations are better able to learn material which confirms their opinions than material which contradicts them and that they remember more of what they have learned if they agree with it.[23] In these experiments one may question the extent to which the ego is involved, but in others the material more definitely impinges upon conceits instead of ideas. Some, for example, have been designed to probe sex pride. Groups of men and women were asked by Zillig to learn and remember aphorisms half of which expressed opinions flattering to the female sex, the other half deriding it. In their recalls only 37 per cent of the aphorisms remembered by the men were favorable to women, whereas 63 per cent of those recalled by the women favored their sex. In a still more refined experiment Wallen used forty personality- or character-defining adjectives which he asked his subjects to use to rate themselves. Having obtained the self-ratings, he subsequently showed each of his subjects a bogus rating alleged to have been made by an unidentified acquaintance. The bogus ratings were constructed by the experimenter and were falsified according to a definite plan. A few days later each subject was asked to reproduce his bogus rating, which he thought was genuine. The results revealed that "when bogus ratings are presented as genuine, recalls of these ratings tend to be altered in such a way as to make them more compatible with the subjects' opinions of themselves."[24]

Like other defensive mechanisms, selective forgetting posits values which set a pattern. Just as a person's hates or fears may be given a social expression that is acceptable to others, so may the defensive memory distortions that are prompted by his estimates of himself or his group. Thus, precedents or charters for group action are unconsciously manufactured.

All the foregoing wants are subject to variation under stress. They are continually being warped in this direction or that by adventitious influences of greater or lesser duration and intensity. External impingements, variable

[23] Jerome M. Levine and Gardner Murphy, "The Learning and Forgetting of Controversial Material," *Journal of Abnormal and Social Psychology*, 1943, 38:507–517.

[24] R. Wallen, "Ego Involvement as a Determinant of Selective Forgetting," *Journal of Abnormal and Social Psychology*, 1942, 37:39.

in their force, may have transient or enduring effects upon the perceptual and recall organizations of the individual. Food requirements, for example, have a noticeable effect upon perception. Hungry people unconsciously, if not consciously, think in terms of food if they are free to build upon the stimuli which confront them; people "see" food in ambiguous and incomplete figures more insistently when they have abstained from food than when they have not. Pictures presented so that they can be seen only through a ground-glass screen more often look like something to eat to hungry people than to those who are satiated.[25] The degree of physical relaxation also introduces a regulative factor; fatigue alters perception, recall, and judgment. A mental state of expectancy or hope can also have a marked effect upon perception. Everyone has heard of the hunter who shoots at a bush, seeing it as a rabbit. Almost as common, and more spectacular, are the miracles that are experienced by the intensely devout and suggestible. Each year the news magazines report some of the more remarkable of these, but by no means all of them.[26] Fear and anxiety have also their synthetic terrors, such as ghosts in the shadows and burglars on the back porch, found especially in the dark or in other unstructured or malleable situations. The intensity of the distorting influences has a bearing upon the degree of their effectiveness for different individuals. Some people are less susceptible than others, or their threshold of tolerance is higher.

It is important to note that while external influences usually produce only momentary fluctuations in mental functioning, they may be persistent enough to induce a continuous and characteristic warp in interpretation. A system of rewards and punishments can do this. Several experiments have shown that autisms may be molded in this way in accordance with some arbitrary decision of the experimenter. Subjects have unconsciously shifted their perceptions in the direction of those for which they have been rewarded in a conditioning period.[27] Situations involving rewards and punishments are not, of course, peculiar to laboratory experiments. They are a part of everyday life. So are other influences, such as group approval and deprivations of all sorts which have the same effect. Food habits and other prejudices undergo insensible and permanent alteration because of changed conditions. David Livingstone relates that after living with African natives for a long time "one feels ashamed of the white skin; it seems unnatural, like

[25] R. Levine, I. Chein, and G. Murphy, "The Relation of the Intensity of a Need to the Amount of Perceptual Distortion: A Preliminary Report," *Journal of Psychology,* 1942, 13:283–293.

[26] For example, "Reactionary Miracle," *Time,* Feb. 20, 1950; "The Vision of Necedah," *Life,* Aug. 28, 1950.

[27] Harold Proshansky and Gardner Murphy, "The Effects of Reward and Punishment in Perception," *Journal of Psychology,* 1942, 13:295–305.

blanched celery or white mice." [28] H. M. Stanley experienced the same revulsion upon his first meeting with Portuguese travelers after his long habituation to his black-skinned companions: [29]

As I looked into their faces, I blushed to find that I was wondering at their paleness. . . . The pale color, after so long gazing on rich black and richer bronze, had something of an unaccountable ghastliness. I could not divest myself of the feeling that they must be sick; yet, when I compare their complexions to what I now view, I should say that they were olive, sunburnt, dark.

Social and economic status imparts a slant that is in varying degrees subliminally acquired. It can even mold the very perceptual organization of a situation. Thus, Bruner and Goodman have found experimental evidence for their hypothesis that the greater the social value placed upon an object and the greater the individual need for it, the more marked will be the perceptual enlargement of it. They have found that coins appear larger than cardboard disks of the same size; that the greater the value of the coin, the greater the deviation of its apparent size from its actual size; and that the children of poor families overestimate coin sizes considerably more than do the children of financially secure parents.[30]

The cultural effects of central subliminal wants are elusive. Ego demands are so subtle and their molding influences so intangible that it is much more difficult to demonstrate their reality as an innovative mechanism than it is to show that the desire to bring a moving vehicle to a stop at will, for example, has been responsible for the development of brakes of various descriptions. Yet subliminal wants, it would seem, have been far more potent in determining the course of cultural development as a whole because they operate to establish value systems. They embody perspectives which contribute to basic world views. They comprise axioms beyond which reason cannot go and which it cannot touch. Ego demands are so essential that they set up fundamental postulates for behavior and interpretation. In their subtle and dogmatic way they segregate the important from the unimportant, the real from the unreal. Their significance for cultural diversification can scarcely be overestimated.

[28] David Livingstone, *Narrative of an Expedition to the Zambesi and Its Tributaries.* London, 1866, p. 379.
[29] H. M. Stanley, *Through the Dark Continent.* . . . New York, 1878, Vol. 2, p. 462
[30] Bruner and Goodman, *op. cit.*

CHAPTER V

DEPENDENT WANTS

Linkage. The wants that were considered in the last chapter yield innovations that are by-products of the desire. Their satisfaction necessarily entails some changes, but only incidentally as instruments, not as ends: the undervalued person wants personal recognition and has to innovate to get it, or the tense individual demands relief and is unable to obtain it by standard means. In the present chapter we shall be concerned with still other innovations that are indirectly inspired. As in the case with the preceding novelties, the need for them, when it can be said to exist, is preceded and conditioned by the need for something else. In these instances, however, more than one desire is involved, and circumstances prevent their isolation and independent fulfillment. Their linkage in time, place, or function necessitates a novel solution to the dilemma that their conjunction presents. One induces another, or both spring from the same set of circumstances. In any event, one want is entangled with another, and the pressure of the resulting impasse is resolved by an escape in novelty.

Convergent Wants. Because human beings are never motivated by lone and isolated desires, it frequently happens that two or more wants of different origins converge upon a single activity with innovative consequences. As far as the individual is concerned, the coincidence of the wants is accidental. The wants themselves may be explicit or subliminal, but their conjunction at a given moment is unpremeditated, and may even be embarrassing and unwanted. The innovation which results is therefore not a new solution to the dominant need of the moment, and it may be rejected as unsuitable for the subsidiary and conjoined ones as well.

There are several relationships that can exist between convergent wants, but in general it may be said that they either reinforce or oppose each other. It sometimes happens that one want in the course of its satisfaction evokes another. The evoked want may have little or no intrinsic or historical connection with the dominant one. It may have existed previously, satisfied or unsatisfied; or it may be induced by the specific circumstances that are provided by the satisfaction of the dominant and preoccupying want. In the first case the preexistent secondary want is merely alerted. It may have been pressing unsuccessfully for satisfaction at other times but been pushed aside under other and perhaps routine demands. A particular conjunction of events revives it because they produce a result that is the answer to its requirements.

The by-product of another want provides the solution to the latent problem, and as such it is an innovation or can provide the key to one.

Many professional inventors declare that solutions to problems that they have set themselves often come to them in this indirect and unexpected way. Some assert that their best ideas have occurred to them while they have been preoccupied with something else and had the least reason to expect them: when they were dressing, bathing, tying a shoestring, watching a motion picture, reading, conversing, or listening to a sermon or a concert. Sometimes they find a new idea startling because it occurs when there is no connection between it and what they are doing. Indeed, some men who make their living by inventing follow the practice of putting an unsolved problem in the back of their minds after they have gone over it thoroughly to await the fortuitous thought that will solve it.[1]

The history of mechanical inventions contains specific instances of a search for a problem solution being ended by some element in an unrelated preoccupation of the discoverer. It is reported that Edison, after testing thousands of vegetable fibers for an acceptable carbon residue for his lamp filaments, one hot day picked up a Japanese fan as he walked around his laboratory. As he inspected the fan, he noticed that its edge was bound with bamboo. He peeled off a strip and had it tested. It ultimately proved to be the best fiber for his purposes that he could find. Goodyear's accidental discovery of vulcanization comes to mind in this connection. He made many blind experiments in efforts to cure rubber, some of which were partially successful. Eventually he bought the rights to Hayward's process of "solarization," using sulfur to treat rubber exposed to the sun. His discovery of the real significance of heat in the process of curing came when he was boiling a mass of decomposed rubber articles and some of the stuff fell on the stove. The discovery of synthetic indigo had a similar origin. Many efforts had been made to find a catalyst to oxidize naphthalene for this purpose before a thermometer burst and released its mercury to produce the desired reaction. A chance use of iodine in gasoline in the General Motors laboratory led to the discovery of the true cause of engine knocks.[2]

Discoveries are just as commonly made when there has been no preexisting search for them. They appear under the pressure of other wants entirely and are mobilized or induced in their discoverer's mind only by his recognition of the value or possibilities of what he has incidentally accomplished. He cannot be said to have had a prior need for his fortunate discovery, but one is induced if he is sufficiently motivated to preserve the results or repeat the process that produced them. In some instances the induced want is only gradually activated or, more accurately speaking, reoriented by a new kind

[1] Joseph Rossman, *The Psychology of the Inventor*. Washington, D.C.: Inventor's Publishing Co., 1931, pp. 101–107.
[2] *Ibid.*, p. 126.

of satisfaction. A man who has previously satisfied his desire for exercise and relaxation by playing handball may, for business reasons, take up golf and find in time that this game is as adequate for his physical needs as is handball. A student who takes a course because it is required or is the only one available at a certain hour sometimes develops a lasting interest in it. In his youth Faraday was a bookbinder's apprentice. In the beginning, books for him were merely objects to which certain things had to be done; but in time he became interested in their content, especially in the subject matter of those that dealt with electricity. In his case and in others an adventitiously inspired want, slowly organized and matured, eventually led to discovery and invention.

In many instances a want is suddenly induced or deflected from its existing satisfaction by an event that is integral to another need system. Thus, one inventor's idea for making soap chips was inspired by an incident that is familiar to most men. One day while shaving he became interested in an article in a nearby newspaper. He forgot about his shaving while the lather dried on his face. When he returned to it the flaky character of the dried soap gave him the idea of devising an apparatus that would dissolve and aerate soap so that thin chips would be formed as it dried.[3] The offset method of printing developed from an alert observation of Ira W. Rufel. The feeder of his lithographic machine once failed to pass a sheet of paper through at the proper time so that an imprint was left upon the printing cylinder instead of upon the paper. The next sheet that went through therefore received an impression on both sides.[4] Calcium carbide and the acetylene gas that it produces were invented as the result of a combination of blind experimentation in search of a process to extract aluminum from clay by T. L. Willson, a wary approach to his tests of Willson's results by the chemist Morehead, and a concern for their company's shaky finances by its treasurer, E. F. Price. All three of these men had other motivations than the desire to create calcium carbide. In fact, they did not know that it had been done until Price decided to find out whether the gas that it emitted was hydrogen by applying a flame to it.[5] Logan found that blackberries and raspberries had crossed themselves to produce "loganberries" in his garden, where he was intent upon crossing a wild and a cultivated variety of blackberry.[6] Discoveries of two sugar substitutes have been made in remarkably similar and unpremeditated ways by two chemists. One discovered the sweetness of saccharine as the result of eating his lunch without washing his hands. Noticing the taste in his sandwiches, he traced it back to the

---

[3] *Ibid.,* p. 51.

[4] *Ibid.,* p. 126.

[5] Waldemar Kaempffert, *A Popular History of American Invention.* New York: Charles Scribner's Sons, 1924, Vol. 1, pp. 560–562.

[6] *Literary Digest,* Sept. 5, 1925, p. 27.

chemicals with which he had been working that morning. Then one day in 1937 a chemist at the University of Illinois noticed that his cigarette tasted unreasonably sweet, and he too was prompted to find out why. His chance observation led to the commercial production of a new synthetic sweetner called Sucaryl Sodium, which has properties that give it some advantages over both sugar and saccharine.[7]

Whether they are due to revived or to induced wants, the list of ex post facto innovations is impressive. They are usually called discoveries, and their cause is referred to as accidents. They have occurred in geographical exploration, medicine, mechanics, astronomy, chemistry—indeed, in practically all fields including the social. Safety-first programs and devices, for example, were developed as a by-product of the desire to reduce insurance costs, and this as a by-product of the demand to ameliorate the physical and financial losses of workmen engaged in hazardous occupations.[8] The lucrative trademark Chicken in the Rough, with all the privileges that go with it, is reported to have had its origin in a grumpy remark by the wife of an Oklahoma restaurateur. One day in 1936, so the story goes, as she and her husband were eating a box lunch while riding over a bumpy road, she commented that they were "really eating chicken in the rough." It struck her husband that her remark would be a good slogan for a dish and a way of eating it that would appeal to the American public.[9]

Convergent wants may conflict with instead of reinforcing or complementing each other. We are dealing here, not with the blocking of a need by something or someone whose interference is not wanted, but with the interference of two or more antithetical demands that are both desirable. The resulting compromise may or may not be considered desirable, but the conflicting needs which condition or necessitate it are nonetheless equally or almost equally valued. It is their simultaneous demands that make the individual uncomfortable, embarrassed, or bewildered. Either the satisfaction of one desire is confused with the satisfaction of the other, or one takes the place of the other. In either case the solution is peculiar and without precedent. It may set a precedent itself; that is, it becomes a typical response in such situations for the originator and for other people.

At certain times in their lives most human beings have simultaneously experienced the urge to act and the demand not to, with unique results compounded of the two urges, or compromises that in some degree satisfy both. There are a great many Americans who know that magic is nonsense but who nevertheless practice it in secret or in modified form. They agree that it is irrational to avoid black cats or wear amulets and are ashamed of

[7] *Time,* June 5, 1950.

[8] J. R. Commons, *Industrial Goodwill.* New York: McGraw-Hill Book Company, Inc., 1919, p. 60.

[9] *Time,* May 15, 1950.

their impulses to do so; yet they cannot entirely suppress their desire to secure themselves against misfortune. Consequently they devise numerous and devious means to satisfy their demand for supernatural protection without embarrassment to their rational conceits. College students do not ordinarily rely upon rabbits' feet to carry them successfully through examinations; instead they wear old ties, sleep with their lecture notes under their pillows, or avoid thinking that a test will not be easy. Tozzer's collection of themes written by college freshmen upon the subject of their superstitions is enlightening as well as entertaining. The subterfuges and the rationalizations which they reveal emphasize the fact of individual variability under the pressures of belief and disbelief.[10]

The conflict between socially approved behavior of any sort and individual desires has produced a great many innovations. The desire to act in accordance with legal or other socially sanctioned norms and the private urge to ignore or by-pass them have always been a prolific source of cultural change. Personal wants often produce ingenious compromises with respectability. The obverse of outward conformance to the Eighteenth Amendment to the American Constitution during the years when it was in effect was a proliferation of evasive innovations such as rumrunning, speakeasies, and home-brews. And now, even though the use of liquor is entirely legal, some people whose reputations are at stake have devised their own private patterns for furtive or concealed drinking.

Sometimes conflicts arise, not between the demand to do or not to do, but between alternative and contrary ways of doing the same thing. Such dilemmas emerge on the purely procedural or technical level with great frequency. They can be expected in individual cases whenever alternative methods, actions, or materials are available and their use is in some ways rewarding. They are scarcely less frequent on the value or policy level where ideological contrarieties demand opposing allegiances. The Palauans have a form of money, made of vitrified clay, that is used for the traditional validation of social and political position. It is still an indispensable correlate of power and status, but American coin has become more important in purely economic transactions because it is necessary for the purchase of imported commodities that are now so essential to the natives. A conflict therefore exists between the demands for the one type of money and those for the other, with various tentative compromises and adjustments taking shape and gaining favor at the present time. Illustrations of the same sort could be cited from almost any society that is being modified by alien contacts. In southeastern Africa Christianized natives not infrequently get married in every way known to them—just to be safe, it seems. According to native

[10] Alfred M. Tozzer, *Social Origins and Social Continuities*. New York: The Macmillan Company, 1925, pp. 242–266.

custom, marriage must be validated by a transfer of property in the form of cattle from the groom's relatives to those of the bride; after that the couple usually feel compelled to be married by a minister of the church and then by a certified official of the government. Christianized Filipino rice farmers hold harvest festivals according to ancient custom, yet the celebrants assemble for a feast in honor of the Catholic patron saint of their locality. A cross is set up and devotions offered; but first the cross is sprinkled with rice wine, a traditional offering to Filipino gods and spirits. And before the feast proceeds, a native religious functionary calls upon the ancestral spirits of the dead to partake of the essence of the food before its substance is consumed by the assembled guests. Not many years ago, some of the Hupa Indians of northwestern California resolved their doubts about an appropriate funeral service for their dead by holding two, one on the white man's pattern, and one that was traditional with them; in some instances, a single rite was performed that contained elements of both the alien and the native patterns. Just as the college student does not believe in magic, they were dubious of the value of the white man's preaching as a send-off for the Indian soul; but it provided additional insurance at little extra cost.

We need not go so far afield to find innovative conflicts among alternative wants. In our own society a businessman needs to practice Christian ethics if he is to maintain his reputation and prosper for long. Yet he cannot permit them to override practical considerations in his commercial transactions. He must be shrewd as well as fair, firm as well as polite, persuasive as well as sincere, alert to opportunities as well as honest. In consequence he has developed a compromise, a code of so-called business ethics, that is amenable to an infinite number of shadings, inflections, and outright modifications to meet individual needs in particular situations. Another example in the area of value systems pertains to our conflicting demands of generosity and thrift. We attempt to inculcate both these virtues in our children and try to exemplify them ourselves—with some odd results when they simultaneously make opposing demands upon us. We deplore the stingy and the selfish quite as much as the improvident and the spendthrift, and the distinctions between these extremes and the virtues of frugality and generosity allow for many private interpretations as well as group emphases. Our favored solution to such dilemmas, like that of other people, is to compartmentalize our virtues by making them applicable in mutually exclusive situations. This is an ingenious solution itself, but it will not always work. Consequently, as individuals and as groups, we thread our way through our value conflicts in patterns of adjustments that are remarkable for their variety if not their cleverness.

The conflict of simultaneously acting wants and demands produces many innovations that are unpremeditated and unwanted. They are called errors, and their originators are more likely to be ashamed of them than otherwise, unless they strike the popular fancy. The need to act or speak quickly often conflicts with the need to think slowly and in advance of the act. Emergencies call for sudden decisions; the desire for social approval in some situations where competition is involved puts a premium upon time in performance; and the desire to gain or maintain a reputation stimulates the need for a display of speed and alertness in speech and behavior. Any of these requirements may at times push the individual beyond his capacities, that is, beyond the demands of his physical and mental equipment. Hence the slips of the tongue, the word salads, and the spoonerisms known to everyone. As a rule these novelties are ludicrous, if not infelicitous; and they die, their originators hope, with the least possible attention given to them. Nevertheless they are novelties; and some men, furthermore, have acquired a modest renown on account of some of their mistakes. Some radio commentators and newsmen are better remembered by the public for their involuntary word confusions than for their ideas. One Hollywood columnist says that he became famous the day a linotypist garbled his column heading "Behind the Makeup" to read "Makeup the Behind."[11] Errors as such have scant chance of being imitated; but they can become immortalized, and with them, their authors.

Errors in perception also occur under the pressure of conflicting needs for haste, for whatever cause, and needs that operate in opposition to it; or the need to save energy and the need to take care; or the need to see or think about two different things at once. Proofreaders' errors are common experiences under the pressure of the need for haste and accuracy; so are interpretations based upon "glimpses" and peripheral vision. Haste, preoccupation, and divided attention not infrequently lead to visual distortion; and while the results, like other errors, scarcely survive their discovery, they constitute cues to action and belief of greater or less consequence and permanence. Some advertisers make the most of the public's tendencies to misread labels; and there are people who characteristically report and vigorously maintain the reality of their first impressions.

The conflict of incompatible needs also produces innovations when an individual, acting in accordance with one of them, prematurely anticipates the requirements of the other. The resulting confusion of reactions is an everyday occurrence in bodily behavior and speech. The slurring of phonemes is sometimes due to such a conflict; so is the transposition of syllables and phonemes in words and of words in phrases or in sentences. Sturtevant describes the process and gives examples of its results: "praying on the street" for "playing in the street," "it outveighs in value" for "it outweighs in value."

[11] *Time*, Mar. 13, 1950.

It must be emphasized that such mistakes can become conventionalized under certain conditions; that is, they become the rule rather than the embarrassing oddity. Expressions such as "I wanta do it," wherein the final "t" of the word "want" is elided under the anticipation of the following "t" of the word "to," are common tendencies in careless speech. Indeed, this process of slurring—or, technically, the assimilation of one phoneme by its consequent—is a rather pervasive phenomenon in the speech of most of us. As Sturtevant points out, "cupboard" was once pronounced as it is spelled, but a premature vocal preparation for a sounding of *b* while the speaker closed his lips for *p* has led to the pronunciation of a double *b*. He remarks that the assimilation of contiguous consonants is of "great linguistic importance." Frequently only one characteristic of consonants is involved, as when a voiced consonant before an unvoiced one loses its vocal quality, or vice versa. Less frequently the anticipation of a consonant results in its partial assimilation of a preceding vowel: the Latin word for "nine" appears to have been changed from "neven" to "novem" on account of this. Anticipation has also led to the assimilation of one vowel by a succeeding one: Latin "rotundas" became "rutundas" under the influence of this tendency.[12]

The premature initiation of one response before the completion of its antecedent is evident in gestures, in bodily movements, or in any other prescribed series of acts. In haste or in impatience we often slur the passage from one discrete movement or sound to another. We abbreviate and "cut corners" in all manner of ways under the dual demands of conforming and of performing an act with the least amount of effort or time expended. Salutes, handshakes, rituals, handwriting, and manual operations of all descriptions tend to "degenerate," that is, lose the discreteness of their parts, unless the demands for their stabilization are continually recognized and emphasized. Strictly speaking, the discreteness of the elements is not lost; one kind of discreteness simply replaces another. But in any event, important changes can take place even though the transition is by insensible steps.

Finally it may be mentioned that a conflict of wants sometimes results in dilemmas that do not admit of a compromise or fusion of their respective satisfactions. The issue is between the satisfaction of the one or the other. In itself this does not produce anything new, but if the impasse is intolerable or if the issue cannot be evaded some unique way of escaping it may be demanded to afford satisfaction. One Yakima Shaker uses the Bible to resolve his dilemmas. When he cannot decide which of two courses to adopt, he opens his Bible at random. He claims that he always finds the answer to his question somewhere in the text on the pages that are thus exposed to his view. His rationalization is that his hand is divinely guided. Doubtless there

---

[12] E. H. Sturtevant, *Linguistic Change.* New York: G. E. Stechert & Company, 1942, pp. 46–48.

are many solutions of the kind that never get beyond the status of half-secret idiosyncrasies. Others of similar origin have become customary. Some people go for a walk to resolve their problems; others "sleep on it." Some pray, some seek religious advice or visit fortunetellers and astrologers; others cut cards, draw straws, or flip coins. All these and many other devices have had their inception in the mind of some individual and consequently once were novelties, although now they are mere commonplaces.

Compensatory Wants. In the instances that follow, the innovator wants what he cannot get, so his desire is displaced. His original demand may be of any sort: the use of things, the control or consumption of them, social participation, or social approval. For some reason its satisfaction is denied him, either temporarily or permanently. The necessity for its sacrifice may be due to other people, things, social conventions, or self-conceptions; to physical, mental, situational, or cultural deficiencies. In any case the denial prompts the individual to adopt an alternative or a subsidiary want; and in attempting to satisfy it or his original desire, he creates a means or an end that is new to him and may be novel to others. In short, we shall consider here the innovative characteristics of substitutes for frustrated wants, whether transient or enduring and whether subliminal or consciously appreciated for what they are.

The existence of a frustrated want presupposes that the thwarted individual has reason to think that it should be satisfied. In other words, the blocked goal is within the framework of his experience, real or imaginary, and is expectable to him at least. Consequently, some standard governs his level of aspiration. This standard is the norm for other people under normal conditions at normal times. But with reference to it, the frustrated individual may adopt one of two attitudes in orienting his aspirations. He may, on the one hand, aspire to the achievement of the norm. If so, he wants to be like other people, to do now as he has done in the past, to have now what he is accustomed to having, or to do here what he used to do there. In brief, he wants to equalize his behaviors and opportunities, and to do so he must surmount certain obstacles. In this category would fall the aims of the physically or mentally handicapped, the castaway, the marginal man, the visitor in a foreign land, the man with inadequate tools, and many others. On the other hand, some frustrated individuals are such because they want to exceed the norm. They are dissatisfied with existing techniques, devices, modes, or conventions and want to be or do the supranormal. Among them may be counted the pioneers in new areas and in new endeavors, the trail breakers, the adventurers, the reformers, and the self-styled progressives, not to mention the egomaniacs, the indispensable men, the prophets, the moon voyagers, and the inventors of perpetual motion.

Sometimes the frustrated individual is, or believes himself to be, responsible for establishing his aspiration level. The fact that he has done so does not prevent his being frustrated if he refuses to relinquish his impossible goal. Thus, there are perfectionists in almost every field of human endeavor. They are never satisfied with their own performances or with those of others because of an ideal that sets goals always just beyond accomplishments. Others who set their own goals at a level that is frustrating include professionals or specialists in highly competitive fields and idealists with selfish or humanitarian motives. Political and social reformers and those with dedicated lives often find themselves in this position, too. So does the self-obligated individual: he who takes a dare or accepts a challenge, gives a promise, or makes a brag that must be vindicated. Professional inventors, scientific researchers, and professional problem solvers of many kinds also deliberately and repeatedly set goals for themselves that keep them moving through a cycle of alternate frustration and accomplishment.

More often the frustrated individual feels that his level of aspiration has been imposed upon him by circumstances beyond his control. His goals are not of his choosing, but he feels that he must adopt them. They have been established by group conventions, by the circumstances of his personal history, by his physical and comfort requirements, by other individuals, and even at times by his sense of divine plan or injunction. Emergency situations can thus be thwarting because they depart from the normal. The hungry or thirsty man who is lost or otherwise deprived of the customary sources and means of satisfying these physical wants is frustrated through no desire of his own. Droughts, famines, fires, and other catastrophes may similarly affect whole populations. Social situations which impose unfamiliar and unexpected demands contain an unwanted source of frustration: what to do upon meeting an utterly alien stranger, what to do in case of a breach of etiquette. All of us have experienced comparable situations, have been thrown upon our ingenuity, and have devised solutions of greater or lesser importance.

The expectations of others all too frequently establish a frustrating situation for some individuals. The goals set up by parents for their children are often impossible of accomplishment, especially when they represent ideals never achieved by the parents themselves. Loyalty, gratitude, and pride nevertheless motivate the children to struggle to at least approximate their parents' desires. In varying degrees the expectations of teachers, sponsors, colleagues, employers, teammates, coaches, and political constituents make the same unreasonable demands, often prompted by irreproachable but ill-considered motives.

As has been mentioned in connection with ego needs, some psychologists distinguish between adaptive and maladaptive behavior. They regard the displaced wants that result from frustration as maladaptive because such responses do not alleviate the basic needs. Regardless of this fact, the satisfaction of a substitute want can be and frequently is innovative. There are several kinds of inventive reactions to the blockage of a want, but in the broadest terms there are three; namely, circumvention, attack, and the setting up of new goals. To the extent that psychological mechanisms are drawn into the following discussion of these responses, it is relevant to insist that they do not of themselves equalize or regularize human behavior everywhere that they are operative. Even though they are universally human, their operation does not everywhere have duplicative consequences. The mechanisms themselves are not equally valued from society to society, and they always permit individual variations in their specific manifestations wherever the resort to them is permitted or encouraged. These individual variations constitute the jumping-off points that may or may not become socially sanctioned just like any other innovation.

In circumvention the frustrated individual nullifies the effects of a blockage by finding a way to arrive at his goal in spite of it. He discovers or invents new paths, methods, materials, or behaviors that overcome his deficiencies or permit him to remove or evade the barriers to his goal. He may be able to surmount the obstacle, or he may have to be content with a compromise with his desire. In practically all cases the substitute is desirable only because the customary means to the goal is impossible; it is a second choice, but it may in time become as satisfactory as that which it replaces if the individual can resign himself to it. Sometimes the blocking of a want is merely temporary; there is an emergency, and the innovator has to make use of whatever is available to him. He utilizes sticks, stones, and bailing wire in place of hammers, pliers, saws, and bolts. During the Second World War the Americans besieged a Japanese armed force on Babeldaob, the largest island in the Palaus. During the prolonged stalemate the Japanese soldiers expropriated the possessions of the natives and forced them to live a precarious existence in the hills. They had little food, and families were disrupted. One old woman who had to care for an infant made a preparation of coconut milk for it that was original with her. The survival manuals that were published for the use of our armed forces during the war contained information of this sort that was culled from various sources. The compilations are impressive testimonies to inventiveness under deprivation by the originators of the ideas in the regions to which they pertain.

Compensatory innovations are also evident when physical deficiencies constitute the blockage to routine, normal, or customary satisfactions. The adaptations of the physically incapacitated usually exhibit individual "twists" in such behaviors as talking, walking, or shaking hands. Nor must we forget that false teeth, eyes, and limbs, crutches, braces, and the other mechanical and medicinal aids to the normal functioning of the human organism are compensatory inventions, though not necessarily conceived by the deprived individuals themselves. Closely related are other compensations for organic inadequacies, such as the custom of adoption—which is not known to all peoples—and the even less popular idea of artificial insemination.

Even the demand for amusement and play seeks satisfaction in substitutes at times. An illustration of this is provided by Spencer's study of the origin of an aberrant form of handball that has come to be known as Oregon ball. This game was invented on the campus of the University of Oregon by a series of modifications of the regulation game that began in 1926. The initiating circumstance was a reduction in the size of the ball court that was occasioned by the lack of adequate building facilities. The devotees of the game were forced either to play it on the smaller courts in a frame structure that had been built for other purposes or not to play it at all. They accepted the smaller playing areas and proceeded to adapt the game to the requirements of this condition. Ultimately a new kind of ball, a new mode of service, and new rules were instituted and came to be preferred by many players. The game is now a recognized sport on the Oregon campus.[13]

Individuals who have been frustrated in their desire to acquire status sometimes adopt devious means of satisfaction. Failing to get the recognition that they feel they deserve in customary ways, they divert their demands to linked goals that may themselves become stereotyped. One means of linkage is through identification with a socially valued object or person. For some people mere passive identification is enough; but not infrequently this leads to peculiar behaviors that are expressive of the conceived identity. The identifying individual may exhibit a sympathetic, defensive, or proprietary concern for the thing or idea with which he associates himself. Or, if the valued object is a person, imitation will often follow. If imitation were ever sheer duplication, nothing new would result from this. But as we have seen, this is never so. Imitation always entails variation, often to the extent of caricature. This is the more certain the more ignorant the imitator is of the real values of his paragon, and the more so the more the conceived paragon is a composite of several ideals. The peculiar results of such imitation are well illustrated in Palau, where the young men affect what are to us ludicrous combinations of civilian and military dress in the belief that they are acting like their ideals, the Americans.

Some people achieve a satisfaction otherwise denied them by identifying themselves with a self-substitute. In this case the association does not involve imitation. Rather, the surrogate for the self is manipulated in ways that give expression to otherwise unrealized and unrealizable desires. The manipulated thing or person is the vehicle for an indirect and subtle self-expression, and sometimes the lengths to which a person will go to accomplish this and the means he uses are remarkable. Many American parents unconsciously use their children for this purpose, and no end of novelties result; some men use their wives in the same way. Objects may serve the purpose equally well

[13] R. F. Spencer, "Oregon Ball: The Evolution of a Game," *Western Folklore*, 1948, 7 (No. 4):342–348.

and better for some people. The motorcycle fan's pride in his gaudy accessories, the antics of "hot-rod" drivers, the amateur gardener's pride in his roses, and the scientist's and artist's involvements with their ideas and products are common illustrations of displaced identifications with things that are productive of innovations.

Another means to circumvent blockage to a goal is by resorting to the spectacular. This means is often employed if the goal is social approval; but the device is not restricted to the achievement of thàt end, as is evident when men cultivate a dramatic display, or at least do not shun it, in their efforts to convince others of the truth or worth of their ideas, whatever they may be. It is, however, a subliminal demand of many who yearn to be personally valued by their associates and feel that they are not. Hysterical seizures are sometimes induced by such wants and serve the unconscious purpose of gaining attention and influence. Characteristically, hysterical symptoms are sensational; and if their victims are able to give any explanation of the attacks at all, the causes that they ascribe to them are dramatic, fictitious, fanciful, and therefore creative. An excellent example is provided by Johnson's study of the "Phantom Anesthetist of Mattoon." This is an analysis of the wave of excitement and fear that swept over an Illinois town in 1944 because of alleged attacks upon innocent and unsuspecting people by a madman using a gas spray.[14] Hero arsonists fall into the same category. They are pyromaniacs who set fires for the sake of being praised for turning in the alarms and helping with the rescue work which follows. A case of this description was recently noted in the press in connection with a disastrous fire in a Philadelphia sanatorium. One of the inmates set the fire and then energetically aided the firemen, several times receiving first aid himself in consequence of his daring.[15]

Out of the pathological category, but still employing dramatic techniques to gain recognition, are those individuals who adopt extravagant behaviors in place of customary means that are beyond their grasp. This device is practically universal among the frustrated members of minority groups whose activities are not rigidly controlled, and it is unquestionably productive of innovations. In large part it explains the exhibitionistic demonstrations of our adolescents who feel, rightly perhaps, that their adult cravings are misunderstood and smothered by parents from whose dictates they have no redress. Hence the startling fads in dress and speech, the antique automobiles laden with gadgets, and the zany amusements resorted to by American high-school children and others of the same age. The following description of male fashions as of January, 1950, among the "drapes"—those among the

[14] Donald M. Johnson, "The 'Phantom Anesthetist' of Mattoon: A Field Study of Mass Hysteria," *Journal of Abnormal and Social Psychology,* 1945, 40:175–186.
[15] *Time,* Apr. 10, 1950.

adolescents who pride themselves upon their "sharp" dressing—gives an idea of the inventiveness of these young people:[16]

In Baltimore last week, the true drape wore his hair seaweed-long. His shirt was pastel pink and buttoned at the throat (no tie); the jacket was loose, wraparound and without lapels. But the distinctive mark was the black zaks—slacks, that is, that are sharply nipped at the bottom to a narrow cuff. The effect was something between a sagging pair of plus fours and badly fitting jodhpurs.

The costume here described is not to be confused with the "zoot suit." Those who call themselves "drapes" resent the identification, for to them the zoot-suiter is a "bum, a draft dodger, or a guy who hangs around street corners." In other words, the zoot-suiter is an outcast, a marginal man, often a member of a minority group. The distinction in point of class membership is real, but the psychological mechanisms which produce the two extremes of behavior are practically identical. The same tendency toward flamboyant dress and bizarre mannerisms can be observed among Filipinos in San Francisco, Negroes in Los Angeles, Indians in Oregon, and Mexicans in Arizona. It is, moreover, a typical sight over much of Oceania among partially acculturated natives.[17] All are manifestations of compensatory wants that have emerged when these marginal individuals have been denied the avenues to social approval that are open to members of the dominant group. These second-class citizens, like our peripheral adults, have had to get around the blockage and satisfy their demands for self-importance in an indirect and striking way.

Aggression is another compensatory response to thwarted desires. When this takes place, there is a direct or an indirect attack upon the source of the frustration. The obstructing thing or person itself may be attacked, or the target may be some substitute for it. In any event, the aggressive act can take a variety of forms; and it may be most ingenious, either in its conception or in its execution. The humiliating and destructive tortures of the Nazis were certainly ingenious, however diabolical. So, too, have been innumerable plans for personal revenge. Most observant parents will agree, also, that the aggressive machinations of their frustrated children are frequently extremely clever, even if not commendable. In some ways it is a pity that we cannot be objective enough to appreciate the ingenuity and the subtlety of our children in their undercutting of our heavy-handed controls over them.

A Manus native of the Admiralty Islands thinks that the spirit of his dead father protects him, aids him in his fishing, and in other ways brings him what he desires. Most human beings fear or at least respect their spiritual helpers, but the Manus man takes a very mundane view of his. If

[16] *Ibid.,* Jan. 30, 1950.

[17] Felix M. Keesing, *The South Seas in the Modern World*. New York: The John Day Company, 1941, p. 78.

he is unlucky or otherwise fails to get what he wants, his ancestral spirit gets the blame. The skull of the deceased individual whose spirit has failed him is unceremoniously thrown out of the house with imprecations.[18] The Kwakiutl Indians of Vancouver Island gave expression to their hates and envies, not by physical attacks upon those who angered or belittled or thwarted them, but by hurling insults at their enemies in formally established ways. They did this under the sanction of the potlatch, an institution whereby a man validated his claims to greatness and shamed his detractors by lavish gift giving. Enemies and rivals for social positions "fought with property," each man attempting to eclipse and humiliate his rival by publicly and formally presenting him with more property than he could return, or by destroying more in his presence than he could assemble for the same purpose.[19]

In many cases aggressive acts are valued in proportion to their cleverness. That is to say, the type of attack is already socially established and expected, but a premium is placed upon originality in its execution. This is so for malicious cartooning, lampooning, caricaturing, and joking. Political jokes jibing at officials and party systems aim at discrediting the opposition by making it ludicrous; or if not that, they serve at least for the venting of spleen in a way that is acknowledged as clever even by the opposition. Aggressive releases in the guise of humor probably occur everywhere that interpersonal or intergroup tensions exist. They arise not only out of the resentment and frustration of deprived groups but also out of the interest collisions and value differences of coordinate groups as well. Interracial, interclass, and international caricatures are common expressions of the urge to express aversions in a high-spirited manner. Such reactions have also been experimentally induced, as happened when one subject during a sleep-, food-, and amusement-frustration test idly drew a series of gory sketches that he later said represented the activities of psychologists. The desultory comments of other subjects during this same experiment, which lasted for twenty-four hours, also contained sardonic expressions of their hostility toward their persecutors, the experimenters.[20] In this connection, the imaginative character of vicious gossip and insinuation must not be overlooked. Neither should the weird constructions of aggressive fantasy thinking. Often both these types of aggression have important social consequences, and they may become charters for group belief and action.

[18] Margaret Mead, *Growing Up in New Guinea*. New York: William Morrow & Company, Inc., 1930, p. 99.
[19] H. G. Barnett, "Nature of the Potlatch," *American Anthropologist*, 1938, 40:356–357.
[20] Robert R. Sears, Carl I. Hovland, and Neal E. Miller, "Minor Studies of Aggression: 1. Measurement of Aggressive Behavior," *Journal of Psychology*, 1940, 9:275–295.

That unique aggressive reactions are in their nature no different from any other innovation is shown by the fact that they can become stereotyped. The Manus and the Kwakiutl examples cited above are illustrative of this. So are certain socially approved patterns of aggression that are peculiar to our own culture. Thus, under the cloak of freedom of speech, Americans are permitted to give expression to their envy of, and their displeasure with, celebrities and public officials in any way they wish, short of legally defined slander and libel. In their impotence individually to do much about political corruption and graft they release their wrath in verbal attacks. Resentful of the alleged frivolity and aloof antics of Hollywood aristocracy, the convention-bound individual revels in the scandals of movie idols and rejoices in pointing out that they have feet of clay. Our aggressive behaviors toward minority groups are also stereotyped, as is the case when a Negro is denied the honorific term of address "Mister." Rivalries in our culture, as well as in some others, may lead to a polarization of differences. In other words, mere variations in point of view are set up as militant opposites, as has happened in our political-party structure. Shadings are converted into contrasting blacks and whites.

The forms assumed by aggressive demands, like those of any other want, seem entirely natural if not inevitable to those who are accustomed to them. Their arbitrary and novel character appears only by contrast with other behavioral systems. In this connection, Dollard's analysis of culturally sanctioned forms of aggression among the Ashanti of West Africa is instructive. According to him, the public execution of offenders and the human and animal sacrifices that were so characteristic of these people may be regarded as an approved outlet for aggression. Another institution that served the same purpose was the court jester. This privileged character was permitted to ridicule anyone, even the king, to the obvious enjoyment of others. In addition, an Ashanti father not only was permitted to whip his child but was scoffed at if he failed to do so in his capacity as a disciplinarian. Thus he was provided with an approved means for releasing his pent-up hostilities. Storytelling served the same purpose. Stories were told at specific times and in ways that permitted the relater to ridicule even very sacred objects and respected individuals. To mention one further illustration, the Ashanti held an annual eight-day ceremony during which the celebrants were permitted several kinds of license that were tabooed at other times. One of these freedoms gave a person the right to tell anyone else, including the highest official of the government, just what he thought about him, with impunity.[21]

There is some experimental evidence which seems to show that inventive potential decreases under frustration. In a study of children ranging in ages

[21] John Dollard *et al.*, *Frustration and Aggression*. New Haven: Yale University Press, 1939, pp. 183–190.

from two to six years, the results indicated that a majority of the subjects whose play wants were thwarted exhibited a regression in constructiveness in the activities permitted them.[22] Twenty-two children showed less constructiveness in the frustrating as compared with the nonfrustrating situation, three did not change, and five proved to be more constructive. It was further discovered that those who showed an increase in constructiveness were actually weakly frustrated. The implications of these data from the standpoint of innovation is uncertain. For one thing, it may be doubted whether "constructiveness" as defined by the experimenters is the equivalent of inventiveness, especially since the children's activities were multiplied and diversified under frustration. This very characteristic may be considered to be innovative, whereas the experimenters judged it to be less constructive because it was "primitive, simple, and little structured." Furthermore, the innovative characteristics of the aggressive acts of the frustrated children were not the focus of the experimenters' attention. Throughout the observations their concern was with the organization of the children's activities rather than with their newness. Nevertheless, there may be some connection between constructiveness and culturally effective newness. Very likely the activities of most frustrated people are too diffuse and shifting for patterns to be crystallized out of them. At the same time a minority of such people, perhaps those who are less confused by the frustrating situation, do doubtless evolve new and effective responses to it. Incidentally, this experiment revealed that the frustrated children did not simply forget about their inaccessible goals; they made repeated tentative efforts to reach them while getting some satisfaction out of those that were accessible to them.

A third type of innovative reaction entails the diversion of wants to satisfactions in new goals. Perhaps, as the conclusion to the preceding paragraph suggests, the redirection of a desire never completely divorces it from its orientation toward the primary satisfaction; but there are degrees of this, and some persons act as if a new goal were just as satisfying as the one denied them. It could also be maintained that the setting up of a new goal is in reality the same as devising a way to circumvent a block to the original one; that, for example, the adoption of exhibitionistic behavior to achieve recognition amounts to the resetting of a goal. This may be, but since we are concerned with innovations and not with the systematic classification of wants and their realizations, it does not matter. In general, however, in the category of circumventions the question was one of means, whereas in the resetting of goals the emphasis is upon ends.

[22] Roger G. Barker, Tamara Dembo, Kurt Lewin, and M. Erik Wright, "Experimental Studies of Frustration in Young Children." In Theodore M. Newcomb and Eugene L. Hartley (eds.), *Readings in Social Psychology*. New York: Henry Holt and Company, Inc., 1947, pp. 283–290.

The adoption of a new goal because of frustration may ultimately have relatively happy consequences. This is true to the extent that the thwarted individual is able to turn to an interest wherein he has strength. In our society, persons who have physical handicaps and those who are disappointed in competitive struggles demanding superior physical strength not uncommonly turn to books for their satisfactions. In the same way, men with indifferent success in business and industry sometimes take refuge in laboratories, libraries, and the academic life. Many become original and outstanding scholars. Contrariwise, the intellectually insecure are prone to contrive compensatory behaviors to shield their weaknesses. Some of these reactions are tactical maneuvers. Their authors use them as smoke screens, lures, and distractors. Women who find themselves at a disadvantage among intellectual friends are sometimes able to obviate the comparison by developing their talents as gracious hostesses, by exploiting their beauty, by making the most of their ability to dress attractively, or by conforming to the ideal of a devoted wife and mother. Men and women who are lacking in attractiveness to the opposite sex or who are blunt and gauche frequently capitalize upon their shortcomings by accentuating and elaborating upon them. They become the impersonal clowns, the life of the party. Intellectual pretenders and others who are insecure in their limited knowledge guard their weaknesses by an elaborate deployment of their superficial knowledge and protect their flanks by an habitual monopoly of conversation. Their strategy, partly unconscious, is to manipulate discussion so that its subject matter falls within the areas of their control. They often acquire the reputation of being entertaining if not brilliant conversationalists.

A new goal may be a symbolic substitute for the one that is unobtainable. Wolfe emphasizes this mechanism in his analysis of reactions to balked desires. He distinguishes between conservative and radical symbolism in the forced shifting of interests. In the former, the thwarted person transfers his attention to socially approved activities—especially, in America, to trite social conventions and to religious endeavors. On the other hand, the aggressive person, when balked, embraces any radical social movement or ideology because it is symbolic of the condition which has distressed him.[23]

There is no doubt that the setting of symbolic goals is a recurrent process and that it accounts for some peculiar behaviors as well as cultural patterns. It is obviously the explanation of the indirect approach in imitative magic, both in its individualized and in its traditionally sanctioned manfestations. The idea behind magic of this kind is that the rehearsal of an act in symbolic and abbreviated form will necessarily lead to its realization in fact. Usually there is a desire for this sequence of events; supernatural forces are coerced

[23] A. B. Wolfe, "The Motivation of Radicalism," *Psychological Review*, 1921, 28:288–294.

by the dramatic enactment of the wish. The magician sticks pins in an effigy of his enemy in the conviction that the latter will be stabbed; rain will fall upon your field if you ceremonially sprinkle a few shoots of grass in it. Sometimes, though, the magical sequence is automatic, regardless of intent: "Do not walk on crutches in fun, or you may walk on them in sorrow." All these beliefs set new goals as symbolic substitutions, though in the thinking of the magician the substituted thing may contain the vital essence of that which it replaces for the purpose of the imitative ritual. The use of a substitute act or object is imperative because the desire is impossible of human accomplishment. Enemies are not slain in effigy if they can be killed with impunity in the flesh; a selected corner of one's cornfield is not sprinkled in the hope that rain will do the rest if it is practicable to sprinkle or irrigate the whole thing. The ends sought in imitative magic are beyond mortal control, hence the frustrated desire is turned toward a symbolic replacement for them.

At times the shift to a new goal amounts to a lowering of the aspiration level of the frustrated individual; failure upon a more expanded horizon impels a reorientation on a less ambitious scale. The individual may not admit that the shift is to a lower plane, or he may rationalize it; but inwardly he realizes his defeat, and the goal that he devises or adopts is treated as second-rate by those who have succeeded where he has failed. The highly competitive nature of American culture forces this compromise upon a large number of people and produces some stereotyped behavior sets. Failures in leadership provide us with a plethora of local politicians, workers for causes, and busywork organizations of one description or another. Such failure has also produced the familiar phenomenon of the little frog making a big splash in a little pool. Many people find real satisfaction in universes that are cut to their measure; and it cannot be denied that their struggles for preeminence sometimes place a premium upon their ingenuity. Merei's study of play-group dominance among children reveals the operation of this device in an experimental situation. As a condition for this experiment certain day-nursery children were selected for their observed cooperative tendencies in their spontaneous play activities. They were chosen because they were neither leaders nor followers. They were then placed together and permitted to work out their own adjustments to each other. This they did rather quickly by establishing conventions concerning such matters as toy proprietorship, seating arrangements, games to be played, and activity sequences. The second step was to introduce into the group a child who had exhibited leadership traits in the original nursery situation. In every instance the newcomer carried his dominant behavior over into the established group and tried to modify its routines. In a very small minority of cases he succeeded. At the other extreme were a few instances in which he abandoned his attempts and was merged into the group. In most instances he was compelled to accept the traditions of the group but asserted his leadership within their framework. He did this by playing the role of a director, a proprietor, or a "diplomat." The director gave obvious orders; he told the rest what to do when they were going to do it anyway. The proprietor claimed rights, but they were in conformance with group patterns. The diplomat accepted the traditions of his new friends, then began to alter them by introducing minute changes that were incidental to the main design or goal of the activity. In most instances, then, the frustrated leader invented some means of satisfying his demand for making an impression upon others.[24]

There are men and women who perforce come to the painful realization that they are unpopular either with the members of their own sex or with those of the opposite sex. There are several possible reactions to this frustrating situation, ranging all the way from complete resignation and withdrawal from it to an obstinate refusal to admit defeat. The situation itself may be solely a product of culturally determined conditions. This is uncertain, but there is little doubt that the reactions to it that are familiar to us are not the only ones possible. Misogynists, spinsters, and bachelors, for example, are not to be found universally. Neither are the Don Juans who flout the ideals of their own sex and make the most of their appeals to the other nor the Samsons who adopt the opposite course and preen themselves before the members of their own sex. Beyond that, it is to be noted that there are individual variations upon all these patterns. No two people respond exactly alike in the redefinition of their sex goals any more than they do in setting up new goals of other sorts.

The retreat from an impossible goal to one that is achievable may take the form of a cynical catering to the vain, vicious, or clouded hopes of others. Disgruntled and discredited professional men sometimes abandon conscience and respectability with the abandonment of their original goals. Well-known instances would include disgraced doctors who sell their services to criminals, shabby lawyers who accept any case as long as it brings money, and professional athletes who permit themselves to be manipulated in illegal ways. There are many others whose misfortunes and moral weaknesses lead them to exploit their knowledge and talents in chicanery and subversion. Medical quacks, seers, faith healers, character builders, and occultists practice their deceptions upon others as thwarted but not as shrewd as themselves. It hardly needs to be mentioned that these charlatans are clever; their number and the variety of their deceits appear to be without end. Traitors, renegades, and fifth columnists are another category of frustrated men with devalued goals. In bitterness they sell their knowledge and bend their efforts to undo the social and political systems that they have found unrewarding.

Another aspect of goal lowering appears with the introduction and acceptance of imitations of inaccessible ideals. Such shifts are a prolific

[24] Ferenc Merei, "Group Leadership and Institutionalization," *Human Relations,* 1949, 2 (No. 1):23.

stimulus to innovation, though not always on the part of those who themselves demand the unobtainable originals. Setting aside the many imitations that are developed to cater to the demands of others, there remain a great many substitutes that are created by those to whom the more desirable originals are impossible. Among them are the many kinds of "homemade" objects of the frugal and the poor and the second-choice copies of prohibited originals, such as the clubs that are organized by groups of individuals who are excluded from membership in those already established.

The most drastic resetting of goals occurs in regression. Like compulsions, aggressions, and hysterias, this reaction is an unhealthy one from the standpoint of the individual. As described by psychologists, regression is an atavistic phenomenon. The regressed person becomes more "primitive" and childlike in his responses. His thinking is disordered, irrational, and inconsistent. His behavior is unstructured and unpredictable. His emotional releases are diffused through unorganized channels. Regression is most likely to develop when the frustrated need is central and the whole ego system is threatened, as it was in the case of the Nazi prisoners in Bettelheim's study (p. 114).

It may be questioned whether the Freudian interpretation of regression as a return to an infantile mental condition is a legitimate characterization of it. But granting for the moment that it is, it must also be admitted that such behavior is novel. An adult's acting childish or using childish means to attain adult ends is as innovative as a man's resort to sticks and stones to build an animal trap when the commercial article is unavailable to him—and perhaps no more of a *return* to a primitive level. Some societies tolerate more of this kind of behavior than do others, and its specific manifestations are unquestionably culturally determined. The Palauans would find the regressive behavior of some congressmen incomprehensible in the context of their council meetings of chiefs; and the "going home to mother" reaction that we tolerate on the part of frustrated brides would surely strike them as very strange. In other words, what is called regression is not merely the duplication of some previous behavior. It is new behavior, new in the sense that the individual who resorts to it has never done it at all before or new in that it, as a familiar response, is introduced into a new context.

We must not be blinded to the innovative characteristics of regression by the evaluative connotations of the term. From an objective standpoint regressive behavior is merely behavior that is different from the normal. Even if it is interpreted as entailing a loss, it still embodies change regardless of whether we deplore the passing of that which is abandoned or not. The arbitrary and evaluative character of our concept of loss appears when it is considered that we do not feel that the invention of pliers has caused us to lose the use of our bare hands but that the machine tooling of things like cabinets does represent a loss of a valued kind of hand craftsmanship. In both instances one thing has been substituted for another, and the substitute is an invention.

The characterization of regression as a substitutive instead of a duplicative phenomenon has a bearing upon our understanding of what has happened to cultures like those of most American Indian tribes that have "disintegrated" under the influence of new ideas and arbitrary controls introduced from the outside. These cultures may be said to have regressed, meaning that the individual members of their societies have done so. And typically the individuals in such groups do exhibit the symptoms of regression. Their behavior is characterized by frustration, aggression, confusion, inconstancy, and emotionalism. Now, from the standpoint of innovation, it must be borne in mind that this condition does not just happen. It does not simply evolve as an indiscriminate mass phenomenon. Each act that can be called regressive is initiated by some individual; and when he performs it, he is making a break with preexisting norms, no matter how unnoticeable or unconscious the breach. His action entails the neglect ot renunciation of the existing mode in favor of an alternative of his own creation. It happens that in regression the substituted behavior is less controlled by the demands of group convention. The change is toward more spontaneous and willful behavior; it gives more direct satisfaction to the innovator than do the customary practices. But it does not mean an abandonment of patterns. It is a substitutive mechanism.

That regressive innovations in detribalized or disintegrated cultures are nearer the animal level is not to be denied. They certainly give more direct expression to wants; there is a minimum of cultural detours and a maximum of satisfaction of individual whims. But this condition in itself represents standardization. Whim satisfaction becomes the rule, and there are accepted ways of accomplishing it. And somebody started it all.

Entrained Wants. It remains to be pointed out, as a final example of the way in which the interdependence of wants leads to innovation, that the satisfaction of one want enriches the soil out of which others spring. The fulfillment of one need establishes conditions out of which others emerge. Rarely are these emergent wants previsioned by the people who experience them. In most instances it is impossible for people to foresee them even if they try. People's prophets are notoriously untrustworthy and are usually more alarmist than realistic. Objective observers with experience and foresight are in a much better position and are consolidating it more all the time; but at present even their prognostications of future wants must be prefaced with qualifications and hedged with probabilities. But setting aside the question of their exact predictability, entrained wants are a consistent feature of motivational stresses for cultural change. The emergence of one want out of the fulfillment of a previous one is to be related to that part of our discussion which emphasized the importance to innovation of a change in a dominant correlate. The more that wants are satisfied, the more they proliferate. This does not necessarily mean that the emergent wants are categorically different from their antecedents, because the former may be merely subdivisions or refinements of the latter. Neither does it mean a crescendo of wants without numerical end, for the rise of a new want is often correlated with the subsidence of an old one.

The emergence of new wants is a characteristic concomitant of the progressive assimilation of added experience. The fulfillment of a demand leaves its mark upon the individual's psychological field. He is never again what he was before that experience, because it in some way becomes a part of him. This alteration and the new demands that it brings are an inevitable aspect of the maturation process. The reorganization that experience entails, not its cumulative effects, necessitates a shift in values. Willy-nilly a person sees things differently and has different desires with the constant reconfiguration of his mental and emotional complexes. "When I was a child, I spake as a child, I understood as a child, I thought as a child; but when I became a man, I put away childish things." Experience permits and even forces a new set of demands to stabilize it, and to this dynamic process there is no end. Experience requires an individual to be constantly readjusting his sights and it alters his level of aspiration in large and small degree. Its peremptory demands extend to minutiae as well as to major goals. A man who struggles for financial security integrates new wants with his achievement of it; from satiety emerge wants not experienced in hunger.

The consequences of entrained wants appear in all departments of culture. Sometimes they are spoken of as repercussions that are due to the integrated nature of culture. Ogburn's analysis of the effects of the airplane, the automobile, and the radio upon American culture exemplifies the phenomenon, so that little more need be said about it.[25] A few detailed illustrations will suffice. When a man buys an automobile, the investment has enough value that it is worth protecting. From this single circumstance there has developed a series of far-reaching entrained wants. The owner, wishing to guard against the sudden loss of his investment, needs insurance against fire, theft, and damage to his car. In order to protect himself against damage suits in case of accidents he needs personal and property liability coverage; and if he has reason to fear incapacitating injury to himself, he needs life and hospital insurance. If, further, he is anxious about his continuing ability to keep his policy in force in the face of hazards that might cut off his earnings, he feels the need for insurance to protect his insurance, such as premium waivers and additional policies. Theoretically, there is no end to this entrainment. It is like the picture within a picture in an advertisement for pancake

[25] William F. Ogburn, *The Social Effects of Aviation*. Boston: Houghton Mifflin Company, 1946. W. F. Ogburn and Colum S. Gilfillan, "The Influence of Invention and Discovery." In *Recent Social Trends in the United States*. New York: McGraw-Hill Book Company, Inc., 1933, Vol. 1, pp. 130–158.

flour. Then to protect his property from deterioration and minor damages, the modern car owner can obtain—and in the recent past was forced to buy —shields and guards of various descriptions for different parts of it. His bumpers protect the body of his car; but to protect the chromium on them, guards have become standard equipment. Seat covers are now generally regarded as indispensable to preserve the automobile's upholstery; but many owners, having paid a handsome price for handsome covers, feel the need for spot covers for the seat covers, especially in the driver's compartment. The same is true for the plush floor covering that appears in de luxe models. The wheel fenders protect other parts of a car as well as riders and passers-by. Lately a protection has been devised for them, a metal finger that warns the driver before he scrapes them on the curb. Paint and chromium protectors are also available for the man who, for social or economic reasons, needs to keep his vehicle looking well.

Each of these entrained need satisfactions has initiated innumerable others at its point of supply. Catering to the wants of the car owner has set up wants in the designer, the manufacturer, and the insurer. The latter wants have, in turn, required innovation, mechanical skills, additional personnel, and materials—which have set up their own chains of demand for tools and men. Even these entrained needs do not exhaust the list that is dependent upon car ownership; they have to do only with the protection of the investment that it represents. There are so many others stemming from the use of the vehicle, for example, or its social implications that it would be tedious to list them.

Our knowledge of entrained wants is greatly advanced by observations of the impacts of one culture upon another. Under these conditions it is possible to study the effects of the introduction of one alien idea into a closed system. The ramifications are frequently as amazing to the observer as they are unsettling to those who have to live with them. Primitive peoples without iron have almost universally wanted it upon first contact with the Europeans, but they have not foreseen, and have been unprepared for, the wants that iron articles have brought in their train. The need for the metal has stimulated the desire for means of getting it, which has meant a demand for money, and that in turn for labor that will produce it, and that in turn for marketing channels, and so on. The acceptance of the iron itself has created a need for working it and a lapse of the need to work in stone or other native substitutes. Its greater efficiency has disposed of the need for the greater patience and skill required by the native tools, and this has led to less magic, and so on endlessly.

Entrained wants, like most of the rest so far discussed, expose the lack of adequate words in our language to express the nuances of motivation. There is no appropriate word to convey the sense of the car owner's feeling toward the things mentioned above. He wants them because he feels compelled to want them. He needs them only because he does not want what the lack of them will bring. He demands them only because they afford controls over events that are hostile to his best interests. They are forced desires, and they frequently make him unhappy. This ambivalence makes it seem to the individual that he is caught in a vise of social forces that are beyond his control. Actually his wants are an expression of himself, not of anything outside him. They are manifestations of internal tensions, and tensions have the double aspect of at once straining in opposite directions. The individual can retire them, or he can keep them at work. We are constantly doing both.

The entrainment of wants is due in part to the dynamic quality of the physical universe. All things change under the constant interaction of natural forces: iron rusts; winds blow and subside; men are born, grow old, and die; and the seasons change. Human wants are correlated with these alterations as well as determined by their own dynamics. Human beings wish for stability or for change, for more security or less of it, as the individual case may be. The achievement of any one desire merely sets another complex of forces to work, for which again there is a demand for greater or less stability. The more man manipulates these forces by the creation of the apparatus that we call culture, the more dynamic becomes his immediate universe; and the more intimate its impingement upon him, the more demands he makes upon it. The continued stimulation of one flux within another, the construction of an arbitrary universe within a natural one, has unending consequences.

CHAPTER VI

THE DESIRE FOR CHANGE

Voluntary Wants. Contrary to popular belief, change for the sake of change is a relatively infrequent motivation for innovation. As the data of the preceding chapters indicate, a large number of wants call for satisfactions that require change if they are to be realized, but the primary desire is not to alter existing conditions. The aim is not newness, freshness, or modification. The impetus is neither a liking for a novelty nor a dislike of the prosaic. The initiating want has other orientations; and if it could be satisfied without disrupting or changing anything, that would be enough.

It is otherwise with the wants now to be considered. They are directed toward change, and nothing less or other than the particular manifestations of change that they have in view will satisfy them. They involve preferences, because they reject a customary usage in favor of a new alternative. Like other wants, they spring from dissatisfaction and discomfort; but unlike the wants previously discussed, they arise from dissatisfaction with the accepted mode itself, not from displeasure with the circumstances that prevent the continued performance or operation of it. In a sense they are therefore voluntary or self-imposed wants. If a compounding of complexity can be excused, it may be said that they are wanted wants instead of forced wants.

Creative Wants. In a 1950 address before the American Chemical Society a business executive in charge of research scientists for a nationally known drug laboratory told the convention what he looked for in seeking men who are likely to make real discoveries. In his opinion a potentially valuable researcher is one who, on the intellectual side, can leap the barriers between the narrow specialties of his field because he is not himself a narrow specialist and because he has the ability to see relationships between things that seem unrelated to other people. On the motivational side, the productive researcher should, he maintained, be impelled by "the esthetic satisfaction he obtains in bringing order out of chaos." [1]

There are a great many inventors, both professional and amateur, who would agree with this emphasis upon the creative urge in scientific discovery. They have other ways to express it, and some may not like the artistic implications of the term "esthetic." Despite preferences for shades of meaning, it would not be difficult to get rather general agreement that, as far as pure re-

[1] *Time,* Apr. 24, 1950, p. 65.

search is concerned, the basic drive is accomplishment for its own sake; and, as is well appreciated, out of pure research come many discoveries. This motivation has long been honored in the arts and crafts, in which all manner of novelty and extravagance has been justified on the ground that self-expression is its own reward. Whatever may be an individual's motivation in espousing the doctrine of art for art's sake, it is the activity itself that pre-occupies him. It is an end in itself. The same motive is evident in the social sciences and in the humanities. The study of history, psychology, or philosophy is its own justification; just doing it is satisfying.

It is noteworthy that the motive most frequently mentioned by the professional inventors queried in Rossman's survey was the "love of inventing." Out of 854 responses, there were 193 references to this incentive. The "desire to improve," with 189 testimonials to its importance, was not far behind.[2] These two incentives are closely related, if they are not in fact identical. Since very few inventors in this survey would consider that their efforts are not directed toward progress, the two judgments would appear to differ only in their phrasing of a common motive, namely, the desire to create. This urge has been described in many other ways, and its importance has been emphasized by students of invention as well as by inventors themselves. Kroeber calls it the "play impulse." He says,[3]

Generically, all the discoveries and innovations of pure science and fine art—those intellectual and aesthetic pursuits which are carried on without reference to technology or utility—may be credited to functioning of the human play impulses. They are adult sublimations, onto a largely supermuscular level, of the sensorily exploratory and kinaesthetic activities that constitute play in children and mammals. They rest on the play impulse, which is connected with growth but is dissociated from preservation, comfort, or utility, and which in science and art is translated into the realm of imagination, abstraction, relations, and sensuous form.

Hart expresses the idea in his phrase "the joy of functioning," by which he means the "pleasure of the inventive process, the zest of pitting one's powers against a puzzling obstacle, the fun of using one's mental and mechanical abilities, the satisfaction of rendering a service to one's fellow-men. . . ." This, he considers, is the desire that "keeps the typical inventor going."[4] While not ignoring economic and other motivations, Taussig states that "it would seem that no satisfaction from pecuniary success or worldly

[2] Joseph Rossman, *The Psychology of the Inventor*. Washington, D.C.: Inventor's Publishing Co., 1931, p. 152.

[3] A. L. Kroeber, *Anthropology*. New York: Harcourt, Brace and Company, Inc., 1948, p. 357.

[4] Hornell Hart, *The Technique of Social Progress*. New York: Henry Holt and Company, Inc., 1931, p. 655.

recognition equals the absorbed interest of trial, experiment, novel problems, happy solutions." [5]

Taussig, like most other serious students of inventors and their motivations, goes on to make the relevant observation that the drive (he calls it "instinct") to creative activity is generic; that is, it is not satisfied by one creative act, and it is not confined to a restricted area of interest. He points out that, although the names of Howe, Cartwright, Watt, Bell, Edison, and Fulton are associated in the popular mind with only one or two inventions, "their biographies show that they were constantly experimenting on all sorts of schemes, promising and unpromising; sometimes with money making intent, sometimes in a spirit of scientific research and sometimes merely in sport." Hart illustrates this theme by summarizing Cartwright's accomplishments: [6]

Cartwright is remembered as the inventor of the power loom and the combing machine. Actually, he never ceased inventing. He published a scheme for rendering houses fireproof; invented bricks on a geometrical system; made a machine for biscuit-baking; helped Fulton with his first steamship models; brought chemistry to bear upon the science of agriculture; introduced a new three-furrow plough; got the Agricultural Board's gold medal for experiments in manure, and their silver medal for an essay on the culture of potatoes; and obtained patents for calendering linens, making ropes, and cutting velvet pile. In his old age he sent to the Royal Society a paper propounding "a new theory of the planetary system, as far as it relates to the power by which the planets are impelled around the sun." Being sent to Dover, in his eightieth year, for warm sea-bathing, he invented a method by which the bathman saved the labor of two men in pumping up the water. A day or two previous to his death he wrote an elaborate argument to a friend on a plan he had discovered of working the steam engine by gunpowder instead of steam.

Rossman sums up the idea by saying that "chronic inventors will invent anything from a safety pin to a locomotive, and will obtain the impetus by almost any casual remark or by seeing some device which appears to them clumsy, unworkable, impractical or in any way open to improvement." [7]

The significance of these facts is that professional inventors are to a very large extent more interested in creation than in the thing created. This does not mean that they are uninfluenced by other considerations, such as the economic, for often they are. Neither does it mean that they throw themselves at random into any creative endeavor. Their interests are channelized by the traditional definition of areas wherein creative efforts are accredited and not condemned as unrespectable or vicious. It does mean that, after all allowances

---

[5] F. W. Taussig, *Inventors and Money Makers*. New York: The Macmillan Company, 1915, p. 22.

[6] Hart, *op. cit.,* p. 656.

[7] Rossman, *op. cit.,* p. 38.

are made for these controls and incentives, there remains a drive to manipulate things and ideas that characterizes the professional inventor and distinguishes him from other people who accept things and leave them as they find them. Nor is the creative drive limited to professionals. It is just as characteristic of the amateur and the hobbyist who putters and tinkers with everything from archery to horticulture. The man with a set of woodworking tools or a machine shop in his garage that he uses after work hours and on Sundays for his personal satisfaction is often motivated by nothing beyond the urge to create. Just what he makes is relatively unimportant to him, and he passes from one enthusiasm to another.

There is a strong element of challenge in the projects which absorb the energies of the inventor who labors for invention's sake. Such men are not content with solving easy and routine problems. They ignore obvious and facile solutions because such exercises offer no resistance to their will. Like musical virtuosos, they not only constantly seek new trials for their abilities but deliberately construct situations that are stimulating precisely because they are difficult. The manufactured challenges that are accepted are of many kinds. Frequently refractory materials are chosen for experimentation when existing materials satisfy almost everyone else, solely because they demand the utmost in skill in handling them. Methods and techniques, on the other hand, may constitute the essence of the problem. Painters, musicians, sculptors, architects, choreographers—in fact, artists and artisans of all kinds—are notable for their deliberate excursions into difficult and untried areas of techniques and materials. But artists are not alone in pushing back the boundaries of the impossible. Physicists, chemists, biologists, and just plain men of high enthusiasm constantly do the same. Explorers and adventurers who might otherwise have stayed at home in comfort have been goaded to discoveries because they have fancied that nature offered a challenge that they could not resist. Clever men who for one reason or another turn their talents to criminal activities not infrequently come to look upon law-enforcement devices as a challenge to their cunning. In spite of their inversion of values they, too, seek a fillip for their creative wants. On a more prosaic and acceptable level the same gratuitous acceptance of challenges to ingenuity is quite evident in games and contests of all kinds. A game is, in fact, an artificial situation which is designed to force the player to draw upon all his resources of a particular kind in a particular way. The obstacles, rules, handicaps, and penalties that are imposed are man-made challenges that must be accepted by the contestant if there is to be any game. Within the universe bounded by the rules, resourcefulness is at a premium. Outside of it, none is needed. Anyone can "beat the game" by ignoring the rules; and unlike the rules of nature, they can be evaded and modified at will. Nevertheless, the universal popularity of games is a testimonial to the universal appeal of a challenge to skill.

The fascination of a challenge is important for an understanding of innovation, because it is the manifestation of a mental tension that cannot be discharged except by the fulfillment of the act that is indicated by the challenge. The tension represents an urge to completion. Once a goal has been adopted, there is a restless demand for its accomplishment. The imperious and abiding qualities of such demands are commonplace experiences for most of us, and their compulsive character has been demonstrated experimentally in situations that involve incompleted tasks. In many instances the failure to achieve a goal results in repeated attempts and an obstinate refusal to admit defeat. If these efforts are still unavailing, the urge to completion is not dissipated; it is merely held in abeyance or "put in the back of the mind," where it is still latently active and may manifest itself as uneasiness, as absent-mindedness, or in many other ways. Its continued residual functioning accounts for many of the sudden insights and the solutions to old but unforgotten problems by professional and other inventors. It also accounts for the obsessions of men with particular problems, like Goodyear, and for the perseverance that Rossman's professional inventors rated as the most necessary qualification for success in their field.[8] The urge for completion is all the more compelling because the ego frequently becomes involved. That is, the failure to meet a challenge sets up a tension not only because it activates the urge to complete a task but also because it is damaging to the self-respect of the person who accepts the challenge.

Creative wants, then, have wide and deep ramifications. They have not been dealt with exhaustively here because they have received so much attention by others and because their effects are so well known. The comparatively short space that has been devoted to them is not to be taken as a measure of the importance that is attached to them. Rather, the aim has been to concur in the conclusions regarding their importance by other students and to add a few additional comments. Beyond that, suffice it to say that creative wants are the only explanation for some of the most spectacular human achievements; namely, those requiring consummate patience and skill.

Relief and Avoidance Wants. Innovators many times want a change of existing conditions because they experience physical or mental discomfort with those conditions. The motivation of such individuals is therefore to escape customary means, ends, and conditions by creating an alternative that is more congenial to their personal ideals or endowments. There are several kinds of these relief and avoidance demands; and in noting them and some of the innovative results of their realizations, it is advisable to keep in mind that there is a distinction between them and those that have been reviewed under the heading Compensatory Wants. Both spring from feelings of depri-

[8] *Ibid.,* p. 40.

vation; but with compensatory wants the innovator needs to find a goal, or a way to a goal, other than the one that is known but denied to him. His frustration is occasioned by an adventitious or an arbitrary interference with what he regards as his due. In relief and avoidance wants the desire is for some nonexistent means or goals. In the one case there is a way to satisfaction, but it is not available to the individual, and he feels the need to devise one of his own. In the other case, the means of the desired relief is not known to anyone. In the former instance the want is forced by external circumstances, whereas in the latter it is voluntarily espoused and cultivated.

The desire for relief from boredom and monotony has culminated in many innovations. The individual who craves a change because of this incentive is "fed up" with some routine, repetitive activity. He is satiated and oppressed, but not because the distasteful situation is too laborious or because it fails to bring honor, pleasure, or compensation. It is unpleasant just because it is dull and stultifying. No small measure of this feeling exists as a component of the creative urge just discussed, but it can functon independently as a dominant drive. Routine occupations and manual or mental operations and techniques at times engender a sense of futility and oppression that bursts forth in rebellious aberration. Even though things like paper plates and dishwashing machines are sold under the name of laborsaving devices, their greatest appeal is the relief that they give from a monotonous activity. The same is true of a variety of other household appliances, such as vacuum cleaners, food mixers, and window cleaners. They give relief from dull jobs either by eliminating the jobs altogether or by shortening them. It cannot be said whether or not the inventors of these things experienced this demand, but it is likely that they did. It is also probable that many innovations in production technique have been stimulated by a surfeit of repetitive activities. No doubt our industrialized technology with its increasing trend toward reducing machine operators to the level of automatic machines themselves has produced innumerable innovative revolts against monotony. Most accounts that are published concerning such reactions depict them as strivings to save labor. It may be suspected that a closer analysis would put a different complexion upon some of the alleged motives for change in assembly-line production, for example, where the actual energy output is often inconsiderable by comparison with many other labor activities.

There are other examples of change that reveal even more clearly the demand for relief from boredom, for the innovations that are produced require as much time and effort as the activities which they replace. Verbal expressions are notoriously subject to alteration under the demand to introduce color and variety and to avoid repetition. This holds for voice inflection, for vocabulary, and for syntax changes. To some extent the desire for variation accounts for slang expressions and neologisms. The avoidance of monotony is also a marked motivation in the spontaneous organization, that is, the invention, of games. People "with time on their hands" on trains, in parlors, in waiting rooms, and in many other places devise forms of amusement to relieve the tedium of their waiting for something else to happen. Furthermore, recognized games are extremely liable to modification when they are played for their own sake but with tedious regularity or continuity. Anyone who has played a card game for fun for several hours at a time or who has had to play a game with his children for prolonged periods will appreciate the force of this contention. It is not surprising, though it is bewildering, to find that there are so many local and familial versions of card games. They are inherently boring to some people.

Another relief demand is the desire for release from restraint. This is not necessarily the same as relief from boredom, although the two may be intertwined. In itself it is felt as a need for relaxation of a given mental, physical, or emotional posture; and it emerges in situations that require protracted application, attention, concentration, mood preservation, or physical stance. It is experienced, for example, by people whose preformed habits or proclivities run counter to the demands of an incompatible situation. Thus, left-handed people living in our right-handed world must work out some adjustment to their need to manipulate things in a way most natural to them. Their individual adaptations are highly distinctive, as can be observed in their writing mannerisms and in their writing itself. Skillful individuals who undertake unfamiliar and awkward techniques also need to make singular adjustments of this nature. And then, for all of us, the need to be as relaxed as possible and at the same time to accomplish designated ends produces a host of individual peculiarities in walking, talking, sitting, and gesturing. These adjustments are, moreover, subject to standardization in families, local groups, and nations. Physical postures of relaxation are ethnically variable. Not all people rest their chins on their hands, place their hands on their hips or in their pockets, or fold their arms as Americans do. The peculiar storklike posture of the Nilotic Negroes, who rest the sole of one foot against the knee of the other leg, would provide no relaxation at all for most of us. The stroll or relaxed walk of the Palauan is difficult to describe, and its description will not be attempted. It is sufficient to say that on a dignified American it would be ridiculous.

Innovative relief responses often derive from excessive physical or mental demands upon the human organism. Ceremonies, either secular or religious, that require some stereotyped activity or prolonged quiet or inactivity can become almost physically painful. That the requirements of being polite, gracious, and unfailingly genial at formal parties is a strain will hardly be denied by anyone who makes a practice of attending them. The rebels who deviate from the artificial demands of such etiquette are asserting their need for relief, at least. The same holds for religious observances. The constraint of the Puritan Sunday so common a few decades ago has suffered so many breaches under the need for relief that in many homes today it has been re-placed by another kind of stultifying monotony. Church services have also been shortened, reduced in number, and in some instances considerably en-livened, in sensible response to fidgeting and drowsing among parishioners.

Several widespread cultural behaviors are to be interpreted as devices de-signed to provide for relief wants of the nature just mentioned. Our custom of having intermissions in theatrical productions and our recesses and rest periods in schools answer this purpose. So does the custom of having a siesta or of taking five-o'clock tea or ten- and three-o'clock coffee or "coke." The Palauans sit cross-legged on their dwelling and clubhouse floors, and they are accustomed to doing so for what seem to be endless hours during their councils, feasts, and business negotiations. In attending these functions and in trying to conform, I found it indispensable to excuse myself for personal intermissions. This could have established a precedent, at least to the extent of requiring a break in the proceedings until my return, if I had made an issue of it and played upon my prestige as an American.

The comedy relief in sustained dramatic productions, in the speeches of popular speakers, and in tense interpersonal situations are illustrations of another mechanism for relaxation from constraint. Even a most solemn and reverential occasion may be interspersed with humorous interludes. The Hopi Indians of Arizona spend much of their time in religious activities. They are a devout people, with a full and intricate annual calendar of cere-monies, some secret and some public. They have fraternities of men whose function it is to make spectators and participants laugh during these cere-monies. The duties of these ceremonial clowns are regarded as a sacred obli-gation; but their humor is of the most mundane and sacrilegious sort. They are privileged characters, saying and doing things which in others would be considered shameful or blasphemous. Their comedy is slapstick and, by the white man's standard, often vulgar and indecent; but for the Hopi it is both funny and devotional. They have achieved a harmonious and not a dis-ruptive integration of their need for emotional release during a tense situa-tion.[9] Ceremonial clowns are not peculiar to the Hopi. They were to be found among many Indian groups in the western part of the present United States.

Another means to achieve relaxation from constraint is to reserve times and places for personal privacy. Every cultural system has to make provision for this human need. The constant demands that social living makes upon the individual to conform to conventions puts a strain upon him. Having always to accommodate to the interests and requirements of his associates—the essence of a social situation—a person is left with no time "to be him-

[9] Leo W. Simmons (ed.), *Sun Chief. The Autobiography of a Hopi Indian.* New Haven: Yale University Press, 1942, Chapter 9.

self" and serve his own purely selfish interests. Even the most sociable people in the most socialized societies demand relief from having to listen to, answer to, and provide for others. The solution is to adopt devices that will allow for personal release in private. Individual solutions are varied, but there are also culturally standardized means. All the sanctuaries which actually or figuratively bear the notice "private" are preserves for the satisfaction of this need. Other withdrawal patterns typical of Americans are taking a walk, going fishing, and woolgathering. Among some American Indian groups, as well as among "cowpunchers," the same end is achieved by simply remaining silent and respecting the silence of others in a group—something that sophisticated Americans find boorish.

These relaxation mechanisms are established customs. The assumption is made that at one time they were innovations and that they originated in response to the same demand that they now satisfy. This is a reasonable assumption, especially in view of the fact that we have knowledge of the origins of parallel phenomena. When John Slocum, the founder of the Shaker cult, first began to hold services for his followers, he required them to kneel for long periods with their hands clasped before them in silent prayer. For a while this was acceptable, but soon some members of the congregation began to complain about the hardness of the floor and stiffness in their knees. Mud Bay Louis, an early leader in the church, introduced the practice of having the congregation stand while each person prayed successively. This change was objected to on the grounds that two hours (*sic*) was too long to pray. In time this sentiment gained enough support to force a shortening of this feature of the service. It now lasts only a few minutes, and the praying is done by everybody, out loud and simultaneously. A second relief demand led to the shortening of the total time for the Sunday morning service. Until about 1905 the service began around ten o'clock in the morning and lasted indefinitely, sometimes until two or three o'clock in the afternoon if enthusiasm for it continued unabated. There were objections to this, too, and finally a Yakima minister decreed that the service should stop at twelve o'clock; and with dramatic emphasis to enforce his ruling he placed his watch on the altar and closed the meeting promptly at noon. His precedent, without the watch, is followed today. As a final example of ritual change due to relief needs, it may be mentioned that members of the Shaker congregation now sit down while they are giving the welcoming handclasp to those who enter the church after they have arrived. Formerly everyone stood in his place until the last straggler wandered in. The discomfort of having to stand idly by their seats for fifteen minutes or half an hour eventually motivated those who made a habit of arriving on time to abandon the custom.

At this point we are on the borderline of conditions that are physically painful. It is not essential for our purposes to demarcate them and distinguish between a discomfort and an ache. It is enough to say that pain or the anticipation or remembrance of it is always a powerful stimulus to action, and that it is to be expected that the desire to avoid it has produced and continues to produce an almost endless number of escape mechanisms. Frequently reactions to it are blind and improvident; but effective solutions have been devised everywhere. In this category would fall all the devices and programs designed to prevent disease and injury, such as health aids, safety and sanitation programs, and the legal restrictions upon hazardous practices. Likewise to be included are protective innovations, ranging from shelter and clothing to battle tactics and armor. Also to be noted are palliative measures and materials, such as anaesthetics, surgery, medicinals, and placebos.

In addition, there is the whole area of psychological conditioning wherein the reality of pain becomes a function of the mental posture of the individual. Thus, men in our society, because of their conditioning to an ideal, ignore or refuse to acknowledge the existence of painful stimuli that are avoided and lamented by women and children. For the same reason pressure tests on American Indians, Papuans, and Ainus revealed that on an average their men experienced pain at a higher threshold than that of the average white man. Their estimate of what constituted discomfort severe enough to demand relief enabled them to exhibit more fortitude than could the white person with a different avoidance threshold.[10] Also, it is well known that pain may be psychologically avoided by the mechanism of self-abstraction or withdrawal; the sufferer makes a distinction between himself as an unfeeling observer and himself as a hurting thing. This mechanism, along with others, makes the endurance of flagellations of many sorts possible. The mechanism of outright denial of the existence of pain is an avoidance pattern that finds expression in some forms of magic, faith healing, and mysticism.

Distasteful things and conditions can be fully as repellent as an aching pain, and persistent urges to avoid them are often incentive enough to innovation. Here again the spectrum of the unpleasant presents gradations into the really painful. Thus, the noises that accompany our mechanized and commercialized technology are frequently so strident, harsh, and loud that they are disturbing if not physically injurious to some people. In many industries little attention is given to their control, but in others noise-reducing features are deemed essential or at least conducive to efficient workmanship. It is on the consumer level, however, that most attention is given to this need. The appeal of quiet is catered to by efforts to reduce distracting sounds and vibrations in radio, in sound pictures, and in automobiles, typewriters, electric fans, air conditioners, furnaces, and a multitude of other pieces of machinery. Recently a perforated propeller blade was patented that is more nearly noiseless than is the solid kind.

[10] R. S. Woodworth, "Racial Differences in Mental Traits," *Science,* Feb. 4, 1910, p. 177.

Innovations aimed at the elimination of qualities of things that are offensive to the other senses have not been wanting. Demands are constantly being expressed and satisfied for the removal of undesirable tastes, odors, and sights. In addition to health considerations, these demands have been a pressing incentive behind garbage- and sewage-disposal programs, the zoning of stockyards and private stockpens and stables, and the pressures upon industrial plants that employ fuels that contaminate the air or discharge useless by-products that do so. Complaints against indiscriminate expectoration are similarly motivated and have led to campaigns against it by Americans at home and abroad. Both the Japanese and the Americans have tried to modify the betel-chewing habits of the Palauans on health grounds, but both experience as much disgust at vulgar spitting as hygienic fear of its consequences. Ideals of beauty and a distaste for the ugly are to be held accountable for as many if not more cultural changes. These ideals undergo changes themselves, and with them comes a demand for the modification of things that embody them. In consequence, we experience the urge to alter machines, houses, and clothing design, with trends in this direction or that. Frequently large parts of cities are remodeled at considerable expense to satisfy this urge in conjunction with others. In the same way, cleanup programs, city zoning, highway advertising restrictions, and public or private landscaping plans originate with the desire to eliminate features that are aesthetically offensive.

Behavioral patterns are sometimes initiated or eliminated only because of their pleasant or unpleasant associations or because they are inherently appealing or distasteful to the innovator. In so far as they apply specifically to avoidance or relief, reference may be made to the previous mention of phobias and compulsions in our discussion of central subliminal wants. Whether on the subliminal plane or otherwise, irrational avoidances of things and situations can provide origination points for new mannerisms or action systems. John Slocum had a deep fear and distrust of the medicine men of his own people as a result of his unpleasant, and some say fatal, experiences with them. He constantly censured them and attempted to exclude them from affiliation with his movement. In particular, he berated them for charging fees to help the sick and for killing innocent people. These obsessions were incorporated into his creed and became basic tenets of Shakerism. Another Shaker started a campaign to do away with the custom of signing with the cross because this reminded him of his dead child. He tried to initiate a new kind of gesture signature. He failed, but that is another story. Some people, both as individuals and as members of ethnic groups, are revolted with the idea of eating eggs or drinking milk. Whether the Burmese and the Palauan avoidances of these food objects ultimately go back to a queasy feeling about them is entirely speculative; but it is evident that these peoples and others as well view our taste for milk and eggs as a perverted one. In the sphere of social relations numerous techniques have been devised to avoid embarrassing interpersonal contacts. Among various primitive peoples, brothers and sisters must avoid each other; and among others, familiarity with one or the other parent-in-law must be avoided by a man or his wife. Where these customs prevail, means must be provided to express the avoidance concepts, and indirect channels must be invented to mediate the necessary social adjustments between the tabooed individuals; for even though they may not confront each other, they must communicate and coordinate their activities. Face-saving devices, such as the Japanese custom of using intermediaries in delicate negotiations and the Kwakiutl use of the potlatch to reinstate esteem, are other examples of means designed to avoid the distasteful.

The existence of penalties establishes another motivational framework for avoidance innovation. Like the other stimuli being discussed, penalties are, of course, distasteful or painful; but they are in a special class because they are contingent upon something else that is valued enough to tempt seekers after it despite the punishment that goes with it. The penalty avoider attempts to evade or nullify the unpleasant consequences of some act or benefit that he enjoys. The penalty may be in the form of corporal punishment, social disapproval, arbitrary handicaps, fines, or deprivations of several sorts.

With this avoidance motivation we are in the thick of cunning and deceit. It seems that there will always be men, perhaps the majority of them, who will attempt to escape the unpleasant consequences of their acts, whether the latter be premeditated or forced by circumstances beyond their control. Some believe escape to be their natural right, others undertake it in desperation. Some even make a gamble, with the anticipated penalty as a stake. For one reason or another, there is no end to the variety of evasions, misrepresentations, subterfuges, circumventions, diversions, blockages, surprises, and other escape mechanisms that have been conceived to avoid forecasted punishments. There is a host of complicated maneuverings that we call strategies that are used to disarm opponents who, if not blocked, would initiate a penalty process. Strategies are known to the members of social, commercial, and domestic circles as well as to military men. Even if we confine our attention to means within the law, there are still a great number of such ingenious evasive mechanisms.

The practice of law is to a large extent a game of strategy between opponents who seek respectively to make the most and the least of it for private or public interests. Setting aside unscrupulous efforts, it must still be admitted that cleverness in interpreting the law is one of the most valuable assets that an attorney can have; and there are men, both in the profession and outside it, who exert themselves to fabricate legal but unforeseen evasions of legislative intent. Some of these circumventions practically nullify the law; others conform to its demands only in a perfunctory way and in a minimum degree. Courtroom procedure itself is a good half of justice, and

it has been a fertile field for the functioning of ingenuity. It is for this reason as much as any other that a layman is well advised to put his case in
the hands of a competent attorney rather than to try to handle it himself.
He can lose merely by telling the truth at the wrong time.

A large number of legal penalty avoidances have become stereotyped.
Among them are legal fictions, such as the establishment of residence in a
state by satisfying some arbitrary requirement on duration, and the divorce
and breach of promise complaints which allege the required extreme mental
cruelty and irreparable emotional harm to satisfy the legal requirements.
Others are immunity cloaks in the name of human rights. In 1949–1950,
United States Congressional investigating committees of several kinds found
that they were being balked by a varied array of subpoenaed witnesses who
declined to testify on the grounds that it was their constitutional right to
refuse to give testimony that might incriminate themselves. In a very short
time this refusal became such a patterned response that new controls had
to be instituted. The legal concept of "extenuating circumstances" covers
another range of ethnically sanctioned penalty avoidances based upon humanitarian considerations.

There are a number of penalty-avoidance patterns of a generic nature that
are widely applicable and offer latitude for individual variations. Faking,
bluffing, and imposturing are frequently practiced to avoid the punishing
consequences of truth. These devices have trivial and innocuous uses as well
as others that are serious, unethical, or illegal. It is probably safe to say that
they are universally used and that every adult has resorted to one or another
of them for protective purposes at some time in his life. When a penalty
is attached to ignorance, the gamble of a guess is preferable to failure; and
the result is frequently novel. Every teacher has a collection of "prize boners"
that he has found or knows have been found in the examination papers of
students who considered that taking a chance was better than saying nothing. Forced guessing of this sort also warps the courtroom testimony of
witnesses and that of anyone else entrusted with valued information or
somehow supposed to be in possession of it. The pattern of the "white lie"
is an acknowledged tradition with us. It is condoned because it is unselfish
and protects those whom we think deserve some special immunity. Several
venerable self-defense mechanisms that aim at avoiding punishment appear
in new and colorful guises with altered circumstances. One such is the
argument *ad hominem* which resorts to personal attacks upon an opponent
to distract attention from the threatening ideas or principles that he represents. Closely related is the technique of issuing a cross complaint or making
a countercharge which seeks to turn attention away from one's own vulnera-
bility by exposing and magnifying the weaknesses of an opponent. The "red-
herring" technique is also a tactic to confuse issues and disorient attackers.
The resort to devices for the suppression or conversion of damaging infor-

mation or opinions is a common practice where it can be brought into play. Suppression need not require anything more original than the application of force; but the need for security has at times evoked remarkably subtle and diversified methods of gaining and maintaining information controls, ranging from propaganda to blackmail. The nullification of damaging rumors and opinions by supplanting or converting them also calls for talent, as when an individual or a political party accepts an epithet hurled in malice and turns it into an asset or deflects it and causes it to boomerang. An example of an effort to discourage unfavorable publicity occurred when the Association of American Railroads decided to offset the popularity of the song "Casey Jones" by sponsoring another that was more flattering to the industry. The fact that the song commemorated a disaster was deplored, so a folk-song writer was commissioned to write another which eulogized the bravery of a conductor who succeeded in stopping a runaway logging train after the rest of the crew had jumped to safety.[11] Sublimation is another kind of conversion that is used to avoid punishment. With it a shameful motive or goal is translated into a socially acceptable form. Cowardice or brutality in certain situations may thus be converted into heroism, or hostility may be diverted into crusades against evil and given expression as righteous indignation. An example is provided by Lasswell's data on the political agitator who unconsciously hated his older brother and resented his father's demands upon him, in consequence of which he became a champion of the masses and a bitter critic of dogmatism and authoritarianism.[12]

It must not be overlooked that there are avoidances founded upon intellectualistic considerations as well as those that are more definitely grounded on self-interests. With them the need is to eliminate doubts, absurdities, and logical conflicts. The innovator feels compelled to reject an existing idea in favor of one that he has conceived, or he must evolve a compromise that will make two or more conflicting ideas compatible. This has been an extremely important incentive in philosophy and in the sciences. Within these areas the creative urge, the importance of which has already been emphasized, is governed and guided by this incentive in a peremptory way that it is not in the arts. Scientists and artists are concerned with different orders of compatibility. The former seek logical consistency and are unhappy with formulations which do not meet this ideal. The scientific attitude compels an avoidance of the irrational, so much so that pure science, *e.g.*, mathematics, is pure reason.

Planck postulated the existence of quanta of energy because that was the only conception of it that could be described mathematically. No one had

[11] *Time,* May 15, 1950.

[12] H. D. Lasswell, *Psychopathology and Politics.* Chicago: University of Chicago Press, 1930, Chap. 6.

been able to set up an equation to describe the emission of light from a luminous body as a continuous stream of energy, and Planck could not do so either. On the other hand, when he made the assumption that the energy was emitted in infinitesimal bursts, the formula demanded by his mathematical reasoning would describe the phenomenon precisely. The contradiction between the requirements of logic and the existing theory of the nature of energy transmission finally compelled Planck to reject the stream theory and to postulate that radiant energy is emitted in pulsations or quanta that vary in amount with the frequency of the light. With the acceptance and elaboration of this view the fundamental units of physics became blobs of energy and not things; and out of this conception developed the theories and researches of Einstein, Bohr, Rutherford, and others to revolutionize the Newtonian concepts regarding matter and its motion.

Social scientists have their intolerable dilemmas too. One that has not let them rest is their dualistic conception of the molding forces in human behavior, what is usually called the problem of heredity versus environment. As long as the explanation of human beings is phrased in terms of this antithesis, as it continues to be, men will be prompted to find some resolution of the logical contradiction it presents. One solution, of course, is to deny that there is a contradiction. In recent decades this problem has received increasing attention under the dichotomous heading of the individual and his society. Laymen and professional men alike have their views regarding the prepotence or impotence of the individual in shaping his own personality and ideals within the framework of the cultural imperatives that bear upon him. The dilemma of double determinatives demands some theory of their interrelationship by anyone who considers the subject seriously. Hence the numerous theories about instincts and drives in human behavior and the many experiments that have been conducted to determine the effects of social environment upon behavior.

The demands for rational adjustments occur widely in the everyday experience of any individual. He must repeatedly evaluate the logic of the demands made upon him and adopt a course that he can justify to himself at least. No person deliberately behaves or thinks in ways that he considers stupid; on the contrary, he feels impelled to avoid them. If he cannot avoid behaving irrationally, he finds some reason for his inability to escape doing so. Rationalizations are attempts at such justifications, and they can be novel. They emerge when a person is induced to think objectively about some habitual behavior, usually because its rationality has been questioned by others. Such rationalizations are significant, not only because they are fictitious, but because they become charters for belief and action. They are cultural preservatives, because they are supported by logic if not by evidence. The avoidance of the irrational also produces skepticism, the opposite of a rational defense of the habitual. Personal doubts of faith in the existing order call for a thesis that is more compatible with reason as the skeptic understands it. The straining of credence has provoked rebellions against all manner of dogmas and opened the way for new conceptualizations.

The avoidance of the irrational manifests itself in the rejection of meaningless and ridiculous customs. The Palauans are in the process of abandoning their native dances because these activities are isolated survivals of a past era. They have lost their meaning because the context wherein they were elaborated has disappeared. They are no longer expressions of a need for artistry, relaxation, or conviviality. They are artificial and are looked upon as work rather than play. Moreover, the young men who are required to dance, comparing themselves with Japanese and American men, have come to think that dancing in the Palauan way is a silly thing for grown men to do. Comparable attitudes are easy to find among young people in our own society. Venerable traditions often strike them as absurd; and if they could, they would abandon them. There are, for example, a number of college professors who look upon the wearing of academic gowns as an exhibition of childish and vainglorious mummery. At the University of Oregon, for the past ten years at least, there have been periodic attempts to rescind or neutralize the faculty legislation which makes the practice mandatory at commencement exercises. Typically, the proposals to take such action have come from newcomers to the campus and to the field of college teaching.

The Desire for Quantitative Variation. Many changes are welcomed because existing mechanisms do not provide enough of something that is valued. An alternative is wanted which will increase or decrease the requirements or the limitations of a customary thing or usage. The goal is therefore a quantitative change of some kind; it can be expressed in terms of wanting more or less of this or that, meaning more or less of the same. Increments and decrements can, of course, be effected by quantitative alterations in existing mechanisms: more money can be made by increased investments, more light can be produced by adding more electric bulbs, more intense pain can be created by an application of greater pressure, and so on. However, this way of initiating change is not innovative according to our definition. Our concern is with constructs that are qualitatively distinct from those they replace. Therefore, in this place we are to consider qualitative changes that produce, require, or permit desirable quantitative changes. Something new is perferred to the old because it involves more or less people, things, money, space, time, behaviors, ideas, efforts or the qualities of these things.

As this brief prospectus indicates, innovations that are conceived out of a desire for quantitative variation cover a wide variety of phenomena. Their number and diversity is great because, for one thing, human beings are strongly motivated to vary the quantitative aspects of their experience. All of us must function within limits, and we are frequently made acutely aware of them. Consequently, premiums are placed upon the ability either to extend the hampering limits or to make gainful compromises within them. Values become attached to ranges and margins; prizes are offered for increments and decrements in terms of prestige, comfort, possession, subsistence items, or other goods. An important mediating value for some people, such as ourselves, is money; that is, shrinkages and extensions of time, space, things, and effort are worth money, and money can be converted into other satisfactions. The lure of it is therefore a strong incentive to excel or surpass the potentialities of existing means. In other words, credit wants, compensatory wants, creative wants, and others impinge upon and may dominate the desire for quantitative variation. The latter becomes a means to achieve the former.

Another reason for the prominence of quantitative variation wants, in our society particularly, derives from the concept of progress. This philosophical principle has been a respectable rationalization for the desire for change for almost two centuries in the Euro-American cultural system. The basic premises of this ideology are that progressive change is natural and normal, that it leads to a state of perfection, and that obstacles in the way of its realization should be eliminated.[13] Innovators, especially technological inventors, have brought their creative and avoidance urges to bear at points where the changes that they suggest will be accorded this interpretation. Their desires to reduce or to augment are cultivated in the name of progress —an unassailable aegis, because nobody can be against it. It has been noted that professional American inventors give prominence to their urge to improve. If asked, almost any other American would characterize his new idea in this way. The point is that creativeness of any sort can be viewed in this light and must be if it is acceptable. Furthermore, quantitative variation is a most acceptable kind of change because it manipulates premium aspects of existing values. In brief, the idea of progress encourages men to seek quantitative change by providing a moral justification for their doing so in areas of demand.

For these reasons and probably others, proposed increases or decreases represent gains or advantages in the mind of the innovator. The gains may relate to the production requirements of the innovation, to the characteristics of its operation, or to the effects that it has upon other things. Each of these concomitants has several aspects that are subject to quantitative alterations. Many of the facets have overlapping effects. The treatment of them that follows is intended to be illustrative rather than exhaustive; a thoroughgoing description would be tedious and no more enlightening.

Quantitative changes in production variables are sought for financial, aesthetic, and other reasons. An innovation is desirable because it requires

---

[13] Frederick J. Teggart, *Theory of History*. New Haven: Yale University Press, 1925, Chap. 8.

more or less of something to produce it as compared with that which it is designed to replace. Under this heading would come reductions in the amount of money, time, labor, and power, or in the number of individuals, techniques, or appliances required. In other words, the aim of such an innovation is the conservation of some resource. Motive power is one valued resource, and the incentive to conserve it has numerous manifestations. It would be inaccurate to say that human beings are lazy and that they always do the least amount of work that is possible. It does seem to be true, however, that they will avoid any labor that is unnecessary to achieve the goal that they have in view. Some goals, of course, are deliberately labor consuming, but even with them there are limits and instruments of least effort that are valued over those that call for a wanton expenditure of labor.

We are all aware of the need to save effort and know of innovations prompted by it. It is quite apparent in the adaptation of mechanical substitutes for human motive power. Simple and complex engines of all descriptions serve this purpose. So do gauges and calculators. Electronic machines now save human beings hundreds of hours of routine calculations. Recently a telescopic sighting apparatus was invented that eliminates the necessity of sending linesmen out on a football field to take measurements on close decisions. All these devices tend to shift the work loads from human beings to things. There are others that enable one person to shift his burden to another person. Wage labor, slavery, the indenture system, and all the variations upon these customs come into view here. Nor should we overlook the clever ruses that our friends and enemies employ to get us to do their work for them—or vice versa. Then there are the "easy-money" artists who often spend more time devising new ways to avoid work than the work itself would require of them. It cannot be denied that gamblers, extorters, speculators, confidence men, counterfeiters, and others who acknowledge a preference for "rackets" are inventive, even though their originality may be confined to variations upon old patterns.

Stereotyped bodily movements also undergo alteration that is due to the need to conserve effort. This is one reason for the "degeneration" of precision routines that become perfunctory. In spite of the importance of keeping it unambiguous, handwriting becomes illegible unless a real effort is made to manipulate the hand in specified ways. Handcopying of any kind is certain to lack fidelity; and a good share of the resulting alteration is due to a relaxation of effort, especially in situations where exactitude is a secondary consideration. The American custom of shaking hands is for some people no more than a flabby touch. Our hat tipping is also reduced by some men to a mere salute or any like gesture that requires the least amount of effort. Other movements, even those requiring whole body manipulations, are vulnerable to change unless a deliberate effort is made to preserve the parts that require stops and hesitations, inflections and reverses, and other

effort features. Dance steps and ritual movements are thus subject to modification under the universal urge to "cut corners" in the absence of a positive
demand not to do so. Speech habits show the same effects of laziness. Sapir
points out that this is one of the reasons for the growing preference for
"who" over "whom" in such expressions as "Whom did you see?" It is not
easy to make the "m" distinct in certain sound combinations like this.[14]
Finally, it is a common observation that we all slur our words and phonemes
in colloquial speech if we are not careful. Real effort is required to enunciate
clearly, and sometimes we do not feel up to it. We often make ourselves
unintelligible out of sheer laziness.

All the foregoing innovative tendencies or inventions are doubtless labor
savers for those who use them. More to the point in some cases, however,
is the question as to whether it was the desire to conserve effort that actually
motivated their inventors. It must be admitted that often we do not have
explicit statements that would constitute unequivocal evidence on this essential point. Nevertheless cases are known. Humphrey Potter made a name
for himself solely because of his innovative laziness. He was hired to open
and close the steam and water valves in the crude Newcomen pump; but
finding this dull and laborious, he constructed a rocking beam to make
them operate mechanically, thus introducing an essential step in the development of the modern steam engine.[15] The Andrus rotary saw filer, used to
sharpen large circular log saws without removing them from their shafts,
was developed as a labor saver. The inventor, B. R. Andrus, relates that it
was a "streak of laziness" that led to the idea. He was a saw filer and "got
tired of pushing a file back and forth, back and forth." [16] During the Second
World War the Delaware Red Cross acquired a patent for a semiautomatic
bandage folder because a certain individual, Philip Burnham by name, found
the hand operation tiresome. Substituting for his wife at the Wilmington
Red Cross center one evening, he was "bored stiff" and went home convinced that there must be an easier way to make gauze pads; so he made
a simple and cheap folder out of wallboard that did the job in one-fourth
the time required by hand.[17] It is interesting to note, too, that in the Rossman
survey "laziness" was mentioned six times by professional inventors as a
motivation for their endeavors.

The desire to save effort is only one conservation demand. Time is another value that prompts new conservation measures and devices. We hear

[14] Edward Sapir, *Language*. New York: Harcourt, Brace and Company, Inc., 1921,
pp. 171–172.
[15] Kaempffert doubts the authenticity of this story, but his reasons for disbelieving
it are no more compelling than the reasons for accepting it. See Waldemar Kaempffert,
A Popular History of American Invention. New York: Charles Scribner's Sons, 1924,
Vol. 1, p. 475.
[16] *Eugene* (Oregon) *Register-Guard*, Aug. 12, 1948.
[17] *Time*, May 3, 1943.

so much of the need to save time in our society and are individually made so fully aware of the virtues of doing so that it is unnecessary to develop this point. It is enough to mention that our age has produced hundreds if not thousands of devices, schedules, and operational schemes in the communication and transport fields alone that answer the need to gain time. Speed and time are "of the essence" in these and other industries.

Space is another resource that calls for conservation. There is always a limited amount of the best of it for any operation, and the demand to make the most of what is available sometimes reaches a critical point. Even if they are not always imperative, space savers represent valuable gains in many sectors of our culture. Our urban life puts a premium upon building space; hence the invention of the skyscraper and the modern apartment house. The limited areas within these buildings and within modern buildings generally have led to such singular features as built-in cupboards, furniture, and appliances. Contemporary American architecture has been greatly influenced by the need or supposed need for space conservation. Automobile designers have likewise been motivated by this demand. Limitations upon transportation space, coupled with its high cost, have also inspired many new ideas in the packaging and arranging of shipped goods. The invention of the folding airplane wing is but one example. Compacted objects are a prominent feature of our contemporary life. We have, or are striving to get, a variety of "vest-pocket" editions of everything from radios to flashlights.

The desire to conserve valuable materials is universal, unless by their waste some supraordinate value is gained. Preservatives of all descriptions come under this heading, and doubtless the number of them that have been invented runs into the thousands when the world and all its valued goods are taken into consideration. The salvaging of waste products is another aspect of this need, especially the discovery of uses for the byproducts of the meat-packing, mining, lumbering, and other major industries in our culture. Very often the invention of a means to convert a waste product, such as sawdust, into a useful substance or the discovery of a new method to extract a theretofore irrecoverable material, such as low-grade ore, has not only bolstered the economy of the mother industry but has led to new ones as well. The discovery of more abundant and cheaper materials has been motivated at times by the scarcity of premium goods; and in individual cases the need to conserve limited supplies of necessities, such as food and fuel, resolves itself in the use of substitute things and in new patterns of consumption. During one famine period the peasants of the Ukraine began to mix bark with their flour to give it bulk and make it last. Before the emergency was over, they had acquired a taste for the mixture and continued to use it when normal conditions returned.[18] Fractionat-

[18] William I. Thomas, *Primitive Behavior*. New York: McGraw-Hill Book Company, Inc., 1937, p. 31.

ing and cutting and mending procedures are conservative measures of wide utility. Merely cutting something in a certain way can effect a major gain in materials. Finally, programs designed to conserve natural resources may be mentioned. We hear a great deal of this at the present time, and many of the measures to which we have been introduced in recent years are new in application if not in principle. Thus, the concept of sustained yield in forest production is an old idea but is relatively new to the timber industry. It involves the planting of timber trees and the cutting of the mature stock in ways that will not destroy the productive potential of the native forests. Soil-conservation programs involving such modifications as contour plowing and restrictions upon grazing have come as novelties to most Western farmers—meddling novelties as far as some of them are concerned. Soil-conservation measures of other kinds are ancient and widespread; so also are the related devices, such as fertilization and crop rotation, that help preserve the vitality of farm lands.

Before concluding this discussion of conservation, it is to the point to mention that by no means all inventions are prompted by the desire to vary the quantities and properties of goods in one direction. It is not always desirable to lessen the expenditure of time, labor, money, and other resources. On the contrary, new means are often sought that will do just the opposite. In the matter of time, a value may be placed upon a means to extend it, especially when more of it is needed to accomplish a predetermined goal. Our familiar "time payment plan" and the lending of money at interest are in effect means to prolong deadlines. In other contexts the making of excuses, the resort to delaying tactics, and means of temporizing or "stalling for time" are conceived to accomplish the same purpose. Premiums may be placed upon such expansive and inflationary mechanisms within any area, even with respect to the amounts of labor and material expended or the cost of producing or operating something. Busywork refinements are well-known means of prolonging a job and making it seem more important and the worker's service more valuable. During the Second World War, in order to induce industries to undertake production ventures that were financially risky or unrewarding, the government adopted the "cost-plus plan" whereby the manufacturer was assured of operating costs plus a stipulated profit. The result was that labor and other costs ceased to operate as controls for both the worker and the employer. Indeed, the more labor the better from their viewpoints.

It is, however, in the area of luxury goods that increases in time, labor, difficulty, and ultimately cost are consciously cultivated and it is in this area that novelties that will accomplish this end are most prized. As long as there is a market to absorb them, expensive innovations will be made as readily as their counterworks. They are important in our culture in connection with our homes, home furnishings, automobiles, clothing, jewelry, and other items that we use for the conspicuous display of our wealth. In these things pride is taken in expense, in prolonged and difficult craftsmanship, and in the amount of waste that is involved. The most valuable of these goods are those that take only the heart out of a valued resource, those that will use prodigious quantities, or those that require tedious and marvelous exertions. Innovations, such as the "new look" in women's dresses of a few years ago, that somehow manage to accomplish this waste of time and materials in a conspicuous way are well rewarded.

Some innovations effect quantitative changes in the usefulness of an existing object, or they are themselves more useful than the objects they are intended to replace. Combination tools and appliances have the latter advantage, although some have gone to such extremes that the gain is a dubious one. English sportsmen of a hundred years ago, for example, were fond of pocketknives that had as many as eighty blades that could serve such varied purposes as cutting beards, opening oysters, and sawing wood.[19] Our boy scout knives are modest attempts at such versatility. So are our adjustable tools, such as the Stillson, the crescent, and the monkey wrench. Detachable handles and grasping implements such as tongs, tweezers, and pliers have comparable merits. Universal garments such as reversible raincoats, convertible furniture such as davenos, and combination gear such as the English shooting stick and the cane-encased dagger are other examples. The ideal of a universal drug or elixir has motivated a search for it by many men from ancient times to the present. The discovery of penicillin, a recent approximation to the ideal, did not come about in this way, but for a time repeated demonstrations of its efficacy held out this hope.

The ambition of some inventors is to produce something that will have superior resistance under longer, harder, or less expert use. More rugged machines are the desideratum under variable conditions of weather, handling, or application. More desirable materials are sought that will better resist fire, oxidation, and decomposition. The copper and aluminum industries have been greatly expanded in the past fifty years in response to this demand. New developments in paint and synthetic-dye chemistry have made the use of inferior natural ingredients to a large extent obsolete. The same trend is evident in the proliferation of composition woods, plastics, glasses, and synthetic fuels. The increased adaptability of these substances adds considerably to our resource potential. Not only are they more versatile, but their invention has also decreased our dependence upon resources as they occur in the natural state.

While we are on the subject of usefulness in things, it is advisable to note again that innovation is not always inspired by the desire for an in-

[19] *Time,* Apr. 3, 1950.

crease. Many innovations in the category under discussion are intended for restricted use because of their specialized characteristics. Thus, implements like surgical knives and forceps have specific and extremely limited uses. So do the tools of any other trade, such as that of an automobile mechanic. An interesting example of a new tool of restricted use is the Philips screw driver. Its popularity with many manufacturers renders the single-bitted screw driver almost useless in some kinds of repair work because the Philips bit requires a special type of screw that will not accommodate the ordinary tool.

People as well as things are the object of quantitative variations in manipulations of the use factor. In other words, some inventions are made with the idea of either increasing or decreasing the number of users, participants, or receivers. Thus, it is often the purpose of a technological improvement to extend the use of a piece of equipment to women or to others who are uninterested and unskilled in mechanics. This end can be achieved by a simplification of an apparatus, but usually the requirement of simplification in operation means a complication in the machine itself. A machine takes over some human function; and normally the more it relieves the individual of the necessity for acting, the more intricate it becomes. Regardless of this point, a great many modern mechanical inventions are made with the idea of increasing the utility of a given object by making it possible for more people to handle it. Touch controls are a significant contemporary development; our era is sometimes referred to as the push-button age because so many important things can be accomplished, even by children, by the mere pressing of a lever or the throwing of an electrical switch. Only slightly more burdensome are such things as hydraulic brakes and fluid gearshifts on automobiles. Neither strength nor skill is required to operate them. There are numerous other inventions that reduce the elements of strength and skill to a minimum, often to the point of requiring their operators to act solely in a discretionary capacity: calculating machines, radar, automatic steering devices, clocks, levels, and gauges, to mention only a few. "Foolproof" compensators are also aimed at wider uses for machines because anyone assisted by them can be an operator. This trend is evident now in private airplane design. The adaptation of procedures requiring a specialist's handling so that they can be controlled by untrained persons provides a further illustration. Innovations in this category aim always at wider uses. Patent medicines and home cures, treatments, and applicators do this. A recent instance has been the development of the home hair-wave kit; its rapid and wide acceptance has been a serious blow to professional beauticians. To give but one other illustration, a home car washer was contrived by a man who felt that there was a market for it after contemplating the expensive machine used by professionals. His invention can be fitted to the doorway of a private garage and costs only a tiny fraction of the price of the prototype.[20]

Some innovations function to restrict the number of users or adherents of an existing thing or idea. Esoteric and secret devices are commonly developed with this intention. Key and combination locks are obviously in this category. So are codes like those used by diplomats and military strategists, and the private signals and jargons devised by brotherhoods and secret orders of all kinds. The creation of selective mechanisms that are designed to screen the participants in some desirable activity may also be noticed here. There is a large number of them, some crude and stale, some subtle and clever. The discriminatory techniques used to disenfranchise or dislocate the members of minority groups are numerous and sometimes are noteworthy because of the indirection of their application. Fraternal organizations also utilize a variety of screening devices. Schools resort to them through examinations and by numerous formal and arbitrary requirements. In business they manifest themselves in freeze-outs, monopolies, and cartels and in preferential rates and trade agreements. In fact, there are very few goal areas that are not hedged by requirements that are prompted by the desire to prevent their indiscriminate enjoyment by all people.

Another field for the play of quantitative variation that invites innovative manipulation is instrumental effectiveness. Stated otherwise, a means is wanted to increase or decrease the effects produced by an existent thing or process. In many instances the goal is a greater or lesser degree of the same effect. In technology, power mechanisms that utilize new principles are frequently able to achieve this end. A few examples out of many would include the recent application of jet propulsion for aircraft, the adaptation of the shaped or conical explosive charge principle for antitank projectiles, the replacement of mechanical brakes by air or hydraulic pressure systems, the use of atomic energy for the making of more destructive bombs, and the envisaged use of bacterial infection in mass warfare. On the other hand, mechanisms that will counteract the increased effects of things like bombs are in demand, and this want in turn produces counteractive devices and plans. Also on the negative side are the heating, cooling, and lubrication systems that prewarm or cool engines; the clothing, air conditioning, and heating installations in dwellings and vehicles that moderate temperatures for human comfort; and the improvements that reduce jar and friction in machines. Alfred Nobel made dynamite because pure nitroglycerin was too dangerous to handle and to transport. A short time ago a butcher in Lebanon, Oregon, patented a knife-sharpening attachment for his meat grinder. He was motivated to do so because the grinding wheels used by professional knife sharpeners revolve so fast that they take the temper out

[20] *Life*, May 1, 1950, pp. 106–107.

of blade steel. Some instruments like rheostats are made for the purpose of varying the intensity of power at will.

The desire for increased degree of effect results in many new ideas in the nonmaterial as well as in the mechanical aspects of culture. The institution of the labor union is a means for more effectively satisfying the demands of the workingman against employers. And within this structure, methods of achieving stated goals have been devised, some long ago and some in recent years. Among them would be included the strike, the sit-down, the slow-down, cost-of-living dictates, and the "no contract no work" slogan—each one of which has itself taken on novel colorings at times. Prestige wants are often insatiable in their demands for increased degrees of effect; hence a premium is placed upon new ways to gratify them. One tactic is to copy an impressive behavior system—with some odd results as far as the model is concerned. Children who ape their elders attract attention, but usually not the adult response they crave. Their age mates are more receptive of some of their pretensions, and this is sometimes the audience to whom they are directing their efforts. The same holds for natives who try to enhance their status by imitating foreigners and for the members of lower classes who adopt the mannerisms and ideals of their superiors. All innovate to make a greater impression, although they are rarely conscious that they are making an original contribution.

Demands for increased and decreased effects are sometimes focused upon range rather than degree when these two aspects can be dissociated. The designers of stratosphere aircraft and of powerful explosives and guns have range as well as degree of effect in view. Communication and transportation channels call for clearance and booster aids in their expansive phases. Greater or lesser penetration and infiltration powers are sought for things like projectiles, gases, and fluids and figuratively for ideas and for people. The demand for more precise extension controls over people, things, and influences gives rise to regulators and specific activators as widely different as selective indoctrination schemes, divisionistic tactics, and local as opposed to general anaesthetics.

Effects may be judged and desired in terms of their number, and so the purpose of an innovation may be to reduce or multiply them. The desired effects may be manufactured items or other units of production, in which case techniques and contrivances that result in absolute or proportional increases are in demand. New sampling and prospecting devices, such as the Geiger counter, contribute to this end. More efficient resource-extracting machines and procedures, such as pneumatic drills and deep-shaft operations, help to increase yields. Manufacturing industries have been able to produce large quantities of highly standardized items through the precise delimitation and coordination of mass effort in what is known as the assembly-line technique. Other efforts at increased production lie in the psychological field, as is evidenced by the inauguration of workers' incentives in the form of bonuses, piecework payment, profit sharing, pensions, holidays with pay, and sundry other inducements. Much research has been done on this problem in recent years, and in consequence many new ideas have been proposed and tried. One point of attack has been upon employer-employee relationships, as is evident in experiments with employee suggestion boxes and labor-management councils. The now famous Hawthorne experiment led to unexpected results concerning employee incentives and to recommendations for increased production based upon them.[21]

Because the control of wealth is so important to so many people, the means that have been contrived to obtain it are almost numberless. It would be futile to attempt a full exposition of them, but attention should be called to a few generic patterns of wealth acquisition. One is the augmentation of income through increased or strategically applied labor. In a sense this approach covers a good share of the activities already discussed, and the innovative variations upon it attest keen insight and real genius. There are easier ways to acquire wealth than by working for it, however; and men have not failed to exploit them. One way is through a redefinition of property rights. Specific devices include the modification or contesting of inheritance rules; the declaration of ethical claims on certain property like heirlooms; the adoption of community property laws (which some states tried a few years ago for the purpose of gaining on Federal income-tax exemptions); and the assertion by employees that they have an inherent property interest in the products of their labor even though they have been paid for it. Then there are the various assessment devices by which claims are made upon the property of others. Among them would be confiscation, fines, damages, and alimony.

When the objective is to affect an increased number of people, a mere geographical extension of available devices is often inadequate. Qualitatively different approaches are needed to reach different ideological levels and to appeal to different personalities. There are many facets to this need. They range from the desire to have and influence more friends to the impersonal craving for political power over masses of unknown people; and each has been prolific of artifices to satisfy the specific demand. One particular manifestation to which we may give attention for purposes of illustration is the desire to increase or decrease the number of people who share in given responsibilities or privileges. The American ideal of mass education has necessitated departures from the European educational system in such matters as the standardization of teaching methods and materials, public support, and the evaluation of proficiency. It has also given rise to special means of

---

[21] Committee on Work in Industry, National Research Council, *Fatigue of Workers: Its Relation to Industrial Production*. New York, 1941, Chap. 4.

ensuring mass literacy: minimum age for voluntary withdrawal from school, truant officers, and methods to overcome the disabilities of handicapped students. Another of our ideals, that of social, economic, and legal equality, has inspired a great number of instrumental devices, especially in the last twenty years. Our efforts to narrow the gap between the rich and poor has resulted in a scaling of income-tax liabilities, in inheritance taxes, social security, minimum wages, crop support, and in proposals to initiate various old-age payment and group-health plans. The ideal of equalization has also produced rationing systems for essential goods and impartial military conscription.

Another order of desire for greater or lesser effects relates to certainty or accuracy. Some people are uncommonly unhappy with crude and unreliable tools; and those who are sufficiently frustrated or who foresee credit for themselves or relief for others undertake to do something about their displeasure. Watt, who was an instrument maker by training, could not tolerate the crudity of the Newcomen pump; it was too cumbersome and wasteful to suit him. Peter Camper, an artist, was so annoyed with the artistic convention of his day that pictured Negro and Caucasian profiles as being just alike that he devised a means of measuring the facial angle, *i.e.,* the degree of slope of the upper face. Such refinements of means and implements have been going on rather continuously throughout cultural history. Measurement devices and systems have exhibited this trend. The solar year has replaced the lunar calendar; time guesses have given way to sun dials, and they to clocks and stop watches; scales, rulers, and numbering systems have had to keep pace with technological refinement. Observational techniques have been made subject to the same demands for greater accuracy and particularity, so that there has been a succession of instruments and approaches that have penetrated the plane of the superficial and the obvious. Correlatively, analytical concepts and tools have given greater certainty to conclusions in everything from crime detection to chemical assaying. The demand for greater accuracy has been responsible for new means of testing and evaluating human potentials in psychology and thing qualities in mechanics and chemistry. The demand for more exact characterization of relationships and affiliations has resulted in revisions of first approximations and guesses, as is evident in Einstein's reformulation of Euclidean geometry and in the improved sampling techniques of contemporary poll and census takers.

An increase or decrease in the duration of effects has been the motivation for some innovations. Preservatives and preservation processes are by their nature inspired by this desire. The successive developments of food smoking, salting, canning, and freezing have been motivated by an ideal of perfect fixation of quality and utility. Comparable goals are evident in other sequential developments with such diverse aims as record keeping and embalming. Rewards and punishments are conceived with this idea in mind. With an emphasis upon lasting effects considerable ingenuity has gone into the origination of durable incentives and deterrents to sanctioned and proscribed behavior.

Finally, the ideal of immediacy and directness of effect has been responsible for an extremely wide range of eliminative innovations. Quite apart from the time they waste, detours and indirect linkages can be insufferable to the impatient goal seeker. Roundabout ways and remote controls fail to give the most desirable effects or the required aesthetic satisfaction demanded by some individuals. They offend people who are sensitized to economy of means or materials or those who crave the sensation of unmediated personal power. Whether or not it is compounded with the desire to save time or labor, this value motivates the efficiency expert, the authoritarian, and the aesthetician. For some individuals unilateral decisions and automatic mechanical sequences are valued above adjusted opinion and diffuse reactions. To them, legislation by fiat, the administration of justice by decree, and automatic response to command are preferable to debate, exploration, and reflection. The ambiguities of communication systems are sources of irritation to those who demand of them vehicles for the direct expression of meaning. Social scientists are harried by the fuzziness of their means of expression and envy the univocal rigor of mathematical descriptions. The semanticists are even more exercised about the sound and fury of stereotyped and meaningless verbiage that commonly passes for descriptions of reality. A great many men, great and small, have sought more direct connections between places just because for them circuitous routes were distasteful as well as wasteful. Apart from the economy of effort that they represent, perfect timing and the coordination of movement have an aesthetic appeal for many who strive for means to achieve them. Within limits and subject to the priority of other demands, directness and immediacy of effect have a universal appeal; and the desire for them has prompted many changes.

In concluding this discussion of the desire for quantitative variation, it seems advisable to point out that the rational ordering of the desires in distinct categories does not have a direct counterpart in fact. The subject has been treated analytically in order to emphasize the range and multiplicity of innovative wants and to give clarity to the exposition. In any given situation, there is no such isolation of wants. There are always linkages, either between the wants themselves or between their effects. Consequently, most innovations probably entail a hierarchy of wants so that the gaining of one enables the innovator to achieve others that are subordinately linked. Motives are complex, and it is undeniable that most of them have a selfish component that may in fact be the most important although not the most obvious one. Furthermore, it is not possible to segregate the qualities of a thing or its effects, even if this were desirable. Often, then, an innovation necessitates the sacrifice of one desire for a more imperative one; which means that the innovator accepts a system of priorities for his needs. Thus a faster means of travel is usually a more expensive means, a labor-saving plan requires higher maintenance costs, and a more powerful machine is more self-destructive. The recognition of such necessary linkages may itself be the motivation for an innovation. In other words, the objective may be the balancing of wants; the innovator, for example, may aspire to a relatively inexpensive, easy, and fast way to travel.

Vicarious Wants. It is not essential that a want have its genesis in the ego system of the innovator, and a great many in fact do not. By implication at least, this fact has been recognized in the data of the preceding chapters, but it is well to make it explicit at this point. Professional inventors provide the best illustration of the transference of wants from those who personally experience them to others who impersonally adopt them. Men who make their living in this way consciously inquire into the wants of others or strive to discern and even to manufacture them. Unlike the vast majority of innovators, professional inventors live by their vicarious endeavors; but such identification is not limited to them. It is in fact a common thing for one person to exert himself to protect, to give advantage to, or to solve the problems of some other person. The altruistic concerns of friends, social reformers, and missionaries should be considered in this connection.

There is nothing distinctive about vicarious wants as wants. They are identical with those that have been described already and so might be anything from self-demands to the desire for greater effect. They differ only in their history. They are adopted or voluntarily assumed needs taken over from other people. They are not in the beginning native or integral to the need system of the innovator. They are secondarily his, but they are nonetheless compelling. Once accepted, they have all the compulsion of an autochthonous want, as is clearly shown in the case of prohibition leaders and religious proselytizers.

The motivations of those who voluntarily assume the wants of others are tangential to our main interest. They overlap with innovative incentives to a considerable degree but have other origins and ends as well. Their treatment would make a study in itself.

Part Three: Innovative Processes

CHAPTER VII

THE BASIC PROCESSES

Configurations. When innovation takes place, there is an intimate linkage or fusion of two or more elements that have not been previously joined in just this fashion, so that the result is a qualitatively distinct whole. The union is a true synthesis in that the product is a unity which has properties entirely different from the properties of its individual antecedents. If we may use a biological analogy, an innovation is like a genetic cross or hybrid; it is totally different from either of its parents, but it resembles both of them in some respects.

In innovation the fusion takes place on a mental plane. The linkage is between the ideas of things. This means that the process and its result are something quite different from a union of the things themselves. Mental images are not necessarily involved; in fact, usually they are not. Neither is the fusion solely an intellectualistic process; sometimes there are ingredients other than ideas involved. Perhaps this is always so. The innovative union of ideas is a complex commingling of perception, cognition, recall, and affect.

Fundamental to this point of view is the assumption that any innovation is made up of preexisting components; and, secondly, that new combinations are entirely the products of mental activity. No innovation springs full-blown out of nothing; it must have antecedents, and these are always traceable, provided that enough data are available for an analysis. An innovation is, therefore, a creation only in the sense that it is a new combination, never in the sense that it is something emerging from nothing.

It may be readily admitted that what has just been said holds for most innovations. At the same time there is likely to be some doubt about its having universal applicability. And even if universality is allowed, most readers will probably question whether any mechanisms can be discovered that will comprehend all the various kinds of fundamentally new ideas. It is the purpose of this chapter to suggest that there are such universals and to indicate their nature.

It is certainly true that as long as we continue to organize our thinking on this subject along traditional lines there can be little hope of discovering any universal regularities. If we are to make progress with this problem, it will be necessary for us to free our minds of certain preconceptions about the nature of the data that are involved. We are accustomed to thinking in terms of things, somehow supposing that things are the materials for innovation and that they are more stable and absolute than the ideas that we have about them. The truth is that the reverse is the case. We tend to regard a table as a unit because it has substance and because it is segregated from other things around it. Actually, however, the existence of the table is real only because we have mentally segregated it and given a discrete reality to it. It has no more internal consistency than we are wont to give it. Obviously there are times when we regard it, not as a discrete whole, but as a mere assemblage of lesser parts, themselves at the moment wholes. Clearly these differences are due to mental operations, in which ideas define the nature and the extent of things.

Ideas are mental activities no matter to what they relate. This means that the idea of a thing with substance can react to the idea of another thing of substance, or to the idea of some intangible; or even to the idea of an idea. The concept of a table is no more substantial than is the idea of fatherhood. Neither is more permanent, or stable, or definitive than the other. The idea of a table is subject to the same rules of mental functioning as is the idea of fatherhood. They have the same properties and the same potentialities. If a table can be said to have shape, then it is equally defensible to speak of fatherhood as having a shape with bounding characteristics that set it apart from other ideas. Each, of course, has its own distinctive features; but these features are nevertheless properties of ideas, not of things. In view of these considerations, it will be of advantage to abandon the concept of a thing and to substitute for it the idea of a configuration, meaning by this a mental configuration.

Under this interpretation a configuration is any unified pattern of experience. Configurations may be large or small; they may be elementary or composite; they may be generic or most specific and discrete. They may be vague and signify nothing more than "something"—which is to say that they may have uncertain, vacillating, fragmentary, or elusive characteristics. They may be nothing more than an organized setting or schema, such as is suggested by Bartlett.[1] But in all cases they are organized; their elements stand in certain definite relationships to each other so that they make up a whole that is configurated by an arrangement of its parts.

Configurations are as varied in character as are human experiences involving organization. They can entail the ideas of things, of people, of ideas, or of the self, or of groups of things, ideas, and people. They may take an infinitude of forms. They may represent things, in the conventional under-

[1] F. C. Bartlett, *Remembering. A Study in Experimental and Social Psychology*. New York: Cambridge University Press, 1932, pp. 201–202.

standing of that term, or groupings of things conceived as a configurated whole. They may be a rule or a principle or a theory. They may constitute a stereotype, or a dogma, or a belief that is organized on the basis of past experience. They are all normative thought patterns, even though they may have fluctuating and evolving limits. Although they may be changing and vague, they are standards of thought. They may be standardized for the individual only or for a social class or an ethnic group. Their relative character is indicated by their variation from individual to individual and from group to group. As norms they are systems of reference, datum points for the evaluation of incoming sense impressions. They mold and channelize these impressions, and they order the thought processes of the individual.

Basically, configurations are mental activity systems that are somehow the counterparts of external referents.[2] But any perceived quality of a thing is a *mental* composition. It is a configuration, an organization of lesser activity systems. Atoms acting in a specific way are known to us as redness, in another as blueness. Our ideas of color, brilliance, and temperature are mental compositions of imperceptible action systems external to ourselves that evoke comparable activities in our sensory apparatus. We compose sensory activities on another level. The same holds for our conceptions of hardness and permeability. The arrangement and organization, spatially and temporally, of these submicroscopic activities constitute the shape, which is the mental configuration of the thing. The patterned activities of these unsensed movements give what we call properties or qualities to some more inclusive entity. Certain organizations of atomic actions are so distinctive and important for configuration that we, by a process of abstraction, have given them names: edge, corner, surface, hole, pit, notch, bulge. More inclusive wholes also have names: spheres, squares, and tubes.

On a grosser level of analysis, combinations of configurations of lesser activity systems can similarly be organized into a larger configuration: the weight of a thing is a sensation that results from the perceptible activity of an observable whole; sound is the sensation of a demonstrable action by a distinguishable thing. As with colors and sizes, there are degrees of frequencies of these motions of gross wholes for which we have words, such as "pounds" and "tones." These words name movement patterns of supra-atomic wholes which can be sensed by touch and hearing.

[2] No answer is here sought or given to the question of what a configuration is in neurological terms. That problem is independent of our present concern with an analysis of the phenomenological characteristics of a configuration. Although majority opinion seems to run to the contrary, configurational theory is not committed to the thesis of isomorphism as that term is generally understood. There is no necessity to predicate a geometry of percepts or concepts which parallels or duplicates the geometry of the things which stimulate them. There is, in fact, much to be said against such a view, and configurational explanations are just as conformable with alternative theories of brain functioning.

Finally there are other activity systems that give properties to still more inclusive configurations. These movements are also patterned in conventional ways, such as up, down, north, and circular. For them, however, our nomenclature is limited. These action systems are so slow and ponderous that we can see them and define them geographically. We say, for example, that an object moves from A to B. The motions of the included configurations ("things") are so slow that they seem a part of the activity system to which we belong. Consequently their action systems do not impart qualities to larger wholes, unless we fixate our gaze and let them cross our field of vision —which is to say that their motion is permitted to have its sensory effect. It is obvious that a thing in motion is entirely different from what it is at rest. We endeavor to discover "what a thing really is" by attempting to nullify the effects of its motion. In effect we analyze the larger whole of which it is a part by devices for stopping its motion. The fact that we can do this makes it appear that gross objects, with relatively slow motion, are not parts of larger wholes. In nullifying their action we make them appear to be isolated and are aware of their movement as such. We do not think of them and their activities as properties of larger configurations. And yet there are borderline cases, sensed movements of things which impart qualities to larger wholes. The flight of an arrow appears as a streak; spinning propeller blades appear as gauzy circles; spinning colors have whole properties that are quite distinct from those of the individual configurations; a waving field of grain has the quality of an undulating surface that is something quite different in its whole properties from that of the individual grain stalks. The rapid pulsing, tapping, or oscillation of a thing can be so rapid that it presents a *surface* to the touch; and a form or configuration is experienced that has the quality of hardness which is quite distinct from any quality exhibited by the thing at rest. Similarly for the feel of a file drawn through the fingers or the sound of a ratchet wheel whirling against the edge of a piece of cardboard.

A mentally organized group of what are otherwise considered to be distinct things can in the same way constitute a shape or a configuration on another level. Thus a ceremony or a football play can be said to have a shape or a configuration no less than the things that go to make it up. It is not the quality of the component things that imparts wholeness to the ceremony or to the football play, precisely as it is not the inert atoms that give redness or extension to an object; it is the sequence, the order and arrangement of the activities of the component things. Just as we could never know the qualities of objects except for the subsensory activities of atoms, so we could never have a ceremony or a football play without activity on a much grosser level.

Configurations, therefore, are made up of the activity systems of their component parts, the qualities of the configuration being distinctive to it and different from the qualities of its components. Whether, as in the case of a ceremony, we regard these large configurations as shapes or not is irrelevant. We may do so if we choose, for logically there can be shapes or configurations beyond the customary range of applicability of these terms.

Every configuration can be analyzed. It can be reduced to distinct configurations or subwholes within itself. Thus the concept of fatherhood has its component parts, just as does the idea of a table. Oppositely, every idea can be incorporated with other ideas as a subwhole in a larger configuration. The idea of a part is relative to the idea of the whole. A part is such only with reference to other parts. When perceived or conceived itself, it is a whole, a unit that is at that instant indivisible, with properties that pervade all of it. If it is analyzed, these whole properties disappear to be replaced by the properties of the individual components. Thus when we think of "family," we have in mind a whole entity with properties that are peculiar to it and distinct from the properties of "husband," of "wife," and of "child." When the focus of attention is directed to any one of these components, it is evident that it has characteristics peculiar to it that tell us nothing of the characteristics of a family. The components are parts in so far as we think of them in relation to each other; but with respect to themselves they are wholes which can in turn be analyzed into still lesser wholes, each with its own distinctive characteristics. Whether a conceptual unit is considered to be a part or a whole is dependent entirely upon our level of analysis.

The purpose of the preceding discussion is to emphasize the point that our experience can be organized in an infinite variety of ways. It is essential to understand this in order to appreciate what happens in innovation. The individual who analyzes the conventional configurations to which he and others have been accustomed so as to provide possibilities for new organizations takes the first and indispensable step in innovation. In order to understand the innovative process, we must be prepared to analyze ideas in any fashion and without limit, even to the point of absurdity, so that we may follow the ramifications of recombination as they actually occur. We cannot deal with the gross stereotyped wholes of conventional thought only. If we are to gain insight into innovative reconstructions, we must treat conventional ideas, such as those of tables and men, merely as more or less stable organizations of experience that can be torn down and reassembled in the wink of an eye.

In all the sciences we have come to expect very detailed analyses of data for purposes of classification. This lead, however, has not been followed by students of invention. In the main, they have continued to deal with stereotyped conceptions and with "things" as they are ordinarily conceived. While in comparative studies we are prepared to take the greatest care to examine things for their differences or similarities, in trying to understand inventions it is common practice to deal with such gross units as automobiles and buggies or power looms and spinning wheels. The attempt to understand one of these complex wholes in terms of the whole of another will give us no insight into their true relationships. We must view the inception of each one in terms of a detailed analysis of its component parts.

The linguists long ago recognized this necessity, and students of linguistic change do not hesitate to break down sentences, words, parts of words, and parts of these parts. They have analyzed the mechanics of human speech in great detail and have shown how one sound production process can become another because of their near relationship. Most significantly, they have tied up linguistic processes with mental processes. They have insisted that vocabulary and grammar are inherent in human thinking. They have therefore been able to enunciate certain laws and probabilities of linguistic change. Their microscopic analyses are likely to appear trivial to the person who is interested in tracing the evolution of human transportation or technology; but it must be stressed that theirs is the only means of arriving at an understanding of these larger consequences. There is no short cut to this end that will yield a real understanding of the innovative processes. The approach must inevitably involve a preoccupation with minutiae. The linguists are very much aware that the data of human experience are not organized according to any natural law but are configurated by the mental mechanism of the perceiver. They appreciate the importance of thought categories in defining the units of experience, so much so that they insist that people see things in terms of their linguistic conceptualizations. This view is entirely in harmony with the one that was expressed a few paragraphs above.

All in all, there can be no question that linguists are far ahead of the rest of us in their understanding of the mechanics of cultural change. We can learn much from them, and we can make comparable advances if we adopt their approach. This is the more certain because language is after all an aspect of culture; and there is no reason why in other areas of culture another kind of reality should prevail.

The importance of detailed analysis for the problem of innovation should be evident from the fact that any configuration, whether it represents a thing or an abstraction, has a multiplicity of characteristics and hence a great number of potentialities for combination. In any particular context only a limited number and kind of values and qualities are significant. Only one of the innumerable qualities of a thing may be relevant and effective. This is one reason why discovery and innovation are difficult. The quality that is potentially effective in another context is latent within the existing context. Experimentation is a technique for discovering potentials by the controlled nullification or elimination of irrelevancies. Insight consists in discovering new potentialities that can be made manifest in other configurations.

When a configuration is analyzed, its parts are recognized as being bonded together by specific relationships. They, in fact, give distinctness to the parts. They are also essential to a configuration while it is a whole; they give it shape. They are infinitely varied in their nature, as varied as the human mind can conceive. It is important to realize that they are of human origin; they are mental constructs. They are the guides for the organization of experience. They occur in all dimensions. A part may be conceived to be related to its associates spatially: it is above them, or to the left of them, or to the north of them. Or two parts may be temporally bonded (*A* precedes *B*), or ordinally combined (*A* is second to *B*), or comparatively related (*A* is heavier or better or more costly than *B*). There are innumerable other broad categories of relationships, including the genetic (*A* generates *B*), the causal (*A* initiates *B*), the correlative (*A* varies with *B*), the incorporative (*A* is one of *B*), and the attitudinal (*A* inspires a mental set on the part of *B*). In addition to being numerous themselves, each of these relationship dimensions has an indeterminate range of nuances and inflections within the area of its applicability: *A* is beside, just under, slightly ahead of, substantially equal to, proportionally better than, reputedly the progenitor of *B*. Furthermore, the relationship between two associates may be characterized by a complex variability, either within one dimension or as a result of an interplay of more than one.

Some of the most routine experiences of our lives involve very complex interdependencies of relationships among the correlates of unitary phenomena: the relationship of an axle to a wheel, of a child to its father, of a needle eye to the needle shaft, of trousers to a man's body. We have a very much underdeveloped terminology to express all these possibilities and permutations, and the mere attempt to verbalize them has awkward and often ridiculous results. The main reason for this inadequacy is that there is no need for an elaborate terminology except in discourses such as the present one. We grasp relationships, even though we do so impressionistically or intuitively; we take them into account in our every act, even though it is impossible for us to characterize them. Behavioristically they are present. They must be, in order for us to function at all. Certainly the innovator must be aware of them even though he does not conceptualize them. In describing what he does it is unlikely that we can do better in characterizing them than he does. Nevertheless we must make them as explicit as possible and, in any event, lay stress upon their importance by giving them a prominent place in our analysis.[3]

The preceding outline must be taken as a minimum for an understanding of what follows. It is impossible to do justice to a conceptual framework such as this in a few paragraphs, but a more thorough discussion in this place would be distractive. The interested reader will find an exposition of the theoretical orientation sketched above in the Appendix.

[3] Cf. C. Spearman, *The Nature of "Intelligence" and the Principles of Cognition.* London: Macmillan & Co., Ltd., 1923, Chaps. 5 and 6.

Recombination. Above it was said that an innovation is due to the hybridization or cross-referencing of two preexisting configurations. By this it is meant that what was formerly a part of one configuration has been united with what was formerly a part of the other to form a new configuration with properties distinct from those of either of the two preexistent wholes. It may further an understanding of this process if we schematize the basic situation with the simple diagram in Figure 1.[4] In it AB represents one of the configurations involved in innovation. It is a recognized unit of

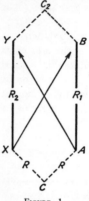

FIGURE 1

some description, such as the idea of a table or the idea of a family. As long as it remains a unit, it is without parts; but as a prelude to its inventive recombination, it must be analyzed into its parts A and B. When this happens, inevitably some relationship will be perceived between parts A and B. In the diagram this relationship, whatever it may be, is symbolized by R_1. The other configuration, XY, is similarly conceived, so that at the moment of analysis its two components stand in some relationship, symbolized in the diagram by R_2. This latter relationship may or may not be the same as R_1; very commonly they are different. When innovation takes place, X is combined with B in the relationship R_1 or R_2; or A is combined with Y in the relationship R_1 or R_2; or X is combined with Y in the relationship R_1; or A is combined with B in the relationship R_2. These six patterns are basic, although they have variants and complications to be noticed later. One or another of them appears to be fundamental to any innovation.

The foregoing possibilities, and others, are not randomly conceived. Neither are they always, or even commonly, arrived at by a rational or deliberate manipulation of the variables through all their possible permutations. Quite often the new combination is made spontaneously; in other cases it is the result of calculated explorations. Sometimes the new idea has an instantaneous birth; it comes with a "flash of insight" or a "flight of the imagination." Just which innovative combination will occur depends upon the characteristics of XY and AB as they are apprehended and interpreted by the innovator. His inventive reorganization of these data rests upon three intimately related but distinct processes that will be treated under the headings of identification, substitution, and discrimination.

[4] In order to avoid misunderstanding, it may not be amiss to emphasize that this figure is neither a sketch of a configuration nor a charting of an innovative brain process. It is not a picture or a map of anything. Like the other figures which follow, it is nothing more than a model that has been devised as a visual aid in the exposition of some rather complicated material.

Identification. Granting that XR_1B, or AR_1Y, or XR_1Y is an innovation, what then? If the joining of X and B is a chance phenomenon, as is so often believed, we are little ahead in our attempts to understand the process. The question that we need to answer is why precisely XY and not some other configuration has been brought into conjunction with AB and crossed with it. Why not *any* two configurations? The answer is that X can be combined with B when X and A are regarded as equivalent. Conversely, A can be united with Y, if Y and B are considered to be equals. The two configurations, XY and AB, are brought into conjunction in the mind of the innovator either by design or by accident. Their juxtaposition may be the result of a deliberate search for correspondences, but in the majority of cases their coming together is spontaneous and without premeditation as far as the innovator is concerned. In any event, unless X is perceived to be similar to A, or Y similar to B, there can be no contacts between the two configurations and there will be no possibility of cross combination.

At this point we are confronted with a paradox. It is evident that equivalents are interchangeable. If X is the "same thing" as A, there is no reason why it cannot be combined with B in the same way that A is. Indeed, this happens all the time. But what is there that is new about it? How can the result be an invention? Obviously it cannot be, if X is indubitably identical with A. But here is the crux of the problem. Can any two things ever be identical? And are there not various kinds and degrees of similarity, with different individual interpretations of them? What are to be the criteria for assessing equivalence? Clearly this is a fertile area for interpretation and reinterpretation, and unquestionably maneuverings in it are crucial for innovation. In fact, interpretations of equivalence make the difference between ideas that are judged to be routine and those that are called innovative. Moreover, there is an unbroken continuity in judgments on this issue, a continuum ranging from assumed identity to complete difference, that makes for degrees of newness and puts innovation in its proper place as simply one manifestation of a normal and routine mental function. Throughout this study it has been emphasized that in innovation we are not dealing with something *sui generis*. This is one of the fundamental reasons why. Innovation does not draw upon some special mental faculty or process; it is a term used to cover an arbitrary range of recombinations at one end of a continuous series.

The problem now has a different complexion. The X and the A of our diagram occur at different times and places in our experience. They are independent of each other; they have different correlates, Y and B. We want to know how the present experiencing of one of them can lead to the reexperiencing of the other. As stated above, their identification is essential; but the differences between them raise questions about how this can be done.

There are three ways in which the gap between X and A can be bridged. One is direct. We may call it the axiomatic method. It utilizes generally accepted truths about identities; that is, the two subwholes X and A are recognized as being equivalent by convention. This means that X and A are parts of another configuration; they are subwholes of a third and independent configuration that are bonded by the relationship of sameness or similarity. We shall consider the genesis of such configurations of equivalence later. At the moment they can be taken as given, because they are so accepted by the innovator and other people as well. Configurations of equivalence exist in all cultures in large numbers. They are traditionally accepted equations of various kinds and modes. Their existence establishes the rather poorly defined and fluctuating limits of classes of things.

Every people have such a taxonomy of their experience, as indeed they must have, for it is impossible for any being to treat every part of its experience as discrete and utterly different from every other part. The discrete entities comprised within the concept of "child," "adult," "clock," "love," "jealousy," and so on are regarded as equivalent within their categories despite their individual differences. Symbols, too, are an important kind of equivalents. Sometimes they are of the same order as the things for which they stand. Frequently, though, they are on a different ideological level; words, for example, may stand for things, and gestures may stand for abstract ideas.

Conventional equivalences are recognized only with reference to specific contexts. They are not universally and absolutely valid. Men and women may be recognized as equivalent in the family situation, but not in a political or a labor context. A father may be the equivalent of his son as far as legal responsibility is concerned, but not otherwise. Sons and daughters may be regarded as equivalent in point of property inheritance, but in other respects they may be treated as quite different in accordance with dictates regarding sexual differences. A clock is the same as a watch for purposes of keeping time, but otherwise they have numerous connotations and associations that differentiate them. Likewise with symbols: one cannot indiscriminately equate a thing and the name for it because they have different properties. The thing itself is used in the context of other things, whereas names are used for purposes of communication, that is, in the context of other words. It is possible, of course, to make a more complete equation of a thing and the name for it in the specific context of communication. One may demonstrate or display a thing in place of using words for it or vice versa. But this still does not make them universally and at all times equivalent.

The relativity of equivalence is an important consideration in innovation. It establishes the limits of sameness with reference to any given correlate of a thing, idea, or behavior. If X is traditionally equal to A in so far as A's relationship to B is concerned, then there is nothing novel about relating X

to B in the same fashion. If B is a person seeking to know (R_1) the time, a watch (X) is as serviceable and appropriate as a clock (A), his usual referent for this purpose. On the other hand, if he is looking for a weapon, the clock's range of equivalents would only doubtfully include a watch.

The resort to equations presumes that configurations of similarity are already available to an innovator. Since they already exist, their employment does not in itself create a new combination. They do nonetheless play an important part in innovation because they make the first step possible. A linkage of equivalence between X and A provides a ready-made bridge between them, which means, psychologically, that the thought of one can arouse the thought of the other. They are associated because of their similarity. Questions relating to the origins of this linkage are fundamental, and they pose a very complex problem that has not been adequately treated. It will be discussed here as the indirect method of linking X with A by means of *analysis* and *incorporation*.

The question now becomes: How can two things come to be regarded as the same when they have heretofore been treated as different? How is an ideological bridge established between X and A when they have not been previously configurated by the relationship of similarity? The answer that is accepted here emerges from an interpretation of experimental data that is too involved to be presented in a general work. It is frankly theoretical, but it has much to recommend it beside the clarification that it gives to the problem of innovation. The theory of innovation and the theory of sameness are independent, however; the one may be accepted or rejected without prejudice to the other.

Summarized, the relevant part of the theory of sameness is as follows. No two things are ever exactly the same, yet we constantly treat variants as if they were identical. The fact that we have group names for things and react to a range of particulars as if they were the same is evidence that we are constantly equating the data of our experience by overlooking the differences which inevitably occur among them. Our common treatment of the many different objects that we call pencils means that we ignore the innumerable variations among them and disregard the quantitative and qualitative changes that they individually undergo by the minute and the hour.

Perfect identities are impossible. But some pairs of things are admittedly more different than others. We are able to draw this distinction because those that we regard as the same have some element in common. In the pronouncement of sameness this common factor is prepotent. Its existence is sufficient to override such differences as are inevitably there. Concentration upon the common factor enables us for the moment, and for given contexts, to ignore differences. Often they are not even perceived. The whole of the one configuration is equated with the whole of the other on the basis of their partial similarity. Under these circumstances, the equation of selected parts takes precedence over the segregation of disregarded parts.

This characterization may be accepted as a common-sense view of sameness, but a psychological justification is needed to give it standing as something more than a logical construct or a guess. The idea maintained here is that before one configuration can be equated with another, some part of a present stimulus configuration must revive the part-in-common that it has with a memory record organized by an antecedent experience. Contact with this "trace-part" of a previous experience may be made either by a sensory stimulation or by the "trace-part" of one previous experience activating the common part of another previous experience. In other words, a configuration may be evoked either by some extant sensory stimulus or by a memory stimulus. In any event the aroused configuration is functionally present; the "trace" is reactivated.

It is further assumed that the reactivation of the "trace-part" of a previously experienced configuration will, under given conditions, lead to the reinstatement of the whole of the previously experienced configuration in such a way as to make it seem to be actually present in the stimulus field. A stimulus is converted or metamorphosed into something that it is not because it is assumed to be identical with the reactivated, mentally existent configuration. The conditions under which this falsification can take place are multiple; they depend upon the mental set of the individual, as defined by his attitude, his intention, and his instant orientation, as well as upon the characteristics of the stimulus situation. In addition, and fundamental to this conception, is the requirement that the activating common part bear with it, as an inherent aspect of itself, its relationship to the other part of the stimulus configuration. This is essential because the relationship gives the part its distinctness; the activating common part can be an entity only if it is set off from its context by the relationship that it bears to this context. Furthermore, concentration upon the common part of the stimulus makes possible the obliteration of the rest of it, namely, its differences from the previously experienced configuration. The requirement that the activating common element bear its relationship with it limits the possibilities for its contacting a previously established configuration, for the assumption is that it can reactivate only those elements having the same relation to their contexts. In short, common parts must have common relationships to their contexts in order for one to activate the other. The differences between the contexts are ignored, the recalled context taking precedence over the disregarded context of the stimulus.

The aroused trace-part-in-relation is energized, not only in the sense that it is again actually present, but also because it is dynamic in itself. It is unstable because of its incompleteness. Its open-ended character sets up stresses that impel the automatic restoration of its context, that part or those parts with which it has been related in the past. In other words, there is a strong impetus for the revived "trace-part" to recall its correlate or associate. The whole of a previous experience is reinstated as a synthesized unit, without parts, by a process which may be called redintegration.[5] Redintegration will not always take place, especially if there are other intrusive stimuli, but for recognition to take place, it must. It must also occur if an identification is to be made between the thing present and the thing recalled.

The result of redintegration is that a memory record, or a "trace," of a previous configuration is restored in its entirety by the stimulation of part of it by a present experience. Consequently that which is inwardly experienced is referred to that which is only partially presented, with the conclusion of sameness being consciously or unconsciously drawn. The conclusion of sameness thus rests upon an individual's disregard of the context of the stimulus common part, which disregard enables him to equate the whole of an extant stimulus with the whole of a previous one. There is consequently always some falsification in identification, whether it is realized or not. Often this error is spontaneous and unwitting, but it may be the result of deliberate effort. Sometimes it is never realized that there has been falsification. At other times reexaminations and reevaluations are made that disclose discrepancies. These rechecks may be ignored or passed off as inconsequential, or they may lead to a rejection of the first suggestion of identity. Reevaluations are prompted when suggestions of identity are contested and also by situations that demand rigorous methods of analysis and classification.

It has been said that no two configurations are ever absolutely identical, yet a common factor is perceived in all cases when a conclusion of sameness is reached. Since a common part implies a partial identity to start with, it would seem that a contradiction is involved. Logically there is, but functionally there is not. Resolution of the dilemma lies in the fact that sameness is always relative to the level of analysis. As we have seen, configurations are made up of mental-activity systems that are bonded by definite relations. That is to say, *analytically* this is so. But while they are configurations, and as long as they are such, they are without parts, elements, or relations. They are undifferentiated, unitary, homogeneous masses of activities. A good example is the musical chord, which, as long as it is a chord, is utterly different from its component tones. It does not even have tones until it is analyzed. Indeed, one cannot say that it is a synthesized whole until this is done; otherwise it is an elementary phenomenon. Furthermore, it is not a unit itself unless it is perceived as a part in relation within a larger configuration. In analysis the moment a relationship is conceived between constituent elements within a configuration, the latter dissolves, and the component parts appear as

[5] This term has been borrowed from Hollingworth and others, though they do not interpret the process that it describes as I do. H. L. Hollingworth, *Psychology: Its Facts and Principles*. New York: Appleton-Century-Crofts, 1928, pp. 4 and 5.

wholes-plus-relations. Then if these subwholes become the focus for further analysis, they too disintegrate into their elements-plus-relations, and their properties as wholes disappear. Thus, the unitary common factor at one level of analysis always turns out to be a complex with elements of dissimilarity at another level.

If two objects are recognized as tables because each has four legs and a flat top, this does not mean that their legs and tops are identical. But at the level of integration which yields the concept "table," legs and tops are without parts. They are taken to be identical. It is as if they were; and for all immediate purposes they are. They are unitary and undifferentiated wholes bonded together by certain relationships that make a table. Now, if attention is directed to their parts-in-relation, there is no table; it has dissolved under the analysis of *its* parts. If then the tops, corners, and tenons of legs are analyzed into their parts, not only has the table disappeared, but also the percept and concept of "leg." In its place are certain leg characteristics, such as the space relations of its parts that make up the concept of roundness or squareness. And at that level, leg may be equated with leg, but not table with table. The dissolution of more inclusive configurations with a progressive analysis of their parts and subparts becomes the more obvious the more intensive or detailed the analysis. If, for example, table legs are analyzed to determine their material composition, all concept of table, leg, and roundness is lost. In microscopic or near-microscopic examinations we cannot see a table or its legs or even think of them within the framework of that level of analysis. Each individual part of any configuration has its own qualities when isolated and considered in itself. When viewed as a part, along with other parts, they, all together and by their very arrangement, give other qualities to the more inclusive whole.

Common factors, then, are to be perceived only at the level of analysis that leaves them unreduced to their elements. And nothing can be affirmed of their sameness or difference at this level. At the instant of their functioning as units, they are merely mechanical activators or inducers on a physiological level unmediated by configurational processes. In order for us to apprehend anything about them they in turn must be analyzed. This is a necessary prelude to the judgment of their sameness, just as it is necessary to an understanding of what they are.

Sameness, then, is between wholes, not between their parts, though it is the parts that are replaceable. Paradoxical as this is, it is a fact well appreciated in practice, as is the case when we interchange the parts of standardized contrivances or replace the worn-out parts of a machine. If we observe the letters *B* and *R*, we may find that they are the same to the extent that they have a common part which approximates the configuration of the letter *P*. This makes *B* and *R* similar. But on this level of analysis we must take the over-all characteristics of *P* as a whole and ignore such differences as would appear upon a closer analysis of those two parts of B and R that correspond to it in this first judgment. If one sees a cow in a pasture, the whole configuration may seem familiar to a previous scene because a cow is common to both experiences; but nothing can be said of the sameness of the two animals involved unless and until the stimulus "cow" is analyzed and related through the mediation of some common part with a previous experience called "cow." The conclusion, impression, or conscious acceptance of similarity equates the whole of one stimulus report with the whole of the record of another through the mechanism of redintegration.

If we relate this discussion to the diagram of Figure 1, it will be evident that, if X cannot be directly identified with A because of a preexisting configuration of similarity that makes the one the equivalent of the other in a given context, then they must be analyzed so that a common factor appears to establish a connecting link over the gap that separates them. This common factor is symbolized in the diagram by the letter C. In conformance with the requirement discussed above, it will be noted that C bears the same relationship R to both X and A. If, then, X can be analyzed so that it contains a C that is likewise discoverable in A, and if the relationship is likewise conceived as identical, it will be possible for the part stimulus C of CX to reinstate the unit CA. In consequence, CA is taken to be CX. There has been, so to speak, a convergent analysis of X and A.

The possibility of making such analyses is ever present, and it is constantly being realized in the thinking of everyone. However, some configurations are more resistant to analysis because of group conventions that reiterate their stability. Some configurations, called "things," seem to bear witness to their absolute unity and distinctness, whereas other configurations seem tenuous and more loosely bound together. This, however, is a relative matter that depends very much upon individual point of view and purpose and upon group conventions. There is a tendency to suppose that things are more tightly bonded together and more resistant to analysis than are groups of things. Offhand one might think also that things are more coherent and therefore more resistant to analysis than are nonthings like movements, behaviors, beliefs, and social groupings. In fact, these configurations often are not regarded as unitary phenomena at all. This is because "things" have density, mass, and therefore a boundary. It is also because they do physically cohere; that is to say, to the naked eye their parts are fixed in their relationships and are not subject to relationship variation, such as is a string of beads, a circle of chairs, a conventional seating arrangement, or a gesture. Nevertheless, it must be stressed again that it is with the *ideas* of all these phenomena that we have to deal, not with the things the ideas symbolize. And as far as their properties as ideas are concerned, all are the same. This means that parts of things are just as easy to reassociate mentally as are things themselves, given the innovative attitude toward them; and that means, fundamentally, a nontraditional view of them.

The cohesion of the parts of a mental configuration, and hence of the parts of their objective referents, is to a large extent culturally determined. This is manifestly true of artifacts, as well as of intangible forms of human creation. They are conceived and maintained in cohesion by the expectation and insistence that they shall be. There is a conviction that they are units. We customarily see things as wholes because this is the way that they have been presented to us. They are given names and in other ways are set apart by arbitrary conventions. This is true, though less obviously so, even of natural forms. Our very concept of "tree" is an arbitrary unit; it is arbitrary in its inclusiveness, in its boundary characteristics, in its size requirements, and in many other particulars. Our ideas of a "waterfall" are conventional, as will be recognized when it is noted that we accord it certain character- istics to distinguish it from other bodies of water. The same may be said for our definition of "snow" or "cow." In these latter instances there are people, such as the Eskimos and some African native groups, who make absolutely different categories of what we regard as variants falling within these single term designations.

Even though the cohesiveness of the ideas of things is reinforced by the physical properties of their objective referents, mental unifications of intan- gibles and action systems assert themselves with just as much inflexibility and with comparable feelings of naturalness. Even though their parts—such as the people in a behavior set, or a hand raised in a salute—may be only momentarily bonded in the physical sense, and may enter into innumerable other configurations, they remain as ideas-sets with a rigidity that is often extreme.

The identification of "things" by convergent analysis rests upon the ex- istence of what are generally called formal resemblances between them. Two segregated wholes have a property, an aspect, or a quality in common that leads to the judgment of their sameness within the context that is given. These characteristics are inherent in each of the two configurations. They must be abstracted by an analysis. This is a very common procedure, but there is an alternative to it that provides the same foundation for identifi- cation. This is what may be called convergent *incorporation*.

In incorporation, identification is made possible, not by breaking down two familiar wholes, but by building up two new ones so that they include a common denominator. This process provides a kind of a detour that ex- actly parallels the situation set up by analysis. Two distinct configurations, A and C of the diagram, that are otherwise recognized as discrete wholes become synthesized into a unit in which they become subwholes that are bonded by a specific relationship. At the same time, another pair of con- figurations, X and C, one of which is common to the first pair, is unified with the same bonding relationship between them. It will be evident that this yields the same situation as that which results from analysis and common-denominator abstraction. The configurations CX and CA are real units, but the fact that they are synthetic often makes them easier to analyze, an important consideration because this is a prerequisite to their identification as wholes. Very often their unity is frail and fleeting. Their unification may strike many people as highly artificial and not compelling, and it may be affirmed that such unifications are not "things" at all. In short, it is just as difficult and as novel to incorporate and synthesize as it is to analyze, and either result may appear to lack genuineness in the eyes of anyone except the innovator.

Synthetic wholes nonetheless have a real psychological justification. They are as real to their configurators as are other wholes, even though they may be physically very unstable because of the absence of physical and chemical bonds between their parts. At their inception they are only different sectionings of the flux of experience; they are alternate groupings of an undifferentiated continuum. Those that have been long established and accepted do not occasion doubts about their reality. Regroupings of *these* conventionalized syntheses may seem specious, but they are as real psychologically speaking as are those that are commonly accepted. A moment's thought will show that, although incorporations may be unconvincing at their inception, their parts can become as firmly bound together as can the parts of a thing. The absence of one of the subwholes that go to make them up can be just as unsatisfying as the absence of a part of a familiar thing. In both instances a partial presentation arouses a feeling of incompleteness and a straining toward fulfillment.

Many synthetic wholes are highly individualistic and remain so. Given a specific context, some people, for example, feel that they must have a cigarette with a cup of coffee; others appear to be convinced that fried chicken and mashed potatoes are inseparably bound together; and ladies of fashion feel only partly dressed when wearing gloves and not carrying a purse. And then there is the case of the woman who claims that she did not know that her neck and her ears were distinct parts of her anatomy until she was adolescent, because when she was a child her mother always washed her neckandears.

Many synthetics are solidified by custom. All the so-called adhesions and complexes spoken of by anthropologists and sociologists fall into this category. The universal custom of assigning different occupations to the sexes is a case in point. Throughout a large part of history the making of pottery with the aid of the potter's wheel has been a male occupation; metallurgy has had a similar history. In Palau the women farm the taro fields, while the men do the fishing; the two activities and their sexual associations are kept rigidly distinct. Food habits reveal similar unifications of discrete entities; the Chinese or the Hindu food complexes are quite distinct from those of the western European or the American. Implements and techniques for their use exhibit ethnically diverse combinations selected out of the total range of possibilities: the knife and fork of the American, the chopsticks and bowl of the Chinese; the needle and thread of the European seamstress, the awl and thread of many other people; the hoe-farming complex of much of Africa, and the plow-farming areas of Europe and Asia. Many linguistic associations constitute synthetic units: clichés and idiomatic expressions, such as "to and fro," "topsy turvy," "in the long run," and "by the way."

It is this phenomenon of incorporation that makes the context of a configuration so all-important for an understanding and evaluation of it. The association of a thing with its setting is often gradually and unwittingly formed; but it may be deliberately inculcated. We are all aware of the significance of this kind of synthetic association of things. An object will not seem the same to us if it is out of context, which is to say, when it is associated with something with which it customarily is not. Thus, we find that evening clothes are out of place in broad daylight or on a streetcar; one does not behave in the home of a friend as one does when relaxing in one's own household. We feel, as we say, that there is a time and a place for everything. The existence of these synthetics permits us to adhere to some curious contradictions in our ideology and behavior. Thus we can condone homicide during times of warfare when the victims are members of an enemy group, but not otherwise. We adhere to unwritten laws regarding theft and violence when there are, as we say, extenuating circumstances, the latter being appropriate contexts for the acts.

The importance of context is also evident in perception. An apple on a dish is "not the same thing" as an apple on a tree; a red traffic light is not the same as a theater exit light; a friend's face in a crowd of strangers may not even be recognized because of its unfamiliar setting. Feingold and others have pointed out how important the factor of background or setting can be in courtroom identifications. Evidence and persons presented there for recognition by witnesses have quite a different appearance than they have in the context of the events to which they relate. Hence stems the advisability of having witnesses revisit the scenes of crimes in order to minimize the possibility of unconscious falsifications of testimony.[6]

Often the unsuspected existence of a synthetic configuration in the mind of one person is puzzling, disconcerting, or frustrating to another. In these cases there is a conflict between differential syntheses of the total situation that is presented to the one individual and the other. This factor must be taken into account in psychological experiments on both animals and human

---

[6] Gustave A. Feingold, "The Influence of Environment in the Identification of Persons and Things," *Journal of Criminal Law and Criminology*, 1914, 5 (No. 1):47–48.

beings. Wary experimenters know that efforts must be made to keep every element in an experimental situation the same, except for those that are deliberately to be varied. Changed contexts have marked effects upon both perception and recall. Carr found in his experiments with rats that the rotation of their mazes, alterations in room illumination, and even a change of position by the experimenter had detrimental effects upon their learning potential.[7] In summarizing the results of experiments that bear upon this issue, Pan concludes that the recall of material is favored by the presence of an environmental factor which has some associative connections with that material, and in the absence of such an association the environmental situation is likely to be unfavorable to recall.[8] We shall see the importance of differential incorporation and its multiple possibilities in the matter of innovation when we come to discuss discrimination and acceptance.

Although convergent incorporation presents the same schematic picture as does convergent analysis and although it has the same potentialities for promoting identification, the two are psychologically quite different phenomena. The starting point in the identification process through incorporation is with one of the dissimilar subwholes, whereas it is with the common-denominator subwhole in the case of analysis. In terms of our diagram the stimulus point in the case of analysis is C; in the case of incorporation, it is X. In incorporation the sight of a pencil on a table may lead an observer to recall that he has previously seen a hat on the same table. The activator of this sequence is the pencil, and the bridge to the hat is "the same table." The subwhole of attention, the orientation point, is the pencil. In analysis, seeing *this* table (with a pencil on it) evokes the thought of *that* table, seen before with a hat on it. The initiator of this sequence is the common denominator of this and that table.

Convergent incorporation is not in itself adequate for an identification. It is rather a prelude to what is essentially an analysis. The latter is the direct approach to identification; incorporation is an indirect approach because analysis is required in addition to it. Analysis is disruptive in the sense that with it there is a divergence of configurations away from the common factor. In incorporation one configuration leads to the common factor and another away from it. The sequence is halted and, so to speak, "doubled back" on itself in order to make the identification.

Analysis is the basic and indispensable process, even though it may have to come after incorporation. We are not always aware that we are analyzing, even though we are constantly doing it. We observe wholes, and only infrequently are we conscious of their having parts. We do nonetheless habit-

[7] Harvey A. Carr, "Maze Studies with the White Rat," *Journal of Animal Behavior*, 1917, 7:271.

[8] Shuh Pan, "The Influence of Context upon Learning and Recall," *Journal of Experimental Psychology*, 1926, 9:490.

ually break up the materials of our experience. As Bartlett says, "although perceiving is rarely analytical or piecemeal in its method, yet it *is* a kind of analysis, since always there are some features of the perceptual situation which take a lead over the others. These dominant details are a kind of nucleus about which the rest cluster. They set the stage for remembering." [9]

The significance of incorporation as a mechanism for identification lies in the fact that it can establish what seems to be an equation between two totally dissimilar wholes—that is, dissimilar when they are considered alone and in themselves. As the term incorporation implies, the configurations that are established by this mechanism are artificial constructs, artificial in the sense that their subwholes are not physically bonded and bounded. For this reason an explicit demonstration, an argument, or a rationalization on the part of the conceiver is often required to convince others of their acceptability as true units. Incorporation binds together previously unconnected wholes, and these traditional groupings do not easily lose their identities in a larger configuration in the minds of most people. Because of their physical detachability, they tend to maintain their isolation and distinctiveness. This is especially true when the wholes are things, configurations with objective referents that have easily distinguishable boundaries. The reason for the difficulty in accepting proposed equations of synthesized configurations is that the focus of attention is upon the dissimilar subwholes and not upon the incorporated and detachable common factor. The connection between the dissimilar things and the common ingredient has the appearance of having been manufactured; and the existence of the common factor, although admittedly there, seems to be extraneous to the issue of similarity. It is relatively easy to apprehend by analysis that a hat seen with a feather on it yesterday is the same as the hat seen today with a veil on it and to get general agreement on this point, with a tacit appreciation that "details" are inconsequential. On the other hand, it is not so easy to perceive that a *feather*-with-a-hat-attached-to-it is the same as a *veil*-with-that-hat-attached-to-it, or to get support for the view, because in this case the focus of attention is upon two different things, feather and veil.

Incorporation brings out clearly a consideration that has been stressed previously and one which is only vaguely appreciated in analysis; namely, that it is not the subwholes that are judged to be the same. It is the undifferentiated wholes into which they are fused that are equivalent. Whole qualities are the critical consideration in identification, even though these can be appreciated only by analysis. It is not X that is equivalent to A; it is CX as a whole that is equivalent to CA, and at the moment of the judgment of sameness they are apperceived as complete and undivided. To revert to the above illustration, it is not feather that is equated with veil, but

[9] Bartlett, *op. cit.*, p. 32.

feather-on-hat with veil-on-hat. It is obvious that, if these configurations can be equated at all, their differences have to be ignored; and there are always such differences. But it is easier to ignore them when they are not the stimulus points, the focus of attention. It is therefore easier for the analyst to gather conviction for his identification than for the incorporator to do so. But in reality both must do the same thing; they must equate wholes, not parts.

In identification by incorporation, as in analysis, any kind of relationship may function. The bonding relationship R of our diagram can be of any description, including all those modes or dimensions and their qualitative and quantitative variations that have been previously mentioned. And similarly, any kind of mental representation can serve as the common factor C. It can be specific or general, very inclusive or very restricted. It can be the total environment, or some aspect of it; it can be the setting or the ground for X and A, or some particular element in this total environmental field. It can be an abstract or generic idea of which X and A are specific manifestations, *i.e*, X and A may be members of a category of things. Serving as the common factor may be what we are inclined to call the meaning of X and A, for it will be appreciated upon reflection that meaning is not any special or mystical attribute of ·a thing, or a vaporous halo about it. "Meaning" is the term that we give to the associations of a thing, the other ideas with which it has specific relationships. A thing does not have meaning in isolation, only in context. It has significance only in terms of some larger configuration of which it is a part. Its "partness" gives it meaning. A thing may have an indefinite number of meanings depending upon the number of associates that it has in the mental field. It is for this reason that synonyms can be substituted; they are identified because the synthetic wholes of which they are parts include a common referent which is their meaning. The opposite is the case with homonyms because their linkage is due solely to formal resemblances; if they are to be identified, they must be analyzed—as they are, in what we call confusion or error.

Identification by convergent incorporation is what is generally termed a confusion of differences. It might just as well be called equation on a basis of common meaning. It strikes us as quite different from common-denominator analysis because of the overriding considerations of form. But there is no difference in the end result. Neither is there any difference mentally speaking between a synthetic configuration and one that has been analyzed. It is as justifiable to consider a thing *and* its meaning or other context as having form, shape, boundaries, and properties as it is to think of qualities only in connection with some physical isolate. That we typically do not so consider them is again a comment upon the impress of our concept of thingness. The reader will find an elaboration of this idea in the Appendix.

The real adhesive between the member parts of any configuration is habituation. The innovator is the person who either consciously or unconsciously reconfigurates the conventional associations that are known and accepted by his group. His rearrangements are dissociative from the standpoint of tradition. They are extrusive or extrapolative; they diverge from the associative sequences of the customary thought responses to a given stimulus. They take off on their own divergent course from a point which until then has been embedded, hidden, or so firmly integrated in one context that the thought of it almost automatically leads to the thought of that context only.

As far as analysis is concerned, disruptive potentialities are compounded of two ingredients in the mental functioning of the innovator: his analytical capabilities and his resource potential. In practice these two factors are not to be differentiated. Analysis and recombination are mutually dependent; one cannot take place without the other; they are merely two aspects of the same phenomenon. But it is clear that each factor has its own degree of variability, its own limits, and its own conditions.

With respect to analytical potential, the following observations are relevant. Some people are more capable than others of analyzing configurations that are customarily regarded as irreducible. Sometimes these wholes are as familiar to the innovator as to his associates and have been accepted as units by him until the moment of his fresh insight. Sometimes they are unfamiliar to him, their unitary character having been established and maintained by a group of which he is not a member. More accurately speaking, it should be said that the innovator's analytical potential depends upon his freedom to make some noncustomary analysis, because any reaction to a stimulus field involves some kind of organization of it. Even in recognition the implied attribution of sameness is dependent upon analysis. The point is that the analysis of the innovator has a new orientation; in it there is a different starting point or a different slicing of experience. The percept, concept, or memory record that is the activator for his response is interpreted in a new way, which means that it arouses a different configuration in his mind.

The boundaries between what is judged to be an old and a new analysis have no objective referents. They are determined solely by popular consensus. Individual interpretations are constantly shifting and wavering around a norm. The conventional boundaries, if they can be said to exist, are elastic, with many individual excursions of doubtful status. Instead of boundaries there is more accurately speaking a zone of idiosyncratic departures, many of which are only dubiously accepted, if at all. Beyond this zone of uncertainties, there are the clear-cut departures that are novel by common acclaim or disclaim.

The resources of an individual are intimately linked up with his analytical ability in the over-all measurement of his innovative potential. He must have available some configuration that will make his new analysis significant. His point of departure in his analysis must connect with some divergent association; some configuration must intrude to interrupt the customary redintegrative pattern that is contingent upon the revival of the common factor. The common factors are pivots or switches; and the intersecting configurations, brought together either by analysis or incorporation, are alternative courses for the redintegrative process. The more of these alternative courses that there are at a person's disposal and the more flexible the switches at their junctions, the more likely will he be to think of some new combination. Hollingworth exemplifies these prerequisites by the use of letter configurations. He says,[10]

Consider the contexts *ABCDE, ABCDF, ABCHJ, ABKLM, AMNOP*, and the constituent details [*i.e.*, the letters] which as parts might function symbolically for them. If so slight a cue as *A* is adequate, it may function for any or all five of these contexts. The system [*i.e.*, the individual] to whom *A* occurs, as effective antecedent, thus has a rich array of consequents, or varied combinations, which may be evoked. For we have seen that consequents simultaneously evoked may combine according to their various compatibilities. The resultant of such combination is thus likely to be novelty, originality, initiative.

If, however, so subtle a cue as *A* alone is inadequate, some larger constellation of details is required for any consequent to occur. Thus if *ABC* is required, only three; and if *ABCD* is required, only two, of the past contexts will be represented. The completely unimaginative or literal minded individual will require the whole of some one pattern, and his repertoire of response will be limited to the duplication of some previous action. Novelty, originality, will be missing.

While all this is certainly true, a multiplicity of available configurations is not the critical measure of innovative ability. Even if few convergent configurations are available and even if there is no great diversity among them, a person may still create striking departures from familiar patterns. He will not be so prolific as some other individuals; but he can be radical, even without trying to be so.

As the last statement implies, analysis or incorporation is at times accomplished with effort; at least, it happens with awareness or by design. Consequently we speak of inventive insight. With reference to analysis we mean by this that the innovator has been able to abstract common denominators. This abstraction is a most critical accomplishment in cultural elaboration. As Thorndike has said, the progress of knowledge is far less a matter of acquaintance with more and more situations in the world than it is a matter of insight into the constitution and relations of long familiar

[10] Hollingworth, *op. cit.*, pp. 283–284.

ones.[11] In a similar vein William James has defined genius as the capacity to see similarities in a background of diversities, because under certain conditions it is extremely difficult for a person to perceive similarity in diversity. Often this difficulty is due to the composition of the objective field. Secret codes and camouflage take advantage of this fact. It is well known, too, that the position of a common element in two configurations has a bearing upon the possibility of its being recognized. Yum, for example, found that when nonsense syllables were employed in recognition tests, the likelihood of recall varied with the locus of the common letters.[12] The essential factor here, of course, is the difference in relationship of a common letter in the learning context and in the test situation. Feingold has attempted to show that the ability to discover common ingredients is dependent upon their quantity or extent in proportion to their context. He maintains, with doubtful justification, that the common element must amount to at least 20 per cent of the whole if identification is to take place.[13] It is doubtful whether quantity as such has much to do with this question, because as we have seen this is merely a matter of the level of analysis. The real difficulty in abstracting common elements arises from their multiple and diverse aspects, hence from the arbitrary character of their definition and the almost infinite possibilities they offer for reconfiguration.

Incorporation at times also requires deliberate effort, because of the already mentioned fact that conventionally recognized wholes do not readily yield their identity to larger wholes. Customary realities are adamant, even though they be made up of intangibles. Even ideas such as "democracy" and "slavery" take on all the certainty of things.

The character of the objective field, then, is a factor determining the facility with which it can be reorganized. At the same time, this is just as much a matter of the attitude of the observer. His orientation toward the stimulus field, his emotional involvement with it, and his incentive in considering it are all directive forces. His orientation may be determined by internal conditions or by external circumstances. It may be conditioned by instruction or by requirements, such as the task attitude in the laboratory, or by other coercives in ordinary life situations. Gottschaldt has shown, however, that there are limitations upon the possibilities for a directed organization of a stimulus field. His experiments indicate that a search attitude will

[11] Edward L. Thorndike, *Educational Psychology*. New York: Columbia University Press, 1913, Vol. 2, p. 27.

[12] K. S. Yum, "An Experimental Test of the Law of Assimilation," *Journal of Experimental Psychology*, 1931, 14:79.

[13] Gustave Feingold, "Recognition and Discrimination," *Psychological Monographs*, 1915, 18 (No. 2):87–88.

reveal hidden figures but only within certain limits imposed by the characteristics of the data of experience.[14]

Effort may also have a bearing upon the intellectual resources available to an innovator. Some people are, as we say, more imaginative than others. They have a wealth of mental associations that occur to them upon stimulation. Some individuals are predisposed to experience imagery, others cognitive material, others kinesthetic. At any rate there are individual differences in richness of association. It is true, too, that the mental inventory of any individual has blind spots. Some of his associations will be incomplete, or he may experience poorly defined or vaguely formulated ideas or connections. These gaps in his resources may be due to misunderstandings, faulty memory, previsions of needs not yet realized, and many other disabilities. No one is completely facile in calling up recollections and connections with past experiences.

Individual differences in availability of materials may be due to a cultivated mental habit, as appears in the contrast between the undisciplined mind and that of the scientist, the professional inventor, and specialists in other fields. With these last three groups the greater availability of alternate and divergent configurations is due to past effort, to training, to education, and to observation; it is also due to present effort in the form of alertness and tenacity in reviewing and marshaling data of past experience.

It is evident, then, that an exploratory, analytical mental set or a unifying incorporative associative tendency is an aid to reconfiguration; but it is just as certain that these attitudes are not prerequisites for it. Many analyses and incorporations are made spontaneously, without effort or design. Very often, in fact commonly, they are effected unwittingly and without the desire to do so. The so-called projective tests of psychologists are sufficient evidence of this. Such effortless reconstructions may be conditioned by an undisciplined, relaxed mental set or by conflicting aims that result in what we call mistakes. They may also be conditioned by the frame of reference that is foremost in the mind of the observer at the moment of his interpretation. Some of these frames of reference are quite personal; they are established by the fears, hopes, doubts, and other emotional complications within the individual.

The importance of such orientations is very evident in the way in which individual Shakers have interpreted the meaning of their religion. One ardent member is something of a philosopher, and he consistently gives a mystical interpretation to the historical events that have marked the development of the cult. Another individual has had quite a bit of Christian train-

---

[14] K. Gottschaldt, "Über den Einfluss der Erfahrung auf die Wahrnehmung von Figuren. I," *Psychologische Forschung,* 1926, 8:261–317.

ing and is literate. He interprets the same facts in the light of Biblical accounts and pronouncements. One of the earliest converts was frustrated in
his desire to become a shaman. For him Shakerism was merely another way
to achieve this goal; he said, "A good Christian man is a good medicine
man." Another individual, a Yakima Indian, has compounded this conviction with anxiety and suspicion toward most of his fellows. He finds evil all
around him in unsuspected quarters and spends all his time casting out
the devil. He has only an incidental interest in the dogma and the ritual
of the cult. He never goes to church but travels constantly from one reservation to another, curing the sick.

Frames of reference are also important in understanding the sectionings
of experience that are typical of groups of individuals. Bartlett noticed that
the subjects he used in his experiments on remembering made interpretations and reconfigurations of their materials under the influence of the wartime anxieties then prevalent in England.[15] As another example, it may be
noted that certain features of the innovations in Shakerism derive from the
fact that it is a religious cult. The essential processes are the same within
this frame of reference; but because it is a religious phenomenon, the changes
that have taken place have been anchored upon certain presuppositions. To
be specific, the sanction for changes is alleged to be divine; consequently
visions suggesting modifications are taken to be charters of their truth and
merit. The so-called "teachings" enunciated by leading Shakers have a compulsive value for the visionary and for others because of the credence placed
in allegations of their divine origin. Because it is a religious cult that accepts,
in good part, Christian dogma and ethics, moral values (as opposed to hygienic, hedonic, economic, or rational values) are points of reference for the
evaluation of behaviors and innovations. The goal and the ideal is heaven,
so relations of things and persons in heaven are models for things here on
earth. The polarity of the desirable and the undesirable—which, of course, is
found in any system—is here phrased in terms of God and the devil. All
these anchors give orientation to this particular system. In another universe,
such as the economic, the same scheme of goals, opposites, and sanctions
would hold, but with different points of reference.

A frame of reference is an area of orientation with its own particular
values. A great variety of particular thought configurations may be organized within it, but it gives color or quality to them. It sets up the basic premises about values that give meaning and order to the various configurations.
These frames or settings are determined by bias, habit, modes, and stereotypes, by a complex interweaving of conceptual and perceptual material.
They color the interpretative organization of the individual without his
being aware of it.

[15] Bartlett, *op. cit.,* pp. 53 and 128–129.

The spontaneous analysis or synthesis of the data of experience may also be conditioned by familiarity or lack of familiarity with it. Things and events may be taken for granted, or they may not. This variation is dependent in part upon the recurring nature of the thing in the observer's experience. Also, and very importantly, it is dependent upon the degree of his identification with the thing. He may accept it, as others do, as being natural because of his habituation to it. Or, if he is not familiar with it, he may maintain a more objective attitude toward it, thus freeing himself for a reanalysis of it. Hence the innovations of strangers, children, and foreigners, and of the frustrated and alienated individuals to be considered in a subsequent chapter.

Substitution. Although identification is a prerequisite to innovation it is not sufficient to create one. Even though it always involves some error, this alone is not innovative. Identification is not a cross combination, which we have assumed by definition to characterize an innovation. More fundamental is the fact that mere identification does not bring anything new into existence. If the innovator mistakes CA for CX, he is merely drawing upon something that is familiar to him to account for something that is presented to him. Both CA and CX preexist his confusing of them. Neither has been originated by him. Furthermore, a real "confusion" of two ideas means something more than a passive neglect of differences. It means that they are treated alike in some respect. They are given the same meaning, or they have the same functions. In brief, one substitutes for the other within the framework of some prototype.

The prototype is simply the configuration that serves as a datum or reference point in the associative sequence that is assumed to be relevant by the observer. For the sake of consistency we shall always refer to the CAB of the diagram of Figure 1 as the prototype, and to CXY as the stimulus configuration. CA then is the analyzed or synthesized mental referent which is taken by the observer to correspond to the stimulus. It is the evoked memory record of a past experience. CX may also be a memory configuration; or it may be a sensory stimulus. As a configurated whole, CA has all the properties of configurations discussed at the beginning of this chapter. An especially relevant attribute at this point, however, is its normative characteristics. The prototype gives charter or warrant for the interpretation of new experiences. It is a resident and latent system in the sense that it is evoked by stimulus CX, or more specifically by C plus its relationship to X. It must be emphasized that this is not a simple mechanical reaction, because, as has been noted before, the arousal of CA is dependent upon a complex of conditions involving the attitude of the individual, his purposes, his retention of past experiences, and the frame of reference upon which he draws at the moment. As Bartlett says,[16] the dynamics of evocation

[16] *Ibid.*, p. 85.

is emphatically not merely a question of relating the newly presented material to old acquirements of knowledge. Primarily, it depends upon the active bias, or special reaction tendencies, that are awakened in the observer by the new material, and it is these tendencies which then set the new into relation to the old. To speak as if what is accepted and given a place in mental life is always simply a question of what fits into already formed apperception systems is to miss the obvious point that the process of fitting in is an active process, depending directly upon the pre-formed tendencies and bias which the subject brings to his task.

Once CA is evoked by CX, it is dynamic and has a preemptive and assertive quality. It carries the conviction that it *is* that which stimulated it. This must be so because it is all that the mind knows about the objective referent. The mental thing is the objective thing. Consequently when identification takes place, CA *is* CX. This conviction is induced by the fact that C, upon being actively revived by direct stimulation, spontaneously elicits its correlate A because of a previously established and accustomed association with it. In short, identification is established by the redintegration of prototype CA.

From that point on, more than one development is possible. Sometimes nothing more happens; at times there is not even a recognition of the thing observed because, as some psychologists believe, this involves a relationship of self to the evoked idea. Upon other occasions additional stimuli will intervene, and there may be a reanalysis or some other kind of an adjustment. Of the several possibilities that follow upon identification, two are significant for innovation because they prepare the way for a cross-referencing or a hybridization of XY and AB, which, in effect, amounts to a substitution.

One of these possibilities results in what we shall call *assimilation*. The first step is the one just described; namely, that CA is redintegrated as a whole. It is reconstituted spontaneously, and it is without parts; it is CA, not A related to C. Then the redintegrative process proceeds by another step so that CA becomes incorporated as a subwhole in a more inclusive configuration. This develops when CA recalls some correlate or associate, B, to which it has been bonded in a previous experience by the relationship R_1. The prototype then becomes CAB. This opens the way for either a deliberate or an unconscious substitution of CX for CA, because CX *is* psychologically CA. From the observer's point of view, "*that* is this." Without further thought CX may be taken to be CA, *in the context B*. Or even if the observer "stops and thinks," the suggestion of substitution has been implanted and can be acted upon. Whether the substitution is deliberate or unwitting, we may speak of CAB assimilating CX because the latter is synthesized with B in the same way as is CA. Thereupon the new configuration CXB spontaneously takes shape, or there is a conviction that it can. This development is indicated in the diagram by an arrow drawn from X to B.

It is important to note that in the process of assimilation CX is joined to B in the same relation as is CA. This is so because CA carries with its apperception as a subwhole its relationship to B. This is essential to its evocation of B rather than another one of CA's many associates. Therefore, with the fusion of CX and B, R_2 and Y are ignored. The result is something quite different from either of the two preexisting configurations CXY or CAB. For, as we have seen, CX is never identical with CA; R_2 may be, and usually is, different from R_1; and Y is different from B.

Assimilation is a most important innovative mechanism; perhaps it is the most important in terms of its frequency. It happens constantly in the reactions of any organism to its environment. It occurs in situations that are not regarded as productive of innovations at all. It happens when we treat things as the same even though we know that a detailed exploration would show that they are not. It happens when we recognize things and people. Feingold says that this reaction is the most common source of error in recognition.[17] It also receives expression in formal logic as the syllogism: A stands in relation R_1 to B; X is A; therefore, X stands in relation R_1 to B. It appears also that assimilation provides an acceptable explanation for the conditioned response. In the psychological literature it has been variously labeled. It has been called assimilation, generalization, or transfer. Thorndike terms it "response by analogy"; Bartlett discusses it under the captions of "importation" and "rationalization."

The routine nature of assimilation recalls the point made earlier about judgments of sameness. The statement can be expanded now by saying that there is no definite boundary between innovative and noninnovative substitutions. Assimilation, an innovative process, is a commonplace event. It is a routine phenomenon. If we do not have a hammer available when we need one, we use anything like a hammer that we can find; it may be our fist, a stick, a stone, a wrench, or a shoe heel. Or we may take advantage of some other power device, which is by so much like the strength of our arm—perhaps a falling rock, the force of water action, or the force of expanding air—and so replace our arm. Köhler's ape, Koko, was inventing when he substituted a plant stalk, then a stone, a stick, a straw, a drinking bowl, and finally a shoe for the stick that he had been using to obtain food.[18] Our impression of newness in what we call an innovation is a function of the degree of similarity that we accord the substitute with reference to that for which it substitutes. And it is obvious that the measure of similarity is individually and culturally variable. By convention we polarize the assimilative continuum about the extremes of the innovative and the noninnovative, with

[17] Feingold, "Recognition and Discrimination," *Psychological Monographs*, 1915, 18 (No. 2):53–59.

[18] Wolfgang Köhler, *The Mentality of Apes* (trans. by Ella Winter). New York: Harcourt, Brace and Company, 1927, p. 36.

further subdivisions or nodings of an arbitrary character that we call inventions, discoveries, mistakes, and so on.

The second innovative sequence mentioned above is what we shall call *projection*. In this process CA is likewise redintegrated by CX, but at that point the redintegrative development is interrupted. CA does not evoke correlate B. Instead, the stimulus Y obtrudes as a second activator following upon the presentation of CX. Nevertheless CA is mentally present and is apprehended by the observer as CX. It is taken to be CX: "*this* is that." This opens the way for a substitution of CA for CX, either spontaneously or by calculation. CA is, after a manner of speaking, projected upon the stimulus field, whether this is internal or external in origin, in place of CX. It is *there* in the context of the second stimulus Y. In the diagram the formation of the new configuration CAY is indicated by an arrow from A to Y.

Projection is also a very common process. Feingold says that it is less frequent in recognition than is assimilation, but its occurrence accounts for many types of so-called errors. It happens when a hunter thinks he sees a rabbit in a bush; or when other anxious people see ghosts in shadows; or when "imaginative" people find a man's face in the moon. It also accounts for the misreading of labels, for the proofreader's error, and for other false apprehensions and remembrances of occurrences. All these things are innovations. They may be called mistakes and so be rejected, even by their innovators; but they do not differ in process from projections that may be, and that at times have become, standardized and acceptable. Even these "mistakes" become customary. People in all societies do not see ghosts as wraiths around graveyards at midnight. Neither do they all see a human face in the moon; some find dogs, frogs, and mythical monsters.

In order to appreciate that something qualitatively new is involved in projection, it is necessary to bear in mind that the configuration CAY has the same relationship between CA and Y that CX had to Y. This relationship is R_2 and not R_1. This fact, plus the added one that CX is not identical with CA, nor Y identical with B, makes the new configuration qualitatively distinct from either CXY or CAB.

In stressing the fact that in assimilation CX is taken to be CA, it is not to be assumed that CA is thereby banished from memory. Assimilation has this momentary effect; but CA is not obliterated, and it continues to be available in the context B. Identification means that no distinction at all is made between CX and CA; either will serve equally well in the context B. In other words, they become alternatives. The same observation holds, of course, in the case of projection.

In most of the instances cited, assimilation and projection take place instantaneously and without an awareness of substitution. The observer "makes a mistake" which he may or may not later correct by a reanalysis of the stimulus. It very often happens that, even though there is a correction (or even if there has been no real confusion), the suggestion of an identity leads to an actual substitution. This may be only a partial replacement; and it may be only gradually effected. Under the compulsion of the suggestion of sameness the stimulus is modified and comes in time and in some ways to resemble the prototype.

Word labels have this imperious effect. If two things look alike or have other properties in common, giving the name of the one to the other may bring about a more complete identification of them. This convergence may result in a modification that tends to duplicate the formal aspects of the thing that is assimilated to the prototype that originally carried the name. Thus, our use of the word "leg" to designate the supports for chests, tables, and couches has in the past led to the construction of these articles of furniture with foundations that resemble the legs and feet of animals.

Word imperialism need not result in formal modification to bring about identification. The transfer of a name may bring about the further identification of similar things by incorporation: the assimilated thing assumes more and more of the correlates of its namesake, the prototype. When John Slocum allegedly returned to life, he told his followers that he had been promised some kind of "medicine" for the Indians by God. Later on, when his wife's hysterical tremors were said to have cured him, the faithful proclaimed that this was the medicine. From that time on, shaking began to assume all the curative virtues that the generic term "medicine" implies. It has been used to "cure" everything from smallpox to hernia.

Assimilation and projection under the aegis of word labels are only a special case of a much more general phenomenon. Any two configurations or any two more extended wholes compromising them will tend to become alike if they have some point in common. The existence of a common denominator C will encourage more B's to be held in common, and vice versa. We shall pay particular attention to this development later.

Logically, assimilation and projection are complementary; one may be said to be the internalization of an error and the other its externalization. But they are psychologically distinct phenomena. It is not easy to say which has happened just by observing or studying an innovation, because one must know which of the two original configurations was the prototype. In many cases a guess can be made on the basis of other evidence or by resorting to certain assumptions. We can, for example, assume with some justification that, generally speaking, the prototype is the configuration that is the most familiar to the innovator or the one that is typical of his group or class. This will not always be so. There are other considerations to be taken into account, especially when it is impossible to say that one configuration is more native than another to the individual who has crossed them.

The difference between assimilation and projection and some indication of the reasons for the occurrence of the one or the other may be illustrated by the following example. Once while reading headlines in a newspaper, I noticed one which I construed as "Filmland Offers Contract to Russia." When I began to read the article—because the idea seemed odd—I found that the text did not have any relation to the headline. Glancing back, I discovered that what the headline actually said was "Finland Offers Contract to Russia." This was a projection of an error; for I had connected my prototype "filmland" with the context "Russia," which was a second external stimulus. If I had misread the headline as "Finland Is Bankrupt," I would have internalized an error; for "is bankrupt" would have derived from some memory prototype, such as "Europe Is Bankrupt," and I would have assimilated "Finland," substituting it for "Europe." Which of these alternatives can happen depends very much upon the relative strength of the demands of the prototypes and of the stimuli. More specifically, it depends upon the pressures of the two contexts. If a certain configuration of shadows suggests "bear" to me, I may project this idea and refer it to the context of the stimulus and so believe that there is a bear *there;* or I may muse upon the idea and let it lead me on to thought associations about bears in general, about one bear of my experience, or even about the oddity of the thought of a bear having been suggested to me by the stimulus. To a large extent these possibilities depend upon my frame of mind, my mood, and my alertness or lack of it. They depend also upon my training, my attitude toward my sense impressions, my ego involvement, my frame of reference, and many other influences of enduring or transient effect.

Just so with whole groups of individuals. Apparently there are societies of people who are either predominately assimilative or mostly projective in the majority of their reactions. This follows as an inference if we accept the general truth that individuals take their own indigenous configurations as reference points or prototypes. Thus it appears that the Zuñi Indians are mainly assimilative, whereas their neighbors, the Navajo, are predisposed to projection in most of their identifications. Typically, when the Navajo individual identifies himself with an American, he expects to behave like an American; that is, he reacts to American situations like an American. During the Second World War, for example, Navajos accepted selective service and treated warfare in the same way that their white buddies did. On the other hand, the Zuñi's, when they identified themselves with whites at all, treated the situations into which they were thrown as if they were extensions of the Zuñi universe. Four out of five Zuñi men who were questioned about their religious observances while serving in the armed forces said that they carried sacred corn meal with them; several of them admitted carrying amulets and other objects of alleged protective power with them during the war.[19] The same kind of contrast appears to hold for the Yapese and the Palauans. The people of Yap have consistently refused to identify themselves with foreigners; and in the few areas where imported substitutes have been accepted they have been fitted into the context of native life. Importations have been assimilated in so far as they could be made to fit in with Yap prototypes. The Palauans have manifested the opposite attitude. They have always been receptive to outside influences; and they are prepared to project their concepts of themselves, and other configurations of their indigenous culture, into introduced situations or contexts.

So far we have spoken as if only CX and CA can be identified. It often happens that configurations XY and AB provide no basis for identification at X and A by way of either analysis or incorporation. This does not necessarily prevent a cross combination of them, because Y and B may afford points of identification. In this event there must be some common factor, C_2, established by analysis or incorporation to make the one substitutable for the other. Someone, for example, may conceive that it would be an attractive novelty for women to wear men's hats in place of their own. Two alternatives provide a basis for such a replacement. If a man (A) and his hat (B) constitute the prototype, a woman (X) may be assimilated to it on the basis of some such reason (C) as "the equality of the sexes" or the acknowledged formal resemblances of male and female despite their differences. In other words, men and women are equated; and one can be substituted for the other. This identification of the sexes may be repellent, as it once was. In this event, the same effect can be achieved by an identification of men's and women's hats, provided that the prototype, the datum for assimilation, is a woman (X) and her hat (Y). It may be maintained that a man's hat (B) is "no different" from a woman's and consequently may be adopted by her. In this case a man's hat has substituted for a woman's hat.

At first thought it may seem that this alternative is inconsequential. It may appear that an identification of Y and B produces a result no different from an identification of X and A, because in either case there is a cross linkage between the two initial configurations. If X is identical with A, it might be assumed that they are interchangeable, so that the new combination would be either CAY or CXB; and if Y is identical with B they, too, would be interchangeable, so that the same new combinations would result. If ideas were manipulated as checkers can be, this might be so. But the fact that X is the equivalent of A does not make them universally interchangeable; likewise for Y and B. The reason is that relationships are involved. Furthermore, it makes a difference whether the prototype is XY or AB.

[19] John Adair and Evon Vogt, "Navaho and Zuni Veterans: A Study of Contrasting Modes of Culture Change," *American Anthropologist*, 1949, 51:547–561.

In practice it is easy to see why these alternative possibilities spring from different conditions and have different consequences. The difference is simply illustrated by the inventions of the ape Koko, already mentioned. He had been in the habit of using a stick to draw near to him bananas that were out of his reach. This, incidentally, was an invention that he made through substituting a stick (X) for his arm (A). Later he used the stick to pull in a pail of water. This amounted to an identification of the pail and the banana of his previous experience; in terms of our diagram he was equating Y with B. Upon another occasion, when bananas were his objective and his stick was not available, he resorted to the several things mentioned previously, such as the plant stalk and the shoe. These substitutions were due to equations with the stick, that is of X's with A, the stick having become A with its regular substitution for the ape's arm.

Another example may be drawn from the Shaker material. In their churches the Shakers employ a plain wooden table as an altar. In the beginning, it was used only in the church building. In time, however, pieces of furniture of identical manufacture were to be found in the homes of devout Shakers. They were called by the same term as the altar; namely, prayer tables. There does not seem to have been anything in the home that could be equated with an altar; there was no A with which altar X could be identified and substituted as a means of introducing it in the home. It was possible, nevertheless, for an identification to be made between Y, the church, and B, the houses of devout Shakers, because they thought of the two buildings in much the same way. Both, for example, were considered to be houses of God, and many religious activities were carried on in homes. This made it possible for the altar (X) to be used in the home (B) just as it was used in the church (Y).

The hypothetical case of men's and women's hats illustrates one important aspect of alternatives in substitution: if one is not feasible, the other may be. The Shaker example reveals another significant fact about alternatives in substitution. It shows that a superficial view of some innovations will lead to the conclusion that something may be introduced that is not a substitute for anything. In the above example it would be the prayer table. In such cases, because the concern is with the introduction, other pertinent factors are ignored. A little reflection will show that this conclusion is due solely to the focus of attention. In the above instance, there has been projection; but it has been due to an identification of what seem to be mere backgrounds. The background or context is nevertheless the functional part of the innovation, despite its seemingly secondary nature.

The same may be said about cases where there has been a substitution of one thing for something that it is totally unlike, even in the mind of the innovator. Thus, in recent times we have witnessed the invention of many devices that make use of photoelectric cells. There have been traffic counters, door openers, mechanical umpires, and automobile-steering devices that keep a car on its side of the road guided by a painted line and a "seeing eye." It is obvious that in all these cases the reacting devices have practically nothing in common with the human eye except the name. They have not been modeled upon the human organ, and yet they have substituted for it in certain contexts. The point is, of course, that these contexts have been equated. The situations wherein these artificial devices and the human eye have some specific role have been analyzed and found to be the same. Consequently, something totally unlike the eye can take its place. It is to be noted that this usually happens in assimilation or projection. When X is identified with A and substitutes for it, B is at the same time substituting for Y—and B and Y are almost always unlike. At any rate, their likeness or their unlikeness has no bearing upon the feasibility of the new combination.

Discrimination. Identification is not the only prelude to assimilation. Differences as well as similarities may function as foundations for substitution, although in different contexts. If X is admittedly different from A, it is not an acceptable substitute for it; but the relationship of *difference* makes of them a configuration that has other potentialities for innovation. If A is heavier than X, the whole of AX may be substituted for the whole of some other configuration ZX (wherein Z is heavier than X) in some context, such as P, that is new to AX.

Configurations of difference are as common as the configurations of similarity that are used in making the direct equations in identification. They parallel the latter in that they comprise conventionally recognized distinctions. They are ready-made configurations with relationships between their parts that range over all the differentials that customarily serve to discriminate one idea from another. The differences between a child and an adult, between a man and a woman, or between a tree and a bush may be drawn upon in sundry ways to lead off an innovative sequence quite as much as can their similarities. A special category of configurations of difference are those which embody the relationship of "opposite," such as our night-day, right-left, north-south, and up-down units. These polarizations of subwholes are, of course, culturally determined, as a familiarity with the ideologies of peoples other than ourselves will readily reveal.

Discrimination as a process takes place when a configuration of difference emerges from a previously undivided whole. In this case the initial pattern and the result are the reverse of those which characterize identification. The starting point is a configuration wherein X, C, and A are compounded as a unit that stands in relationship R_1 to B. Strictly speaking there is no X, no A, and no C, but some such entity as $\times$. Discrimination and segregation are possible with the aid of either analysis or incorporation, but in this case they operate disjunctively instead of conjunctively as in identification. Commonalities are ignored in favor of differences. The common part of X and A

is not abstracted as it is in identification; with discrimination the common part does not appear because it is retained as an inherent part embedded in each. Were it not that C (or any other symbol in its place) denotes an element of commonness, we could say that ✗ becomes XC and AC; as it is, with C not being recognized, we must symbolize the discrimination process by saying that XCA becomes X and A.

Analysis and incorporation dissolve the unification of ✗ by drawing its parts off with other linkages in disparate configurations. They operate divergently instead of convergently. Divergent analysis is the complement or reverse of convergent analysis. It selects the part of ✗ that is not A to become the common-part activator of a prototype with which it is identified. Thus, if we observe the biologist's symbol for male and female we can, if we are so minded, find by convergent analysis that they have a common element o. On the other hand, if attention is otherwise directed so that their ↗ and their + parts are more significant, they can be discriminated. This is accomplished when ♂ and ♀ are analyzed so that ↗ and + initiate divergent prototypes, such as an arrow for the one and a cross for the other.

Divergent incorporation reverses the dissociative results that occur when X is divorced from Y by its convergent incorporation of C preliminary to identification with A. For in this, the X part of ✗ is bonded by some relationship R_2 into a configuration XY that segregates it from its initial connection with A. Its C ingredient is ignored and provides no basis for further unification with A. A may also be divergently incorporated with B to form a unit without a C component. In the end, XY is free of AB, the beginning situation for identification.

As with equations, differences are always understood to exist with reference to a specific context. No two things are absolutely and unequivocally different; they are different with respect to some frame of reference. X is unlike A with reference to Y, but not with reference to B. A clock is different from a watch in many respects, and the two timepieces are treated as different in those contexts wherein their differences are significant, such as those that relate to their sizes or their portability. Women are different from men physically, and they may be so regarded in some social, economic, or political contexts. This relativity of difference, like the relativity of equality, is always an important consideration in understanding innovation as well as other psychological processes.

Discrimination in itself does no more than reclassify. In this respect it is like identification. Seeing resemblances and differences is not innovative because they are already inherent in the stimulus field. The judgment of like and unlike alters the segregative pattern of experience, but it does not cross-relate the segregated wholes. It may be said that a person *discovers* a difference; that he, for instance, finds a given substance to be not an element but a compound. It is true that he has revealed a new fact; but it has no cultural significance until the differentiation takes on meaning, which is to say, until it is *assimilated* to some aspect of the artificial construct that we call culture. Discrimination, like identification, is just a mediating step for innovation. By contrast with identification, it shifts the locus of attention. It provides a new take-off point for a redintegrative sequence that proceeds again by identification and substitution in some prototype other than the one from which it has been differentiated. Assimilation cannot take place in the context of a configuration that has been established as different. If X has been distinguished from A, it is not a substitute for A. X can, however, be assimilated to some other prototype.

It is not essential that the segregation of X lead to its linkage with some configuration other than AB. For one thing, if it is found to be linked with Y in the R_2 relation and if B is identified with Y, X can then be linked to B in the new relation R_2. Thus, even though X has been clearly differentiated from A, it is still possible for it to become a different kind of substitute for A as far as B is concerned. By this process, if initially X and A had been used indiscriminately with reference to B, in the end X would be linked with it in one special relationship, whereas A would be linked with it in another. Secondly, it is possible, and it often happens, that X upon being differentiated from A dispossesses the previously undifferentiated unit, AX, of itself and A. AX then becomes obsolete, lost, or out of favor in the context of B. This development, incidentally, also explains how a part can come to substitute for a whole, a matter to be considered later on.

Discrimination may result in the undoing of an existing configuration that has been built up by, or is conceptually equivalent to, an assimilative sequence. It may have happened that in the past X became identified with A, and the two came to be used indiscriminately with reference to B. Discrimination of them and their reassimilation in other contexts destroys this arrangement: X and A are no longer alternatives. Discrimination is therefore conceptually the breaking up of an assimilative nexus, and often this is a historical development. Children very often configurate the particulars of their experience in large categories that only later become subdivided. They begin with generalizations that are progressively reduced in accordance with cultural dictates. Thus it is that children only gradually differentiate adult men into categories of "daddies" and "nondaddies," and/or "daddies" and "husbands."

Discrimination and reassimilation are very common occurrences in everyday life, for people continually discriminate as well as identify. Frequently, when we examine more closely experiences that at first seem to be like others that we have known, we find that we have misjudged them. Or we wish to make certain of our identification because it is important to be precise. We listen more closely to a sound or scrutinize an object with greater care after a first glimpse of it. The process is also called into play in many experimental situations, either deliberately or inadvertently. Pavlov's dogs quickly learned to discriminate between the variety of stimuli that surrounded them in the laboratory. At first the animals responded to a touch at any point upon their bodies and to a number of sound stimuli; as the experiment progressed, they learned to react to the critical stimulus as determined by the experimenter.[20]

While we are not concerned at this point with the conditions favoring discrimination, it is relevant to point out that rewards may lead to it and that, furthermore, the use of rewards may confuse the question about innovation. It should not be overlooked that in many laboratory situations, such as the one mentioned above, the discrimination process is one which is artificially stimulated and manipulated by a source external to the organism in which it is being studied. The experimenter, through the use of punishments and rewards, has fixated a substitution in the mind of his subject. He has decided upon achieving this effect in advance, which means that it is he who has conceived of the possibility of discrimination or identification. In other words, it is he who is the inventor, not his subject.

Gain and Loss. Innovations are commonly discussed with reference to whether they effect an increase or a decrease in a given cultural inventory. This is merely a way of looking at the processes that have just been described. Cultural addition, unlike mathematical addition, is not a process; neither is elaboration, obsolescence, simplification, elimination, or any other quantitative description of cultural change. All these expressions are simply formulations of observations which reflect the observer's interest in presences and absences, in sizes and amounts. There is no cultural or psychological machinery which can be specified by such terminology. There are no disembodied calculators to augment or to lessen the content of a given cultural universe; and innovators, unlike mathematicians, do not employ additive or subtractive formulas or procedures to produce their creations. At the same time, there is no good reason to shun a quantitative terminology as long as it is understood for what it is; namely, a way of interpreting some of the interesting and culturally important consequences of the innovative processes of assimilation and projection. It is necessary to bear in mind that gains and losses are relative judgments, that they are not mutually exclusive results, and that they are always the by-product of a substitution.

It is evident that gains and losses must be defined with reference to something that gains or loses; and if innovation proceeds by identification or discrimination, and always by substitution, then those referents must be the contexts of the features that are involved in the substitution. Furthermore, since the action is substitutive, every gain is attended by a loss that is either

[20] I. P. Pavlov, *Conditioned Reflexes* (trans. by G. V. Anrep). New York: Oxford University Press, 1927, p. 115.

complementary or compensatory, depending upon the referent; and the algebraic total of the plus and minus variations occasioned by the substitution adds up to zero. In other words, there is no absolute gain or loss, only shifts that are proportionate and the obverse of each other. In assimilation, when the X of Figure 1 replaces A, it loses and is lost by Y; and by the same token and in equivalent degree, it gains and is gained by B, and B loses and is lost by A. The amount of these proportional gains and losses ranges from something slightly more than zero at the inception of the innovation to 100 per cent with the exclusive association of X and B and the consequent complete severance of their connections with Y and A. Components X and A may coexist indefinitely and in any proportion as alternative associates of B, or X may preempt B and cause the obsolescence of A in this particular connection. If a woman (B) decides that the hat (X) of a man (Y) is not essentially different from her own hat (A) and proceeds to act upon the conclusion to which this reasoning leads her by wearing her husband's hat, it may be said that she has acquired a new piece of apparel for her wardrobe. To the same extent she has also lost, that is, given up the use of, her own hat. A concurrent shift in affiliations must to some extent take place with respect to X, Y, and B, with B either sharing its newly acquired associate with Y or taking it over completely to the exclusion of Y. The hypothetical husband and wife in the above illustration may both wear a man's hat, or he might withdraw and turn to another style of head covering or go without any. The two sets of reconfigurations do not of necessity parallel each other: X may completely replace and so eliminate A, while at the same time maintaining its customary association with Y. The wife in the present paradigm may completely abandon female hat styles without dispossessing her husband of the one that is customarily associated with his sex. Whatever happens, Y and A are the vulnerable components of the whole pattern of change; and it is with respect to their dissociation from X and B respectively that we can speak of cultural loss, elimination, obsolescence, abandonment, and decay.

Simplification and elaboration are merely refinements of the loss-and-gain interpretation of change. At this juncture it is important to keep in mind that we are not concerned with the simple reduction or multiplication of identical features. The problem is to explain changes which introduce or eliminate component elements of a configuration, not to account for changes in their size or number.[21] The innovative product that is called elaboration may result from the fact that component B is a more inclusive or complex unit than is Y so that its configuration with X gives the appearance of an over-all gain in complexity for X. Someone might, for example, equate an outboard motor (X) with an automobile engine (A), analyzing the totality of the two machines in such a way that the hand-starting mechanism of the

[21] See the definition of innovation in the Introduction.

outboard motor amounts to Y and the self-starter of the engine to B. The resulting suggestion of a self-starting attachment for the outboard motor might then be considered to be an elaboration upon the customary hand starter or upon the motor assembly as a whole. Just as often, the impression that an elaboration has been created results from the fact that the Y component is seemingly nonexistent. It is there, but it does not obtrude in the consciousness of the innovator or in the evaluation of those who interpret his creation as an elaboration. To them it is mere background or setting for X; or it is some affiliate of X which is not considered to be a part of or intimately connected with it. Thus, if X is a wheelbarrow, A a lawn mower, and B a small gasoline engine which propels the lawn mower, the inventor to which this particular conjunction of configurations occurs may adapt the engine for the propulsion of his wheelbarrow. The latter is thereby elaborated on without any very evident Y component figuring in the inventive process, the reason being that Y in this case was not a part of the wheelbarrow. It might have been the general setting of wheelbarrow and lawn mower, or some particular function of the former, or, more probably, the inventor himself who got tired pushing his wheelbarrow and wanted a mechanical substitute. In any case, the vagueness, unimportance, irrelevance, or detachment of the Y component gives the illusion of an absolute addition to X, a gain without a correlated loss.

Simplification results when the opposite set of relationships exists between the two configurations XY and AB; that is, when the Y component is more complex than B, or when Y has been regarded as an intimate part of X but B is only the setting, ground, or some detached associate of A and consequently of X. In this case A is identified with only a part of what is normally considered to be X, while the remainder is ignored and relegated to Y. With the loss of the remainder being compensated for only by the lesser gain of a detached or indifferent B, there is the appearance of a reduction or a simplification in the new configuration XB as contrasted with XY. If X were a commemorative pillar at a street intersection and Y a heroic statue at its top, a tourist in trying to sketch or describe the scene from memory would have to relate it to some memory prototype. Simplification would result if in the prototype the recalled pillar (X) were to evoke the image or thought of a similar pillar (A) surmounted by a marble ball (B) seen elsewhere. Or the memory record might simplify the original experience if there was a recall of an unadorned monument (A) in the same or in a similar street setting (B). If a man equates his office (X) with his home (A) wherein he habitually wears a shirt (B) but no tie, he is in a fair way to abandon the more complex shirt-tie unit (Y) which he has in the past associated with his office.

It will be noticed that the conditions for simplification will present themselves if the stimulus-prototype status of XY and AB are the reverse of that which brings about an elaboration; that is to say, if the configuration which functions as a stimulus in the first instance becomes the prototype configuration in the second. If a lawn mower with an engine is assimilated to a hand-propelled wheelbarrow, it will lose its engine and also be hand-propelled. While elaboration and simplification are thus the reverse of each other in point of the status of the two initial configurations, as well as logically, they do not normally evolve out of each other by a switch of their positions. Change so produced would be circular and meaningless; but describing the mechanics of elaboration and simplification in this way illustrates the essential point that whether the one or the other takes place depends upon the level of the analysis which produces the X and the Y and the A and the B components of the initial configurations. The innovation XB appears as a simplification of XY when B is only a part of Y or when it is only a secondary associate of A. The assimilation of X to B thereby eliminates a part or the whole of Y. Elaboration occurs when B is more inclusive than Y or when it is an integral part of A. It then adds to the total composition of X in the process of assimilation.

It must not be overlooked that discrimination can also initiate an innovative sequence and so result in losses and gains. In this instance B gains X and at the same time loses an undifferentiated XA through the substitution of the former for the latter. If two things, X and A, are related to the same context, B, in precisely the same way so that they are inseparable, either formally or otherwise, they are a unitary phenomenon with respect to that context. They constitute a homogeneous whole in that reference, irrespective of how they might otherwise be regarded. To the extent that they are indifferently used or necessarily conjoined in association with B, they are not, in fact, two entities at all. This must be so regardless of whether they can be shown to be different, whether they are mutually exclusive physically, or whether they are differently associated in other contexts. The layman who calls all large plant growths with trunks "trees," the chemist who unknowingly uses a compound while supposing it to be an element, and the writer who indiscriminately employs two forms of the letter r are all dealing with whole phenomena within the respective limits of the contexts of each. But as soon as discrimination takes place, one homogeneous unit becomes two; which is to say that, in terms of Figure 1, X becomes segregated from XA, and of the two units only X is considered to be appropriate to B. Hence the undifferentiated X and A, which only now appears as a composite, is rejected or lost. Or, viewed in another way, a part replaces a whole, and there is consequently a simplification or a reduction of the original configuration XAB as compared with the innovation XB. In this way adulterants, irrelevancies, variants, and superfluous elements are "weeded out" of what was originally a unit.

A historical example of simplification through discrimination is the case of the emergence of alphabetic writing. For centuries Egyptian scribes used a dual system to record the sound elements of their language. One was basically pictorial and made use of the name-sounds of the things pictured, while the other was purely symbolic and employed arbitrary signs for elementary sounds. The two kinds of characters for the same sound were employed collaterally and uncertainly, the one serving to complete the identification of the other. As Kroeber says, it seems that Egyptian authors felt they risked being misinterpreted unless they made doubly certain of their intent.[22] Finally, sometime prior to 1500 B.C. it must have occurred to someone that only one of these systems, the purely symbolic, was essential to convey meaning; for inscriptions of about that date have been found on the Sinai Peninsula which lack the pictorial elements. From a practical and objective standpoint only these elements were lost with this invention of alphabetic writing. Nevertheless, since originally the pictorial forms (A) could not function independent of their alphabetic mates (X) it was this whole unit of XA that was replaced by the psychologically distinct unit of X in each given context of sign meaning, B. In the beginning X and A were as much a part of each other as is the vertical line and the dot over it that makes the English letter i. This illustration loses force precisely because it presents a close parallel: Americans may be well on their way to the "loss" of this dot. Perhaps a better example would be the letter t. In any event, the upright lines and the dot and cross of these two symbols are not independent marks, even though they can be physically separated. Psychologically a vertical line without a dot over it or one without a horizontal dash through it is not simply an undotted i or an uncrossed t. It is something entirely different, and it is not possible to lose one of the component parts without losing the other.

There are some instances of loss which on first thought seem to require another kind of explanation. These involve changes whereby something is abandoned without evidence of a positive replacement. Something gives way to nothing. A thing, a behavior, or an idea is renounced, avoided, or neglected so that inactivity seemingly follows upon an activity. Examples would be the breaking of a habit, the abandonment of a tool, the repudiation of a goal, or the emergence of a disbelief. In order to understand that these cases are no different from the rest, it is necessary to revert to what has been said about the nature of cultural data: namely, that they are not things or overt behaviors but the ideas of things and of overt behaviors; they are mental representations rather than objects and acts so represented. When cultural realities are seen in this light, there is obviously no distinction to be made between a thing and a nothing, between the thought of doing something and

[22] A. L. Kroeber, *Anthropology*. New York: Harcourt, Brace and Company, Inc., 1948, p. 371.

the thought of not doing it. The idea of cessation is as positive a fact as is the idea of continuance, and they have equal potentialities for cultural change. The renunciation of a thing or an act is not to be confused with the thought of renunciation. This being so, the idea "stop it" can replace or displace the idea "do it"; and the conclusion "it should not be" can supplant the conviction "it should be." In consequence, losses may, in a very real sense, be acquired and so constitute gains, despite their negative manifestations from the standpoint of gross overt behavior. Nothing, as symbolized by the X of Figure 1, is therefore often either a direct substitute for something, A, or the necessary entailment of the assimilative process which indirectly causes B, representing nothing in another situation, to displace the antecedent something represented by a lost Y.

The circumstance which leads to the misapprehension that substitution is not a relevant process in the last-mentioned instances is that the term "nothing" often has connotations of emptiness in this as in other connections. It connotes a void without substance or activity. This is a philosophical notion, and it obviously cannot define a state of being of an organism. When a human being stops doing something which he has been accustomed to do, there is no abysmal breach in his thinking or in his behavior. Instead he does something else; that is, he substitutes one thought or action for another. As was noticed in the last paragraph, this substituted activity is sometimes the logical opposite of its predecessor; but just as often it is another alternative that is merely different. The man who stops smoking may supplant the thought and the act of smoking by determined—and real—thoughts not to smoke, or he may substitute chewing gum, sweets, or finger exercises when the urge to smoke comes upon him. In any event, he does not experience or substitute a blank in his thinking and acting at these junctures.

The mechanics of substituting opposites, like the exchange of something for nothing, is to be considered later. At the moment it is sufficient to say that this can be accomplished directly in some cases and indirectly by displacement in others. It can happen directly if the doing and the not doing of something is a matter of indifference to a particular individual, if he, for example, does not care whether he has a cup of coffee or not or goes swimming or not. Alternatives of this sort, even though they are logically and physically incompatible, are equivalents to the unconcerned individual. More often, however, nothing supersedes something indirectly through the equation of their associates or contexts. Thus a man who succeeds in giving up smoking may do so by equating every situation with those in which he was accustomed not to smoke in the past. In other words, he goes without smoking at all times, not just sometimes, the latter being his prototype and model.

It appears, then, that loss and gain are ways of viewing the consequences of assimilation and projection and that they are not processes themselves.

They are interpretations of innovative effects and are not clearly differentiable in this connection because of the hybrid character of innovations. Loss and gain presume to dichotomize cultural data; and since innovation mixes rather than sorts, they are not adequate for a rigorous analysis of change. No harm comes from their use, however, as long as their true character and shortcomings are appreciated.

CHAPTER VIII

RAMIFICATIONS

The Range of Substitution. In the preceding chapter it has been pointed out that assimilation and projection are fundamental to any innovative combination. Innovations are so varied in content that it may be difficult to see how they could all conform to a few basic patterns and rest upon the same processes. It is the purpose of this chapter to demonstrate how they do, in terms of assimilation and projection, and to show how every innovation has a prototype, substitution for or by which accounts for every kind of new idea.

In the discussion that is to follow, no attempt will be made to distinguish assimilation from projection. The reason for not doing so has been given earlier; namely, that it is not possible to distinguish these processes unless the particulars are known, or unless certain assumptions are made that must at times be suspect. For simplicity's sake, all instances, unless otherwise specified, will be called assimilations. Reference to Figure 1 (page 88) continues as illustrations are offered. No consistent effort is made to characterize relationships, for if this were done the presentation would become tedious as well as complex. It should be kept in mind, however, that precision and specificity are their essence. The letters that appear in parentheses in the text agree with those in Figure 1 and are intended to relate the analysis of the illustrations to the identification and substitution scheme symbolized by the diagram.

Language. Language changes offer many illustrations of substitution. It is easy to point them out when they have taken place across ethnic boundaries. Rarely are there complete correspondences over the range of phonemes that are in use in one language and those that are familiar to the speakers of another. When an individual attempts to pronounce foreign words, he identifies alien sounds (X) with those most nearly like the ones (A) with which he is familiar, and then projects the latter into the context of the rest (Y) of the borrowed word. As a result the Frenchman is likely to pronounce our word "pin" in a way that sounds to us more like "peen," while in pronouncing French words we substitute our own approximations for his nazalized *n* and trilled *r*. People who do not have a sonant *th* sound in their language may say "dis" for our "this," while we, with only one *l* sound in our language, identify all the variants upon it with this one form. The Palauans have a sound in their language which the Germans have consistently written and pronounced as the harsh *ch* known to them. The American ear finds this sound to be much less rasping and more like *k̯*. This difference in interpretation parallels the experience of an individual who tries to pronounce a foreign sound that is intermediate between two that are familiar to him. He vacillates between his two prototypes, now hearing the foreign sound one way, now the other.

It is true that cross-cultural sound projections do not lead to changes in the donor language. But they are innovations, nonetheless, and they may become standardized and so affect the speech of the borrowing group to the extent of their incorporation in it. Such incorporation will be the more significant if the adopted word comes to be related to something in the borrowing culture by a still more inclusive process of projection. When this happens, a foreign word (Y), such as "taboo," is adopted as a label for an idea-set (A) that has something of the same meaning as the idea-set (X) to which it originally belonged. The discrepancy between the realities (X = "forbidden" and A = "illegal") that is ignored in the identification process is a measure of the aberration of such cross-cultural innovations. The mediating mechanism has been identification through the incorporation of a common referent (C), either the meaning of the idea-sets, as suggested above, or some act or thing, such as murder or a religious object.

Of more significance, perhaps, are internal vocabulary changes. The mechanism is no different, but the prototype for the substitution is more restricted in that it is peculiar to a certain group or class among those who speak a common language. The most obvious innovators in this connection are children. While they are attempting to learn the language of their group, they are constantly substituting strange or difficult sounds to conform to their repertoire. Many American children find *r* a difficult sound to pronounce. They make shift with such substitutes as *w* or various modified vowels, the choice depending upon the position of the *r* with respect to other sounds. Sturtevant relates that until his thirtieth year he pronounced "trough" as "trouth," not realizing until that time that other people were saying "trouf." [1] He considers it not unlikely that permanent phonetic changes have come about from such "defects" in hearing and articulation. Actually, these are also cases of projection.

Word substitution also occurs in the vocabulary building of an individual during the course of his associations with playmates and friends. The person who has been taught to say "pretty" and who eventually adopts the word "purty" in its stead has assimilated it to the contexts appropriate to "pretty" because it either sounds the same to him or "means the same thing." Similarly for the person who begins to say "ain't" in place of "is not." The two expressions are identified by common meaning; to him they are synonymous.

[1] E. H. Sturtevant, *Linguistic Change*. New York: G. E. Stechert & Company, 1942, p. 34.

Expressions involving not only words but sentences and paragraphs may also be taken out of their accustomed context by assimilation to a new one. During 1950 a new kind of newspaper made its appearance in Jerusalem. It is styled by journalists and has the conciseness and the phrasing of modern news reporting. The content, however, is very ancient history; it tells the stories of the Old Testament. The forms of the Biblical accounts—the actual wording (A)—are different from the forms (X) in the newspaper ("Queen of Sheba Arrives; Lovelier Sight Never Seen"); but the meaning (C) is the same. The contexts (B) to which both forms relate are the other particulars of the occasion (the date, the questions put to Solomon by the Queen of Sheba, her offerings to him, etc.). This assimilation of the modern by the context of the ancient makes for the novelty of this kind of dead-news reporting. It "enlivens" the past.

Various coded forms of speech employ direct equations of phonemes or syllables. In other words, two different sound sets (X and A) are arbitrarily equated; and whenever one occurs in normal speech, it is automatically replaced by its stipulated equivalent. Such "secret" languages are common among children in many countries. Jespersen has assembled a bibliography of them. One illustration given by him is the "Ziph" gibberish in which "wa" is substituted for the first of two initial consonants. Sometimes a phoneme or a syllable is equated, not with another sound, but with vocal breaks between them. Thus, in the "*M*-gibberish" mentioned by Jespersen the *m* sound is introduced between the syllables of ordinary speech: "going out today" thereby becomes "goming mout tomdaym." [2] The so-called pig Latin of American children is only one such linguistic invention.

Technology. It is evident that assimilation is a consistent process in what is ordinarily called invention, even though it may involve numerous complexities and ramifications. In the illustrations that follow no attempt is made to be exhaustive. Rather, the intention is to indicate the range of assimilation in this field. Throughout the remainder of the chapter, and in subsequent ones as well, additional instances will be discussed as they bear upon particular problems.

In the first place, it is instructive to take notice of the fact that our technology, for all its varied manifestations, plays many an old tune. It is replete with what in other contexts we would call clichés and old reliables. These constants are threaded through a wide variety of different associations, and this reassociation is the only thing that makes them new when they first make their appearance in such connections. In short, they have been assimilated or projected from one context to another on the basis of some similarity between themselves (X) and the things (A) they replace or on the basis of an equation of their correlate (Y) and the correlate (B) of the thing they replace.

[2] Otto Jespersen, *Language*. New York: Henry Holt and Company, 1922, p. 150.

The use of wheels is an example. Whatever their original burden (A) may have been, they (B) have become a universal fitting for any object (X, X_1X_2,X_3) that needs to be moved in a particular manner. More recent than the wheel itself has been the progressive assimilation of a part of it by all its specific manifestations: the inflated rubber tire has been assimilated by an indefinite number of "kinds" of wheels, ranging from monstrous road builders through wheelbarrows to baby buggies and toy tractors. The automobile wheel (B), beginning like its ancestor the buggy wheel with a solid rubber tire (A), soon assimilated the inflated tire (X) of the bicycle wheel (Y), and in its turn became the prototype for the numerous other adoptions that are continuing to pop up as novelties.

The same processes have been at work in the motorizing of movables of all descriptions: ships, automobiles, trains, lawn mowers, lawn sprinklers, car windows and tops, garage doors, and toys—in time we may expect motor power on wheelbarrows and baby buggies. Other devices that have been assimilated widely include tripods (on windmills, scaffoldings, cranes, well drillers, transits, cameras, furniture, etc.), ball bearings, locks, hinges, cushions, electromagnets, and so on, in what tends to become a rather dull procession seen in this light. It becomes evident that almost anyone can think up an "invention" of some description by simple equation and substitution. Whether it would be useful is another question—or whether it would be allowed to be dignified by that name. There is also the important requirement of making it work once it is conceived. This is only another aspect of the same phenomenon, but it does demand more resource and ability because of the narrowing of possibilities due to the requirements of a particular situation. This problem aspect of innovation will be considered later on.

A few specific inventions will serve to bring out some further points. It is related that Arkwright got the idea of drawing out cotton thread by mechanical means while he was observing hot iron rods being thinned as they passed between two pairs of rollers, one set revolving faster than the other. This sight recalled his problem requiring the roving of fibers. The substantial resemblances between the fibers and rods were nil; but they had the common property of extensibility (C). On the basis of this abstract equation, the fibers (X) were substituted for the rods (A) and assimilated to the mechanism (B) used to elongate (R_1) them.

Recently an engineer of the Rheo Motor Company developed a lawn mower that operates by remote control. According to news releases, the mower consists of a motor-driven blade controlled by a hydraulic mechanism which is activated by a radio receiver. The transmitter broadcasts signals up to 500 yards, thus enabling a man to sit on his porch and mow his lawn. Although the particulars of this invention are not available, there is not much doubt that it has been modeled upon other motor-driven vehicles, such as airplanes, whose courses are controlled by radio signals. In this invention, then, a lawn mower (X) has been identified with something like a pilotless airplane (A) and has been substituted in its context; namely, that of a radio transmitting and receiving set (B) that manipulates (R_1) steering controls.

Since the war several new types of automotive vehicles have made their appearance under the pressure of economy in operation. In Japan a cross between a tricycle and an automobile has been developed in which the body has been modeled upon the automobile and the wheel base upon that of some vehicle such as a tricycle delivery cart (Y), or the landing gear of an airplane (Y). The three-wheeled chassis (X) has been substituted for the four-wheeled support (A) of the automobile body (B).

A man in Munich has converted his motorcycle sidecar into a miniature automobile body by adding a windshield and convertible top and by installing a steering wheel and motor controls there in place of the customary handlebars, seat, and controls on the motorcycle itself. Leaving out the details—which must themselves be novel—we can say that this innovation represents at least a two-part sequence of ideas. In the first place, the handlebars (A) of the motorcycle (B) have been identified with the steering wheel (X) of an automobile (Y). This was possible not because of their formal resemblances, of course, but because of their common relationship (R) to a common thing (C), such as the steering parts of the two vehicles or the wheels they turn, or simply because of their common meaning as steering devices. With this identification the redintegrative sequence has stopped. The steering wheel has not been assimilated by the prototype, because the aim has not been to install it on a motorcycle frame. Instead, another sequence was initiated that took advantage of the result of this identification. In it, the sidecar (X) was equated with an automobile body (A) having its steering wheel (B) on the left side (R_1) of the driver's compartment. Thus, the sidecar was substituted for the automobile body—or it was "assimilated" by the wheel of the latter. The two steps in this development are essential in order, first, to dispose of all controls on the cycle and, second, to install a new kind of control on another part of the total vehicle.

The invention of devices for "sand sailing" and "ice sailing" has entailed a similar eliminative and dislocative sequence of substitutions. Sand sailers are low-slung, wide-beamed, three-wheeled rigs with a mast and a 100-square-foot sail. They speed over dry lake beds or other level courses under sail—and handbrake—control. It is obvious that this simple idea has involved at least two major substitutions. First, there has been an equation of sand (X) and sea (A), on the basis of certain formal resemblances, with the resultant suggestion of a boat (B) riding (R_1) over a sandy surface. Then a vehicle (X) has been identified with the hull of a boat (A) and substituted for it in its relations with a sail (B). It is very probable that there has been a third step by which a four-wheeled chassis has been replaced by the tricycle gear.

Practically every invention does in fact necessitate more than one innovative step. The initial conception may be simple, but its realization usually entails numerous contributory adjustments that draw upon the substitutive processes.

Behaviors. Innovators often treat themselves and other human beings as thing or object configurations. They must do this when new behaviors are invented. In such instances the innovator identifies himself with another person or some nonhuman organism that is accustomed to doing something that he is not. He in effect puts himself in the place of the other being; he substitutes himself (X) for someone else (A) who does something (B) that previously has been alien to his own behavior.

This process is the basis for all imitation. The implication is that one person does not imitate another unless he identifies himself with that person either explicitly or implicitly. This identification is what makes some imitations ludicrous to those for whom the imitated behavior is well established. Children imitating adults can be very amusing; so can unsophisticated adults trying to ape their paragons. The same fact accounts for the irritation that some imitations provoke. Some people resent being imitated by others precisely because there is a presumption that the imitators regard themselves as their equals. Children can provoke this attitude if they do not "act their age," and members of despised social groups may do so if they "get out of their place."

Identification of the self with others or of the human body and its features with the bodies of other beings because of some apprehended similarities between the two selves or bodies is a very widespread and recurrent process. People configurate themselves as they do other things. They analyze themselves and incorporate themselves with other things to form subwholes and more inclusive configurations. When a few years ago Palauan chiefs (A) began to wear sun helmets (Y) they were doubtless identifying themselves with American naval officers (X) and projecting themselves into an alien context and, incidentally, abandoning the headgear (B) to which they were accustomed. They did the same sort of thing many years earlier when they first acquired umbrellas. At the present time most of the Palauans are identifying themselves more and more with Americans and hence are adopting the clothing, gestures, linguistic expressions, and other behavioral traits that characterize American culture.

The same process has, of course, gone on all over the world and is still going on. In Africa the natives have adopted the farming practices of the European and have taken up occupations, behaviors, and attitudes that have been introduced. In the Palau Islands, as in many other areas, young people have identified themselves with introduced prototypes and have become policemen, clerks, schoolteachers, boatmen, and machinists. The Shaker church has been organized on a Presbyterian prototype; hence the leaders of the cult have become ministers, missionaries, elders, and deacons.

Attempts to hurdle class differences within a society are frequently made by the same mechanism of imitation. Individuals in one class equate themselves with members in another and project themselves into the behaviors of that class. They attempt to acquire the same possessions, to adopt the same gestures, and to take on the same attitudes as those they imitate. In many instances their projective attempts are stigmatized, and they are rejected by the other group. At times, however, their efforts are judged to be praiseworthy; and if they are sufficiently encouraged, a leveling of class differences occurs through the abandonment of those features which formerly characterized the imitating group.

Among the Yakima Indians there are marked differences of attitude and behavior between the conservative and progressive factions in the tribe. The conservatives make a deliberate effort to dress and act like Indians. The men wear their hair in long braids, refuse to farm, and adhere to a nativistic cult that is antipathetic to the whites. They have refused to identify themselves with white men, and hence they reject the associated behaviors. The others have broken with tribal tradition in varying degrees. Their cross-cultural identifications have led to the assumption of attitudes that make it impossible for them to participate in the native lifeways. Specifically, their adoption of individualistic attitudes has taken them out of the orbit of family and tribal privilege and responsibility, and has made some of them asocial as well. This tendency was more marked in the early days of contact, when the models of their fathers and grandfathers were unscrupulous and irresponsible white men. Cross-cultural identification with disruptive effects is by no means confined to the Yakima. It is practically worldwide.

Labor recruiting in Africa and in some of the Pacific Islands has, in the same way, engendered a new ideal-man concept. In both areas it has become almost indispensable for a young man to accept a term of service away from his home village, not because he needs the money paid for his work, though that is important, but because of the sophistication that it gives him. And sophistication is a pathetic imitation of the ways of the local Europeans or their native imitators. Some degree of such identification is essential to make the whole man. Otherwise he fares badly in the marriage market and in other situations where status and favor count.

The Nilgiri Hills tribes of southern Indian rank low in the esteem of their caste-conscious Hindu neighbors in the lowlands. Among these tribes four groups have until recently formed a self-sufficient cultural enclave. These four, the Todas, the Badagas, the Kotas, and the Kurumbas, each have their own occupational and other specialties that are mutually interdependent. The Kotas, for example, serve as ceremonial musicians for the other groups. In keeping with their superior status and its aloofness, the Hindus have refused to have anything to do with this system of services. Recently, some of the Badagas, hoping for a reevaluation of themselves in Hindu eyes, have also rejected Kota musicians.[3] This process of identification with members of a superior caste, with an assimilation of its behaviors, is not unique to the Badagas. Neither is it of recent origin. It happens all over India.

Sometimes the identification of human beings results in an assimilation that is degrading in a class structure. This is the obverse of the situation just described, and it is a common development in colonial areas where the dominant group is class conscious. Thus the Japanese equated the Palauans (X) with the Okinawans (A), a despised group at home. Using this prototype, they insisted upon stereotyped expressions of inferiority (B) for the Palauans, such as segregation in hospitals, busses, and boats.

Sex differences play an important role in person-for-person identification. Usually the discrimination between male and female is so positive that their equation is regarded as a more radical departure than any man-for-man identification. In spite of this, innovative equations of the sexes are made. In frontier situations or in emergencies or other unusual circumstances women occasionally assume the occupations of men. There is, for example, the case of the Yurok woman who became a competent bricklayer in the early days of contact with the whites. Linton relates that in one tribe in Madagascar women gradually took over the art of pottery making from the men. This instance parallels developments during the past fifty years in the United States, where women have been gradually assuming men's skilled vocations and their occupations in the wage-labor industries; they have become stenographers, clerks, lawyers, doctors, bank tellers, bartenders, and, during the war, soldiers, sailors, railroad workers, and metalworkers—all occupations formerly regarded as provinces of the male sex. In South Africa married Bantu women have gradually come to assume more and more of the responsibilities and the freedoms of their husbands. This equalization tendency has been promoted by the prolonged absence of men who go to work for Europeans in towns, in mines, and on various plantations.[4]

Under the influence of Christian doctrine—and a particular interpretation of the meaning of equality—missionaries have persistently tried to equate the statuses of men and women in the so-called primitive societies.

[3] David G. Mandelbaum, "Culture Change among the Nilgiri Tribes," *American Anthropologist,* 1941, 43 (No. 1):21.
[4] I. Schapera, "Present Day Life in the Native Reserves." In I. Schapera (ed.), *Western Civilization and the Natives of South Africa: Studies in Culture Contact.* London: Routledge and Kegan Paul, Ltd., 1934, pp. 46–47.

In Palau, for example, the sexes are rigidly differentiated, and the women are given a status inferior to that of the men. A few years ago a missionary attempted to rectify this error by preaching the equality of men and women in the sight of God and insisting that women be treated with more respect and consideration. He said that a man should not walk down the road with his wife and children following him like a drake trailed by his hen and ducklings; his wife should walk by his side, just as another man would. In this innovation the missionary has asserted an equality between a woman (X) and her husband (A) who walks abreast (R_1) of another man (B) and has insisted that the woman have the same privileges as her husband, including that of walking abreast of another man.

In the preceding instances one individual has been identified with another, either by himself or by some observer, with the conclusion or suggestion of imitation. There has been a person-for-person substitution. In other instances behavior innovation results from the alternative means of achieving the same end: a person acquires a behavior, not by imitation, but by identifying one situation (X) with another (A) and then introducing the act (B) that is normally appropriate to the one (A) as the correlate of its equivalent (X). If the reactions of individual visitors to museums, art galleries, enclosed memorials, and other historic buildings are observed, it will be noted that many people show an indecision about some of their particular behaviors. It is clear that some treat the interiors of a given building as they would their own homes; there are others who treat them as more public places. Some react to them as if they were entirely secular; others as if they were hallowed places. Some people speak in hushed tones, as they would in church; others comport themselves as they would in an amusement park. Some men remove their hats as they would in a private home or a church; others identify these public buildings with any other kind of public building, such as a store. The prototype that is elicited by certain selected aspects (C) of the situation determines the response.

The same kind of situational identification results in innovations that we label *faux pas* or the improprieties of the ignorant. Individuals who find themselves in unfamiliar situations and who must nevertheless act in some way draw upon the only prototypes that are available to them, these being the reactions and the behaviors to which they are accustomed or those that they have read or been told are appropriate to the strange situation in which they find themselves. Since neither of these categories of prototypes is adequate in some cases, the individual may commit breaches that others find ridiculous or barbarous. He may use the "wrong" piece of silverware, make "mistakes" in introductions, use the "wrong" forms of personal address, and so on. The same holds true for situational mistakes made by the absent-minded individual when he (B), for example, lights his cigarette and throws (R_1) it (X) away in place of the match (A).

The development of Shaker ritual and doctrine reveals many instances of behavioral innovations that rest upon the assimilative process. Numerous individuals in the history of the cult have identified themselves with religious figures and have attempted to act like their prototypes. Historical accounts show that at least two Indians in the early days of the cult identified themselves with Christ. One of them rode a horse through the streets of Olympia, Washington, proclaiming that he (X) was Jesus (A), that his wife was Mary, and that sinners must hearken to his forecast of doom (B). In another city in Washington another Indian allowed his hair to grow untrimmed, wore a long garment, and in other ways attempted to imitate his idea of Christ. John Slocum, the founder of the cult, equated himself (X) with a Catholic priest (A) and so initiated the practices of listening to confessions (B), using a hand bell (B) to mark intervals in the ritual that he introduced, and wearing a white vestment (B). Innumerable individuals have either consciously or unconsciously identified themselves with the prototype of the aboriginal shaman or medicine man, as a consequence of which most of the behaviors and curing practices of the medicine man have been assimilated by the Shakers.

Church ritual has been elaborated by the same mechanism. Shakers hold what they call prayer meetings in their homes. These meetings were originally distinct from the regular services held in the church on Sunday. Parts of the rituals associated with the two meeting patterns have been interchanged because of an identification of the one with the other. Some attempts at innovations involving these two services have been rejected; others have succeeded in introducing into the home upon the occasion of a prayer meeting certain phases of the Sunday worship, such as preaching, confessing, testifying, and handshaking.

There is at least one recorded instance of a transfer of a part of the Sunday ritual to a secular situation.[5] At one point in the Sunday service it is customary for the minister or for any member of the congregation to make any kind of announcement that he wishes. Usually these announcements have to do with church business or with plans for activities by the congregation. Upon one occasion a village council was convened to consider a question of interest to the entire community. Several Shakers were present, and one of them suggested that before the agenda was taken up they open the meeting with the same preliminaries that serve to initiate a Shaker Sunday service. Evidently, the proponent of this suggestion had equated the business part (A) of a Shaker meeting with the business (X) to be taken up by the council (Y) and had therefore suggested the recognized associate (B) of the former.

[5] O. C. Upchurch, "The Swinomish People and Their State," *Pacific Northwest Quarterly*, 1936, 27 (No. 4):294–295.

The Shaker practice of confession has several times been identified with other religious activities and has been elaborated in accordance with the correlates of these other institutions. One innovator found a resemblance between confession and the offering of testimony and made an unsuccessful attempt to force the assimilation of the former into the context of the latter. Testimonials are offered during the Sunday service by anyone who feels so prompted in the presence of all those who are assembled. The innovator therefore suggested that instead of a person's confessing in private to a minister, he should declare his sins before the congregation. Another individual equated confession with prayer; and since it is customary for a Shaker to light the candles on his prayer table before he kneels to pray, this practice was initiated when a minister heard the confession of one of his parishioners. This same individual equated a confessant with a sick man, asserting that, if a person has sinned and comes to confess, he is ill. Consequently, he should be treated as a sick man, which in practice meant that the confessor should brush him with his hands as Shakers do to heal the sick.

Other Shaker innovations involve the treatment of things of ritual importance. According to belief, one cause of sickness is the loss of the soul. When this misfortune occurs, the healer must recover the soul and restore it to the patient's body. Before he rubs it back into place, he warms it in his cupped hands, sometimes with the aid of his breath. Some individuals now use a candle flame for this purpose. The initiator of the custom doubtless equated the warmth of the hands and of the human breath with the warmth of the flames of the candles that are kept on the altar during Shaker services. Very early the Shakers adopted the Christian practice of holding a ceremony to dedicate their new churches. Eventually this same ritual came to be used for what they call the dedication of several other objects connected with their worship; these include the garments that are worn by some of the more ardent members of the cult and the large hand bells that are used to set off phases of the services and to accompany the dancing. Because of their common associates (C), all these objects have been equated. Regardless of their formal unlikeness, convergent incorporation has made the correlate (the dedication, B) of one of them (the church, A) appropriate for the others (X). The same thought process very early brought about an identification of the Shaker church with heaven. Obviously these two configurations are not intrinsically alike, but both are holy and have other common meanings that make them equivalent by convergent incorporation. Consequently, behaviors that are appropriate to the one are appropriate to the other. This was the explicit reasoning offered by the individual who first encouraged the use of "garments." He told others that he had had a vision of heaven wherein he saw Shakers dressed like angels and that, since the church was a place where they practiced to become angels, they should wear the same clothes; namely, long white robes with blue crosses sewn on the front.

Ideas. There is no clear-cut distinction between the invention of a behavior and the development of a new idea, for behaviors and things are manifestations of ideas. There is a degree of overlapping between pure idea-sets that do not call for overt action and those which exist for that very purpose. On the other hand, some conceptions have no other purpose than to formulate configurations of intellectual interest. In the illustrations that follow the aim is to demonstrate that even in the area of abstractions the same principles hold as in the invention of things and behaviors; no effort will be made, however, to keep the abstract distinctly separate from the behavioral.

Beliefs, convictions, or theories may become fixed because of assimilation. The process is essentially what we call deductive reasoning: the prototype AR_1B is the major premise; the minor premise is the identification X equals A; and the conclusion is the innovation XR_1B. The "truth" of the conclusion depends upon the validity of the prototype, especially if the prototype asserts some universal, such as "all A are B" or "A is always B." Apart from that, the "truth" of the conclusion depends the justification for the identification of X with A. If the identification has the impress of reality, a new belief can be established by transferring ideas appropriate in one to the other. Sometimes such transfers are made deliberately, sometimes not.

Several theories that serve to justify Shaker practices have taken shape by this process. In aboriginal times individuals could obtain supernatural help from a spirit. This help enabled a person to heal the sick or to succeed in any precarious or difficult undertaking. Shakers tend to identify the power that they claim to get from God (X) with this older type of spirit power (A), even while maintaining that they are not the same. Though different, both are supernatural power (C). Consequently, individual Shakers say that God's power, which they call their "shake," tells them what to do and empowers them (B) to do it. This same identification of spirit power and God power has led to the belief that, when a Shaker is in an ecstasy of rapport with God, he must be permitted to do anything that he likes—or, more strictly speaking, anything that God directs him to do. This precept rests upon the aboriginal prototype which asserted that it was harmful for anyone (B) to interfere with (R_1) the free expression of a person (A) in such states because it was not he but the spirit that manifested itself in his actions. It was also believed that if a person revealed the nature of his supernatural experience to others, he would "weaken" his power. The Shakers identify the spirit aspect of this aboriginal power with sin. While admitting that their kind of power is like the old kind, they reject the source of the old type. Aboriginal power, like sin, comes from the devil. Therefore, since disclosures about the old type of power weakened it, the same kind of disclosure, namely, confession, can weaken sin. Another aboriginal belief was to the effect that there were some people who had died, gone to the land of the dead, and then returned to life with messages about what was to be found there. Several legends of this character were prevalent among the Indians in the area where John Slocum lived, and he was undoubtedly acquainted with them. This seems to be the explanation for his alleged death and resurrection, with the significant modification that he went to heaven. In short, he identified heaven (X) with the Indian land of the dead (A) and assimilated it into the context of a belief in death and resurrection with a message for the living (B).

Objections to new ideas are often founded upon assimilation. When Dr. Channing of Boston first attempted to use ether to alleviate the pain of childbirth, he was opposed on the grounds that to do so was to undermine the instinct of mother love. One objector stated, in effect, that the very suffering (A) that a woman undergoes at this time is the cause (R_1) of the love (B) that she has for her offspring. In this argument the proponent was, in a hazy fashion, equating the sacrifices and the concerns (X) that accompany motherhood with the actual physical suffering that sometimes goes along with it.

The practice of generalizing from one known instance to another is very common in human thinking, and it is founded upon the deductive process of simple assimilation. It is in this way that we are able to attribute the properties of one thing to all the members of the class to which it belongs. Classes are made up of specifics that have something in common, so it is possible to equate them and to assign to all the correlates of any one of them. Thus, if in the experience of an observer one Negro has outstanding musical ability, it is relatively easy for him, if he is not cautious, to attribute that ability to all congeners of the instance he knows. He may therefore formulate the generalization that all Negroes are musically inclined.

Scientific theories, good, bad, and of uncertain status, are not infrequently formulated by the same process. Their contents and the controls exercised in their selection may be different, but the new combination of ideas resulting from deductions follows the pattern of simple assimilation. Sauer's theory of American Indian domesticated plant origins provides an example. He is impressed with the fact that the inventory of aboriginal American Indian plant foods included a preponderance of starchy composites, such as corn, manioc, and the sweet and white potato. To him it does not seem reasonable that all these foods could have been brought under cultivation in the same area by one Indian group, precisely because they all are carbohydrates. His major premise for this argument is that people will not take the trouble to domesticate a new plant food if they already have a well-developed one of the same kind. He begins with the conviction that "if one successful starch food was already at hand, it is unlikely that effort would be expended on the improvement of a wild plant serving the same ends."[6] This prototype has been derived from other observations, perhaps by analogy; and it is presumed to be applicable in the case of the American Indian plant foods. Sauer reasons that carbohydrates such as corn (X) and potatoes (A) are equivalent, because they have similar compositions (C); therefore an Indian group (B) that was already cultivating (R_1) potatoes would not undertake the domestication of their equivalent, corn. He concludes that the places of origin of these and other starch foods were different.

Theories concerning the origins of other aspects of American Indian culture and of the Indians themselves are also based upon deductions. Most students of this subject accept the proposition that the New World was populated by emigrants from the old; and the majority of these students also subscribe to the idea of a Bering Sea passage as the most logical route. Their reasoning rests upon their experience that a person (A) or a group of persons, with crude means of water transportation (C) or none at all, cannot cross (R_1) large bodies of water (B) such as the Atlantic or Pacific Oceans. This is the major premise or prototype, and it approximates a truism. The minor premise, also supported by good evidence, asserts that at the time when the New World was populated, some 10,000 to 15,000 years ago, the immigrants (X) must have had only primitive boats (C), if any at all. Therefore since XC equals AC, these Neolithic invaders could not have come across the Atlantic or Pacific Oceans.

Some students hold the contrary view, especially as it relates to the explanation of the high cultures of certain South and Central American Indian groups, such as the Incas. They begin with the unassailable fact that at the time of their discovery by Europeans, Easter Island, Hawaii, and other South Pacific Islands were inhabited by Polynesians. Their major premise asserts that the Polynesians (B) sailed (R_1) between these widely scattered and remote spots (A); so there is no reason why they could not have reached the coast of South America (X), bringing their culture with them and implanting it in the New World. In other words, the 2,000 miles (C) of ocean known to have been traversed in several instances by the Polynesians in their colonization of the island world are no different from the 2,000 miles that separate Easter Island from the nearest point on the coast of South America.

A third view regarding pre-Columbian cultural connections with the Americas begins with another kind of contradictory proposition. Its major premise maintains that the Pacific Islands were not populated by a southern

[6] Carl Sauer, "American Agricultural Origins: A Consideration of Nature and Culture." In *Essays in Anthropology Presented to A. L. Kroeber*. Berkeley: University of California Press, 1936, p. 291.

Asiatic people in an eastward migration but by early inhabitants of the New World sailing westward. Here we have an instance of an alternative of the kind described in the next chapter. The Asiatics (CA) are differentiated from the alleged New World voyagers (CX), who must have had some of the same characteristics and yet have been different. The ancient Peruvians (X) are said to meet these requirements because they possessed among other things a fairly large seagoing craft (C) that is supposed to have been capable of reaching the Galápagos Islands (Y). Hence, if they are able to sail that far, there is no reason why they could not have gone on to other islands (B) to the west. By this reasoning, the migration of the island colonists is reversed in direction, first by a rejection of an alternate identification (Asiatics with Polynesians), then by a reidentification (Polynesians with American Indians), and finally by a conceptual substitution on the basis of an alleged equivalence of achievements (sailing to one island with sailing to another).

A few years ago further deductive support was offered for this theory. Six men built a duplicate of the balsa-log raft that was used by the ancient seagoing Incas and sailed it from Peru to the island of Raroia in the Tuamotu Archipelago.[7] The leader of this expedition, in maintaining his theory, equates the native seafarers (X) with his party (A). If the latter reached (R_1) a remote island in the Pacific like Raroia (B), so could the former.

As has been mentioned, moods and attitudes play an important part in certain configurations. It is likely that they always have some effect upon the redintegrative process. To some extent the ego must be involved and make itself felt in the character of the prototype that is evoked at any given instant of contact with an experience. Sometimes, however, attitudes are essential to a configuration. They form relations between its parts. When this is the case, the "I" or the "me" of an individual's thinking is related to the thought (B) of something in some definite relationship (R_1), such as "fear," "anxiety," "identification," "admiration," or "love."

Theories may be constructed upon such a prototype by the identification of things similar either to ego or to the object with which it is correlated. If I (C) dislike a sequence of events (A) for which someone else (B) is responsible (R_1), I am inclined, if it is possible to do so, to attribute anything else that I dislike (X) to the same person. Or, if I (B) dislike one thing (A) that an individual (C) does, I am prepared to dislike something else (X) that he does.

The Shakers (C) are antagonistic to medicine men (A) of the aboriginal type, and they accept as a prototype the allegation that the medicine man is sponsored (R_1) by the devil (B). Individual Shakers have mani-

---

[7] Thor Heyerdahl, *Kon-Tiki*. Chicago: Rand McNally & Company, 1950.

fested a tendency to throw all things that they dislike into the category of the distrusted and hated medicine man and to attribute their origins and support to the devil, not because these things resemble the medicine man, but simply because both are disliked or distrusted. Thus, at one time or another someone has equated kerosene lamps, electric lights, particular curing techniques, new songs, new regalia, and other departures (all X's) with medicine men. Then, simply because they as individuals were opposed to the innovations, they have rationalized their dislike by assimilating them to the context of devil origin (B).

Errors of fact, rather than "errors" of classification, are often made at the juncture of an identification of X with A. Whereas a person may not be swayed from his conviction in equating two phenomena with which he is fully conversant, he may be made to see an error of fact if he learns more than he did when he first made his identification. Very often fictions become established because their creators have only a fragmentary knowledge of the X-configuration in their identification. They proceed to fill in the blanks, using something that is known to them. In such cases the known material of the prototype overrides the weak or incomplete stimulus material. The uncertain data "must be" or "very probably is" the same as the certain. The known is projected into the context of the indefinite or vague.

Fictions of this character are common in rumors. They are also evident in constructive recall. Individuals who do not definitely know about some past event proceed to model it upon something known to them. They fill in the details and the gaps in accordance with what they think the event ought to have been, this being determined by its similarity with the known. Their incomplete knowledge may be due to faulty information, to lack of interest, or to memory lapses. In any event, there is retroactive inter-polation, based upon the prototype which they call into service. Bartlett gives some excellent illustrations of this process in his experiments upon recall by repeated reproduction. He distinguishes two mechanisms which he calls transference and importation. Both these operate under the controls of what is here being called a prototype.[8]

Individual accounts of the history of Shakerism contain a multitude of falsifications of this character. There are all kinds of substitutions of details that are to be explained by the relator's idea of what would be appropriate, as judged by his own experience in comparable situations. When John Slocum rose from the dead, the first thing that he asked for, according to those who were present, was some water with which to wash his face; next he wanted a bed sheet to wrap around him. Other people, recounting these events, state variously that he went outside the house to a rain barrel,

[8] F. C. Bartlett, *Remembering. A Study in Experimental and Social Psychology.* New York: Cambridge University Press, 1932, pp. 57–58.

or to a creek, to wash his face; some substitute the beach and salt water for the creek and fresh water. One individual declared that he asked for a "garment"—obviously a substitution for the bed sheet and a patent error because it is certain that the use of these garments came much later in cult history and were introduced by someone else. One informant related that John's wife brushed his body with her hands as he lay sick before he died; this too, is an interpolation that is clearly inaccurate because it was only later that this behavior was associated with healing.

The accounts of Shaker history reveal many substitutions of one personage for another because of some specific or generic resemblance between them. One of the most widespread fictions of this nature credits John Slocum with being the first Shaker, *i.e.*, the first one to tremble. Those who know at first hand about the initiation of the ecstatic state and the shaking of the hands that accompanies it agree in saying that it was Mary who first manifested it as a result of what we would call an hysterical attack brought on by grief over the presumed death of her husband. Those who are not acquainted with these details, yet know that it was Slocum who died and returned to life as a founder of the religion, tell the story so that he is made the initiator of the "gift" of shaking and healing the sick. The personages who were associated with him and with Mary during the first years of the cult's existence have all, at some time, been confused with one another. Some people affirm that Dr. Jim, a medicine-man friend of Slocum, killed him; others say that Dr. Jim tried to make him well. In the one case Slocum is being identified with other individuals whom Dr. Jim was supposed to have killed; in the other, he is being identified with people whom this shaman had helped, perhaps Slocum himself. Several ardent disciples of Slocum were jailed by government officials because of their activities in the early years of the cult's history. The most reliable evidence goes to show that Slocum himself was never persecuted in this way, mainly because he was timid and abandoned the real leadership of the movement to others. In the telling of the history of this period some Shakers now have it that Slocum was jailed along with the others. In the same way, things that happened to one prominent local leader of the cult will nowadays be found to be associated in the minds of many people with some other leader.

Shaker cult history, as now related by contemporary adherents, contains many illustrations of what Bartlett calls rationalization. These are manufactured connections between internal events that put a more acceptable interpretation on them than their fragmentary character allows.[9] Again, we are dealing here with prototypes which fill out the gaps of incomplete knowledge. All accounts agree that soon after Slocum's resurrection he asked his followers to build a church within a stipulated time limit and that a part

[9] *Ibid.*, pp. 84–85 and 89.

of the roof was not finished when the first service was held in it. Most individuals who tell the story feel impelled to give an explanation for this detail. Their interpretations are quite varied, but they all hinge upon familiar and similar circumstances (AB) that could explain the unfinished roof. Some say that there was not enough lumber available; others that the time was too short; others that it was God's will that it should be that way. Many Shakers feel that it is necessary to give an explantation for the inception of shaking. This, too, is rationalized in terms of what it might logically have been. So are the causes of Slocum's death and his return to life. Some say that he was killed by medicine men; others that his neck was broken by a falling log; still others that it was because he was so sinful. One individual explained Slocum's resurrection by saying that it was not his time to die. The fact that Slocum was not buried soon after his alleged death has also called up several rationalizations. According to some accounts it was necessary to await the arrival of relatives for the funeral; other sources affirm that no coffin was locally available, so men had to go to Olympia to procure one; one individual has it that, before he died, Slocum told his friends not bury him.

The descriptions of alien behaviors and beliefs that are written by superficial observers contain falsifications that derive from similar faulty equations with stereotypes. It is for this reason that we find travelers' accounts of primitive customs laden with characterizations of ceremonies as "devil dances," "voodoo worship," and "sun-god sacrifices." The implication is that all heathens have these rites; consequently, any particular behavior that approximates the stereotype is assimilated to it in name and in interpretative detail. The same reading-in of prototypes or stereotypes has occurred when sympathetic white people with only a superficial knowledge of its details have given accounts of Shaker history. Thus we find one writer stating that John's wake was attended by "witch charms, tom toms, rattles and bells." Another reports that Mary "had a vision of the Savior vouchsafed to her" while John lay dead. Another sympathetic historian states that when John died "he was prepared for burial amid wailings and passionate lamentations of the tribe"; that he "went to the Pearly Gates and met St. Peter"; and that he came back with a "message he had received while in heaven from God himself." In instances of this sort it is obvious that the historian has drawn upon some prototype that is familar to him and has identified parts of it with similar parts in Shaker history, so being enabled to attribute the correlates in the prototype to the similar parts that have been assimilated.

The Necessity of a Prototype. In Chapter VII it has been maintained that the fundamental processes of identification and substitution are dependent upon the existence of a prototype configuration which reacts with a stimulus configuration to form a new idea. Ideas do not occur directly and spontaneously linked together in innovative combinations. There can be no direct combinations unlike anything that has existed, or irrespective of any that have occurred.

The idea of spontaneous origin has been fostered by popular notions that invention is due to some special faculty, that it is the product of imagination, and that only geniuses are capable of it. Setting these fancies aside, a serious question remains. Several aspects of the problem will be treated in an effort to demonstrate that prototypes in some form are essential to new combinations of cultural significance.

Analysis and incorporation alone can hardly be creative. At most, analysis discloses already existing parts and their relations, and incorporation asserts a connection that is preexistent to its realization. If two things are found together, either in nature or artificially joined, the mere noting of this conjunction is not innovative. Conversely, the mere conceptualization or verbalization of linkages that are already inherent in a phenomenal field does not alter the situation but only brings it to the level of awareness. An additional step is essential in either case to introduce the element of the artificial, which is the hallmark of things cultural. Some meaning must be given to a discrimination of parts or to the unification of wholes. The reconfiguration of existing data must be related to the rest of the cultural body before it can become a part of that body. This integration is accomplished by means of precedents or prototypes as mediating mechanisms. If Satan and the devil, or blue and gray, are discriminated, the distinction is insignificant, if not meaningless, unless it is somehow reflected in the intellectual or behavioral repertoire of those who make it.

In addition to this consideration, there is serious question that an analysis or an incorporation can be made at all without some standard of reference. It is doubtful that conceptual wholes can simply fall apart or decay, just as it is questionable that they can be put together in a similarly mechanical fashion. In any event, conscious probing, exploring, examining, and analysis presuppose some mental control or prototype to explain the activity; at the very least, some concept of "parts." This control or prototype may be only vaguely formulated, and it may exist below the threshold of awareness. Also, the distinguishing of parts presupposes a recognition of them, and this in turn presupposes some prototype with which they are identified. The same reasoning applies to an arbitrary synthesis of two configurations that have never before been joined in the experience of the innovator. There must be some precedent, reason, or rationalization that contributes to their consolidation into one configuration. There must be the idea of joining them. There is at the least the preexistent concept of "combination," and this is derived from prior experiences that serve as models.

This requirement holds even though the analysis or synthesis has been accidental. The awareness of the cultural value of two things that are brought together by an accident of nature entails insight. So, too, does an appreciation of the significance of two ideas that get combined without fore-thought and of two things or ideas that emerge out of what was one thing or idea. Discovery is not a passive process. The discoverer can be such only if he is alert to the possibilities of his observations. His insight rests upon his ability to see the implications of what he observes in terms of his cultural background. Chance combinations must be fixed by relating them to some-thing that is already known. They take on meaning in a context of some existing standard; only in this way can they become conceptual entities. The truth of this becomes evident when we consider that a multitude of natural conjunctions and disjunctions take place and pass unnoticed every day; or, if they are noticed at all, it is only with a passing wonder or surprise.

Basic to all these considerations is the fact that recognition itself requires a prototype. It is inherent in this situation that some prior configuration plays a part in the knowing about the extant stimulus. The latter is what it is made by a record of the antecedent experience. This record is certainly modified by adventitious circumstances, but it, as a prototype, is essential to orderly reactions to incoming stimuli. Recognition is itself a process of assimilation or projection.

One day as I lay on the sand at a beach resort I felt the need of a pillow. I turned over on my side and drew a rather large inflated rubber ball under my head. As my ear pressed against it I heard a cacophony of muffled noises within. The noises surprised me, and I tried to understand the meaning of them. My first evanescent effort was directed toward determining the character of the sounds. I tried to recognize them by asking myself what they were like. I recall thinking first that they resembled the muted noises of a machine shop. But they were not quite like that either. An instant later I noticed that there were irregular pulsations which I connected visually and audibly (through my other ear) with the voices of people and other external sounds around me. Then I immediately realized that the continuous surging of overtones inside the ball was a reaction to the roar of the nearby surf. This reminded me of the conches to be found in many middle-class homes years ago which, when held close to the ear, emitted the "roar of the sea," as some people said. This identification led to thoughts about resonating chambers and their acoustical properties; and I wondered whether the characteristics of a vibrating sphere had ever been studied and whether such a study might not have significance for the theory of sound transmission and, perhaps also, practical applications in music and acoustics.

Nothing came of these thought ramblings. Like tens of thousands of others that occur daily, they rolled through an indolent and inept mind. But the point is that they, or their kind, would have been indispensable to the conception of something new in theory or application. An experience has to be related to something in the past if it attracts any attention. For this to happen it must be analyzed, if ever so fleetingly and impressionistically.

An identification always involves some disregard of details, some error in the affiliation process. A discovery must elicit the thought of something that it is not before it is a discovery.

One day a young woman art student at Carleton College happened to get a daub of bright-colored oil paint on her denim trousers. This accident was disconcerting, because the pants were too good to throw away. Accidents of this sort have happened to thousands of people before and since; but this art student quickly resolved to make a virtue of her mishap. Typically, it was integrated with one of her main interests at the moment. The daub suggested a design, and she immediately began to work it into a decorative pattern. The result struck the fancy of her campus mates, and almost overnight another college fad was on its way. Her friends appealed to her to design their fatigue jackets, milkman's overalls, work gloves, and rough sports clothes. With the fillip of some national publicity to urge it on, the idea spread to other colleges. For a time, coarse garments with curious designs, slogans, and pictures painted on them were smart if not comfortable apparel among certain members of the younger set in schools.[10]

Pasteur discovered his immunization technique by accident while trying to find a cure or preventive for chicken cholera. During the course of his experiments he was accustomed to feeding chickens a few drops of a broth containing cholera bacillus to induce the disease. The animals always died. In order to keep his germ culture alive and growing, he had to replenish the liquid part; otherwise the organisms died. Once he happened to give some of his chickens drops of broth from a stale culture. They sickened for a few days but survived. Surprised, Pasteur then fed them drops from a fresh culture of the germs. They were not affected by this, although others were killed by it. Those that had received some of the first batch of the weakened germ culture had acquired an immunity to the cholera bacillus.

In this discovery Pasteur's prototype was the customary dosage of *active* bacilli (A) which invariably killed (R_1) chickens (B). When he gave one group of chickens a dose of partially dead bacilli (X), he had no reason for making a distinction between it and the other dosages in so far as its virulence was concerned. He expected those chickens to die like the rest. For him the doses were the same; X equaled A.

Americans very often say "nop" for "no." This is the result of laziness or carelessness. The speaker allows his lips to close prematurely and smother the vowel of the word, thus forming a final p. It is also customary for some people to conclude the word with an abrupt cessation of the o sound, especially if they want to be emphatic or unyielding. Such stoppage of vowel sounds is a recognized speech element in many languages. It is produced by an abrupt closure of the glottis and is called a glottal stop. Again, it is

[10] *Life*, July 1, 1946.

common for some individuals to express surprise by a prolongation and inflection of the *o*.

Now, the first of these endings on the word "no" is due to an unpremeditated action; and the others might once have been and may still be in individual cases when the special meanings mentioned above are not attached to them. In any event, all of them are substitutions (*Y*'s) for the speech element, an aspiration (*B*), that is the standard and proper correlate of "no" (*A*). In short, the *p*, the glottal stop, and the prolonged *o* have been identified with the relaxed and silent expulsion of the breath properly following *o* in the prototype and have been assimilated to it. All the expressions convey the meaning of negation and to a large extent are interchangeable. The variants must be related to a prototype before they can have this commonality of meaning.

Unrecognized Prototypes. It sometimes happens that a prototype is obscure, vague, or not consciously appreciated. There are also times when it is difficult to see how there can be any prototype at all. This is especially true the further back one goes in time in an innovative series. Technological developments over the centuries afford a pertinent illustration. It may be easy enough to see how one invention is founded upon another and elaborates upon its predecessor. But, theoretically, if we go back far enough we must come to the first invention in the series—and then what?

Much of the difficulty that is presented by this line of reasoning will be eliminated if we bear in mind that nature is replete with things and parts of things that are amenable to reconfiguration. And here again it must be stressed that the human body and other organisms are to be considered as raw materials for invention no less than sticks and stones.

It is unquestionable that in many instances the human body has been the prototype for a cultural elaboration. The earliest human beings used their own bodies and natural objects as tools. They employed them in ways and for the same purposes that we now use hammers, pliers, knives, weights, measures, counters, lifters, twisters, and so on. But we do not have to imagine man's reactions in his primordial, cultureless state to justify this assertion. At the present time there are people with meager technological resources who use their own bodies where we use the artificial, extraorganic constructions that we call tools and implements. And we ourselves resort to these elemental prototypes when we lack weapons and tools and turn to biting, scratching, clawing, kicking, and pounding.

All this is not to say that human beings have necessarily copied their body shapes in the making of cultural devices or have attempted to duplicate the processes and the action systems of other objects in nature. There have been inventions that have made use of natural models, but relatively few have been outright imitations. Leonardo da Vinci attempted to construct a flying machine with flapping wings; and there have been other devices, such as gliding attachments, that have been modeled directly upon the anatomical features of flying creatures. Swimmers have also tried to copy the adaptations of aquatic animals, as in the case of the rubber flippers that are attached to the feet in simulation of the webbed feet of frogs. It is said that Howe spent about a year trying to invent a machine that would imitate the sewing movements of the human hand before he finally abandoned this approach. Whitney in his efforts to develop a mechanical cotton-seed extractor tried, among other things, wire claws that passed through slits in a coarse wire screen, on the analogy of human finger culling. A Norwegian engineer and polar explorer, Daniel G. Martens, designed an automotive sledge for a proposed French expedition to the North Pole in 1927. The traction principle utilized was derived from the tread of a dog, and it was conceived to accomplish what caterpillar and other treads cannot do in ice and snow. A wheel jutting from the front of the sledge was provided with feet which gripped into the ice. The wheel was connected with a motor the exhaust pipes of which were carried along the bottom of the sledge to warm it.[11]

Substitutes for body parts need have very little resemblance to their human prototypes in the thinking of most people, and ordinarily they do not. Obvious exceptions are those artificial devices that are intended to imitate the body parts that they are intended to supplement or to replace. They would include artificial teeth, eyes, and hair and various types of body padding. In these instances the aim has been to simulate natural features as closely as is possible. When no value is placed upon a literal copying of human features, more is to be gained by paying no attention to the shape characteristics of the substitute and aiming at performance rather than appearance. Consequently most body-part substitutions have so many qualities that are different from the organ they are designed to replace that they seem utterly unlike it. Even though the body part has been a model, there is often a wide difference between it and its replacement. Nevertheless, in these cases the discoverer or inventor has perceived some resemblance, some common quality that is significant. As has already been noted, it is this ability to see sameness in diversity that characterizes the innovator. When a thing is recognized as having some attribute in common with a body part, even though this overlap may be obscure, the thing can replace its organic prototype part by assimilation.

But things with common attributes are not the only source, or even the most usual one, for body substitutes. The replacement may be modeled upon some prototype entirely unlike the body part and yet serve as a substitute because all three, the body part, the substitute, and its prototype, are related to some correlate in the same way. There is a similarity between the correlates of a thing and its substitute, not between the thing and its substi-

[11] *The New York Times,* Feb. 28, 1926, p. 1.

tute. Or, a substitute and that which it replaces may be formally quite different, but alike in that they both include a common referent by incorporation. One does not need to replace his fist by its formal duplicate in stone or metal. The common quality of hardness, not the outline, is the important consideration. Stones and metal slugs can hurt men or fracture objects even better if they are not shaped just like fists. Mention has already been made of "seeing-eye" devices. One of them is the "electronic umpire." This device was developed by the General Electric Company and was installed at a baseball training camp in Florida in 1950. Its immediate purpose was to improve pitching and batting techniques. It consists of a complex of photoelectric cells, lenses, and mirrors that signal when a ball passes through the strike zone over the home plate. This contrivance was certainly not modeled on the human eye, but it replaces one of the functions of the eye in a specific context.

Sometimes innovations operate upon the same principles as do organic mechanisms even though the latter have not been prototypes for the former. Instead there has been a convergence through a roundabout and independent development of the innovation based upon unrelated models. Evidently radar functions in the same way as a bat's flight-control mechanism; but it has had a history unrelated to this fact. It has had other prototypes, such as marine depth-sounding devices; and perhaps all the series could ultimately be traced back to a recognition of the mechanics of an audible echo.

Whether or not an invention copies the shape of a human body part, it is clear that the innovative process makes no distinction between the body and other things. The human body and other organisms are considered objectively and take their place along with the other objects of nature. In cultural development things replace body parts, and body parts replace things. It is also clear that the whole course of technological innovation has been a succession of inventions that serve as body substitutes and supplements. The human body has been retired from many of its natural functions by the invention of attachments and replacements for its feeble or worn-out parts.[12] We commonly call such devices labor savers, comfort devices, conveniences, mechanical aids, supports, protectors, and strengtheners. They are substitutes for human power, organs, and appendages and for physiological and psychological functions. Calculating machines, typewriters, recording devices, written records, communicating devices, artificial limbs, medicines, clothes, houses, weapons, diets, vaccination—all these do what the human mind and body have done in other times and places or on a smaller scale.

Typically when these innovations make their appearance, they inspire distrust, disgust, horror, or ridicule. They inspire distrust and resentment

[12] H. G. Barnett, "Cultural Growth by Substitution," *Research Studies of the State College of Washington,* 1942, 10 (No. 1):26–30.

because they are so personal. Their adoption might be detrimental to life or health, because, as in the case of vaccination, new drugs, and reducing diets, they are untried. They inspire disgust or horror because they are "unnatural." They are literally not a part of the natural order; they are not for human beings because they are derogatory or they are presumptuous; they degrade the human being or they exalt him beyond his proper expectations. Often, too, there is a component of fear in the feeling of unnaturalness, a fear of the results of tampering with nature. Usually this fear is one of supernatural vengeance. In Berlin, for example, street lighting was opposed because it was a "presumptuous thwarting of Providence, which had appointed darkness for the hours of the night." In other places iron plows were rejected because they were against the will of God and poisoned the soil; lightning rods were considered evil because they flew in the face of divine will; and there were protests against the use of chloroform in obstetrical cases because to alleviate childbirth pains was to "avoid one part of the primeval curse on woman." In 1848 the school board of Lancaster, Ohio, objected to the use of a schoolhouse for a debate on the use of railroads because "such things as railroads and telegraphs are impossibilities and rank infidelity." The school board went on to say that there was nothing in the Bible about them and that if God had intended that his creatures travel at the "frightful speed of fifteen miles an hour by steam He would clearly have foretold it through His holy prophets."[13]

Innovations that are designed as replacements for body parts or their functions may be ridiculous because they seem so unnecessary. People have gotten along for centuries without their use; and they imply that a normal, healthy individual is incapable of taking care of himself. Patents have been issued for scores of antisnoring devices, and recently a kit containing several has been placed on the market in New York City. This kit contains snore cuffs that prevent the sleeper from turning on his back, antisnore gums that force him to breathe through his nose, a mask to hold his mouth shut, a ball which, when clipped to his pajama back, whistles if he rolls over—and fourteen earplugs as a last line of defense. An English tavern keeper has devised a support for his cigar that encircles the crown of his head and supports a holder before his nose. This allows him the free use of his hands for card playing and other things. Other interesting innovations that relieve the body of some of its routine functions include a golf putter with a two-handed grip and a leveling gauge, contrived to ease nervous tension and to mechanically perfect muscular precision in crucial shots; an apparatus that arouses the drowsing motorist by blowing ammonia vapor in his face when he relaxes his grip on the wheel; an inflated rubber bicycle seat; a motor-driven fan for removing the foam from beer glasses; a self-propelled electric iron;

[13] William I. Thomas, *Primitive Behavior*. New York: McGraw-Hill Book Company, Inc., 1937, pp. 727–728.

an electrically heated toilet seat; an ejector for removing butter from forks; a lip exerciser for the players of wind instruments; and an automatic mirror wiper for vanity cases.

All these things in their conception conform to the pattern of assimilation or projection. Sometimes the human body part has been the prototype, but more often it has not. The thing is formally quite different from the human organ it replaces, and the similarity lies in a convergence of effects upon things with a common quality. The golf-club gauge, mentioned above, was certainly not modeled on a human organ but, rather, upon something like a carpenter's level. Yet it has the effect in this context that some body mechanism has upon muscular coordination. The instance of the vanity-mirror wiper is comparable. Undoubtedly the prototype in this case was an automobile windshield wiper, the similarity between the glass of the mirror and of the windshield accounting for the identification and for the assimilation of the wiper by the vanity case. The shapes of artificial limbs now have as their prototypes the shapes of the human members; but the peg legs of the past, as well as canes and crutches, were modeled upon supports of other things that were equated with the human body, all with the common attributes of an unstable mass.

Lost Prototypes. Very often no one except the innovator knows the prototype for his creation, and often even he is not consciously aware of it. We hear very little about antecedents in the history of invention because the tendency has been to glamorize the process. Most accounts make it seem that an invention has been a creation *ex nihilo.* The details essential to an understanding of precisely what has happened are passed over because they are too mundane and prosaic. When prototypes are mentioned, they are likely to be speculative or spectacular and of doubtful authenticity. Unless they appeal to the popular fancy, they disappear from history.

Very often, too, it is impossible to recover a knowledge of original prototypes because they are forgotten by an innovator in the course of his experimentation. A first suggestion is found to be impractical, and it is abandoned in favor of a second that it suggests. Or another approach entirely is made. In any case, the thought which prompted the departure disappears; and the result is a gap between the initial concept and the ultimate result. This may happen even before the world learns about an invention. Almost every inventor finds that he must modify his initial conception before it becomes workable. He has to "eliminate the bugs" by trial-and-error experimentation. Rossman lists this step as an essential one for most technological innovations; and, as he says, the final result may be entirely different in form from the first idea, although the two very likely will have something in common.[14]

[14] Joseph Rossman, *The Psychology of the Inventor.* Washington, D.C.: Inventor's Publishing Co., 1931, pp. 61–62.

The end result of a long innovative series may be so far removed from the initial conception that it gives no clue to the characteristics of its ancestor. Successive elaborations upon it make devious turns so that it is impossible to see any resemblance between the contemporary product and its early beginnings. In such cases it is futile to look for prototypes in contemporary forms. If history permits us to go back to the first tentative efforts, however, the picture changes. An article that appeared some years ago in the *Literary Digest* is informative in this connection: [15]

Twenty-five years ago, a mechanical horse, "with measured iron step" and hinged jaws honking, advanced up a Fifth Avenue lined with rows of gaping spectators. The animal appeared to be pulling a "horseless carriage," altho in reality it was propelled by the vehicle. The New York Sun, in an article reprinted from the Kansas City Star, tells us that this odd contraption was "the obvious remedy to the 'horse wanted' appearance of the early motor-vehicle," and goes on to say that:

"This new breed of colts was produced by men like John Doyle of Hoboken, Thomas J. Thorpe of Chicago, and Henry Hayes of Denver and Emil Langrenne in an attempt to combine and reconcile the esthetic and the mechanical."

Where the motor was located in its body, the dummy horse could be hitched between the shafts of a carriage, the same as its living prototype. Doyle devised a system of levers for "mechanically imitating the step of a horse," while Thorpe created a mount which could be used on the bridle path "as well as for pulling a carriage."

Where the motion was communicated to the horse by a motor in the vehicle which it was intended to pull, its interior was used as a storage place for tools, extra tires, and other equipment for the automobile, as well as the saddle, which in the emergency of an extra guest, furnished a comfortable seat on the horse's back.

Steering was accomplished by a pull on the reins, and at night lamps inside the animal's head transformed colored lenses into flashing eyes. Indeed, these mechanical horses lacked only the ability to balk when they met vehicles of the purely "horseless" variety. . . .

We read that the issue of October 2, 1845, of *The Scientific American,* bore on its cover a picture of what was probably the first motor-car ever invented. "It looked exactly like an open carriage with a smokestack on the back, and it even had reins to do the steering." Later inventions also followed the line of the carriage, and possibly Yankee frugality accounted for this. The story continues:

"Some responsibility for the refusal of the public to accept the motor-vehicle in its true guise doubtless rests on the makers. There was the consideration that by using horse-vehicle forms they could use horse-vehicle parts, and thus save time, money, and work by not designing something special when regular parts were to be had in the market. There was also the conservatism born of generations of contact with the oxcart, the Army mule, and the horse.

"It is necessary to ponder the extraordinary attachment which mankind has for the familiar, the usual, the tried, and to remember how satisfied men are

[15] *Literary Digest*, Dec. 11, 1926, pp. 58–59.

with things as they are, in order to appreciate the doubt and indifference, often the hostile opposition, through which the automobile blazed its trail.

"The first body designs were copied line for line from forms long associated for style and beauty with the horse-drawn carriage. They consisted of an ordinary phaeton with the shafts removed and a motor placed on the running gear.

" 'The very suggestion of internal motive power is avoided as tho it were a breach of good taste,' observed an editor of the time, 'and often the machinery is so placed that it is necessary to twist oneself out of shape or take the whole vehicle apart to get at it.'

" 'The Public does not understand machinery,' replied the makers, and carefully concealed the mechanism. Only in the course of time did increased experience demonstrate that the automobile was not a carriage and had no more excuse of imitating a horse vehicle than a locomotive."

If our historical records were less complete, and the memory of man shorter, the body of the modern automobile might strike us as a conception without antecedents instead of a direct transfer of an existing form to a new context—or, to put it in the language of our formula, an identification, by synthesis, of an internal combustion engine (X) with a horse (A) as a source of motive power (C), and then its assimilation to the context of the vehicle (B) that had previously been associated with the horse. There are numerous other evolutionary sequences that depart widely from their ancestral forms, and hence from their prototypes. If we knew less about the history of alphabetic writing, we would be at a loss to find prototypes for our particular letters among all the variants that exist today. If indigenous religious beliefs or prestige ratings are disregarded, the numerous local syncretisms and distortions of western European ideologies that now exist must seem perverse and entirely fortuitous. An acquaintance with native prototypes gives meaning to this chaos, just as the prototypes have given meaning to the importations for the people who have accepted them within the framework of their understanding of them.

It is impossible to know the conditions surrounding the inception of some of our common cultural possessions. We do not know what prompted the conception of the wheel, or the bow and arrow, or most of our social conventions. At this date they do not seem to have had any natural prototypes; but it is as rash to declare that they had none as it is to speculate upon what they might have been. In this matter, as in others scientific, it is better to deal with known quantities.

The Relativity of Prototypes. Every individual has an indeterminate number of prototypes at his disposal. Some of them are personal; some he holds in common with other individuals. Of those that he shares with others, some may be restricted to his family circle; others extend to members of his social class, his age or sex group, or his national or ethnic group. In conformance with this multiplicity of prototype resources some innovations draw upon group stereotypes, some upon idiosyncratic models. All these stereotypes distort objective referents in line with the habitual thinking of the observer. Mental habit systems in the form of redintegrative sequences assert themselves in both perception and recall. The variability of these systems from individual to individual and from group to group is characteristic of them.

Some years ago Rice reported upon the influence of stereotypes in an experimental situation wherein subjects were asked to characterize several individuals whose photographs were shown to them. From the reports given by the subjects, it was obvious that their interpretations were influenced by stereotypic conceptions of what constitutes the facial contours and expressions of bankers, bootleggers, politicians, and other status and professional groups. It is the existence of prototypes of this character that leads us to think that we can pick out examples of racial and criminal types. As Rice says, "The process of filling out our actual sense perceptions in this manner takes place in our face to face estimates of people, no less than in the case of estimates made directly from photographs." [16]

The material cited in a previous section relative to the need for ego defense still further illustrates the intrusion of individual prototypes and the ensuing shaping of interpretations.[17] The meaning that Shakerism has for individual adherents also reveals coloration that is due to idiosyncratic prototypes. Myth versions and other fictional accounts are likewise notorious for their reflections of interests and biases. The contents of stories are elaborated upon or reduced in conformance with individual stereotypes that dictate what the teller considers important or interesting to relate. Frequently stories, like rumors, undergo marked distortions under the impress of personal patterns of meaningfulness. Among the many specific illustrations of this development that could be cited, the instance of the Apache Indian discussed by Opler will suffice. He noted that one storyteller minutely described the progress of a deer hunt which in versions by others was only an incidental and unelaborated feature of the story. Opler's acquaintance with this individual led him to conclude that this emphasis was due to the personality and the personal preferences of the teller.[18] This particular Indian had interpolated his knowledge of hunting practices at the point in the story where the hunt was mentioned. He had projected his prototype (*AB*) into the con-

---

[16] Stuart A. Rice, " 'Stereotypes:' A Source of Error in Judging Human Character," *Journal of Personnel Research,* 1926, 5 (No. 7):275.

[17] See under central subliminal wants.

[18] Morris Edward Opler, "Three Types of Variation and Their Relation to Culture Change." In Leslie Spier, A. Irving Hallowell, and Stanley S. Newman (eds.), *Language, Culture, and Personality. Essays in Memory of Edward Sapir.* Menasha, Wis.: Sapir Memorial Publication Fund, 1941, pp. 154–155.

text of the story (XY) on the basis of a detail (X) with a minimum of resemblance to his principal interest (A).

The gestalt psychologists and others who have followed their lead try to explain cognitive reorganizations like these on the basis of certain principles. Gestalt theory holds that some configurations are inherently better structured than others; some have form and organization, while others lack it. Constructions that are supposed to have good shapes are more stable than the others, and as a consequence they are less liable to modification in perception and recall. Sometimes those that are less vulnerable to distortion are called "simple" or "regular" configurations. It is asserted by some writers that poorly organized figures become better structured through the mechanisms of "sharpening" and "leveling."

Most students of cross-cultural phenomena will probably feel that the concept of a stable organization has validity only within the limits of a given cultural framework. That which is stable in one traditional setting will not be in another. That which is simple or good for one ethnic group will not be for another. While experimental evidence is unfortunately lacking to support the statement, on a priori grounds it seems entirely unlikely that a circle, for instance, will be universally regarded as a "better" configuration than an ellipse or a scroll or a swastika. There is experimental evidence to show that there are characteristic ethnic differences in the interpretation of the same schematic and thematic material in recall. Nadel told a short story to some Yoruba and Nupe children and then asked them to repeat it. Pictures were also presented to them, and they were asked to tell what they saw. The Nupe children showed a decided tendency to retain details, regardless of their import as far as the plot of the story was concerned. Their reports were detached and objective; they were given in a matter-of-fact manner. The Yoruba children, on the other hand, tended to be selective in their recollection of particulars, being far more concerned with the over-all trend of the story. They seem to have felt impelled to give meaning to the details that they included; and where details appeared to have no significance, they omitted them. In short, the Yoruba were strongly rationalistic in their interpretation, filling in the gaps under the compulsion of an organized stereotype which they had formulated when the material was presented to them or which had evolved in their minds during the interval between learning and reproduction. The Nupe prototype was organized, not in terms of its internal characteristics, but with reference to extrinsic factors, such as enumeration or order of presentation.[19] Differences of the same order have been revealed by thematic apperception tests given to the Hopi and Navajo Indians. It appears, then, that a stable organization is one that conforms to any well-defined prototype, however it might be formed; or, in the case of

[19] S. F. Nadel, "Experiments on Culture Psychology," *Africa*, 10 (No. 4):421–435.

successive recalls by one individual, to a succession of prototypes that fluctuate around a norm.

Sharpening and leveling are elusive concepts. The interpretations given to the terms are not always consistent or clear-cut. Efforts to define them do not relieve the difficulty of distinguishing between them. In reality they appear to be two aspects of the same phenomenon. Leveling is said to result from the omission of details, whereas sharpening is the "selective perception, retention, and reporting of a limited number of details from a larger context." They are admitted to be "reciprocals"; one cannot take place without the other.[20]

In the specific applications of these concepts there are, moreover, overtones that appear to be derived from the geometric implications of the terms: leveling implies "smoothing out," whereas sharpening embodies the idea of contour emphasis. Thus, in referring to an experiment by Wulf in which subjects were asked to reproduce certain geometric figures, Krech and Crutchfield say:[21]

If Wulf's subjects had been presented with simple figures instead of the irregularly formed figures, their memory of the original forms would have been much more accurate, after even a long interval of time, than it was under the conditions of his experiment. On the other hand, if the original perception is of a figure that lacks form and organization, then, during the retention process, such sharpening and leveling will tend to take place. Similarly, if you recount a very detailed and complicated story of a riot or accident or any other incident, your hearer will "trim down" the story to a simple, well-organized, and meaningful whole. If you wish your story to be repeated essentially as you told it, you must make it coherent, simple, with only the essentials included. It is not a question of how much can be remembered but what will be remembered.

It cannot be affirmed as a universal rule that the reproduction of complicated memory material will always result in a reduction of the original. It is true that this has been shown to happen with some kinds of material under some conditions. It was a noticeable development in most of the serial reproductions reported by Bartlett. Allport, on the basis of his studies, finds that it is also characteristic of rumor transmission. On the other hand, it is well known that elaboration can take place in the retelling of stories, as it did in the case of the Apache Indian mentioned above. Furthermore, students of the evolution of art forms have shown that there can be a progression from the simple to the complex as well as the reverse; or that one complex form can be metamorphosed into another complex form through copying and

[20] Gordon W. Allport and Leo J. Postman, "The Basic Psychology of Rumor," *Transactions of the New York Academy of Sciences*, 1945, Series II, 8:72.

[21] David Krech and Richard S. Crutchfield, *Theory and Problems of Social Psychology*. New York: McGraw-Hill Book Company, Inc., 1948, p. 131. Quoted by permission of McGraw-Hill.

successive reproduction. And as for trimming down complex incidents, it is likely that this is an individual—or group—matter that depends upon whether or not the teller of the story has an interest in such things as riots or accidents.

From an objective standpoint it is difficult to see how one figure can be more irregular or simpler than another. It is so only by cultural definition. Some training must be required for one to say whether leveling or sharpening has taken place, a circumstance which indicates that this concept is itself a stereotype or a prototype. In so far as these terms have relevance to the view expressed in this chapter, they relate to reverse aspects of the identification process. They pertain to analysis in which there is a choice of one aspect of an experience as the most significant and critical (sharpening) with an inevitable ignoring of the differences (leveling). Sharpening would then amount to the choice of a common denominator, while leveling would signify the neglect of differences between the X and the A of our diagram.

Ambiguous Stimuli and Ambiguous Prototypes. In the discussion of constructive recall it was pointed out that a fragmentary stimulus and a well-defined prototype can give rise to an innovation in the form of a distortion of fact. When there is inadequate knowledge of what actually "was," the existence of a prototype permits and encourages the conviction that the event "might have been" or that it "must have been" in accord with the known similar instance included in the prototype. The fragmentary stimulus poses a problem, whether it is consciously realized or not, until it elicits an acceptable redintegration. The person who is trying to recall an event is in one way or another asking himself, "What was it?" In order to answer the question, he taps his memory record and tries one possibility after another for a response to the incomplete stimulation.

This tactic is a kind of problem-solution seeking. James has given a subjective but a vivid description of what happens when we search our memories for a forgotten name: [22]

The state of our consciousness is peculiar. There is a gap therein; but no mere gap. It is a gap that is intensely active. A sort of wraith of the name is in it, beckoning us in a given direction, making us at moments tingle with a sense of our closeness, and then letting us sink back without the longed-for term. If wrong names are proposed to us, this singularly definite gap acts immediately so as to negate them. They do not fit into its mould. And the gap of one word does not feel like the gap of another, all empty of content as both might seem necessarily to be when described as gaps. . . . The rhythm of a lost word may be there without a sound to clothe it; or the evanescent sense of something which is the initial vowel or consonant may mock us fitfully, without growing more distinct.

[22] William James, *Principles of Psychology.* New York: Henry Holt and Company, Inc., 1890, Vol. 1, pp. 251–252.

Such tentative stimulation by an incomplete activator is not confined to memory attempts. Ambiguous, sketchy, or incomplete stimuli may set up the same testing procedure when something that is not available is needed to accomplish a predetermined goal. A person "racks his brains" to find a solution to his problem. This is a common pattern in deliberate innovation. In such cases the innovator wants "something" to effect a given purpose. He knows "in a general way" what it is that he is seeking. This is another way of saying that he knows some of the essential or salient characteristics of the solution that he desires. He knows that it must have certain attributes and not others, even though he cannot round out his demands with particulars.

This situation parallels recognition, wherein there is always only a partial activation by a total stimulus configuration. There is a *de facto* analysis in both cases; but for the problem solver, it is an involuntary analysis. His stimulus configuration is too sketchy to instigate a prototype, even supposing that an appropriate one is available to him. The stimulus presents itself in a fragmentated state with relations between its parts too uncertain to evoke a familiar prototype. He has no resident configuration that will put it together because of his inability to grasp precisely its organizational pattern. He nevertheless applies the stimulus in trial-and-error fashion, just as does the person who is trying to remember the particulars of a past event. He tries to evoke some appropriate prototype either in his mind or, if he chooses, in the mind of someone else to whom he describes what he needs as best he can.

Let us suppose that a man wants to fill large cracks that have appeared in the plaster in the corners of his living room. He begins, let us say, by using a putty knife to force new plaster into the cracks; but he finds that this is an awkward method and not very successful. He wants a substitute (X) for the putty knife (A), but something that is entirely unlike it, to force (R_1) plaster into the cracks (B). He knows that the thing he needs has certain properties: it must be tubular and have some kind of mechanism for forcing a supply of plaster through the tube and into the cracks. These requirements take his thoughts away from anything resembling the putty knife. Instead, they become a rather ambiguous probe that he uses to elicit something that has a likeness to it in his mental inventory. This probing may result first in the instigation of a thought of an eye dropper or a syringe. A mental or an actual testing of these suggested substitutes will probably make them and still other solutions turn out to be impractical. Let us suppose that the man finally thinks of a cake decorator, one of those contrivances with a spout and a canvas bag out of which the frosting is forced by hand pressure. This becomes his substitute (X) with its correlate (Y) the cake frosting, and there is an easy identification of frosting and plaster with the resultant assimilation of the decorator, or a modification of it, to the context of the cracks.

The foregoing interpretation has much in common with Duncker's analysis of problem solving.[23] According to him an individual with a problem first sets up a general hypothesis that eliminates all the negative aspects of the desired solution; it establishes the general framework *within* which the goal is to be found. This would be the step in the above account where the putty knife is rejected. Then, according to Duncker, functional hypotheses within this general range are suggested that more nearly fulfill the essential requirements of the thing needed, until a very specific and final solution is reached. In these suggestions, such as the idea of using an eye dropper or a syringe, the individual is assisted by his past experiences, *i.e.,* his prototypes.

The case of the crack filler is taken from life. So is another example, that of a home-made osteometer. It happened this way: a physical anthropologist was telling some of his friends at lunch about his need for a cheap device to measure accurately the long bones of the human skeleton. He was not satisfied with the devices at his disposal. He wanted something that would be light in weight, simple, and easy to manipulate but still have an accurately calibrated scale to which could be attached two adjustable but rigid stops between which the bone to be measured could be placed. These essentials offered only a sketchy stimulus (X) for his listeners; but two of them immediately offered suggestions. One said that the anthropologist should have something like the extensible calibrated rod (A) that is used in measuring human stature (B). The second man suggested the extensible device (A) used by shoe salesmen to determine shoe sizes (B). The merit of these suggestions is, of course, not in question. The point is that the two listeners immediately recalled prototypes established in their minds by past experiences that had elements in common with the essentials (C) of the ambiguous stimulus configuration presented verbally by the anthropologist. They projected the recalled devices (A) into the context of skeletal long-bone (Y) measurement.

Problem solving can also entail the interaction of an unambiguous stimulus and an incomplete prototype. This is the reverse of the situation in the preceding instances, and the distinction between them rests solely upon whether the ambiguous configuration has temporal primacy or dependency with respect to the appearance of its counterpart. Basically this is a question of whether the incomplete configuration has an active or a passive role. If the ambiguous configuration—that which is wanted—is the instigator, it is a stimulus as in the above cases. On the other hand, if it is the instigated configuration, it is the prototype. In the latter case the innovator wants some indefinite, inchoate thing and cannot find any response in his mental inventory. He nevertheless keeps a mental record of his desire "in the back

[23] K. Duncker, "On Problem Solving," *Psychological Monographs,* 1945, 58 (No. 5).

of his mind," and if his need is continuous, he becomes observant and alert to all possibilities. Finally, something that he experiences evokes the fragment. The stimulus may come at a time when he least expects it. He may not be thinking of his problem at all and may be engaged in some entirely unrelated activity. But however and whenever it appears, the person with the problem knows that "this is it." The stimulus activates his incomplete prototype and revives the context in which it is needed. Many of the inventors queried by Rossman attest that solutions to problems that had worried them for some time came to them in this way.

These two aspects of problem solving may already have been recognized by the reader. They are assimilation and projection in another guise. With an ambiguous stimulus, projection takes place; with an incomplete prototype, there is an assimilation of the extant stimulus into the context of the desired but unknown thing.

Symbolic Prototypes. An interesting kind of innovation occurs when things and behaviors are assimilated by a prototype that consists solely or partially of ideas of abstractions and intangibles. The result is a reification or materialization of the mental configuration or some part of it. There is, in effect, a translation of pure ideas into things and behaviors that have the same organization as the mental pattern.

This objectivizing process begins with a prototype that contains one or more nonsensory components. They may be the relationships (R_1 and R) between the terms of the configuration or the terms (C, A, and B) themselves. The prototype may consist of a piece of imagery, an abstract statement, a principle, a law, a moral truth, a shibboleth, or a cliché. Things and behaviors are identified with one or more of its components and assimilated to it. The identification is made on the basis of some recognized equation, including symbolic ones; on the basis of similarities that are due to incorporation; or on the basis of alternates that are alleged to have something in common.

The identification process frequently draws upon some very frail and dubious equations. The linkage between X and A is tenuous and often highly artificial. Frequently it revolves upon what we call a play upon words. Figures of speech and the equation mechanisms upon which they rest have a prominent part in this. Similes, metaphors, and personifications permit the substitution of things for words and of one thing for another by perfectly conventional linkages. A physical surrogate for an abstraction or the substitution of one abstraction for another may be acceptable because of some axiom, tenet, or cliché which equates a part of one thing with its whole. Thus, in the synecdoche "hands" may be substituted for "labor," "cloth" for "clergy," and "rifles" for "infantrymen." The metonymy is likewise very useful; a physical thing may be a substitute because it is the embodiment or customary associate of the abstract idea, as it is when we substitute "chair" for "professorship," "bar" for "legal profession," and "board" or "table" for "meals."

Verbs and other relations can also be reified, either by some symbolic substitution or by being literalized. Substituted movements and gestures may be merely partial and indicative, or they may be direct transfers of movements that have the same name in some other context. The Shakers, for instance, "scoop out" sin, or they "brush it off"; they "chase" the devil; and they are afraid of shamans who "shoot their power" into them. These expressions are obviously adopted from contexts where they apply to movements directed toward material objects. The devil (X) is identified with something like a man (A), who can be chased (R_1), and so he too can be actually chased; sin (X) is identified with something like dirt (A) so it can be brushed or scooped off (R_1) a person (B) just as the substance dirt can be.

We are familiar with literal transpositions of this sort in many aspects of our culture. The allegory and the ballet are based upon such devices. So is the game called the charade. Ideographic writing employs the same techniques: footprints mean "travel," lines issuing from the mouth of an individual mean "talk," crossed roads signify "town." Rebus writing makes use of homonyms to provide the common denominator of meaning (C) that is linked to different configurations $(X$ and $A)$ in the same way: the number 2 means "two," "too," or "to"; a picture of an ant may mean the insect or may mean "aunt, a mother's sister," or "aunt, a father's sister."

Other examples of reification will appear when we come to discuss the formation of analogies and parallels. They occur with greater frequency in those instances because the whole of an abstract idea can be translated into the material sphere.

A Posteriori Prototypes. It is unquestionably true that unpremeditated or accidental combinations of things and ideas occur that in time become standardized. Individuals do see new configurations in the course of their experience with natural events. It is also true that many behavioral changes begin, as has been noted in Chapters IV and V, without forethought or design. Individual actions that originate in this way may be adopted by other people. These are merely configurated action systems that have been selected out of the multiplicity of diverse reactions to internal and external stimulation that occur daily. Quite often they are purely neurophysical in origin. They ease physical and mental stresses. As has been noted in the consideration of random activity, they are subconsciously directed or may have an even lower level origin. They are on the order of automatic responses and reflexes. Closely related to these muscular reflexes are the spontaneous probings and manipulations of ideas that take place merely because man in his conscious state has to cerebrate. A host of mental ramblings are novel and unpremeditated. Only a small number of them ever become objectified.

Few ever attain to the level of a realization of their newness, and fewer still achieve the status of a shared reaction.

It is true, then, that all kinds of innovations can originate without their being organized by a controlling prototype. Nevertheless, it would be a mistake to assume that prototypes do not function in these cases. They are always brought to bear, but in these instances they come into play after the event instead of before it. They are ex post facto applications of a standard configuration. They serve to define and to organize the activity. They standardize it. They are also essential in that they explain it, justify it, and give meaning to it. Otherwise the innovation fails to materialize as a norm; it goes the way of the multitude of other combinations of activities that never become crystallized.

Examples of spontaneous innovations have been noticed in the discussion of impulses, random activity, and conflicting wants. It is unnecessary to review them here. The purpose at the moment is to bring them within the framework of the processes described in this chapter and specifically to show that they entail a posteriori identifications and assimilations to recognized prototypes. The significant point about them is that, while they have not themselves been modeled upon a prototype, their linkage with the context wherein they erupt necessitates their inclusion within a more comprehensive prototype. They are assimilated to it because of a retroactive appreciation of their similarity with another configuration associated with the context or because of the similarity of this context with another that was previously linked with them.

The question here is not why an impulse or some other unpremeditated thought or action occurs. Reasons for this have already been mentioned. The inquiry now becomes: How does the intrusive idea or behavior become fixed in the new association? Basically this is a question of acceptance, but this time acceptance not by others but by the initiator himself. He must, consciously or unconsciously, justify his act to himself, if not to others. There must be some rationale for it if he is to repeat it. It must seem appropriate to the context if he has conviction enough in it to revert to it upon succeeding occasions.

Many times a belief or behavior "just grows." It develops without anyone's being aware that it is becoming a custom. The fact of gradual growth—it is really a misnomer—should not mislead us into thinking that the practice had no definite beginning. Gradualness is a function of acceptance, not a measure of the degree of abruptness of a departure from a traditional mode. All innovations, impulsive or otherwise, are abrupt. Smoothness in acceptance is an indication of tacitly acknowledged propriety; the innovation fits the situation by common consensus.

For innovations of this nature no justification is needed and often none is given. Their reason for existence is self-evident. They suit the popular mood and are satisfying in themselves. They appeal because they provide an answer to a commonly recognized problem or because they are otherwise emotionally gratifying. They conform to likes and dislikes, to predispositions and prejudices. The trembling, stamping, bell ringing, and hand movements of the Shaker "under power" are examples of this. These behaviors were injected spontaneously and fortuitously into the religious system advocated by John Slocum. But their incorporation was sealed by ex post facto theories of their relevance. Because of chance associates with which they were configurated, they were identified as healing ingredients in the "medicine" God had promised the Indian people. Upon one occasion during the early days of the cult's development, Mary's shaking (X), taking the place of a "medicine" (A), was alleged to have stopped a nose hemorrhage (B). This rationalization and others like it that were called upon to establish such practices are unknown to a great many contemporary Shakers. They do not know why they do what they do at their healing ceremonies. If put to it, they manufacture any reason that seems acceptable at the moment.

This tendency brings up an important point: prototypes need not be brought to the level of awareness and certainly need not be clearly set forth unless the propriety of an innovation is called into question. This development is most instructive because it reveals the need for a model, whether it is there to begin with or is summoned up as a defensive rationalization. During the past twenty years a schism has developed in the Shaker church over a controversy between those who favor using the Bible as a source of truth and those who put their faith in direct revelation. The Bible advocates are relatively young, and they are literate, which most of their opponents are not. To meet the challenge of the Bible readers, the conservatives have wheeled up their defensive prototype: they maintain that John and Mary Slocum, as well as their disciples, received their inspirations from God, unmediated and pure. This resort to fortuitous precedents out of the past has happened repeatedly in Shaker history under the challenge of changing times. It has been employed by the conservatives in their opposition to such things as the introduction of electric lights in the church buildings in place of candle lighting and the wearing of high-heeled shoes and the bobbing of hair by women.

The reverse may happen, too: the propriety of a new custom is questioned and thus stands in need of a model. Some invulnerable concept is then conjured to satisfy the need. At the present time married Bantu women consider that adultery is justified during the absence of their husbands from the village. This attitude has developed in consquence of the labor-recruiting practices in South Africa whereby men are taken away from their villages for months at a time to work on plantations or in the mines. The idea that a woman should have freedom in her sexual relations as well as in other ways because of the absence of her husband has crystallized only very gradually. Now license and freedom for married women have the sanction of popular opinion. Adultery is rationalized by saying that there is a need to keep up the population and the strength of the tribe. This reasoning draws upon an ancient and approved prototype for many of the habit systems of the Bantu.[24]

It is even more illuminating to observe what happens when a spontaneous act or thought is met with indifference, skepticism, or disapproval. If the initiator himself has no conviction of its worth or propriety, he renounces it, perhaps ashamed of his "mistake." On the other hand, if his impulsive reaction is gratifying to him and seems worthy of incorporation into the context where it occurred, he proceeds to justify it to himself and to others. There are several techniques that will serve his purpose, but the most interesting ones employ tenuous identifications and specious deductions. The innovator must *find* a reason to back up his conviction, and often he clutches at straws. The anchor of his reasoning is some tenet of belief, some axiom of behavior, or some truth or rule which has the sanction of popular approval. This is the major premise or prototype that he evokes. Then his minor premise equates or compares in a convincing way the thing, the act, or the idea that he is trying to justify so that it may in effect be substituted for its equivalent in the major premise. His conclusion is that, since his act is no different from that which is now the practice, it should be acceptable as an alternate or as a replacement.

The crucial step in this demonstration is the identification line. The prototype is acceptable. It is true, it will work, it is satisfying. But the question is whether the case advocated by the innovator is relevant. This is the point where persuasion and ingenuity are needed to confront the opposition. Sometimes a simple assimilation serves to justify a proposed action or counteraction. Thus a Yakima woman several years ago declared that she was opposed to members of the congregation spitting on the church floor. In order to establish her prejudice as a rule she argued that the church (X) was just the same as Christ's body (A) and that, since no Shaker (B) would consider defiling (R_1) the body of Christ, he should feel the same way about the church. The same sort of argument has been developed to justify the carrying of lighted candles by Shakers at certain points in their services. One of their apologists declared that Christ is the light of the world and draws the faithful to him. The candles that the Shakers carry are lights (X) like Christ (A), and therefore they draw (R_1) converts and devotees (B) to the church.

At times argumentation is not sufficient to establish an identification. It must await proof in the eyes of the skeptics. For some people such proof is given by a dramatic event. The identification is then vindicated; and the

[24] Schapera, *loc. cit.*

new idea can be assimilated, at least by those who have been convinced by the alleged objective evidence of its truth. Thus, one individual asserted that a Shaker who fell from grace was the same as a sick person and that, if he did not reinstate his faith, he would die just as would a person who had a fatal illness. The proponent of this doctrine gained enough attention to establish the idea by pointing out that certain individuals who became ill, and some who died, were flagrant backsliders. The acknowledgment of the curative properties of praying, singing, bell ringing, and other behaviors has had the same history: their proposed identification with medicine has been accepted because of some selected observation of co-occurrence. At one time the church was almost split over the question of whether the ritual circuit by the congregation during a part of the service should continue to be in a counterclockwise direction or whether it should be reversed, as one member suggested, on the basis of what he called a divine inspiration. In 1903 the members of one congregation in Washington were making their ritual circuits in a clockwise direction, contrary to the established pattern elsewhere. When the local minister was rebuked for this by a visiting member, he replied that his congregation had made the change because it was the way that was advocated by Mary Slocum and that two events had compelled him to conclude that she was right. He had himself received a revelation to cure an insane white man by leading him by his left little finger three times around the room in a clockwise direction and had followed these instructions with success. Secondly, a local girl with a stubborn illness was cured when she followed her inspiration to pray in the four corners of the church, moving from one to the other in clockwise fashion. The visitor, a person of some importance, was not convinced by these arguments. He maintained that God's way was counterclockwise; and when he led the service later during his visit, he insisted upon following the practice. The local leader refused to participate; but not many months after that his son died, as a consequence of which he recanted.

Often an innovator is not very resourceful in trying to justify his impulses; or there is no adequate prototype upon which he can draw. Sometimes he wishes to introduce only a thing and not a behavior, so only a part of his prototype is suitable for his purposes. At other times he may wish for a certain action to be instituted or a quality or a state that he dislikes to be eliminated; so he converts only relevant parts of his prototype, leaving the identification incomplete and of dubious value as a convincer. It may have force, however, because of emotional overtones that are connected with the truism or precept upon which he draws for sanction.

Shakers have adopted the custom of placing flowers upon their church prayer tables. One Oregon Shaker objected strenuously to this practice. He said scornfully that he did not think that a Shaker altar should be covered with "brush." But his real argument against flowers ran thus: the heart (A)

of a Shaker should be *clean* (B); an altar (X) is like a heart (A); therefore our altars (X) should be *clean* (B). It will be noted that his stress was upon cleanliness and that there was an unannounced switch from the spiritual to the material implications of the word. The linkage between the heart and an altar was arbitrary and entirely dependent upon a metaphorical point. Another individual objected to the way in which Shakers crossed themselves, Catholic fashion. The truth is that this gesture reminded him of the death of his son, but his argument ran otherwise. He said: We do not want to *cut* our lives short; crossing ourselves is like *cutting* our lives; therefore we should cease crossing ourselves. In this there was a metaphorical use of the word "cut" and a symbolic equation of it with some action like that of a sharp instrument. One other innovator objected to the use of artificial flowers on altars. He reasoned: We do not want to be *imitation* people; these *imitation* flowers make us that way; therefore we should not use them. In this case, there is again a play upon words with indiscriminate switches in their meanings.

Often the prototype is a cliché or a truism so timeworn that it is not clearly formulated when it is drawn upon to justify an impulse or a prejudice. Consequently an arbitrary substitution in the missing part is not so shocking because there is nothing that it definitely replaces; and the emphasis is upon the other part where the word play is effective. Thus, one individual's justification for the use of lighted candles during a healing séance ran in this fashion: Shakers can *see* what is wrong with a sick person; candlelight helps us to *see* better; therefore candlelight helps us to *see* better what is *wrong* with a person. In this argument the word "see" is used for "know," and there is an implication that seeing inside a person is like seeing in the dark, but this is left to be filled in by the listener. All these conversions rest upon a play on word sounds and their diverse meanings; they use the material significance of a word of double or multiple meaning and impute to it the function of the thing named.

Some rationalizations require an identification with more than one of the terms of the requisitioned prototype. During a part of a Shaker service all of the participants circle around the room as they stamp and sing to the accompaniment of a clangorous ringing of hand bells. Several years ago a leader in one congregation tried to speed up and intensify the fervor of this movement. He urged everyone to stamp harder and move faster. This resulted in everyone's crowding upon the heels of the person in front of him. Many objected to the innovation for this reason and others. The innovator defended his idea by saying that the participants should close up the gaps between them so as to keep the devil out. In this he was equating the devil (X) with a human being (A) by personification and identifying the file of participants (Y) with something like a fence (B). Another individual in his rationalization for the use of hand bells during the services asserted that they

(X) were like telephone bells (A), but they rang up God (Y), whereas telephone bells summoned people (B).

It has long been the custom for a person who enters the church before a service to pass around the room and shake hands with those who have assembled before his arrival. Many years ago a prominent member of the Yakima church announced that this was all wrong. He had received a revelation to the effect that people should go straight to the altar and cross themselves before shaking hands with other members of the congregation. This was so, he said, because when you die you go straight to God to be judged and then get acquainted later. Consciously or otherwise this man was equating the altar, or the assumption of divine presence near it, with God and the members of the congregation with people in heaven. The most prominent disciple of Slocum, Mud Bay Louis, maintained that Shakers should wear only plain white garments because in heaven angels are dressed alike and in white. For him there was an identification of the church with heaven and of the congregation with angels. Conversions of this description differ in some degree with others that have been described. In order to understand them it is necessary to describe the formation of analogies. This will be considered in the next chapter.

CHAPTER IX

COMPOUNDED PROCESSES

Analogies. So far we have considered in detail innovations that result from an identification of either X with A or Y with B and their single or alternative assimilations to AB. There is no reason, however, why both these identifications, and consequently a total assimilation of XY by AB, should not occur. This does, in fact, happen with considerable regularity. Strictly speaking, some of the innovations previously noted more properly belong in this category, for reasons to be mentioned shortly.

The process of double projection or double assimilation (as a result of double identification) results in a pairing of duplicates or equals. There is always a familiar configuration, AB, which is the datum of reference, the model. The equations of the members of the two pairs of equivalents, AX and BY, take place as in other identifications by conventionalized equations, by analysis, or by the incorporation of common denominators.

It is important to realize that when double assimilation takes place, the relation, R_1, between A and B is the new bond between X and Y. Otherwise nothing new would result. But with the combination XR_1Y, there is something new. Double projection or assimilation can be defended rationally by stating that if two things are identical they may stand in the same relation to two other identical things. We know, however, that the alleged equivalence of X and A, and of Y and B, is faulty, so that there is always some measure of change.

The importance of this compounded process lies in the fact that there is a sameness of relationship with the prototype but a substitution of its component parts. These parts may be things, or they may be behaviors or ideas. In any event, there is a change of the content of a prototype but a retention of its shape or form because of the retention of relationships. The result is a "square of similarity," or an analogy. This is what happens when something, such as a gesture, a sound, or any activity system, is arranged so as to exhibit some pattern, such as a rhythm or any other interpart relation, that is already exhibited by another form. The compounding of assimilation thus accounts for such things as the ramification of ritual numbers and the composition of different words for the same tunes. New expressions in a variety of media may be constructed upon the relationship pattern of the prototype: if you sound a church bell three times, you likewise ring a hand bell three times, make three ritual circuits of a room, or recite a prayer three times. Configurations that have been organized on other grounds may be justified by an appeal to analogies, as is evident in the rationalizations that were mentioned at the end of the preceding chapter. There has been a substitution of new forms in an old relationship framework. The shape of a total configuration persists, although there has been a change of content.

Spontaneous analogies occur when the innovator is unaware that he is confusing X with A and Y with B. The whole of the new combination XR_1Y is substituted in a still larger configuration in which AR_1B was appropriate. This substitution is not essential as far as innovation is concerned, because something qualitatively new has been created with double assimilation and the organization of XR_1Y. Whether it will happen or not depends upon the ease with which the identification is made.

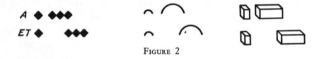

FIGURE 2

Analogies may be worked out deliberately, too. The process is the same, but a conscious effort is made to find or to construct an XY out of parts that have not up to this point stood to each other in the R_1 relationship. Figure 2 is intended to illustrate how this can be done. The prototype upon which each of these series is based is the conventional Morse code symbolization for the letters A and ET. It will be apparent that each of the patterns has only one aspect in common with the prototype. It is the length of the horizonal lines; not their thickness, color, straightness, or any other quality of the figures. Yet any one of the three patternings can be an acceptable substitute for its conventional counterpart because of this common quality. The actual shapes of the subwholes differ, except for this one aspect or quality of length; but their interrelationships are the same as those of the prototype. The subwholes are known in other contexts and with other relationships existing between them, but as far as is known they have not been hitherto configurated in just this fashion.

The difference between a simple assimilation and an analogy is that in an analogy B, as it exists, usually cannot be combined with X as it exists. Not B but something like it is required. This is a very common occurrence in innovations that are at first suggested by, or start out by being, simple assimilations of CX by CAB. Not infrequently it turns out to be impracticable to link B with CX because, although theoretically the combination is possible, some adjustments are necessary. These adjustments take the form of a modification of B or of CX or of both, whichever is the more feasible. I may get the idea of having my old dog wear spectacles, by identifying him (X) with myself (A) and by visualizing my spectacles (B) on his nose in place of mine. If I were to try this out, I would find that the spectacles would not fit his profile and most certainly would not accommodate his visual needs. Something (Y) like my spectacles, though, could be devised for him—and the idea is not too absurd when we consider the many ways in which pets have been identified with and been treated as human beings.

This kind of readjustment of parts is the usual thing in technological inventions. We have taken notice of this fact before in stating that it is a step in the perfection of most inventions. It is a forced step; for B often will not harmonize perfectly with X, because of the latter's differences with A. There is almost always some misfit with things, at least; so in a sense all mechanical innovations are analogies. However, many start off as simple assimilations. Real analogies begin and end with double identifications. That is the original plan of their initiators.

The most obvious, and perhaps the most common, analogies are those that entail an identification and a substitution of substance in a thing. We call these innovations that retain the form but not the content of the prototype imitations, especially when there has been an effort on the part of the innovator to substitute a material that is, in one or more of its qualities, as much like the original substance as possible. In these instances an element of deception is involved, whether it is selfishly or otherwise motivated. The intent of the innovator is not relevant in this place, but it may be noted that we have a vocabulary for evaluating intent with reference to his products; they are called imitations, substitutes, ersatzes, phonies, fakes, or counterfeits, depending upon the social implications of their use. Somewhere in this range fall the "mink" coats that are made of almost everything save mink fur, dime-store jewelry, patent leather, stage props, lead dollars, chicory, oleomargarine, wax and plastic objects of many descriptions, such fabrics as pongee and shantung—the list could be made almost endless.

All analogies may be said to be imitative to the extent that they are designed to replace their prototypes in some larger configuration of use. This intent is aside from the issue of deceit. The replacement may be desirable, or it may not; in any case the more it simulates the original, the better. Hence such phenomena as the battle between the producers of oleomargarine and the dairymen. The latter have insisted that the oleomargarine manufacturers refrain from making their product appear any more like butter than it naturally is by adding a yellow coloring and dispensing it in packages and cuts resembling butter cubes and squares.

Before leaving the subject of deceptive analogies, it should be noted that they are not confined to substance replacement. They may involve subtly concealed ideological or behavioral differences with a prototype. These differentials, occurring between X and A and Y and B, are masked by the compelling similarities of the analogies that are due to preemptive proportions or influences resident in the common parts, C and C_2. Hence the care that must be exercised in accepting products that are labeled "Strucky Like Cigarettes" and "Lydia Dinkham Compound."

Some analogies—in fact, many—are amusing. The following quotation is an example. Unfortunately its author is unknown. Its prototype is obvious; and what make it an analogy are the common elements ("Our fathers brought forth . . .") with common relationships between them that preserve the form but only a small part of the content (the words) of the original.

"One score and sixteen years ago our fathers brought forth upon this nation a new tax, conceived in desperation and dedicated to the proposition that all men are fair game.

"Now we are engaged in a great mass of calculations testing whether that taxpayer or any taxpayer so confused and so impoverished can long endure. We are met on Form 1040. We have come to dedicate a large portion of our income to a final resting place with those men who here spend their lives that they may spend our money.

"It is altogether anguish and torture that we should do this. But in the legal sense we cannot evade—we cannot under-estimate this tax. The collectors, clever and sly, who computed here, have gone far beyond our power to add and subtract.

"Our editors will little note nor long remember what we pay here, but the Bureau of Internal Revenue can never forget what we report here. It is for us taxpayers rather to be devoted here to the tax return which the government has thus far so nobly spent. It is rather for us to be dedicated to the great task remaining before us—that from these vanished dollars we take increased devotion to the few remaining; that we here highly resolve that next year will not find us in a higher income tax bracket.

"That this taxpayer, underpaid, shall figure out more deductions; and that taxation of the people by the Congress, for the government, shall not cause our solvency to perish."

Communication devices provide more serious examples of analogical innovations. The Morse code as it comes from a telegraph receiver is a series of specific sounds of unequal duration that are patterned by time relations between them. A number of analogies may be constructed upon this prototype, either by analysis of its sensory report and the report of other things or by a convergent incorporation of them, so that any stimulus in any sensory mode can be substituted to convey the same meaning as long as the intervals or time relationships of the prototype are preserved. Any other sound, such as that made by a buzzer, a bell, a pencil tap, a bugle, or the human voice, may be broken up into X and Y intervals on the pattern of AR_1B ("long, short, long," etc.). Light stimuli (lines, blocks, and lights) may be treated the same, as may gestures with the hands.

In connection with the last-mentioned possibility, an interesting communication analogy is reported for the Aleuts. About 1900, Afenogen

Ermeloff, an Aleut of Umnak, Alaska, invented a semaphore system that is distinctly different from the model upon which it is based.[1] Ermeloff, like most Aleuts, was literate, having been schooled in the writing of his native language by means of the Russian alphabet introduced in the area by the missionary Veniaminoff in 1828. Ermeloff was also acquainted with the outward appearance of the semaphore code employed by the United States Coast Guard personnel in its off-shore operations in the vicinity of his home island. These two facts, plus the additional circumstance that Ermeloff supposed that the Americans were signaling by making body signs shaped to represent letters of the Roman alphabet, led to his invention of an Aleutian analogy. In his system the arms and upper body of the signaler were configured to approximate as nearly as possible the forms of the various Russian letters. In the conception of this innovation, Ermeloff obviously thought that he was doing what the Americans were doing. Just as they fixed their arms (A) in positions to represent the shape and signify the meaning (R_1) of a given Roman letter (B), so he placed his arms (X) in positions which were intended to reproduce and signify (R_1) a particular letter (Y) of the Russian alphabet. The analogy was made possible because of the common characteristics (C) obtaining between pairs of body shapes on the one hand, and other common features (C_2) allying pairs of their written counterparts on the other.

Musicians make extensive use of analogies. The most obvious instances occur when the same tune is played by different instruments or the same song is sung by different voices. In the same way, an analogy is created when a score is transposed from one key to another. The substitution of different words in the same tune is, of course, an equally common occurrence. In all these cases the form has remained the same but the precise characteristics of the content have changed. The tonal relationships of the words are the same as in the prototype; but the content, the actual sounds, are different.

The Shakers offer an interesting variant upon this widespread pattern. In their preaching and testifying they very early adopted the singsong intonation that was so typical of the old-fashioned preacher's exhortations. They affected a monotonous undulation of their voices as they praised the means of their salvation and cautioned sinners to repent. Now, as has been mentioned before, there is an interval in their Sunday service that is reserved for secular announcements. Many individuals have acquired the habit of making their announcements in the same singsong voice, interlarded with appeals to "my dear brothers and my dear sisters." The words themselves (X and Y) and their import differ in the two instances; but the tonal ar-

[1] Jay Ellis Ransom, "Aleut Semaphore Signals," *American Anthropologist*, 1941, 43 (No. 3):422–427.

rangement (R_1) of the announcement is modeled upon the preaching stereotype (AR_1B).

Something directly parallel has happened to produce a rather remarkable Shaker document. It was compiled a few years ago by members of the Bible-reading faction with the idea of establishing a written record of some of the important events in cult history. The interesting part about it from the present standpoint is that its phraseology bears unmistakable resemblances to the language of the King James version of the Bible or of analogies modeled upon it. The following sentence is illustrative: "There were times when the spirit of God brought such heavy conviction upon the heart of John Slocum, that he fell prostrate upon the skid roads while at his work; but being ignorant of the will of God, temptations overcame him, and he continued in the ways that were not convenient." In this quotation the particulars (John Slocum) that are relevant to Shaker history are substituted for those (Jacob, Solomon, etc.) in the Bible; but the elements that they have in common with those of the Bible ("the will of God," "temptations," etc.) and the interrelationships of these elements ("brought such heavy conviction," "fell prostrate," "continued in the ways," etc.) are retained.

Nowadays we are very familiar with a kind of analogy in the "forms" that we have become accustomed to filling out in applying for jobs, rations, credit, and so on. These forms are well named because they maintain their interpart relationships regardless of content substitution in the "blanks that are provided." The specific data are the X's, A's, Y's, and B's of our formula, while the common parts are the printed words. The relationships between them are maintained regardless of the filled-in data.

Behavior systems can also be created by analogy. The patterning of acts, such as handshaking, dance steps, football plays, or ritual movements, are cases in point. In the same way there can be rationalizations for impulses, as has already been mentioned. The concept of numbers involves the recognition of a set of relationships between the units in any series of numbered things; and the transfer of the number description, verbal or otherwise, to another series of things constitutes an analogy. Numerically the relationship between one person and two is "one-half of," or "twice that of," depending upon the point of reference. Or, if there is a succession of units, the units are related in terms of "another" or "first" or "prior," etc. If the symbol "one" refers to one of these configurations and the symbol "two" refers to the other, and if these symbols are applied to similar configurations of other things, it is by a process of double identification or analogy.

Memory distortions may come about as the result of an intrusion of prototypes that function as analogues. Bartlett gives some good examples of this when he shows that his subjects were seeking to interpolate meaning into their memory record of some strange story material. In trying to recall an American Indian myth his English students read explanations into their memory fragments that would justify them in terms of the rationale of their English background. Bartlett calls the interpolated elements in these reproductions "explanatory particles and phrases." [2] They are the relationships that have been drawn from the prototypes of the storyteller.

There are many examples of falsification that are due to analogical reasoning in the individual accounts of Shaker history. Very often there are false attributions of ritual numbers. Typically Shakers will now recount events or describe situations of which they have no direct knowledge in terms of either three or seven. Both these mystic numbers were introduced with Christianity.

Children and other people who are not familiar with our speech idioms commonly build words and phrases by analogy, using some prototype with which they have become familiar through the use of other linguistic correlates. Mistakes in the formation of the past tense of some verbs come to mind in this connection. To one who knows that "spring" (A) is the present tense (R_1) of "sprang" (B), the thought of "bring" (X) leads logically enough to "brang" (Y) as its past tense. The "ring" of the stimulus word is not only the common element (C) in the words "spring" and "bring"; it also helps to evoke one of the words upon presentation of the other through a clang association. The same is true of the "rang" (C_2) of their correlates. Other analogies in linguistic constructions depend not upon common elements, but upon the common meanings or contexts for two sets of words or phrases. The pairs are brought together by convergent incorporation. Thus, the prototype "hands (B) is the plural (R_1) of hand (A)" may evoke the analogy "foots (Y) is the plural (R_1) of foot (X)." Or the tense pattern of "move—moved" may produce the analogy "catch—catched."

Four-year-old Susan's middle name is Marie, but so far she has heard it applied to herself only when her mother scolds her. To a large extent it is synonymous for her with "don't" or "for heaven's sake!" When a second term follows explosively (R_1) upon "Susan" (A), in her experience it can be either "don't" (B) or the assimilated word "Marie" (Y). With this as a beginning she has evolved an analogy by identifying other (C) assumed proper names like "mommy" and "daddy" (X) with "Susan." Hence she reprimands her mother and father with the expressions "Mommy Marie!" and "Daddy Marie!"

Novel words and phrases are constantly being constructed upon the same pattern, not only by children and the unlettered, but by anyone in search of more adequate or colorful expressions. There is, for example, a pressure, which is due to the compulsion of prototypes, to create nouns from verbs

[2] F. C. Bartlett, *Remembering. A Study in Experimental and Social Psychology.* New York: Cambridge University Press, 1932, p. 86.

of certain kinds. Almost anyone can appreciate the meaning and the usefulness of words like "hammerer," "clasher," and "renewer" on an analogy with
other nouns derived from a prototype which correlates a verb (A) with a
noun (B) as a prefix (R_1) to "-er." The bridge between each pair of words
derives from incorporation; the members of one pair are verbs, and the other
are nouns. The case is comparable with nouns ending in "-ation" and
"-ment." Words like "yieldment" and "surrenderation" are immediately
comprehensible though unorthodox. Such constructions follow the pattern
of a proportion, with linkages established over detours of incorporated
equivalences. The verb "invent" is to the verb "desire" as the noun "invention" is to the noun "desiration." The R_1 relationship in these cases is that
of a verb prefixed to "-ation."

As Sturtevant points out, it is sometimes impossible to say whether such
constructions are due to simple assimilation or to analogies.[3] He uses the
illustration of the unconventional pronounciation of the word "national."
In simple assimilation a part of "national" is identified with "naytion" on
the basis of formal identity in spelling. "Naytion" (X) is equated with the
"nation" (A) part of the prototype which ends (R_1) in "-al" (B), and is
assimilated to it. On the other hand the unconscious reasoning of those who
say "naytional" may be based upon an analogy such that "naytion" is to
"nation" as "naytional" is to "national." As Sturtevant says, both processes
may be at work supplementing each other. The same holds for any comparable instance in any aspect of culture. Simple assimilation, as noted previously, may be a rarity; theoretically it exists, but practically it may not.

As these linguistic illustrations indicate, analogies may be phrased as proportions. Some proportions are analogies; some are parallels, as will appear
later. Proportional analogies are those that are concerned with the relationship between similar pairs of phenomena. Sometimes innovations spring
from the interpolation or extrapolation of paired correlates, as in the foregoing linguistic examples. The prototype provides the basic two terms, and
a relationship between them. Some third term is presented and affiliated
with one of the other two on the basis of similarity. The fourth term may
then be determined solely by its similarity to the other term of the prototype, in which case its relationship (R_1) to its correlate is postulated or interpolated by translation from the prototype.

Some analogical innovations are not due to the interpolation or the extrapolation of a new term or a new relationship. The terms and their interrelations may already exist, but the innovation consists in asserting the existence of the R_1 relationship between the *common elements* of the two pairs
of correlates that are brought into conjunction for this purpose. Correlates,

[3] E. H. Sturtevant, *Linguistic Change*. New York: G. E. Stechert & Company, 1942,
p. 43.

or alleged correlates, are assembled and paired, and a correlation of some description (the R_1 relationship) is asserted to exist between their abstracted common parts or their incorporated equivalents. This is the method of induction.

Theories arrived at by induction thus involve four variables instead of the three that are essential for deduction. They make use of analogies instead of simple assimilation and are concerned with relationships between the common elements of paired correlates. In place of assuming that all Negroes are musical just because they are Negroes, the suggested correlation between negroid characteristics and musical ability is tested by repeated observations. Each successive individual (X) is treated as a discrete instance having something in common (C) with the first individual (A) noticed, although differing in numerous particulars. In the same way each succeeding manifestation (Y) of musical ability is regarded as a phenomenon distinctly different in time, place, and characteristics from that (B) of the prototype; yet it has something (C_2) in common with it. These common denominators are essential to the theory because the interrelationships between the two sets of correlated phenomena are stated in terms of them. The other and unique features of each phenomenon are irrelevant. If repeated observation yields a correlation between musical ability and the possession of characteristics associated with the Negro race, the alleged correlation must be between common denominators of the two sets of phenomena, the individuals observed and their performances.

Since the theory of the nature of invention herein proposed is innovative it must itself conform to one of the innovative patterns described. I believe that it has been arrived at mostly by induction and that its basic idea rests upon analogical reasoning. It is an analogy on a second level of abstraction, as it must be, because it comprises the first-level abstractions that we call inventions or innovations. It is an innovation about innovations. Its characteristics are presented schematically in Figure 3. The block of letters on the left side represent one invention, while those on the right represent another. They have the same characteristics, and the diagram indicates their parts and the relationship of hybridization or assimilation between the two original configurations XY and AB that is the alleged characteristic of any innovation. The dotted lines represent abstractions of common factors that obtain between successive instances of hybridized configurations. The C which is common to all instances of XY is "a *stimulus* configuration of analyzed subwholes X and Y." The C_2 which is common to all instances of AB is "a *prototype* configuration of analyzed subwholes A and B." The relationship (R_1) between these two common factors is "hybridization" or "assimilation." The theory is that when C is assimilated or crossed with C_2 an innovation results.

It will be noted that this theory follows the pattern of an analogy the subwholes of which are themselves complexes with subwholes. This is as it must be, for the theory presumes to be inclusive of processes like itself. At the same time it should be pointed out that the breakdown of the subwholes indicated in the diagram is for the sake of clarity in presentation and of necessity in demonstration. As far as the over-all theory is concerned, there are only two parts to each included invention. The XY configuration on the left is conceptually subwhole X, while XY on the right is subwhole A. Similarly, the AB on the left is subwhole Y and the AB on the right is subwhole B. In other words, this is a general theory in which particular values can be substituted in accordance with these four equations for X, Y, A, and B.

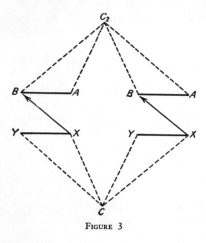

FIGURE 3

Pasteur's theories reveal a series of inferences based upon analogies and parallels. It is exceedingly risky to attempt a reconstruction of the development of a man's thinking without detailed knowledge of it, and no such attempt will be made here. It is not necessary to know the numerous and particular steps in Pasteur's reasoning to justify the assertion that he proceeded by analogy. Those details are included in a larger theoretical structure, the outlines of which are fairly evident. "Their logical sequence is such an instructive feature of Pasteur's researches, that it would be wrong not to point out how the researches on fermentation led to the investigation of diseases in wine and vinegar, and how from the conception of epidemics of yeast and other benign organisms, Pasteur was led to the conception of the cause of epidemic disease in plants, in animals and man." [4]

Pasteur began his investigations of fermentation with the idea that its causes were organic. He thought of the process in terms of a double analogy: yeasts (X) consume sugar (Y) as organisms (A) consume their appropriate foods (B); and secondly, yeasts (X) eliminate alcohol and carbon dioxide (Y) as plants and animals (A) eliminate their waste products (B). It cannot be said with certainty whether his immediate prototype in this reasoning was the plant and animal configuration or the proposition independently propounded by de Latour, Kützing, and Schwann that yeasts

[4] *Encyclopaedia Britannica*, 1946, Vol. 9, p. 177.

are living things. It does not matter, because Pasteur's own microscopic observations of the budding of yeast were sufficient to evoke directly the thought of either the biological parallel or the general proposition arrived at in the same way by his predecessors mentioned above.

Pasteur drew conviction for his theory from another set of analogues that resulted from his work with tartaric acid crystals. He noted that a certain mold (A) consumed one kind of racemic ammonium tartrate and left (R_1) another kind (B) with an asymmetrical crystalline structure (C_2). Analogously, in wine fermentation some substance (X) acted in the same selective way (R_1) to produce the by-product amyl alcohol (Y) that also had an asymmetrical structure (C_2). The active agent (X) in the fermentation process must therefore be something like a mold (A), *i.e.*, an organism.

Pasteur thus took the first step on the way to hypothesizing a living substance as the sufficient cause for fermentation. Simultaneously he noted a contrasting analogy which provided him with reason for asserting that organisms are also a necessary cause. He found that by a laboratory technique (A) he could syntheize (R_1) a form of amyl alcohol (B) that had a symmetrical structure (C_2) similar in its reaction to light to that of undecomposed racemic acid (Y) that was formed (R_1) naturally and, hypothetically, by some chemical means (X) similar to his laboratory technique for making the alcohol. The difference between these two analogical pairs, which involved different forms of the two substances and their origins, permitted him to set up a parallel (see later) that took into account both their similarities and their differences. The conclusion may be stated in the form of a proportion: symmetrical structuring is to asymmetrical structuring as chemical compounding is to organic causation. Organic matter, Pasteur therefore believed, had a selected action on the materials in which it lived.

From this point onward, Pasteur's resort to assimilations, analogies, and parallels for his theories on fermentation and infection is even more evident. When he had developed his immunization technique, he proceeded to establish its universal efficacy by simple assimilation, or analogy, depending upon one's interpretation of it. Probably for him it was uncomplicated assimilation. When he first noticed that a group of chickens did not die of cholera infection if they had first been given a weakened dose of the bacilli, he proceeded to repeat this sequence of exposures to the germ on a number of other fowls. Each repeated immunization (X) was modeled upon the original (A), and so it was a duplicate to the extent of having the necessary common elements (C). In actual fact, of course,, each repetition was different, as any duplication must be, although to him they were identical. So, too, were the characteristics of the animals that he used. All were healthy chickens, and to that extent they were the same; but they, too, were necessarily different in their individual characteristics. His conclusion was the generalization that the essentials of his technique would immunize any healthy chicken.

Subsequently Pasteur proceeded to apply his immunization prototype (AB) to other animals (Y), including man, by further analogies. If cholera vaccine (A) immunized (R_1) chickens (B), then anthrax vaccine (X) should immunize (R_1) sheep (Y). The similarities and differences between these four subwholes are evident. The formal differences between the members of a pair are irrelevant if abstraction can produce a residue of sameness. If it cannot, the identification, by incorporation, of chickens and sheep as members of a class called animals and of cholera and anthrax bacilli as disease-producing organisms provides ready-made channels for the linkage of the pairs of equivalents.

Parallels. Up to this point in the discussion of compound processes the emphasis has been upon equivalences between the two pairs of terms X and A, and Y and B. Innovations occur, however, in which equivalence is a secondary consideration or of no concern at all, the interest being centered upon the differences between the members of the two pairs and their connection in the relationship R_1. There are several variations upon this pattern. They grade into each other and into the pattern of analogies just described. We may call them parallels.

Parallels, like analogies, may be conceived as proportions; but, unlike analogies, they deal with the differentials rather than the resemblances between paired correlates. They involve hybridization, but not as the result of an assimilation of terms. Instead, the R_1 relationship of the prototype AB is interpolated or projected into another set of data XY. It ties X and Y together in a way not previously conceived.

The establishment of a parallel begins with the recognition that A has some relationship to X as well as the relationship R_1 to B. The XA relationship may be of any description apart from one of similarity. Its existence discriminates and thereby sets X and A off from each other. In other words, they constitute an analyzed configuration that already exists when the process starts; the thought of A may therefore suggest the thought of X. A previous configuration of Y and B is likewise demanded. Then Y is evoked as a correlate of X with the relation R_1 existing between them.

Sometimes the thought of X may lead to a seemingly uncontrolled extrapolation of Y by the transference of R_1 to X. A tentative, open-ended XR_1 is thus produced. Y then may be anything as long as it is different from B. The thought that a window (X) is the opposite of a door (A) and that a door is in (R_1) a house (B) may lead someone to the thought of a window in something as completely different from a house as a hat (Y). Such combinations can be thought of ad infinitum, either deliberately or in a kind of a freewheeling, uncontrolled manner. For the most part the results are so unrealistic or so extravagant that they are meaningless. Still, it is not to be denied that new combinations, such as a window in a hat, can be so conceived and that they have been. Furthermore, they have been accepted.

Parallels ordinarily take shape under more precise controls. Not only is there a recognized relationship between X and A but there is a specific one between Y and B. Moreover, the relationships between X and A and between Y and B, whatever their natures might be, are in some way conceived to be similar. X and Y are thus set off from A and B by the same measure; and they are, of course, linked with each other in the same way (R_1) as are A and B. This leads to a parallel with recognizedly different subwholes instead of the duplications, imitations, or interchangeables that characterize the subwholes of analogies. These double discriminations produce symmetrical constructions, but not of equivalents; there is a square of difference instead of the square of similarity figured by the analogy.

Parallels may be established when there are two things, ideas, or behaviors that are regarded as distinct but as having common potentialities, requirements, or functions. They are often constructed upon the initial framework of sex differences. Thus, it may be noted that women in many societies organize clubs that are parallel to those of the men. The existence of the numerous ladies' auxiliaries in our culture is a case in point. The persistent phenomenon of a sexual division of labor, wherein the activities of the women are complementary to those of the men, belongs in the same category. In Palau men do all the fishing to support the household economy, whereas women are exclusively responsible for the production of taro. In the same society men have one kind of "money" that is exclusively theirs, and the women have another.

Class differences are also responsible for the development of parallels. Ideologies, entertainments, and possessions reveal paired cleavages that are practically confined to different economic or other social levels. Our expression, almost amounting to a formula, to the effect that "X is the poor man's A" illuminates this process, since it by implication sets the poor man off from the rich by a contrast of their associated and parallel activities, beliefs, and identifications. Champagne, yachts, polo, marlin fishing, opera, symphonic music, Picasso, and Einstein have their counterparts on group levels where they themselves are not appreciated or available.

Above it was stated that similarity is not a critical consideration in the formation of parallels. It is not *the* bridge or focus of attention that leads from the thought of A to the thought of X. Nevertheless this does not mean that it cannot be present. It may be. Moreover, it may be essential, even though its fundamental character is obscured by the emphasis upon differences. Very often parallels are formed under the dual controls of identification and discrimination, so that X and A are at once similar and different and so are Y and B.

This situation may develop when there is, so to speak, a cleavage of an analogy. This means that X and Y come into view as a result of their being discriminated from A and B. The new configuration XR_1Y is set up as an offset or as a counterdictate to the configuration AR_1B because of a stressing of their unlike aspects despite their similarities. The perception of differences between X and A and between Y and B does not destroy their similarities, and the relationship between them is the same as it was before they were discriminated. The casual observer may, for example, put gills and lungs in the same category because they look somewhat alike and both are used in "breathing." The anatomist, however, will insist upon a distinction between both gills (X) and lungs (A) and upon the water (Y) and the air (B) that passes over (R_1) the tissues of the gill and lung membranes. He finds a superficial resemblance, a parallel, where less acute observers see an identity. Much of what we call science consists in pointing out parallels in place of what are here called analogies by "splitting" the latter. The result is innovative because parts are substituted for wholes: X takes the place of *X and A*, and Y takes the place of *Y and B*, to form two different configurations. The process has been described in the section on discrimination in Chapter VII.

Many imitations of the kind mentioned under analogies have become parallels in this way; that is, through a discrimination of the potentialities of their parts. Nylon, for example, was at first a silk substitute. In time the very qualities which differentiated it from silk recommended its use for other things than the manufacture of flimsy garments. These divergent qualities led to its assimilation in configurations independent of those involving silk. To cite but one instance out of many, the Canadian government has recently perfected a secret process for making nylon fur coats for the use of its airforce personnel. In time this new kind of piling may be a competitor for real fur by reason of its assimilation to that context; in any event nylon has been taken out of the category of silk. Its differences from its former competitor have become its virtues in this particular frame of reference.

Parallels with common denominators have origins other than the splitting of identities. They can be "triangulated" from a standpoint of commonality and difference between X and A and Y and B. Differences are sought or admitted only within the area, confines, or framework of similar things. Under these demands, X's and Y's of parallels are not randomly selected; they occur within a universe of the same class of things. This, in fact, gives meaning to their being differentiated; there is no point in differentiating them unless there is some prospect or certainty of confusing X with A and Y with B.

Parallels, then, may be built up with a dual orientation of similarity and difference. Sometimes our children want to "help" us at our gardening, knife sharpening, or house cleaning. They identify themselves with us and insist upon doing as we do. The reluctant and resourceful parent is a good parallelist. He not only distinguishes between himself and his energetic child but invents some proportional activity that simulates or is complementary to his own in a way that is convincing to the child. It is different enough to suit the parent and like enough to satisfy the child. The relationship of the parent to his activity is preserved in the "busywork" pattern that he constructs.

Mud Bay Louis introduced the wearing of "garments" at Shaker services. According to him they were to be white robes with blue crosses on the front. Mary Slocum, the wife of the founder of the cult, was Louis's rival in church leadership for several years; and she repeatedly opposed his dictates. At one time she claimed to have had a revelation in which it was made manifest to her that men and women should not dress alike in church. She maintained that since the sexes were different, they should wear different robes; the women (A) should wear white (B), and the men (X) should wear black (Y). It is obvious that her differentiation between the sexes was based upon a concept of opposites.

A few years ago a patent was granted for a retractable saw-tooth bar that could be thrust out beneath the wings of an airplane to cut enemy planes to pieces. This device, it is said, was suggested by the sharks' teeth that were painted on the Flying Tigers' P-40's during the Second World War.[5] In this we have an instance of a parallel that had its origin in a picture. The picture of a shark's head aroused the idea of a real shark (A) that can damage (R_1) a human being (B) with its teeth. This evoked the parallel of a mechanical device (X) that had some attributes (C) in common with the shark and that could damage (R_1) fighter planes (Y), which are unlike men except that both are vulnerable things.

Sometimes similarities between the contrasting members of two parallel sets are acquired. The two configurations preexist, but someone lines them up as parallels and adduces similarities among the differences that characterize their respective parts. They are joined, not built up; and they are made to approximate an analogy. A common denominator, by analysis or synthesis, can be made out for any two things, even though they are quite diverse; and this fact can be played upon to establish parallels of greater or less appeal. Previously unassociated things may become parallels through the use of homonyms, similes, metaphors, and high-level abstractions pointing to previously unrecognized resemblances. The newness lies in the juxtaposition and integration of the preexistent wholes at their points of sameness. Sometimes such juxtapositions require real insight; sometimes they are specious or merely clever.

[5] *Time*, May 1, 1944, p. 72.

During 1950 a nationally known petroleum company conducted an advertising campaign for one of its products that ingeniously exploited parallels. In its ads two quite different animals (X and A) were so pictured that at first glance they seemed to have much (C) in common. Furthermore, the animals were so chosen that their names (Y and B) sounded alike (C_2). The eye-catching quality of this device was carried over into a parallel with sales value: the reader was told that, just as there is a great difference between a coon and a loon, for example, so there is an immense difference between one kind of gasoline and another.

Parallels that simultaneously take into account the resemblances and the differences of their member parts often give rise to correlations that advance our knowledge or lead to theoretical speculations. The study of the demographic distribution of cancer has progressed in consequence of distinctions made between its different manifestations and its diverse associations. It appears, for example, that American Negroes (X) manifest a lower percentage (Y) of skin cancer than the percentage (B) that is revealed among American whites (A). Furthermore, among whites, the incidence (Y) of all forms of cancer exhibited by those who live in the South (X) is higher than the incidence (B) manifested by those who live in the North (A).

A study of the history of cultural growth reveals that frequently the particular manifestation of a given belief or artifact that is the oldest is also the most widely distributed in space. This time-space correlation rests upon the fact that it takes time for an innovation to diffuse from the point of its origin and upon the observation, or supposition, that related innovations later conceived at the same or some adjacent point of origin will diffuse at about the same rate as did the first and so will be more restricted in their distributions. Consequently, earlier manifestations will be found to be marginal to later developments. This age-area principle, employed in biology and paleontology as well as in cultural-history reconstructions, is based upon parallels. For example, the bow and arrow (A), as a weapon, now survives only in remote areas (B) by contrast with the gun (X) and its use by peoples of the civilized world (Y) and those in contact with them. The principle can be stated as a proportion: the older trait is to the younger trait as the greater distribution of the first is to the lesser distribution of the second.

It may be that all true parallels are characterized by member pairs that are at once similar and different. It is possible that all such alignments that are not just "thought up" as an exercise have this dualistic character. In any event, many, if not most, of them are linked by bonds of similarity beyond the common relationship R_1 between their parts. Emphasis upon the similarities or the differences then gives them the complexion of a parallel or a duplicate in accordance with the attitude adopted toward them. If the double similarity becomes a paramount consideration, if it outweighs differences, amalgamation can take place. An emphasis upon similarity makes

XR_1Y unstable and is conducive to its confusion with AR_1B. There is a tendency to complete the identification, so that the whole of one configuration is assimilated to the whole of the other.

Such assimilation not infrequently happens, in spite of cautions against it. Of late years we have heard much of elaborate machines that are called mechanical brains. We are told that they can think, forget, and even get worried and go insane. It is unquestionable that these intricate mechanisms can produce some results that duplicate the products of human thinking. They can do this faster and more accurately than can the human brain. But it is something else to say that they are brains and that they function in the same way. To attribute "decisions" and other human functions to them is to confuse a parallel with what we have been calling an imitation or an analogy.

It is not surprising that such confusions occur. The coexistence of common denominators and differences in two pairs of a parallel series often makes it difficult to draw a clear line of distinction between double assimilation and double discrimination. At times sameness and difference are really only two aspects of the same phenomenon. In fact, that is the quality which gives them virtue in many contexts. Their dual and contrary aspects can be exploited, and they frequently are. In many imitations, as we have seen, the idea is to make the innovation two-valued. Substances are substituted in some imitations with the idea of making the analogy cheap but expensive-looking. In the case of fraternal organizations the parallels are not the same, but they are enough alike to be satisfactory for those who want to imitate the patterns followed by others out of their class. A new code also has a double value: it is the same as its prototype for the insiders, but different for those who do not know its secret.

A consideration of these facts reveals that there is no absolute distinction between parallels and analogies. Whether something should be called a mere parallel or a true analogy depends very much upon the purpose of the innovator and the uses conceived for his innovation. It depends upon whether he intends to distinguish two parallels or whether he hopes that they will be identified and so be made interchangeable.

Alternatives. Identification and discrimination can operate together to produce a new combination. They do so by "pulling" X and Y in opposite directions with respect to the prototype AB: the configuration X is differentiated from A, but Y is identified with B. This is a very common pattern, especially in deliberate innovations when the hope is for an alternate solution to a problem or when there is demand for a new idea that differs from the existing mode. This motivation is typical of those innovations in which something, X, differing in specified ways from A, is sought as a replacement for A. Improving innovations and those mentioned under "quantitative variations" in Chapter VI fall in this category.

The conditions set up for these innovations are that X be discriminated from A but that it stand in the same relationship as A to B; it must satisfy the same requirements with respect to B that A does but have stipulated differences. Since the sought-for "something" might otherwise be anything, more positive directives or controls are needed to establish the characteristics of X. One such control lies in the qualifications that are demanded of it. These requirements permit it to be identified with something like it in some other configuration, such as C_3ZY in Figure 4. Y can be a second orientation point if it is configured with Z in the required relationship and if it is at the same time similar to B. These two controls will "locate" X. In short, Z, of some known configuration ZY, is identified with X and assimilates it to Y; and Z is in turn assimilated to B because of a similarity between Y and B.

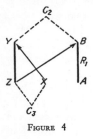

FIGURE 4

Suppose that "something" (X) that is not salt (A) is wanted that will keep a person from slipping (R_1) on an ice-coated pavement (B). It must be something light that can be attached to shoes. The clue to its character is provided by "something" of this description (Z) that is used in connection with something similar to ice, namely, slick logs (Y). If this line of reasoning were followed, then Z, and consequently X, would be the calks or spikes used on loggers' boots.

Sometimes alternatives are forced by the observation that the desired "something," X, is directly connected with Y. Then the characteristics of X must be deduced without the intermediation of Z. The fact that upon one occasion Pasteur's chickens failed to succumb to a cholera bacillus infection brought this configuration into conjunction with the expected pattern of the prototype established by previous experimentation. An explanation in terms of their difference was consequently indicated. Pasteur was called upon to discriminate, either between the chickens that had survived and those that had died, or between the character of the doses that he had given to them. The first alternative would have signified that some chickens (B) died of cholera bacilli (A) while others (Y) did not. Thus, by identifying the doses, X and A, and projecting A, the configuration AR_2Y would result, meaning that the same bacillus affected different chickens differently. This was not reasonable in view of Pasteur's previous experience with his flock. There was more evidence for discriminating between the germ cultures CX and CA while maintaining the identity of the chickens Y and B. In other words, B was equated with Y and assimilated to its context to form the more reasonable configuration XR_2B, meaning that a moribund bacillus culture would not kill any chickens.

It will be observed that this situation does not differ from the one already described in Chapter VII with reference to alternatives in assimilation.

There it was said that if no similarity exists between X and A, then Y and B could be identified with the same results. Here the only added consideration is that X and A *must* be different to satisfy the requirements of the situation. Consequently, there must be an indirect substitution, a detour instead of a direct approach.

This pattern of innovation also bears upon the contention that discrimination is an ancillary mechanism, an assisting or a stage-setting device, not the basic process that identification is. It should also be pointed out again that this pattern gives the appearance of a substitution of differences even more so than when there is no conscious segregation of X and A. In effect, the result is just that; the aim has been to substitute something that is entirely different, but it must be accomplished indirectly and incidentally. Psychologically the process is due to the substitution of equivalents, Y and B.

Crosses. So far we have proceeded on the assumption that the two configurations that enter into a new combination do so (1) when a subwhole of one is identified with a subwhole of the other; or (2) when the two subwholes of one are identified with the two of the other; or (3) when the two subwholes of one are discriminated from, but have a definite relationship to, the two subwholes of the other. In the first instance a cross-referenced combination results; in the second there is an imitation or an analogy; in the third a parallel is produced. It remains to be shown that cross-referenced combinations can also result from a double identification.

This kind of combination can happen when there is a third common element in the two configurations, one in addition to that which appears upon the analysis or convergent incorporation of X and A or of Y and B. There is a common factor, a kind of a convergence point, somewhere in between X and Y and in between A and B. This point of overlap may be fully recognized antecedent to the innovation, or it may be factored out at the moment that the innovation takes place. In any event, and in terms of our diagram, this means, schematically, that XY crosses AB at some point along its extension. The two lines converge and diverge; they are not parallel.

As an example of an innovation that takes place under these conditions, we may suppose that I want to say, "We must avoid that man," but that I say instead, "We must evoid that man." I have obviously mixed the two words "avoid" and "evade." The reason for my confusion lies in the fact that these words are to some degree synonymous; they can be used interchangeably in some contexts. This is their meaning, their common denominator by convergent incorporation. They are both present in my thinking almost simultaneously, but I begin with one and later shift to the other. The shift comes at their second common point; namely, on the v sound. There is another divergence after this, which is due to the differences between "-oid" and "-ade." Then finally there is a convergence in the common context, "that man." Figure 5 symbolizes these interwoven relationships. In common parlance, I have confused the words "avoid" and "evade"; in the technical terms of the linguist, one of these words has interfered with the other. The common element v acts as a kind of a switch—or since we deplore the result, a better term for it would be a derailer or a shunter. At first I am thinking of a but I say e; then I am thinking of "-ade" but I say "-oid."

In terms of the theory maintained here, two interpretations of such mistakes are possible. One is that there has been a double identification and assimilation combined with a switch in prototype. Either e has been identified with, and assimilated to, a, and "-oid" likewise with "-ade"; or the re-

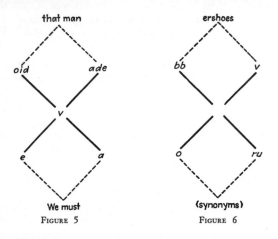

FIGURE 5   FIGURE 6

verse has taken place, depending upon whether initially "avoid" was the prototype or whether "evade" was. The switch in the prototype, and a repetition of the identification process—perhaps in an unconscious effort to readjust—occasions a double confusion. One identification only (e with a) and a switch of prototype (to "-ade") would have created nothing new; in fact one confusion would have compensated for the other.

A second interpretation would be that there has been a retention of one prototype throughout but that in the beginning there was an assimilation and later a projection. If the prototype were "avoid," then the result could be explained as being due to an identification of e with a, with a subsequent projection of "-oid" onto "-ade." The opposite would hold true if the consistent prototype were "evade."

There is something to be said for each of these interpretations. Perhaps now one and now the other is operative, depending upon the circumstances. In any event, this compound process produces results the reverse of an analogy. Analogizing builds up equivalents out of paired hybrids. Crossing builds hybrids out of paired but crossed equivalents. This kind of compounding is not the same as simple or double identification, because the common middle term plays a critical part in the process. The middle term is an added feature, and it occasions the duplication of identification.

The above example is the simplest kind of cross because it rests upon an obvious switching point. There are, however, many more subtle involvements. We may take another linguistic example to illustrate one of these complications. Figure 6 schematizes what happens when a person who intends to say "rubber shoes" says either "ruver shoes" or "obber shoes." Again we are dealing with words that are brought into conjunction because of the similarity of meaning and the possibility of their being interchanged in certain contexts. The switching point in this case, however, does not depend upon an obvious identity in the middle of the two words; it represents a realization of *some* phonetic similarity between the sounds b and v. An abstracted common factor occasions the crossing over.

There are examples of confusions of this sort that involve more than one cross in the middle of words or phrases. Figure 7 is intended to schematize the error made by a person who intends to say "weak and feeble" but who says instead either "feak and weeble" or "weeble and feak."

Finally, there are examples of asymmetrical crosses. In these cases the two expressions do not have their common point in the middle of each prototype. It may be in the middle of one word and at the beginning, or at the end, of another. The two thoughts are brought together as in the preceding cases, but schematically there is a blank at one of the points of divergence. This does not mean, however, that psychologically there is nothing there. There is some psychological entity, something that fills in, not an absence of mental functioning. This blank may be considered to be something in the nature of a pause or a preparation for what follows. In any event, there is some mental appreciation of it; it is a filled interval, comparable to the concept of zero or nothingness. Figures 8 and 9 schematize examples of these asymmetrical crosses. The question mark symbolizes the blank just discussed.

Innovation by crossing can take place when, for any reason, two configurations with more than one common element are juxtaposed. The fact that there is a fundamental difference between them at X and A and that this difference is linked with distinct correlates, Y and B, makes their confusion innovative. The differences between them are interwoven between their similarities. This interlacing may be spontaneous, as it is in mistakes like those just illustrated, or it may be worked out deliberately. Crosses are not by any means confined to verbal expressions. Many of them are due to divergent demands of any sort that simultaneously require expression. The phenomenon of crossing therefore explains many of the innovations that were noticed in Chapter V under the heading of conflicting wants.

Crossing is not necessarily dependent upon resemblances between X and A and Y and B. These pairs of terms may be linked by any relationship that will serve to bring about the apposition of the two prototypes. In other words, crossing over may take place between the two configurations of a parallel if they have, in addition to their discriminating relationships, an element in common that operates to join and confuse them. If I am accustomed to eating my dinner (X) before attending lodge meeting (C) on Thursdays (Y) but not (A) if I attend meetings (C) that fall on Mondays (B), it is probable, if I am not careful, that I will appear at lodge headquarters on some Thursday without having had my dinner.

The crossing of prototypes consistently occurs in memory lapses, just as do simple assimilations and analogies. The acts of individuals, the parts that they have played in certain events, dates, and other details of the past, get mixed up because of several points of resemblance between two different idea sets. New interpretations and beliefs thereby

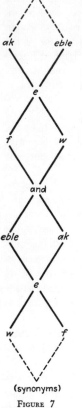

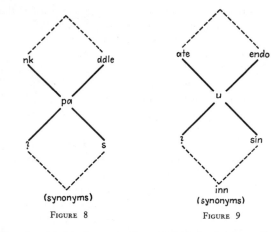

(synonyms)   (synonyms)   (synonyms)

FIGURE 7   FIGURE 8   FIGURE 9

have their inception. Crossing is also the cause for certain behavioral modifications. Shaker ritual has undergone several alterations because of confusions of this character. To give one example, a certain ritual performance called for the participants to march in from the right side of the room, turn around once, and then begin to sing. Another maneuver called for them to march in from the left, turn around once, and then begin to pray. These two patterns became confused, perhaps because of the common marching pattern, but more certainly because of the second element of similarity, the turning around. Consequently, it developed that the participants came in from the right, turned around once, and prayed, instead of singing as they should have done in accordance with the old pattern.

It may seem that crossing is a form of innovation at variance with others described. It has been assumed throughout this chapter that there are only two subwholes in configurations whose parts are recombined. It has been maintained that at the instant of analysis, or incorporation, there is one subwhole that is focused upon and another from which it stands out and which gives it its distinctiveness as a subwhole. This conception is adequate to explain all instances that have been considered, including crossing, if we keep in mind the fact that a configuration is such at a given level of analysis only. It may be broken down an instant later or resynthesized; and in the case of crossing this has happened. In crossing there is no persistent configuration such as XY, but subgroupings within it that are themselves complexes with interrelated subwholes at one moment. At the next instant there is a regrouping. In short, we have here a sequence of analyses and identifications within XY and AB instead of just one.

Part Four: Acceptance and Rejection

CHAPTER X

THE ADVOCATES OF CHANGE

Innovation and Acceptance. From the standpoint of social consequences the fate of an innovation is as important as its conception. Many new ideas are stillborn, and countless others are ephemeral and perish without a trace. Some are only casual thoughts; others become cornerstones of faith. Some affect only the innovator himself; others, millions of individuals. Some are bitterly resisted, others are welcomed. For some the welcome comes early, for others it is tendered late. These are clearly matters of importance, quite apart from questions concerning origins. Illuminating as they are, the latter probe only a small part of the problem of cultural change, and from some points of view the least important part. For an understanding of many changes a knowledge of ultimate origins is irrelevant, as it is when Christianity, for example, is introduced into remote corners of the world. Also, from a practical standpoint, it is not sufficient to comprehend the mechanism of innovation and the conditions which stimulate or discourage it. Subsequent events are equally if not solely important to the salesman and to the culture historian; and a definition of alternative possibilities with an analysis of the conditions affecting them may have both practical and theoretical implications. In brief, a study of cultural change takes us beyond the appearance of a new idea into a consideration of its acceptance and rejection.

In discussions of this subject a distinction is sometimes made between the acceptance of a new idea by people within the cultural sphere of the innovator and acceptance by those of other ethnic groups. The growth in popularity of a new idea within the society of its origin then comes under the heading of "adoption," "acceptance," or some similar term, whereas the passage of an idea across ethnic boundaries is usually referred to as its "spreading," "borrowing," or "diffusion." Or, if considerable parts of the cultures of two ethnic groups are involved in the transfer, the equalization is called "assimilation" or "acculturation." These are useful distinctions and serve to highlight certain aspects of cultural change. At the same time these varied phenomena are merely manifestations of the same process. In the last analysis the question always comes down to the particular relations between two individuals, the donor or carrier of an idea, for whom it is more or less habitual, and a

potential receiver or adopter, for whom it is more or less alien. Idea transference requires some means of communication between a person who
already has the idea in question and another person who is to be made acquainted with it. Consequently, whether it be a matter of idea transfer from
an American innovator to his next-door neighbor or to a Samoan or from
many Americans to many Samoans and from the latter to many Tahitians,
the essential mechanism must be the same. The possessor of the idea reveals
his acquaintance with it in some way, and those to whom it is revealed either
accept or reject it for themselves. Diffusion, acculturation, and faddism are
all therefore manifestations of the same phenomenon. They are varied patternings of the process of acceptance. Each has its own conditions, and so the
final result is different; but they come about through the differential operation of acceptance and rejection on the individual level. Diffusion is acceptance and acceptance is diffusion, the one term being conventionally appropriate to the description of a collective response to a new idea, the other to an
individual reaction. Psychologically there is no difference.

Many of the observations already made with reference to innovation also
apply to acceptance. Sometimes, for example, the conditions that are conducive to innovation also stimulate acceptance. The cultural areas of anticipated change are also areas favorable to the acceptance of new ideas. Frequently, too, the motivations and the characteristics of acceptors of novelties
are much the same as those of innovators. Furthermore, the boundaries of
novelty establish the areas of controversy about accepting them. As we have
seen, substitutions within the range of "sameness" are not recognized as innovations. Correlatively, there is no question of accepting or rejecting them;
they are not regarded as departures, so they raise no issues. Finally, it is to
be noted that acceptance is imitation, so that what has been said of imitation
applies equally to acceptance. This means that since imitation is inevitably
innovative, acceptance is also.

While the problems of innovation and acceptance thus join at many
points, the two phenomena are distinct and have different determinants.
Although the conditions, attitudes, and consequences that relate to them
overlap in some degree, they also diverge. In some instances the conditions
which produce the one will not produce the other. Thus, a multitude of innovations are made that are never accepted, many by men who know in advance that they will not be and do not care. In many other instances of
change there is no question of innovation; from the viewpoint of the individuals involved, the issue is solely one of acceptance. Thus, once an innovation is made, the issue is whether to accept it or not, and this confronts many
more people than does the question of whether to invent or not. In large part,
too, the psychological characteristics of innovators and acceptors are different,
although they may be said to be complementary. Some men want to lead and

can; others, while preferring the new, need a leader. On the other hand, many innovators are reluctant pace setters and need follower-advocates. Finally, even though imitation, or acceptance, is actually innovative, it is not motivationally so. From the standpoint of their own attitudes and of the attitudes of others toward them, the distinction between innovators and acceptors is clear-cut.

For these and other reasons it is advisable to treat acceptance apart from innovation. It is easy to do so and saves confusion. In the present section we shall therefore be concerned with the characteristics of situations, persons, and things relative to the acceptance of new ideas and with the processes by which it takes place. In this and the next chapter attention is given to the advocates of new ideas. This is a significant, though not always a clearly conceptualized, aspect of the problem of acceptance. Innovations require an advocate of some description if they are to make any social impression. The categories of advocates treated below are not intended to be exhaustive, nor are they mutually exclusive. In general they comprise different motivational complexes. All the advocates considered champion change in some way. Even though they do not seek the acceptance of a novelty by others, they pose social problems by adopting it themselves. That which they sponsor need not be new to them, and frequently it is not; but it is new from the standpoint of others. Whether or not a custom is lately acquired by its advocate is a question of some significance, but the emphasis upon advocacy as such relegates it to a subsidiary status in the discussion which follows.

Innovations without Advocates. Before proceeding to characterize advocates, it is well to note again that many innovations have none. This remains true even though we set aside the countless aberrations that fall within the range of conventionally established identities. Obviously a departure from tradition needs no champion if it is not considered to be a departure; but there are numerous instances in which a recognized novelty has no social consequences because no one, not even its author, will support it. We have given attention to some of these innovations in the discussion of conflicting, subliminal, and compensatory self-wants. There it was noticed that innovations appear involuntarily or in desperation and that frequently no one, least of all their originators, wants to adopt them as habitual responses. Or, if they are subsequently resorted to, this and their authorship itself are disclaimed or admitted only reluctantly. Such denial can be expected whenever the innovator is ashamed of his creation; that is, when he regards his aberration as substandard rather than as merely variant or as supranormal.

Innovations like those just mentioned lack advocates because they are held to be mistakes or misguided ventures. There are others without this stigma which nonetheless are abandoned at their conception. Sometimes a new idea, even though admittedly a good one, or potentially so, never acquires a sponsor. We have to do here, not with failures under competition, for competing novelties must necessarily have at least the advocacy of their creators, but with new ideas that are forgotten. In these instances there is a lack of motivation on the part of the innovator. For some reason he is not interested in clarifying his idea, in building upon it, or in incorporating it into his behavior system. This may be because he is lazy, careless, or preoccupied with other things. His idea strikes him as a good one, but he does not have the energy or the time to give it further consideration. Or he may think that it is sound and useful but has only trivial implications. The results that may be expected from many innovations are inconsiderable by comparison with the effort, money, or time that would be required to put them into effect. They may save time but are too costly; or the gain that could be expected from their operation would not be a sufficient reward for the habit and other changes that would be required for their adoption.

Embryonic innovations are frequently put aside through a lack of perseverance. Comparatively few people have the persistence repeatedly to rework a basically good idea until it can meet the tests of practicability or logical consistency. Most people lose their enthusiasm for their novel conceptions with a few discouragements. Then, too, many do nothing because they know that innovators are seldom honored and are often ruined, financially and otherwise, through being identified with their ideas. The way of the innovator is hard, and some men know this in advance. They are willing to leave such hardships to others.

A great many novelties begin and end as individual peculiarities. They are valued by their originators but no attempt is made to secure their general acceptance. In the ordinary meaning of the term, they, too, lack advocates. It is likely that all of us have such idiosyncrasies that we have invented and that we never think of asking others to adopt. In many cases the suggestion would be disconcerting, because we consider them to be personal possessions that others can have no good reason for wanting to imitate. Obvious aping can be embarrassing if not irritating. It may be taken not as flattery but as sycophancy or as an invasion of privacy.

Some innovations are by the circumstances of their origin individualized prerogatives. They are not intended to be popularized because they are symbols of distinction. They put the stamp of uniqueness upon their originator and have this function only. They are in a sense trade-marks and are valued for that reason. Some men, for example, affect a particular style of hat, others a speech mannerism, others an irascible disposition. Artists are especially prone to adopt some peculiar posture as their symbol, but they are by no means alone in this propensity. Thus, over against the temper of G. B. Shaw, the dripping watches of Dali, and the sombrero of Joaquin Miller may be set the stance of Napoleon, the pearl-handled pistols of George Patton, the "My Friends, . . ." of F. D. Roosevelt, and the thunderous jeremiads of John L. Lewis. No one could or should imitate these personal signatures. They are private property.

Still other idiosyncrasies remain such because their innovators have conceived them solely for their own pleasure. They have given satisfaction either in their conception or in their private use. With this they have accomplished the purpose for which they were designed, and that is the end of it as far as their originators are concerned. If others are interested in adopting them they may do so, but that is an irrelevant consideration. This attitude is intimately linked with the creative wants of those individuals who putter, probe, or try their capacities against manufactured obstacles. Such people do not need to convince others of the worth of their ideas and are indifferent to the question of their general acceptance.

Finally, some innovators reject the role of proselytizer for themselves. They may consider that their ideas are good for others as well as themselves but shy away from carrying the torch to prove their conviction. They may be selfish or indifferent toward others, or they may simply lack the reformer's spirit.

It would be a mistake to believe that innovators whose creations remain individual peculiarities have no cultural effect. Though they make no effort to gain acceptance by others, their unusual behavior is certain to have some consequences for their associates. A man who sleeps for only four hours each night would have to be a recluse to pass unnoticed. At the least he must be tolerated; at most everyone with whom he has close relations must make allowances and sacrifices for his eccentricity. These allowances will obviously bear most heavily upon his most intimate associates, his family and his fellow workers—if he has any. But even beyond this range idiosyncrasies have repercussions. They establish reputations, and legends cluster about them. They encourage identifications by other people and give vicarious enjoyment in the ego magnification which they inspire. Furthermore, iconoclasts and lone wolves can cut a wide swath without anyone's wanting to be like them, particularly if they are in positions of power and influence. It seems that the intimates of Ivan the Terrible, Rasputin, and Hitler were not attracted by the personal peculiarities of these men, but their lives and the lives of millions of others were vitally affected by them.

Professional Advocates. Almost all American and European inventors of 30 to 100 years ago were their own salesmen. Goodyear spent most of his life trying to convince others of the commercial possibilities of cured rubber. He took out patents on almost every conceivable use of rubber except, unfortunately, for pneumatic tires. He spent $50,000 on a display of rubber goods at the Paris Exposition in 1855. Edison spent almost as much getting his incandescent lamp to burn for forty hours and not long after put on a successful demonstration of his laboratory and street-lighting systems in Menlo Park, New Jersey, for some 3,000 people who were brought by special trains from New York. Sholes was an ardent advocate of his typewriter idea, so much so that he had no trouble getting collaborators to help him remedy the defects of his first crude machine. Morse had to give repeated public and private demonstrations of his telegraph to get enough money to continue with his work upon it. He exhibited it to an indifferent public in New York and Philadelphia, demonstrated it to members of Congress, and sent and received messages between Washington and Baltimore with observers present, in order to sell the idea to the government. Selden tried to get investors on both sides of the Atlantic interested in his automobile patent, a procedure forced upon many inventors before and since.

Nowadays most professional inventors relinquish their advocacy to professional surrogates. This applies to literary and other artistic creations as well as to technological inventions. Because of competition and the complexities of marketing a new idea, people who make their living by their creative efforts usually find it advisable to leave the advocacy of their innovations to representatives who are specialists in this field. The categories of specialists who are available are as varied as are the approaches to publicity in our publicity-conscious era. This field itself has, in fact, become an area for ingenious elaboration. If an innovator is lucky or influential, he may be able to get a boost through the interests of news reporters, talent scouts of various descriptions, or exploiters of the "human-interest" field. An example is provided by a United Press story, under a 1950 Washington, D.C., date line, of a young man in Detroit afflicted with cerebral palsy. Although he has had to work under extreme physical difficulties, this young man has spent his time inventing things to help other people. According to the news story, he hopes that some of his inventions will be accepted because his ambition is to "help others to an easier way of life."[1]

Professional innovators cannot depend upon a stroke of luck for the general acceptance of their ideas. Those who are determined to maintain an investment in their creations may, if they are financially able, employ an agent or attorney to represent them and to promote their interests for a consideration. Alternatively, they may try to find a collaborator or an investor with the necessary funds to support their researches and to market their ideas successfully. Failing that, many sell their ideas outright or work at a fixed salary for an industrial organization the business of which is to promote research and to sell its practical results. Amateur innovators are also forced to resort to these methods to get backing. The impecunious inventor of whatever sort often has no other recourse than to delegate the

---

[1] *Eugene* (Oregon) *Register-Guard,* Dec. 20, 1950.

advocacy of his ideas to others. As Rossman says in his remarks concerning the inadequacy of our patent system:[2]

The Government has taken no direct interest in the welfare of the inventor except in granting him a patent and the value of this patent depends entirely on the skill and ability of his patent attorney and not on the merits of his invention. The many conditions adverse to the inventor which prevail today have, therefore, forced most inventors to enter the employ of large organizations in order to live. The simplest inventions require the expenditure of thousands of dollars, the services of many experts and specialists before the invention is actually marketed. Very few inventors can meet such rigorous requirements and their only recourse is either to interest some promoters or to drop their brainchild, for the Government is utterly indifferent and has no facilities to give him expert advice or assistance. As one inventor has said, "We are nothing but intellectual serfs."

The result of this system of delegation of sponsorship is that the innovator seldom gets a name credit for his ideas. He is bought out, and his sponsor becomes the innovator as far as the public knows or cares.

To some extent this outcome must be anticipated by the majority of innovators at the present time regardless of the initial patronage that they receive. In Europe and America sponsorship has become so commercialized that it requires a considerable amount of planning and organization. It is a business and must be handled like any other commercial venture. Consequently, whether an innovator continues to be identified with his ideas or not, his personal advocacy of them counts for very little. The promotion of their acceptance is turned over to an impersonal organization that uses highly specialized techniques to reach and influence the public. Promotion requires skill and money and does not encourage pride in accomplishment so much as it does an awareness of what can be done through publicity and sales techniques. Even though the innovator's name continues to be associated with his impersonally sponsored product and even though he retains some control over its promotion, he is at some remove from its actual presentation to potential acceptors.

Promotional organizations and schemes advocating changes are a common feature of American life. A great many of them are initiated by individuals seeking profitable investments. No small number, however, are backed by groups of individuals who already have a vested interest in the success of a proposed change. These include professional societies, political parties, ethnic classes, fraternal associations, citizen groups, producer or consumer organizations, and so on indefinitely through the range of interest groups which make up our society. Public-relations experts, apologists, and salesmen of various kinds are employed by such groups to act as their

[2] Joseph Rossman, *The Psychology of the Inventor*. Washington, D.C.: Inventor's Publishing Co., 1931, pp. 161–162.

contacting agents with the public. Advertising in all its varied media is an indispensable adjunct. Pressure-group tactics that include political threats, bribery, and *quid pro quo* concessions are effective "sales" techniques at one —and often the most critical—promotional level. The practice of lobbying, both for and against change, has become an accepted adjunct of the legislative process at the state and national level. For the favors that they found it worth while to render to national congressmen in Washington, 256 lobbying groups expended approximately 8 million dollars in 1949. Much of this was spent by organizations, such as the American Medical Association, the National Association of Margarine Manufacturers, the United World Federalists, The Townsend Plan, and the National Association of Real Estate Boards, whose membership was either supporting or opposing some new idea.[3]

Governments as well as private groups among their citizens utilize promotional machinery to advance or suppress new ideas. Autocrats occupy an enviable position in this respect; but the heads of democratic governments operating under popular mandates, however acquired and interpreted, act as surrogate advocates with a powerful organization at their disposal. Promotional methods differ; but whether the authorization for a change is a Hitlerian decree or a parliamentary enactment, its face-to-face protagonists as far as its acceptors are concerned are the personnel of the governmental agencies assigned to institute it. Although the praise or blame for reforms is directed at corporate bodies, such as political parties and administrations, the real advocates must take the shape of individual human beings who represent them and individually subscribe to their programs. Bureaucrats and other public servants therefore make up an important category of paid advocates of change who, like investors and professional publicists, are interested as much in the fact of acceptance as they are in the social consequences of it. In other words, getting the idea across is a job for them. They are professional advocates.

Professional advocates are experts in persuasion. Their activities, more than anything else, support the popular fancy that inventions are prompted because people need them. In actual fact, as has been pointed out, need is an individual condition, and a mass concentration of it is a relatively infrequent occurrence. In by far the majority of cases only the inventor needs what he invents. If this were not so, his creation would require no advocacy. A simple announcement of its availability to a waiting world would be and sometimes is sufficient. But when organized advocacy by specialists and vested interests is called for, it can scarcely be maintained that group necessity is the mother of invention. On the contrary, inventions of this character, far from satisfying wants, are actually unwelcome. Those who undertake their

[3] *Time,* Mar. 6, 1950.

sponsorship, especially if this is their business, contrive to stimulate an atmosphere of acceptance. They actually create wants for the thing they have to sell. They make the housewife feel abused to be obliged to wield a broom when she, like other normal women, could have a "Whiz" vacuum cleaner; they make her conscious of her scrub-reddened hands when she, too, could have that appleblossom complexion by using "Sno-Soft" hand lotion. Without slandering competitors, they make it obvious that the "Woolsey Lambsie" mattress is far superior to the one with the unwrapped spring. They make the new multiple injector a necessity, and cheap at "less than $5," although its sales price is marked as $4.99. They invent wants to match the qualifications of the inventions that they advocate.

Financial difficulties are not the only consideration impelling a transfer of sponsorship. Financial necessity, after all, is a special case dependent upon a rather unique set of circumstances that have developed in recent times in our own historical tradition. More often the innovator shuns the role of advocate for his concept because he is temperamentally unqualified for it. He realizes that he is lacking in the personal attributes that promotion techniques demand. He may be reticent, uneasy among others, fearful of ridicule or failure, lacking in practical sense or tact, or easy to discourage. This is not an uncommon situation. There seems to be an incompatibility between a personality make-up that is likely to be creative and one that is suited to the vigorous dissemination of ideas. There is, of course, no rigid demarcation, but some people build better than they sell, and vice versa. There is much to substantiate the popular stereotype of the impractical dreamer and the absent-minded scientist. The inventors who were contacted in Rossman's survey rated business ability high on the scale of requirements for success in their profession—and 176 patent attorneys reported that in their opinion the lack of it was a noticeable characteristic of them.[4] The same thing may be said of innovators in other areas of culture. In fact, if there is any difference, social innovators are likely to be even more reticent than the inventors of things, so that surrogate advocates for them are even more common.

Surrogates who assume the function of advocating a new idea may have one of several possible relationships with the innovator. They may have a business agreement whereby the obligations and the benefits of each are stipulated in advance, as obtains in the case of the inventor who sells the rights to his idea to a manufacturer. On the other hand, there may be no direct contact between the innovator and his advocate at all. They may not be acquainted or have any personal interest in each other. It is the idea alone which interests the advocate. In still other cases the personal element is pronounced, and the advocate identifies himself with the innovator.

[4] Rossman, *op. cit.*, p. 39.

Sometimes the distinctive relationship between the two is that of a superior and a dependent, a leader and a follower, or a master and a disciple. Then the advocate praises the genius of the innovator, celebrates his achievements, and urges others to do likewise.

It is remarkable how often the master-disciple relationship has developed in the arts and the sciences and in philosophy and religion. It often happens that scholars and artists whose particular methods or interpretations attract a student following are more embarrassed than pleased by their apotheosis. They hesitate to publicize their achievements. They are discomfited by the flattery of being called the leader of a "school," and if their praises are sung, it must be done by their disciples. It is not simply self-consciousness that is involved. More fundamentally, the kind of innovator who attracts proselytizing disciples is different in temperament from them. Innovations which inspire such personal adulation for their originators are not trivial conceptions realized on the spur of the moment. On the contrary, they are evolved out of mental turmoil and wide understanding, and they are pregnant with implications for the existing order. It would seem that the man who is capable of profound and revolutionary thought is seldom equipped to propagandize it as effectively as is some aggressive admirer. The disposition to think rigorously and persistently is not often combined with the urge and the ability to convince others of its worth to them. Put in another way, there are men who are primarily thinkers and others who are at their best as executors. Individuals cannot be dichotomized within this frame of reference; it merely brings into relief certain polar characteristics which may be integrated in varying proportions. But it is remarkable how often the master-disciple relationship functions on a creator-proselytizer axis.

This relationship has been a recurring phenomenon in religious innovations. Frequently the prophet, the thinker, is overshadowed in the public eye by the dynamic personality of a convert who acts as his advocate and without whom the new movement would either fail or be accorded only a very limited acceptance. Moreover, the disciple advocate, whether knowingly or not, inevitably injects his own interpretation into the doctrine of his master and modifies it to some extent. The spread and the survival of many religious revolutions have been dependent upon the appearance of such evangelists. Thus Jesus, for all his appeal to the crowds that flocked to hear him, left only a small and a bewildered group of followers at his death. It was Paul of Tarsus who gave them a theology, who gave meaning to the crucifixion, and who was the spokesman for Christianity to the world beyond Galilee and Jerusalem. Mohammed had his militant and steadfast advocate in Abu Bekr. Of the roles of these two men in the early history of Islam, H. G. Wells has written:[5]

The true embodiment of the spirit of Islam was not Muhammad, but his close friend and supporter, Abu Bekr. There can be little doubt that if Muhammad was the mind and imagination of primitive Islam, Abu Bekr was its conscience and its will. Throughout their life together it was Muhammad who said the thing, but it was Abu Bekr who believed the thing. When Muhammad wavered, Abu Bekr sustained him. Abu Bekr was a man without doubts, his beliefs cut down to acts cleanly as a sharp knife cuts.

To choose another example, if the fate of the Shaker cult had depended upon the proselytizing ability of John Slocum, the movement would scarcely have survived him. He was a timid man, temperamentally unable to carry out his divine commission to tell the Indian people of the blessing God had bestowed upon them. Informants who knew him say that he was "afraid" or "bashful." From the time of the announcement of his message, his importance to the cult rapidly diminished, while first his wife and then Mud Bay Louis took over its leadership. Unlike many of his early converts, he was not considered important enough to be courted or persecuted by the cult's opponents; and when the Shaker church was organized in 1892, he was made only an elder. At the present time nobody knows just when he died. While differing in particulars, the history of the Modekne cult in the Palau Islands presents a parallel development. Temudad, the visionary who founded this syncretized Christian-Palauan religious revival, was little more than a curiosity in his home village until he was joined by a militant organizer and protagonist, Ongesi. The dominant personality of Ongesi soon led to a dual leadership whereby Ongesi became the spokesman for Temudad, who was the spokesman for God—subject to reinterpretation by Ongesi. Under his apostle's influence Temudad's version of puritanical Christianity became a reactionary revival of pagan practices with a pronounced antiforeign orientation that led to its suppression by the Japanese. At present, apologists for the cult stress Temudad's teachings in defending it before outsiders; but it is evident that the real meaning that it has for them bears the imprint of Ongesi's personality.

Out-group Advocates. When an idea or a custom diffuses from an ethnic group wherein it is familiar to one wherein it is new, acceptance takes on a different complexion. Alien acceptors are the counterparts of the acceptors of indigenous novelties, and the two have much in common psychologically. Both are in some measure advocates of that which they accept, although the out-group acceptor, like his in-group counterpart, may have no desire

[5] H. G. Wells, *The Outline of History* (3d rev. ed.). New York: Garden City Publishing Company, Inc., 1929, p. 582. Quoted by permission of G. P. Wells.

to propagandize his associates to follow his lead. Each by his adoption of something new is by so much an advocate of it in the eyes of others, and each is made aware of his position upon every occasion that summons him to act upon his conviction. Nevertheless, in most instances, there is an important distinction between the roles of these two categories of advocates and the attitudes of their fellows toward them. The difference stems from the fact that in the one case a single ethnic group is involved, whereas in the other there are two. From the viewpoint of the advocates this may make little difference, or it may be most important; but more often than not the fact that one of their number has adopted a specifically alien custom makes a major difference to most of the members of the group. In other words, imported novelties are commonly regarded in a different light from indigenous ones. They may be held to be better or worse, but they are not the same; and their advocates participate in the credit or discredit that is assigned to them. This is often the incentive or the deterrent for acceptance or rejection in cross-cultural diffusion.

Some alien advocates are such because of circumstances over which they feel they have no control. This is true of individuals who have for one reason or another found it necessary, interesting, or expedient to spend some time in close association with foreigners and then later to rejoin their home community. Inevitably foreign contacts, unless they have been brief and wholly superficial, produce some change in the tastes, the behavior, or the ideological orientation of repatriates. Frequently such changes, which are in the nature of partial assimilations to the norms of an individual's alien associates, take place subtly, by degrees, and beyond his awareness of them. Then it is only upon his return to his previous cultural environment that he and his fellows appreciate the extent and the depth of his acculturation. Deliberate assimilation, whether undertaken out of preference or necessity, is, of course, equally common among such exiles. They are out-group representatives until they are assimilated by their new cultural environment, whereupon they become alien advocates within the context of their home situation if they return to it.

The cultural effects of out-group advocacy by repatriated individuals may be undiscernible and ephemeral, or they may be lasting and significant for the stay-at-homes. The vigor and the extent of advocacy by repatriates depend upon the motivation of the homecomers, the degree to which they have been acculturated, and the local conditions to which they return. Their effectiveness also depends upon their number. These are matters to be considered in another connection. Just now we may note that the "native returned" is a frequent vehicle for diffusion and a more universal one than is sometimes supposed. He is to be found wherever there are facilities, incentives, or coercives to pass freely across ethnic boundaries of any kind. The disposition of many Americans to leave home, combined frequently with a later nostalgic yearning to return, yields a high percentage of voluntary or involuntary interregional and international advocates. The New England relatives of a person who has spent a few years on the Pacific Coast are likely to be disturbed by the oddity of his speech if he revisits them, just as his Western friends come to find it more understandable. The same holds for any local mannerisms and customs that are transplanted by the urge to see new places, to enjoy exotic experiences, or to seek greater opportunities. In American society, and in others, the desire to escape the limitations of a provincial existence has led to a heterogeneous influx of the curious and the ambitious into metropolitan and industrial centers and to a disproportionate ebb of partially denaturalized repatriates to the farms and the villages of the hearthlands. The last war drew a great number of American people out of their accustomed routines, reaffiliated and reindoctrinated them, and then released them with perspectives that frequently made them advocates of change in large or small degree among their previous associates. This has been particularly true of war veterans, especially those of minority groups, but to some extent it affected most people who directly experienced the upheaval. Cross-cultural marriages sometimes result in alien advocates at home. They may if they do not endure and one of the ex-spouses ultimately returns to his or her homeland after a substantial interval of foreign residence; or if the children of such a marriage maintain contacts with the nonlocal side of their families. Field scientists, governmental representatives, and adventurers are also in a position to act as culture importers following a term of residence among outlanders. Several American families in the Palau Islands have adopted the Japanese (and the native) custom of removing their shoes before entering their own homes, and one individual has carried this practice back to the United States. He, his wife, and his children wear stockings but no shoes when they are alone at home. Moreover, the neighborhood playmates of the children have, with a little encouragement from the mother, also taken up the practice.

Advocates of foreign customs are likely to appear with any conjunction of cultural differences, and they do so with considerable frequency in the contacts between members of an invading and a resident society. From the time of their discovery by white men, individual natives of some of the Pacific Islands have been drawn into close association with Europeans for limited periods of time, after which, in most cases, they have of necessity if not by choice been compelled to return to their home villages. In the early days of European contact young men were employed or were taken away by force to serve as seamen or as plantation or mine workers. The indenture system, or something very like it, still exists in several parts of the area. Moreover, natives are now employed in considerable numbers all over the region as day laborers, house servants, policemen, or personal attendants by planters, prospectors, explorers, and governmental agencies. A few have been sent away to school or to some laboratory set up for specialized training in skills like nursing. Some understanding of the alien culture to which they are introduced is inevitably imparted to all such individuals. Indeed, in most instances they know far more about the customs of their teachers and employers than the latter know about theirs.[6] Furthermore, many adopt these alien customs as their own and become their advocates at home. Those Palauans who have been on the most intimate terms with the Japanese, and later with the Americans, at once stand out in their native communities by their dress, by the houses they build, and by their mannerisms. Their aberrant inclinations are still more crucial, though less evident, in their ideological conflicts with the less acculturated individuals of their communities. They are, as forcefully as they dare, advocating changes in Palauan culture that are based upon the Japanese and the American models that appeal to them, especially those which would grant them individual independence and security.

It is sometimes difficult to distinguish between individuals who are genuinely acculturated and those who parade an alien posture before their fellows for some real or supposed private advantage that it gives them. It is not easy to differentiate between behaviors that are adopted because they are in themselves satisfying to their acceptors and those that are welcome for their instrumental value alone. Nevertheless, it is evident that at times foreign traits are exploited rather than enjoyed by their acceptors. They are used by their advocates to achieve some personal goal. The aim may be to curry favor with the members of the out-group from which the custom has been taken or to acquire power or prestige within the value system of the in-group. At one extreme among these opportunists are those who cast their lot with the out-group and support its values and interests at the expense of in-group welfare. Into this category of self-seeking advocates would fall the renegades, fifth columnists, apostates, traitors, turncoats, and collaborators whose names are anathema to the majority of their own people. Yet even among them it is not always possible to say whether selfish interests are uppermost. Doubtless many deserters not only are more satisfied personally with the alien values that they espouse but genuinely believe that their group as a whole would benefit from their acceptance. Many workers for the Communist cause in the United States are unquestionably sincere in their conviction that the collapse of the capitalistic system would represent a gain not only for them but for everybody. Despite this, their goal, like that of other reformers, is rejected by most Americans because it has been determined by unilateral decision; and their advocacy,

[6] Stephen W. Reed, "The Making of Modern New Guinea," *American Philosophical Society Memoirs*, 1943, 18:231.

more than that of an alien, is resented because they have set the values of an out-group above the values of their own. They have gone over to the opposition and sold out their own people.

Less objectionable—because they are nonreformist—are the opportunistic advocates who adopt an alien behavior for the impression they hope to make upon their fellows. Pseudo sophisticates, bohemians, and dilettantes use this technique to advertise their cosmopolitanism, to excite the envy of their associates, or to make themselves conspicuous. Idiosyncrasies serve the same purposes but not so well for some people under some conditions. Alien novelties may be more effective because they come from a group with a high prestige rating, because they are symbols of wide experience, or simply because they are exotic. Pseudo sophisticates borrow across all sorts of ethnic boundaries, including those of class and caste, when they are able to do so. The affectations of social climbers, the cosmopolitan pretensions of small-town hostesses, and the posturing of the "international set" draw upon alien patterns for in-group prestige. Such borrowing has been a rather common occurrence wherever Euro-American culture has invaded primitive areas. The members of the upper classes in Chamorro society in Guam at first looked upon the adoption of Christianity as an aristocratic prerogative. They resisted its introduction among the common people because their exclusive possession of it enhanced their superior position.[7] When the Yurok Indians first became acquainted with American dress, the men who could afford the luxury of long red underwear solemnly wore suits of it as prestige symbols upon formal occasions. Palauan men at the present time wear high rubber boots obtained from the Americans for the same purpose. They take them off when they come to a stream that must be waded.

The advocacy of alien customs can easily fit into, or develop into, competitive contests. At one time certain Maori villages in New Zealand vied with each other in the building of bigger and better flour mills. Other Polynesians have adopted church buildings and other appurtenances of Christianity as vehicles for prestige competition.

Many a South Sea village has one or more huge cathedral-like structure, while the tumbling ruins of abandoned earlier structures are a familiar sight everywhere. In some instances, missions have had to set limits upon competitive church building to prevent their adherents from saddling themselves with crippling debts and obligations, and at least one government, that of American Samoa, has regulative laws on the matter.[8]

[7] Laura Thompson, *Guam and Its People*. Princeton, N.J.: Princeton University Press, 1947, p. 180.

[8] Felix Keesing, *The South Seas in the Modern World*. New York: The John Day Company, 1941, p. 124.

The exploitation of the outward symbols of Christianity and of European learning occurred also in the Bismarck Archipelago in the early days of white and native contact there. A missionary at Port Hunter finally succeeded in inducing the natives of the village where he resided to build a church. News of this soon spread, and within a few weeks seven other groups, not to be outdone by the first, erected churches in their villages.[9] In the same district a head man of one community sent an appeal to the resident missionary for a teacher for his people. At first this request was gratifying to the missionary, but he later learned that the chief looked upon the presence of a teacher in his village as a social privilege and not as a source of enlightenment. Hostilities broke out between the followers of this chief and the people of another village when the latter were also promised a teacher.[10]

Although pseudo sophisticates do not intend to reform their associates, the example they set by their advocacy of alien customs often has this effect, especially if their borrowings are from a group with generally recognized prestige. Their friends feel that they must follow suit or lose face. Thus, the laplap or waist cloth very early became, and continues to be, a symbol of sophistication in parts of Melanesia. Nakedness or near nakedness was the rule over much of this region in pre-European times, but after the arrival of the missionaries the laplap became a visible token of civilized shame. The use of this covering has spread from one native group to another as a result of the ridicule of the sophisticates who have adopted it.[11] For the same reason some of the tribes of the interior of New Guinea who are not yet fully under governmental control, and who are not therefore required to pay a head tax, do nonetheless importune officials to tax them because this has become a hallmark of civilization. Reed says of the Kwoma that it is worth 10 schillings to their vanity to be to this extent like the more cultured inhabitants of the Sepik River. Some villages in this region boast of the amount of head tax they pay because this is a measure of prestige.[12] The natives of Malaita in the Solomon Islands now expect a young man to take employment away from home for several years as a necessary part of his education. Hogbin says that "a man who has not seen Tulagi and one or two other islands is looked upon almost as if he has not been correctly brought up, and his contemporaries refer to him contemptuously as 'man belong bush.' "[13]

[9] Reed, *op. cit.*, p. 107.
[10] *Ibid.*
[11] *Ibid.*, p. 109.
[12] *Ibid.*, p. 180, footnote.
[13] H. Ian Hogbin, *Experiments in Civilization*. London: Routledge and Kegan Paul, Ltd., 1939, p. 161.

There is one characteristic that all out-group advocates have in common: whether by choice or force of circumstances they are eclectics. They straddle two ways of life. They are not content either with their own native culture in its entirety or with the whole of the culture from which they borrow. There are obstacles or disabilities that deter them from throwing in their lot completely either with their own group or with the out-group. They do not want to expatriate themselves—as their critics often suggest that they should. Instead they want to live in their homeland and enjoy whatever satisfactions they find in their indigenous culture; but at the same time they want to introduce certain specific customs that other people have and that are more to their liking than are the local counterparts. And, as we have seen, sometimes this introduction is impossible unless they are able to convert or to betray their fellows, for acceptance in many cases cannot be an individual matter. Out-group advocates, then, are selective; they choose what they believe to be the best from two or more cultural systems and attempt a fusion of their choices.

Conservative Advocates. Up to this point we have considered the advocates of novelties presented either by innovation or diffusion. Such advocates accept a change that is new to them as well as to their associates. Theirs is a significant kind of advocacy; but it must not be overlooked that there are advocates of conservatism as well as of change and that what is constancy for one person may mean change to another. In other words, although conservatism is usually thought of as a reaction against new ideas originating at home or abroad, the situation may be reversed and conservatism may itself take the initiative and become a proselytizing force that demands change by nonconformists. The imperialistic animus of conservatism is aroused when it comes into contact with anything that differs from it, whether new or old. The advocate of conservatism may thus be intent, not only upon the preservation of the *status quo* as he knows it, but also upon its extension to and its acceptance by others. The issue to him is not one of self-change, but of change on the part of others to bring them into agreement with himself. Unlike the advocate of a novelty, he remains unchanged. Whether the idea that he opposes is an innovation of his own group or is presented to him as a part of the habit system of an alien group, he demands its abandonment and a substitution of that to which he is accustomed. The conservative advocate is, in other words, an ethnocentric protagonist. He is uncomfortable with novelty, and he mans the bastions of his cultural system along its frontiers.

All of us are upon occasion and in varying degrees advocates of conservatism, as indeed we must be if we are to have any faith or security at all. No one is so disengaged from his culture that he will not stand as its representative in at least a passive way. As products of our social microcosm we have no choice other than to exhibit its impress in all save a limited range of recognized idiosyncratic behaviors. The significance of this truism is not

evident until we are confronted with some alternative to our accustomed behaviors. Then we must decide whether we are to continue as we have done,
to change, or to advocate change by those who differ from us. It is probably
true that every mature individual has at some time and in some way been
confronted with this issue, for there are universal as well as special conditions which bring it into relief. Furthermore, in our reactions to it, none of
us is either wholly conservative or completely malleable. Each of us has
experienced behavioral variability and has reacted in part positively and in
part negatively to it. Everyman is a conservative as well as an innovator.

Parents obviously play the role of advocates of conservatism—some more,
some less. In this capacity they are not mere paragons posing for the imitation of their offspring. They are not passive exemplifications of one way to
live but aggressive protagonists of *the* way to live. They are ethnocentric
and militant advocates supporting their conventions on the frontier of a new
generation. The members of the new generation, moreover, are not colorless,
habitless, aimless organisms waiting to be molded and directed. They are an
aggregation of spirited and wayward animals who are always taking off in
the "wrong" direction, ignoring or flouting the arbitrary and incomprehensible demands of their elders. They constantly press the issue of change or
stability upon their parents and force them, whether they like it or not, to
be advocates of conservatism.

The members of kinship groups, including the conjugal family, also develop into ethnocentric protagonists of their particular folkways. The members of a closely knit in-group, such as a family, almost inevitably evolve
habit patterns which differ in some degree from those of other comparable
units. Such intergroup differences are more marked perhaps in societies like
ours than in others, but it seems probable that they are to be found in some
measure everywhere. Among us, family customs differ markedly in such
details as eating and sleeping routines, food preferences, household management, ideas of child training and discipline, relations between husband,
wife, and children, verbal expressions, and mannerisms. Anthropologists and
other social scientists are prone to overlook the significance of these family
traditions. There is no agreement among them about the size or the composition of an ethnic group, but by implication at least they always consider
it to be larger than the kinship unit. Yet a little reflection will make it evident that family traditions are in every respect like those shared by larger
groups and that they are just as significant as any others within the framework of their sameness or difference. Family differences are highlighted in
neighborhood antipathies and in the unsettling effects of interfamilial dif-
fusions among children. It is not to be denied that there is a great deal of
cross-familial assimilation, with one family adopting the habits of another.
At the same time there is always a limit to this assimilation and a point at
which the members of one family assert their folkway independence. The

Browns may have "supper" at six o'clock in the evening, but the Whites will insist upon eating "dinner" at that hour; the Jones children may be allowed to roam the neighborhood at all hours, but the Black children are certainly not going to do so. The more intimate the relationship between families, the more significant become the similarities and the differences between their traditions. They can be ignored, and commonly are, unless there is a need or a wish for families to work or live together in close cooperation. There are usually mutual surprises in store for families who go on camping trips together for the first time.

Whole families may act as advocates in neighborhood contacts, or individual family representatives may carry their home-grown customs much farther afield. Weekend guests and college roommates often find themselves living with people who do some very queer things which, besides casting their own practices into relief, very often serve to strengthen their conviction in their own ways. Family cultures take on real significance when their conflicting values are brought together by their individual protagonists in marriage. Personality clashes make marital adjustments difficult; so do variant family ideals. Each spouse carries over to the new home situation certain orientations that are accepted norms in the one that he or she has left. Some of these are overt and some covert, as in any other cultural situation.

Spouses will insist upon perpetuating some customs while agreeing to make concessions on others, as will advocates in any meeting of divergent traditions. Some of the differences may be judged trivial by outsiders; but, as has been maintained throughout this book, triviality is a measure of an attitude, not a quality of a behavior or a thing. Husband and wife can and frequently do make major issues out of the acceptance or rejection by each other of trifles—whether to read newspapers at the breakfast table, whether to open Christmas packages on Christmas Eve or on Christmas Day, whether to go visiting or to stay home on Sunday. Husbands in our society frequently expect their wives to cook their eggs or hang up their trousers just as their mothers did, and wives expect their husbands to accept the household traditions to which they themselves are accustomed. A bride whose father treats her mother's views with respect is likely to find it difficult to adjust to a husband whose family tradition asserts the unequivocal and unilateral dominance of the male head of the house. Some of the more obtrusive of these clashes make their appearance in the engagement period, when they may be resolved, ignored, or magnified to the point where they are intolerable. A large number of them, however, appear only after a period of intimate acquaintance and daily association.

Immigrants are another category of ethnocentric culture carriers. Like the advocates of conservatism just discussed, they may be the conveyors of familial, regional, or national traditions; and at times they are identical with spouses and parents. In a sense all these individuals are immigrants who move into an alien cultural environment. However, in the ordinary meaning of the term immigrants are people who cross cultural boundaries that are more distinct than those which usually separate families, neighborhoods, adjacent towns, and provinces. There is, moreover, an emphasis in the term upon displacement, upon a definite and a decisive removal from a homeland to a new habitat. Immigrants voluntarily dissociate themselves from accustomed scenes, routines, and personal contacts. They sever many ties and have to make many new adjustments. At the same time, they inevitably transport much of their native culture with them. This they may in part abandon, modify, or insist upon maintaining in their new home.

The importance of immigrants as advocates of conservatism depends upon factors which permit, facilitate, or hamper individual mobility. The question of mobility has relevance not only to international movements of people but also to interregional migration within the borders of a single political unit or linguistic area. In the United States immigrants have introduced whole complexes of customs from abroad and have been able to maintain them by living in close and exclusive association with other individuals who have the same or similar backgrounds. Only a minority of the population of the ethnic enclaves thus formed—usually the second-generation residents—need to make any major adjustments to the culture of the dominant group in the midst of which they live. Many individuals among them know no English and have only intermittent and secondhand contacts with the manifestations of American culture around them. Aside from this well-known phenomenon, however, there is the fact that within what is called American culture itself there are marked regional variations and a high degree of individual and group mobility back and forth across the diffuse zones which vaguely define these ethnic provinces. Intersectional importations are obvious all over the nation in the behaviors of the migrants who have made a temporary or a permanent shift in residence. They are evidenced by introduced food preferences and cuisines ("southern-style dinners"), speech provincialisms, dress habits (men carrying umbrellas or going without hats), home construction and decoration ("ranch-style" homes, houses with or without basements), attitudes (political views, racial discrimination), and many other variants that stand out in the local scene because they are not indigenous to it. Rural and urban as well as sectional customs also have their advocates who, when they change their residence, continue in varying degrees to believe and to behave as they have been accustomed to doing.

Colonists, administrators, missionaries, teachers, and entrepreneurs in alien lands are conservers of the traditions of their homeland, and sometimes aggressively such. They may do no more, but they usually endeavor to live in their new habitat much as they did in the old. Americans in the Palau

Islands, Hong Kong, and Arabia dress, speak, and act as they do in the United States; and they have, if they can, radios, washing machines, refrigerators, overstuffed furniture, and air-conditioning machines. They practice their accustomed ideals of interpersonal relations, manifest a pride in the accomplishments of their compatriots, and exemplify their traditional ideologies in their behaviors. Some individuals in foreign service are, by the very nature of their occupations, bent not only on conserving tradition in their personal behavior but on advocating its extension among local inhabitants. This is the aim of missionaries, and it becomes the adopted role of the native catechumens trained by them. It is also the aim of representatives of custodian or colonial governments that administer the affairs of dependent peoples. When treaties were being made with American Indian tribes, part of the benefits that the Indians were to receive in return for the cession of their lands consisted of things and techniques that were valued by the white man. Beginning at that time and continuing into the present the government, where it has fulfilled its part of the agreement, has introduced on reservations a variety of resident advocates of American culture. Among them have been missionaries, blacksmiths, carpenters, farmers, physicians, matrons, and schoolteachers. All these people have attempted to make the Indian more and more like the white man.

It is sometimes overlooked that underneath the diffusion that has taken place as a result of the movements and the commerce of protagonists of European and Asiatic traditions, there has been a great deal of cultural mixing instigated by the human flotsam that has been caught in the eddies of these larger currents. The Shaker cult has spread from one group to another in the Pacific Northwest solely by individual Indian advocates using channels of communication opened up by whites and to a large extent as a by-product of the periodic interminglings of Indian laborers working for whites in harvesting operations. Native neophytes in Oceania have been widely used by missionaries to spread Christianity and the secular European and American traits that have everywhere accompanied the invasions of this religion. The Wesleyan Mission established in 1875 in the Duke of York Islands in the Bismarck Archipelago consisted of its leader, George Brown, and nine Samoan and Fijian converts, with six of their native wives.[14] Inevitably native immigrant converts like these Samoans and Fijians have imported certain elements of their culture into the new lands where they have taken up residence. Keesing reports that Tahitian missionaries in proselytizing other islanders have used their native tongue so exclusively that their converts now speak Tahitian rather than their own language.[15] The Palauans now have so many songs and dances imported from Guam, Yap, Ponape. and Truk

[14] Reed, *op. cit.,* p. 105.
[15] Keesing, *op. cit.,* p. 71.

that they seldom resort to their own. These foreign features have all been introduced by natives who have moved about the area working for the Germans or the Japanese. Many of the Pacific Island ports, such as Suva, Papeete, and Rabaul, have become minuscule cosmopolitan centers from the standpoint of the diverse native cultures that are represented there. Natives from the same districts cluster in small colonies within these seaport towns. Like the immigrant enclaves in the United States, these colonies are conservative outliers or isolates in the midst of an alien environment. Their component individuals are advocates of the *status quo* to the extent that they remain culturally differentiated from those within the other groups around them.

CHAPTER XI

ADVOCATE ASSETS

Acceptance Controls. The reception given to a new idea is not so fortuitous and unpredictable as it sometimes appears to be. The character of the idea is itself an important determinant. Also, when either an innovation or an alien importation first makes its appearance, it does not do so in a vacuum. There are certain situational features connected with it which predispose those to whom it is introduced either to accept or reject it. In particular instances the values placed upon these features may either reinforce or nullify each other. Moreover, as we shall see in a subsequent chapter, there are also determinants among the range of potential acceptors. The permutation of these differentials often creates a very complex interplay of forces that contributes to a resultant of acceptance or of rejection. Complexity, however, differs from a random conjunction of events when the variables in any given complex are finite in number and their individual effects can be calculated. Acceptance is governed by definable controls, and their existence may be ascertained in advance of a given introduction. One set of such controls relates to the auspices of the presentation of a new idea, specifically to the personal and the social characteristics of its advocate. There are several variables that fall under this heading.

Prestige. It is sometimes said that the prestige of the advocate of a new idea is a decisive factor in its acceptance or rejection by others. This is true, but only with important reservations. The proposition does not provide us with a sufficiently refined conceptual tool to probe the effective elements in the situation. On the one hand, this statement is likely to be misleading and, on the other, it does not bring to the surface the advocate characteristics that are pertinent. Prestige is a blanket term that covers a heterogeneous assortment of discrete attributes. Eminence is, in the last analysis, an accreditation of competence. It therefore attaches to many qualifications the differential effects of which are masked by their all being referred to simply as prestige factors. All advocate characteristics which bear upon acceptance can be subsumed under the rubric of prestige or the lack of it if one wishes, but this gives no insight into the issues in the acceptance situation.

It is often taken for granted that a chief, a king, a politician, or a social leader exerts influence under any and all circumstances, but only a little analysis is required to reveal that this is not true. In fact, anyone can adduce multiple instances to the contrary drawn from his own experience and common knowledge. Attention to particulars will soon disclose that the prestige ratings of the same person are varied. They vary with reference to particular situations, particular groups, and particular areas of behavior. Bernard Baruch is a venerable statesman whose views upon national and international affairs have influenced United States policy and practice for many years. He is considered to be an oracle in high places; but there are many Americans who have not even heard of him; or if they have, his preeminence in politics has meant nothing to them. He is certainly not the ideal of the teen-agers. His dress, speech, ideas, and pleasures are not theirs; and any change that he might advocate along these lines, unless it were to coincide with their views, would have little or no effect upon them. The Duchess of Windsor has enormous prestige in certain circles, and her social appearances are given international publicity. At the same time the new gowns that she wears and the life that she leads do not constitute models to be imitated by the Iowa or the Washington farmer's wife. These women look to other paragons to set the pattern for their ambitions within their own circles. Outcasts and marginal men, such as hobos and criminals, without question have paragons different from those of the successful merchant.

In dealing with alien peoples whom they want to influence, missionaries, traders, and administrators usually make contact with priests, kings, and aristocrats, hoping to secure the cooperation of these powerful men in gaining popular acceptance of their goals. They attempt to play upon the prestige of local leaders even though they themselves might be in a position to bring force to bear upon the populace. The theory is good, and sometimes it works. Seldom does it work perfectly, however, for it is premised upon the faulty generalization that prestige is the exclusive property of the elite and is co-extensive with authority. Almost never is a leader universally admired and looked upon as a model to be voluntarily copied by all ages and classes within the domain of his control. There will always be some individuals for whom the doings of their headman are a matter of indifference or something to be scorned, because they do not identify themselves with him or with his ambitions. He is not their ideal man, or he may be so only in limited areas.

In trying to understand this complex situation it should be kept in mind that we are dealing with distinct prestige structures as well as with hierarchical ratings of individuals within each. Two complementary facts, then, are relevant to leadership on this basis: first, no person serves as an exemplar in the particular area of his preeminence for everyone who knows him; and second, no one is so versatile that he is a universal exemplar in every area of interest that is valued by those who know him. From the viewpoint of potential acceptors this means, first, that they are free to choose among protagonists in particular areas, such as political activities; and, second, that they acknowledge different exemplars in their different areas of interest, such as the political as contrasted with the scientific. In both instances prestige rests upon competency; but in the first it is a matter of degree of prestige, and in the second a matter of kind of prestige. In the first, there is a choice of claimants for leadership at the option of the acceptor; in the second, there is a distinction between experts in one field and experts in another. In the first, prestige hierarchies are established; in the second, prestige structures remain discrete with their own hierarchies of individuals within them.

Within any area of interest it is rare to find everyone agreed upon the ratings to be assigned to those who manifest an ability in coping with it. Individual judgments based upon different criteria of excellence give rise to discrepant prestige hierarchies, even when personality clashes are at a minimum. When personality differences play a dominant role in interpersonal relations and when other contingencies are permitted to impinge upon the weighing processes, as they usually are, the results tend to become still more diversified. The more competitive the striving to gain adherents, the more certain this is to be true; but even when there is no overt contest, or none at all, personal evaluations of actual or potential protagonists can vary greatly. In a society like our own the number of individuals in any given field, such as athletics or politics, who are the foremost favorites of somebody is certainly enormous. The ratings of nationally known celebrities are not less extreme, though the number of persons that are involved is necessarily less. The labor leader who commands the respect of one group of workers is a scoundrel in the opinion of others, and the news commentator who functions as an oracle for one segment of the populace is an irresponsible mischief-maker in the estimation of those whose favorite is another.

Popularity, like authority, can be a misleading guide to advocate effectiveness because of the range and variety of individual allegiances. The individual with the most impressive reputation may be statistically the most effective advocate of an idea, but he is not the only one who can produce an effect. He may be able to influence more people than can some lesser light, but the latter is equally powerful within the smaller circle of his admirers. Prestige is, after all, a matter of interpersonal relations, and anyone can be the idol of at least one other person. Close friends, relations, and others whose names are unknown and whose virtues go unappreciated outside the restricted circle of their acquaintances are commonly far more effective advocates of change—or of conservatism—than are those who have been elevated to the pinnacle of popularity or command by reason of birth, selection, or accident.

Prestige ratings of the principals within a single area of interest are therefore a function of individual evaluations which seldom are in perfect agreement. Beyond this, there is the second fact mentioned above; namely, that no person can achieve the status of a paragon in every activity that is recognized as important by those who know him and have an opportunity to accept his advocacy. The reason for this is that prestige may rest upon any value, and no one is so versatile or Olympian that he can range over all the interests of a society with equal ease and proficiency—even if he were permitted to do so. Prestige accrues to excellence in any area of endeavor; and for physical reasons if for no other, it is almost impossible for one person to be rated as universally superior. Men cannot excel in the activities or the ideologies habitual and appropriate to women without in effect being rated as women. In the same way, men reared in an aristocratic tradition rarely excel in middle-class virtues, even though they may be paragons for those who aspire to go beyond them. Consequently, an advocate of change has influence only to a limited extent and with reference to his specific proficiencies; and one expert defers to the prestige of another in an area beyond the range of his competence.

The advocacy of experts not only sets off new waves of acceptance; it also frequently kills or attempts to kill them by counteradvocacy. Stern, among others, has called attention to the damaging effects that the opposition of men with prestige has had upon medical discoveries. Vesalius was attacked by his contemporaries because he challenged the authority of Galen on human anatomy. He was called a madman, and his resort to dissection to acquire knowledge was labeled impious. Harvey met with opposition of the same sort, and on the same grounds, with the publication of his researches upon the circulation of the blood. At least twenty authorities upon anatomy challenged his views in print, and many others ignored his discoveries or abused him personally. Lister's insistence that antisepsis would prevent the suppuration of wounds provoked attacks from many quarters, and for several reasons; but the really damaging contentions were those of medical authorities, such as James Simpson and James Morton, who either denied his method any originality, belittled its effects, or advocated some other causes for the good results that he was able to demonstrate. When Semmelweis announced his theory that puerperal fever was a contagious disease and was not due to any supernatural influences, he was violently assailed by members of the medical profession and experts in related fields. Virchow ignored him with pontifical disdain. Others fell upon him with ridicule, misrepresentation, and personal vilification.[1]

Groups as well as individuals are ranked according to their abilities as these abilities are judged by their evaluators. Again, the estimates are selective. Scarcely any group of people is granted eminence in all aspects of its behavior. Palauan chiefs yield prestige to American administrators in governmental affairs, but they are not so eclipsed in matters pertaining strictly to native customs or native welfare. Thus, for changes in custom

---

[1] Bernhard J. Stern, "Social Factors in Medical Progress." In Faculty of Political Science of Columbia University (eds.), *Studies in History, Economics, and Public Law*, No. 287. New York: Columbia University Press, 1927, pp. 37, 44–50, 66–70, 80–89.

that are demanded by adjustments to the outside world, such as those in trade and law, the people, including the chiefs, look to American officials for guidance; for internal changes, such as the adjustments between native factions and family members, the chiefs are relied upon for leadership because the background of the Americans does not qualify them to offer reasonable decisions, a fact which is appreciated by the Americans themselves.

Although the prestige of an individual or a group seldom if ever extends over every area of interest of an evaluator, there are approximations to this condition. The more complete the identification of an admirer with his paragon, the more extensive will be the prestige accreditation. Very often a new idea is accepted or rejected solely because of the group affiliation of its advocate. Loyal partisans accept it because it is sponsored by one of their group, as happens when relatives, age mates, co-workers, or political-party members identify themselves with the prestige of their leaders. On the other hand, independents embrace new ideas that are advocated by out-groups just because of the prestige of such groups, as is the case when the members of lower castes, classes, or minority groups, for example, accept the leadership of their acknowledged superiors. Stated otherwise, some individuals are predisposed to rate their own group as universally superior to out-groups, whereas others are inclined to do the opposite.

These predispositions to acceptance have their obverse in patterns of rejection. Some people reject a new idea just because it is advocated by one of their group, while others are prone to reject anything that is sponsored by a foreigner. Most of the nativistic cults which have evolved as a reaction to submergence by invading cultural influences have a strong element of this negativistic attitude. Their adherents reject anything of foreign origin just because it is foreign. Conservative Shakers want no white man, nor any white man's idea about the way in which their service is to be conducted, to influence them. Theirs is specifically an Indian religion.

The sex of an advocate is always an important factor in acceptance because of distinctions between the interests and ideals of men and women and because of prejudices favoring one sex or the other. Sometimes such biases lead to pervasive prestige differentials that approximate completeness over the whole range of culturally established interests. Not infrequently the superior rating of one sex does extend over all the group interests that are considered most important. In any instance of a novelty introduction there will be some men and some women who will favor its adoption if it is advocated by a male instead of a female, and there will be others of both sexes who will react oppositely. Nevertheless, the proportions will usually be significantly different for the two sponsors, the difference depending upon the generally accepted bias in favor of one sex or the other, usually the male. In most societies men have a higher prestige rating than do women, perhaps because they can enforce it. They also have a habit of belittling or usurping female leadership in important matters; and women, except for militant feminists, are accustomed to submitting to their bullying. In places where the prestige differential is marked, as in Palau and in the United States, there is in consequence a decided prejudice in favor of accepting the advocacy of males as contrasted with that of females for precisely the same novelty. This predisposition affects members of both sexes more or less equally, so that women, revealing the bias of their husbands, fathers, and brothers, will grant leadership in novelty to men but not to members of their own sex. Palauan women have a markedly lower prestige rating than do their menfolk in the estimation of both sexes. Consequently, they do not function as leaders either in advocating the new or in maintaining the old. American women fare only slightly better in those areas of our culture, such as science, business, and politics, that are considered important enough for men to want to dominate them. In other areas of interest where free and indiscriminate participation by both sexes occurs, there is no such consensus in favor of advocacy by either men or women.

In evaluating the preceding observations, it must be kept in mind that there is a distinction between prestige that rests upon innovative ability and that which rests upon other competencies. It is obvious that prestige which is based upon ingenuity mobilizes support for itself and establishes a following for those who exhibit it. In other words, people who admire an innovator or a radical just because he is the advocate of something new will follow his lead. It has been noted that in most societies, if not in all, there are certain areas wherein novelty is rewarded for its own sake. Naturally in these aspects of culture eminence is defined in terms of ingenuity. Prestige is accorded an innovator precisely because he does introduce new ideas. Hence the fame of Edison, Marconi, Volta, Einstein, Burbank, and Ford and the following that their creative leadership inspired. Novelty is also valued in the field of art, and consequently coteries of admiring imitators gather about painters, architects, and musicians. This fact also explains leadership in fads and dress fashions. These, too, are areas wherein change per se is valued. Freshness and novelty are prized in and for themselves in women's dress, slang expressions, and amusements. An advocate of change in these areas is therefore doing what is expected of a leader and consequently can be expected to be followed. If Mrs. William-McWilliams uses the new "Glow Shampoo" or if Laruthy Glamour wears "Shear" or if a Distinguished Gentleman smokes "Malvert," others will welcome their advocacy. In all these instances the elite are the radicals. That is the basis for their being defined as leaders. Their prestige ratings depend upon their support of novelty within a limited framework of expectancy.

The concluding statement of the last paragraph needs to be emphasized. The advocacy of a novelty is a precarious venture, and it jeopardizes the prestige of its sponsor quite as much as it is supported by it. Esteem is based upon past performance, and this fact establishes a liability as well as an asset. An eminent man owes something to his admirers, and one of his obligations is to meet their expectations of him. These expectations may be imposed upon him because of the status accorded him by birth, or they may be extrapolations based upon his achievements. In either case they impose restraints upon his behavior and forbid radical departures from the norm that has been determined for him or that he has evolved for himself. A reputation is an obligation to conform, and it permits little freedom in advocating novel ideas. This is true even though the reputation is founded upon originality, because in such cases the prized deviations are always demonstrations of originality within bounds. They are expected nonconformances. Radical departures, those which exceed the bounds of expectability for their originators, must be advocated at the risk of prestige loss.

This is one important reason why the elite are seldom in the vanguard of cultural change. It cannot be denied, of course, that radical changes are sometimes inspired by preeminent individuals. Royalty and nobility have brought about social revolutions, as in the case of Peter the Great of Russia and the Emperor and the upper classes of Japan who initiated the Meiji reform in 1868. There are many other examples of men of high station advocating reforms, among them Hitler, Kemal Ataturk, and Mussolini. It is to be noted, however, that the success of programs of this sort has been ensured by the power prerogatives rather than by the prestige potentials of their sponsors. The acceptors had no choice but to submit, regardless of what the coercion did to their estimates of their leaders.

Over against every instance of a radical change that has been carried solely by the prestige of its advocate there could be set several others that have resulted in prestige collapse. This has happened to several political leaders of international prominence in recent decades. King Edward VIII of Great Britain and King Leopold of Belgium were forced into exile partly because their subjects, or an effective nucleus of them, refused to accept their determination to marry commoners. Leopold's estrangement was compounded by the fact that his prestige was not coextensive with his realm to begin with, and by his submission to an alien order represented by the Germans during the Second World War. Syngman Rhee experienced the disaffection of many of his people for somewhat the same reasons when he tried to form a United Korean Republic. Many Koreans, after first welcoming him as the embodiment of their hopes for national unity and independence, rejected him because of his foreign orientation. During a thirty-year period of exile, much of which was spent in the United States, Rhee had acquired an Austrian wife and a preference for occidental dress, speech, and political thinking. These sources of irritation were played upon with considerable success by his political opponents.

Little-known and long-forgotten examples of prestige failure that has resulted from the advocacy of new ideas could be drawn from all parts of the world. Ikhnaton, the Egyptian Pharaoh who attempted to abolish polytheism and to institute the worship of one god in its place, failed to influence popular beliefs even though he had absolute power and was considered to be divine himself. The innovation was too radical for all save a small coterie of intellectuals, despite the fact that most Egyptians of the time were cynical of the old religion and disgusted with the corruption and the hypocrisy of its priests. In 1819 the high chief Liholiho of Hawaii dramatically renounced the taboo system which, among other things, forbade women to eat certain foods and men and women to eat together. Except among the small group of his inciters, his revolutionary action was shocking. He, like Ikhnaton, was divine and his power absolute; but this status did not induce his subjects to embrace his blasphemy. On the contrary, he was denounced by many and had to fight a civil war to maintain his position, a war that he was able to win only because of a superiority granted him by the possession of alien firearms.[2] The man who came to be known as Pomare, King of Tahiti, had a very similar history. In 1813 he publicly broke taboos to the awe and consternation of his attendants and brought upon himself the ridicule and persecution of not only his political rivals but his own family and friends. In 1815 he too had to fight a war to reestablish his control over Tahiti.[3] Several chiefs in Palau have lost face and favor among their people because they have become the advocates of alien ideologies and behaviors. By adopting English clothing and mannerisms Aibedul, the high chief of the islands during the early years of intensive European contact, alienated his followers and provided a rival with a political weapon for his defeat. He was scoffed at as a "half-white man." The present ranking chief of one of the northern districts in the islands is accused of being an upstart and a renegade because of his amenability to alien suggestions, and he is able to maintain his position only by continuing to identify himself with American administrative aims. When a member of one of the elite Yurok families identified himself with the whites by adopting some new custom or by renouncing an old one, his peers and social inferiors were more inclined to repudiate him than to follow his lead. His defection was far more shocking to everybody than was that of a low-class person. It was so incomprehensible to the Yurok that a rationalization was invented to explain it: the apostate could not really have been a legitimate lineal descendant of elite ancestors; his alienation was proof that he had an unknown or a forgotten flaw in his genealogy.

[2] James Jackson Jarves, *History of the Hawaiian or Sandwich Islands.* . . . London: E. Moxon, 1843, pp. 197–200.

[3] William Ellis, *Polynesian Researches.* . . . London, 1820, Vol. I, pp. 191–192, 197, 245ff.

Advocate prestige is important in influencing acceptance, but there are clear-cut limitations upon its effectiveness. As far as any particular advocate is concerned, there is first of all the fact that he is rated differently by different potential acceptors; in addition, his prestige is confined to one or a few fields of acceptor interest; and, finally, the degree of originality that can be successfully supported by his reputation is relatively minor. Advocate prestige is not a peculiarity of the novelty situation. Like many other phenomena that we have been considering, it is a floating variable which may come into play in a variety of associations. It is effective in any situation wherein persuasion is important. It mobilizes opinion upon any issue, pro or con, new or old. It is only one attribute of an advocate, and it is only one ingredient in the compound of influences that affect the acceptors of new ideas.

Personality. The personality of an advocate plays an important part in promoting or blocking the acceptance of the novelty which he supports. His personality is something apart from the prestige that an advocate may have or lack. As with prestige, its influence upon potential acceptors is not confined to novelty situations. It is a crucial asset or a liability for any man who would influence others on any issue. A suggestion—any suggestion—made by a person whose manner, bearing, or attitude creates antagonism is likely to be rejected by most people, regardless of the essential merits of the proposal. Advocates whose personal characteristics are offensive create such an uncongenial atmosphere that the antipathy which they personally inspire suffuses the idea which they propose, irrespective of its brilliance, common sense, or suitability. The man and not the idea is the offender, but both become the targets of attack by those who are offended. The latter identify the thought with the man and are from the beginning negativistic to the one just because of the other.

An appealing personality is a major asset in securing the acceptance of an idea, whether new or old. A good half of salesmanship lies not in knowing what you are selling or in selling a desirable thing, nor yet in believing what you are saying, but simply in being an engaging person. Many people buy things that they do not need or want or accept new things or new ideas solely because they have been attracted by the personalities of advocates. Sometimes they are aware of this all along and do not care. At other times they realize it with humiliation or indignation when it is too late. Traveling teams of salesmen making full and sometimes unscrupulous use of their personal appeal are organized to conduct swift and intensive campaigns in towns and small cities in various parts of this country. When they overstep the law, their sobered clients may be resentful enough to seek to turn it upon them, as happened in the case of a magazine-soliciting crew whose activities were reported in a local newspaper. Several disenchanted subscribers in this case complained to the city authorities that they had been "high-pressured" by fast sales speeches, misrepresentations, and engaging female blandishments. The manager of the crew answered the charges by stating that a display of "personality" was a recognized part of their business.[4]

To refer again to Stern's analysis of factors that have influenced medical history, it may be noted that personality difficulties have accounted for more opposition to new ideas than scientists, objective as they are alleged to be, are willing to admit in their own behavior. The most outstanding example of an unfortunate personality is offered by Pasteur. Even his most sympathetic biographers seem to be agreed that he struck the majority of his contemporaries as an insufferable egoist with not a little of the paranoiac about his behavior. He was dogmatic, cocksure, conceited, contentious, and extremely sensitive to criticism. De Kruif says of him that he was "bristling, curious, and impatient." His personal unpopularity almost cost him a seat in the Free Association of the Academy of Medicine; he was elected to it by a majority of only one vote, despite the fact that he was the first on the list of eligible candidates. There is no doubt that his offensive mannerisms inspired violent antagonisms toward his brilliant discoveries. It seems that personality difficulties were also a significant factor in the reactions against Semmelweis's views on puerperal fever. One biographer characterizes him as "irascible, impatient, and tactless." The controversy over the acceptance of vaccination was also emotionally toned by personality clashes. Jenner was jealous of his role in introducing the practice and resented any suggestion of sharing honors with others that would detract from his exclusive claim for credit. He was dogmatic, sensitive to criticism, and ready to attack anyone who differed with him. Benjamin Waterhouse, who introduced vaccination into the United States, was also disliked, partly because of his demeanor. He antagonized his colleagues by the air of superiority and patronage which he affected as a result of his training abroad.[5]

The spread of the Shaker cult has been much affected by personality factors. It was mainly because of them that the cult was poorly received by the Yurok during the first years of their contact with it. The first man to proselytize among them was converted on the Siletz reservation in Oregon. He was a timid and an emotionally unstable individual who had led a confused and unhappy life up to that point. He was not liked by most of the Yurok people, and he had a speech defect which became the butt of their ridicule when he tried to preach to them. Two of his first converts were a man and wife who were also disliked, because they were vicious gossips. They almost turned the Yurok against the cult because they converted it into a vehicle for the expression of their aggressions. They estranged some

[4] *Eugene* (Oregon) *Register-Guard,* Jan. 17, 1951, p. 1.
[5] Stern, *op. cit.,* pp. 58, 59, 68, 71–72.

of the most influential individuals from the beginning by accusing them of being witches, devils, drunkards, and philanderers, which knowledge they claimed to have had revealed to them while they were under divine power. The converts who eventually joined the church did so in spite of the initial protagonists and mainly after these advocates had been superseded by other leaders.

An appealing personality is a more valuable asset for an advocate than is prestige, because it is more flexible and can therefore be manipulated more easily. It does not depend upon something already accomplished and evaluated; it is dynamic and hence adjustable to the circumstances of the moment. Its immediacy gives it precedence over personal estimates made on other scores. Personality traits are, moreover, inescapable elements in the acceptance situation, and the potential acceptor must have some reaction to those of an advocate. These individual and personal evaluations are more emotionally toned than are estimates of things and accomplishments, so they can ignore or preclude prestige rating.

Personal Relations. Still another variable that bears upon the effectiveness of an advocate is that of his personal relations with potential acceptors. There are many kinds of such relationships of greater or lesser intimacy and consistency. One is acquaintanceship or friendship, with its varying degrees of intensity over a wide range of interpersonal relations. People will often accept a recommendation if it comes from a friend and reject it if it is proposed by a stranger. This differential response is quite independent of the nature of the idea being advocated. The merits of the novelty do not enter into the decision to adopt or to reject it, or do so only secondarily. They may not even be known; but the motivations of a friend can be relied upon, whereas those of a stranger are not above suspicion. After I had lived in a Palauan village for several months, I was often asked for an interpretation of some new American regulation, such as the request that polygyny be abandoned or the order that fallen coconut logs be burned to destroy beetle larvae. The natives were uncomprehending and sometimes distrustful of the motives behind such requirements. They felt more assured that they should cooperate with the officials if I could find nothing inimical to their interests in the law. They had the same confidence in a particular naval officer on the administrative staff. He spoke their language and understood their customs and was therefore the best possible official advocate of American policy.

Where, as is usually the case, the personal relations between relatives are more intimate and take precedence over the attachments between nonrelatives, kinsmen are effective advocates of change and kinship linkages act as channels for diffusion. Allowance must be made for domestic rivalries and animosities; but even without this reservation it is a noteworthy fact that acceptance runs in families. It is, of course, social and not biological kinship that is here involved. Families include spouses and both consanguineous and affinal kin, brothers-in-law as well as brothers, stepchildren as well as progeny. The data on the subject reveal that this patterning of acceptance happens with greater than chance frequency, no matter what the particular novelty is. Instead of an independent assortment of individuals, whole families, or large proportions of them, tend to become acculturated. Husbands and wives, fathers and sons, and brothers and sisters are predisposed to react to new proposals as a divisible but viscous unit. In the acceptance of foreign ideas among the Yurok, Tsimshian, Yakima, and Palauans it is remarkable that there have been, so to speak, accepting and nonaccepting families. Conversions to the Shaker cult have also been threaded along kinship ties. The religion has established a foothold in new communities in this way. The initial convert in each locality has ordinarily been able to convert members of his own family before, or more certainly than, members of other families. Family nuclei of converts rather than randomly distributed individuals have consequently formed the spearhead of new growths in new areas.

The most consistent kin-group clusters of acceptors among the Yurok, the Tsimshian, the Yakima, and the Palauans have been those of parents and children and husbands and wives. This is quite understandable because of the close association of these individuals and because of male dominance over households in all four of these societies. When the head of one of these households adopts a new custom, it is expectable that his wife and children will follow his lead, whether they are equally motivated to do so or not. A more fundamental fact, and one that has much wider implications, has already been emphasized in another context; namely, that a family is a cultural microcosm whose members have more in common among themselves than they as a group have with other families. They have common sympathies, reactions, and beliefs and are more likely to be affected in the same way by the same stimulus than is a heterogeneous assortment of individuals. This is but another instance of a social phenomenon that is not specific to cultural change. Musicians and Republicans tend to run in family lines, too—a fact which is independent of, and has significance in contexts other than, innovation and its acceptance.

Some personal relations are structured on a framework of dominance and submission. This is another alignment of significance where advocate and acceptor are concerned. It often happens that an advocate of something new has authoritarian controls over those whose acceptance he seeks. As has been noted, subjects and subordinates may revolt and refuse to follow their leader along new paths, so that formal control does not always mean absolute and unquestioning acceptance of a leader's decision. The effectiveness of his leadership in this respect depends upon the particular circumstances and upon how real his control is. At times and for some people the advocacy of a trusted, idolized, or feared leader is enough to win support for his views regardless of the intrinsic merits of the proposal. Palauan chiefs and clan heads have autocratic powers bestowed upon them by tradition and, until recently, by the common consent of those whose public and private affairs they administer. Although the younger men are now discreetly and privately questioning their authority, the chiefs are still the undisputed masters of their people. No one dares to be disrespectful to them or openly to defy their orders. Consequently, they are the conservers of custom as well as the authoritarian advocates of certain changes, principally those that are being initiated by American administrators. Requests and demands are transmitted through the native hierarchy of chiefs, and seldom does anyone have the temerity to refuse to acknowledge them. Privately there has been grumbling over work conscriptions for new projects, such as water systems and building programs, but this discontent has not stayed the changes in native culture that the projects have initiated. The chiefs of the Bantu tribes in South Africa also have exercised authoritarian controls over their subjects with respect to the introduction of alien ideas. These tribal leaders traditionally have extensive powers. They inherit their positions, and they are the executive heads and supreme judges in their domains. They take the advice of councilors, but they rule by decree. They are priest-kings who are responsible for the spiritual well-being of their subjects, the spirits of their ancestors giving guidance and protection to all. They become tribal gods after their deaths. Consequently, chiefs are respected and obeyed. Schapera states that "the active support of the chief is a powerful influence in insuring the success of any new measure, while his opposition or indifference invariably creates obstacles and difficulties." In Bechuanaland the Ngwato chief became an enthusiastic convert to Christianity and abolished the tribal initiation ceremonies for young men and women, whereas the head chief of Swaziland has remained a pagan and so have his people. Some Bantu chiefs have used force to compel Christian converts to undergo the tribal initiation ceremonies.[6]

These instances of authoritarian controls over acceptance are not unique. In fact, wherever political domination carries with it some real threat of punishment for disobedience, or the withdrawal of protection, its administrators make powerful advocates of reform or conservatism in virtue of that control alone. Political bosses and the Exalted Dragons of secret societies possess such power. So do the heads of totalitarian states, recent and modern, who have held in their hands the ultimate threat of death for disobedience of their dictates. Religious leaders are not infrequently in a position to promulgate arbitrary decrees that demand conformance of the faithful upon

---

[6] I. Schapera, "Cultural Changes in Tribal Life." In I. Schapera (ed.), *The Bantu Speaking Tribes of South Africa*. London: Routledge and Kegan Paul, Ltd., 1937, pp. 362, 382–383.

threat of excommunication or supernatural retribution for failure to comply. Usually the reforms that are advocated by spiritual leaders are within or rather directly impinge upon the religious domain as they conceive it. But there is not always a clear-cut separation of church and state, or of the sacred and the profane; and authoritative religious leaders sometimes demand entirely secular reforms, as did Pope Gregory XIII when he sanctioned a calendar reform in 1582 and as did the Sacred Congregation of the Holy Office in 1951 when it decreed that no Roman Catholic priest might thenceforth be a member of the Rotary businessmen's club.[7] Native Christian pastors in South Africa and in Oceania have used the threat of eternal punishment to secure their converts, as have evangelists and sect leaders in other parts of the world. The founders of such cults as the Modekne and the Shaker have instituted beliefs and practices with similar sanctions. John Slocum told his first converts that he would die again and abandon them to their sinful ways unless they followed his admonitions. Either he or one of his close associates also announced that unless the Indians accepted his revelation they would not see their dead relatives in the next world. Temudad, the Modekne messiah, decreed that everything fit to eat was given by God to His people and that therefore the Palauans should cease to observe the dietary taboos associated with their clan membership. American Indians who refused to join the messianic ghost-dance religion which swept through the native populations of the Western states just after 1890 were threatened with dire consequences by its advocates. Unbelievers were told that they would "grow little, about a foot high, and stay that way. Some of them will be turned into wood and be burned in fire."[8]

Traditional patterns of domestic authority, quite apart from other considerations, offer ready-made channels for the expression of advocacy. Palauan men are undisputed masters in their homes, and their receptive or rejective attitudes dominate their households because neither their wives nor their children dare take issue with them. Japanese men exercise comparable controls in the households of which they are heads. In cross-cultural marriages this matter of domestic authority has a significant bearing upon the cultural identification of the children. On the frontiers of a geographically expanding cultural system, men rather than women are the invaders of new lands and become the coparticipants in mixed unions. The influence that such men are able to exert upon their offspring is dependent upon several factors; but where male dominance in the household is traditional, foreign men make a decided impression upon their children. Among the Yurok, the Yakima, the Tsimshian, and the Palauans the children of white men and native women have revealed a consistent bias toward their fathers'

[7] Time, Jan. 22, 1951.

[8] James Mooney, "The Ghost Dance Religion," Bureau of American Ethnology, 14th Annual Report, 1892–93, Washington, D.C., 1896, Part 2, p. 784.

way of life. This inclination has doubtless been reinforced in most instances by an original predilection of their mothers, who by preference have associated with white men rather than with men of their own group.

As another aspect of the personal relationship structure, it should be mentioned that rejection or acceptance is often dictated solely because of the preexistence of rivalries, feuds, and estrangements between an advocate and other potential acceptors. The perversity of human beings frequently leads them to do something that an enemy does not, or not to do something that he does, simply because he is an enemy. We are not dealing here necessarily with personality conflicts, but with any disagreement prior to the particular issue of acceptance in question. Antipathies previously conditioned for any reason may suffuse the acceptance issue and polarize the adherents of its advocate and those of his rival. The political convictions of both Waterhouse and Semmelweis had much to do with the rejection of their respective advocacies of vaccination and the causes of puerperal fever.[9] Many a new idea has been used as a political football in our own and in other countries, the outs opposing the ins as a matter of principle as much as because of anything else. Factionalism has played havoc with new ideas in all parts of the world and at all levels of cultural sophistication. In Samoa and Tahiti the fact that one clique adopted Christianity caused rival groups to reject it.[10] Myron Eells, the Protestant missionary on the Skokomish Indian reservation at the time of Slocum's alleged death and resurrection, relentlessly opposed Catholicism. Because of this opposition and some related matters, Eells had, previous to Slocum's experience, antagonized several other Indians, including one called Billy Clams. When he attacked Slocum's pretensions, Eells found himself resisted by Clams and his cohorts, just as he had been many times before on other issues. This resistance was substantial enough to defeat Eell's efforts to suppress the cult. A great many Indians joined Clams in his support of Slocum and became believers in the new faith for no other reason initially than that they disliked Eells. This pattern has repeated itself upon several subsequent occasions elsewhere, both within and outside the cult membership.

Majority Affiliation. As a final item it may be mentioned that the support of a majority is an asset to an advocate. In actual numbers the supporters of a new idea need not constitute a majority or even approximate it. They need only give the impression that they are or must inevitably become the majority. Their advocacy is strengthened by their making it seem that opposition to their idea is futile, unreasonable, or stubborn. The technique of the advocate is to overwhelm the objector by summoning a

---

[9] Stern, *op. cit.,* pp. 59, 68.

[10] Felix Keesing, *The South Seas in the Modern World.* New York: The John Day Company, 1941, p. 231.

mass verdict the logic of which, just because it is a consensus, is alleged to be irresistible.

In this technique, as in the exploitation of other advocate assets, use is made of a valued attribute that is extrinsic to the nature of the novelty. The mere number of those supporting the advocate of the new idea is a compelling consideration for many people who waver between accepting and rejecting it. People are made conscious of the views which they hold with minorities; and unless they are highly self- or group-centered, they are susceptible to the pressures of majority opinion. Nobody wants to be out of step; and unless he can convince himself that it is not he but others who are in the wrong, he is vulnerable to suggestion. If nothing else, mass advocacy is intimidating. On the rational and practical levels it is also a difficult thing for the isolated doubter to live with, the more so the more emotionally toned the issue is. In short, many people accept a new idea because "everybody else" is doing so. The multitude must be right; even if it is not, there is no use contending with it.

CHAPTER XII

NOVELTY CHARACTERISTICS

Intrinsic and Extrinsic Values. The sponsorship of a novelty is only one component of the acceptance situation. Very often it is the critical factor in influencing others, but it never functions in isolation. A novelty advocate always supports some specific change; and the precise nature of the change is as important to a potential acceptor as is the background, the attitude, and the personality of its sponsor. Novelty characteristics that have a bearing upon this problem fall into two categories. There are, first of all, those features which are inherent in the novelty itself as they are envisaged by the potential acceptor. They give it significance in terms of his background; and the understanding that he has of it in the light of this background either gives or fails to give it a particular appeal and a place in his behavioral system. Beyond this there are considerations having to do with the feasibility of adopting the novelty provided that it is in itself acceptable. These considerations are of another order, because they are extrinsic to the nature of the new idea. They bring into question the value of the novelty and are frequently as important for its actual acceptance as are its inherent characteristics. In this chapter we shall consider reactions to the novelty itself, and in the following chapter attention will be given to its evaluation.

Innovation in Acceptance. Novelty acceptability is often discussed with reference to the concept of compatibility. This is a useful concept provided that its meaning is made clear and provided that its definition affords an analytical tool and not merely another name for acceptability. A first step in this direction requires the distinction made in the last paragraph between the intrinsic and extrinsic values of an idea. It is also imperative to bear in mind that compatibility or its opposite entails a specific referent. An idea or a behavior, new or old, is adaptable or harmonious with something known, believed, or done by a potential acceptor, not with abstractions like statistical averages, consensuses, trends, common denominators, or cultural patterns. These abstractions summarize or describe compatibilities. They do not determine them. They are delineations of compatibility, but they are not the reactions which comprise it.

Basically, compatibility from an acceptor's standpoint is a question of the possibility of a substitute in a particular situation. As far as intrinsic characteristics are concerned, this means that the acceptor admits an equation between something new and something old. Either he identifies the novelty with something familiar to him, so that it can be substituted in the context of the familiar entity; or he identifies the correlate of the novelty with something familiar, so that the latter is an appropriate substitute for the former; or he identifies both the novelty and its correlate with a familiar form and its correlate, so that there can be a double substitution. Unless one or another of these possibilities presents itself, either spontaneously or through explanation and persuasion on the part of its advocate, the introduced idea must remain alien and unacceptable as far as the particular acceptor in question is concerned.

It will be recognized, perhaps, that the same processes are at work here as in innovation itself. There is identification with its consequents, assimilation and projection, or a compounding of them on the pattern of analogies and parallels. Acceptance operates within the same perceptual and conceptual framework as does innovation. Everything else may indeed be different—the motivations, the conditions, and the precise data; but the processes, the mental mechanisms, are repeated with each individual case of acceptance, beginning with the innovator himself, who is only a special, the first, acceptor of the novelty. As far as thought processes at the instant of conception or acceptance are concerned, innovation and acceptance reveal no distinctions. This is why, when allowances are made for the prior existence of a novelty, the conditions which prompt and favor the one set the stage for and stimulate the other. It is also why it must be granted that acceptors, by the act of acceptance, are innovators, regardless of the fact that they build upon a recognized break with tradition rather than upon some aspect of it. It was noted in the first chapter that copies are never perfect and that imitations are always, in small or large degree, innovations. Acceptors are simply imitators of novelties, and they must therefore be innovators even if they do not try to be such or do not know that they are. Both the acceptor and the imitator try to conform, the one to a form that is new to him and to his associates as well, the other to something that is new to him but not to his associates. Both fail in some measure and by that token create a variant.

In his treatment of diffusion Kroeber proposes a distinction between acceptance which does not involve an alteration of the diffused idea and that which does. He refers to the first as ordinary diffusion and to the second as stimulus invention, idea diffusion, or stimulus diffusion. In the first category he places such things as the spread of the knowledge of the planetary week, the arch, the automobile, and the Australian ballot; while in the second he includes the Chinese stimulus to the invention of porcelain in Europe in the eighteenth century, the devising of local alphabets in several parts of the world under the stimulus of the European form, and the discovery of Japanese grammar by Motoori as a result of contacts with Western grammatical treatises.

Attention to particulars will reveal that there is no real distinction between these instances as far as alteration in transmission is concerned. In all cases acceptance has entailed creative modifications. This fact can be overlooked only if we arbitrarily treat certain modifications as "insignificant," or if we ignore the change of context and association that is inevitably connected with the adoption of an idea by one person from another. A fruitful analysis forbids both of these oversights and requires our dealing with specific manifestations, no matter how trivial their details may seem in the long sweep of history. Even though the contemporary English alphabet may be said to be "essentially the same" as the ancient Phoenician or Greek, it has nonetheless been greatly modified both in itself and with respect to the sounds that it has symbolized and does now symbolize in numerous languages. Even if it were granted that a given letter has not been altered, which is not so, its meanings, its correlates, certainly have. The bodily transfer of a thing, even if it remains intact, does not mean that acceptance has been passive and noncreative; for the integration of a thing demands that it be embedded in a new context which has varying degrees of resemblance to, but never complete identity with, the one out of which it was taken. Singer sewing machines have been transported to Palau and have been accepted intact by the natives. Despite this fact two considerations must not be overlooked; namely, that the imported machines, regardless of the retention of their form, are not the cultural realities that they are in the majority of homes in the United States where they are found; and, secondly, that any attempt by Palauans to replace their outworn machines by manufacturing imitations of them or their parts is certain to result in changes in the forms of the replacements. Some of these machines in Palau are used for sewing, some are not. The majority of them are placed by front windows to be used as impressive display items whether they function mechanically or not; and men as well as women operate those that do work. In point of associations and meanings their acceptance has made something new of them, and in point of form they remain identical only so long as they do not undergo native repair. Persistence of form should not mislead us into assuming passive acceptance, and imitations should not be taken as identities. Both assimilation and copying are innovative.

While the concept of stimulus diffusion recognizes the innovative character of acceptance, it is necessary to be on guard against one interpretation of it as an explanation for modification. It is not altogether clear whether Kroeber thinks of this kind of diffusion as requiring a specific or generalized stimulus. He says that "it occurs in situations where a system or pattern as such encounters no resistance to its spread, but there are difficulties in regard to the transmission of the concrete content of the system. In this case it is the idea of the complex or system which is accepted, but it remains for the receiving culture to develop a new content." [1] If this means that only a specific manifestation, the X of our paradigm of Figure 1, can diffuse, and that the abstraction of a likeness, C, between this and some local form, A, is done by the receiver himself, there can be no objection to the concept. On the other hand, one gets the impression that Kroeber means something else; namely, that generic ideas like "democracy," "pottery," and "grammar" as such can be diffused independently of their specific manifestations. This is especially true of his speculations upon historical linkages between things and institutions in which *he* sees common elements. The question is not merely one of just who sees the common feature between two specific manifestations of "the same thing." More fundamental is the fact that it is impossible to transmit a generic idea to another person without exemplifying it. No special circumstances are required to appreciate the impossibility of conveying the meaning of such abstractions as "sin," "authority," and "parenthood" to children and others who are unacquainted with them, except by specific illustration. In diffusion' it is equally impossible to transmit the "idea" of X without presenting X itself. Views to the contrary derive from an unwitting substitution of an observer's concept of similarity for those of the participants in the acceptance situation. Only by this rationalistic approach can the incautious synthesizer of cultural data be led to speak of the "idea" of a class, a scheme, or a pattern diffusing apart from, and being accepted in place of, the things and institutions which go to make them up. They are abstractions which have existence only in his mind, and hence could not have figured in the mental processes of the acceptors themselves.

All acceptance is diffusion, and all diffusion is stimulus diffusion when the acceptance of a new idea is understood as a mental process of the acceptor and not as a logical construct to explain resemblances. Innovation is characteristic of acceptance, whether it takes place inside a single cultural system or involves a conjunction of parts of two different ones. In every case innovation and acceptance are stimulated by some XY, and in every case this is modified under the controls of some prototype AB that is previously resident in the mind of the innovator or acceptor. As far as the process is concerned, it does not make any difference whether XY is or is not a part of the innovator's or the acceptor's culture. From the standpoint of oddity of the result as judged by people who are familiar with XY, it may make a difference, but innovations are always odd from the standpoint of existing familiarity with unmixed AB's and XY's. Even when both the stimulus XY and the prototype AB have existed independently in the same mind as familiar ideas the thought of crossing them is strange from the standpoint of either one. There is a continuous gradation of circumstances

[1] A. L. Kroeber, "Stimulus Diffusion," *American Anthropologist*, 1940, 42 (No. 1):1.

from this hybridization of two familiar ideas to the joining of a familiar one to an utterly alien one, and the latter circumstance prevails as widely within what we call a single culture as it does on the borders of two different ones. It can occur any time that an idea familiar to one person is conveyed to another to whom it is new. In some cases there is more likelihood of this happening across cultural boundaries than within a single one, but this is by no means the rule. Cross-familial, cross-class, and cross-regional assimilations and projections provide exact intracultural duplications of the innovative process.

The acceptance of a new idea does not recapitulate the procedure of the innovator in the latter's conception of it, but it does require another innovative sequence. The starting points of the two sets of processes are obviously different, though they as processes are identical. The innovator finishes his creative act with the innovation, whereas the acceptor begins with it. They therefore have different stimuli and different prototypes, the end product of the innovation becoming the stimulus for the acceptor. To revert to our paradigm of Figure 1 again, the innovator's prototype CAB is evoked by XC to result in CXB, whereupon CXB becomes for the acceptor an X which must make a contact with some one of his prototypes that is like it. The man who begins to make use of a motorized wheelbarrow following the lead of its inventor does not need to perceive a resemblance (C) between a wheelbarrow (X) and a motorcycle (A) with its gasoline engine (B) as the innovator did. If he makes a copy of the invention he merely identifies his wheelbarrow (CA) with the one observed in use (CX) and mentally projects it into connection with the motor observed (Y). If he buys or borrows the novelty (Y), he identifies himself (CA) with the man (CX) he has seen using it; or he equates its observed uses (CX) with the uses (CA) to which he has been accustomed to putting his wheelbarrow (B). The man who decides to abandon the wearing of ties at his office need not rehearse the thinking which led its innovator to the idea. He need do no more than identify himself with the innovator.

Stated in this way it seems that acceptance is much easier than innovation. The truth is, though, that no such distinction can be made. Even though the context of their thinking differs, both the innovator and his imitator identify and assimilate or project. Sometimes this is easier for the innovator; sometimes it is easier for the acceptor.

The acceptance situation duplicates the one that characterizes innovation with the novelty acting as a stimulus, the X in the context of Y of our diagram of Figure 1. The acceptability of the novelty depends, first, upon whether either X or Y or both can evoke an A or a B of some familiar configuration; and second, if this happens, upon whether the resulting XB's or AY's are contrary to or conformable with existing values. There are several aspects to each of these possibilities. They may be discussed in terms of novelty characteristics as those characteristics relate to the elements in the existing cultural inventory to which the acceptor refers them.

Meaning. To be acceptable a novelty must provide some basis for an identification which will permit assimilation or projection to proceed. It must be associable with some previous experience of the acceptor. There must be some A to which the introduced X can hook on. Some connection between the two, either by analysis or incorporation, must be appreciated and must be real to the acceptor. Many of the results of laboratory experiments on the transfer of learning or performance are best understood as failures of identification on the part of the subjects of the experiments. At one time it was generally supposed that it was possible to teach students to think logically, or to be obedient or industrious, with respect to one situation and that they would carry the pattern over to another situation. Experimental tests failed to verify this hope or supposition. It turned out that neatness learned in the preparation of arithmetic papers, for example, was not transferred to the writing of English compositions.[2] Evidently the subjects found no connection between the two tasks. Arithmetic was not related to English composition; hence neatness, the learned correlate of arithmetic, was not a consideration in the writing of an essay. In other words, composition was not assimilated to the neatness context of arithmetic. Many other experiments upon transfer have been misconceived and misinterpreted because those who have made them have strait-jacketed their subjects by their own preconceptions of what should constitute an identification. Seldom have experimental subjects been allowed to make their own judgments and so voluntarily to assimilate a novel form presented in a test series to a prototype of their past experience, whether the latter has been given to them in the learning situation or otherwise acquired.[3] These laboratory situations are manufactured acceptance situations. They demonstrate what can happen when the observer rather than the participant formulates concepts of sameness, and they reveal clearly the error that can develop from the use of the concept of stimulus diffusion in the interpretation of culture history. When more attention is paid to the mood, the mental set, and especially to the prototype inventory of laboratory subjects, much may be learned that will be useful in understanding the process of acceptance. Surely one essential is that a novelty must make contact with a mentally resident configuration. If this is not possible, there can be no response whatever.

Another way of stating that a novelty must be associable is to say that it must have meaning to its acceptor. Meaning is the insight which comes when the idea of the presented thing is referable to the idea of some past

[2] Edward L. Thorndike, "The Psychology of Learning," *Educational Psychology.* New York: Columbia University Press, 1913, Vol. 2, pp. 415–417.

[3] Robert S. Woodworth, *Experimental Psychology.* New York: Henry Holt and Company, Inc., 1938, Chap. 8.

experience. It is an evidence of contact, the idea of the one thing being understood in terms of its mental associates. In so far as unfamiliar experiences are concerned, meaning is evoked if some familiar configuration is aroused either directly or indirectly, either spontaneously or by search and effort. There is always some intermediating *C* to make the contact, whether it be a common thing or a common aspect or property bonding the stimulus and its resident affiliate. The activating configuration, the stimulus, has to be fitted into the context of the known in some fashion. Often the linkage is circuitous. In a passage that is relevant at this point, Bartlett summarizes some of his conclusions concerning experiments on the repeated reproductions of an American Indian myth by his English subjects: [4]

There is a marked and well-known distinction, both in perceiving and in remembering, between direct reaction to what is literally present and reaction under the guidance of some tendency which gives to what is presented a setting and an explanation. The latter tendency is present to some extent in all perceiving and in all remembering, but may vary greatly in importance and in prominence from case to case. Sometimes, in these experiments, reasons were definitely and explicitly formulated and introduced into reproductions to account for material which had been presented without explanation. Sometimes, without any definite formulation of reasons, the material was so changed that it could be accepted by the observer without question and with satisfaction. The first process appears to be a special instance of the second. Both have the same general function in mental life, and I shall discuss both under the head of rationalisation.

Identification must take place if a novelty is accepted, even though the new idea is embedded in a highly charged emotional field that interferes with a circumspect estimate of it. Meaning is not necessarily a total or a logically defensible placement of a new experience. It is merely some kind of orientation with reference to the background of the individual that is more or less satisfying to him. Meanings are often assigned under emotional stress that would be rejected under less disturbing conditions. They may be fantastic by other standards, but they serve to provide some rationale for the acceptance of the idea which evokes them. "The Invasion from Mars" provides an illustration. Those who believed that an invasion was taking place had inwardly to justify their belief. They either provided the links themselves or were given them by the remarks of the radio announcer to whom they were listening. For some individuals the dramatic reality of the account provided a meaning. Most listeners, however, had to supplement their emotional identification with the announcer by casting about for explanations that would fit in terms of what they knew or had heard at one time or another in the past. Thus, one woman who could not fit

[4] F. C. Bartlett, *Remembering. A Study in Experimental and Social Psychology*. New York: Cambridge University Press, 1932, p. 84.

the alleged events of the moment into any other explanatory scheme labored with the idea that this must be the end of the world, even though she had aways supposed that when the end came it would be sudden and unannounced.[5]

If no meaning of any kind can be assigned to a novelty, it has no chance of surviving in and of itself. This explains why many Christian concepts fail to pass over ethnic boundaries. Even an allegedly Christian cult like Shakerism lacks prominent elements of Christian creed and practice. The Shakers as a group have never understood the Trinity, communion, baptism, or hell. Some Christian ideas had meaning for Slocum but not for other Indians; and the further away from him the cult's adherents have been in time and place, the less these ideas have meant to them. Among such ideas that have fallen by the wayside are confession, sin, salvation, Christian love, and the millennium. Lack of meaning often manifests itself in scorn or humor on the part of prospective acceptors. Some individuals are inclined to condemn the meaningless, others to laugh at it. Some American Indian informants have reported that they found praying a ridiculous act when as boys they were required to do it in boarding school. It made no sense to them. The Palauans have the same attitude toward kissing. A few of them have become acquainted with this custom through association with American servicemen. Most of them think that it is funny. Upon one occasion a young man who had been to Guam introduced the throwing of a kiss as a novelty feature in one of the dances referred to in the discussion of expectation of change in Chapter II. The participants and the spectators found this ludicrous. But more to the point here, it did not survive as a part of the dance during the three days of the festivities. Those who copied the gesture from its introducer maimed it beyond recognition in the beginning because they did not understand it; and gradually all of them ceased to reproduce it during successive repetitions of the dance.

A suggested meaning that is deemed to be misguided or impossible is as inimical to acceptance as is no meaning at all. The crux of the issue, the point about which there is doubt and argument, is in the identification. Thus we come back to the essentials of assimilation and projection, which is innovation itself. An advocate does what an innovator does, though not necessarily with reference to the same value or prototype; and the limits of convincing sponsorship, like the limits of innovation, are established by the limits of a definition or a redefinition of sameness. Sometimes the assertion of sameness is secondary; it is a rationalization, as it is with importations across cultural boundaries. The advocate of a novelty reasons deduc-

[5] Hadley Cantril, "The Invasion from Mars." In Theodore Newcomb and Eugene Hartley (eds.), *Readings in Social Psychology*. New York: Henry Holt and Company, Inc., 1947, p. 620.

tively: we all want X because it is good, this is X, therefore. . . . In this way the advocates of changes in Shakerism have urged their acceptance upon others: we all want to follow the word of God, the Bible is the word of God, therefore . . . ; we would not spit upon the body of Christ, the church floor is the body of Christ, therefore. . . .

The opponents of change deny such identifications. That is their main argument against the proposal to accept something new. They also resort to identifications that have antithetical values to combat the advocates of change. Some proposition that states a truth that is generally accepted as undesirable is called upon and the rejected proposal is identified with it; or a truism is stated, and the new proposal is declared to be its antithesis. Much of the opposition, past and present, to human dissection has been argued in this way: any mutilation of the human body is sacrilegious, dissection is mutilation, therefore . . . ; an incomplete body cannot be resurrected on the day of judgment, dissection makes for incompleteness, therefore. . . .[6] Lightning rods, iron plows, street lighting, bathtubs, railroads, and many other things have been opposed by the same resort to an undesirable meaning: we do not want to question the will of God, and we want to preserve our health; these things are sinful and unhealthy; therefore. . . .[7]

Asserting that meaning is à *sine qua non* for the acceptance of a novelty is not to imply that the requirement holds for all the analyzable parts of the novelty. Acceptance, like perception and conception, is by configurated wholes. Wholes as such are accepted or rejected; and to refer to what has already been emphasized, wholes are artifacts, not pieces of nature. They are made rather than found, so their inclusiveness and their characteristics depend upon the observer and acceptor. Consequently clusters of traits conceived as units are accepted or rejected without reference to their parts, details, or aspects as these might appear from another analytical approach. What from an advocate's point of view might be a complex of ideas may be accepted because it appears as a whole and has meaning only in these terms to an acceptor. All of us accept ideas in this way; that is, not because their details have meaning but because the idea as a whole has. Or the reverse might happen: we reject parts because they lack meaning. The Indians who became Shakers accepted what to us are only selected parts of Christianity. The rest was meaningless and failed to be carried over. New converts to the religion did the same within the framework of cult doctrine and ritual as it passed from one to another acceptor. Contrariwise, converts have taken whole blocks or segments of cult ritual whose parts in themselves had no meaning. Thus, very few contemporary Shakers can give any

[6] Bernhard Stern, *Social Factors in Medical Progress.* New York: Columbia University Press, 1927, pp. 34–35.
[7] William Thomas, *Primitive Behavior.* New York: McGraw-Hill Book Company, Inc., 1937, pp. 726–728.

rational explanation of how their actions "under power" heal the sick; they just do. Similarly, the hand movements in this ecstatic state are, as isolated units, meaningless to them. They have no theory to account for them.

The significance of a novelty must be understood to be the meaning that it has for the acceptor. This is not necessarily the meaning that it has for its introducer. Unless this essential is kept in mind in judging novelty acceptability, there is the same danger of misinterpretation that has been noted for the concept of stimulus diffusion. The identifications of an introducer or of an observer need not and often do not coincide with the equations made by individuals who are the acceptors or rejectors. Aboriginally the Yurok were not a farming people. Their women gathered acorns, roots, and berries, while the men fished and hunted. The student of culture, given to formulating abstractions, might say that the Yurok women were the producers of "vegetable food." Yet when the whites introduced agriculture, which was also a technique for producing "vegetable food," it was not the Yurok women but the men who became farmers. Evidently the concept "vegetable food" provided no link between their accustomed activities and those introduced in connection with horticulture. This inference is borne out by the fact that the Yurok assert that there is nothing in common between acorns and wheat. The two foods look different, they taste different, they are prepared differently, and they grow differently. Similar considerations relate to the observer's abstraction "wood-getting activities." Yurok women collected firewood, using bone wedges and mauls for splitting it. When metal axes were introduced, the Yurok men, not the women, began to use them to obtain firewood as did the Caucasian men whom they copied. To give another example, the Yurok held celebrations during which wealthy families publicly exhibited their valuables, including long obsidian blades, upon which their prestige depended. We may therefore say that they held a "wealth display dance." Yet when they began to acquire gold coins and other "valuables" from the white man, they did not display these treasures along with or in place of the native "forms of wealth." The reason is obvious: they had no conceptualization of the order of "wealth" which comprised coins and obsidian blades. These two things were not the same in their minds, their formal differences placing them in different categories. Neither did the Yurok have an abstraction such as "gambling" which would comprise their own betting in a game of guessing and our betting in connection with introduced card games like poker and contests like horse racing. None of the indigenous associations of their "games" were transferred to such introduced forms. Indeed the suggestion that the two were after all the same struck informants as a novel idea.[8]

[8] H. G. Barnett, "Culture Processes," *American Anthropologist*, 1940, 42 (No. 1):33–37.

A number of examples of this kind could be cited, but perhaps these few are sufficient to demonstrate that only confusion and artificiality can result from a structuring of acceptance issues in terms of the thought processes of an observer or a novelty introducer rather than in terms of the mental prototypes and identifications of the actual acceptors and rejectors. The observer's fallacy, or the error of rationalism, is one against which all of us must be on guard. It is easy to succumb to it unawares. Sauer's conclusion that there were probably as many distinct centers of starch-plant domestication in aboriginal America as there were distinct starch plants is an example, since he argues that a group of human beings would not spend time domesticating a new starch plant if they already had a good one. Apropos of this he asks, "Would generation after generation of cultivators in one locality give their attention to the breeding, let us say, of a grass, a nightshade, and a morning glory in order to have a multiple source of starch food?" [9] They might very well do so—even considering that they did not want to duplicate their efforts—if they did not know, as Sauer does, that a grass, a nightshade, and a morning glory, which are all quite different in other respects, are chemically compounded of the same elements of carbon, hydrogen, and oxygen. The end would be identical, as Sauer affirms, only if they had knowledge of this chemical fact. It is quite probable that the Indians did not, since comparatively few contemporary Americans are aware of it, nor do they care. Lowie offers a similar explanation when he says that the Chinese very likely rejected the white potato because they already had "an adequate counterpart" in rice, whereas the Maori accepted it because they probably held it to be superior to their sweet potato.[10] This explanation would be valid only if the Chinese and the Maori envisaged the potato in the same way that Lowie does.

Malinowski has enunciated the concept of the "common factor" as "the clue to all the discussions of change and contact." Speaking of cultural change in Africa, he says that "the common factor exists wherever there is a long run identity of interests between Europeans and Africans, as well as competence and knowledge on the part of the whites in carrying out a well-planned policy." [11] This mixing of compatibilities and competencies is confusing, as is his subsequent attributing of intergroup cooperation to the presence of a common factor and of maladjustment to the functioning of

[9] Carl Sauer, "American Agricultural Origins: A Consideration of Nature and Culture," *Essays in Anthropology. Presented to A. L. Kroeber.* Berkeley: University of California Press, 1936, p. 291.

[10] Robert Lowie, "The Transition of Civilizations in Primitive Society," *American Journal of Sociology,* 1942, 47:530.

[11] Bronislaw Malinowski, *The Dynamics of Culture Change.* New Haven: Yale University Press, 1945, p. 66.

a "negative common factor." There is some clarification when he says [12] that the concept of common factor "is the direct corollary of our principle that human institutions are commensurable across the dividing line of culture . . ." and that

the ultimate reality in culture change thus hinges on the fact that corresponding institutions in two cultures satisfy analogous needs in different ways and with different techniques; but in the process they have to use the same human and natural resources: land, capital, labor, politically organized force, the impulses of human reproduction, and also the standardized emotions, values, and loyalties specific to each culture.

Malinowski here seems to suggest that it is always possible to discover common factors cross-culturally and that we should direct cultural changes along the lines of basic human needs in accordance with them. This is an attractive thesis as long as one deals with it on an abstract plane detached from concrete instances. When the concept is shifted to real problems, it will be found, for example, that even though all people have a religion, it is extremely difficult to get most of them to recognize that their ideas are after all the same as others and that any variant is as acceptable as the one thing they cherish. It is true, as Malinowski says, that "the African family and type of marriage are equivalents of the European marriage and family"; but this fact does not seem to convince the Englishmen that polygyny is an acceptable substitute for monogamy, nor does it convince the African native of the reverse. The truth is, of course, that polygyny and monogamy are quite different practices, even though by a process of abstraction we might all be able to agree that they embody the common factor of "marriage." At another level of abstraction, so do certain relations in chemistry and physics.

It is significant that some rationalists who attack the problem of acceptance find that novelties are welcomed because of common features with preexisting customs, whereas others find that they are rejected for exactly the same reason. The explanation of this contradiction lies in their abstract, ethnocentric approach. Any two things can be placed in the same category at some level of abstraction and in accordance with some criteria of identity —or they may be segregated. The pertinent issue is whether the actors rather than the audience have done so.

Incongruence. The meaning that a novelty acquires as a result of its being identified with something familiar is a necessary step in its ideological acceptance, but in many instances it is not the only one. Often identification really only sets the stage for the mental reaction that is for or against it. It establishes an innovative configuration XB or AY—an introduced X that is meaningful in the familiar context B or a familiar A that is meaningful

[12] *Ibid.,* pp. 70–71.

in the introduced context Y—which then poses the problem of acceptability. The housewife who contemplates purchasing a vacuum cleaner to replace the broom to which she has been accustomed must first of all identify herself (A) with, and project herself into the place of, another woman (X) who uses one; or, alternatively, she may identify the vacuum cleaner (Y) with her broom (B) and assimilate it to the context of herself. In either case all that she has done so far is to visualize herself using a vacuum cleaner. This may or may not be acceptable to her; it may or may not conform to her concept of herself in her housecleaning capacities, regardless of how she feels about other women using vacuum cleaners. Without the identification of one of its components XY remains totally unintelligible and alien; with identification the assimilated X's and Y's, or the projected A's and B's, present a conjunction of ideas which may or may not be congruent with the value system of the individual who makes the linkage. Specifically, the question for him is whether the new configuration XB or AY controverts or agrees with the valued AB with which it is inevitably linked.

The question of XB or AY congruence forces itself upon the potential acceptor whenever there is a question in his mind about identifying the other two terms of XY and AB. If there are reasons for making a complete identification, and if this identification produces a contradiction between XB or AY and AB, the novelty will have little appeal to the individual who values the custom represented by the mental configuration AB. This can happen if the relationships between X and Y and between A and B are different and if a double projection is suggested or demanded, because the result will be an AR_2B that is contrary to the accustomed AR_1B. Aiyappan's account of cultural change in India contains illustrations of this kind of incongruity. In a discussion of compatibility he warns against the hope for success of English experiments with democracy in India in these terms:

Authority diffused among the populace is a foreign element to Hindu tradition. Those skeptical observers who know that a dominant trait of Hindu culture is a sense of reverence for authority divine or human, and therefore think that dictatorship has better chances of success in India than democracy, may not be absolutely wrong. Nationalism in India may be regarded as a corollary of acculturation, but the mould in which it is cast is Indian, colored by the all-pervading religiousness which is another important trait in Indian culture. The administrator in order to avoid blunders has to take full cognisance of this law of cultural compatibility.

Aiyappan finds another illustration of the "working of the law of compatibility" in the Hindu opposition to European courtship patterns:[13]

[13] A. Aiyappan, "Theories of Culture Change and Culture Contact." In J. P. Mills (ed.), *Essays in Anthropology Presented to Rai Bahadur Sarat Chandra Roy.* Lucknow, p. 44.

Young Indians brought up in western traditions are nowadays anxious to adopt courtship of which they read so much in English literature and by the romantic charm of which they are naturally overcome. But Indian tradition, opposed to any pre-marital familiarity between young men and women, does not provide the social opportunities for the fascinating contacts preliminary to marriage in the West. Unless Indian society and mentality undergo revolutionary changes, courtship will not be adopted in Hindu culture.

In both these cases the incompatibility is between relationships. The acceptance of Occidental concepts of leadership and courtship would require the identification of individual Indians with individual Englishmen and a mental projection of the former into the places of the latter. Objection to this arises in these particular conceptual frameworks because the required changes in relationship between a Hindu suitor and his prospective bride and between the Hindu leader and the populace are unacceptable.

Comparable instances of the juxtaposition of antithetical relations brought to the fore by a double identification of the component subwholes of an introduced and a resident configuration could be cited from almost any acculturation situation. To give but one: Palauan men do not eat with their womenfolk upon formal occasions, which means when a group of men are assembled for any purpose and a feast is held for them. Despite this, the head chief of the district in which I lived decided that upon the occasion of a certain marriage he would like to honor American custom for my benefit by having the bride join her father and the other men in eating the food that was customarily served only to men. It was so ordered, but it was obvious to all that neither the man nor his daughter enjoyed the novelty. They were tense and embarrassed. They did no more than make a gesture of eating and were glad when the whole thing was over. The new relationship between father and daughter that was forced by their identification with an American father and his daughter was intolerable because it was directly opposed to the Palauan concept of the proper relationship between these two individuals.

In the immediately preceding instances an incongruity results from a double identification and projection which introduces an unacceptable relationship between the components of an indigenous configuration. Things considered to be food by one person are often rejected by another because this occurs. The introduced item is refused because it recalls a nonfood substance the thought of eating which is repellent. The Yurok were at first revolted by the sight of white men (X) eating rice (Y) because rice looked to them like maggots (B). The thought of identifying themselves with the eaters of these things prevented the Yurok from regarding rice as food. Similarly, many Americans are repelled by the slimy consistency of boiled okra or by the partially cooked white of an egg. In these instances it is not just the identification of the substance with something nasty that occasions the revulsion. The substance is rejected specifically as a food, which means a suggested identification of the self with someone who uses it as such. It is the suggested shift in relationships (from not eating to eating) between the projected self and the unpalatable stuff that is repugnant.

Another obstacle to acceptance appears when the initial identification that gives rise to XB or AY suggests a second or a third that is objectionable to the potential acceptor. The relationship factor presents no difficulty in these cases, but the suggestion of contravening customary differences does. Thus, if X is identified with A and assimilated to its context B, the linkage XB may suggest or imply an equation of Y and B that is considered to be invalid, improper, or impossible. What this means is that one component of AB (in this instance, B) is restrictive. It forbids the inclusion of Y in its class as far as its relationship with A is concerned. The secondary identification presumes to violate the reality of the segregation of Y and B.

Rejections are common when they thus secondarily entail an undesirable identification of the sexes in a particular context. The Japanese tried to induce Palauan men to follow their example and engage in the cultivation of rice. The suggested identification of a Palauan man (A) with a Japanese man (X) who cultivated rice (Y) was agreeable enough, but rice cultivation in the Palauan mind was identified with taro cultivation (B) because of common cultivation techniques and growing conditions for both. It was this secondary identification that made the acceptance of the custom impossible, because only women (another A) cultivate taro and men make a point of having nothing to do with this activity. It is something which clearly sets women apart from men in Palauan society. When women's hats with ostrich-feather plumes were introduced among the Yurok, their women were barred from accepting them because by aboriginal custom only Yurok men could wear any kinds of feathers on their heads. The identification of Yurok women (A) with white women (X) and their projection into the context of wearing hats with plumes (Y) was acceptable, but not the suggested identification of the plumes with native types of feathers (B) which were reserved for males (another A). It will be observed that this line of reasoning would make Yurok men and women identical (both A's), a conclusion that was not acceptable to the Indians. In the early days, Yurok women refused to wear corsets for the same reason. Aboriginally their men (A) wore a waist and chest protector (B) made of wooden slats (C) when they went to war. Quite apart from other considerations, then, a woman (another A) who identified herself with her white sister (X) and adopted this garment (Y) violated a prejudice, for she tended by so much to identify herself with a Yurok warrior.

The same concatenation of projection and assimilation forestalls acceptance when class or in-group and out-group differences are overridden by secondary and derived identifications. The use of iron was only gradually accepted, and it met with considerable opposition for several centuries after its discovery despite the fact that it made a better tool and weapon than did its predecessor bronze. Opposition to it developed from the fact that bronze (A) had become entrenched as a treasure item, a possession of kings and aristocrats (B), and it was, moreover, embedded in ritual contexts (B). Iron (X) was by comparison a plebeian metal, and its social connections (Y) outweighed its superior physical properties in the thinking of people who were in a position to do the most about advancing its widespread acceptance.[14] Iron and bronze (X and A) were identifiable, but their human or other associates (Y and B) were not. The Ashanti people of the Gold Coast made beautiful decorative cloths that were worn by their chiefs and aristocrats. Some enterprising foreign traders had exact duplicates made and imported to West Africa for sale. There were no native buyers, however; for unprivileged men would not brave the ridicule of wearing them since they were not entitled to do so, and rich and privileged men had no need of availing themselves of these cheaper imitations.[15] In this case there was little doubt about the identification of the cloths (X and A) from the two sources; but the two classes of individuals (Y and B) could not be equated, as they would have been by implication if common men had taken to the wearing of the imported fabrics. The Palauans have refused to eat corn in recent years although the American authorities have encouraged its acceptance by them. The reason for its rejection is that the Palauans regard it as "Chamorro food," that is, as being associated with the natives of Guam, whom they regard as inferior to themselves. Putting themselves (A) in the place of Americans (X) who eat corn (Y) would also mean identifying themselves with the Guamanians (another A) who likewise eat corn (B). To the extent that corn eating implies this equation to a Palauan man, he refuses it. The Yurok have until lately refused to follow their white neighbors in their use of oatmeal for much the same reason. Oats, they say, is horse food and is not fit for human consumption. To some extent this is perhaps a rationalization, but the mental processes which have led to just this formula for rejection and not some other are of the same character as those in the previous instances. One acceptable identification forces another that is objectionable.

Situational segregations also forbid acceptance when this double identification process is at work. Another way to put this is to say that people often refuse to project a familiar thing or activity (A) into a new setting (Y) when the logic of identification (of X and A) would force them to do so. The natives who have moved into urban centers in South Africa for the most part do not carry on with the ritual activities traditionally associated with

[14] A. L. Kroeber, *Anthropology*. New York: Harcourt, Brace and Company, Inc., 1948, pp. 726–727.

[15] Melville Herskovits, *Man and His Works*. New York: Alfred A. Knopf, Inc., 1948, pp. 559–560.

their life-crisis ceremonies. The majority of those who do continue with them at all resort to their ancestral home where the ceremonies are appropriate.[16] Although the ceremonies (A) could be performed in almost identical fashion in the two places, the projection of them into the town setting (Y) implies an equality between it and the home scene (B) that is generally regarded as inadmissible. This, incidentally, explains why many customs are abandoned: the permanent elimination of the original setting for a thing leads to the extinction of the thing, too. Situational segregation also reveals the inaccuracy of saying that customs have been renounced when they are merely relegated to the context that was originally appropriate to them and have not been carried over into new settings. The Hupa Indians, who are neighbors of the Yurok and aboriginally had much in common with them, rejected the use of metal pots and spoons for the preparation and eating of their acorn gruel in religious ceremonies until quite recent times. The explanation offered for this by some individuals was that the imported utensils made the gruel "taste like iron"—an obvious rationalization, because they did not hesitate to use them for other foods. A little probing reveals that the real objection has been to the equation of a secular setting (Y) with a religious one (B), metal spoons (X) being appropriate to the first, whereas wooden or shell spoons (A) were traditionally associated with the second. The Yurok were repelled by the American custom of setting up Christmas trees in houses, because aboriginally they brought a fir shrub (A) into the house only in connection with a mourning and purification ritual (B) for a recently deceased member of the household. The manifestations of gaiety (Y) associated with a Christmas tree (X) could not be reconciled with the solemn acts (B) connected with the fir shrub that resembled it. It was for the same reason that older Yurok individuals objected to bobbed hair for their women when this became an American fashion a few decades ago. According to native custom a woman cut her hair short only if she were in mourning for her deceased husband or a near relative. A Yurok woman (A) whose bobbed hair (C) identified her with a white woman (X) would be out of place in any context of amusement (Y).

It will be recognized that incongruence, as the term is used here, develops when an unacceptable analogy is suggested by the introduced configuration. A double projection, or a combined assimilation and projection, leads to an idea pattern that is incompatible with a preexisting norm. The acceptance of the novelty would entail an admission that AR_2Y or an AR_1Y is the equivalent of AR_1B. In the first, the equation is not granted because R_2 does not equal R_1; in the second it is not granted because, although X equals A, Y does not equal B. The analogy fails because it is forced. Its parts are

[16] Ellen Hellmann, "The Native in the Towns." In I. Schapera (ed.), *The Bantu Speaking Tribes of South Africa*. London: Routledge and Kegan Paul, Ltd., 1937, pp. 414, 418.

preformed, one half coming from each of two cultural systems. The fact that the advocates of the novelty see a true analogy in the artificial conjunction of the two parts is not convincing to the potential acceptors.

Independence. Objections that arise from incongruities are obviated if the introduced idea evokes the thought of another which it complements but does not antagonize. When this happens, the novelty is not identical with the familiar form; neither does it propose a contradictory pattern. It preserves its character and is acceptable because it represents an independent standard of behavior. It has meaning because one of its terms, X, has contacted a term, A, of a familiar configuration; but the issue of incongruence does not come up because the Y and B correlates of these identified terms maintain their separation. This can come about through a single projection: A is projected into the context Y to create an AY that is isolated from AB.

The independence of AY develops in more than one way. At its simplest it occurs when a familiar subwhole is projected into the context of an introduced complex on the basis of a single identification and with a complete disregard of the accustomed correlates of the projected entity. The X of XY contacts the A of AB, but Y and B do not figure in compatibility demands because the characteristics of B, and its relationship to A, are ignored. This is what takes place in simple innovation by projection. From the standpoint of acceptance it represents an advantage, because the novelty XY, which by identification becomes AY, does not have to meet the requirements of AB. It has meaning but is completely independent because A is independent. There are no complicating factors introduced by B.

This pattern of independence is manifest whenever a person sets himself or something that is familiar to him within the framework of an unaccustomed construct. It therefore comprises one pattern of alien imitation; specifically, the one wherein a person identifies himself (A) with a foreigner (X) and proceeds to do the alien things (Y) that his model does irrespective of his own accustomed behaviors (B). The African chief who has adopted the European administrator's custom of collecting taxes from his subjects for the purpose of subsidizing schools and well-drilling operations is an example. So is the European missionary who, identifying himself with local chiefs and priests, assumed the function of advising the natives upon internal political matters, prayed for rain for their crops, took part in their life-crisis ceremonies, and held thanksgiving rites in connection with their harvest ceremonies.[17] The Fijian who shakes hands with an American is likewise projecting himself into an alien context with a new correlate and its relationship. In many parts of the world it has been the custom to wear little or nothing that could be called clothing in the European sense. This has not pre-

---

[17] I. Schapera, "Present Day Life in the Native Reserves." In I. Schapera (ed.), *Western Civilization and the Natives of South Africa: Studies in Culture Contact.* London: Routledge and Kegan Paul, Ltd., 1934, pp. 42–43 and 54–55.

vented the diffusion of garments into those areas, because prior associations need not play a part in projection. The naked native, or one who is accustomed to wearing nothing except a breechcloth, has only to identify himself with a European to envisage himself in shirt and trousers without prejudice to or question about body covering as such. The same holds for religious syncretisms of the type whereby a local deity is identified with a foreign god and so takes on new attributes, functions, or ritual associations. Finally, in the sphere of inanimate things, there is the Palauan invention of a coconut-leaching machine. This device was taken over bodily from the Japanese who used it to wash rice. After the war a certain Palauan recovered one such machine from a pile of debris and began to use it to wash the oil from shredded coconut. The machine and the method (Y) were unrelated to the customary technique of hand squeezing (B); but, by the innovator's own account of his invention, there was a resemblance between rice (X) and shreds of coconut (A).

A novelty may be granted another kind of independence. In this it is not so free of internal controls, but it is compatible because it is self-contained. This occurs when the Y and B correlates of A are not ignored, but need not be because they are segregated from each other. They are regarded as distinct, and A's divergent affiliation with them is acceptable because it does not pose a dilemma or suggest an impossibility. The AY which results from an identification of A with X and its projection into the context Y is set apart from AB because Y and B are held to be different and A's relationships to them are different. There is thereby an acceptable identification of two of the terms of XY and AB and an acceptable segregation of their correlates. Palauan women will permit no one except a sister or other near female relative to attend them at childbirth. The prohibition upon viewing a woman's nakedness is very strong, and most women feel it keenly today. Most parturient women now refuse to go to the local hospital for delivery because native female aides and nurses are assigned to take care of them there. The significant point is, however, that they do not object at all to American physicians examining them or delivering them. Neither did they object to Japanese midwives doing the same. The reason they give is that Americans and Japanese are "different." The taboo does not hold for them. What we have in this case, then, is a Palauan woman identifying herself with an American or a Japanese woman in pregnancy and then isolating their correlates (physicians and native nurses). This is a case of a novelty's taking advantage of an indigenous class or in-group and out-group distinction instead of overriding it.

The segregation of in- and out-group representatives is a phenomenon that has been noted repeatedly by ethnographers in all parts of the world. It is, moreover, a fact of common observation within our own society where group differences are involved. It happens so consistently in the contact of peoples that it can be expected to account for many instances of alien idea acceptance. One additional illustration at this point will suffice. As has been mentioned, Palauan women never walk abreast of their men; they always trail them respectfully. At the same time I experienced no difficulty in getting some of them to walk beside me after a few trials. When this was tactfully called to the attention of a few women who had slipped into the habit (or the trap), they replied that I was not a Palauan; and one woman expressly completed the paradigm by asking, "That's what American women do, isn't it?" This woman had consciously identified herself with white women and had segregated me from Palauan men. Consequently she (A) could walk with (R_2) me (Y) without doing violence to her tradition of not walking with (R_1) native men (B).

Things and places as well as people are fitted to this pattern of independence by segregation. Labor recruiters in the South Seas found that they could not hire natives to work on plantations in or near their home villages but had no difficulty if the place of employment was in a foreign locality.[18] The native (A), identifying himself with others (X) who worked for pay in distant places (Y), regarded this as entirely distinct from doing the same thing at home (B). South African schoolboys have taken up the European custom of carrying the bundles of girls—but only at schools, not in their home villages where the opposite relationship is appropriate.[19] The Samoans still adhere to their traditional pattern of hospitality and generosity, but they tend to draw a distinction between native goods (B) and foreign goods (Y) in this connection. Along with the latter they have adopted an individualistic, proprietary attitude "and an unwritten law seems to be arising that such articles belong to the person who took the trouble to purchase them; they may be borrowed but not taken. . . . Food, drink and shelter, however, are always freely available."[20] This development has been very common elsewhere.

It will be noted that this pattern of identifying one set of terms, X and A, and of segregating the other set, Y and B, conforms to the pattern of an alternative as it has been discussed under innovation in Chapter IX. The only difference is that in this case the novelty forms a ready-made part of the paradigm. The latter emerges from a conjunction of two established traditions rather than being drawn out of previously unrealized connections within one. The conditions are therefore different, but the results are the same; and acceptance depends upon whether the novelty permits a fit in

[18] William Wawn, *The South Sea Islanders and the Queensland Labor Trade*. London: S. Sonnenschein, 1893, pp. 23–24.

[19] Monica Hunter, "The Effects of Contact with Europeans on the Status of Pondo Women," *Africa*, 1933, 6:269.

[20] Felix Keesing, *Modern Samoa*. Stanford, Calif.: Stanford University Press, 1939, p. 326.

terms of the requirements of a combined identification and segregation. From the standpoint of the identified thing, A, there are alternative connections with its differentiated correlates Y and B.

Alternatives can be rather unstable. In many instances, because of the status of Y and B as alternatives, and sometimes also because of their resemblances, a question is raised concerning their identity, and hence about the propriety of the novelty. Are Palauan men and American men really different or different enough to be put in isolated categories? Similar doubts may be raised about the initial identification. Are Palauan women really the same as American women and so entitled to associate in the same way with American men? It usually happens that there are individual differences of opinion upon these issues and consequently different reactions to the same novelty. Furthermore, the same individual may vacillate in his responses because he is uncertain of his interpretations. This frequently happens in acculturation when there are forces operating both for and against cross-cultural equations, although it is by no means restricted to such situations. Doubts and waverings about interindividual identifications are especially prominent, the upshot of this being that one person tentatively identifies himself with another individual at one moment and refuses to do so at the next. Quite often a native will behave alternatively as a native and as a foreigner with whom he makes a provisional identification. Sometimes this vacillation has an element of security seeking about it, especially in anxiety-producing situations. It is now quite common for some South African natives to get married in every way known to them—native style, by Christian service, and by civil code. The Yurok for a long time, and to some extent today, held both their kind of funeral and a Christian burial service. They were uncertain about their identification with white men and questioned whether an Indian could go to the white man's heaven. They considered it best to take the chance upon the identification and at the same time to fortify themselves by continuing with their native practices. Very commonly natives the world over accept scientific medication as do white men yet continue to resort to their local magicians in times of crisis. The sick man is dubious about identifying himself or his disease with the white man and his diseases, or about the validity of segregating the physician and the medicine man. If he feels that he can clearly differentiate his ills into native and foreign types, his decisions can be much more satisfying.

Some novelties fit a third pattern of independence that is more stable. In it the initial identification of X with A establishes the meaningful configuration AY, both terms of which are segregated from preexisting AB's. The result is a parallel of the same description as has been discussed under innovation: A is discriminated from something that is like it—some other A —and Y is likewise set apart from the correlate—another B of this second A. The best examples of this rest upon clear-cut distinctions such as those which set off sex, class, and other dichotomies. Natively, Palauan women were the farmers in their society. They are still solely responsible for the planting, weeding, and harvesting of indigenous crops; but the men have, in part, undertaken the cultivation of such introduced crops as sweet potatoes, beans, and manioc. The tending of plants of both types remains the obligation of women; but men do not shun sweet-potato fields as they do taro patches, and some of them take pride in their knowledge of alien crops and introduced cultivation techniques. They are able to maintain this parallelism because they have identified themselves (A) with the male farmers (X) who introduced the alien food plants (Y) and at the same time have differentiated the latter from taro (B) and themselves from their women (another A) who are associated with its cultivation. Palauan men, but not women, have also learned to bake bread and to prepare certain Japanese dishes, following the pattern of professional male bakers and restaurant owners whom they observed in the town of Koror. Except for feast foods like turtles, however, native cooking is a responsibilty of the women. In South Africa native men (A) can be employed to do household chores for Europeans (Y) because this employment is doubly distinct from the familiar pattern of a woman (another A) performing such services for native families (B). In one tribe of this region women (A) are responsible for making the thatching (B) for native-style houses. Since the advent of the Europeans, native men have learned to make thatching—but it is the kind (Y) that was introduced by the European men (X) along with their own style of house construction.

It is probable that in most instances the acceptor of a parallel does not see it as such at all. Rarely would he judge its acceptability by setting off its terms from an indigenous counterpart. Yet a segregation is recognized in the very fact that identifications (as between native women and foreign men) are not made indiscriminately. Furthermore, the awareness of segregated sets does rise to the surface if they are for any reason challenged. The young Palauan man who worked for me volunteered to do the cooking for our household, but it turned out that he meant only the cooking of American food. He could not be prevailed upon to cook taro or other native foods. He said that was a woman's business and that he did not know anything about it. He identified himself (A) with me (X), whom he had observed cooking, but clearly distinguished foreign (Y) and native (B) foods. This segregation was essential to him in order to preserve his distinction from women (A) whose duty it was to prepare his traditional foods. The suggestion of overriding the dictates of segregated pairs evoked an awareness of them in his mind even though he may never have recognized them as such before.

That there is an awareness of the double segregation inherent in parallels compounded from two cultural systems is evidenced by the failure or the refusal to see or to treat the introduced configuration XY as an appropriate substitute for the indigenous configuration AB. The two halves of the parallel are compartmentalized and as units are embedded in larger configurations which do not overlap. In short, they are not viewed as analogies. Aboriginally the Tsimshian had clan names with which were associated certain specific property rights. When these Indians became acquainted with alien goods and conventions, they began to take or to be given European family names and also to acquire new kinds of property whose ownership was tied up with the names. Nowadays the two configurations constitute segregated sets, the native style names and their associated rights making up one inheritance system, the foreign family names with their ownership correlates comprising another. Among the same people tribal affairs used to be administered by a group of hereditary chiefs. Toward the end of the last century a missionary among them decided that an elected council of progressive and competent individuals would better serve community interests, and he succeeded in getting the idea adopted. This did not result in the elimination of the older administrative body or in any considerable loss of its functions. The chiefs continued to deal in traditional ways with traditional matters just as they always had. The elected council, which had some of the same men on it, deliberated new issues, such as entertainments and sanitary regulations, and managed new enterprises, such as school and church construction.[21] The two institutions paralleled each other in composition (X and A) and in functions (Y and B) with little tendency for one to overlap or conflict with the other. This was relatively easy because of the dual segregation; one political body was associated with the new and the other with the old. The same process accounted for parallels in the material culture of the Tsimshian and others. The Tsimshian accepted rowboats but kept them in a separate category from their native canoes. The two craft remained distinct in use, manufacture, and associations. Some Palauans have adopted the use of chairs, but not in association with native-style dwellings; chairs go with the Japanese- and American-style homes with which they were imported. The Yurok accepted knives and forks and tables and chairs and linked them in the same way with American-style foods and dwellings.

These parallels recall other examples given in the discussion of rationalistic interpretations of acceptability (p. 339). Those illustrations are also parallels resulting from diffusion, and what has been said in the present connection applies to them as well. The significance of this statement is that parallels are acceptable because they are different, not because they are the same. Although we, and perhaps some acceptors, perceive linkages of similarity between the components of an introduced and an indigenous part of a parallel, this similarity is not the reason for the welcome given to the

[21] H. G. Barnett, "Invention and Cultural Change," *American Anthropologist*, 44 (No. 1):24–25.

former. On the contrary, it is precisely because of their differences that both can be supported without friction or confusion. The "common factor," if it is recognized at all, is an obstacle in the way of acceptance instead of a facilitating feature when parallels are involved. And as we have seen, parallels are involved when an introduced configuration has terms which, according to the acceptor's system of values, must be segregated from the terms of a preexisting form.

Structuralization. The process of projection figures prominently in setting the stage for the acceptance of novelties that recommend themselves because they do not get entangled with existing values. The same freedom from complication facilitates acceptance when it can be accomplished by simple assimilation. As in innovation, this process introduces a variant in the guise of an identity under conditions which do not disturb existing values: X is equated with A and takes its place as a correlate of B. The Y correlate of X, the introduced novelty, is ignored; hence any possible relationship that it might have with B is irrelevant. There can be no conflict between XB, the meaningful metamorphosis of XY, and AB because X and A are regarded as identical. The shock of accepting novelties that can be treated in this fashion is minimal, and it may not be sensed at all. It is the easiest kind of acceptance.

This pattern of acceptance is the obverse of that established by simple projection as exemplified in the first part of the preceding section. The results of the two processes appear in quite different lights to the advocate and to the acceptor of a novelty. In projection the advocate is not aware of the creative character of acceptance, and he is usually puzzled by resistance to its adoption. To him acceptance is mere copying, which he considers to be a passive act. But from the projector's standpoint a meaningful identification always entails the inclusion of something new in his experience, the Y of our diagram. With acceptance by simple assimilation it is the other way around. The assimilator is not aware of his creative act in acceptance, but the advocate is. To the advocate's surprise he finds his X configurated with the acceptor's B, which might be quite different from Y, its proper correlate in his experience. This is why many intergroup borrowings, made in all naturalness and innocence by their acceptors, strike their donors as bizarre or ludicrous. Strange things do happen in this way. The first coins that came into the possession of the Yurok were handed over to their children who thought them ideal substitutes for the flat pebbles they used to throw so that they would skim the surface of the river. The first flour that the Hupa saw was left at a camp site of an exploring party. They used it in place of chalk for face paint. The Tsimshian and other Indians around them found a resemblance between the first buttons and thimbles that they saw and the shell and dewclaw ornaments which they sewed to their ceremonial garments, so they replaced the latter with the former. Not so long ago a Hupa Indian who aspired to become a shaman initiated the practice of healing patients while he was under the influence of liquor. When he attended a patient, he brought along a jug of wine which he proceeded to drink while he worked himself into the proper ecstatic state by singing and dancing as genuine medicine men did. He claimed that he got his supernatural help in this way, and it appears that he sincerely believed that his abnormal mental state was the equivalent of that of the orthodox shaman.

It is evident that such freely assimilated novelties cannot be as firmly embedded in their alien matrix as they are when projection is the mechanism for substitution. The assimilated component of the introduced configuration must be detachable from its proper correlate. Detachment is, of course, not a property of anything. It is a function of perception and not of the thing perceived, so it depends upon the prior experience of the perceiver. This dependence is as true of projection as of assimilation; but, as we have seen, there are more stimulus controls in projection than in assimilation. With reference to acceptance this means that assimilation presumes a minimum of requirements imposed by the conditions of the novelty presentation. The assimilator is free to organize his stimulus field (the novelty and everything about it) in any way that is meaningful and appealing to him.

The utmost freedom is permitted when a novelty has no advocate at all; that is, when there is no one to interpret it or to insist upon its being accepted. This occurs when a new artifact or substance is discovered out of its accustomed contexts of use and users, as is the case when a person finds a lost or a cast-off object. The Hupa assimilation of flour to the context of a face paint is an example. So was the Palauan use of bottle glass. The first pieces of this material acquired from Europeans were identified with one variety of native money, and in the beginning they were acceptable substitutes for it. Later they were rejected, both because there was a difference between the two substances and because bottle glass soon threatened to flood the market and produce a financial crisis.

The freedom to assimilate at will is also invited when a novelty is manifest in the behavior of an individual who has no intention of promoting its acceptance by others and hence does not think about or take the trouble to explain it or to define its limits for them. Since a novelty always appears in some context, the uninformed acceptor is free to analyze it or the total field of which it is a part in accordance with his understanding of it. Innumerable traits have diffused under these conditions, as occurred when the Yurok adopted red underwear for formal attire. Another instance was my social placement by the Palauans. Upon my introduction to the community where I was to live, I endeavored not to give the inhabitants any clue about my conceptions of what their attitudes toward me should be. I neutralized myself as much as possible. More accurately stated, I gave many diverse cues but did so in a tentative and unobtrusive way and then followed where the native interpretation of them led me. I wanted to avoid giving my impress to our interpersonal relations so that I might see how the Palauans would structure an unorganized or disorganized presentation of myself. As might be expected, the results were diverse and individualistic. Most of the people treated me either like a Japanese or an American. Others found special niches for me in accordance with their private prototypes.

The same opportunity to assimilate a novelty by "free association" is inherent in situations wherein the stimulus field is well structured but is not understood by the acceptor. Language difficulties, advocate antipathies, and other barriers to full understanding often produce assimilations that are disconcerting to interested advocates. Following the Second World War doctors in certain parts of Italy initiated a campaign to get pregnant women to take prepared vitamins. In one town the plan seemed to be working out satisfactorily until two women who had been following the prescribed regimen had twins. Immediately several others decided that they wanted no more of the pills. Evidently they equated the vitamins (X) with something (A) known to them in folklore, or perhaps entirely unknown and only postulated, as the cause of multiple births (B). They did not comprehend the nature of the real effects (Y) of the vitamins, even assuming that these had been explained to them. Administrators in South Africa, as elsewhere, have had to contend with similar difficulties that have been due to misunderstandings; that is, unanticipated interpretations by the natives of the meaning of the novelties which the administrators have tried to introduce.

The compulsory dipping of cattle, *e.g.*, has been interpreted by natives in many parts of South Africa as a device to kill off their animals and so impoverish them still further; the compulsory branding of cattle in infected areas to facilitate control of their movements is resented as "marking them off as government property"; proposals for land development are rejected for fear that if it improves too much the white man will take it away; while suggestions for the formation of farmers' associations are regarded as just another scheme for robbing the people of their money.[22]

In this connection we may note that not all misunderstandings are accidental. Some are deliberately contrived and disseminated by interested parties in an effort to defeat new proposals. Canards are circulated to influence legislation, to delay new projects, and to undermine initial confidence in any new idea.

Free assimilation is most common when the contacts between a novelty advocate and a potential acceptor are limited, indirect, sporadic, or impersonal. It is therefore characteristic of initial, fleeting, and isolated contacts such as those which take place on the frontiers of two cultural systems that are meeting for the first time. The possibility of it lessens with the development of more frequent and more intimate contacts between their repre-

[22] I. Schapera, "Cultural Changes in Tribal Life." In I. Schapera (ed.), *The Bantu Speaking Tribes of South Africa*, pp. 362–363.

sentatives. It is reduced to a minimum when the representatives of one system endeavor to proselytize members of the other and are able to direct and correct interpretations made by the acceptors.

The rigidity of the structuralization of a novelty is thus a very important control upon its acceptability. Structure patterns often determine not only how a new idea will be integrated into the receiving culture, but also whether it will be accepted at all. It is a prepotent factor in all cases of acceptance, including those discussed under incongruence and independence. The difference is that with projection the structuring of the novelty field has been done by individuals to whom it is familiar, whereas in free assimilation this is a function of the acceptor. The same data present entirely different acceptance possibilities depending upon whether the advocate or the acceptor is permitted to do the structuring. A few examples will make this clear.

Among the Swazi of South Africa, women aboriginally were primarily responsible for farming. Their main implement was the hoe. In the ordinary course of events they were not supposed to have anything to do with cattle tending, for this was an occupation that was a man's special interest. Since the introduction of the ox-drawn plow by Europeans this implement has tended to supersede the use of the hoe in native agriculture. As might be anticipated from what has already been said, Swazi men, not the women, now use it.[23] This is because the plow was introduced, not in isolation or in a display window, but as an integral part of a man-ox-plow unit that offered no basis for an identification with the women-hoe configuration. The insistence upon the three-part linkage, by European example and perhaps by precept, permitted the native man to idenitfy himself (A) with the European man (X), or to identify his man-cow unit (AC) with the European man-ox unit (XC), and so to envisage himself in the place of the foreigner operating a plow. By the same token it was not possible to break this configuration down and to disregard its correlates in such a way that plows (X) and hoes (A), or plow-tilling (XC) and hoe-tilling (AC), could be identified and so be assimilated to the native woman's (B) activities. When metal axes were introduced to the Yurok, white males, of course, were their principal users. Yurok men took them over because of this sex linkage, despite the fact that Yurok women traditionally had the task of collecting firewood, one of the uses to which their menfolk put their newly acquired axes. The imported man-ax configuration was compulsive and so did not permit a native woman to identify herself with a white man. Neither did it permit a reconfiguration so that an ax-firewood (XC) grouping could be identified with its native wedge-firewood (AC) counterpart and the ax and this use of it thereby assimilated to the context of women's (B) use. In contrast to these two illustrations there is the case of the Shakers who have insisted upon a re-

[23] Bartlett, *op. cit.*, p. 262.

configuration which from the beginning has been resisted by the Christian missionaries who have worked among them. Both the Shakers and the missionaries have acknowledged that God can bestow supernatural power and insight upon a person. However, the missionaries have played this configuration down and have stressed other attributes and functions of God which they consider to be more appropriate. The Shakers have refused this structuring of the introduced theology. Stressing the gift of supernatural power (C), they have equated God (X) with aboriginal spirits (A) and have therefore been able to assert that God's power can effect all the miracles formerly claimed for shamanistic spirit power, including the healing of the sick and clairvoyance (B).

It is obvious that a configuration which is a unit to one person can be for others a compound of elements or merely a fortuitous aggregation of particulars. This fact helps to explain the phenomenon of adhesion, which is the term given to persistent linkages between idea-sets as they diffuse across ethnic boundaries. Artifacts of this sort are called complexes because the analyst finds them to be made up of more than one component. This structuring, however, is merely his characterization of them, and it cannot be taken as an insight into the way in which the actual participants have viewed them. In fact, there is every reason to assume that acceptors see such a complex, not as an adhering cluster of different things, but as a whole. It has a unitary aspect to them, and so they place it in a context which preserves its unity. Sometimes it has its unitary character because of the way in which it has been presented to them, sometimes because of their own configuration of the novelty field. In any event acceptance, like innovation, is by units regardless of how complex they seem to others than the acceptors.

CHAPTER XIII

NOVELTY VALUES

Incompatibility. The emphasis in the last chapter upon agreement between old and new idea characteristics may make it seem that this conformity is a necessary and a sufficient requirement for the acceptance of a novelty. It is, in fact, neither. With some novelties it is an inescapable consideration for the potential acceptor, but in itself it does not compel acceptance or rejection. There is always something beyond the question of novelty compatibility as judged by the dictates of the established custom that is thrown into relief by its appearance. There must be something by which to judge both novelty and custom, not in terms of their agreement, but in terms of their desirability. This something beyond is a supraordinate criterion by which credit or discredit is assigned to the familiar custom, and hence to a novelty that conforms or disagrees with it. In brief, the whole of a novelty and the whole of the custom which gives it meaning must have a place in a more inclusive value system, and novelty concordance or the lack of it provides a basis for making the evaluation.

Lack of conflict, then, can be no more than a minimum recommendation for a novelty. New things, ideas, and behaviors are evaluated, not only with reference to their intrinsic merits or demerits, but also by comparison with existing usages which can be measured on the same scale. Sometimes the comparison is with the custom that is highlighted by the question of compatibility; sometimes it is with another quite unrelated custom. It is obvious that the evaluation of a new idea cannot be made by reference to some near or partial equivalent when the thought of the latter is not evoked by the mental presence of the former. As was illustrated in the last chapter, this condition is typical of certain patterns of assimilation and projection, as is evident when a native identifies himself with a European and begins to wear a sun helmet. The fact that there may be no indigenous custom formally like it does not mean that the novelty cannot be evaluated, however. It is simply judged with reference to something else, something to which it is conceived to be related and against which its virtues are measurable. There may also be alternative, multiple, or ordinal systems of values wherein different criteria of excellence apply. Thus the acceptance of a vacuum cleaner may be conditioned by its comparison with the mechanical instrument, the broom, that it is designed to replace or with some prestige item like a piece of jewelry for which it can likewise be regarded as a substitute or perhaps as a

357

compensation. In any event, there must be some basis for comparison and some resident configuration with which the novelty can be compared.

The evaluation of a novelty, like its conformance with a familiar counterpart, may be taken as a measure of its compatibility. The two ratings have different standards, but they may be connected. Although in most of the last chapter, and most of this, the datum of reference in the discussion of acceptability is the modal behavior for a social group, it is evident that this standard gives an incomplete picture of the problem. Specifically, it leaves out of account the well-appreciated fact that the value systems of potential acceptors differ, even in the same society. That which is unacceptable to one person may, for exactly the same reason, be welcomed by another. With particular reference to novelty compatibility this means that a new idea may have acceptors just because it defies conventional rules of equivalence and difference. Merit lies with incongruence because the conventional mode has a negative value. Compatibility is not a necessary condition for acceptance. On the contrary, incompatibility is a sufficient recommendation because it accords with a valued antithesis. It becomes a novelty asset rather than a liability.

Few customs have the unqualified support of everyone who follows them or at least admits them in the cultural inventory of his ethnic group. Some are personally rejected by certain individuals who regard them as absurd, unjust, vain, or untrue despite a general concurrence to the contrary. To such objectors familiar customs may in effect be alien and their opposites desirable. For them a novelty which contradicts a despised norm is more welcome than one which conforms to its requirements. Furthermore, it is their receptivity to opposites that most often raises the question of incompatibility. Except for their advocacy most contradictions would pass unnoticed as alien and irrelevant behaviors. Their sympathy makes manifest what would otherwise be only latent and hypothetical incompatibilities.

Acceptability from the standpoint of the custom-alien individual is the reverse of acceptability as already discussed. The incongruities of the preceding chapter were cited as illustrations of rejections, but it is evident that they were not or need not have been wholly that. Indeed many of them presuppose the welcome of an incongruous novelty by individuals who valued its challenge or abrogation of conventional modes. Thus, the citation from India indicates that not all Hindus find European patterns of government and courtship objectionable and that some of them certainly approve of these foreign customs just because they are different. The same is true of the novelties characterized as rejects because they presumed identifications that were intolerable by customary standards. While most Yurok people undoubtedly resented any suggestion of an equation of the sexes, it is equally certain that others, especially women, did not. Most Palauans rate the Chamorros as a low-class people and do not want to be identified with them even indirectly. But this is not an absolutely universal attitude. A small minority of the Palauans have had Chamorro friends and consider the popular rating foolish and unjust. They reject the stigma that attaches to corn eating even though they may not like the taste of corn. And finally, it is a fact that some Yurok women did proceed to bob their hair and some Hupa did begin to use metal utensils at their religious ceremonies despite the frowns and admonitions of their tradition-bound associates.

As has been implied, novelty congruence is generally judged to be an asset. It has merit in itself, and it is often demanded as a least condition for acceptance. But this is seldom a sufficient reason for embracing a change. It is not enough for a novelty to be neutral toward or coincident with honored patterns of equivalence and difference. There must be some additional quality to recommend the novelty and give it precedence over available usages. It must have a superior rating on some scale by comparison with an existing custom in order to make the change worth the effort of accommodating it. Values are measured from several different points of view, which means that there are usually advantages and disadvantages that attach to the adoption of anything. For a particular individual the benefits may or may not outweigh the liabilities, or they may cancel each other. Some adoptions entail initial disadvantages and long-term gains, others only temporary benefits. Here again the variables are multiple, and the remainder of the chapter will be concerned with the part they play in determining acceptance over and beyond congruence. They represent different scales of values by which novelties are judged in comparison with familiar forms that are their functional alternatives.

Efficiency. One consideration is the effectiveness of a new thing or idea. Many innovations, just because they are untried, are clumsy, inefficient, and untrustworthy. Their uncertain or disappointing performance under test leads to impatience and skepticism among persons who would otherwise welcome them. Prospective acceptors are not willing to take a chance or serve as experimental subjects or dupes. They do not want to invest in white elephants or to accumulate gimcracks. New methods, materials, and technological devices raise objections of this sort, especially when something very important like personal safety or welfare is at stake. Vaccination was resisted, for one thing, because in the beginning it was often administered so carelessly that complications developed. Also, too much was claimed for it by advocates who did not want to retreat from their earlier claims that it afforded permanent immunity. Antisepsis was rejected by many doctors who, not understanding all the precautions that were necessary, failed to achieve the results claimed by Lister. In fact, by 1875 repeated failures by medical men in England, Germany, Belgium, and Holland had led to reaction against its use. Lister's advocacy of a carbolic acid spray for the atmosphere around a patient's wound created a side issue that was obstructive, too, because the spray was useless and could be harmful. The first automobiles were cumbersome and unreliable. One early manufacturer insisted upon equipping each machine with a whip socket. When the designer objected, he snorted, "Every one of these newfangled things is going to need a horse to pull it home sooner or later." [1] New ideas as well as new things are viewed with skepticism before they have been tried out. Witness the objections of many people to current efforts to establish some kind of world government, especially if the proposal presupposes a renunciation of national sovereignty. Objectors are doubtful that the scheme would work on a world design.

Cost. The cost of acquiring or using a novelty may be prohibitive as far as some potential acceptors are concerned. This is an obvious deterrent to the widespread adoption of a host of modern innovations and importations in both the technological and the ideological realms. A great many people in the world today are ready to accept—in fact, psychologically they have already accepted—television, electric lights, electric dishwashers, radiant heat, rest cures, sanitation programs, modern house designs, and many other changes, but they are unable to afford them. The practical realization of a new idea is very often a costly undertaking. Putting the idea into operation calls for labor and materials; so, ordinarily, does its introduction to potential acceptors. Initially, very few individuals are in a position to have or do what is required in accepting it. In technology the aim of mechanized production and efficiency research is to lower the requirements for actual acceptance so that more people may become acceptors. In some instances the cost of a novelty is so great that no one can afford it. The idea is acceptable and has important implications, but the returns to be expected are not commensurate with the investment required to produce it. Such is the present status of atomic power for industrial uses.

The restraining effect of novelty costs is evident when they are absent. It is relatively easy to get people to try something if doing so entails no loss to them. They may think that it is no good or harmful just because it costs them nothing, but they are more likely than not to accept it just because it is free. This is quite evident in America, and industrial concerns play upon the inclination in their advertising campaigns. Only the person who is suspicious that there might be some "strings attached" to a sample will reject it and fail to give it a trial. Trying it does not commit him—and what can he lose? The sponsors of bank nights, radio giveaway shows, lotteries, box-top contests, and auctions capitalize upon this appeal and win often enough to make the gamble a sound business practice. When treaties were made with the Indians in Washington and Oregon in the middle of the nineteenth century the representatives of the United States government stipulated that schools, sawmills, work horses, farming implements, and other items conducive to

[1] *Literary Digest*, Dec. 11, 1926, p. 59.

"civilized life" were to be provided as compensation for Indian land ceded to the government. In most instances the Indians did not value these things; they took them because they were pressed or were forced to do so in order to get something else, such as food, that they really wanted. Nevertheless, when the government failed to supply the stipulated goods and services they were demanded just because they had been promised. In the beginning, converts were attracted to Shakerism because it offered them something for nothing. Slocum made much of the fact that his "medicine" cost nothing, as contrasted with the services of a shaman; and the testimonials of those who claimed to have been healed and saved by God's power emphasized this feature in praising the benefits of this religion. Free "medicine" was a selling point that brought many a doubter into the fold.

Cost is a relative judgment. It is a function of an individual's economy of preferences. The price of a novelty in goods or labor is measured by a prospective acceptor's reference to his total wealth, by his comparison of its cost with the cost of some alternative, and also by his estimate of the pressure of his need for it. The man who can afford a yacht may still find the price of a new lawn mower excessive; yet the sick man considers that any sacrifice is not too great to secure relief. An American mortgages his salary to buy an automobile, whereas the English workingman considers this price too high for him to pay.

Advantage. Some novelties are welcomed primarily because they give the acceptor a material or an imponderable advantage not otherwise obtainable. The advantage may be direct or indirect. In this the motivations for acceptance directly parallel those for innovation that were discussed in Chapter VI under the heading The Desire for Quantitative Variation. In other words, novelties are accepted because they give the acceptor priority over someone else or because they represent a gain in some way over available things or techniques. A great number of phenomena fall within the framework of this appeal; only a few instances need be cited to indicate its range. In the technological field it is sufficient to recall that inventions and importations are welcomed if they are rated as superior to existing devices in saving time, labor, money, space, or any other valued resource. Or, in technology or out of it, novelties appeal if they give some social or political advantage. Businessmen, politicians, social leaders, and native chiefs embrace the new if it augments, consolidates, or protects their position. Kings, princelings, rebels, and ambitious underlings in all times and places have eagerly seized upon new ideas to forward their aims and save themselves from disaster. Apart from familiar examples that will occur to most readers there are many others that could be cited from ethnological literature. Both Kamehameha I of Hawaii and Pomare I of Tahiti had the good fortune to control those parts of the islands upon which they lived that provided the best anchorage for European ships. Consequently they were well situated to acquire a virtual monopoly upon trade goods and foreign favors. Both of them seized the opportunity to improve their political positions. They sought firearms and the assistance of European blacksmiths, shipwrights, and military advisers to aid them in their drive to subjugate their rivals. The present head chief of Ngarard district in the Palau Islands has chosen the same course for the same reason. He works closely with the Americans, accepting their recommendations for change, in the hope of making himself the preeminent power in the islands.

The lure of prestige gains is as attractive as the prospect of increased power or material advantage in inducing acceptance of a novelty. Something has already been said of this in the consideration of out-group advocates. One or two further illustrations drawn from non-European sources may not be amiss. William Duncan, the missionary among the Tsimshian in the 1850's, preached his first sermon in the house of a chief who was looking for an opportunity to get even with a rival. The Indian sought to make political capital of Duncan's patronage and succeeded in doing so. First his rival and then other chiefs invited Duncan to preach in their homes. This show of wholesale acceptance was heartening to Duncan; but he was soon to learn, if he did not suspect it in the beginning, that something other than repentance was motivating his eager sponsors. The truth was that they were attempting to use him rather than to understand him.[2] The Germans, and later on the New Zealanders, who have administered Western Samoa have succeeded in introducing several changes by playing upon the natives' pride in invidious accomplishment. Villages were encouraged to compete with each other in expanding their footpaths and in building roadways. The construction of community water systems was also drawn into this competition, so that practically every village now has an assured water supply. Accolades were conferred upon local health committees and sanitation teams, with the result that medical knowledge became a prestige commodity rather than a stimulus to community welfare. Children have learned to read and write under the same competitive drive for village prestige.[3]

A special case of vantage seeking occurs when one novelty is accepted because it is a requirement for obtaining another. The prerequisite is not wanted for its own sake or because it is an alternative means to a familiar goal. It is made- necessary in order to get something else that is new and desirable. The two novelties are linked together either because of some inherent connection between them, or, more commonly, because they are arbitrarily joined by their advocates. Such linkage is familiar to Americans as a result of some modern merchandising campaigns and is known as the "tie-in sale." In this the purchaser must buy one thing in order to get another

[2] H. G. Barnett, "Applied Anthropology in 1860," *Applied Anthropology*, 1942, 1 (No. 3):20.

[3] Felix Keesing, *Modern Samoa*. Stanford, Calif.: Stanford University Press, 1939, pp. 298, 304, 382–383, 393, 417.

that he really wants. The technique is just as common in novelty-acceptance situations. The term "rice Christians" conveys the idea and has come to be widely employed beyond the field of religion to denote people who accept a nuisance in order to get an essential. Reverend Wilbur, who was for many years the resident missionary and the government agent among the Yakimas, was accused by the Indians of employing this device by officially favoring those who made the gesture of becoming members of his Methodist congregation. Regardless of the truth of this charge, it is clear that many Yakimas went to church just to be certain of getting on the preferential list for teams of horses, rations of beef, clothing, and other valued goods that were dispensed through the agency office in fulfillment of treaty obligations. Many native peoples in Africa and Oceania have accepted Christianity because they have wanted to learn to read and because missionary teachers have been the only source of instruction available to them.

Sometimes a connection between imported novelties has been established by their recipients rather than by their donors. In these instances an acceptor has interpolated an integral relationship between two things and has felt that one is a necessary condition for the other. Thus, a Samoan chief is reported to have urged his people to become Christians because it appeared to him that the Christian god was the giver of desirable things such as ships, guns, and knives. He said: "Now I conclude that the God who has given to His white worshipers these valuable things must be wiser than our gods, for they have not given the like to us. We want all these articles; and my proposition is that the God who gave them should be our God." [4] This is a typical Samoan reaction, but the reasoning has occurred repeatedly among other peoples at their first contacts with Europeans.

Just as the prospect of an advantage offered by a novelty is conducive to its acceptance, so is the lack of promise a deterrent. If a new idea appears to be more of a handicap than a gain over existing alternatives, or if the gain that is alleged for it seems trivial, its appeal will be negligible. This fact is obvious when it is possible to sum up neatly the advantages and disadvantages of a novelty, but sometimes evaluations are made with different standards of reference. In particular, the advantages that an innovator claims for his idea may seem vain or unrealistic to others. Very often a novelty is ridiculous because it seems to be so much ado about nothing, or because there seems to be so little return on the cost, labor, or inconvenience entailed in its utilization. This is very likely the reaction that most people can be expected to have toward the shoe attachments invented by a man of Tarbes, France, to make it easier to walk up and down hills. He has spent fourteen years on this project and now has an apparatus constructed to keep the feet

[4] Felix Keesing, *The South Seas in the Modern World*. New York: The John Day Company, 1941, p. 230.

level on inclines by means of a "gearshift" which sets the walking surface of the attachments at different angles and so keeps the shoe soles of the walker on a horizontal plane.[5] More or less in the same category are the following inventions for which patents were granted a few years ago: an overcoat provided with built-in electrically heated elements and a carrying case for batteries; sinkers frozen in ice cubes to keep them away from the lips of highball drinkers; a mechanical wiper for fogged spectacles; and a metal casing which is designed to fit over the toes of shoes to prevent their being scuffed.[6] These inventions recall those mentioned under the heading of Unrecognized Prototypes. The fundamental reason why all of them seem funny to most people is that they tacitly allege an advantage over existing controls where none is, in fact, felt by potential acceptors. Another way of saying this is that they create a want instead of filling the void that is experienced when a real want goes unsatisfied.

Pleasure. Hedonistic considerations enter into the determination of novelty values, and frequently they are the deciding factors in acceptance or rejection. It is self-evident that something which is enjoyable is more appealing than something which is not. This truth is an unexceptionable one, however, only if the widest implications of the term "enjoyable" are understood. For one thing, it cannot have an absolute and universalistic meaning. The judgment that a thing is enjoyable must be made by the person experiencing the thing, not by some other person. Specifically, the judgment cannot be based upon the value system of an advocate as opposed to that of the acceptor. Secondly, it must not be assumed that unpleasantness or even pain cannot be enjoyable. A great many people enjoy or are ambivalent toward excursions into the shocking, the painful, or the terrifying. Witness the appeal of murder mysteries, ghost stories, strenuous sports like football and ice hockey, the terroristic performances of the Kwakiutl Indian dancers, the Plains Indians' sun dances, and the mortification of ascetics, not to mention the self-punishments of neurotics. Finally, it cannot be said that the immediately pleasurable thing will always be preferred if it leads to an ultimately unenjoyable end. To put it another way, the enjoyable will not necessarily take precedence over its opposite unless their rewards are judged to be equivalent. A man will not accept leisure in place of work unless he can continue to eat; and a conscientious artist will not use a machine to substitute for his manual skill unless the machine product meets his aesthetic demands.

There are all degrees of enjoyment, and several modes of pleasure and its antithesis, that are pertinent to the question of the acceptance of novelties. The amount of effort required to make a change from the old to

[5] *Eugene* (Oregon) *Register-Guard,* Feb. 20, 1950.
[6] *Time,* May 1, 1944.

the new is one aspect of pleasure which affects decisions. The course of least effort to achieve the same end has a preponderant appeal. The validity of this proposition depends upon the definition of "same end," and as has been stressed above, the determination of this must be left to the acceptor. Such equations are made spontaneously with great frequency, especially in technology. Commonly the appeal of least effort is illusory in that the immediate gain must be compensated for by added effort in some other quarter. The Palauans are now replacing wornout hand-wrought planks and timbers in their dwellings by milled lumber because it is easier to get material this way than it is to log and hew it. For the same reason African natives are giving up ironworking; it requires less effort for them to buy implements of European manufacture. Of course, in order to buy lumber in Palau or to buy hoes and plows in Africa one must have money, and to get money one must labor at other things. The effort is merely displaced; and there is often a loss rather than a gain, but this loss is concealed or is rated as a secondary consideration by the native who does not want to cut wood or to mold plow shares. The focus of attention and the appealing measure of saved effort are with respect to the acquisition of the article in question. When the issue is weighted in this way, it is obvious that for most people it is more pleasant to buy something than it is to make it.

This situation grades into those where actual physical comfort is involved in accepting or rejecting something new. The Palauans find sitting on chairs uncomfortable, just as I found sitting cross-legged on the floor tiring. Each of us returned to our accustomed posture with relief. Many of the older Yakima people still sleep on the floors of their dwellings. They say that beds are unsteady and that mattresses are too soft, yielding, and enveloping. They feel that they are suffocating, especially on feather mattresses of the variety that was known to them when they first became acquainted with our beds. Palauan canoes are being abandoned and replaced by rowboats because the canoes are very narrow and cramp their passengers. Women especially favor rowboats for this reason. Aboriginally when a Palauan woman had her first child she had to undergo a prolonged ritual treatment to purify herself and to introduce herself and her child to the community. The private part of the ritual imposed seclusion, food taboos, and daily baths in a steaming herbal infusion. Very few women submit to this treatment at the present time. The few who are compelled to do so by their conservative relatives dread the ordeal because it is physically painful. This is particularly true of the bath, which calls for water as hot as the woman can bear it. At one time the Shaker minister of a Washington congregation got the idea of insisting upon a very fast tramping of the participants as they circled the church room. He accelerated the tempo of the stamping to a point where the older members of the congregation objected because they could not keep up or found that it was too exhausting if they did. The innovation, which necessitated others in consequence of it, did not survive his advocacy of it. It was unpopular because it required too much physical exertion. When asked why they have not become Shakers, a considerable number of Indians state that their introduction to cult practices was accompanied by unpleasant or physically painful experiences. They complain of the confusion and of the deafening noise created by the vigorous stamping and the incessant ringing of the large handbells by the participants. One prospective convert said that he had had enough of the religion when he was induced to ask for help to cure his pneumonia and one woman "under power" beat his back and chest with her fists. "It was too much like fighting," he said. Another convert was lost when the healers who milled around him burned him and dropped candle grease on his head and neck.

In these last-mentioned cases the unpleasant feature seems incidental to the main issue of acceptance. Even so, it can weigh heavily, both for and against acceptance. Keesing notes that church music has been an attraction with significant consequences in the spread of Christianity in the Pacific. The same is true in America. Many Christianized Indians attest that they went to church in the beginning because they liked to hear the singing and to sing themselves. Shakers find one of their main satisfactions in the fact that active membership in the cult involves much traveling from reservation to reservation participating in conventions, reunions, and feasts.

Introductions that are considered to be exciting take precedence over those that are dull and routine, whether new or old. This fact goes far toward explaining the widespread acceptance of new games and amusements as contrasted with novelties which require isolated and concentrated effort aimed at some future reward. Presumably this is what Hart means by "the facilitation of new functioning" as an incentive for the acceptance of novelties.[7] Card games, American music, and American dancing were adopted almost immediately by the Palauans, the Yurok, the Yakima, and others. It is rather startling to hear Palauans playing a rasping recording of "Redwing" on one of the antique phonographs they have obtained from the Japanese or to catch the refrain of the Japanese version of "Chinatown" being sung to accompany a novelty dance. Horse racing with its concomitant, betting, found equal favor among the Indians almost from their first acquaintance with it.[8] The Palauans are very adept at staging dramatizations of anecdotes, called "shibais" after their Japanese prototypes, and the spectators thoroughly enjoy them. Games like soccer and baseball have been accepted and eagerly played by natives in remote areas all the way from the hill country of Luzon to the upper Skeena River in British Columbia. Motion pictures have, if

[7] Hornell Hart, *The Technique of Social Progress*. New York: Henry Holt and Company, Inc., 1931, pp. 607–608.

[8] H. G. Barnett, "Culture Processes," *American Anthropologist*, 1940, 42 (No. 1):36.

possible, an even greater fascination. The Palauans flock to them even though they can understand not a word of the dialogue and have only a slightly greater comprehension of what is being portrayed on the screen. Keesing's comment that motion pictures are very popular among Pacific Islanders and that "above all, exciting Wild West pictures with racing horses and gun-handling heroes are favored" would have an almost universal application.[9]

It is not difficult to get people anywhere to accept a holiday, provided, as has already been noted, that its adoption does not compromise other values, such as the need to make a living. Notwithstanding this reservation, it is remarkable how readily people the world over have taken to the idea of periodic breaks in their daily routine when these intervals are not made mere blanks or periods of enforced idleness in their existence. It is true that Sunday has often been rejected, but mostly because those who have sought to introduce it made of it a day of taboo and restraint instead of one of recreation and relief. There was never any difficulty in getting the Yakima, the Yurok, and their neighbors to observe Sunday as an interval to be filled with visiting, feasting, horse racing, and gambling.

Introduced behaviors that offer freedom of action where there was none before have a strong appeal and are acceptable if penalties do not attach to their adoption or if the relief that they offer is valued above the punishment that they incur. There is no question that one of the most potent appeals of Shakerism is its permissiveness. Its dogma is a perfect warrant for the expression of individualism in almost any form as long as it does not contravene the beliefs upon which the warrant rests. Any person, regardless of sex or station in life, can claim sanction for being a prophet or a remodeler. Shakerism is an excellent vehicle for the relief of the depressed, the thwarted, and the unsatisfied. The church affords an ideal theater for exhibitionists. The function of the faith as a spillway for dammed-up emotions is evident in the behavior of many regular participants in the shaking parts of a ceremony. They attend the service for this exercise alone. They are impatient of the sermonizing and other preliminaries. They readily become ecstatic and just as matter-of-factly regain their composure and go home.

It is a common belief that religious sanctions are among the most powerful conservers of tradition. A comparison of the survival qualities of taboos and secular behaviors does not bear this out. On the contrary, taboos, which are restraints upon activity, appear to be quite vulnerable to suggestions of their abandonment. Food taboos seem to be especially threatened when the temptation to ignore them is implanted by the example of nonconformists. Of all taboos, they seem to be the first to go when natives come in contact with Europeans, though possibly this is because the incongruity of the ritual

[9] Keesing, *The South Seas in the Modern World,* p. 195. See also Raymond Kennedy, *The Ageless Indies,* New York: The John Day Company, 1942, pp. 84–86.

food habits of two peoples is more conspicuous than is the disparity of other religious differences between them. The taboos surrounding life-crisis observances are also noticeably insecure. Despite the lamentations over their loss by the older natives, very few of them remain among the Palauans, and still fewer have survived among the Yakima, Yurok, and Tsimshian. To cite but one example, the Yurok have been quite willing to allow Caucasian undertakers to care for their dead, the reason being that aboriginally Yurok corpse handlers had to submit to a five-day period of taboo and purification which they did not relish and would not undertake except for close relatives. Hellmann relates that although native girls in the towns of South Africa are still required to undergo a seclusion ceremony upon arrival at puberty, they regard it as "a tedious and unwelcome imposition" and that food taboos upon women after childbirth are nowadays seldom encountered.[10]

The converse of the foregoing must also be true; that is, novelties which obstruct satisfactions more than do their alternatives are unpopular. The efforts of missionaries to impose blue laws on Sunday are an example. So, too, are their advocacy of sexual restraint and their insistence upon the virtues of thrift and hard work. The Polynesians have been hard to convince of the virtues of chastity; and the Africans and many others have abandoned polygyny, when they have, with reluctance. The renunciation of feasting, visiting, dancing, and singing has also been regarded as a high price to pay for the blessings of European civilization. In Tahiti the cult of the Areoi dedicated its adherents to a life of sensuous pleasure and unrestrained license in the name of the god Oro. One requirement of its members was that all children born to them had to be destroyed because, among other things, children were a nuisance and an obstacle to full participation in the carefree life expected of an Areoi. The early missionaries to Tahiti epitomized their difficulties in converting the natives as a struggle between themselves and the devotees of this cult. They ostracized the wife of Pomare from their company because she was adamant in pursuing her intention of killing an infant born to her. She wanted other things that the missionaries had to offer, but she would not accede to their interference with her freedom.[11] The Shakers hold annual conventions during which meals are prepared and served in a cookhouse adjacent to the church. Because of the number assembled, they are usually obliged to set second and third tables to accommodate all those present. At one such meeting a few years ago an enthusiastic member initiated a church service at table while others were waiting to eat.

[10] Ellen P. Hellmann, "The Native in the Towns." In I. Schapera (ed.), *The Bantu Speaking Tribes of South Africa*. London: Routledge and Kegan Paul, Ltd., 1937, pp. 413, 418.

[11] James Wilson, *A Missionary Voyage to the Southern Pacific Ocean*. . . . London: S. Gosnell, 1799, pp. 156–157.

This novelty showed commendable fervor, but it was not enjoyed by those who were hungry. The innovation did not survive the convention, because everybody wanted to eat at the first table.

Finally, under the heading of hedonistic considerations, there are the doubts and fears for personal security that are inspired by some novelties and which dictate their acceptance or rejection. Automobiles, airplanes, and other pieces of complex machinery are terrifying to the uninitiated individual, especially to one who believes himself to be too old to learn to master their controls. Few people over forty look forward to the day when they will be the pilots of their own airplanes even though they could afford them. Some people are afraid to use electric heating pads and blankets, gasoline stoves, and insecticides. Fear is the ultimate reference in some of the antipathies already mentioned. The reason why many people are reluctant to embrace new medical discoveries is that they fear for their personal safety. The public may be cautious about new drugs because experts disagree on their value, but basically because people are afraid that they might be more injurious than the diseases that they are alleged to prevent. Fear likewise gives force to taboos. Taboos that have divine sanction carry with them the threat of supernatural vengeance for their infraction; and negativistic mores, sometimes called taboos, are observed because ignoring them brings social sanctions to bear that can be as frightful as divine punishment. When individual Palauans, Hawaiians, and Tahitians decided to break their dietary taboos, they did so in defiance of an awful penalty. Contrariwise, threats to unbelievers and heretics have brought many converts into religious congregations through fear of personal harm.

With reference to the relief aspects of a novelty it should be emphasized again that this estimate of them must be made by the acceptor himself, not by an observer. If it is the custom to repress aggressive impulses and to relieve them by displacement or by some other indirect means, an attempt to introduce patterns of direct relief will find favor with only a limited number of those who follow the custom; namely, those who feel repressed in spite of the permitted means of expression. Those who experience no repression with existing release mechanisms will see little advantage in a change from this standpoint. They are, in fact, repressed only by an observer's definition.

Mastery. Any usage makes certain performance demands upon those who adhere to it, and these requirements can be the central consideration in the acceptance of a new one. Activities that require concentrated and prolonged effort to master them or to gain an understanding of them are at a disadvantage compared with some alternative that does not. The difficulty of reconditioning oneself or of relearning something sets up an insurmountable obstacle to many proposed changes even though their desirability may be generally agreed upon. Hence, in large part, stems the opposition of adult Americans to a phonetic revision of our system of spelling. For the same reason several variations introduced into the Palauan dances that have already been described failed to be incorporated in the final selections; that is, they were admittedly too intricate to be worth the trouble of learning them. Shakers who have a history that reveals an interest in Christianity have turned away from churches with predominately white congregations and have joined the Shaker faith because they are more at home in the surroundings in which it flourishes. They say that they do not want to dress up to go to church, or to attend reverently to a sermon, or to be polite and proper to other parishioners. In short, our church-going behavior patterns are uncongenial to them and are not worth the effort necessary to accommodate them. All this is apart from their being made to feel unwelcome as members of a barely tolerated minority.

Behaviors and beliefs which assess minimal requirements for participation in them must obviously be more popular in a quantitative sense than are those that are exclusive. The conformance demands of some customs are much more rigid and relentless than others. The acceptance of some requires strict adherence to predetermined rules and conventions; others permit more freedom in individual interpretation and manipulation. Novelties that have stringent and inflexible requirements for their mastery will have an appeal to fewer people than those that are less dogmatic or restrictive. There is a great difference between the acceptance of Christianity and the accept-ance of ship bread and molasses from the standpoint of performance de-mands on the part of those to whom they are new. For the same reason there is a major difference between becoming a Catholic and becoming a Shaker. Quite apart from the greater effort required to understand the one as com-pared with the other, more care must be exercised in acting the part of the one as compared with the other. There are broader limits and more choices in the one case than in the other. It seems that this is why the Congrega-tionalists have had greater success in missionizing the Samoans than they had among John Slocum's fellow Indians. In Eastern Samoa the demands upon converts have been made far less rigorous than those which Myron Eells sought to impose upon his charges on the Skokomish reservation. For him there was no compromise with the basic tenets of the church as he under-stood them, and in consequence few Indians were prepared to meet the test of conversion. By contrast, the Samoans have been permitted to adapt Christianity to their understanding of it.[12] So have the Shakers and the members of other cults like it. Speaking of the popularity of a contemporary Maori cult, Sutherland writes: "All the members of the congregation take part and today every member of this church is competent to conduct a service.

[12] Margaret Mead, *Coming of Age in Samoa.* New York: William Morrow & Com-pany, Inc., 1928, p. 270.

Up to the beginning of this century a very large proportion of the congregation in the Maori Anglican Church could do the same. . . ." [13]

The demand aspect of a novelty applies to the inherent qualities of things as well as to arbitrary rules and definitions of propriety. This means, among other things, that something easy to do or understand invites wider acceptance than does its opposite. This makes for a wider appeal of the simple as contrasted with the complex, these characterizations referring, of course, not to the things themselves but to the requirements for manipulating them. A testing device or a tool which requires only one adjustment is preferable to one which requires several from the viewpoint of the operator, especially if the adjustments necessitate a careful and laborious balancing or regulation of their setting. Hence derives the appeal of automatic devices and push-button controls. Complex behavior patterns, while they may be intriguing to some individuals and may be deliberately cultivated for their own sake by virtuosos, are certain to attract fewer people than will simpler ones.

Penalty. Penalty attachments are a deterrent to acceptance. Obviously if a person fears some punishment as a consequence of adopting a novelty, he is constrained to reject it regardless of its appeal for him. Threatened or anticipated punishments for accepting a novelty have sanctions that are as varied as are those for any other interdicted act. Among them may be mentioned political pressures, public censure, and supernatural prohibitions. Laws or decrees are a common means of curbing the acceptance of innovations or importations. Such restraint is, in fact, the function of much of the contemporary legislation in countries like the United States; many laws are aimed at stopping the spread of new ideas and practices that are against the public interest because they are fraudulent, hazardous, predatory, or subversive. With autocratic and paternalistic governments the protective aegis of the controlling power may extend widely indeed. Authoritarian leaders often prohibit or regulate closely the acceptance of foreign ideas, as Japanese rulers did up until 1868 and as the heads of totalitarian regimes in Europe have done in recent years. Colonial powers administering the affairs of dependent native peoples have also followed the practice of prohibiting all but a selected range of novelties to be made available to their wards. Examples are the widespread prohibitions upon native acceptance of liquor and of trade goods that have not been guaranteed by the controlling authority. Sometimes political leaders reserve certain novelties for themselves and punish presumptuous underlings for usurping their assumed prerogatives. Most American naval officers in the civil government in Palau wore sun helmets; and when these hats first became available to the natives, the chiefs preempted them for themselves. They made it known that they regarded helmets as

[13] Apirana Ngata and I. L. G. Sutherland, "Religious Influences." In I. L. G. Sutherland (ed.), *The Maori People Today*. New York: Oxford University Press, 1940, pp. 368–369.

symbols of power and forbade their sale to common men by native store-keepers. Umbrellas also became the prerogatives of chiefs when they were first introduced to the islands by the Germans. European kings and dictators have been known to act upon the same principle. This practice, in fact, seems to be a regular concomitant of autocratic regimes.

Adverse public opinion in the form of ridicule and blame has the same penalizing effects upon the acceptance of some novelties. Many Americans have secret urges to participate in new activities but are afraid of what other people might say or think about them if they did. This is true of those who feel that they have a reputation to maintain or a dignity to preserve. It is equally marked in the aged and the timid. Many would venture to try fresh excitants and experiences if, as some confess, they "only had the nerve." The same compulsion to conform, with real or imagined public sanctions behind it, constrains acceptance by certain individuals everywhere. The son of one of the highest ranking Yurok chiefs in historic times has all of his life remained faithful to his father's teachings concerning the obligations of the Yurok aristocrat. He lives by standards that no longer have any appeal for his associates. Now in his sixties, he has never married because his anachronous ideals require too much of him. His position calls for marriage with a woman possessing the virtues and the ideology of the Yurok elite of times past; and as he has grown older, there have become fewer and fewer women with those qualifications until now there are none. He still has the set of native valuables that was given to him by his father to pay for his bride; but they long ago lost for others the meaning they have for him, and he therefore prefers to keep them and to remain single. Noblesse oblige.

Fear of supernatural punishment for abandoning a custom is a powerful brake on change in certain specialized areas of behavior. This is the most important reason why magical acts are among the most resistant to change of all cultural phenomena. By magic is meant the ritual acts or thoughts that are supposed to have supernatural potency in securing desired ends of either a positive or a negative sort. These acts, as opposed to the taboos already discussed, are not considered to be oppressive. On the contrary, they are clung to as the only means of obtaining protection and success in situations that are beyond human comprehension or control. They are conceived to secure the practitioner against bad luck, ill health, or some specific misfortune; and their renunciation in favor of mundane controls raises the specter of self-doubt and dread of failure. Supernatural powers threaten the apostate and the flouter. Examples of this fear and its conservative influences appear on every side where a materialistic and a mechanistic philosophy encroaches upon areas previously dominated by faith in absolute and willful causation. Perhaps no illustrations are needed beyond a reference to the superstitions that are well known in any civilized country today.

Repercussions. Because a culture is made up of interdependent parts, the acceptance of something new always entails stresses and dislocations; and because of these involvements the desirability or the undesirability of a novelty itself may not be the paramount consideration. This is the case when the acceptance of the novelty suggests or demands a change in some linked feature which the potential acceptor treasures more than he does the novelty. Rejection is likely even though the linked feature is not of superior value if changing it would require an effort that is not worth the advantage to be gained by accepting the novelty. These controls upon acceptance relate directly to the conditions for innovation discussed under the heading The Modification of a Dominant Correlate. There are several facets to the problem of intertrait linkage that have been reserved for treatment at this more appropriate juncture.

There are, first of all, physical conditions that must be fulfilled for the continuance of some custom clusters. A change in one feature requires a change in its correlate because there is a material dependency of one upon the other. Thus, Welsh copper miners in Montana abandoned their custom of chanting at their work when air drills took the place of hand drills because the former had no relation to the work and song rhythms and also because they created a deafening noise. Some of the natives who have taken up residence in Johannesburg, Africa, attempt to carry on their tribal customs in the town setting. The older women at least still insist upon the birth ritual which requires a seclusion of the mother and her newborn child. Under tribal conditions the seclusion period lasts for as long as three months, during which time the father, the mother, and the child are taken care of by relatives. Since kinship groups are not always well represented in town, and since strangers cannot be expected to substitute for them, women have to reduce the seclusion period to a minimum.[14] This situation has a rather close parallel in American society where there has been a marked reduction in the size of families and a tendency for conjugal units to set themselves up independently and often at some distance from the parental home of either spouse. Young couples at the present time must hire baby sitters to care for their children in place of grandparents and other near relatives who used to perform this function. Other examples, already cited, further illustrate this point: Japanese- and American-style houses in Palau will not permit the natives to continue with certain customs, such as prestige seating arrangements, because the buildings are too small by comparison with indigenous dwellings; and the construction of larger and heavier motor vehicles in the United States in recent decades has made the building of larger roadways, bridges, and garages a physical necessity.

[14] Hellmann, *op. cit.,* p. 413.

Besides physical linkages there are arbitrary connections that have been established solely by tradition; and even though no physical necessity regulates their interdependence, the bond is as firm in the minds of their adherents as is the size of a house and the number of polite people it can accommodate. The connection that exists in Christianity between theology and ethics provides an excellent illustration of an ideological bond the severance of which is generally regarded as fatal to the whole structure. Christians do not admit that there can be a substitution of some other kind of morality in place of the one which is historically associated with their belief in God. It is un-Christian to condone murder and adultery, just as it would be to advocate polytheism. Some of the more puritanical Christian sects have gone further. They have held that going naked, smoking, and living improvidently are offensive to God. Consequently to accept deviation in these respects would, in their thinking, demand a reorientation which they have not been prepared to make. There are many other ideological connections of such a character that a change in one of the associated features "logically" demands a correlative change in the other.

Social complications contingent upon the acceptance of a novelty stand apart from the linkages considered so far in that they derive from the integration of social units. They develop because acceptors initiate effects upon others with whom they are associated as a result of the mutual adjustments of behaviors that are a prerequisite for any social situation. The social effects, however, differ in accordance with the nature of the novelty involved. One distinction of significance is between what might be called individual and group involvements. Some customs by their nature require only the commitment of an individiual, whereas others presuppose the commitment of all the members of a society or of a subsociety. And the point with respect to the acceptance of a novelty is that it is obviously easier to secure the assent of a single individual than it is to get an agreement of many upon any issue. Furthermore, from the acceptor's standpoint it is easier for him to act unilaterally than with some required support.

Some behaviors allow more individual choice of action than do others. This is the reason why, as Reed says, "in the process of acculturation, purely social features of aboriginal life are usually the last to be affected by alien contacts." [15] Institutions which require reciprocation in kind, or cooperation, or agreement upon values, ends, or means, diffuse much more slowly than do ideas and behaviors that can be enjoyed in private. The vocabulary or other aspects of a foreign language cannot be used for communication by a single individual. Legal concepts are in the same category. To be effective, laws must hold for at least two individuals—in fact, for all people

[15] Stephen W. Reed, *The Making of Modern New Guinea.* . . . Philadelphia: American Philosophical Society, 1943, p. 260.

within the social universe where they apply. Political ideologies must be of the same character. Within the same political structure diverse patterns cannot function, and a change from one to another goes beyond a single individual's choice. The same is true of ideas concerning kinship reckoning, property inheritance, monetary values, and a variety of other mutually agreed-upon standards. At the other extreme are introductions which demand only individual conformance, among them ideals of personal beautification, the use of medicines or other healing practices, and the employment of tools and appliances. It is also possible to make a relevant distinction between conviction and realization; that is, between belief in institutions as opposed to the practice of them. It is easier for an individual to embrace the ideal of democracy, for example, than it is for him to live by its principles if his fellows insist upon clinging to an autocratic regime.

Several acculturation studies seem to show that the tangible aspects of any culture are more readily diffused than are purely ideological or behavioral aspects. Usually the differentiation is made in terms of the material or thing aspects of a donor culture and its nonmaterial or social aspects. There is a substantial body of evidence to support this generalization, but so far there have been few suggestions offered to explain why it is true. The explanation appears to rest upon the factor which we are now examining. That is to say, the different performance demands which material items place upon their acceptance as contrasted with the requirements of nonmaterial customs make the former easier to assimilate than the latter. There are three differences between material and nonmaterial customs that are pertinent.

First, it is much more difficult to explain an idea than it is to demonstrate it; and the more abstract and intangible a usage is, the less amenable it is to overt presentation. It is exceedingly difficult to explain philosophical concepts, feelings, and theoretical constructs. It is not much easier to expound an idea of government or the meaning of marriage, even though there are certain visible manifestations of these institutions. Even the acting out of a behavior is subject to misinterpretation because the overt features of an act do not contain any objectively verifiable connections between them. Meanings are their essence, and these must be verbally expressed or conveyed in some indirect way. Where there is a language barrier, as is usually the case, the difficulty is greatly multiplied. There is no distinction between conveying the meaning of a handshake and the meaning of an ax, but more is needed to supplement a demonstration of the one than is needed for the other by a potential acceptor. To put it another way, a large part of the meaning of an ax or of a rowboat is inherent in what it does, whereas the meaning of a handclasp or of a wedding ceremony is purely conventional.

This fact relates to a second point of difference; namely, that the advantage or disadvantage of one thing over another is more obvious than is the advantage or disadvantage of one institution over another because the potentialities of a thing are more closely related to its physical properties. It is, for example, much easier for anyone to see that an iron knife is more durable than a stone knife; but it is difficult if not impossible to demonstrate that one religious belief is superior to another or that monogamy is better than polygyny. The real point here is that knives are judged by the same standards, whereas religious and marital customs are not; and this is true of all things to a greater extent than it is of all institutions.

The third aspect of difference between material and nonmaterial culture items is even more significant for acceptance. It stems from the fact that things are impersonal and their use makes no counterdemands upon their user. There is a one-way reactive system. The adopter is the volitional agent, the actor or the doer; and he exploits the object as he sees fit without emotional entanglements with it or without ethical considerations entering into his use of it. There can therefore be a maximum of the experimental attitude toward things and a minimum of personal commitment to them. The commitment to use a thing can be tentative and unfeeling. An acceptor may try a new object and cast it off in a way that he could not engage and disengage himself from other human beings in social relations wherein two wills and two sets of rights and obligations are necessarily involved. A man can take up and leave off with a thing without any of the preliminaries, the scruples, or the consequences which inevitably enmesh him when he decides to become a party to an interpersonal constellation of attitudes and behaviors. He is, as much as he can ever be, a free agent in accepting or rejecting things.

A second social complication arises when an accepted novelty requires a behavior on the part of the acceptor which indirectly affects his associates. It is not that their acceptance of it is required, as in the preceding cases, but that they must make some compensation to accommodate the change embraced by one of their number. Their resistance to this demand may force a potential acceptor to forego his desire. The lone acceptor of an idea is always subject to some social pressures to cease and desist. His forwardness is cause for adverse comment, curiosity, gossip, ridicule, or condemnation; but as long as he is willing to tolerate such abuse and as long as no one else is involved, his acceptance is his concern alone. On the other hand, if his friends, relatives, or co-workers become implicated, another factor is introduced. Even though there is no question of their disapproval of the idea itself, they may object if it places new obligations upon them. The young Palauan men who want to establish independent households when they get married are confronted with this difficulty. They do not care whether other members of their clans do likewise, for this is not essential.

But their hopes clash with the interests of the conservatives who do not want to relinquish their right to manipulate the lives of their dependents to gain prestige and power. Taboos provide another illustration of social repercussion. Among the Yurok almost all supernatural prohibitions carried sanctions against the violator alone. Only the transgressor of a taboo would be punished, not his family or other members of his community. Consequently, if he were willing to risk his own safety by a violation, that was up to him. The result was that most of these taboos fell rather rapidly after white contact. At the opposite extreme are prohibitions like that of the Eskimo against offending the goddess of game animals. A violation of this taboo is conceived to do harm to everybody in the village, so the compulsion to observe it is much greater. Another example of minor consequence but of equal theoretical interest comes from Shaker history. A certain individual conceived the carrying out of a special act of obeisance before the cross on the altar of the church as he passed it in the file of worshipers circling the room. In order to do this he held up the others and slowed down the ritual movement. It was on this basis that the other members objected; not because it was wrong for him to have his own private ceremony, and not because he advocated that they should adopt the practice.

Obviously social complications like those just described depend upon the characteristics of the social situation into which they are introduced. At the same time, there are classes of behaviors and ideas that are universally less entangling than are others. As an illustration we may revert to what has already been said about the distinction between material and the nonmaterial customs and say that an additional reason for the greater acceptability of the former is that on the whole they create fewer, and in many cases not any, social complications. As has been pointed out, the acceptance of a thing primarily involves only a relationship between a person and a nonperson; consequently this situation is fundamentally a nonsocial one. Not only does an acceptor act unilaterally with respect to the thing which he uses; in most cases he need not consult other people if he decides to do so. He may be ridiculed, but again it is his business; and unless his use of an object interferes with the peace or accustomed routines of his associates, his satisfaction is all that he need concern himself about. Hence derives the relative ease of adopting new tools, appliances, home, and dress styles. The same observations would hold, of course, for the acceptance of nonfunctional ideas about social institutions; that is, those that are accepted as private convictions but are not put into practice.

CHAPTER XIV

ACCEPTORS AND REJECTORS

The Problem. In the four preceding chapters attention has been given to the conditions for acceptance as they relate to the advocacy of a novelty and to the characteristics of the novelty itself. A wide range of variables was reviewed, and an attempt was made to assess their effects upon acceptors in terms of conventional values. It is the purpose of this chapter to explore the problem of individual variability in response to the presentation of novelties and to attempt to bring some order out of the bewildering complexity of data that are available on the subject. The question which calls for an answer is: Just which individuals in a given group are more likely than others to accept a particular novelty? The problem now is to find out, not why a novelty or its auspices has an appeal, but why it appeals more to one person than to another, presuming that everything else is as constant as it can be. If, for example, a new mousetrap in all ways makes the same demands upon everybody who wants to eliminate mice, which individuals would be disposed to adopt it and which not? If everyone is equally influenced by its advocate, who will accept and who reject it? What attitudinal biases characterize the acceptor as contrasted with the rejector when all the other variables of the acceptance situation are held constant? This is another way of asking why people react differently to the element of newness in their experience. Clearly, there are individual differences in this respect. It is a fact of everyday experience. The question is, Why? An answer should seek to probe the genesis of attitudes toward novelty as they manifest themselves in specific ways and in specific contexts.

The generalizations that are to be offered comprise three interlocking hypotheses which have been in part inductively and in part deductively established. The first is that an individual will not accept a novelty unless in his opinion it satisfies a want better than some existing means at his disposal. Stated in terms of a comparison with other members of his group, which is our frame of reference now, the thesis is that a novelty has less appeal for those who are enjoying the benefits of its functional alternative than for those who are not. This does not necessarily mean that the likely acceptor is absolutely dissatisfied with the custom for which the novelty can be substituted; it does mean that for some reason he does not get all the satisfaction out of it that others in his group do. By contrast with some of his associates he is unsatisfied, although he may not be definitely dissatisfied.

The second hypothesis is that there are biographical determinants for the lack of satisfaction that is characteristic of individuals who are predisposed to accept a substitute for some accustomed idea, and that these determinants result from the interplay and adjustment of an individual's conception of himself and the events of his life history. Whether or not such biases are personality traits may be argued; but the essential point is that people develop tastes and preferences under the influence of particular experiences, and these orientations are significant for the acceptance or rejection of new ideas. In the present inquiry the emphasis is upon a search for precontact causes of acceptance; not upon the effects of synchronic influences, such as artifact and advocate characteristics, that operate at the time of the presentation of a novelty. The events in a person's life unquestionably affect his attitude toward the conventions of the society in which he lives. It is highly probable that no one ever gets complete satisfaction from all the customs of his group. The present problem is to generalize upon the circumstances which contribute to the personal indifference and dissatisfaction with the *status quo* that are antecedent to the appearance of suggested changes in it. This is one approach to the question of relative receptivity; and while it requires intimate and detailed knowledge that is hard to get, it provides the kind of information that is essential for predicting responses. This is the reason for the concern with biographical data; ideally, a knowledge of them should provide a basis for forecasting. The stress upon antecedent attitudes does not deny that people who have no prior record of unsatisfaction accept novelties. It is quite evident that they do. As the analysis of novelty values and advocate attributes was intended to show, people are often swayed this way or that by these concurrent influences. Many people accept a novelty just because their friends do, or because they are convinced of its superior value either by a salesman or by their own comparisons. Others are turned against a new idea that they like because of its sponsorship and for many other reasons that have already been mentioned. These historically synchronous variables are important because they can *make* a person unsatisfied with what he has or with what he could otherwise have. Dissatisfaction is fundamental to acceptance in all those cases, too; but our interest now is in preexisting attitudes rather than in those that are organized by contemporaneous influences. They are the biographical determinants.

The third hypothesis is to the effect that dissatisfaction or unsatisfaction may be a pervasive attitude in some individuals. It then colors their view of relatively large but variable sectors of their culture. It may have had its genesis in repeated specific disappointments; or it may have emerged under indoctrination; or it may be due to a compulsion to generalize an attitude from a single or a few intense or prolonged disillusionments. Those who manifest such a diffuse attitude of apathy or dissatisfaction tend to be universal acceptors. They are most likely to be the impersonal friends, the reluctant participants, and, if they have the courage, the chronic dissenters and escapists. They are the truly marginal individuals.

Despite the fact that a person may be rather generally unhappy with life in his group, he nevertheless experiences specific wants. He feels the need of satisfaction at particular times and places and with respect to particular things, ideas, or behaviors. The same is even more obviously true of more completely adjusted individuals. This is a fact which must be kept in mind in evaluating the significance of the first hypothesis. If it has any meaning for action, satisfaction or the lack of it is directed toward *something*. There is not simply displeasure or the absence of enjoyment, but displeasure or apathy with respect to something that is definite enough that it can at least be differentiated from something else. The appeal of novelties is to be correlated with these specific avoidances or repulsions; that is, with their functional counterparts in the preexisting system. Otherwise there can be no rationale for acceptance.

It should be clear from the foregoing discussion of the problem that, with the possible and partial exception of marginal individuals, there is no category of acceptors as opposed to a category of rejectors. These terms cannot be used to impose a dichotomy upon humanity. They do not designate absolutes. No one is wholly or persistently an acceptor or a rejector. He is simply more or less so than is somebody else and with reference to a specific idea. For any given novelty the incidence and the rapidity of acceptance may be high or low in a certain society; but there will always be some individuals who lag behind others in giving their approval to it and some perhaps who never do. There are relenting as well as die-hard conservatives, slow and reluctant as well as quick and eager acceptors. Our attention must be focused upon the relative placement of individuals anywhere along this continuum, whether they fall at its extremes or in contiguous sectors. Relatively speaking, there are acceptors and rejectors all along this line; and at any given moment that is the pattern which presents itself in spite of the fact that the rejectors of today often become the acceptors of tomorrow. That shift merely changes the proportions, not the pattern of acceptance versus rejection. As far as our problem is concerned, and from a practical standpoint also, the important phenomenon is the lag in acceptance.

Four orders or categories of acceptors are recognized below. They are defined in terms of their attitudes toward the novelty equivalents traditional with their group. In accordance with the first hypothesis all the labels express a neutral or a negativistic mental set. The characterizations represent an effort to classify as broadly as possible while retaining fundamental distinctions. There could be further subdividing or further synthesis, depending upon the degree of distinctness that the subordinate attitudes are believed to have. Other definitions of attitudes would do as well as the one proposed; so would some other appropriate nomenclature for them. The essentials, which are the biographical determinants that give rise to them, would remain unchanged in any classification scheme. The important point is that the same or comparable biographical events occur widely and repeatedly, with the same or comparable attractions or repulsions for novelties growing out of them.

The Dissident. There are substantial reasons for believing that there are individuals in every society who have consistently refused to identify themselves with some of the conventions of their group. They may give lip service to certain customs to avoid punishment, but they mentally or symbolically shun them and would dispense with the necessity of conforming with them if they could. The more courageous and independent these dissenters are, the more they openly rebel and withdraw from participation in the offending customs. Regardless of whether or not this is a universal phenomenon, it is a sufficiently common one in contemporary American life and in many other societies to create no surprise when it manifests itself. Rather, there is some expectancy of the attitude, if only a limited tolerance of it. It is obviously a potential source of irritation for both the conformers and the dissenters, depending upon the tolerance of the former and the aggressiveness of the latter. But whether or not there is discord between them, the dissenter is certainly more likely to be attracted by a new alternative for the custom in question than is the person who is satisfied with it. This is not to say, of course, that a noncomformist will accept any new alternative. He has the freedom of choice with respect to novelties just as does anyone else. The contrast to be made is between the conformer and the dissenter, not between novelties; and when this is done it is evident that acceptance probabilities are weighted on the side of the dissenter. This observation recalls a part of the last chapter where it was maintained that the compatibility of a novelty is not a recommendation for its acceptance for some individuals although it might be for most. As was mentioned, the opposite can be true: incompatibility, just because it is that, may be welcomed by a person who refuses to acknowledge the validity, the reality, the appropriateness, or the satisfactions claimed by others for existing customs.

Dissenters are set apart from others who are alienated from certain aspects of their culture in that they have never accommodated themselves to specific cultural demands. They have always held aloof or have maintained a mental distance between themselves and the things that they dislike. People in this category often absorb their negativistic attitude from their teachers and personal paragons. As children either they are deliberately taught to be skeptical or dissident by their parents, or they model upon parents or someone else because they admire them. Protestant gestures of any sort may be perpetuated in family lines by an early and consistent conditioning of each succeeding generation, as is evident in the persistence of ideas such as states' rights, pacifism, atheism, and monarchism.

There are other forces at work to produce dissidents apart from example and training. It is difficult to escape the conclusion that some individuals are born with nervous organizations that are fundamentally retractile, protective, cautious, and negativistic to certain kinds of stimulation rather than neutral or receptive to it. We need not ask whether this is after all the result of conditioning on the prenatal level; it is sufficient to know that some children react negatively to suggestion, whereas others do not, and that this attitude causes them to be more fastidious, tentative, and tardy in extending their sympathies and in consolidating their convictions, if they ever do. They are independent, sensitive, tortured, and alone. Their a priori rejection of a group norm leaves them unhappy because they have nothing to take its place. Moreover, their abnormalities are evident to them in the face of satisfactions had by others where they have none. They feel "left out"; and regardless of whom they blame, themselves or others, they would welcome some answers to their wants other than those that are available to them. It would please them to be like other people, and they would if their own predispositions and conceits did not thwart them. They would like to be sociable save for what sociability entails. They would prefer to love and to be loved if they could give affection and have it on terms other than those that are expected of them. Many an agnostic would like to have a faith.

It is essential that a distinction be made between dissenters who are unhappy with certain customs but have no alternative save to endure them and objectors who have a solution to their wants in the practice of a congenial substitute. The dissent of the latter, if the term is applied to them, does not have the same significance, because they do have their satisfaction. It is merely different from that of the conformists who are in the majority. Their disagreement is not an incentive to change, for they like what they themselves have. Thus, American children who are reared in strictly puritanical families learn in their infancy to avoid many behaviors and associations that are regarded as sinful by their parents, but they are given compensatory satisfactions in return. They are convinced that they have the real enjoyments at their disposal. Fundamentalistic sects may be called dissident minorities, but not in the same sense as frustrated individuals who have no recourse from the smothering of their wants. The Old Order Amish of Pennsylvania are extremely conservative, and they abhor and prohibit the use of automobiles, telephones, and electric power in their communities.[1] Their children are taught to eschew these and other worldly frivolities and abominations from infancy, but they are provided with satisfactions in lieu of them. As a

[1] John Gillin, *The Ways of Men.* New York: Appleton-Century-Crofts, Inc., 1948, pp. 209–220.

group the Amish are not, then, more receptive to new ideas than are people who derive great pleasures from the automobiles and other technological developments known to them.

Nonconformism may be generalized, especially if it is grounded in a perverse ideal. In most of the native groups in which I have worked I have found individuals who come to mind at this point. Our meeting and subsequent friendships have not been mere accidents of random selection. Such individuals are attracted to foreigners, and sympathetic foreigners are attracted to them. They make excellent informants because they have an objective attitude toward their culture that is not to be found in the average individual. They therefore have something in common with the ethnographer, but their centrifugal tendencies may land them in the camp of any tolerant alien. One old Palauan man affixed himself to me like a humble and undemanding satellite, paying me the respect and tribute that belong to a Palauan chief. All that he got out of it were a few presents—much less than the chiefs got—and the gratifications of the association. By Palauan standards he was a nobody, one important reason being that he was very early orphaned and bereft of the kind of social sponsor who is essential to success in Palauan life. Other Palauans of better station could not understand why I tolerated him. They said that he knew nothing about the things that I was interested in, which was to a large extent true simply because he had all his life been a dissenter and therefore a nonparticipant. He was either skeptical or critical of Palauan customs, and he praised those of foreigners. He was contemptuously called "the professor" because years before he had fastened himself upon a German botanist much as he was attaching himself to me. He wanted to talk about America rather than Palau, which he denounced constantly as a worthless place in which to live. Even at his advanced age he wanted to leave Palau, preferably to go to the United States but, if not that, then at least to go to Guam. Another much younger Palauan repeatedly compared his people to animals. He deplored their laziness, talkativeness, incompetence, and ignorance and said that they should be kept in pens like hogs. He prided himself upon his industry and reflectiveness. He was widowed but refused to marry again because he was attached to his children, whom by Palauan custom he would have had to abandon upon remarriage. He, too, had a long history of independent thinking, but in his case it was coupled with a fierce self-righteousness. I have often thought that knowing him was the nearest that I ever came to meeting a head-hunter, and that he would have chosen that course to vindicate himself had he lived a few generations earlier. As it was, he turned to alien satisfactions. Under the Japanese he staked his future and that of his children upon an acceptance of the goals that the Japanese set up as models for Palauans to follow. In their being defeated by the Americans, the Japanese had failed him; as a consequence he was dispirited, recognizing that it was too late for him to start over under the Americans. But he was determined that his youngest son should make the readjustment and affiliate himself with the new order. The son, age seventeen, was just as strongly motivated by the same ambition. He volunteered to do any kind of work for me just for the advantage of associating with me. He was sadly alienated from his own people and even more pathetically determined to become an American. Almost certainly he is destined for deep disappointment.

Comparable instances drawn from their own experiences will come to the minds of most readers who have lived among a foreign people. Unfortunately there are few published documents detailing the personal backgrounds of centrifugal individuals. Mandelbaum's analysis of a particular religious innovation among a village of Kota people in southern India emphasizes the role of personalities in cultural change and brings to light a persistent dissenter in the person of a man named Sulli. This individual was the only person in the village in 1938 who had learned to read and write English, who held a government post, and who had extensive contacts with Hindus and Europeans. Both his father and his grandfather were flouters of Kota traditions; and when he was a boy, he ran off to join a missionary with the aim of being converted to Christianity. He was brought back by force, but he has been a rebel and a reformer ever since. "He is everlastingly advocating change. He wants to alter tribal dress and diet, to abandon old occupations and take up new. He has scant respect for some of the most venerable taboos of the culture, wants to abolish certain phases of social behavior which are now right and proper." [2] After a social crisis precipitated by a severe epidemic of relapsing fever in 1924, another aberrant individual, Kusvain, initiated the worship of a trinity of new gods. The names of these divinities were drawn from the Hindu pantheon, and the ritual of service for them included elements found in Hindu temples. Sulli supported Kusvain because of his own abhorrence of certain Kota customs, such as carrion eating, that were reviled by Hindus and which Sulli regarded as symbols of Kota inferiority. The source of the alien worship coincided with Sulli's own predilections and permitted a more complete identification with the Hindu values which he esteemed above those of his fellow Kotas.

Random observations, taken from life and made as circumstances dictate, are certain to be sketchy and loaded with variables the effects of which cannot be isolated. The data upon which they rest have the advantage of not being artificially controlled, but by the same token they leave many questions unanswered. The optimum condition is provided when conclusions drawn from a circumscribed experimental situation and those abstracted from their

[2] David G. Mandelbaum, "Social Trends and Personal Pressures: The Growth of a Culture Pattern." In Leslie Spier, A. Irving Hallowell, and Stanley S. Newman (eds.), *Language, Culture and Personality. Essays in Memory of Edward Sapir*. Menasha, Wis.: Sapir Memorial Publication Fund, 1941, p. 229.

natural setting can be matched. Merei's study of children's play groups, cited in another connection, is relevant at this juncture. It will be recalled that he was interested in the formation of traditions in prearranged play units and in the emergence and influence of leadership with respect to those traditions. He also concerned himself with group solidarity and cooperation and with individual identification and allegiance to group standards. It was in this connection that he noted the emergence of withdrawn individuals whom he called marginals. The behavioral traits that he lists for the marginal child can be taken as a description of the essential characteristics of the dissenter. In Merei's words such an individual "does not collaborate, he only serves; has no contact with the group's activities, only with single members, and then mostly by serving them; will be the first to join a newcomer; will be the first to capitulate to a new leader because he is held least strongly by group custom. He is 'tradition alien.' " [3] The centrifugal tendencies of the marginal individual that are evident from this description deserve to be stressed. They lend support to the argument that dissenters are preeminently inclined to be acceptors of change.

The Indifferent. Many individuals are prepared to accept new ideas because they have not dedicated themselves irretrievably to a custom or to an ideal of their society. Their receptive attitude is not due to a dislike of existing conventions, nor can it be said that they fail to participate in them and receive some gratification from them. On the other hand, while they may be participants, they are not enthusiasts. They do not achieve complete identification with the ideas and behaviors expected of them or experience an anticipatory or a lasting satisfaction from them. They are neither antipathetic nor emotionally involved with the custom or with specific parts of it. They are ambivalent or indifferent; and, not being committed unequivocally, they find no contradiction in adopting alternatives or in abandoning what others value. They are more open-minded and objective than are their opposites, those who have committed themselves.

The greatest number of individuals in this category are children, all of whom everywhere are indifferent to the values of their elders until and unless they have become indoctrinated by them. There are individual differences, of course, depending upon cultural background and personal experience; but young people in any society are inevitably less securely bonded to their culture than are their seniors, if for no other reason than that they have had less time to understand and to be conditioned by it. Questions of personality and background may be set aside in a contrast between old and young people in this respect. Infancy and youth are not dedicated to the satisfactions of the aged, nor are children dedicated to the role assigned

[3] Ferenc Merei, "Group Leadership and Institutionalization," *Human Relations,* 1949, 2:34.

them as immature adults by their elders. They have to be domesticated; and until they are habituated by this process, the vagaries of their own imaginations and those of their wild relatives are as appealing as the arbitrary standards of their elders.

Indifference to custom is more marked among children than in advanced age groups, but it is not confined to them. Indeed, there are, generally speaking, gradations of it from one extreme at infancy to the other at senility; and, again speaking generally, the younger a person is, the more flexible and receptive to change he is. There is a progressive consolidation of preferences with habituation and therefore with advance in age, provided that the habituation has been constant. Harvey remarked that no man over forty years of age accepted his discovery of blood circulation when it was first announced. If exceptions are made for the rare individual who makes an effort to "keep an open mind" and for the special instances where patronage and personal biases enter, a statement of this sort could be made to characterize the response to any novelty. The age levels would vary with the kind of novelty, but the fact of an age differential in acceptance would remain.

Animals other than man exhibit the same progressive commitment to habit with advance in age. Stefansson took notice of this in connection with his efforts to break the food prejudices of his sled dogs in the arctic. The animals had been raised on seal, caribou, and fish. Upon one occasion all these foods were withheld and a wolf was killed and its flesh given to them. There were six dogs of different ages. None of them would eat the meat for three or four days; then they began to accept it in the order of their age, the youngest one relinquishing his prejudice first. The oldest dog refused wolf meat for two weeks, and finally it was necessary to secure caribou meat for him.[4]

It is unnecessary to document the role of age in novelty appeal as it applies to the acceptance of internal changes. Americans especially have ample illustration of the receptivity of young people to fads and other new ideas. It is only necessary to mention that this is a universal phenomenon of greater or lesser visibility, depending upon the tempo of change that a culture is undergoing as a result of either innovation or diffusion. It is quite apparent on the frontiers of advancing Western civilization. Young people everywhere have been more susceptible than their elders to suggestions of changes introduced by foreigners. In Palau a very serious but covert struggle has been going on between the old and the young men over questions of changing some of the most fundamental native customs. Yurok, Tsimshian, and Yakima children were always more forward in making contacts with the whites, and more inclined to model upon them, than were their elders. Many

---

[4] V. Stefansson, "Food Tastes and Food Prejudices of Men and Dogs," *Scientific Monthly*, 1920, 11:541.

Indian children were taken into white households or served as farmhands and laborers; others were, by their own admission, mere beggars idling about settlers' homes, stores, and camps, satisfying their curiosity, and hoping for leftovers of food, remnants of clothing, and knickknacks. Missionaries and educators of natives everywhere have acted upon the adage that it is difficult to teach an old dog new tricks and have concentrated upon indoctrinating the young. This policy is the explanation for the era of compulsory boarding schools on American Indian reservations. By this technique children could be isolated from their parents, and their relatively uncrystallized habit structures could be altered and molded in conformance with Caucasian ideals.

Besides the age determinant there is another common cause of indifference to custom which is apparent but which is likely to escape notice because of its very obviousness. It derives from the fact of specialization and from the inability of any one person to span the cultural range with equal intensity and interest. Indeed, in most societies it is impossible for a single individual even to know very much about all aspects of the culture which he acknowledges as his. This means that there are parts of it toward which he is relatively indifferent because they do not directly involve him. They are his, but only vicariously so. He shares in them indirectly as a consumer or a spectator rather than as an actor or a protagonist; and toward them his attitude of proprietorship is more diluted than it is with customs and ideals that serve as his performance directives. We may say that with respect to his own interests he is an active and committed participant, and with respect to the rest he is merely a passive and relatively indifferent participant.

All of us are passive acceptors of large sectors of the cultural universe which we call our own. We claim the totality even though we do not participate in many aspects of it, because those who do participate are recognized as belonging to our in-group and reciprocate in their atttitudes toward us and our activities. Some of these passively accepted customs are outgrowths of the subcultures that are comprised by any social system. Others develop out of an elaboration of diversified interests and so are what Linton calls specialty and alternative traits.[5] The passive acceptor admits that for better or for worse all are a part of his culture, but not for him. It is all right with him if some people want to shoe horses, play golf, watch birds, or listen to Beethoven—as long as he doesn't have to.

The difference between passive and active participation is emphasized by the difference between liking something or wanting it to happen, and liking to do it or bring it about oneself. Sometimes the distinction rests upon personal preference and tolerance; sometimes upon a segregation of emotional and rationalistic predispositions. Thus, I like football as an entertainment and recommend it as a means of sublimating the excess of energy

[5] Ralph Linton, *The Study of Man*. New York: Appleton-Century-Crofts, Inc., 1936, pp. 272–274.

in strong young men, but I do not want to play it. Rationally I believe in hard chairs and dieting, but not with reference to myself. I dislike shipyards because of their noise, but recognize their value and the necessity of some peoples' working in them. For active participation a person must find a personal relevance in the custom. Its dictates apply specifically to him, and it becomes a motivation for action only when he envisages it in this light. In brief, he must participate through personal involvement and with effort. The active participant is prepared to be a protagonist for his custom; he is ready to perpetuate and to defend his interests in it.

Passive and active participations in existing customs have their immediate parallels in the passive and active acceptances of new ideas. In fact, the latter is merely an extension or another way of phrasing the former, for acceptance is participation. There is an important difference between the active and the passive acceptance of a novelty, just as there is between making bread and acknowledging that breadmaking is a part of one's way of life but that it should be done by a neighbor and not by oneself. There is a difference in the hospitality which an individual offers to a new idea in the area of his active interest and that which he offers to one in an area of primary concern to someone else. It is relatively easy for a man to encourage his wife to adopt a new cooking method or for a father to insist that one kind of toy is as good as another for his children. It is more difficult for him to face change in his business practice and in his dress.

Passive acceptance is quite apparent in attitudes displayed toward many novelties, whether they are indigenous or imported. It is often not at all difficult to introduce a custom without objection as long as there is no pressure to get people to adopt it. Many will tolerate it if a few are, in their opinion, crazy enough to want to have it. This laissez-faire attitude helps to account for the proliferation of innovations within the Shaker cult. Any person may act according to his inspiration; and, within limits, his action is acknowledged by the rest as a part of their faith, even though they do not practice it themselves. Passive as opposed to active acceptance is a distinction well known to the religious proselytizer, to whom it is often a source of despair or chagrin. In their efforts to secure conversions, Christian advocates reiterate that it is not enough for a man to admit that he is a Christian and to say that it is good for other people to be Christians. He must act like one. Or, phrasing their appeals in terms used in the preceding paragraphs, ministers of the gospel emphasize that a true convert must accept Jesus Christ as his *personal* savior.

Passive as opposed to active acceptance is exemplified in the following account of an event in South Africa: [6]

[6] W. M. Eiselen, "Christianity and the Religious Life of the Bantu." In I. Schapera (ed.), *Western Civilization and the Natives of South Africa: Studies in Culture Contact.* London: Routledge and Kegan Paul, Ltd., 1934, pp. 78–79.

Some years ago I was doing field work among the Masemola tribe at a time when that part of the country was suffering from a severe drought. The chief had tried to procure rain in the traditional way by first having the fields sprinkled with rain medicine and then organizing a tribal rain hunt, but no rain had come. The outlook was very black indeed—if the rain delayed much longer a bad famine was inevitable. After due consultation with his councillors the chief sent a deputation to the local missionary—in this case a native—to ask him whether it would not be possible for him to celebrate a rain service in the heathen village. Of course the invitation was gladly accepted, and the next morning the whole Christian congregation marched to the chief's village. The schoolboys had brought their drum which they beat lustily. On its way this procession was joined by many tribesmen, and there was a great gathering at the chief's place to listen to the singing and the prayers of the Christian visitors. That same evening there was a terrific thunderstorm accompanied by one of the heaviest downpours I have ever witnessed. The following morning there was great rejoicing and the Christians were most heartily congratulated. I know for certain, however, that not even one heathen sought baptism in consequence of this successful rain service. One might say that the Christian God had become a distant friend of the heathen tribesmen.

In this account it will be noted that the author's view of the situation was quite different from that of the pagan natives. They regarded the singing and the praying of the Christian converts as something to be accepted passively. The Christians proved their abilities and were accepted just as native rain makers were accepted; not everybody can be a rain maker or even wants to be one, so the fact that a new kind of rain magic worked did not suggest that everyone become an active participant in it. In short, the converts were accepted as specialists whose services were valued by their passive beneficiaries but not envied. The same author in another place notes that a Christian missionary took over some of the functions that had previously belonged exclusively to chiefs, so much so that he was accepted almost as a tribal official. This did not lead to mass conversions either. The natives passively accepted his advice and prayer in their benefit; but prayer was his business as a specialist, and they saw no reason for their being required to join him and become Christian practitioners also.

The Disaffected. Some people start out by being active participants in certain aspects of their culture but later acquire a distaste for them. Many experience a change from a positive to a negative attitude as a result of some personalized event or series of events. The change may be rather sudden, or it may develop gradually and almost imperceptibly in the disaffected individual's consciousness; or perhaps it would be more accurate to say that the cause of the estrangement is either discrete and definite or complex and accumulative.

It is not always feasible to distinguish between a person who has achieved and then repudiated identification with a custom and one who has never aligned himself with it; that is, between what is here being called disaffection and dissension. From a behavioral standpoint the distinction does not matter; but since we are interested in the conditioning of negativistic attitudes, it is important to recognize that aversions to custom do have more than one set of biographical determinants. Defections from group norms are often incomprehensible unless they are viewed as an attitude reversal that has sprung from some particular complex of prior events.

If the circumstances are propitious, the mere opportunity of becoming acquainted with an alternative mode of behavior is enough to wean a person away from his previous convictions. The circumstances are conducive to disaffection if alien and antithetical ideas are introduced in such a way as not to arouse initial antagonism, and if they are persistently presented. The techniques that have been used for this purpose are ingenious, and the circumstances that have been capitalized upon are varied. Clever advertising and propaganda in all its modern forms have carried the technique to refined and extremely effective lengths. Formal education, especially when students are isolated from their parents in schools or are practically abandoned to teachers by their parents, as they are in the present American school system, can have far-reaching effects in revolutionizing the world views of young people. The older the student is, the more definite the possibility of an attitude reversal, since immature minds, as we have seen, are not yet committed. Many American college students coming from protected homes with restricted outlooks are genuinely shocked by the ideas to which they are introduced on university campuses. It is surprising how many of them today are deeply troubled by their first acquaintance with the doctrine of evolution or by their first meeting with the notion of cultural relativity and the meaning of the relativity of moral values. A revolution takes place in the philosophical orientation of those who are able to assimilate such ideas after an earlier habituation to contrary conceptualizations.

There need not be any deliberate effort to indoctrinate a person in order for him to experience a reversal of his previous identifications with, and gratifications in, the standards of his group. He may be the active and often unwitting agent of his own disaffection. His native and normal curiosity or some fortuitous event, such as his abandonment among strangers, may lead him gradually and insensibly to a distaste for his former means of satisfaction. Before he knows it, he has become estranged from his old value system, a fact that he recognizes in full force only if he attempts to return to his previous way of life. Time and time again natives who have undertaken a term of service with foreign employers have experienced this metamorphosis. So have Americans and others who have left the scenes of their childhood and later returned. The home town is never what it used to be, and almost always it is a disappointment. More accurately speaking, a person is never what *he* used to be. Over a period of time new excitements wean him away from his former allegiances and make him unhappy if he has to return to them.

If disaffected individuals are denied the new satisfactions that they have learned to want by alien teachings and associations and are compelled to revert to those from which they have become estranged, they make good candidates for other new proposals which offer them escapes. This was the condition of the widows, the orphans, and the illegitimate children of white men who had relations with Indian women among the Yurok, the Yakima, and the Tsimshian in the early days. Such women and children had had a taste of the white man's way of life, enough to make them unhappy with the Indian way; and when they were thrown back to feed upon tribal values, they found them tasteless, bitter, or indigestible. Case histories of individuals of this sort are highlighted by rebellious and delinquent trends, which testify to their suggestibility and to their desperate clutching at any new straw which would enable them to fight against or relieve them of the necessity of conforming to native standards. Half-castes especially are to be counted among these restless malcontents. When they are contrasted with their full-blood relatives, they stand out as a disturbed and disturbing element in most populations. As Keesing says of the natives of the Pacific: "Frequently mixed bloods are to be found in the van of movements for cultural or political nationalism; in the latter case they are usually anathema to the governing authorities." [7]

Almost without exception the Palauans who today are struggling to upset the aboriginal scheme of privilege and control have backgrounds of alienation under Japanese tutelage. The insurgents almost without fail speak Japanese —a mark of schooling under the Japanese regime. But their bilingualism is only a touchstone, an easily discernible key to a revolutionary bias in their thinking. Among those with formal schooling, who as a whole are more estranged than are those who were not subjected to it, there are gradations of disaffection that are regularly correlated with length and completeness of identification with Japanese ideals. Those who were given special vocational training or who lived with Japanese families or who prospered in economic enterprises fostered by the Japanese—these are the foremost among the contemporary advocates of changes. And the important point is that they and their fellow aberrants are ready to accept American standards in place of the Japanese. They have been permanently estranged from Palauan customs, and since they cannot have the Japanese, they are willing to take the American— a second choice, as most of them recognize, but different at least from Palauan.

Disaffection sometimes comes suddenly. Frequently this is the result of a punishing experience at first contact with an idea or behavior. Shocks and disillusionments of this character can have far-reaching effects upon the

[7] Felix Keesing, *The South Seas in the Modern World*. New York: The John Day Company, 1941, p. 289.

avoidance and withdrawal patterns of an individual. The psychoanalysts make a great deal of this kind of conditioning, especially in very early life; but one need not accept their premises or their symbolizations to grant that late as well as early biographical events establish lasting repulsions and distastes. Even leaving out of account those with phobias and compulsions the genesis of which is concealed from them, there are numerous examples of people whose peculiar introduction to sexual, religious, dietary, or personal-contact customs has turned them against further participation in them, or whose fear of such introductions has prevented them from ever experiencing the customs at all. Men have renounced political careers in our own society because they have been disillusioned by the evidences of corruption and selfishness that they have found to be integral to politics. Others have been embittered by the hypocrisy, the shabbiness, and the hollowness of crusades, pretensions of brotherly love, and professional façades and have denounced the organizations that are associated with these things. Some men have become pacifists in recoil from the horrors of modern warfare. Some people never get over the shock of the failure of their parents to support them in times of crisis and tragedy. Funerals, bank failures, injuries sustained at work and in athletic contests, hunting experiences—in fact any dramatic and painful experience is sufficient to disillusion men and to transform them into lifelong avoiders and haters of certain institutions and ideologies. By the same token they are prepared to accept something new in place of these old failures.

A special and spectacular cause of disaffection is related to disillusionment but springs from an essentially different set of circumstances. It happens when an individual, conforming to the norms of his group, finds that his hopes are blocked by a conjunction of events that he cannot control. He has played the game according to the rules, but they have resulted in his being checkmated. He is presented with a dilemma just because he has done what is expected of him. A conflict of cultural values has caught him in a vise not of his making, and he reacts by revolting against them if there is something that he can take hold of. He has been led into a blind alley by his cultural directives; and he proceeds to extricate himself in the only way possible, which is by renouncing them and accepting a new set of rules. Such frustration is the explanation for many boltings and apostasies that are mystifying to the superficial observer. It goes to the root of sudden aberrations by individuals who appear to have everything to lose by their defections. It is conspicuous in individuals who to all outward appearances are well adjusted to their culture and seemingly have every reason to continue to support and to be supported by its rules and their sanctions. It is why men in high places suddenly desert their stations, repudiate their ideals, and abandon their admirers and dependents. William Duncan, the first missionary among the Tsimshian Indians, experienced several instances of this. When he set up his model community of Metlakatla 30 miles from Fort Simpson to siphon off the small minority who were his followers and to isolate them from the rest, he had to start with the dregs and the marginals of Tsimshian society. Then suddenly, within a year after the community was founded, he was overjoyed by the appeal for acceptance by two of the most prominent Tsimshian chiefs and practically all the tribe of one of them. Their apparent conversion was a signal victory; for up until that time these two men had obstructed Duncan's missionary activity, and one had even attempted to murder him. Their submission was therefore not only a supreme achievement; it added prestige to his movement. But what he did not know at this time was that the two chiefs were faced with dilemmas which shamed them in the eyes of their fellows and for which they could find no satisfactory solution within the framework of their native culture. They were pinched by conflicting commitments which they could not repudiate without the loss of highly valued goals. The easy way was for them to abandon the whole situation and to play, ostensibly at least, for comparable stakes according to the new rules. Duncan did not know that this maneuver was in the minds of the two chiefs when he accepted them into his community; and as it turned out, it did not matter. As so often happens, the escapees became enmeshed in the machinery which they proposed to exploit for their own purposes, and in the end the scoffer became a convert.[8]

Repeatedly the Europeans, with their ships and guns and superior knowledge, have been welcomed by checkmated chieftains as the instruments of their reprieve from political eclipse. Both Pomare I and Kamehameha I were able to extend and consolidate their power solely by the fortuitous arrival of Europeans who offered them the means to confound and destroy their enemies. Pomare had an exceedingly tenuous hold upon his little realm and would have had to relinquish it had it not been for the English with whom he fraternized and pleaded for help. For all their flattery of him, the missionaries despised him for his impotence and his fawning upon them. Wilson says this about him:[9]

Thus Pomare (the Otoo of Captain Cook), on whom the favour of the English had drawn many enemies, and who at different times was so chased and straitened by them, that, afraid of his life, he has frequently entreated his visitors to take him off the island, had now, at a very good time, extended his power far beyond all former example, and that without either courage or talents for war comparable to his enemies; so that I cannot but ascribe it to the providence of the Almighty, who ordereth all things after the counsel of His own will, and for the accomplishment of His glory and gracious purposes.

[8] H. G. Barnett, "Personal Conflicts and Cultural Change," *Social Forces*, 1941, 20 (No. 2):164–167.

[9] James Wilson, *A Missionary Voyage to the Southern Pacific Ocean*. . . . London: S. Gosnell, 1799, p. 185.

Kamehameha was also in a precarious political position when succor came from alien sources. He was the stronger character, but he too had ambitions beyond his power when the Europeans appeared to strengthen his hand. He eagerly embraced, in fact took by force, the strange and wonderful things that he could turn to his purposes. In 1790 he made captives of two seamen, John Young and Isaac Davis, and proceeded to exploit their skills to his advantage.[10] Ellis's comments upon the careers of the two men, Pomare and Kamehameha, are pertinent: [11]

In the circumstances attending the formation of his character, and in the commencement, progress, and result of his public career, there was a striking resemblance between Pomare, the first king of that name in Tahiti, and his contemporary, Tamehameha, the first king of the Sandwich Islands. Both rose from a comparatively humble station in society to the supreme authority; both owed their elevation principally to their own energies, and the aid they derived from their intercourse with foreigners; both appeared the main pillars of the idolatry of their respective countries; and both left to their heirs the undisputed government of the islands they had conquered. Each appeared to have possessed natural endowments in high order, and both were probably influenced by ambition. Pomare was distinguished by laborious and patient perseverance; Tamehameha, by bold and daring enterprise. The characters of their immediate descendants were in some respects similar to each other, though both were very different persons from their respective predecessors.

Crises are not respecters of status, and the lofty and the low alike grasp at means of relief which they would otherwise ignore and which other people who are not similarly imperiled do ignore. Desperately sick people are obviously more likely to try unfamiliar remedies than are others, especially if they are chronic sufferers who have found no relief in existing treatments. They, too, have lost confidence in and are frequently embittered by the means that are available to them. Like the threatened chieftain, they are in a more intolerable position than is the carefree individual, and they are therefore more receptive to anything which offers a prospect of escape. Medical research is now being greatly stimulated by urgent demands for cures for poliomyelitis, cancer, arthritis, allergies, and common colds; and distraught sufferers are only too eager to give any drug or treatment a chance. Their eagerness and not their apathy toward the new is cause for concern by the medical profession. Deliberate deception and unproved claims for patented cures thrive upon it. The United States government, operating under the Pure Food and Drug Act, has undertaken to protect the public from its gullibility under the pressure of desperation.

[10] James Jackson Jarves, *History of the Hawaiian or Sandwich Islands.* . . . London: E. Moxon, 1843, p. 135.

[11] William Ellis, *Polynesian Researches.* . . . London, 1820, p. 125.

It is not always easy, nor is it necessary, to distinguish clearly between disaffection which is generated by frustration and that which is provoked by unfulfilled promises as interpreted by disillusioned individuals. It is sufficient to know that many people repudiate an idea because they have made the most of it yet remain unsatisfied by it. At some critical juncture it has not measured up to expectations or to the claims of others for it. Genuine religious conversions frequently take place when the convert feels that no mortal means, or at least none at his command, can resolve his difficulties and give him satisfaction. The appeal for divine help in such extremities is an acknowledgment, an acceptance, of the belief that superhuman means must replace human means. Some conversions seem to be spontaneous and to take place under sudden pressures of anxiety, self-pity, or regret, so that they apparently coincide with the renunciation of self-sufficiency. A large number of the conversions among fighting men during wartime and a good proportion of those which take place at revival meetings are of this character. Others are merely precipitated by a crisis and have a history of misgivings about the reality and the permanence of satisfactions to be derived from an atheistic or an agnostic stand. These may more properly be said to be due to alienation or estrangement resulting from disappointments and inner conflicts. The common phenomenon of conversions among the aged and the infirm as opposed to the young and the self-confident has its roots in the doubts about the adequacy of human power to give ultimate satisfaction. The case histories of Shakers, as well as their own testimonies, bear witness to this yearning for an absolutely dependable source of strength in consequence of disappointments that have resulted from human failures. They are highlighted by refrains of hopelessness, anxiety, bewilderment, and embitterment resulting from a sequence or a conjunction of overpowering events beyond the control or comprehension of the individual. The biographical determinants—chronic illness, thwarted ambition, tragedy, loneliness—reveal no distinction from those that are so familiar in Christian conversions.

Whole communities, tribes, and nations of individuals—or a majority of them—can experience anxiety and hopelessness as a result of large-scale misfortune. Consequently, a new idea that offers prospects of relief may have widespread appeal. Contrasts in receptivity between groups with common cultural backgrounds and diverse historical experiences are especially interesting because they highlight the critical importance of the accidental historical factor. When the Maori of New Zealand began to receive firearms from Europeans, they turned them upon each other; and, as elsewhere, native warfare was greatly stimulated. What had previously been smoldering feuds with sporadic minor engagements became bloody programs of extermination. As always, some groups had the advantage in the possession of more powder and guns. In New Zealand the tribes on the northeastern coast of North Island had this advantage over tribes in the interior and the south, and their depredations on these less fortunate groups were harrowing. Many people of the overwhelmed tribes were either killed or made captive, and the social and economic life of the victims was disrupted. The Christian missionaries who arrived upon the scene made little headway between 1814 and 1837 in their attempts to gain converts among the arrogant and aggressive northerners. "It was among the tribes to the south and their representatives in the north [captives] that the new religion began to appeal, and to appeal primarily for its shielding and protecting influence." Many of the converted captives were highborn men. The missionaries secured their release and, having indoctrinated them, used them as Christian advocates in their own tribes. Many were made catechists.[12]

Eiselen's observations upon the contrast in the receptivity of two large blocks of African Bantu tribes to Christian teachings offer a close parallel to the Maori case. He perceives clearly that there have been historical determinants for the acceptance and rejection attitudes of these natives and that the way to conversion among them was prepared by social disorder with its accompanying uncertainties and fears. Speaking of the success of Christianity in certain parts of South Africa, he writes:[13]

Yet I doubt whether the early efforts of Christian missionaries would have been so successful had not their arrival synchronized with singular events in the history of South Africa. Petty intertribal wars, with little bloodshed, had been common enough among the Bantu, but when the missionaries came to this country it was just one great battlefield. The tribes of the Free State and the Transvaal had been reduced to terrible straits by the wars of Tshaka and his emulators and by the ensuing years of famine. Starving remnants of once powerful tribes were wandering aimlessly about the country in constant fear of attack by some band of cannibals, or they were eking out a miserable existence in some mountain refuge. To these harassed people the missionaries came like so many good Samaritans. Their faith in the ancestral gods had been badly shaken and they were ready to open their ears to the message of love and hope.

The attitude of the victorious tyrants Dingana and Mzilikazi was entirely different. They showed little liking for the gospel and its teaching of brotherhood and tolerance. In fact all those tribes which emerged with flying colours from the chaos of the Zulu wars of the early nineteenth century—the Zulu, the Swazi, and the Amandebele of Mapoch—did not in the beginning befriend the missionaries. Even with the broken tribes of the interior the progress of Christianity became far slower than it had been in the initial stages, when once they had had the opportunity of reconstructing themselves and of consolidating their position in a country which had become peaceful under the Boer regime.

[12] Apirana Ngata and I. L. G. Sutherland, "Religious Influences." In I. L. G. Sutherland (ed.), *The Maori People Today*. New York: Oxford University Press, 1940, p. 339.
    [13] Eiselen, *op. cit.,* p. 68.

Satiety is another specific source of disaffection. In this the estranged individual is a habitué or an addict of that which he finally renounces, and that is precisely the reason for his estrangement. He has enjoyed something to the full and has become dissatisfied with it. It palls on him, and he wants a change. Games, toys, and pastimes grow wearisome after a time for most people, especially with an advance of age; but the same disinterest and surfeit can develop with respect to anything or to an entire schedule of life. The familiarity, the repetition, and the free access to it become tiresome just because participation has been unlimited and the possibilities of the routine have been exhausted as far as the disaffected individual is concerned. He is dissatisfied because he has had too much of it, not because he cannot control it or get enough of it; he renounces it because it has become fatiguing instead of stimulating.

This is a common reaction after prolonged periods of self-indulgence and sensuous gratifications. The debility and depression that come as an aftermath are demoralizing and often carry with them twinges of guilt. The continuous stimulation jades the appetite and engenders a feeling of futility by the cycle of elation and depression. The renunciation of sensuous indulgences most often takes place under this impetus; and if some alternative such as a philosophy, or a creed, or a moral dictate is offered as a substitute, the glutted and forlorn are the first to embrace it if they can understand it. Because the great proselytizing religious faiths of the world have placed great emphasis upon a denial of the flesh and upon spiritual satisfactions in its place, they have consistently appealed to the victims of self-indulgence who have been led, or can be led, to feel the futility of their materialistic will-o'-the-wisps. Offshoots of Christianity like the Shaker and numerous other messianic cults also alert those who have been sensitized to the vapidity and emptiness of their lives. Along with those who feel that they have been let down by their private creeds and limited physical powers, these individuals emerge in bold relief out of the mass of the more emotionally secure. Gamblers, drunkards, and delinquents found solace in Shakerism. Mud Bay Louis expressed the sentiment of many of his fellow converts in these words: [14]

Well my friend we was about the poorest tribe on earth. . . . We would not believe in anything. Minister came here, but we laugh at him. We loved bad habits—stealing—and John Slocum died. He was not a religious man—knew nothing of God—all of us the same. . . . I was worst of the lot. I was drunkard—was half-starving—spent every cent on whiskey. I gambled, raced horses, bet shirt, money, blankets,—we did not know any better. John Slocum brought good to us; his words civilized us. We could see. We all felt blind those times. We lost by

[14] James Mooney, "The Ghost Dance Religion," Bureau of American Ethnology, *14th Annual Report, 1892–93,* Washington, D.C., 1896, Part 2, p. 753.

drowning—our friends drink whiskey and the canoes turned over—we died out in the bay. Today who stopped us from these things?

As this quotation indicates, disaffection can be compounded and so produce a complex pattern of attraction and repulsion. Men like Mud Bay Louis revolt first against their cultural heritage and then in disillusionment recoil from the conflicts produced by their anomalous position. Their rebounds may take an erratic course; but unless there is some third choice, their revulsions have a reverse component so that the second disaffection has a reactionary result. This is true of almost all messianic cults because of the limited cultural perspectives of their founders. In the recoil from the bewilderment and frustration of the new order there is no other course open except a partial return to the native past. The revivalistic component is much more marked in some cults than in others, but in most instances the failure of the present brings a nostalgia for the past. The suppression of warfare and of its impingements upon other aspects of Fijian life left the young men with only relatively tame emotional outlets. One result was the creation of a secret organization known as the Water Babies, which incorporated a number of aboriginal ritual elements and encouraged violent and aggressive behavior among its members at their meetings. The initiates were expected to experience supernatural visitations by a spirit helper. Thompson says that those who were reputed to have passed this test were "all restless, slightly maladjusted, and frequently gifted young men. They had apparently grown dissatisfied with the monotony of modern life and were seeking super-human outlets for their energies." [15] It is notable that their recoil led them to reinstate some symbols of the Fijian past for this satisfaction.

Revivalistic cults and societies are, however, only formalized and preternaturally flavored instances of a more universal phenomenon. Reversion resulting from disillusionment is a very common reaction. It is quite evident in older individuals who have tried to straddle two ways of life. As youths they have reached out to embrace the offerings of an alien system, either with or without encouragement, eagerly or reluctantly, perforce or by choice; but gradually the attractiveness of the foreign way of life fades, hopes are dashed, and the impossibility of a complete identification with it becomes clear. The reaction that sets in sometimes takes the extreme form of an advocacy of a return to the remote and unadulterated past, to ideals that were never experienced by the reactionary but were known only to his ancestors or are alleged to have existed in some golden age long gone. More often, however, the individual who has taken a disillusioning excursion finds comfort and security in the ideals and the goals of *his* past life. Speaking of the Maori, Sutherland says that although the taboo on men and women eating

[15] Laura Thompson, *Fijian Frontier*. New York: Institute of Pacific Relations, 1940, p. 115.

together is breaking down among young people, "it is noticeable that as soon as the young women marry and become matrons they quickly relapse to the model of their mothers and grandmothers." [16] Parallels could be multiplied indefinitely. As Keesing says in discussing the natives of the Pacific who leave home and then come back to scoff at authority and tradition, "As in other societies the world over there are forces of consolidation as well as disintegration, and the young rebel often becomes the conservative elder." [17]

As Keesing's observation implies, there are forces other than disaffection at work in the making of a conservative. At bottom there is the process of progressive socialization with advance in age. The waywardness of the bicultured youngster is merely a magnified version of the normal aberrations of youthful individuals everywhere. His deviations are more arresting because they take a swing through a set of values other than those that are traditional with his group. But it is significant that he returns to his own. He does not veer into the orbit of the alien system and become incorporated into it. Instead, he is repelled by it if he has had time to become habituated to his own way of life and if there are forces of rejection operating to exclude him from the alien system. Furthermore, he retreats, not to remain as he is, but to approximate as nearly as possible what his father was. In other words, there is not merely a return to the present but a reversion to the past.

It is a well-known but elusive fact that a person can hold contrary ideas toward the same thing at different times. This is a truth of general import which, like passive and active attitudes, makes the acceptance of novelties only a special case of acceptance in general. New as well as familiar ideas can evoke opposite reactions, depending upon the circumstances. One common reason for this contrariety is that people are predisposed to act in accordance with their self-interests, and their vacillation is an opportunistic device. They are attracted and repelled, they accept and reject, in accordance with the immediate situation and what it has to offer them. All of us are capable of supporting an idea when it serves our interests to do so and of disavowing it when it does not. The ordinary American motorist finds traffic laws irksome and violates them when he can, sometimes making a game and a joke of his avoidances. For him traffic rules are "something to get around"—until someone else is the offender and he is the victim. Then he becomes an ardent supporter of the rule that he otherwise treats as an infringement upon his personal liberty. The Palauans have the same attitude toward their clan affiliations. By hereditary rule a person belongs to his mother's clan, but he may and often does shift his allegiance to the clan of his father or to any other clan if the change will benefit him financially and socially.

[16] I. L. G. Sutherland, "The Maori Situation." In I. L. G. Sutherland (ed.), *op. cit.,* p. 420.
[17] Keesing, *The South Seas in the Modern World,* pp. 158–159.

Human beings are able to live with their contradictory behaviors because of the facility with which they are able to compartmentalize their thinking. When they are confronted with the fact of their conflicting attitudes toward the same thing, they manufacture some distinction. Fundamentally their reactions derive from ego involvements, and a rationalized distinction is made possible by the critical value of context or association. An act in this setting is not seen as the same as when it occurs in that setting, and there is a strong motivation to see the acts as different if personal interests are at stake.

Opportunistic acceptance and rejection is a noticeable feature of the behavior of individuals who are trying to interlace two cultural systems in a life pattern for themselves. They are eclectic, and they quite naturally want all the advantages of each system and none of the disadvantages of either. This Roman-riding act calls for some nimble footwork, and inevitably upon occasions it necessitates a choice of relying upon one cultural horse or the other, depending upon the support that it gives. Reservation superintendents and others who have worked with partially assimilated American Indian groups are familiar with this straddling by individuals whose interests are best served by their being neither consistently protected wards of the government nor fully independent and personally responsible citizens. Each has its advantages and its disadvantages, and it pays a man to be a part-time Indian. He is not to be blamed; the situation invites an opportunistic attitude. Individual Palauans play the same game with native and alien customs that can be alternated. Both American money and their own are essential to them, and to some extent the two forms of valuables have been equated. They are treated as equivalents when it suits the purpose of an individual to do so, otherwise not. If a man needs cash, he will insist upon its being paid to him in lieu of Palauan money in situations where the latter is due him, or vice versa. This vacillation often leads to disagreements because of conflicting demands. Chiefs at the present time are inclined to take an opportunistic view of the criteria of aristocracy. Aboriginally they controlled all the wealth and could manipulate it without consulting the dependent members of their families. Now the latter earn the American money that is demanded for some types of services like carpentry; and in order to get the cash that they need, the chiefs try to wheedle it out of the young men by calling them chiefs and inviting them to participate in meetings where collections for chiefs' projects are made. But this is the only occasion when the young men are treated as equals, an obvious inconsistency which rankles. The objections of the young men are interesting because they, of all Palauans, are the most opportunistic in their attitudes toward alien concepts of property rights. In their plans for themselves and their children they adopt and reject Palauan inheritance rules with complete disregard of consistency. In making his property claims the ambitious man reverses himself with self-righteous abandon to make the most of the offerings of both alien and native ideas on property ownership and inheritance. He is not embarrassed by contradictions when his interests are involved, but he will indignantly refuse the counterclaims of others made in the same way.

The Resentful. There are very few if any societies wherein there is complete equality of opportunity to enjoy the prized objectives of the group. Indeed, the most highly valued goals are such just because comparatively few individuals are able to share them. The mores of a group always forbid a wholesale and indiscriminate struggle for valued objectives, although some systems more closely approximate unrestricted opportunity than do others. Some people submit to their social placement without complaint, but others feel that they have been unfairly treated and never really accept their assignment and the lesser prizes that go with it. Unlike the dissenter, they are dissatisfied not because they object to the values of their group but because they are denied those that are esteemed the most. Unlike the indifferent individual, they are the have-nots instead of the care-nots. They are negativistic toward their own roles but enamoured of those of more favored individuals. They are envious and resentful of those who enjoy the things which they cannot. They are not resigned to their fate; and by contrast with the complacent individuals whom they envy, they are markedly receptive to the suggestion of a change which will at least equalize opportunities or, perhaps even better, put them on top and their smug superiors on the bottom.

By contrast with his complacent opposite, the resentful individual is more susceptible to a suggestion of change because he has less to lose by accepting it; and in extreme cases he has nothing at all to lose and everything to gain, so even a gamble is attractive. Because there are usually such differential investments in most aspects of a culture, it almost always happens that there will be someone who will be attracted by an innovation or an importation. Scarcely any new idea will go begging because of a complete lack of acceptors. Furthermore, the envious individual, along with the dissenter, is not repelled by a novelty which is the antithesis of the familiar alternate that it threatens to supplant. On the contrary, that characteristic often enhances its attractiveness for the covetous individual as well as for the dissenter.

Invidious distinctions may be made and resented in any area of cultural behavior wherein excellence of possession or performance is rewarded and mediocrity is disabling or ignominious. In some cultural systems a hypertrophy of selected interests has placed a premium upon accomplishment in the activities which promote them that is disproportionate to the rewards for efforts in neglected sectors. Success in manifesting these interests is preeminently meritorious; and prestige is consequently the most rewarding consequence of this success, whatever other satisfactions it might bring. Thus, for the American, the Palauan, and many other people the possession and manipulation of wealth are valued for the prestige they bring, irrespective of other considerations. In Imperial China highly formalized scholarship brought comparable rewards; whereas for the Hindu and the Buddhist, spiritual perfection is the ultimate satisfaction and the source of all honor and privilege. In other societies still other preoccupations mark the highest good. In fact, almost any activity may be so rated and men measured against each other with results that are invidious to some of them.

While the failure to get prestige is a common source of resentment, it is not the only one. Men may be envious of superior achievements of any description by others, irrespective of how their ambitions are integrated with the prestige framework. They match their strength, their wit, their social appeal, their glibness, and a host of other capacities and take galling pride in their triumphs over their less accomplished associates. Consequently, the potentialities for resentment are numberless, and so likewise are the yearnings of those who feel penalized in their efforts to achieve their ambitions. A novelty that will implement their purpose is obviously more appealing to them than it is to those who have done well enough with existing devices.

As these observations suggest, novelty acceptance may be conditioned by failure in competition with a rival. This can happen, of course, only in those areas where prizes are open to competition; and these areas, as has been seen, have their limits in any cultural system. Nevertheless, in most departments of culture disgruntled rivals have frequently been eager agents of change. Reference has already been made to the initial welcome given to William Duncan among the Tsimshian. His sponsor was a chief who had been thwarted in his attempts to outdo a rival by the customary Tsimshian methods. The means that were available to him had not been adequate to his expectations, and his defeat rankled. He grasped at the new instrument providentially placed in his hands by Duncan's eagerness to deliver a sermon under the aegis of a man of influence. His rival, and then other ambitious men, also felt compelled to invite Duncan to their homes to give a sermon. Neither they nor their followers were converted by these gestures, because they had another purpose in mind. Yet, whether they liked it or not, they were introduced to some radically new ideas; and this introduction was enough to set more genuine receptive forces in motion. The Mormon Church secured a following among the Maori under comparable circumstances. Its missionaries did not enter this area until the 1880's, much later than the missionaries of the Church of England. By that time the latter sect had been accepted by the dominant political factions in certain Maori communities, and as a group these converts were not interested in adopting an alternative form of Christian teachings. On the other hand, Mormonism did appeal to the "chiefs and leaders of disgruntled sections of Maori communities, who, to emphasize their breakaway, were willing to embrace a new and rival sect." [18]

Experienced politicians, ethnographers, administrators, and many others are familiar with the pattern of acceptance and rejection that has been dictated by factionalism and rivalry. They know that their ideas, their prestige, and their policies may be accepted and used to implement aspirations that have no intrinsic connection with their hopes or with what they represent. They are accepted and used by the have-nots to gain the prizes that others have and which they covet. It is equally obvious, however, that new devices are employed for the purposes for which they have been intended by their introducers and that disgruntled rivals are more receptive to them than are those who have used accustomed alternatives with success. The incentives for acceptance in these instances do not differ from the motivations for innovation under the same conditions. Envious men innovate to compensate for their physical, economic, or other handicaps; and other envious men who are struggling under the same handicaps find their solutions appropriate and appealing, certainly more so than do their complacent rivals.

Competition induces receptivity to new compensatory mechanisms, but it is not a necessary condition for the attitude. Quite often resentment develops in class-structured societies among individuals who cannot resign themselves to the menial and subordinate positions dictated for them by reason of their inescapable placement in the social hierarchy. Custom has decreed that because of their ancestry, or the order of their birth, or their sex, they have fewer privileges, possessions, and powers than have others who are favored by other uncontrollable circumstances. In any given society at a particular time in its history the majority of its underprivileged members may, if they are given to reflecting upon it, consider their social placement a part of the natural order of things—or they may not. But whether the majority are so disposed or not, lone misfits are usually to be found whose smoldering or flickering resentment makes them ready for a revolutionary change that would give them the advantages that others have and they lack. Among such individuals may be found hybrids, orphans, illegitimate children, outcasts, and the seventh sons of seventh sons. Furthermore, it seems that, whether the masses and the misfits have been previously discontented with their lot or not, it is relatively easy to create dissatisfaction among them when they as a group are compared with the elite and the powerful. This is an important point. Essentially it means that class distinctions are not inherently invidious. They do not naturally evoke dissatisfaction among all members of subordinate classes everywhere; or, if they do, the reaction is not necessarily one of resentment and envy. Discrimination is a concept, a way of evaluating

[18] Ngata and Sutherland, *op. cit.,* p. 369.

the unequal distribution of preferment and prerogative which can either be nurtured and disseminated or disparaged and curbed. Like any idea, discrimination is new to some people and a part of the philosophical system of others. It has had an origin, or origins, and a history. In short, it has been an innovation and has diffused along with means to relieve the discontent which it fosters. This fact has been quite apparent with the diffusion in modern times of the revolutionary sociopolitical doctrines of democracy and communism to increasingly greater numbers of the world's population.

It is a transparent fact that the members of privileged classes have a vested interest in the system on which they thrive and that they resist changes in it which will deprive them of their advantages. Changes which threaten the social, political, and economic prerogatives which they cherish are understandably not welcomed by them. If social revolution has any appeal at all, it will attract the dissident, the indifferent, the disaffected, and the resentful who covet the rewards denied them under the existing system. The consolidation of those in the latter category and their readiness to adopt techniques that will enable them to by-pass, nullify, or destroy the controls of the established interests are prominent features of revolutions and popular reform movements. The political commitments of people in the United States during the recent Roosevelt administration were very largely determined by personal or vicarious involvements in the power and privilege struggle which the New Deal symbolized and brought into the open. The have-nots and their ideological congeners welcomed the social reforms that comprised it, and the haves and their affiliates opposed them. Except for entrenched partisanship, people were Republicans and Democrats almost solely on this basis. As is well appreciated by both their advocates and their opponents, socialism and communism have comparable appeal to those who have learned to attribute their distresses and deprivations to their being exploited by their economic, political, and social superiors. The advocates of reform seek to implant and to cultivate this resentment, and its opponents fear it and seek to block or divert it with compromises. This is a familiar process that has happened repeatedly either by design or by accident.

When cultures meet, the majority of those who switch their allegiances are individuals with the least opportunity for full participation in the most valued activities of their own society. When primitive societies have come under the impress of expanding European culture, it has always been the chiefs and other entrenched individuals who, unless they have been thwarted, have been the most difficult to alienate and who have clung longest to indigenous traditions. A priest among the Yakima in 1860 wrote that in spite of more than nine years of effort it was still unfortunately true that it was the chiefs and the *"les grands esprits"* who remained the infidels and the enemies of Christian morality. The Yurok and the Tsimshian were sensitized by tradition to social and political status that was founded upon inherited privilege and peremptory claims. The person who was not born to advantage had little chance of acquiring it during his lifetime. Characteristically the first to abandon the system and to adopt white customs and beliefs were those who had nothing to lose by their defection—the social props and pawns of the elite. Of his troubles in converting the Tsimshian William Duncan wrote: "I had to deal with a lot of chiefs. Almost all of them were opposed to change—to any progress. Our customs brought to the Indians white man's customs, and the chiefs wanted none of this. I had a great amount of trouble with them." [19] Consequently he concentrated upon children and others who were not entrenched in the system of privilege and power. Some of his early followers were older people, among them orphans, slaves, third cousins, and illegitimate children, for whom the future held no prospect of emancipation or gratification of the social ambitions accredited in the Tsimshian scheme of values. Many others who came to him were disillusioned or frustrated because they found themselves confronted by dilemmas which made any new way of life attractive as an avenue of escape.[20] The conservative Yurok of today, lamenting the anxieties and the misfortunes which beset him, explicitly lays the blame in equal shares upon the white man and the low-class Yurok who in the beginning consorted with and aped him. An analysis of individual histories leaves no room for doubt about the essential truth of this observation made by the natives themselves.[21] In New Zealand the members of ranking families as a group resisted education, whereas those of lesser birth sought it and used it to lay the foundations for a new kind of leadership, one based upon the knowledge of the ways of the foreigner.[22] Analysts of acculturation in Africa and in India report the same developments in those areas. Eiselen observes that social upheaval is inevitable when ordinary African tribesmen adopt European ideas and their kings and priests hold themselves aloof from foreign contacts; and that "this is exactly what has taken place all over the country." [23] Aiyappan reports that the Brahmins of Malabar have despised and rejected English customs, whereas their caste inferiors, the Nayars and the Iravas, have availed themselves of every opportunity to partake of them. "Acceptance of the new culture," he writes, "was inversely proportional to the cultural wealth of the groups named." [24] In point of "cultural wealth"

[19] H. G. Barnett, "Applied Anthropology in 1860," *Applied Anthropology*, 1942, 1 (No. 3):21.

[20] *Ibid.*, p. 22.

[21] H. G. Barnett, "Culture Processes," *American Anthropologist*, 1940, 42 (No. 1):28.

[22] Sutherland, *op. cit.*, p. 403.

[23] Eiselen, *op. cit.*, p. 72.

[24] A. Aiyappan, "Theories of Culture Change and Culture Contact." In J. P. Mills (ed.), *Essays in Anthropology Presented to Rai Bahadur Sarat Chandra Roy*. Lucknow, p. 43.

the untouchables certainly have had the least to lose by renouncing the gradations of privilege and power that are associated with the caste system. Their disabilities have been severe, but so have the religious sanctions which support them. Defiance of the system calls for an extraordinary toughness of character because of the immortal penalties which the philosophy of caste imposes upon malcontents. Nevertheless, the untouchables have broken with the system, and, led by one of their own number, Bhimrao Ramji Ambedkar, they have demanded social, economic, and political equality and are searching for a new religious faith that will accommodate their aspirations. Bhimrao has come to the conclusion that "the enlightened path of the Buddha" is the most satisfying.[25] Finally, it has been noted again and again that the founders of messianic cults and cognate movements have emerged out of social obscurity to proclaim their inspirations. Typically they are men of humble origin with undistinguished backgrounds and colorless careers until their advent as prophets. It would appear that they are merely those few individuals out of the many who, seeking to gain distinction by miraculous claims, attract attention and are given serious consideration because their promises meet the wishes of men in anxious times. Their visions, coming when they do, almost inevitably incorporate alien elements; their claim of being the Chosen One is a vehicle for self-realization, a means of getting attention and perhaps power.

It is very likely true that the equalitarian precepts of Christianity and of political democracy have played a significant part in the development of discontent among underprivileged classes in various parts of the world. Christianity in particular expressly asserts the spiritual equality of men and withholds its sanction from, if it does not openly attack, social inequalities. This, then, accounts in part for the defection of the indignant and the resentful underdog, but it is not the key factor. For one thing, the great majority of the representatives of Occidental cultures who have conveyed Christianity to frontier areas have proclaimed their Christian faith more often than they have practiced its ethical precepts, especially in their dealings with indigenous populations; and their hypocrisy has been obvious and repellent to heathens everywhere. Furthermore, the pattern of aristocratic rejection and plebeian acceptance has occurred irrespective of the ethical and political principles of the invading cultural system. The Japanese assuredly did not seek to implant the doctrine of the equality of mankind among the class-conscious Palauans. On the contrary, they denied it by preachment and example. They taught Palauan children that they as a race were biologically inferior to the Japanese; and they found nothing wrong with the native hierarchy of age and family status, paralleling as it did their own. Yet the acculturation results have been the same as elsewhere.

[25] *Time*, June 19, 1950, pp. 61–62.

Families with a tradition of preeminence are today the conservers of aboriginal custom, and their headmen are its staunchest defenders. At present it is only in the behaviors of these upper-class families that one can observe ancient Palauan customs. Only the aristocrats by native definition make an effort to continue with forms aboriginally deemed to be prerequisites for marriage, funeral, and other ceremonies. These forms have become symbols of status, and their retention is vested with an air of vindication and self-righteous propriety. They are marks of the determined Palauan. The lesser folk long ago relinquished them in favor of German, Japanese, or some compromise behaviors.

It has been affirmed—and denied—that women are more conservative than men. There is no evidence to support the view that there is an absolute and universal difference between the sexes in this respect, but it is defensible to maintain that in specific contexts there are consistent regularities which exceed chance expectations. It is not a matter of different innate propensities; in so far as we know, there are no sexual characteristics of this order. The predispositions which do appear are a function of cultural variables. Specifically, they appear to be correlates of the degree of restraint and obligation that is imposed upon the members of one sex as contrasted with the freedoms and prerogatives permitted for the other. In any society the existence of such contrasts, or the absence of them, is known even if it is not verbalized. Traditions which sanction inequalities may lead, in individual cases, to a resentment of them as discriminatory measures. But whether such dissatisfactions develop spontaneously or not, the introduction of an idea or a behavior which can be construed as a relief for the members of one sex will be more readily accepted by that sex than by the other. Again, it is a matter of a person's accepting a novelty that will compensate for a deficiency that is felt by him as contrasted with the rejection of it by a person who already has his satisfactions. Sex is simply another differential to which unequal behaviors and expectations may be attached by traditional usage. Where they exist and come to be interpreted as discriminatory, members of the sex who are penalized accept an emancipating novelty with greater frequency than do those of the opposite sex.

Male or female conservatism becomes, then, a question of which sex has an advantage and which wants to get it. This often makes women more receptive than men in one situation and men more receptive than women in another, or puts them in opposite positions on the same question in different societies. In South African towns Bantu women are eager to be married according to European custom, especially by civil rites, because this kind of marriage gives a woman an independence that she does not have under the native system, which requires a transfer of cattle to her relatives by her husband and her assuming a humble and submissive role among his people, often as a subordinate co-wife. In addition to their growing resentment against polygyny, most women in town want the assurance of economic support from their husbands. A civil marriage rite theoretically protects a woman against desertion without economic compensation from her husband.[26] Women also favor small independent households, in contrast to the native custom of living in patrilineal kinship groups; for when they live only with their husbands and children, they are not subject to the constant demands for service and respect on the part of their mothers-in-law.[27] Since these gains are made at the expense of male prerogatives, men are understandably less receptive to them. In Palau the reverse situation exists. The young men want to be married without having to hand over Palauan money to their wives' male relatives, for their doing so initiates a long series of such payments, the size and number of which will depend upon the amount of food and service with which their in-laws ply them to increase their capital. Young men complain bitterly about the abuses of this system and want to free themselves of it entirely. By contrast the young women want it to continue because their sentimental ties are with their brothers, not with their husbands. Kinship solidarity is very strong; and whatever comfort, support, and security a person gets comes from his immediate blood relatives, more particularly from his or her siblings. This is the only source of consolation and protection for a woman. Her husband dominates and exploits her. He is an outsider; and unless he is constrained by her male relatives, he can, and frequently does, make life miserable for her. Young women are not willing to cut their traditional ties with security for an uncertain future with a man who has been reared in this tradition.

It is noticeable that wherever Christian morality has been accepted in place of one embodying double ethical standards, female acceptors have outnumbered male. The reason is that nonequalitarian standards, where they exist, usually penalize women rather than men. In practically every society men are in control, and in most of them men exercise their power by demanding preferential treatment and invidious freedoms of many sorts. Christian missionaries have consistently, but not too logically, deplored this condition; and their public attacks upon it have not endeared them to the majority of their male auditors, the less so the more flagrant and numerous the condemned inequalities. It is not surprising, therefore, that observers have noted that Christian congregations in mission areas are made up mostly of women and children. This composition is quite evident at the present time in Palau. Rarely did any men between the ages of fifteen and fifty come to the Sunday services in the Ngarard district in

---

[26] Ellen Hellmann, "Native Life in a Johannesburg Slum Yard," *Africa*, 1935, 8:52.

[27] Monica Hunter, "The Effects of Contact with Europeans on the Status of Pondo Women," *Africa*, 1933, 6:273.

1947 and 1948. Significantly, a few men much older than this came; but the core and the spirit of the meetings were provided by women of all ages, mostly the older ones, and preadolescent children. William Duncan had the same experience among the Tsimshian. Benjamin Danks, the missionary sent to New Britain in 1878, lamented that "we had the greatest difficulty in getting people together for worship. I often sent a teacher to one end of the village with a bell, to ring the people up, and beg them to come to church while I went to the other doing the same. The result was about a dozen or so women and children, possibly two or three men. Sometimes none but our few servants came." [28] In Africa women have accepted Christianity much more readily than have men. Among the Pondo, for example, "they are in the majority in every congregation, and readily take part in religious meetings, speaking, praying and reading in public." This situation is partly due to the related fact, common among other tribes, that more girls than boys have taken to education on the European pattern. Christian and secular teachings together have given the Pondo woman the courage "to demand an independence of judgment and freedom of action which under the old conditions she would never have dreamed of claiming." [29]

The controls which men commonly exercise over the behaviors of their sisters, wives, and daughters can very easily distort the real potentialities of an acceptance pattern as they relate to sex differences. Men are almost always the contacting agents for the transmission of new ideas, except for those which pertain exclusively to women. Men, therefore, have greater opportunity not only to observe and to adopt new ideas pertaining specifically to male behavior, but also to exercise the option in interpreting and accepting those that in any way affect them. Unless there are communication channels between women, as there are inside a society, but as there seldom are on the frontiers of an expanding cultural system, ideologies which pertain to women are filtered through men. Furthermore, men can and do set themselves up as the guardians of their women and as censors of subversive influences as they understand them. This behavior is quite apparent on frontiers where the only representatives of an alien culture are workmen, traders, administrators, or other men. It is only with increasing familiarity with the foreigners that native women have an opportunity to know much about the system that these foreigners represent, irrespective of the way they might react to it if they knew anything about it. As a result, men are usually the first and most frequent acceptors of importations by comparison with their women. Even though they take extremely little,

[28] Quoted in Stephen Reed, *The Making of Modern New Guinea*, Philadelphia: American Philosophical Society, 1943, p. 114.

[29] Hunter, *op. cit.*, pp. 274–275.

this is true. Yet in time this situation may be radically reversed. It very often is reversed when outside men make direct contact with local women, especially, as is usually the case, with young or unattached women. The consequences of this turn of events have been revolutionary wherever they have occurred. Not only do such heterosexual contacts result in the introduction of aberrant mating patterns; in addition, the women involved are offered the opportunity to accept a variety of new satisfactions and freedoms, and because of the intimacy of the contact, they learn much more about the culture of their consorts than do their brothers or their fathers. These women in time become the principal purveyors of new ideas to their group.

Conclusion. Although the preceding characterization of acceptors places an emphasis upon discontent, this should not be taken to mean that only those individuals with a background of estrangement will accept a new idea. Such individuals are preeminently and predominantly susceptible to suggestions of change involving the elements toward which they have a detached or alienated attitude. Their bias, antecedent to the appearance of the novelty, makes them already receptive; but this condition is by no means a prerequisite for acceptance. It is true that the satisfied must also become dissatisfied with what they have before accepting an alternative; but their discontent follows the advent of a novelty, is initiated by it or by other current circumstances, and may have nothing to do with personal background. Their acceptance is therefore due not to a predisposition but to novelty or advocate characteristics.

This fact points up the necessity of taking all three of the components of the acceptance situation into account for an understanding of any given individual's reaction to a novelty. While for purposes of systematic analysis biographical determinants can be isolated from advocate assets and these from novelty characteristics and values, no one of these components can be treated as if it functioned independently. In reality all three are intimately conjoined and are mutually influential. Variables of all three are present in any concrete instance, and from one individual instance to another they have different potentials. A persuasive advocate can "sell" a man a new gadget even though the latter has been quite happy with the one he has; or a novelty, by its superior performance, may sell itself to a man who up until then has found no reason to complain about the thing that it might displace. Oppositely, the unsatisfied individual is seldom if ever an absolutely indiscriminate acceptor. He may be more or less so, but rarely can it be said that a malcontent will accept anything from anyone under any circumstances. He, too, is influenced by the auspices of the novelty and by its meanings and values as he sees them.

ON THINGS

It is a part of the necessary economy of everyday living that all of us assume that there is a constancy about the objects of our experience. We assume that the pencil we used five minutes ago and still hold in our hands is the same thing now as it was then; that the clock we looked at in the morning at six o'clock is the same object that we looked at at ten. The assumption of continuity and stability in such matters not only is essential to our sanity but is a prerequisite for the least measure of effective reaction to our environment. It is also basic to the learning process, because it would be impossible to build on past experience if every moment brought an entirely new order of things. And yet, in actual sensory fact, we all know that an object seen under a green light is not the same as it is when seen under a white light, that a hot poker is not the same as a cold one, that a feather seen as a part of a bird's plumage is not the same as it is when viewed as part of a lady's ensemble. This well-recognized fact is something more than a psychological curiosity. It has a fundamental bearing upon our opinions and our behaviors, and the part that it plays in initiating cultural change is not less important than is its significance in other practical ways.

If everyone at all times viewed a given situation or thing in the same way, there would not only be more harmony in human affairs; it is practically certain that there never would be any alteration of them. Without insight into the unrealized potentialities of a thing, there can be no modification of its use or relations; and insight means that a thing becomes different in some of its sensory manifestations. If the sensory qualities of a stick of wood were fixed and absolute, it could never become anything except a stick of wood. No one could perceive a new use for it within a given cultural setting; nor would its passage over cultural boundaries disclose new potentialities, since there could be only one view taken of it. If this is true, and it is difficult to deny it, the student of change is obliged to face some fundamental questions. It will not do to toss invention off as an act of the "creative imagination." It is imperative to ask what a "thing" is and what constitutes "sameness" in things.

It should be realized at the outset that it is impossible to deal with these questions in a satisfactory manner on the verbal level. The very use of language, because it names things, their qualities, and the relations between

411

them, often prejudges the issues and obscures the importance of the psycho-logical processes that are involved in the judgment of identity. To say that the sight of a pencil evokes the thought of a pencil seems banal. In reality this necessary verbal short cut masks the fact that the given object is not a *pencil* until it has been apprehended as such by a mental mechanism. The manner and the conditions under which this apprehension takes place are the core of the inquiry, but at every step the linguistic detour belittles the difficulty. The demonstrative method—using the objects themselves and pointing at them—eliminates some of the attendant frustration and helps to elucidate the problem. It obviously cannot be resorted to here.

In the attempt to understand why things appear as they do, it is well in the beginning to concentrate upon what we call material objects. These tangible things are known to us, and can only be known to us, through the intermediation of our several sense organs; and in some instances, as with sight and hearing, through the instrumentality of a surrounding medium. In any case, barring parasensory phenomena, there is always some physical contact between the thing and the experiencing individual. It would be strange indeed if this contact were ever of a static character, if the thing simply came together with and rested against the responding organism. And yet for all that our senses tell us to the contrary, this is what happens; and we must have some familiarity with modern physics to consider material objects as anything other than compacted masses of permanently lesser things.

Things have "substance"; they are solid, opaque, pressure-resisting masses of fixed particles. A stone has hardness because of this compacted particle composition; it has color and other visual properties for the same reason. A sound or an odor is wafted to our senses, but it has the same rigid homogeneity within itself. If we attempt to analyze things with our sensory apparatus, we find only that they are made up of smaller things, and these of still smaller things. In short, our untutored senses never get beyond the concept of subdivision as an explanation of real objects.

Nevertheless, by the same necessary report of our senses, we are able to infer on indirect evidence that even the most rigid of objects is made up of motion, not of pieces. Because of the behavior of substances under certain conditions, physicists are convinced that things are what they are because of the existence of a definite number of submicroscopic configurations of energy called atoms. No conception of the structure of atoms along purely mechanical lines seems to account for all the observed effects of their behavior. In the most general way these dynamic figures may be thought of as some kind of infinitesimal planetary system, with one or more energy units called electrons vibrating, revolving, or pulsating about a core or nucleus. There is a temptation to carry on with materialistic notions of the composition of matter and to refer to the energy units in these systems as particles. Doing so is well enough as long as we do not expect these units to be more elemental than the systems of which they are parts. The nucleus, which constitutes the bulk of the mass of an atom, has been undergoing a disturbing conceptual transmutation from something to nothing as a result of its fission. It now appears that not even this core contains a "solid" substance that can be referred to as the ultimate basis of matter. The ultimate source of our experience of things is energy, and this manifests itself in the last analysis in the form of motion.

The relatively stationary objects of our experience must, therefore, be complex systems of activities, whether these be on the molecular, atomic, or subatomic level. It must also be true that these activities are transmitted to the nervous tissues of the living organism without diminution or obliteration of their distinctive aspects. Although these vibrations are infinitesimal and we are unconscious of them as such, they must nonetheless be conveyed in direct fashion to our nervous system.

Two considerations are involved here. On the one hand, there can be no discontinuity between the external activity and its internal counterpart; that is, the nervous system upon sensory contact becomes an integral part of a vibrating continuum which includes the object or medium of stimulation. Secondly, there must be a direct correlation or parallelism between the external activity *pattern* ("thing") and the character of the nerve-cell activity pattern. There does not appear to be any other explanation of our ability to discern the distinctive qualities of things, an accomplishment that is an everyday experience for all of us.

Philosophers have treated form as a fundamental quality of matter; and yet there is no sense modality for directly experiencing this property. Even the kinesthetic sense experiences only the motion of the sensory apparatus and not the form of the sensed thing, although the latter may be deduced from the former. Indeed, all shape experience seems to be an interpretative matter, which means a mental activity. In the determination of shape, however, there is some autonomous mental activity; there is a thought component that is not due to the translation of an external stimulation. The mind experiences successive or simultaneous pulsations of energy with intervals of "nothing" between them. But there is something in our consciousness. Otherwise we could not know the unity and the extension which are necessary to the concept of a thing. An act of organizing the discrete pulsations that make up a thing must take place before it can have distributive aspects. The object must be a unit before *it* can be long, sharp, concave, or round. This is also true with respect to its other qualities, for they are likewise derived only from many discrete impulses. Before an aggregation of impulses can assume the character of a hot, blue, heavy, or hard thing, they must be grouped and bonded into an entity. In fact, these qualities are the only sensory realities, and the quality of extension is mentally derived from them. The precise nature of the primary data—the frequency, intensity, and amplitude of vibration—determines the sensory qualities of a thing. The distribution or arrangement of these activities determines its size, shape, and, in a sense, its location. All coexist, but the latter aspects are clearly separable from the former. Thus different activity systems can inhere in the same shape, as is the case with a lead ball and a wooden one; and the same action system can be manifested in different forms, as in black cats and black horses, or in hot pokers and hot stoves. All qualities are aspects of the whole thing and can have no significance except in extension.

Some philosophers have regarded motion as a primary property. As far as experience is concerned, this view adds little to our understanding of things. All objects are doubtless in a state of motion with respect to some datum, but an appreciation of this fact throws no light on the nature of the object itself. Motion does impart quality, but not to the thing that is moving. All qualities are synthetic; they are compounded of motions, not of "things" and motions. So the motion of an object is not an attribute of the object; but it does contribute to the qualities of a larger whole, namely the system of activities with which the object is mentally integrated. Thus, the electrons and atoms of a chair are not colored by their movement, but the chair is. If a lead pipe is struck with a heavy hammer and dented, the atoms of lead remain unaltered. It is still a *lead* pipe. But the loci of the activities of some of the atoms are altered; and the larger unity, the pipe, is affected. The dent that appears is an aspect of the whole pipe and can pertain to nothing less. The perception "dent in pipe" is the mental synthesis of movements which at once destroys the particularity of the moving parts and creates the qualities of the larger unit that is formed by them.

Things can be of any "size" because there are an infinite number of levels of integration, each resulting in a more inclusive whole without discernible parts. An atom of hydrogen can be such only when it is no longer "composed" of an electron vibrating in a certain fashion around a nucleus; a molecule of water can be such only when it is no longer made of two atoms of hydrogen and one of oxygen; and a glass of water can be such only when it no longer manifests the singular properties of discrete molecules behaving as molecules. Each higher synthesis fuses the activities that characterize the subordinate systems when taken alone and dissipates their particularity in a new unity that has nothing in common with them. Contrariwise, the isolation of a movement as such destroys the quality of the whole of which it is a part and discloses the lesser unities to which the action may be referred. When an atom of hydrogen conceptually becomes an electron moving in a certain way around a nucleus, it is just that and not an atom. In the last analysis, a thing and its movement are simply a more complex order of movement.

A thing, then, results from the synthesis of the discrete activities that are transmitted to the mind by an appropriate compound stimulus. It should be borne in mind, however, that the synthesized activities are those which take place in the nervous matter of the brain, not those which make up the external object. Descriptively, the process of analysis is the apprehension of relations between activities. There is no external counterpart for this function. There is no external source for the concepts of relatedness between things, no stimulus for high, low, first, last, more, or less. That which we call a relation between things is a mental contribution to the external situation. It is an interpretation. And yet it inheres in the nature of the stimulus and is immediately knowable. Spearman lists this fundamental property of the mind as one of his three cognitive principles. He calls it "the eduction of relations," by which he means that the presentation of two or more stimuli at once and spontaneously tends to evoke a knowing of the relation between them.[1] It is an unmediated and a nonseparable aspect of the apperception of things.

If we accept the conclusion that the essentials of mind action are its activities and their conceived interrelations, it is possible for us to take an expanded and more significant view of what a thing is. Common usage restricts the term "thing" to more or less homogeneous bodies of uniform density. This restriction serves a good practical purpose, but we must take issue with it on theoretical grounds. We have seen how elusive a "solid" object may be upon analysis and how unproductive the search is for a satisfying definition of substance in the common meaning of the term. It remains to be shown that the same mental processes are at work in the definition of phenomena other than objects and that the restriction of the word "thing" to this class of experience is the result of arbitrary selection from a wide range of identical processes on different synthetic levels and in different sense modalities.

One important implication of this interpretation is that there are heterologous units or object combinations, which are as real and compelling in human behavior as are single objects themselves. This view is not a novel one, but it calls for an explicit analysis of just what is meant by the idea and a theoretical justification for it. The justification is to be found, I think, in showing that there is no psychological difference between molecular combinations ("things") and inter-thing integrations. The same mental processes are at work in organizing both units, and both have the same impress of reality; they are subject to the same influences, and they display the same patterns of unification, disjunction, and recombination.

[1] C. Spearman, *The Nature of "Intelligence" and the Principles of Cognition*. London: Macmillan & Co., Ltd., 1923, p. 64.

In order to appreciate these facts it is essential to abandon the unfruitful conception of a thing as the only reality. And since the constraints of linguistic usage are restraints upon the adoption of new thought perspectives, it is well to forego the use of the word "thing" and to substitute a term which is more suitable to the entire range of facts that it is to comprehend. Although it has its drawbacks, which derive from diverse loose and private connotations, the term "configuration" is as meaningful and serviceable as any for this purpose. In adopting it we shall understand by it any whole concept which, upon being analyzed, is revealed as a composition of mental activities that are bonded together by definable sets of relations. The concept of an object-thing is, therefore, a configuration; but there are many configurations which are not thing-concepts by common definition, and they differ profoundly from one another in the level, degree, and dimension of their organization.

For the moment nothing further need be said about the nature of mental activities that enter into the formation of a configuration. What has been said before applies at this point as well. A configuration, or any part of it that appears upon analysis, is an integrated activity system. The size of systems and the relations between them are highly variable. With object-things, only a very limited range of relations needs to be considered. They are, for example, supposed to be continuous and to have boundaries. If there is a discontinuity, there are two objects; and if there are no boundaries, there is no thing. There is also the feeling that objects have stability; they remain units unless they are operated upon by disruptive physical forces. The relations that mentally bind configurations of this character together are purely spatial. Their parts, upon analysis, are to the right, below, or adjacent to each other. In such instances the impression of unity is a function of the distance between the component action systems. When two stimuli approximate each other so closely in space as to be no longer distinguishable, they become one; and when a compact cluster of such stimuli exists, the mental result is an object. In point of distance there is a threshold below which two concurrent stimuli are mentally fused into one. We know that this fusion is a mental process on other grounds; but because of the inherent characteristics of the nervous matter which establish the threshold, it is not immediately or directly knowable. It is this spontaneous process that yields the impression of homogeneity and oneness to an object, and because of this fact an object is as much a mental phenomenon as it is a "physical" thing. Indeed, in one sense an object is solely a mental construct; for although the contiguity of separate stimuli can be said to be a physical fact, the property of oneness that unites them is not. We are so much accustomed to thinking of objects as so obviously and undeniably "real" and as so distinct from other mental forms that it is necessary to stress their mental component in order to define the real nature of their distinction from other configurations. This distinctiveness does not derive from a special property called "reality," but from the fact that they are defined in spatial terms. Configurations are object-configurations when their component stimuli are too close together spatially to be discriminated directly by our sensory apparatus.

It might be assumed that in the foregoing we have been talking about only homogeneous objects, that is, things with uniform characteristics throughout their mass. And so we have; but it must be pointed out that all configurations, as long as they are such, are unitary, whole, and uniform, with all their characteristics distributed throughout their extension. It is only when analysis is undertaken that these whole properties disappear and are supplanted by the heterogeneity of parts. An elementary laboratory demonstration of this phenomenon occurs when a piece of paper or a razor blade is placed under a microscope. But there are even more common everyday experiences of the same phenomenon, as when we scrutinize more closely some object by drawing nearer to it or by attending more closely to it with any of our senses with a view toward analyzing or identifying it. Upon closer inspection—that is, upon resolution of its parts and their interrelations—the distant figure of a human being turns out to be a man; and upon further exploration, it proves to be a well-known acquaintance. Or a gray mass that we approach from a distance progressively becomes a tree, an oak tree, and finally a dead oak tree. With each step successive levels of whole qualities are inexorably dissipated as new ones emerge. The immediate sensory qualities which connote the face of a friend are not those which define a human being, nor are the qualities of a tree implicit in a gnarled oak. The qualities of a configuration, a whole, inevitably disappear when its components are realized. As wholes, they are homogeneous.

In the examples given, configurations dissolve as a result of artificial techniques which in effect lower the discriminative threshold. This might be taken to imply that the existence of an object configuration depends upon physical conditions which keep the spatial relations of its parts below the sensory level. This, however, is not true. We experience many configurations in our daily life that retain their undifferentiated whole properties, not because we do not have the opportunity or the ability to resolve them into their parts, but because we do not attend to them with this purpose in mind. The paths that we take upon our routine walks, be they ever so familiar, are lined with objects which have no other characteristics than whole qualities. We know them intimately and deal with them for all practical purposes in an effective manner; but in our consciousness they exist only as "houses," "shops," "trees," and "sidewalks"—we need not know what kind or how many or exactly where. We discover this fact with surprise at those times when we try to recall a familiar scene or when we "see for the first time" an object that we have passed by many times before. If we are "more observing," we have broken down some of the undifferentiated wholes that move by in a familiar pattern, but seldom all of them, and never any of them through all their successive levels of organization. Doing so would require intense application and constant alertness for a lifetime—in addition to some training.

Spatial configurations, then, are as much a matter of attitude as of physical "fact." Their parts may be separated by any distance. The important thing is that we are not conscious of their composite character. Their parts are embodied in wholes directly without any intermediate process and, therefore, without our "knowing" it. When analyzed, the object that we repeatedly see and think of as an automobile has its parts widely distributed; but this fact is of no consequence at the moment of its being apprehended as an automobile, simply because there are no parts to the concept. There is only an extended whole; and there is no limit to the physical size of a system that can be comprehended as a conceptual entity.

It follows that there is no conceptual distinction between objects and groups of objects. All configurations are, when resolved by any means available, heterogeneous. They must be in order to have parts at all. This holds even though the parts are of the same kind. Homogeneity is a whole quality which dissolves when any object, whether a blank sheet of paper or a house, is analyzed. And with reference to spatial configurations, the distance between the parts makes no difference as far as the notion of a whole is concerned. In short, neither homogeneity nor the degree of separation of its parts sets up limits for the definition of a unit. Consequently, there are spatial configurations—objects, if one prefers to extend the term—which in their material manifestation exhibit all degrees of constancy, flexibility, internal diversity, and extension and which are amenable to shaping on an indefinite number of integration levels. That is to say, not only single objects, but sets of objects, and groups of sets of objects, no matter how similar or diverse, or how closely joined, can form units in precisely the same way that a stone is conceived to be a unit. And since a configuration, of whatever kind, is a mental construct, its reality consists in its mental retention or revival; and the forces which influence these processes are the same in all cases.

With the successive reduction of each level of integration, the product is always two or more activity systems bonded by some definite relation. The hierarchy of levels may be quite complex; but at each reduction the parts, no matter what their size or complexity when they in turn are resolved, appear as unitary activity systems at the moment of the realization of their component character. Analytically, these parts may be integrated molecular systems ("things"), groups of things, or arrangements of groups of things.

But in all cases they are unitary activities until an analysis of them causes their whole properties to dissolve into a lesser unit-plus-relation structure.

As a result, not only things but combinations of things have shape. The term "form" is equally applicable to compact objects and to arrangements of them regardless of how permanent their interconnections may be. Understood in this light our extensive use of the word "form" to designate patterns of arrangement finds justification and takes on new meaning. Thus there are architectural forms, application forms, order forms, forms of address, forms of behavior, mechanical forms, pictorial art forms, mathematical formulas, and many others that must be said to have shape no less than a stone. The significance of this expanded interpretation of a "thing" is, of course, that it offers the prospect of investigating configurations of widely diverse character by the same techniques and leads to the expectation that, within appropriate limits, what is found to be true of one will prove to be true of another. For example: in all instances shape is separable from content and may, therefore, inhere in any variety of substance or combinations of substance. Anything may be configurated like anything else. The specific names and addresses of innumerable persons can be set up in the same form. Just as a stone, a piece of metal, and a piece of cloth may be circular, so a line of stones, a string of beads, and an arrangement of human beings can be circular and the one conceptually or actually substituted for the other. Through all the shifting of content the configuration remains intact and as real as the shape of an iron bar.

We should exist in a curious unidimensional world were there just the one organizational factor, the spatial. The potentialities of many others, functioning in the same way, afford the opportunity of projecting our thought configurations into a multidimensional universe; and they add immeasurably to the richness and adventure of thinking. New ones are always possible, either by refinement of others or by sheer discovery, that is, by definition. The units that result differ greatly one from another. Each order of configuration, that is, each dimensional section, is qualitatively distinct from the rest; and we cannot expect them to be amenable to the same conceptual manipulations throughout. Nevertheless, structurally and operationally all of them exhibit features in common with object-configurations. Except for prejudice we could, in fact, call them things.

The temporal relationship is an important configurating factor. It is so fundamental to our thinking that it is commonly supposed to be inherent in the nature of events. In other words, we believe that everything must happen in time. And yet time, like space, is no more than a manner of ordering experience. Its ubiquity derives from the nature of our perceptive and cognitive faculties, not from the nature of things as such. It is futile to ask what it is about things-in-themselves that permit our viewing them in the time dimension, for we can never know the answer. All that we need to know here is that the mind can make this kind of conceptual cross section of experience, with the result that time forms emerge. There are a great many of these time shapes that not only regulate our daily lives but constantly nucleate the flux of events about us. Some are simple and momentary; others conform to persistent and repetitive traditional patterns. The nature and duration of the participating activities are highly variable; so are the intervals between them.

All routine or periodic phenomena, from the marching of men to the sequence of our personal habits, are embodied in time configurations. Grouping in this dimension, like that in any other, is indicative of a need to reduce diversity and confusion. Regularity in events, like stability in things, is a comforting solution. The temporal frameworks which we impose upon the stream of natural events testify to the importance of this factor. So do the schedules by which we order our own behavior and that of the inanimate things over which we have control. Many social forms—all those acts which involve a sequence of events—and all procedural norms are integrated about the time factor. Some are quite simple and brief, as they are when a signal or cue calls for a given response. Others may be lengthy or complex, as is the case in military maneuvers, religious rituals, and the "plays" in various group sports, such as basketball and football. Each completed operation constitutes a configuration, and the nature and duration of the component activities plus the intervals between them give form to it no less than to an object. The two orders of units take shape under the same mental necessities.

Circularity and repetition are frequently characteristic of time configurations because they have the utilitarian virtue of regulating and standardizing behaviors into a comparatively few familiar and predictable sets. A comforting feeling of constancy, from which we derive much of our sense of security, is thereby gained; and the shocks and frustrations that attend the unexpected and the alien are minimized. Also, as a consequence of the standardization of sequences, we are able to divert our conscious thinking processes from a major part of our daily experience and focus them on less routine and more complicated problems. Thus many of our acts and responses become habitual and unreflecting. This means that the situation and the habitual response, like other time patterns, become, at the moment of habituation, undivided wholes. In concept they are unitary activity systems without parts. Hence their "naturalness," their "instinctiveness," and their absolute reasonableness. Their shape is supposed to inhere in the nature of events, just as the shape of a tree is supposed to inhere in the nature of the matter of which it is composed.

While the repetition of time configurations is one of the special reasons for their development, it is not essential to their definition. A sequence of activities may be unique. It may serve a special purpose or none at all. In the dramatic arts special attention is given to this subject of uniqueness; the entire emphasis is upon creating different action sequences. Authors of plays, ballets, and musical compositions are intent upon contriving departures in action sequences for their thought-producing effects. They strive deliberately to transcend the commonplace—that is to say, the habitual—configurations rather than to conform to them. In this, artists do not differ from inventors; and they are similarly constrained by the number of available configurations within their cultural tradition and the degree to which the internal cohesion of these habitual configurations resists their efforts to break them down and reintegrate them into new units.

It is important to bear in mind that in speaking of the rendition of a musical score, for instance, or the presentation of a drama, or the recitation of a poem, we have not departed from the fundamental conception of a configuration as being, analytically, a combination of activities plus relations. Again, as with space-things, there are levels of integration; and what at one moment is considered to be a unit depends upon what the next most inclusive level of combination is. Thus, the tone emanating from a tuning fork is a unitary fact until it is analyzed into its components; then it no longer exists as a whole, and there remain only lesser wholes, called air vibrations, with a specific periodic time relation between them. If a second fork that vibrates twice as rapidly is struck simultaneously, a new unity is sensed, uncompounded, pure, and elemental. And this compounding is a mental effect; for two sounds whose vibration rates are not too close together can pass through the same point in an elastic medium such as air without physically altering each other in the least. The same result is achieved directly by striking a piano key. The ensuing sensation is called a note; yet we know that it is a compound of lesser configurations, each defined by one vibration system among several that act at the same instant along the piano string. And so with octaves on a piano. They are configurations integrated on the more inclusive level of pitch. They are, therefore, sensed as single sounds.

Two simultaneous notes separated by the interval of a fifth yield a "shape" different from that of two that are separated by a third or an octave. As is true of other kinds of configurations, time shapes are transposable. They are abstractions and can be "filled in" by any kinds of activities as long as the relationship between the activities remains the same. There are several pairs of vibration systems that will answer to the definition of a musical third; and if we follow the practice of the physicists and disregard the vibratory limits of audible sound, the number is indefinite.

The shape of a note or a chord is analogous to the shape of an object. All its parts seem to coexist. This is inevitably a quality of all configurations; otherwise they could not be whole things. The totality must be comprehended at once. Yet it is clear that the elements of a note do not coexist. One element follows the other by some interval, no matter how small. If that were not so, we should not be able to state the vibration rate by which pitch is defined. By the statement that an air-wave frequency of 256 vibrations per second is recognized by us as the sound of middle C in our musical scale, it must be meant that each pulsation that reaches our ears is separated by a time interval of $\frac{1}{256}$ second, and hence that they do not impinge simultaneously. Intervals of this magnitude are below the threshold of "conscious" discrimination but not beyond the limits of perceptual segregation. This is obviously so, for otherwise we could not know the difference between middle C with 256 vibrations per second and A with 430. Furthermore, the experimental evidence indicates "that hearing is without question a function in which the various pitches which we know to be necessary in the constitution of difference in timbre or quality are separately perceived, though interpreted as a whole." [2]

We are thus led to a conclusion paralleling the one arrived at with respect to spatial configurations; namely, that simultaneity is not a fundamental aspect of time configurations. It is as illusory as absolute contiguity. There are always temporal gaps between the component activities of time shapes, just as there are always space gaps in objects. Some time shapes seem to be more "solid" than others, but this fact tells us less about these time things than about our sensory abilities. And above the subliminal threshold—the "object" level—there are many experiences that we treat as wholes although it is evident that there are wide time gaps between their parts. Thus, notes in succession, no less than notes in conjunction, can be embodied in time forms. We call them rhythms. In addition, the duration of the individual notes can be organized into distinct shapes. So can their intensities. When these three modalities are combined with pitch shapes, the results are more inclusive configurations, such as musical runs, bars, or measures. These in turn, when conceived as wholes, are configurated into themes, refrains, or movements, and the latter into complete compositions. Regardless of key, the shape throughout remains the same, and transpositions—that is, activity substitutions—are possible.

Perhaps it need not be added that the same analysis could be made of any other composition in sound. The spoken word, for instance, is a configuration. It is a unit, but upon analysis it will appear as a composition of all the time configurations that were mentioned for a succession of notes; namely, those of rhythm, intensity, and duration. And the pitches of its "elementary" forms, the phonemes, will be found to be extremely complex integrations of lesser activities.

Some configured systems disregard one or another of the possible temporal modalities. Signaling systems like the Morse code are monotonous

    [2] G. Oscar Russell, *Speech and Voice*. New York: The Macmillan Company, 1931, p. 32.

and dispense with intensity patterns. Others, like drumbeats, may go further and almost completely eliminate durational patterns. It is worth noting that all these time configurations can, by various systematic translations, be transformed into the spatial dimension. A common convention for this purpose is to equate duration with length.

The same kind of analysis can be made of visual time configurations, such as rituals and plays. With each movement a participant establishes a given relation with some feature of his environment and thereby configurates himself in a definite fashion with it. Taken alone, the act may be regarded as a spatial form; but when it is viewed in relation with the action of another participant or with a later action by the same participant, time patterns and other kinds as well are manifested. It is only through the apprehension of such interconnected sequences by an audience that the action details have meaning. Each detail configurates with others; sets of them build up into scenes, scenes into acts, and acts into a whole performance. There is a progressive synthesis which successively dissipates the details of scenes and acts and leaves nothing but plot or story. That whole is nonetheless pregnant with all the richness of its component parts; all the latter are present at once but without the qualities that they have in their isolation.

It may seem that in making a case for time configurations the implication has been that the mind ignores time differentials. This, however, is not the way that the process must be described. The point is that these configurations, like all others, are without parts at the moment of their conception and hence without relations between parts. With respect to time, this means simultaneity. Simultaneity is the constancy factor in this dimension; and it is as illusory as continuity, the constancy factor in the space dimension. In the one case two things that are separated in time are made to coexist as a result of their being configurated. In the other, two different objects—a chair yesterday and the "same" chair today—are made one by being separated in time.

As a result of their experiments gestalt psychologists have come to the conclusion that there is no psychological difference between so-called stroboscopic or apparent motion and "real" motion.[3] If a small spot of light is exhibited to an observer in a dark room and then extinguished and a second spot made to appear quickly a short distance from the location of the first, the light will seem to move in the direction of the second dot. The psychological effect is well known, and it is utilized in producing "motion" pictures and in such public displays as the news strip that moves around the New York Times Building. All our judgments about motion rest upon our abilities to discriminate the successive positions of an object. And position is, of course, a matter of relations. By the location of an object we mean that the

[3] Kurt Koffka, *Principles of Gestalt Psychology*. New York: Harcourt, Brace and Company, Inc., 1935, pp. 286–288.

object has a spatial relation with some aspect of its environment; it rests at a certain distance from a datum point. A second position means that the same object exists at some other measurable distance from the same datum. When one of these space constellations follows the other by an interval of time, that is, when they are perceived to be organized in a temporal dimension, the inference of movement is the result. This must be so whether the observation is continuous or discontinuous; whether we observe the passage of an automobile from one point to another or see it parked in one place today and another place tomorrow. In neither case is the translation itself a sensory fact; like other relations, motion has no external referent. In this instance, however, the relationship factor is not a simple one. It is not only the product of a relation between relations; it is also an integration of a "thing" in two dimensions.

It is obvious that motion, like other relations, cannot be discerned as long as the configuration of which it is a part is an integrated totality. It becomes manifest only under conditions that enable us to analyze the two-positional, time-spaced phenomenon that it binds together. There are many occasions when such a direct sensory reduction of a whole is impossible. When the time interval between the two positions is short enough, as in molecular and submolecular phenomena, there can be no conclusion of movement; and the resulting time-space configuration is sensed as an undifferentiated whole. Under these conditions time is translated into space; a temporal-spatial phenomenon becomes merely an element all parts of which are simultaneously distributed in space.

We can experimentally synthesize time-space wholes in some instances, and in others we can ascertain their character by indirect methods. When two points of light appear a short distance apart in quick succession, they are not seen as two points. Neither is there a moving thing. Instead there is a motionless *streak;* and we speak of "it," not "them," for we sense a unitary phenomenon with none of the whole characteristics of a point. Similarly, when something unexpectedly flashes across our visual field, the dark band that we sense may be taken to be a bird in flight; but the experience itself cannot tell us this. There can be nothing in common between the two sensory experiences, and we can translate one into the other only on other evidence and by inference from it.

When the conditions are such that we can discriminate between the two positions of an object, that is, when we can analyze both the time and the space configurations, the impression is that movement has taken place. Then the qualities of the moving object are distinct from the qualities of its supraordinate whole. We train our sense organs in techniques to accomplish the reduction of many of our common experiences precisely for the purpose of discovering the nature of their subordinate units. One method, so habitual that it is difficult to resist the urge to follow it, is to move our eyes along certain planes across the dynamic field of our vision. This "stops" the movement of objects that are moving in the same plane and at correlative rates, and we can fixate them and analyze them. This is the only direct way in which we can identify them. Experience and probability can provide a basis for guessing, but only by a secondary process. The act of visually fixating a moving object stabilizes the relations between the eye and the object, and in so doing the larger environmental configuration of which it was a part is disintegrated. One over-all configuration becomes two in space with a time relation between them; the result is an object plus that combination of relations called motion. This is what happens when we actually discern a bird in flight or an automobile speeding past us on the street. It also occurs when we read the letters in the moving strip on the Times Building and follow the sequences of a motion picture, as we noted above.

There are many other relations in addition to time and space that regularly enter into the process of organizing configurations. Among them may be listed the functional, the comparative, the causal, the genetic, the ordinal, the predicative, the symbolic, and the proportional, to mention only a few of the more inclusive categories. Although these relations do not at first thought seem so inescapable as the categories of time and space, they do in fact canalize our thinking in the same imperious fashion. Thus, when any two events fall under our attention, not only do we take cognizance of the time or space interval between them; it is also extremely difficult for us not to regard one of them as preceding the other, that is, to rate one as appearing first and the other second. Similarly, in attending to some object it is almost impossible for us not to think "about" it, which means to predicate or affirm some quality or condition of it. Likewise, if we concentrate upon the figure A——B————C, it is difficult not to think of AB either as a part of—that is, belonging to—AC or as standing in some proportional or comparative relation to it.

These relations serve to organize perspectives across the universe of our experience, each order of relationship being analogous to a plane or a dimension within which a characteristic analysis of the total dynamic mass can be made. The planes may intersect, or the same sets of data may be viewed in more than one dimension and the two perspectives correlated or harmonized. Some relations are more suitable for projection upon another dimension than are others. Thus, it is easy and customary to project causal and ordinal relations upon a temporal framework. Likewise it is easy to project the causal upon the ordinal. In other words, a cause is separated in time from its effect, a first event is separated by a time interval from a second event, and an effect turns out to be second to its cause. These are not identities. The concept of first has nothing intrinsically to do with the concept of duration.

Configurations that are organized in any of these dimensions have the same characteristics as those in time and space. In all of them the relations seem to inhere in the very nature of the things themselves, whereas they are actually intrinsic to the nature of our conception of them. One of two things viewed in the causal dimension must be the cause of the other, or they are unrelated; viewed comparatively, one must be larger, smaller, or equivalent to the other, or it is impossible to think of them at once. The relation inheres in the concept of the thing itself, just as is the case with the mental activities stimulated by objects. The concept of one person as an ancestor inevitably— by definition, we say—involves the conception of another as a descendant. The idea of one thing being darker necessarily implies that another is lighter. The thing, conceived in a given dimension, carries its relation with it as an essential attribute of the thought of it.

Nontemporal and nonspatial configurations are apprehended directly as undifferentiated wholes even though they can be analyzed. It is because of this that we can think of them as a fact, or a situation, or an event, that is, in unitary concepts. To state that one man killed another is to state a single undivided fact; and it will be treated as such in any further thinking that we give the matter—which is to say, in the process of our synthesizing it into more inclusive configurations. Regarded as an event, it is a singular phenomenon, not a pluralistic conjunction. The "details" of the event—that is, its component activities—may be realized upon breaking the total idea down, and they may even enrich it from the beginning; but at the moment of conceiving it as a whole, the characteristics of these postanalytical elements are dissipated.

The whole nature of these configurations is further indicated by the way in which we define them. The terms that we employ are, so to speak, transitive. Even though they point to one member of a pair of components, they necessarily imply the other. They do not describe either member but rather the total situation. Even though we say that one man is the father of another, this statement does not describe either of the men; and it implies something more than the genetic relation between them because it includes both of them. The same is true of the concept that one thing is larger than, superior to, dependent upon, or inclusive of another thing. The nature of the whole or the shape of the configuration is thereby described, but its components are not. Any number of diverse activities can be fitted into the same shape, and one pair may therefore be substituted for another without altering it.

Finally the whole character of these configurations, like those of time and space, is shown by the fact that their attributes are not the attributes of their parts. A stone cast against a window pane will cause the latter to break. That event has none of the characteristics of the moving stone or the shattered pane. It is neither. A description, no matter how detailed, of either action will yield no knowledge of the event as such. There still remains two discrete actions and their connection. Treated as an integrated whole, however, the event loses the traits of its parts and takes on its own unique characteristics that diffuse over the entire unit. The total event, for example, cannot be described in terms of its motion, for it has none; it has time-space coordinates that are different from its components; it can be compared with and set in relation to other events; and it has characteristics, such as instantaneity, that do not belong to its parts. The same may be said of other wholes, such as sentences. The syntax of a sentence is its analyzed shape, and different rules of organization produce different shapes. Moreover, as we all know, a complete sentence comprehended as a unit is something quite different from the meaning of its individual words and is independent of their relative positions. As a whole it produces an order of meaning that cannot be drawn out of an understanding of its word parts or their relations to each other. This fact has led some linguists to assert that nothing less than a sentence can convey a whole thought.

With regard to these configurations it should also be emphasized that we have not departed from the previous definition of a thing. A configuration in the causal or the genetic dimension is a mental activity quite as much as a thing is. The thought that we call "stone" is a unitary activity. The thought that we analytically describe as a "stone-cast-at-window" is also a unitary activity on a more inclusive level. Likewise for the thought "window" and "shattered-pane." Finally, the event which our verbal requirements force us to analyze descriptively as "stone-cast-at-window-shatters-pane" is also a unitary mental activity. It is not easy to establish this point by discussion because the very use of language militates against an appreciation of the concept. If our language contained words for "stone-cast-at-window" and "stone-cast-at-window-shatters-pane," it would be much easier to discuss the subject, and a more accurate characterization of the mental processes that words designate would be available. Perhaps we can agree nevertheless that any event, no matter how complex it becomes upon analysis, is, at the moment of thinking it, the simple undivided experience that is here called a mental activity or configuration.

It may seem to some readers that, these parallels between object configurations and others notwithstanding, there remains the obstinate fact that a thing is in a class by itself simply because it is patently and undeniably in one piece. It is very easy to shake the confidence of anyone who rests his objection upon this argument by asking him to look about his room and enumerate the number of discrete objects in it, but we shall apply ourselves to this question later on. We can meet the objection on other grounds by recalling that our impression of oneness comes from the incapacity of our senses further to reduce an object into parts. Our unaided senses are unable to discriminate activity systems that are operating at submolecular velocities. This limitation, however, is not peculiar to object configurations. It is characteristic of all.

In every configuration there is a threshold below which we cannot directly resolve it into its component activities and their relations. There is, for example, a limit to our ability to dissect the event which we grossly analyze into a cause and an effect. These alleged parts are but the conceptual extremes of what turns out to be a continuum upon closer inspection. For when or where does the cause end and the effect begin? At their conjunction they merge and become indistinguishable, just as two welded metals, separated by a clear line of demarcation to the unaided eye, appear to fuse and intermingle their boundary elements under the microscope. Similarly so for genetic configurations: When or where does the procreator end and the progeny begin? When does the ancestor of a living form cease to be an ancestor and become a descendant? The progeny in some form must be contained within and co-exist with its begetter. At what point are they distinct? The question likewise arises for the predicative relationship: When does a thing cease to be its own self-contained whole entity and become the attribute, appositive, or adjunct asserted of it? Also there is an obvious limit beyond which we are unable to distinguish the first of two events from the second and where the two so segregated become one. And with respect to time intervals we have already seen that the impression of simultaneity is a relative matter.

All configurations, therefore, turn out to be in one piece. In all cases there is a point beyond which closer scrutiny only serves to disclose their ultimate indissolubility. At this threshold two things leap abruptly into another plane and become one. The unit as such is not reportable in terms of its components any more than the sensory experience of a stone is reportable in terms of atoms. As has been said with respect to time and space, the "parts" of a configuration at the moment of their apperception must be coexistent and coterminous, which means that they lose their characteristic qualities and a new form with its qualities exists.

The expression "the whole is not equal to the sum of its parts" has frequently been used to convey the idea of this *de novo* characteristic of a configuration. It will serve well enough as long as it is appreciated that the leap into a new level of integration does not in any way involve the question of addition, subtraction, or division. Configured wholes are, we may say, "made up" of parts. But no amount of adding increments to or subtracting bits from elements will ever add up to the attributes of a totality. The problem is not a quantitative one. It is a matter of relations.

There is no doubt, however, about the truth that the expression intends to assert. Its reality is a matter of everyday experience. If we take the letters *o*, *w*, and *n* and combine them in that sequence, we get a configuration (own) that has a meaning entirely distinct from the three separate unities. Further, if we combine them in the order "won," a new configuration results which is distinct from "own" and also from a third combination, "now." The elements remain the same; their several "sums" are entirely distinct. There is nothing about the appearance of the word "now" that remotely suggests the word "own." It does, in fact, require some conscious trial-and-error manipulation of the elements of a word to work out a simple demonstration of this kind. We see each word as a whole and hence as unrelated to another word which contains the same elements.

Artists rely upon our mental capacities to integrate spontaneously experiences on levels qualitatively different from the substrata of those experiences. They aim at conveying an impression of the total composition, but the observer must play his part by employing some viewing technique to obscure the parts. He must stand back or half close his eyes before the total figure or scene can be comprehended. This is especially true of the works of the "impressionists," and more particularly of Monet and his followers. They insisted that the mind of the observer perform its composing function to its own taste. They attempted a prismatic decomposition of light with their touches of paint and expected the observer to recompose them in the whole view. When this is accomplished, the discrete daubs of paint disappear; and a total shimmering pattern emerges. And the suddenness and the unexpectedness with which this happens is the psychological expression of the discontinuity that occurs between the sums of parts and the whole that exists on another qualitative level.

It should be apparent that when we speak of relations, we refer to those that an individual finds between the subwholes of his experience and not those that someone analyzing his thinking processes might discover. We are attempting to formulate relations of the latter order, using the former; but the two must not be confused as they not infrequently have been by some psychologists. In the mind of the person who contemplates a dog chasing a cat, the mental activity which we label "dog" is *for him* related to the activity we label "cat" by a relation which can be called "follows," "causes to run," or whatever he takes to be the connection between the two objects crossing the field of his vision. The entire activity takes place, of course, in his nervous tissues; but the relation which he envisages between its parts is attributed to the objects outside it. Obviously this is not the same as the relations between his thought sequences. It is possible for him to analyze this internal system by introspection, in which case he is thinking about his thoughts as such and not about dogs and cats. This also is what an experimenter who is using him as a subject does. The relations which the experimenter finds to exist between one of his subject's thoughts and another are quite different from the relations that the subject finds between the objects of which he is thinking.

It is because of this distinction that it is possible to conceive of configurations which are, when analyzed, made up of relations between relations. This possibility exists because a relation, when it is thought about, is an activity. Thus, I can think "causality." I can also think "time interval." And finally, I can think of relations between these two concepts, and configurations defining my views on this subject will emerge. These configurations in turn can be configured on more inclusive levels until an abstract pyramid results, culminating in a final bracketing of all in a single comprehensive definition of relations. This, in fact, is what has happened.

When the distinction between the mind of the subject and that of his observer is appreciated, it is also possible to understand that there can be configurations integrated about the relation of unrelatedness. There is no doubt that I can think of such combinations of ideas as "horse-treasury," "man-pond," and "uncle-universe." To the extent of my awareness the members of these pairs are unrelated. I have been able to put them together only by a deliberate effort to avoid a previously experienced connection. I have invented the combinations. At first such combinations are unstable; but as they become familiar, they can acquire a unity with whole qualities which transcend their meaningless duality. In this way the concept "man-pond" can emerge with no obligations to its antecedents. A configuration is formed with attributes and potentialities of its own. To the critic who objects that the ideas of "man" and "pond" do have a relationship nonetheless because they coexist in my mind, or because the one follows the other when I say them, it should suffice to point out that these are relationships that exist in his mind by which he links together my thoughts and not men and ponds. Or, from an introspective standpoint, my thought of "man" is not the same as my thinking about the "thought of man." The one is a response to an object and the other is a response to this response. In short, it is possible to think about things, and it is also possible to think about thinking things.

We have seen that not only objects but the submolecular activity systems within objects have shapes. They are referred to as the qualities of the thing, such as its color, temperature, hardness, and so on, depending upon which sensory adapter is capable of translating them. These whole properties appear to us to be both static and inherent in the thing because our senses are incapable of breaking down the minute systems and factoring out the time-space relationships that exist between the atomic parts. Since what we call qualities and their apparent static character are wholly dependent upon the limitations of our sensory apparatus, we should be prepared to find that there are more directly perceivable and less stable activity systems that do not differ fundamentally from the submicroscopic configurations that we treat as objects. In particular, we should expect to find the following to be true: First, that while grosser activity systems have shapes and other whole qualities analogous to those of atomic configurations, they should not be expected to be identical with "things." Secondly, that velocities of all magnitudes may characterize the movement of the parts of these larger systems; that the threshold for the discrimination of motion marks the point at which such configurations may be directly decomposed; and that there are configurations at the opposite extreme from the atomic wherein the motion of the parts is so slow that it can readily be factored out and the whole quality of the configuration dissipated. And, finally, we should be prepared to find these gross activity systems united into even more inclusive configurations with shape aspects that are analogous to the forms of objects.

Configurations do exist on all these levels. Some of the most interesting are those the whole properties of which can be demonstrated to be derived from the motion of their components. The streaks that flash across our visual field and which we later discover to have been "caused" by some object cast through the line of our regard belong in this category. Configurations of this sort are so fleeting that their qualities are not easy to define. There are many others, however, which can be controlled and made to persist. This is especially true of rotary motion, wherein the total action can be kept in view. Rapidly spinning propeller blades, spoked wheels, and perforated disks each have their own characteristic shapes and other whole qualities which are entirely distinct from the properties of the motionless objects. The same can be said of rapidly vibrating objects, such as strings and staves. At a more inclusive level of integration the combination of a large number of such discrete activity systems under controlled conditions produces still other shapes. When a breeze sweeps across a field of grain, the individual stalks sway to the pressure; and each of their movements constitutes a configuration. But in this instance many individual activity systems act in unison, with the result that their individuality is lost; and a new configuration appears as a wave or undulation in the mass of grain.

The integration of observable activity systems into large unstable wholes is not confined to visual phenomena. When a file is drawn lightly but rapidly across the surface of the finger, it becomes something quite distinct from the series of ridges that define it when it is at rest. When an oscillating member, such as a string or a vibrating steam pipe, is touched, its qualities-at-rest cannot be sensed; and when the motion is vigorous and sustained, as it is with an air drill or a riveter, the periphery of the activity takes on the aspect of a surface that has contours and hardness in the same way that the surface of an object has these qualities. Similarly so with auditory phenomena. If a card is held against a slowly rotating cogged wheel, a series of distinct clicks will be heard. But when the rotation of the wheel is speeded up, the individuality of these activity systems becomes lost; and a new whole, sounding like a buzz, is the result.

Finally at the other extreme, there are the numerous everyday configurations that depend upon the action of some object but do not seem to have any shape or whole aspects at all. This category would include all our voluntary body motions and the motions of things that we control as a result of them. Thus walking, bowing, and saluting are configurations involving parts of our bodies, an action, and a datum of reference. Each act can be analyzed into smaller wholes or incorporated into larger units. The time-space relations of one-foot-to-the-floor may be a unit of analysis; or the relations of the two legs to each other (the configurations of standing still or walking) may be; or the larger unit of a person and his relation to an entire room (as in moving across it) may be. In short, any act or any combination of acts can form a configuration. Hence, a ritual, a football "play," or a behavior set within either can be so regarded—and are when we call them "patterns" or "types."

This discussion of the nature of a configuration does not provide any criterion by which a whole can be identified, nor does it afford any basis for establishing its limits or contours. Indeed, the effect of robbing "things" of a special place in nature may be quite the reverse. If a continuous boundary cannot be relied upon for the definition of a unit of experience, and if, furthermore, wholes are always subject to decomposition into lesser wholes, often simply by a shift of attention, it does not seem that much is left of stability in the world that we must think of as stable if we are to cope with it realistically. And with the world of things stripped of qualities which impart to it a persistent, detached status, independent of individual point of view, we might seem to have lost the vantage point of objectivity which permits each of us to arrive at the same conclusions about it. Lacking this assurance, we might seem to be on the verge of resting the case on subjective judgments and thus abandoning an essential of scientific procedure.

The need for a common frame of reference and for common tools with which to operate is certainly imperative; but it cannot be said that the acceptance of the notion of a configuration requires the abandonment of a common basis for understanding. Indeed, there is no necessary connection between the two situations. Configurations as they have been described merely define more precisely the nature of our experience. If we find that the consequences and implications are less satisfying than we had supposed, that is the fault of our manner of experiencing, not of the definition. If the latter leads us to discover discrepancies and ambiguities in the former, that discovery, at least, is a step forward. Practically, we can spare ourselves some illusions and the embarrassments that hinge upon them. It may be possible, moreover, by attending to the nature of configurations, to find a more adequate expression of what is real and unvarying.

In any event we can be no worse off than we are now. It is instructive to reflect upon the confidence we place in the unimpeachable status of "facts" and "things" in the face of daily demonstrations that we cannot agree on what they are. We have developed certain operational techniques, such as systems of measure and logic, which reduce the areas of disagreement— which means that we constrain and conventionalize the possible points of view—and abet our delusion that there is something "out there" which is true and real regardless of whether anyone can or does know it or not. We are loath to admit that there are no facts or things, but only interpretations, each one of which is as real and true as any other and beyond which exists no basis for an evaluation of their truth and validity. All who have given thought to the question of the validity of evidence based upon eye-witness accounts must have doubts about the existence of "pure" facts; and anyone who systematically attempts to name, describe, or enumerate the things on his desk or in his pocket will find his confidence in approaching the task receding proportionately with his application to it. The word "thing" is extremely useful, but it is not conducive to clear thinking. It invites the opposite.

The idea of a configuration deserves the same distrust unless it can escape the ambiguities of the "thing" idea. In order to establish a basis for sounder procedure, it is necessary to answer the practical question: How do we know when a phenomenon is a configuration? What qualities does it have by which each of us can independently distinguish it, delimit it, and set it off for common discussion?

It is doubtful that this question can be answered at the present time to the satisfaction of everyone. Those who expect some new formula for describing configurations as if they existed "out there" beyond ourselves will certainly be disappointed. There does not seem to be any way of arriving at an acceptable definition in these terms, which are generally called objective. On the other hand, if we accept the thesis that a thing or a configuration is an idea, there is no reason why we cannot regard our ideas objectively. It does not matter that we cannot directly know the thoughts of another person. It is sufficient that we can compare the impressions of our respective thoughts as they take shape under a common stimulus set. With sufficient exploration of and experimentation with these impressions, we should be able to come to an understanding upon the characteristics of a whole thought or configuration. The gestalt psychologists have given considerable attention to this problem, and some of their conclusions call for notice at this point.

One recognizable characteristic of a configuration is its whole quality. This means that it is homogeneous and without parts. It has no disjunctions, inequalities, partitions or other internal structuring. Every quality that it has pervades all of it; the entire unit is blue, rough, or higher than something else. This much has been said already about a configuration, and more could be. Further exposition, however, is likely to become a purely verbalistic exercise; for it would tend to put the matter on an intellectual level, where it does not belong. It must be stressed that a whole is an experience, and any attempt to give a word picture of it inevitably destroys some of its immediately given characteristics. In large measure completeness rests upon conviction. Few of us in adult life will find ourselves without the concept of a whole and a high degree of assurance that we know one when we experience it. A definition in terms of this attitude is, therefore, probably as communicative of the meaning intended and as valid as any other.

A phenomenon, then, is a configuration when and as long as it is regarded as a whole. There is no doubt that we can be aware of incomplete wholes, sometimes acutely. All of us have had the experience of seeing something and realizing that a part of it is missing although we may not know what. Many times a familiar object appears unaccountably strange or ludicrous because it is somehow "not all there." Often, too, we may realize immediately what the missing part is, as we would in the case of a man who is fully dressed except for a tie. Sometimes a more or less successful search must be made before the answer appears, as happens when we probe our memory to recall the third of three things we were to remember to do. In any case there is a feeling of incompleteness and along with it an emotional disturbance that we can characterize as dissatisfaction in varying degrees of intensity. If we are able in some fashion to bring the configuration to its total realization, our tension relaxes.

Among the many experiments which Bartlett conducted in his work on recall there were some which involved the use of a series of figures which were designed to build up certain preconceived structures by their successive presentations to his subjects. After the first few figures the observers began to sense that the design was developing toward a certain end; they "felt" or "got the impression" that a pattern was building up, and with varying degrees of confidence they felt that they knew where it was trending. The final figures always brought a sense of equilibrium and relief. Of this Bartlett says: "Something that must be called 'an impression of completeness'—or even of 'rightness'—seemed to spread over the whole perceptual situation, setting the attitude of the subject into one of ease and finality. I think that this may have important consequences for many a process of learning and in many a case of recall also." [4]

The gestaltists have developed the concept of "closure" to account for the psychological straining toward the completion of a configuration. According to this view, the presentation of a part of a configuration, either in perceptual situations or in recall, sets up a physiopsychological field of tensions and stresses which seeks equilibrium through supplementation by the missing part. When this missing part is realized, the gestalt is closed; and the subject thereupon experiences a relaxation of the tensions that were occasioned by the incompleted process.

Ellis illustrates the meaning of closure in what I have called the comparative dimension by describing what happens when we judge the weights of two objects like a salt and pepper shaker. He notes that we do not first make an absolute estimate of the weight of the pepper shaker and then compare it with a second absolute judgment of the weight of the salt shaker. Instead, the pepper shaker's weight (kinesthetically) is merely an item that "pulls

[4] F. C. Bartlett, *Remembering. A Study in Experimental and Social Psychology.* New York: Cambridge University Press, 1932, p. 25.

over, stretches toward the coming experience of lifting the salt shaker. Instantly the salt shaker is taken up its place in the whole 'pepper-and-salt-heavier-or-lighter-than' is fixed."[5] Similarly so for the significance of any other perceived object. The object has the particular meaning that it does only when it fills a gap in a particular configuration. Thus, writes Ellis,[6]

A post is a sign post insofar as a given context or whole determines its nature as experienced. This is the sense in which a symbol may be called a "part" closing a gestalt previously unclosed. The gestalt "desire-post-city" is phenomenally (*i.e.,* subjectively) pre-present in crudely general form in the sense that desiring to reach the city presumes some subjective forecast of what and where the city is and what sort of things (*e.g.* sign posts) would presage its attainment. Perception of a sign post under these circumstances is, therefore, perception of a *sign post* as such. Hence we speak of the perception as "closing" the gestalt lying ready for it just as perception of the second shaker is a gestalt-closing perception, *viz.,* the perception which closes the gestalt "judgment of heavier-than."

The gestalt explanation is applicable in other dimensions and levels of integration. Not only do parts of words, phrases, and sentences initiate stresses that call for the completion of their respective wholes; sentences and groups of sentences also set up states of disequilibrium that persist as psychological tensions until the parts that they imply are forthcoming. Any ordered thinking is a fulfillment of such shapes. "From idea to idea there is a certain stretch relative to the whole context under consideration. Relative to such context, ideas are surely not independent units but can be discriminated only post-analytically and in abstraction."[7] Questions are definitely of this character. They "arouse configurational processes which are incomplete and call for closure."[8]

The compulsion that we feel toward the attainment of an established goal or the completion of a task can also be attributed to the operation of a dynamic set of forces seeking a state of equilibrium. To appreciate this tension it is necessary to view the idea of the self as a part of configurations which include ideas of behaviors, the whole self-behavior concept constituting a unit that must issue to completion to discharge the tensions that are set up by the appearance of any part of it. Köhler calls attention to the common experience of "something like a dark pressure somewhere in the field" of our consciousness all the while that we put off doing some accepted task. He refers to certain experiments made by Lewin and Zeigarnik wherein subjects were given a series of short problems to solve. In approximately half

[5] W. D. Ellis, *Gestalt Psychology and Meaning.* Berkeley, Calif.: Sather Gate Book Shop, 1930, pp. 62–63.

[6] *Ibid.*

[7] *Ibid.,* p. 110.

[8] Harry Helson, "The Psychology of Gestalt," *American Journal of Psychology,* 1926, 37 (No. 1):54.

the cases the subject was interrupted by the experimenter before he had completed his assigned task. At the end of the entire series he was asked to name the problems that had been given to him. The tasks that were recalled first were those that had been interrupted, and the total number remembered in this category was much greater than the number of finished tasks recalled. Köhler concludes that the most plausible explanation for this is that a stress is set up by the acceptance of a problem and that this stress does not disappear until the solution is effected or the memory of the problem fades.[9]

A configuration, then, has the attribute of completeness which is directly knowable. Another of its attributes is shape. This is a corollary of the fact that units are homogeneous. Where homogeneity—which is not to be confused with blankness—ends, a thing ends, there is a discontinuity of some kind, and another form begins. This statement does not mean that form is equivalent to area. It may or may not be. It means only that the entire range of possible combinations of elements within a given dimension is not covered by any single configuration. There are always components and noncomponents. Each unit is a constellation of activities the extent of which, since they do not coincide, must give a definite distribution to a whole. Each possible arrangement gives a different shape.

This is one particular aspect of the more general fact that configurations give us the impression of being detached from their surroundings. If a phenomenon fails to evoke the experience of distinctness, it is not a whole. Properly understood, the word "boundaries" can be employed to indicate the impression of detachment, but its application must not be restricted to objects only. Thus a musical note, or a score, has boundaries in the sense that it exists only within a certain range of vibrations beyond which are other notes or a monotonous continuum. So does any complete idea that embodies a configuration in any modality; it is complete because it is discontinuous with the ideational set that precedes, coexists, or follows it. It is, in gestalt terminology, a "segregated whole," and it bears the impress of distinctness on the face of it.

Another particular aspect of segregation in addition to shape is what might be called the protrusion or elevation of a configuration out of its environment. Its homogeneous properties tend to lift it away from its equally homogeneous background. In consequence a segregated whole carries the impression of being solid and cohesive by contrast with its surroundings. This is true even though the configuration itself has vague or shifting boundaries. The "thing," whatever its components or modality, looms out of a background of the nonthing. Figure 10, taken from Köhler, will illustrate the significance of this distinction.

[9] Wolfgang Köhler, *Gestalt Psychology*. New York: Liveright Publishing Corp., 1929, pp. 329–332.

It is possible to see the complex of lines contained in the square as embodying two entirely distinct configurations. In one case a cross like a four-bladed propeller with pointed tips can be seen. As long as this organization of the visual field can be maintained, the rest of the area within the square outline is a blank space upon which the cross seems to rest. Another organization is possible, however. When this develops, the propeller-cross dissolves into background, and the area that previously was blank space now protrudes as a solid figure with the outlines of the heraldic cross patté. The psychological effect of this transformation of the same sensory field is striking, and it illustrates very well the difference between a given complex of stimulations being a thing and a nonthing. It will be noticed that the two possibilities cannot materialize at the same time. Both of them cannot be things at once, and one is a thing only because of the presence of the other. Rubin was the first to describe the relief aspect of a segregated whole. To denote the contrast, he applied the expressive terms "figure" and "ground."

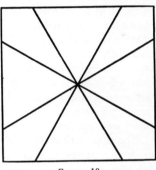

FIGURE 10

The preceding example of a transformation from figure to ground will also serve to open a discussion regarding the conditions under which a whole will appear to have the qualities of completeness, shape, and relief. In other words, if a whole is a vacillating entity, when or why does it appear stable? The answer seems to be that it is a whole only when it is regarded as a subunit in a more inclusive configuration. In practical terms this means that the moment we fix our attention upon a thing, its unity dissolves under an analytic process that is automatic with the attitude of close inspection. The result is always two homogeneous subwholes bound by a relation. With respect to the quality of relief, the figure is one subwhole and the ground is the other; both are homogeneous, but they are connected by a relation which, by the very fact that it is a connection, sets them apart. The only circumstances under which this condition can prevail is when the observer's regard is fixed upon one subwhole-in-relation and not upon either of the two subwholes exclusively. For the moment that a shift takes place that fixates one of the subwholes, its external relation to the other disappears; and it becomes itself a compound of two subwholes with an internal relation between them. This is why relations inhere in the ideas of things.

We express these facts when we say that a thing can have meaning only with reference to some context; that is, some other component in a larger universe. The larger universe is implicit in the definition of a thing although it is largely ignored as a conscious element. We may suppose that we are viewing a thing in isolation, but doing so is never possible because only the data of reference can impart whole qualities to an observed thing. In analyzing a thing by fixating a part of it, we may presume that we are perceiving a unit by itself; but in reality we have shifted the frame of reference as a necessary concomitant of apprehending the lesser unit. A thing must be a whole-in-relation-to-something-else, which means that it is at once a part of a more inclusive configuration. Paradoxically, a whole is such only when it is a part of a greater whole.

The question of levels of organization turns out to be very much a matter of point of regard. A pencil can be a whole only so long as it is regarded in terms of its relation to something else, the top of a desk, for instance. When the "lying-on-the-desk" aspect of the situation is eliminated by a focus of attention on the pencil, it is no longer a pencil but a compound of "eraser-on-a-shaft," "lead-in-a-shaft," "point-at-the-end-of-a-straight-shaft," and so on in a variety of combinations, none of which gives any sensory report of a total pencil. We may "remember" that it is a pencil; but doing so is an interpretation, not a sensory fact. Likewise, a pencil and an inkstand can form a whole with respect to the desk top; but while they do, there is no pencil *and* inkstand.

The characterless aspect of the ground element is, therefore, not peculiar to it; that is one measure of its whole quality. Its recessive aspect is a function of the mutually repellent processes of cohesion within the figure and the ground units. The total field is polarized: its positive component, the figure, is such because the relationship factor is viewed as being contained within it; the negative component, the ground, is withdrawn because it is the datum of reference. Its passive role tends to eliminate it from conscious recognition, hence also to eliminate the larger configuration of which it is a component. All wholes are viewed in this axial perspective; they are the positive poles of larger entities.

A fundamental question comes at this point; namely, Can the ideas of any two things be organized into a configuration? The gestalt psychologists have taken issue with the traditional theories of association on this question. Proponents of the view that mental connections are established between the things of our experience simply because they have been observed in association do, by implication at least, accept the conclusion that any fortuitous combination of things can form a unit. According to this theory, things become associated because they have occurred together in the past, or because they are similar, or for other reasons; and the strength of the connection between them varies with a number of circumstances. Whatever the nature of the association, the bond is established through familiarity with a particular combination. "The organized character of sensuous data is the product of previous experience." [10] If in the past two things have not been associated, they need not be considered so when they are presented in the same sensory field; and the thought of one will not recall the thought of the other. The intrinsic character of stimuli has no bearing on whether they become connected. Furthermore, once a bond has been established by experience, the unit that is thus formed will impose itself upon subsequent presentations of an indifferent set of stimuli. "Past experience transforms the sensuous data by suppression and supplementation." [11]

The gestalt psychologists reject this theory of unification on both counts. Wholes exist, they assert, irrespective of past experience and often in contravention of it; and the past is ineffective in ordering the immediate data of a sensory field. They do not deny, of course, that experience plays a part in mental operations; but they do insist that the memory of it has no power to arrange incoming stimuli. The forces of organization are inherent in the immediate situation. The experience of a segregated whole is due to an actual physiological process in the observer. It is not due to a memorized unification of stimuli into wholes that project themselves on the sensory receptors. There are relations between the millions of minute excitations coming from things "out there," relations such as contiguity, similarity, and inequality; but "organization in the sensory field is something which originates as a characteristic achievement of the nervous system." [12] The field presents a mass of stimuli that are dynamically interrelated by actual forces of mutual attractions and repulsions. Some areas of the field are dominated by forces of cohesion between their respective elements and at the same time by collective repulsions toward each other. This patterning of the sensory field as a result of the dynamic adjustments that are necessary consequents of the perception of it gives rise to the bounded regions that we call things or configurations.

The gestaltists take this stand on the conviction that the organization process is not unique to mental phenomena. It inheres in other natural processes as well. Gestalts are evident in such biological processes as ontogenesis and in physical and chemical processes. [13] Köhler writes, [14]

Take as an example the contact of oil and water. Here interaction is so strong that the form of the surface is determined by it; but this surface as such remains a sharp boundary and the drop of oil remains detached from the water by those same molecular forces which, at the same time, mold the form of the drop. I shall

[10] Harvey A. Carr, *Psychology. A Study of Mental Activity.* New York: Longmans, Green & Co., Inc., 1925, p. 112.

[11] *Ibid.,* p. 114.

[12] Köhler, *op. cit.,* p. 174. To give whole properties an external existence is to commit what Köhler calls the "experience error." *Ibid.,* p. 176.

[13] *Ibid.,* p. 194.

[14] *Ibid.,* pp. 143–144.

assume, then, that in optical processes, contours are preserved by similar forces of antagonistic contact, depending upon differences in the properties on the two sides of the contour.

According to the gestalt view the segregation of wholes, therefore, depends upon the characteristics of nervous activity and not upon experience. Köhler points to the undeniable fact that we can perceive well-defined shapes without recognizing them and even without ever having seen them before. All of us have made out forms through mist at a distance, or in half-light, which are utterly unfamiliar to us, not always because they are poorly delineated. Whether the outlines are distinct or not is a secondary consideration. As wholes they are different from their surroundings and segregated

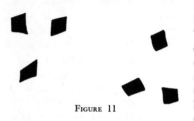

Figure 11

from other things around them. And the very fact that we can ask ourselves, "What is that?" indicates that they exist as sensory facts independent of our familiarity with them. As Köhler says, it will not do to attempt to explain the existence of an unknown form as being due to the generalized knowledge that in past experience a thing hangs together; because in the first place, the hanging-togetherness must exist in perception before experience can be drawn on for an explanation. Furthermore, many perceived units hang together despite the fact that, generalizing on the basis of past experience, they might just as well fall into different groupings. Thus, in Köhler's illustration (Figure 11) there are two distinct groups of spots. Yet on the basis of experience, there is as much reason to see them as six different things, for we know that six persons, flies, or other things can take such relative positions at one moment and disperse themselves widely at the next.[15]

For these and other reasons the gestalt psychologists maintain that forms are the primary data. Forms exist entirely independently of any meaning they might acquire. An object on my desk may not be a pencil to an illiterate primitive, but it is nonetheless a fully segregated unit from the instant it is perceived. Says Köhler,[16]

Such is the conception that *gestalt* psychology offers to defend. It even goes so far as to hold that it is precisely the original organization and segregation of circumscribed wholes which make it possible for the sensory world to appear so utterly imbued with meaning to the adult, because, in its gradual entrance into the sensory field, meaning follows the lines drawn by natural organization. It usually enters into segregated wholes.

[15] *Ibid.*, pp. 154–155.
[16] *Ibid.*, pp. 151–152.

From this point of view some constellations in the sensory field hang together automatically while other theoretically possible alignments do not. Some configurations are more "stable" or "better organized" than others. But, according to gestalt theory, this is not a matter of previous familiarity with them. The concept of better and worse configurations is embodied in the "law of prägnanz," which has been formulated by Koffka thus: "Psychological organization will always be as 'good' as the prevailing conditions allow." By "good" the gestaltists mean the full expression of a given characteristic or aspect. In general, those configurations that are more regular, simpler, or more symmetrical than others and those that are "closed" as opposed to those that are "broken" or "unclosed" are good figures.

Resort to these evaluative terms inevitably introduces the elements of subjectivity and relativity into the definition. The gestaltists therefore make no further attempt to elucidate them but turn directly to optical demonstrations of phenomena that are supposed to reveal immediately the meaning of the law. Thus, a figure such as C would not be a good shape because it is incomplete and unstable; it strives to become a circle. This arrangement of lines $\sim\!\!\sim$ violates the "law of good continuation" because it tends to be broken up by the formation of a series of circles. A circle is stable, not because it is a familiar object of our experience, but because it is inherently a good figure.

The gestaltists have been able to assemble a convincing array of evidence to demonstrate that sensory data manifest stresses toward certain configurations and not others. Their achievement is an important one. At the same time we need not agree that they have as yet proved one of the principal points of contention; namely, that experience is not a factor in ordering the reports of the senses. They and their opponents have conducted a great number of ingenious experiments that were designed, respectively, to support and controvert this thesis. On the face of it, each side has been more or less successful. In consequence the impartial observer is led to suspect that something has gone awry. He is likely to suspect that the source of the contradiction lies in the special requirements of their experiments, the unwitting acceptance of which misrepresents the problem. For all that has been shown by the controversy is that under certain conditions, which could be well defined, previous experience is a critical factor in determining what is perceived, and under other conditions it cannot be operative. The real problem is, therefore, to investigate these conditions.

It also appears that the gestaltists have not proved that chance or indiscriminate combinations of forms cannot be organized into real wholes, even though they have shown that some organizations are more spontaneous or take precedence over others. It is uncertain to what extent they have intended doing this; but they have criticized the associationists for assuming that wholes can be aggregates of "indifferent" material, and by their experiments they have demonstrated that in certain sensory fields some patterns are impossible. Again, however, it must be insisted that the real problem lies in defining the conditions under which this or that combination is possible.

Perhaps we should grant the important point that wholes are dependent upon the existence of internal cohesive forces, and that this has nothing to do with previous experience or unfamiliarity with them. Forms exist because of their own inherent properties; but this does not mean that a particular mass of stimuli can be configurated in only one way. A given sensory field is not set in one rigid and unalterable framework. It is kaleidoscopic in two ways. First, the same total aggregate of stimuli can be organized in more than one pattern; and second, any particular pattern can be broken down into lesser wholes. In all cases the patterns are necessary units as long as they are seen as such; but a reanalysis is always possible, and this can vary the character of a field. Furthermore, the *choice* of one of the possible patterns is frequently if not normally dependent upon familiarity, habit, or previous experience.

Many of the gestalt demonstrations themselves attest to these facts. Their many examples of ambiguous figures, such as that in Figure 10, are evidence enough that the same total field can be organized in different ways, each one as complete and stable as the other. In point of stimulation nothing·has changed; but with a change in the observer's mental posture, remarkable and sometimes startling transformations occur in the visual field. Transformations can also be experienced in other configurative dimensions, as is the case when the same set of sounds suddenly undergoes a transformation from one rhythmic pattern to another.

In such cases, where there is a vacillation between one configuration and another, it is quite probable that the absence of a stabilizing factor is independent of the character of the patterns themselves and is a function of our indifferent attitude toward them. We are without preference; either of the two arrangements is acceptable. Choice, however, is to a high degree dependent upon habit; and it is, therefore, extremely likely that habituation to one alternative to the prejudice of the other will in time result in a preemption of the field by the first to the total exclusion of the second. And, since it is probable that any aggregation of stimuli can be organized in more than one pattern, there is every reason to suppose that the view we take of our daily environment is simply the one alternative among several that has been settled upon by custom or habit.

This is the conclusion that has been drawn from some of the experiments set up to refute gestalt theory. Donahue and Griffitts, as a result of presenting a series of ambiguous figures to their subjects, concluded that the complexity of the patterns was a factor in the alternate perception of two possible organizations, but that familiarity with them was more important. The more familiar the two interpretations were to the observers, the more rapid was the rate of their fluctuation from one to the other, unless there was greater individual familiarity with one than the other, in which case there was a tendency toward stabilization.[17] Using very similar figures, other experimenters have also concluded that their subjects were able to fixate one interpretation for a longer time or more easily when it was less involved and when they were better acquainted with it from previous experience.[18] Each of us can, furthermore, demonstrate to our own satisfaction the stabilizing effect of habit in perception. If we make repeated efforts to see only one configuration in an ambiguous totality, as, for example, the propeller-like cross in Figure 10, it will be noted that the more accustomed to it we become, the more difficult it will be to bring about the mental shift that induces the alternate interpretation. It may be mentioned, too, that Rubin, whose work on figure and ground problems was well received by the gestalt psychologists, found a "figural aftereffect," which means that, once a subject has divided a field into figure and ground, he is likely to see it the same way when he is confronted with it again.

Köhler calls attention to the meaningless quality of outline maps and the utter strangeness of sea charts for the average person. This is indeed a matter of organization; but with maps, as with other ambiguous figures, the experience of meaning reveals the flexibility of the organizing factor and at the same time serves to show the importance of previous acquaintance in determining the selection of one interpretation over another. An outline map is "meaningless" when all that appears to our consciousness is some more or less sinuous lines on a blank page. In other words, the configuration that is present is *line*-on-page, line as figure, page as ground. But this configuration can be dissipated in an instant. It disintegrates when one line is seen in relation to another line, with the result that the area included between them becomes a whole with respect to the blank page. Now, this transformation may or may not eventually occur to a person who has never seen a map or a piece of paper with inked lines on it; but it will certainly occur readily to one who is familiar with the technique of map reading, and it is doubtful whether a cartographer would ever interpret the conventional markings known to his profession as anything save boundaries of land and sea areas. Similar observations hold for sea charts. To a person who is unaccustomed to their interpretation they may appear only as lines on a page; or if he is geographically minded, they may be composed into areal configurations with the cohesive units looking to him like unfamiliar land blocks. It

[17] W. T. Donahue and C. H. Griffitts, "The Influence of Complexity on the Fluctuations of the Illusions of Reversible Perspective," *American Journal of Psychology*, 1931, 43:613–617.

[18] M. F. Washburn, C. Reagan, and E. Thurston, "The Comparative Controllability of the Fluctuations of Simple and Complex Ambiguous Perspective Figures," *American Journal of Psychology*, 1934, 46:636–638.

is unlikely, however, that a sea captain would fall victim to this tricky metamorphosis of the figures of his profession into the ground of the land-lubber.

The existence of alternate modes of organizing the same sensory field and the establishment of a priority of one interpretation through habit indicates one way in which previous experience can affect the perception of wholes. It can also have an effect when more inclusive wholes are dissipated in favor of their components. This is the point at which the gestaltists are likely to enter a vigorous objection, for they have been at some pains to demonstrate that past experience is an ineffectual tool for the analysis of stable configurations. In so far as they mean by this that experience is powerless to organize the data they have presented experimentally, they are probably right. But they have adopted the inadmissible tactic of cutting the cloth to suit their needs and so have accomplished not what was intended but something else. They have set the requirement that previous experience be automatically effective in disorganizing a presented configuration; and yet they have so designed their experiments that, according to the rules of gestalt, this result is impossible. In addition they have further prejudiced the issue by eliminating the factors which would be conducive to bringing the results of experience to bear upon the situation. Obviously this procedure does not prove that familiarity with a given figure has no effect whatever upon the character of a perception. It means only that under the conditions imposed by the experiment this is true.

In order to establish their contention the gestalt psychologists have relied to a great extent upon the difficulty that observers have in voluntarily discovering hidden figures. Gottschaldt performed one of the best known of these experiments.[19] His method was to show his subjects a series of simple geometric figures several times and then later to expose another series of more complex figures which contained the earlier simple figures. No intimation was given that there was any connection between the two showings; the subjects were asked simply to give a description of the members of the second series. In the first trial the simple figures were exposed only three times; in a second trial with new subjects they were repeated 520 times. In both instances the results were practically the same. In over 90 per cent of the individual cases the subjects failed to detect the simple figures contained in the complex ones. The conclusion was that familiarity with a given form in itself has no appreciable effect upon its apprehension when it is geometrically embodied in a whole that is stablized by its own forces of integration. This is no doubt true, and it really needs nothing more than the proof of everyday experience to establish it. What is called for, then, is an elucida-

---

[19] Cited and discussed by Koffka, *op. cit.*, pp. 155*ff*.

tion of the circumstances which explain the conclusion, rather than an unconditional denial of effects being due to previous acquaintance.

The explanation given for our inability actually to see hidden figures, even when we know that they are present, is that the total configuration before us is well organized; or, stated from an analytic viewpoint, the contained figure is absorbed in its environment. Something is to be gained, however, by an exposition of just what is involved in this matter of absorption. It takes place, of course, when the contained figure does not exist perceptually as a discrete whole; but there are two aspects to the difficulty encountered in seeing it as a unit. One of them bears upon the definition of a configuration as being without parts and yet itself being a part-in-relation

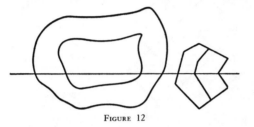

FIGURE 12

to something else. Thus, if two or more contradictory relations exist with the something else, which is the ground or datum for a judgment of its distinctness, there can be no configuration. Because when the same datum stands in two or more mutually incompatible relations to the entity under consideration, the entity must have parts on the basis of these frames of reference. If the whole of the configuration does not have a single relation to the same element in its environment, it does not exist as a whole; instead the common equivalences combine and segregate from the common differences, and what would otherwise be a figure is cross-sectioned to become two new configurations, each containing parts of the original one. This is the essence of protective coloration and camouflage. The same conditions can be discerned to be operative in many of the cases of experimental absorption offered by the gestaltists.

In Figure 12, which is taken from Köhler, some observers will be able to see the contained shape of the number *4*. Others will not, even though they are told to look for it. The difficulty arises partly because the figure (the number *4*) has no single relation to any one of the other possible forms with which it is associated. Its left arm, for instance, is within the curvilinear figure, while its right arm is not. The whole figure is not on, inside of, or adjacent to the whole of any other one thing. Consequently it is broken up into parts, each of its subwholes relating to different elements in the larger configuration. Under such circumstances, therefore, a whole ceases to exist because of the disintegrative forces of its environment. Another way to phrase it is to say that a thing cannot have different relations in the same dimension to something else; it cannot at the same time be both under and over or lighter and darker than another thing.

A second aspect of the difficulty in perceiving hidden configurations derives from their being fused with more inclusive wholes. In order to discern them, it is necessary to analyze the presented whole so that some component may be found on the level of integration of the simple figure to be discovered. Absorption takes place in this instance because the whole of the simple figure coincides with a part of one that is more complex. The task

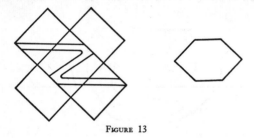

FIGURE 13

that is laid upon past experience under these conditions is to see a semicircle in a circle or to distinguish a drop of water in a lake. Fundamentally this is also a problem in relations. The figure is not lost because of the disintegrative effects of contradictory relations with other parts of the larger whole. It is still intact; but it, as a subwhole, bears a different relation to its correlate when it is embedded in a larger shape than it does when it is isolated. In order for it to have whole qualities, *i.e.,* to be a thing, when it is embedded, it must be related to the engulfing thing. Only in that way can it be set apart as a whole. Now, obviously it is *within* its matrix; that is its relation to its correlate. When it is isolated, *this* relationship is impossible, whatever the correlate might be. Clearly the two phenomena are not the same thing; and it is not surprising that we fail to think of one when we see the other.

The combined effects of disintegration and fusion very nearly serve to rule out completely the possibility of a spontaneous application of past experience. Both effects are involved in Gottschaldt's figures, one of which is reproduced as Figure 13. The hidden figure is the hexagon on the right; it is the "past experience" that is fused in the figure on the left. It is to be noted that it is a thing, a hexagon, because of its distinction from the white paper ground around it. This distinctiveness derives from the fact that it is *on* the paper—or some observers might be able to see it *under* the paper. In any event, it is not contained *within* its environment, as it is in the figure on the left. In that latter manifestation it is, therefore, a totally unfamiliar experience.

The thing that is a hexagon as it stands in isolation is also distorted out of immediate recognition by the disintegrative action of the rest of the elements in the figure on the left. That arrangement of lines is so contrived that there are at least three subconfigurations contending for mastery: two rectangular planes and an unbalanced Z or N. Each is plainly discernible because each in its entirety has a single relation with each of the others. But the hexagon does not; it is pulled apart by the contradictory forces of the others. The Z overlies and overruns it—yet cannot because its outline shows through the Z; it is within one rectangular plane—but cannot be because it is within the other also; it is enclosed by all the rest of the figure—but is not because it is *under* (or over) most of the Z. The only way that it can be seen as a whole is by relating it to one of the easily distinguished subwholes, thus ignoring a contradiction. This, however, requires conscious effort, as does an attempt to compensate for the effects of fusion.

An attitude of analysis on the part of the observer is thus a prerequisite to success in apprehending figures as well hidden as Gottschaldt's. One way to induce the attitude is to suggest the presence of the figures or direct an observer to find them. This condition has been ruled out in the foregoing experiments, and with some justification; for in our everyday experience of things we are not coached to discover subwholes in them or to combine them into larger wholes. At the same time an adequate statement of the problem must include attention to what happens when past experience is in some way caused to be psychologically present as well as when it is not.

The gestalt psychologists have, in fact, given recognition to this aspect of the subject in other contexts when they have not been so eager to demonstrate their case for the independent existence of segregated wholes. Köhler, for instance, discusses the effects of an observer's adopting special attitudes, among them the analytical, toward a given field and even admits that "in many cases a change of organization will be the consequence of such an attitude, and hence 'analysis' of this sort involves a real transformation of sensory facts in gestalt psychology." [20]

Indeed it would be extremely difficult to explain some of the most important psychological facts without reference to the effects that past experience has upon perception. How else explain recognition, or the occurrence of many illusions prefigured by past experience? Considerations of this kind led Koffka to formulate the conclusions of Gottschaldt and others in less dogmatic fashion. We may, he says, interpret Gottschaldt's results as an "absence of an automatic effect of experience" if we care to; but the real explanation is not that a memory record cannot influence a subsequent perception, but only

[20] Köhler, *op. cit.*, p. 183.

that it cannot do so if there is no circumstance which serves to bring the two in conjunction.[21]

The questions of when past experience does bear upon perception and what its effects are lead us to the heart of the problem of innovation. It appears that previous experience structures subsequent perception more often than the principal protagonists of gestalt theory have been willing to allow. It also appears that the ordering of a present sensory report in terms of some past experience like it can be more creative than is generally recognized. The mental interaction between what is and what was, in fact, does provide the only basis for a recombination of natural events; that is, for innovation, the uniquely mental contribution to newness.

[21] Koffka, *op. cit.*, p. 602.

INDEX